Classics of
Organization Theory
Sixth Edition

Classics of Organization Theory
Sixth Edition

Jay M. Shafritz
University of Pittsburgh

J. Steven Ott
University of Utah

Yong Suk Jang
Korea University

WADSWORTH
CENGAGE Learning·

Australia • Brazil • Japan • Korea • Mexico • Singapore • Spain • United Kingdom • United States

WADSWORTH
CENGAGE Learning™

**Classics of Organization
Theory, Sixth Edition
Jay M. Shafritz, J. Steven Ott,
Yong Suk Jang**

Executive Editor: David Tatom

Development Editor:
Drake Bush

Assistant Editor: Rebecca Green

Editorial Assistant:
Reena Thomas

Marketing Manager: Janise Fry

Marketing Assistant: Mary Ho

Advertising Project Manager:
Kelley McAllister

Project Manager, Editorial
Production: Rita Jaramillo

Art Director: Rob Hugel

Print/Media Buyer:
Emma Claydon

Permissions Editor:
Sarah Harkrader

Production Service: Newgen

Copy Editor: Newgen

Cover Designer:
Jeannette Barber

Cover Image: Rowan
Moore/Getty Images, Inc.

Compositor: Newgen

For product information and
technology assistance, contact us at **Cengage Learning
Customer & Sales Support, 1-800-354-9706**

For permission to use material from this text or product,
submit all requests online at **www.cengage.com/permissions**
Further permissions questions can be emailed to
permissionrequest@cengage.com

Library of Congress Control Number: 2004102128

ISBN-13: 978-0-534-63156-7

ISBN-10: 0-534-63156-8

Wadsworth
10 Davis Drive
Belmont, CA 94002-3098
USA

Cengage Learning is a leading provider of customized learning solutions with office locations around the globe, including Singapore, the United Kingdom, Australia, Mexico, Brazil, and Japan. Locate your local office at:
international.cengage.com/region

Cengage Learning products are represented in Canada by Nelson Education, Ltd.

For your course and learning solutions, visit
academic.cengage.com

Purchase any of our products at your local college store or at our preferred online store **www.ichapters.com**

Printed in the United States of America
6   7   12   11   10   09   08

Contents

Chapter 3
Human Resource Theory, or the Organizational Behavior Perspective   145

Chapter 4
"Modern" Structural Organization Theory   193

Foreword

Modern societies are filled with formal organizations. New areas of social life, such as the semiconductor industry or marriage counseling or international consulting, are carried out by organizations. And older social patterns, in the school, hospital, firm, or government, are formalized and managed as organizations. Organizations, once restricted to a few institutional areas in the political and economic systems, are now to be found in every sector of social life.

The modern expansion in organizing is by no means a matter of evolutionary drift. Organizations are self-consciously constructed and managed. This is a matter of definition, since organizations are distinct from other sorts of social collectives precisely in that they are articulated and formalized.

Organizations, thus, are theorized. And they are interdependent with the theories that create them, but that also arise from them. It is a two-way street. The academic theory of organizations develops in good part out of the intellectual examination of life in real-world organizations. But it also importantly drives the kinds of organizations that people build in the real world, and greatly affects the ways existing organizations change. Theorists and researchers analyze organizations, and their analyses, carried into reality by a variety of consultants and trained practitioners, change the organizations that exist.

In this book, Shafritz, Ott, and Jang provide an extraordinary overview of the development of modern organization theory by collecting and integrating discussions in the field that have become classics.

- In part, this overview describes the historical development, to greater maturity and sophistication, of an intellectual enterprise. There is more and better empirical research, and there is a greater variety of theoretical ideas and schemes with which to work.
- But in part, it depicts the development toward more complexity of modern organizations themselves. Organizations arise and expand in more and more settings, carrying out more and more tasks. They thus change. And the theoretical developments displayed in this book change with them.
- And further, social ideas about what activities and domains ought to be brought under formal organizational control expand greatly in the modern system. We want our natural environment to be measured and protected, our expanded human rights as workers or consumers taken carefully into account, and our technical and administrative procedures rendered rational and efficient. So expansions and change in organizational theory reflect not only evolving realities and sophistication in analyzing these realities, but also expanded modern ideologies about what needs to be brought under the systematic control of formal organizational structures.

Thus the theoretical developments displayed in this book's sweeping portrait of the development of organizational theory show increased theoretical sophistication, but also changes over time both in the actual landscapes of organizational life and in modern ideals or fantasies about the social control of uncertainties.

In all three of these respects similar developments occur with the development of the field. Simple formulations become more complex and contingent. More and more inter-dependencies are discovered, created, or desired. And this occurs on more and more fronts, as organizations are seen at once as managing work, people, and relations with multiple wider environments. In an important sense, rational organizations become less simplisti-cally rational.

In fact, these last sentences capture the evolving complexity of organizational theory. Organization, and its theoretical counterpart, is after all an attempt to simultaneously ra-tionally bring under control activity, people, and linkages to wider environments. This is difficult, since each of these dimensions of control poses different demands. It all requires much structuring, and becomes even more difficult as each of the elements to be linked ac-quires more and more complexity. Obviously, the work and activity to be controlled is much more complex than in the past. But so are the dimensions perceived of the people to be controlled, who now are seen as having many more rights and capacities. And the social and physical environments, too, are filled with more and more perceived complexity.

The history, thus, starts with the enlightenment dream, displayed in Chapter 1, of pulling some activities and/or people out of the messy societal environment and struc-turing them in rational and standardized form under the will of a unitary sovereign. The emphasis may vary from the rational structuring of work with a division of labor, to the bureaucratic control of people, or to the maintenance of the effective will of the sovereign.

It turns out, in social history and in the history of the field, that there are inconsis-tencies between the requisite elements of the actualities and ideologies of organization. Structuring work effectively has some inconsistencies with controlling people effectively, and both are inconsistent with maintaining total sovereign control. There is skepticism about the simple rational dream. It is prominently displayed in Chapter 2 of this book, in which theorists raise questions (more than give answers) about the validity of the original dream. The subsequent history of the field takes off from the materials in this chapter.

1. COMING TO TERMS WITH THE HUMAN PARTICIPANTS

One early development was to concentrate on the human dimension of organizing. Orga-nizations in practice have to (or anyway do, or should) take into account that the people in them are participants, not just objects of control. And over time, the human rights and recognized (and schooled) capacities of these people have grown rapidly. Various sacrifices in the rational exercises of sovereign control, or the rational management of work, are necessary in coming to terms with the changing reality of human complexity. Chapter 3 of this book presents the core theoretical materials, in this area, that permanently changed the field.

The people who participate in organizations are not the simple psychological entities of the original formulations. They bring, from wider society, a whole host of cultural mean-ings and interpretations. On the one side, organizations must come to terms with these. More importantly, organizations can (or must, or should) give up some aspects of their rational structuring to use these cultural elements, or build them, or manipulate them. Organizational culture, thus, constrains but also may facilitate functioning. The line of reasoning involved is displayed in Chapters 7 and 8.

2. COMING TO TERMS WITH VARIABLE ACTIVITY

Classical theory had tended to treat the work activities going on in organizations as having a rather simple character, and tended to imagine that fairly simple rules could cover them. But organizational activities vary sharply in their character and technologies. And the variance increases over time as more and more human activities are brought under the control of formalized organizations. Chapters 4 and 5 of this book pull together the major lines of theorizing that tried to come to terms with this central fact. The agenda here is not about the problematics of people, but about the variable difficulties in controlling activity. The effort is to suggest variations in structure that can come to terms with these difficulties. It is understood in these chapters that sacrifices in simple rationalistic models are made necessary by the complexities involved in technical and work interdependencies.

3. COMING TO TERMS WITH VARIABLE SOVEREIGNS AND GOALS

Classical organizational theory had tended to imagine rational structuring around singular goals—say efficient production of work or effective control and standardization of people—under the authority of a single sovereign. Reality is more disordered than that, and with complex modern society becomes more disorderly over time. Chapters 6 and 9 of this book show the lines of contemporary theorizing that result. One dimension of this effort emphasizes the loose power that accumulates within and around organizations, and the constraints (and opportunities) that result. The sovereign is never entirely in command, and must sacrifice rational controls (and unitary goals) to accede to a variety of internal and external pressures. A second dimension is cultural in character—organizations depend on legitimacy to function. They must (or can, or do) use environmentally legitimated forms, and meet socially legitimate goals, whether or not these are most rational or effective. A third dimension is competitive. Any given organization is likely to be highly dependent on the competitive, as well as legitimating, environment. The best and most rational way to do things, in principle, may not be feasible in practice, depending on what competitive and supportive elements the environment supplies.

All in all, the modern discussions of organizational theory keep an interesting distance from the simple rationalistic dreams of the early classical texts. There is more complexity and more skepticism. Sometimes this takes a pessimistic form, as writers emphasize the failures and pretenses of rationalism. Often it is more optimistic, as theorists see gains in overall effectiveness to be produced by sacrificing simple rationality to incorporate environmental supports, the commitment of human participants, or the complex and variable characteristics of the tasks at hand. In any case, the rational organization is seen as a good deal less rational than it once was. Partly the field has gotten more sophisticated, partly organizations themselves have changed, and partly the original mechanistic Enlightenment ideals have matured or eroded.

In any event, the entire history is under display in this extraordinary collection. Shafritz, Ott, and Jang have done students, and the field, a considerable service in creating and updating it, so that it reflects the continuing growth of the field.

John W. Meyer
Department of Sociology
Stanford University

Preface

*C*lassics of Organization Theory is a collection of the most important works in organization theory written by the most influential authors in the field. *Classics* does not simply tell the reader what the "masters" said, it presents their works in their own words. These are theories that have withstood the test of time — the critically acclaimed masterworks in the field. Although this book contains a liberal sprinkling of important current works, its focus is the enduring classics. *Classics of Organization Theory* thus tells the history of organization theory through the words of the great theorists.

This book is designed to help people who are new to the field of organization theory "get into," understand, and appreciate its important themes, perspectives, and theories. We describe and explain what organization theory is, how it has developed, and how its development coincides with developments in other fields, as well as the contexts in which these great works were written.

Each chapter focuses on one major perspective or "school" of organization theory. Readers thus can immerse themselves in one perspective at a time, before moving on to the next. Most of the articles are organized chronologically within the major perspectives or "schools." The major perspectives of organization theory are:

- Classical Organization Theory
- Neoclassical Organization Theory
- Human Resource Theory, or the Organizational Behavior Perspective
- "Modern" Structural Organization Theory
- Organizational Economics Theory
- Power and Politics Organization Theory
- Organizational Culture Theory
- Reform Through Changes in Organizational Culture
- Theories of Organizations and Environments

Several other features that help to make *Classics* "reader friendly":

- The Foreword by John W. Meyer explains the book in the context of the field of organization theory.
- The Introduction explains why there are competing perspectives or frames for grouping theories of organization, and why we chose the particular framework used in *Classics*.
- The Introduction explains how theories of organization reflect what is going on in the world at the time (for example, World War II or the "flower child"/antiestablishment/self-development era of the 1960s); defines the criteria used for including and excluding works (for example, "Should the serious student of organization theory be expected to be able to

identify this author and his or her basic themes?"); and presents the organizing framework for the book.

- The Introduction contains a chronology of important events and contributions to the field of organizational theory from 1491 BC into the 2000s. The chronology allows the reader to see the intellectual development of the myriad themes and perspectives of organization theory, and to comprehend the impact of time and context on the development of perspectives across the field.
- The opening pages of each chapter identify the central themes and issues of the perspective, contrast the perspective with others, and briefly summarize the contributions each article has made to the field.
- Most of the articles have been shortened to make them more readable. The editing helps readers to focus on the central ideas that make an article a classic.
- Each chapter contains a bibliography of the most important books and articles from the perspective (whether or not the works are reproduced in *Classics*).

CHANGES FROM THE FIFTH EDITION TO THE SIXTH EDITION

In our never-ending attempt to walk a fine line between holding this book true to its purpose and thus including only "true classics"— but also including a few important newer areas of theory, we have realigned and repositioned several chapters, and increased the emphasis on organizational economics. As for all editions, readings have been added and deleted.

Systems theory selections have been moved from Chapter 5 to a newly created Chapter 9, "Theories of Organizations and Environments." Thus, the core classic readings on systems theory remain in this sixth edition, including "Organizations and the System Concept," by Katz and Kahn, and "Organizations in Action," by James D. Thompson. The new Chapter 9 now includes these great classics and several more recent readings on organization-environment interfaces by John W. Meyer and Brian Rowan, Jeffrey Pfeffer and Gerald Salancik, and Glenn R. Carroll and Michael T. Hannan. Chapter 5 is now focused exclusively on organizational economics theories, a perspective on organization theory that we believe warrants a chapter of its own.

Chapter 8 has a clearer purpose and the readings in it have been strengthened. Whereas in the fifth edition this chapter was titled "Organizational Culture Reform Movements," it has been changed to "Reform Through Changes in Organizational Culture." All theories presented in this chapter now address organizational reforms that explicitly require organizational culture change, whether the reform is to render an organization more customer friendly or to overcome systemic bias against and underutilization of women and people of color. Thus, we moved Joan Acker's "Gendering Organizational Theory," from Chapter 7 and added "Creating the Multicultural Organization: The Challenge of Managing Diversity," by Taylor Cox Jr.

Although it is always difficult to select inclusions from among the rich choices of newer theories, we hope that we have identified some of the most important—theories that will become classics. The following selections, listed by chapter, have been added and deleted:

Chapter 3. Human Resource Theory, or the Organizational Behavior Perspective
Deletion from the Fifth Edition
Bart Victor and Carroll Stephens, "The Dark Side of the New Organizational Forms" (1994)

Chapter 4. "Modern" Structural Organization Theory
New Addition
> Richard M. Burton & Børge Obel, "Technology as a Contingency Factor" (1998)

Chapter 5. Organizational Economics Theory
New Addition
> Oliver E. Williamson, "Markets and Hierarchies" (1975). This reading was in the third edition of *Classics*, and we brought it back.

Moved to Chapter 9, "Theories of Organizations and Environments"
> Daniel Katz & Robert L. Kahn, "Organizations and the System Concept" (1966).
>
> James D. Thompson, "Organizations in Action" (1967)

Chapter 6. Power and Politics Organization Theory
New Addition
> Robert Michels, "Democracy and the Iron Laws of Oligarchy" (Originally written in 1915, translated into English in 1962).

Chapter 7. Organizational Culture Theory
Deletion from the Fifth Edition
> Meryl Reis Louis, "Surprise and Sensemaking: What Newcomers Experience in Entering Unfamiliar Organizational Settings" (1980)

Moved to Chapter 8, "Reform Through Changes in Organizational Culture"
> Joan Acker, "Gendering Organizational Theory" (1992)

New Addition
> Joanne Martin, "Organizational Culture: Pieces of the Puzzle" (2002)

Chapter 8. Reform Through Changes in Organizational Culture
New Additions
> Joan Acker, "Gendering Organizational Theory" (1992)
>
> Taylor Cox Jr., "Creating the Multicultural Organization: The Challenge of Managing Diversity" (2001)

Chapter 9. Theories of Organizations and Environments
Deletions from the Fifth Edition
> William Bergquist, "Postmodern Thought in a Nutshell: Where Art and Science Come Together" (1993)
>
> Michael Hammer & James Champy, "Reengineering the Corporation: The Enabling Role of Information Technology" (1993)
>
> Janet Fulk & Gerardine DeSanctis, "Articulation of Communication Technology and Organizational Form" (1999)
>
> Edward A. Stohr & Sivakumar Viswanathan, "Recommendation Systems: Decision Support for the Information Economy" (1999)

Moved to Chapter 4, "'Modern' Structural Organization Theory"
> Richard M. Burton & Børge Obel, "Technology as a Contingency Factor" (1998)

New Additions

Daniel Katz & Robert L. Kahn, "Organizations and the System Concept" (1966)

James D. Thompson, "Organizations in Action" (1967)

John W. Meyer & Brian Rowan, "Institutionalized Organizations: Formal Structure as Myth and Ceremony" (1977)

Jeffrey Pfeffer & Gerald R. Salancik, "External Control of Organizations: A Resource Dependence Perspective" (1978)

Glenn R. Carroll & Michael T. Hannan, "Demography of Corporations and Industries" (2000)

ACKNOWLEDGMENTS

This sixth edition of *Classics of Organization Theory* has benefited immeasurably from the advice that we have received from an array of friendly critics of the fifth edition. We wish to thank those who provided ideas and encouragement, including Richard Green, University of Utah; Ralph Hummel, University of Akron; Al Hyde, the Brookings Institution; and E. W. Russell, Victoria University of Technology. Jayne Buchholz, University of Utah, contributed invaluable advice about inclusions, provided editorial assistance, and managed the permissions. The reviewers selected by Thomson—Wadsworth provided worthy suggestions for deletions and new additions.

We thank the authors and publishers of these classics for their permission to reproduce their work. As with the previous editions, we sincerely solicit comments, ideas, and suggestions from the scholarly and practitioner communities. Given sufficient encouragement from readers and support from our publisher—and long enough lives—we will continue to revise *Classics of Organization Theory* as new theories and perspectives gain in importance and others fizzle.

Jay M. Shafritz
University of Pittsburgh

J. Steven Ott
University of Utah

Yong Suk Jang
Korea University

Introduction

This book is about organization theory. By *organization*, we mean a social unit with some particular purposes. By *theory*, we mean a proposition or set of propositions that seeks to explain or predict something. The something in this case is how groups and individuals behave in varying organizational structures and circumstances. This is obviously important information for any manager or leader to have. It is hardly an exaggeration to say that the world is ruled by the underlying premises of organization theory, and that it has been ever since humankind first organized itself for hunting, war, and even family life. Indeed, the newest thing about organization theory is the study of it. Only in the twentieth century were intellectual substance and tradition given to this field, which until then had been the instinctual domain of adventuresome entrepreneurs and cunning politicos. Organization theory lay largely dormant over the centuries until society found a practical use for it: to help manage the ever-burgeoning national (as opposed to local) industries and institutions that increasingly ran the twentieth century. When the problems of managing an organization grew to be more than one head could cope with, the search for guidance on how to manage and arrange large-scale organizations became as noble a quest as the secular world of business could offer. If a commercial society ever had prophets, they were those pioneers of the scientific management movement who claimed that the path to ever-greater prosperity was to be found in the relentless search for the "one best way." They were offering society a theory—abstract guidance for those who knew where they wanted to go but didn't quite know how to get there. They already knew what Kurt Lewin would assert years later: "There is nothing so practical as a good theory" (Marrow, 1969).

Peter Drucker (1954) once observed that the thrust toward scientific management "may well be the most powerful as well as the most lasting contribution America has made to Western thought since the Federalist Papers." Of course, the scientific management movement was just the beginning of a continuous search for the most effective means by which people can be organized into social units in order to achieve the goals of their companies, their governments, or themselves. It was once said of the first atomic bomb and the first U.S. voyage to the moon that they were as much achievements of organization as of engineering and science.

Have the more recent theories of organization kept pace with our industrial and technical achievements? Probably not, although if one compares them with the primitive notions, for example, of the turn-of-the-twentieth-century "scientific management" movement, the answer would certainly be yes. Yet many of the basics remain as givens. The laws of physics and gravity do not change with intellectual fashions or technological advances, nor do the basic social and physical characteristics of people change. Just as those who would build spaceships have to start by studying Newton, those who would design and manage organizations must start with Fayol, Taylor, and Barnard. The future builds upon

1

what is enduring from the past. That is the rationale for this book: to provide those who seek to understand and/or to advance organization theory with a convenient place to find the essentials, indeed the classics, of organization theory. However old some of these articles may be, they are not dated. A classic is a classic because it continues to be of value to each new generation of students and practitioners who study organizations.

The basic elements of organizations have remained relatively constant through history. Organizations (or their important constituencies) have purposes (which may be explicit or implicit), attract participants, acquire and allocate resources to accomplish goals, use some form of structure to divide and coordinate activities, and rely on certain members to lead or manage others. Although the elements of organizations have remained relatively constant, their purposes, structures, ways of doing things, and methods for coordinating activities have always varied widely. The variations largely (but not exclusively) reflect an organization's adaptation to its environment, because organizations are "open systems" that are influenced by and impact on the world around them. The world around organizations includes, for example, their sources of inputs (such as raw materials, capital, and labor), markets, technology, politics, and the society's culture and subcultures. Organizations are inseparable parts of the society and the culture in which they exist and function. Human behavior—and thus also organizational behavior—is influenced by culturally rooted beliefs, values, assumptions, and behavioral norms that affect all aspects of organizations.

Theories about organizations do not develop in a vacuum. They reflect what is going on in the world, including the existing culture. Thus, contributions to organization theory vary over time and across cultures and subcultures. The advent of the factory system, World War II, the "flower child"/antiestablishment/self-development era of the 1960s, the computer/information society of the 1970s, and the pervasive uncertainties of the 1980s and 1990s all substantially influenced the evolution of organization theory. In order to truly understand organization theory as it exists today, one must appreciate the historical contexts through which it has developed and the cultural milieus during which important contributions were made to its body of ideas and knowledge. To help readers place writings in their historical contexts, "A Chronology of Organization Theory," a review of the major events and publications in the field, follows this Introduction.

CRITERIA FOR SELECTION

The editors are neither so vain nor so foolish as to assert that these are *the* classics of organization theory. The academic study of organization theory rests on a foundation of primary and secondary sciences and draws significantly from such diverse disciplines as sociology, psychology, social psychology, cultural anthropology, political science, economics, business administration, and public administration. It draws less, but still importantly, from mathematics, statistics, systems theory, industrial engineering, philosophy and ethics, history, and computer sciences. We readily admit that some important contributors and contributions to the field have been omitted from this collection. Some omissions were particularly painful—especially the readings that we deleted from the fifth edition. However, considerations of space and balance necessarily prevailed.

We have continued to use the same criteria for making our selections. First, we asked ourselves, "Should the serious student of organization theory be expected to be able to identify these authors and their basic themes?" When the answer was yes, it was because the contribution has long been, or is increasingly being recognized as, an important theme by a significant writer. Whereas we expect to be criticized for excluding other articles and writers, it will be more difficult to honestly criticize us for our inclusions; the writers and selections chosen are among the most widely quoted and reprinted theorists and theories in the field of organization theory. The exceptions are the articles chosen to represent the newer perspectives of organization theory, particularly organizational culture and information technology. Obviously, new articles have not been quoted as extensively as those written ten, twenty, or thirty years earlier. Thus, we had to be more subjective when making our editorial decisions about inclusions and exclusions in these chapters. In our judgment, these selections have a reasonable chance to fare well àgainst the test of time.

Although this is a book of classics, we continue to receive requests to include some current and near-current management best-sellers. "How can *Classics of Organization Theory* fail to include 'modern management classics' such as *The Fifth Discipline* and the *National Performance Review?*" Other readers and reviewers, however, urge us to stay true to the book's purpose. "Stay with the time-tested classics. Don't try to be everything for everybody. Let other anthologies keep readers up to date with the current fads." We hope to appease both points of view by including some modern management contributions, particularly in Chapters 7 and 8. Purists can simply pretend these chapters are not included.

The second criterion is related to the first: Each article or portion of a book had to make a basic statement that has been echoed or attacked consistently. In other words, the selection had to be important—significant in the sense that it must have been (or will be) an integral part of the foundation for the subsequent building of the field of organization theory.

The third criterion was that articles should be readable. Those of you who have already had reason to peruse the literature of organization theory will appreciate the importance of this criterion.

The inclusion of articles from the more recent perspectives raises important questions about our choices of chapters for grouping theories and selections. For example, what is the basis for our distinction between the "modern" structuralists and the systemists? And why are some readings included in Chapter 7, "Organizational Culture Theory," while others are in Chapter 8, "Reform Through Changes in Organizational Culture"? The answers to questions such as these reflect our own conceptual and historical construction of organization theory, tempered by the need to limit the size of this volume. It is crucially important, then, to understand where we, the authors/editors, are "coming from." Thus we have written rather lengthy essays to introduce each chapter. Each presents a school or perspective of organization theory, but because there is no universally accepted set of schools or perspectives, a few words of explanation are needed here.

A FRAMEWORK: THE "PERSPECTIVES" OF ORGANIZATION THEORY

There is no such thing as the theory of organizations. Rather, there are many theories that attempt to explain and predict how organizations and the people in them will behave in varying organizational structures, cultures, and circumstances. Some theories of organization are compatible with and build upon others—in what they explain or predict, the aspects of organizations they consider to be important, their assumptions about organizations and the world at large from which they are created, and the methods for studying organizations that work well. They tend to use the same language or jargon. These groupings of compatible theories and theorists usually are called schools, perspectives, traditions, frameworks, models, paradigms, or, occasionally, eras of organization theory. We use these terms interchangeably throughout this book.

Organization theorists from one school will quote and cite each other's works regularly. However, they usually ignore theorists and theories from other schools — or acknowledge them only negatively. In 1961, Harold Koontz described management theory as a "semantics jungle." In 1963, Arthur Kuriloff found that "each [school of organization theory] is at odds with others, each defends its own position, each claims that the others have major deficiencies." But that was 1963, and we have come a long way since then. Or have we? In 1983, Graham Astley and Andrew Van de Ven observed: "The problem is that different schools of [organizational] thought tend to focus only on single sides of issues and use such different logics and vocabularies that they do not speak to each other directly." And in 1997, Lee Bolman and Terrence Deal observed: "Within the social sciences, major schools of thought have evolved, each with its own view of organizations, its own well-defined concepts and assumptions, and its own ideas about how managers can best bring social collectives under control."

It is reasonable to conclude that not only is there no consensus on what constitutes knowledge in organization theory, but there is not likely to be any such consensus in the foreseeable future. Anyone who studies this subject is free to join the school of organization theory of his or her choice and to accept the philosophic boundaries of one group of serious thinkers over another. But before casting your lot with one school and excluding others, consider the options. Examine each school's strengths and weaknesses. See if its philosophy is in harmony with your already-established beliefs, assumptions, and predispositions. You may find that no single perspective deserves your loyalty, that each contains important information and insights that are useful in differing circumstances. Remember, these are schools with no tuition, no classes, and no grades. They exist only as intellectual constructs and as mutual support networks of organization theorists. They have one primary purpose: to organize and extend knowledge about organizations and how to study them.

Just as there is disagreement among the various frames about what makes organizations tick, there also are different views about the best way to group organization theories into schools. Each of the major frames of organization theory is associated with a period in time. For example, the classical school was at its prime in the 1920s and 1930s, and the human resources school in the 1960s and early 1970s. Each school had its beginnings while another was dominant, gradually gained acceptance, and eventually replaced its predecessor as the dominant perspective. Some years later, another came along to challenge and eventually take its position. Once-dominant frames of organization theory may lose the center stage, but they do not die. Their thinking influences subsequent frames — even those that reject their basic assumptions and tenets. Important works from these earlier perspectives become the timeless classics.

This cycling of schools through struggling ascendancy, dominance, challenge by other schools, and reluctant decline is not unique to organization theory. Thomas Kuhn (1970) postulated that this dialectic process is common in all sciences, including physics, mathematics, and psychiatry. It is quite common for frames that are close to each other chronologically to have widely divergent basic assumptions about the object of their theories.

FIGURE 1 • ASTLEY AND VAN DE VEN'S FOUR VIEWS OF ORGANIZATION

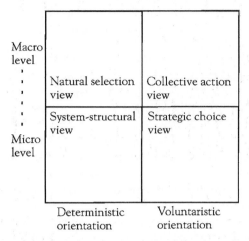

Examples of some representative organization theorists for each of the four views

System-Structural View: Blau and Scott (1962), Fayol (1949), Gulick and Urwick (1937), Lawrence and Lorsch (1967), Merton (1940), James D. Thompson (1967)
Strategic Choice View: Bittner (1965), Blau (1964), Feldman and March (1981), Strauss et al. (1963), Weick (1979)
Natural Selection View: Aldrich (1979), Hannan and Freeman (1977), Pfeffer and Salancik (1978), Porter (1981)
Collective Action View: Emery and Trist (1973), Hawley (1950, 1968), Schön (1971)

Adapted from W. G. Astley & A. H. Van de Ven (1983), Central perspectives and debates in organization theory, *Administrative Science Quarterly*, 28.

Despite their differences, most of the better-known approaches to grouping organization theories into schools have commonalities. First, they group theories by their perspectives on organizations—in other words, by basic assumptions about humans and organizations and by those aspects of organizations that they see as most important for understanding organizational processes and structures. Second, they usually group the theories by the period of time during which the most important contributions were written. Other organization theorists use different approaches for labeling the theories. On the other hand, Herbert Simon, among others, has put forward a solid argument that the use of frames (or schools or perspectives) confuses more than it enlightens (1997, pp. 26, 27).

Graham Astley and Andrew Van de Ven (1983) proposed a useful logic for classifying schools of organization "thought" into four basic views based on two analytical dimensions: the level of organizational analysis (micro or macro) and the emphasis placed on deterministic versus voluntaristic assumptions about human nature. Thus Astley and Van de Ven concluded that organization theories could be grouped into the cells of a two-by-two matrix (see Figure 1). Their voluntaristic-to-deterministic dimension (the horizontal continuum in Figure 1) classifies theories by their assumptions about individual organization members' autonomy and self-direction versus the assumption that behavior in organizations is determined by structural constraints. The macro-to-micro continuum (the vertical continuum in Figure 1) groups organization theories by their focus on communities of organizations or single organizations.

W. Richard Scott (2003) has offered an alternative organizing schema that includes three perspectives of formal organizations: *organizations as rational, natural, and open systems*. The first of these perspectives, *organizations as rational systems*, views organizations as highly formalized rational collectivities pursuing specific goals. The early studies of organizations reflected this rational system perspective. For example, Max Weber (1946) and Robert Michels (1949) studied the rise of the bureaucracy and the expansion of formalized rules and official hierarchies within organizations at the turn of the twentieth century. Frederick Winslow Taylor (1911) and his associates developed the ideas of scientific management as important mechanisms to restructure and rationalize the activities of business organizations. Henri Fayol (1949) and his colleagues articulated a universal set of principles of administration to guide the specialization and coordination of work activities. These early works viewed formal organizations as rationally designed instruments for achieving goals and maximizing machine-like efficiency.

The second perspective, *organizations as natural systems*, views organizations as social systems with multiple interests, informal relations, and participants with subgoals. Organizational theorists and researchers with this perspective argue there is no one best formal way to maximize organizational efficiency. Rather, they emphasize informal structures that include roles and relationships that emerge among individuals and groups of organizations and shape organizational goals and activities. Exemplary work from this natural system perspective include Elton Mayo's human relations notions (1945) and Chester Barnard's conception of cooperative systems (1938).

Finally, the *organizations as open systems* perspective views organizations as systems of interdependent activities embedded in and dependent on wider environments. Whereas the rational and natural system perspectives view organizations and their environments as separate and closed entities with clear boundaries, this separation is not apparent in the open system perspective. Organizations not only acquire material, financial, and human resources from their environment, they also gain social support and legitimacy. The main focus of theory and research from this perspective is on the interactions and interdependencies between organizations and environments. Exemplary works include Hannan and Freeman's organizational ecology model (1977), Pfeffer and Salancik's resource dependence model (1978), and Meyer and Rowan's institutional theory (1977).

Theoretical models of organizations underwent a major change about 1960 when the open system perspective gained support and essentially displaced the closed system models (Scott, 2003). Although these three perspectives developed historically as distinct research paradigms, recent organizational research tends to combine elements of rational, natural, and open system perspectives and stresses the interactions between organizations and environments. The primary focus of research has been shifted from internal characteristics of organizations to external dynamics of competition, interaction, and interdependency.

THE ORGANIZATION OF THIS BOOK

We believe strongly that a historical approach offers clear advantages for students, and the use of schools or frames as the basis for organizing chapters lends itself quite well to such an approach. Organization theory tends to be somewhat cumulative: theorists and schools of theorists learn from and build upon each other's works. Sometimes the cumulative building of organization theory has been accomplished through the adoption of prior theorists' assumptions, logic, and empirical research methods and findings. In other instances, the building process has advanced by *rejecting* prior assumptions and theories (Kuhn, 1970). Thus, we have decided to retain a rather traditional, historically oriented approach that allows the reader to follow the ebb and flow within and between the perspectives. Within chapters, most selections are presented in chronological sequence so the reader can gain a sense of the evolution of thought in the field. Although we have attempted to include only selections that fit into one school, many works span the boundaries, no matter how tightly or loosely they are defined and drawn. Thus, the reader should remember that the schools — and the chapters — reflect periods in time as well as perspectives of organizations. Also, the reader can gain a quick overview of the historical development of organization theory by referring to the "Chronology of Organization Theory" that follows this Introduction.

Our perspectives, or schools, and the corresponding book chapters are:

Chapter 1   Classical Organization Theory
Chapter 2   Neoclassical Organization Theory
Chapter 3   Human Resource Theory, or the Organizational Behavior Perspective
Chapter 4   "Modern" Structural Organization Theory
Chapter 5   Organizational Economics Theory
Chapter 6   Power and Politics Organization Theory
Chapter 7   Organizational Culture Theory
Chapter 8   Reform through Changes in Organizational Culture
Chapter 9   Theories of Organizations and Environments

Each perspective is described and discussed in the introductory essays in the respective chapters.

REFERENCES

Argyris, C., & D. A. Schön (1978). *Organizational learning: A theory of action perspective*. Reading, MA: Addison-Wesley.
Aldrich, H. (1979). *Organizations and environments*. Englewood Cliffs, NJ: Prentice-Hall.
Astley, W. G., & A. H. Van de Ven (1983, June). Central perspectives and debates in organization theory. *Administrative Science Quarterly, 28*, 245–270.
Barnard, C. I. (1938). *The functions of the executives*. Cambridge, MA: Harvard University Press.
Bittner, E. (1965). The concept of organization. *Social Research, 32*(3), 239–255.
Blau, P. M. (1964). *Exchange and power in social life*. New York: Wiley.
Blau, P. M., & R. G. Scott (1962). *Formal organizations*. San Francisco: Chandler.
Bolman, L. G., & T. E. Deal (1984). *Modern approaches to understanding and managing organizations*. San Francisco: Jossey-Bass.
Bolman, L. G., & T. E. Deal (1997). *Reframing organizations: Artistry, choice, and leadership*. 2d ed. San Francisco: Jossey-Bass.
Burton, R. M., & B. Obel (1998). *Strategic organizational diagnosis and design: Developing theory for application*. 2d ed. Boston: Kluwer Academic.
Cohen, M. D., and L. S. Sproull, eds. (1996). *Organizational learning*. Thousand Oaks, CA: Sage.
Deming, W. E. (1986). *Out of the crisis*. Cambridge, MA: MIT Press.
DeSanctis, G., & J. Fulk, eds. (1999). *Shaping organizational form: Communication, connection, and community*. Thousand Oaks, CA: Sage.

Drucker, P. F. (1954). *The practice of management*. New York: Harper & Row.

Emery, F. E., & Trist, E. L. (1973). *Towards a social ecology: Contextual appreciations of the future in the present*. New York: Plenum.

Fayol, H. (1949). *General and industrial management*. London: Pitman. (Originally published in 1916.)

Feldman, M. S., & March, J. G. (1981). Information in organizations as signal and symbol. *Administrative Science Quarterly, 26*, 171–186.

George, C. S., Jr. (1972). *The history of management thought*. Englewood Cliffs, NJ: Prentice Hall.

Gulick, L., & L. Urwick, eds. (1937). *Papers on the science of administration*. New York: Institute of Public Administration.

Hammer, M., & J. Champy (1993). *Reengineering the corporation: A manifesto for business revolution*. New York: HarperCollins.

Hannan, M., & J. Freeman (1977). The population ecology of organizations. *American Journal of Sociology, 82*, 929–964.

Hatch, M. J. (1997). *Organization theory: Modern symbolic and postmodern perspectives*. Oxford, UK: Oxford University Press.

Hawley, A. (1950). *Human ecology: A theory of community structure*. New York: Ronald Press.

Hawley, A. (1968). *Human ecology*. In D. L. Sills, ed., *The international encyclopedia of the social sciences*, vol. 4 (pp. 328–337). New York: Crowell-Collier & Macmillan.

Hutchinson, J. O. (1967). *Organizations: Theory and classical concepts*. New York: Holt, Rinehart & Winston.

Ibn Khaldun (1969). *The muqaddimah: An introduction to history*. Trans. F. Rosenthal. Ed. and abridged N. J. Dawood. Princeton, NJ: Bollingen Series/Princeton University Press.

Kanter, R. M. (1977). *Men and women of the corporation*. New York: Basic Books.

Kanter, R. M. (1983). *The change masters*. New York: Simon & Schuster.

Kendall, K. E., ed. (1999). *Emerging information technologies: Improving decisions, cooperation and infrastructure*. Thousand Oaks, CA: Sage.

Koontz, H. (1961). The management theory jungle. *Academy of Management Journal, 4*, 174–188.

Koontz, H. (1980). The management theory jungle revisited. *Academy of Management Review, 5*, 175–187.

Kuhn, T. S. (1970). *The structure of scientific revolutions*. 2d ed. Chicago: University of Chicago Press.

Kuriloff, Arthur. (1963). An experiment in management: Putting theory Y to the test. *Personnel, 40*(6), 8–17.

Lawrence, P. R., & J. W. Lorsch (1967). *Organization and environment*. Cambridge, MA: Harvard University Press.

Marrow, A. J. (1969). *The practical theorist: The life and works of Kurt Lewin*. New York: Basic Books.

Mayo, E. (1945). *The social problems of an industrial civilization*. Boston: Graduate School of Business Administration, Harvard University.

Merton, R. K. (1940). Bureaucratic structure and personality. *Social Forces, 18*, 560–568.

Meyer, J. W., & B. Rowan (1977). Institutionalized organizations: Formal structures as myth and ceremony. *American Journal of Sociology, 83*, 340–363.

Michels, R. (1949 trans.). *Political parties*. Eden and Cedar Paul. Glencoe, IL: Free Press (originally published in 1915).

Nadler, D. A., M. S. Gerstein, & R. B. Shaw, eds. (1992). *Organizational architecture: Designs for changing organizations*. San Francisco: Jossey-Bass.

Osborne, D., & T. Gaebler (1992). *Reinventing government*. Reading, MA: Addison-Wesley.

Ott, J. S., S. J. Parkes, & R. B. Simpson, eds. (2003). *Classic readings in organizational behavior*. 3d ed. Belmont, CA: Thomson-Wadsworth.

Perrow, C. (1973, Summer). The short and glorious history of organizational theory. *Organizational Dynamics, 2*(1), 2–15.

Peters, B. G. (1996). *The future of governing: Four emerging models*. Lawrence, KS: University Press of Kansas.

Peters, T. J. (1994). *The pursuit of wow!* New York: Vintage.

Peters, T. J., & R. H. Waterman Jr. (1982). *In search of excellence: Lessons from America's best-run companies.* New York: Harper & Row.

Pfeffer, J. (1981). *Power in organizations.* Marshfield, MA: Pitman.

Pfeffer, J., & G. R. Salancik (1978). *The external control of organizations: A resource dependence perspective.* New York: Harper & Row.

Porter, M. E. (1981). The contributions of industrial organization to strategic management. *Academy of Management Review, 6,* 609–620.

Schön, D. A. (1971). *Beyond the stable state.* New York: Basic Books.

Scott, W. G. (1961, April). Organization theory: An overview and an appraisal. *Academy of Management Journal, 4*(1), 7–26.

Scott, W. G., & T. R. Mitchell (1972). *Organization theory.* Rev. ed. Chicago: Dorsey Press.

Scott, W. R. (2003). *Organizations: Rational, natural, and open systems.* 5th ed. Upper Saddle River, NJ: Prentice Hall.

Senge, P. M. (1990). *The fifth discipline: The art & practice of the learning organization.* New York: Doubleday Currency.

Simon, H. A. (1997). *Administrative behavior: A study of decision-making processes in administrative organizations.* 4th ed. New York: Free Press.

Strauss, A., L. Schatzman, D. Erlich, R. Bucher, & M. Sabshin (1963). The hospital and its negotiated order. In E. Friedson, ed., *The hospital in modern society* (pp. 147–169). New York: Free Press.

Taylor, F. W. (1911). *The Principles of Scientific Management.* New York: Harper.

Thompson, J. D. (1967). *Organizations in action.* New York: McGraw-Hill.

Weber, M. (1946 trans.). *From Max Weber: Essays in sociology,* ed. Hans H. Gerth and C. Wright Mills. New York: Oxford University Press (first published in 1906–1924).

Weick, K. E. (1979). *The social psychology of organizing* (2nd ed.). Reading, MA: Addison-Wesley.

Weick, K. E. (1995). *Sensemaking in organizations.* Thousand Oaks, CA: Sage.

Wren, D. A. (1972). *The evolution of management thought.* New York: Ronald Press.

A CHRONOLOGY OF ORGANIZATION THEORY

1491 BC   During the exodus from Egypt, Jethro, the father-in-law of Moses, urges Moses to delegate authority over the tribes of Israel along hierarchical lines.

500 BC   Sun Tzu's *The Art of War* recognizes the need for hierarchical organization, interorganizational communications, and staff planning.

400 BC   Socrates argues for the universality of management as an art unto itself.

370 BC   Xenophon records the first known description of the advantages of the division of labor when he describes an ancient Greek shoe factory.

360 BC   Aristotle, in *The Politics,* asserts that the specific nature of executive powers and functions cannot be the same for all states (organizations) but must reflect their cultural environment.

c. AD 770   Abu Yusuf, an important pioneering Muslim scholar, explores the administration of essential Islamic government functions, including public financial policy, taxation, and criminal justice, in *Kitab al-Kharaj (The Book of Land Taxes).*

1058   *Al-Ahkam As-Sultaniyyah (The Governmental Rules),* by al-Mawardi, examines Islamic constitutional law, theoretical and practical aspects of Muslim political thought and behavior, and the behavior of politicians and administrators in Islamic states.

c. 1093   Al-Ghazali emphasizes the role of Islamic creed and teachings for the improvement of administrative and bureaucratic organization in Muslim states, particularly the qualifications and duties of rulers, ministers, and secretaries, in *Ihya Ulum ad-Din* (*The Revival of the Religious Sciences*) and *Nasihat al-Muluk* (*Counsel for Kings*).

c. 1300   In *As-Siyasah ash-Shariyyah* (*The Principles of Religious Government*), ibn Taymiyyah, "the father of Islamic administration," uses the scientific method to outline the principles of administration within the framework of Islam, including "the right man for the right job," patronage, and the spoils system.

1377   *The Muqaddimah: An Introduction to History*, by Muslim scholar ibn Khaldun, argues that methods for organizational improvement can be developed through the study of the science of culture. He specifically introduces conceptions of formal and informal organization, organizations as natural organisms with limits beyond which they cannot grow, and esprit de corps.

1513   Machiavelli urges the principle of unity of command in *The Discourses*: "It is better to confide any expedition to a single man of ordinary ability, rather than to two, even though they are men of the highest merit, and both having equal ability."

1532   Machiavelli's book of advice to all would-be leaders, *The Prince*, is published five years after its author's death. It became the progenitor of all "how to succeed" books that advocate practical rather than moral actions.

1776   Adam Smith's *The Wealth of Nations* discusses the optimal organization of a pin factory. It becomes the most famous and influential statement of the economic rationale of the factory system and the division of labor.

1813   Robert Owen, in his "Address to the Superintendents of Manufactories," puts forth the then-revolutionary idea that managers should pay as much attention to their "vital machines" (employees) as to their "inanimate machines."

1832   Charles Babbage's *On the Economy of Machinery and Manufactures* anticipates many of the notions of the scientific management movement, including such "basic principles of management" as the division of labor.

1856   Daniel C. McCallum states his six basic principles of administration in his annual report as superintendent of the New York and Erie Railroad Company.

1885   Captain Henry Metcalfe, the manager of an army arsenal, publishes *The Cost of Manufactures and the Administration of Workshops, Public and Private*, in which he asserts that there is a "science of administration" that is based upon principles discoverable by diligent observation.

1886   Henry R. Towne's paper "The Engineer as Economist," read at a meeting of the American Society of Mechanical Engineers, encourages the scientific management movement.

1902   Vilfredo Pareto becomes the "father" of the concept of "social systems." His societal notions would later be applied by Elton Mayo and the human relationists in organizational contexts.

1903   Frederick W. Taylor publishes *Shop Management*.

1904   Frank B. and Lillian M. Gilbreth marry. They proceed to produce many of the pioneering works on time and motion study, scientific management, and applied psychology.

1910   Louis D. Brandeis, an associate of Frederick W. Taylor (and later Supreme Court Justice), coins and popularizes the term *scientific management* in his Eastern Rate Case testimony before the Interstate Commerce Commission by arguing that railroad rate increases should be denied because the railroads could save "a million dollars a day" by applying scientific management methods.

1911   Frederick W. Taylor publishes *The Principles of Scientific Management*.

1912   Harrington Emerson publishes *The Twelve Principles of Efficiency*, which describes an interdependent but coordinated management system.

1913   Hugo Munsterberg's *Psychology and Industrial Efficiency* calls for the application of psychology to industry.

1914   Robert Michels, in his analysis of the workings of political parties and labor unions, *Political Parties*, formulates his iron law of oligarchy: "Who says organization, says oligarchy."

1916   In France, Henri Fayol publishes his *General and Industrial Management*, the first complete theory of management.

            Frederick Winslow Taylor's principles of scientific management are published in the *Bulletin of the Taylor Society* as an abstract of an address given by Taylor before the Cleveland Advertising Club in 1915.

1922   Max Weber's structural definition of bureaucracy is published posthumously. It uses an "ideal-type" approach to extrapolate from the real world the central core features that characterize the most fully developed form of bureaucratic organization.

1924   The Hawthorne studies begin at the Hawthorne Works of the Western Electric Company in Chicago. They last until 1932 and lead to new thinking about the relationships among work environment, human motivation, and productivity.

1926   Mary Parker Follett anticipates the movement toward more participatory management styles in a book chapter, "On the Giving of Orders." Follett calls for "power with" as opposed to "power over."

1931   Mooney and Reiley, in *Onward Industry* (republished in 1939 as *The Principles of Organization*), argue that newly discovered "principles of organization" have indeed been known since ancient times.

1933   Elton Mayo's *The Human Problems of an Industrial Civilization* is the first major report on the Hawthorne studies and the first significant call for a human relations movement.

1937   Luther Gulick's "Notes on the Theory of Organization" draws attention to the functional elements of the work of an executive with his mnemonic device POSDCORB.

1938   Chester I. Barnard's *The Functions of the Executive*, a sociological analysis of organizations, encourages and foreshadows the postwar revolution in thinking about organizational behavior.

1939   Roethlisberger and Dickson publish *Management and the Worker*, the definitive account of the Hawthorne studies.

1940   Robert K. Merton's article, "Bureaucratic Structure and Personality," proclaims that Max Weber's "ideal-type" bureaucracy has inhibiting dysfunctions that lead to inefficiency and worse.

1941   James Burnham, in *The Managerial Revolution*, asserts that as the control of large organizations passes from owners into the hands of professional administrators, society's new governing class will be the possessors not of wealth but of technical expertise.

1943   Abraham Maslow's "needs hierarchy" first appears in his *Psychological Review* article "A Theory of Human Motivation."

1946   Herbert A. Simon's *Public Administration Review* article, "The Proverbs of Administration," attacks the principles approach to management for being inconsistent and often inapplicable.

1947   The National Training Laboratories for Group Development (later renamed the NTL Institute for Applied Behavioral Science) is established to conduct research on group dynamics and, later, sensitivity training.

        Herbert A. Simon's *Administrative Behavior* urges the use of a truly scientific method in the study of administrative phenomena. The perspective of logical positivism should be used with questions of policy making, and it should be acknowledged that decision making is the true heart of administration.

1948   Dwight Waldo publishes *The Administrative State*, which attacks the "gospel of efficiency" that dominated administrative thinking before World War II.

        In their *Human Relations* article "Overcoming Resistance to Change," Lester Coch and John R. P. French Jr. note that employees are less inclined to resist change when the need is effectively communicated to them and when the workers are involved in planning the changes.

        Norbert Wiener coins the term *cybernetics* in his book with the same title, which becomes a foundation concept for systems theories of organization.

        R. M. Stogdill's list of personal leadership traits is published in the *Journal of Psychology*. They include physical characteristics, social background, intelligence and ability, personality, task-related characteristics, and social characteristics.

1949   Philip Selznick, in *TVA and the Grass Roots*, discovers "cooptation" when he examines how the Tennessee Valley Authority subsumed new external elements into its policy-making process in order to prevent those elements from becoming threats to the organization.

        In a *Public Administration Review* article, "Power and Administration," Norton E. Long finds that power is the lifeblood of administration. Managers must do more than apply the scientific method to problems—they had to attain, maintain, and increase their power or risk failing in their mission.

Rufus E. Miles Jr. of the U.S. Bureau of the Budget, states Miles's Law: "Where you stand depends on where you sit."

Air Force Captain Edsel Murphy states Murphy's Law: "If anything can go wrong, it will."

1950   George C. Homans publishes *The Human Group*, the first major application of "systems" to organizational analysis.

1951   Kurt Lewin proposes a general model of change consisting of three phases, "unfreezing, change, [and] refreezing," in his *Field Theory in Social Science*. His model becomes a conceptual frame for organization development.

Ludwig von Bertalanffy's article "General Systems Theory: A New Approach to the Unity of Science" is published in *Human Biology*. His concepts become *the* intellectual basis for the systems approach to organizational theory.

1954   Peter Drucker's book *The Practice of Management* popularizes the concept of management by objectives.

Alvin Gouldner's *Patterns of Industrial Bureaucracy* describes three possible responses to a formal bureaucratic structure: "mock," where the formal rules are ignored by both management and labor; "punishment-centered," where management seeks to enforce rules that workers resist; and "representative," where rules are both enforced and obeyed.

1956   William H. Whyte Jr. profiles *The Organization Man*, an individual within an organization who accepts its values and finds harmony in conforming to its policies.

In the premier issue of *Administrative Science Quarterly*, Talcott Parsons's article "Suggestions for a Sociological Approach to the Theory of Organizations" defines an organization as a social system that focuses on the attainment of specific subgoals and in turn contributes to the accomplishment of goals of the larger organization or society itself.

Kenneth Boulding's *Management Science* article "General Systems Theory—The Skeleton of Science" merges Wiener's concept of cybernetics with von Bertalanffy's general systems theory. This article becomes the most-quoted introduction to the systems approach to organization theory.

1957   C. Northcote Parkinson discovers his law that "work expands so as to fill the time available for its completion."

Chris Argyris asserts in his first major book, *Personality and Organization*, that there is an inherent conflict between the personality of a mature adult and the needs of modern organizations.

Douglas M. McGregor's article "The Human Side of Enterprise" distills the contending traditional authoritarian and humanistic managerial philosophies into Theory X and Theory Y and applies the concept of "self-fulfilling prophecies" to organizational behavior.

Philip Selznick, in *Leadership in Administration*, anticipates many 1980s notions of "transformational leadership." He asserts that the function of an institutional leader is to help shape the environment in which the institution operates and to define new institutional directions through recruitment, training, and bargaining.

Alvin W. Gouldner, in "Cosmopolitans and Locals," identifies two latent social roles in organizations: "cosmopolitans," who have little loyalty to the employing organization, high commitment to specialized skills, and an outer-reference group orientation; and "locals," who have high loyalty to the employing organization, a low commitment to specialized skills, and an inner-reference group orientation.

1958   March and Simon, in *Organizations*, attempt to inventory and classify all that is worth knowing about the behavioral revolution in organization theory.

Leon Festinger, the father of cognitive dissonance theory, writes "The Motivating Effect of Cognitive Dissonance," which becomes the theoretical foundation for inequity theories of motivation.

Robert Tannenbaum and Warren H. Schmidt's *Harvard Business Review* article, "How to Choose a Leadership Pattern," describes "democratic management" and devises a leadership continuum ranging from authoritarian to democratic.

1959   Charles A. Lindblom's "The Science of 'Muddling Through'" rejects the rational model of decision making in favor of incrementalism.

Herzberg, Mausner, and Snyderman's *The Motivation to Work* puts forth the motivation-hygiene theory of worker motivation.

Richard M. Cyert and James G. March postulate that power and politics influence the formation of organizational goals. Their essay "A Behavioral Theory of Organizational Objectives" is a precursor of the power and politics school of organization theory.

John R. P. French and Bertram Raven identify five bases of power—expert, referent, reward, legitimate, and coercive—in "The Bases of Social Power." They argue that coercive and expert power bases are least effective.

1960   Richard Neustadt's *Presidential Power* asserts that a president's—or any executive's—essential power is that of persuasion.

Herbert Kaufman's *The Forest Ranger* examines how organizational and professional socialization can develop the will and capacity of employees to conform.

1961   Victor A. Thompson's *Modern Organization* finds "an imbalance between ability and authority" that causes bureaucratic dysfunctions.

Harold Koontz's "The Management Theory Jungle" describes the current state of management and organization theory as a "semantics jungle."

Burns and Stalker's *The Management of Innovation* articulates the need for different types of management systems— organic or mechanistic—under differing circumstances.

Rensis Likert's *New Patterns of Management* offers an empirically based defense of participatory management and organization development.

William G. Scott's *Academy of Management Journal* article, "Organization Theory: An Overview and an Appraisal," explains the relationship between systems theory and organization theory and the distinction between micro and macro perspectives in theory development.

Amitai Etzioni, in *A Comparative Analysis of Complex Organizations*, argues that organizational effectiveness is affected by the match between an organization's goal structure and its compliance structure.

1962   Robert Presthus's *The Organizational Society* introduces his classification of how individuals accommodate to organizations: "upwardmobiles" identify and accept the values of the organization; "indifferents" reject such values and find personal satisfaction off the job; and "ambivalents" want the rewards of organizational life but can't cope with the demands.

Peter Blau and W. Richard Scott, in *Formal Organizations: A Comparative Approach*, assert that all organizations include both a formal and an informal element, and it is impossible to know and understand the true structure of a formal organization without understanding its parallel informal organization.

David Mechanic's *Administrative Science Quarterly* article "Sources of Power of Lower Participants in Complex Organizations" anticipates the power and politics perspective of organization theory.

1963   Strauss, Schatzman, Bucher, Erlich, and Sabshin describe the maintenance of order in a hospital as a dynamic process operating within a framework of negotiated "contracts" among people and groups with different expectations and interests in "The Hospital and Its Negotiated Order."

Cyert and March demonstrate that corporations tend to "satisfice" rather than engage in economically rational profit-maximizing behavior in *A Behavioral Theory of the Firm*.

1964   Blake and Mouton's *The Managerial Grid* uses a graphic gridiron to explain management styles and their potential impacts on an organization development program.

Michel Crozier, in *The Bureaucratic Phenomenon*, defines a bureaucracy as "an organization which cannot correct its behavior by learning from its errors."

Bertram M. Gross publishes his two-volume *The Managing of Organizations*, a historical analysis of thinking about organizations from ancient times to the present.

1965   Don K. Price publishes *The Scientific Estate*, in which he posits that decision authority flows inexorably from the executive suite to the technical office.

Robert L. Kahn's *Organizational Stress* is the first major study of the mental health consequences of organizational role conflict and ambiguity.

James G. March edits the huge *Handbook of Organizations*, which sought to summarize all existing knowledge on organization theory and behavior.

1966 Katz and Kahn seek to unify the findings of behavioral science on organizational behavior through open systems theory in *The Social Psychology of Organizations*.

Think Magazine publishes David C. McClelland's article "That Urge to Achieve," in which he identifies two groups of people: the majority who are not concerned about achieving, and the minority who are challenged by the opportunity to achieve.

In *Changing Organizations,* Warren Bennis sounds a death knell for bureaucratic institutions, asserting they are inadequate for a future that will demand rapid organizational change, participatory management, and the growth of a more professionalized work force.

In "The Power of Power" (a chapter in *Varieties of Political Theory,* ed. David Easton), James G. March explores alternative definitions, concepts, and approaches for empirically studying social power in organizations and communities.

1967 James D. Thompson's *Organizations in Action* seeks to close the gap between open and closed systems theory by suggesting that organizations deal with environmental uncertainty by creating specific elements to cope with the outside world, which allows other elements to focus on the rational nature of technical operations.

Anthony Downs's *Inside Bureaucracy* seeks to develop laws and propositions to aid in predicting the behavior of bureaus and bureaucrats.

John Kenneth Galbraith's *The New Industrial State* asserts that control of modern corporations has passed to technostructures, and technostructures are more concerned with stability than profits.

Antony Jay, in *Management and Machiavelli,* applies political principles from Machiavelli's *The Prince* to modern organizational management.

1968 Harold Wilensky's *Organizational Intelligence* presents the pioneering study of the flow and perception of information in organizations.

In *Group Dynamics,* Dorwin Cartwright and Alvin Zander propose that the systematic study of group dynamics would advance knowledge of the nature of groups, how they are organized, and relationships among individuals, other groups, and larger institutions.

Walker and Lorsch grapple with the perennial structural issue of whether to design organizations by product or function in their *Harvard Business Review* article, "Organizational Choice: Product vs. Function."

Frederick Herzberg's *Harvard Business Review* article "One More Time, How Do You Motivate Employees?" catapults *motivators* or *satisfiers* and *hygiene factors* into the forefront of organizational motivation theory.

1969 Laurence J. Peter promulgates his principle that "in a hierarchy every employee tends to rise to his level of incompetence."

Lawrence and Lorsch call for a contingency theory that can deal with the appropriateness of different theories under differing circumstances, in

Organization and Environment. Organizations must solve the problem of simultaneous differentiation and integration.

Paul Hersey and Kenneth R. Blanchard's "Life Cycle Theory of Leadership" asserts that the appropriate leadership style for a particular situation depends on employees' education, experience level, achievement motivation, and willingness to accept responsibility.

1970 In "Expectancy Theory," John P. Campbell, Marvin D. Dunnette, Edward E. Lawler III, and Karl E. Weick Jr. theorize that people are motivated by calculating how much they want something, how much of it they think they will get, how likely it is their actions will cause them to get it, and how much others in similar circumstances have received.

Chris Argyris writes *Intervention Theory and Methods*, an enduring work about consulting for organizational change from the organizational behavior/ organization development perspective.

1971 Graham T. Allison's *Essence of Decision* demonstrates the inadequacies of the view that decisions of a government are made by a "single calculating decision-maker" who has control over the organizations and officials within the government.

Irving Janis's "Groupthink," first published in *Psychology Today*, proposes that group cohesion can lead to the deterioration of effective group decision making.

1972 Harlan Cleveland, in *The Future Executive*, asserts that decision making in the future will call for "continuous improvisation on a general sense of direction."

Charles Perrow's *Complex Organizations* is a major defense of bureaucratic forms of organization and an attack on writers who believe that bureaucracy can be easily, fairly, or inexpensively replaced.

Kast and Rosenzweig, in an *Academy of Management Journal* article, "General Systems Theory: Applications for Organization and Management," assess the success in applications of general systems theory and advocate contingency theory as a less abstract and more applicable theoretical approach.

1973 Jay Galbraith articulates the systems/contingency view that the amount of information an organization needs is a function of the levels of its uncertainty, interdependence of units and functions, and adaptation mechanisms in *Designing Complex Organizations*.

1974 In a report for the Carnegie Commission on Higher Education, Cohen and March introduce the phrase *organized anarchies* to communicate why colleges and universities are distinctive organizational forms with uniquely difficult leadership needs and problems. The report was published as the book *Leadership and Ambiguity: The American College President*.

Robert J. House and Terrance R. Mitchell's article "Path-Goal Theory of Leadership" offers an explanation for the effectiveness of certain leadership styles in given situations.

Victor H. Vroom's *Organizational Dynamics* article, "A New Look at Managerial Decision-Making," develops a useful model whereby leaders can diagnose situations to determine which leadership style is most appropriate.

Steven Kerr's article "On the Folly of Rewarding A, While Hoping for B" substantiates that many organizational reward systems are "fouled up"—they reward behaviors other than those they are seeking.

1975   Oliver E. Williamson uses economic market models to analyze organizational decisions about producing products and services internally or purchasing them, and assesses the implications of such decisions on, for example, organizational authority, in *Markets and Hierarchies: Analysis and Antitrust Implications*.

Behavior in Organizations, by Porter, Lawler, and Hackman, examines how individual-organizational relationships emerge and grow, including how groups can exert influence on individuals in organizations and how such social influences relate to work effectiveness.

1976   Michael Maccoby psychoanalytically interviews 250 corporate managers and discovers "The Gamesman," a manager whose main interest lies in "competitive activity where he can prove himself a winner."

Michael Jensen and William Meckling describe an organization as simply an extension of and a means for satisfying the interests of the myriad individuals and groups that affect and are affected by it, in "Agency Costs and the Theory of the Firm."

In "A Concept of Organizational Ecology," Eric Trist proposes a field concept of organizational population ecology. The field is created by the organizations whose interrelations constitute a system; thus, the system is the field, not its component organizations.

Herbert Kaufman concludes in *Are Government Organizations Immortal?* that governmental agencies experience a death rate of less than half the annual rate of business organizational demise.

1977   Hannan and Freeman's article "The Population Ecology of Organizations" proposes "populations of organizations" as the appropriate unit of analysis for understanding organizations.

John Meyer and Brian Rowan stress that the modern world contains socially constructed practices and norms that provide a framework for the creation and elaboration of formal organizations, in an *American Sociological Review* article, "Institutionalized Organizations: Formal Structure as Myth and Ceremony." Organizations as open systems gain legitimacy and support to the extent that they accept these norms as appropriate ways to organize.

Gerald Salancik and Jeffrey Pfeffer's article, "Who Gets Power—and How They Hold On to It," explains how power and politics help organizations adapt to their environment by reallocating critical resources to subunits that are performing tasks most vital to organizational survival.

In *Matrix*, Davis and Lawrence caution against using a matrix form of organization unless specific organizational conditions exist that are conducive to its success.

In *Men and Women of the Corporation*, Rosabeth Moss Kanter examines the unique problems women encounter with power and politics in organizations.

1978   Pfeffer and Salancik explain that the structure and behavior of an organization cannot be understood without also understanding its context in *External Control of Organizations: A Resource Dependence Perspective*. Organizations are not self-sufficient and must engage in exchanges with the environment in order to survive. They must acquire resources from their environment, and how important and how scarce these resources are determines the extent of organizational dependency.

Thomas J. Peters's *Organizational Dynamics* article, "Symbols, Patterns, and Settings: An Optimistic Case for Getting Things Done," is the first major analysis of symbolic management to gain significant attention in the mainstream literature of organization theory.

James MacGregor Burns's *Leadership* introduces the concept of transformational leadership, a leader who "looks for potential motives in followers, seeks to satisfy higher needs, and engages the full person of the follower."

1979   Rosabeth Moss Kanter's *Harvard Business Review* article, "Power Failure in Management Circuits," identifies organizational positions that tend to have power problems and argues that powerlessness is often more of a problem than power for organizations.

Structuring Organizations is published, the first book in Henry Mintzberg's integrative series "The Theory of Management Policy."

1980   Connolly, Conlon, and Deutsch argue that assessments of organizational effectiveness should employ multiple criteria in order to reflect the diverse interests of the various constituencies involved with organizations in "Organizational Effectiveness: A Multiple Constituency Approach."

Meryl Reis Louis's "Surprise and Sense Making: What Newcomers Experience in Entering Unfamiliar Organizational Settings" proposes that sense making by newcomers usually must rely on inadequate sources of information, which can lead them astray.

1981   W. Richard Scott offers three definitions of formal organizations in *Organizations: Rational, Natural and Open Systems*. The first sees organizations as highly formalized rational collectivities pursuing specific goals. The second views organizations as social systems with multiple interests, informal relations, and subgoals of participants. And the third views organizations as systems of interdependent activities embedded in and dependent on wider environments.

In "Organization Development: A Political Perspective," Anthony Cobb and Newton Margulies claim that organization development (OD) has developed more political sensitivity and sophistication than most critics realize, but that political activity by OD practitioners is fraught with serious utilitarian and values problems.

Jeffrey Pfeffer's *Power in Organizations* integrates the tenets and applications of the power and politics school of organization theory.

Thomas Ouchi's *Theory Z* and Pascale and Athos's *The Art of Japanese Management* popularize the Japanese management movement.

1982   Organizational culture becomes "hot" in the general business literature with such books as Peters and Waterman's *In Search of Excellence*, Deal and Kennedy's *Corporate Culture*, and *Business Week*'s cover story "Corporate Culture."

1983   Henry Mintzberg's *Power in and Around Organizations* explains the power and politics school of organizational theory as a coherent theory of management policy.

In *The Change Masters*, Rosabeth Moss Kanter defines change masters as architects of organizational change. They are the right people in the right places at the right time.

Meryl R. Louis's article "Organizations as Cultural-Bearing Milieux" becomes an early integrative statement of the organizational cultural perspective's assumptions and positions.

"Values in Organizational Theory and Management Education," by Michael Keeley, proposes that organizations exist by virtue of agreement on joint activities to achieve separate purposes of important constituencies, not to achieve organizational goals or purposes.

Ian Mitroff's *Stakeholders of the Organizational Mind* describes how the perceptions of internal and external stakeholders influence organizational behavior—particularly decision making about complex problems of organizational policy and design.

Pondy, Frost, Morgan, and Dandridge edit the first definitive volume on symbolic management, *Organizational Symbolism*.

Linda Smircich's "Organizations as Shared Meanings" examines how systems of commonly shared meanings develop and are sustained in organizations through symbolic communications processes and how shared meanings provide members of an organizational culture with a sense of commonality and a distinctive character.

1984   Sergiovanni and Corbally edit the first notable collection of papers on the organizational culture perspective, *Leadership and Organizational Culture*. Sergiovanni's opening chapter, "Cultural and Competing Perspectives in Administrative Theory and Practice," articulates the fundamental assumptions of the organizational culture and symbolic management perspective.

Siehl and Martin report the findings of a quantitative and qualitative empirical study of organizational culture in "The Role of Symbolic Management: How Can Managers Effectively Transmit Organizational Culture?"

1985   Edgar Schein writes the first edition of his highly regarded statement on organizational culture, *Organizational Culture and Leadership*.

In *The Irrational Organization*, Nils Brunsson postulates that rationality may lead to good decisions, but it decreases the probability of organizational action and change.

Administrative Development, by Muhammad A. Al-Buraey, combines western methodology and techniques with Islamic substance, values, and ethics to demonstrate how the Islamic perspective—as a system and a way of life—is a moving force in the process and realization of administrative development worldwide.

1986   Michael Harmon and Richard Mayer write a comprehensive text on public sector organization theory, *Organization Theory for Public Administration*.

Gareth Morgan's *Images of Organization* develops the art of reading and understanding organizations starting from the premise that theories of organization are based on metaphors—distinctive but partial mental images.

Jay B. Barney and William G. Ouchi provide an overview of themes, such as agency theory and price theory, which have contributed to organizational theory, in *Learning from Organizational Economics*.

1988   Michael Keeley combines concepts of multiple constituencies, organizational purposes, systems of justice, values, and organizational worth in the first comprehensive statement of *A Social-Contract Theory of Organizations*.

Quinn and Cameron compile *Paradox and Transformation*, a collection of essays on managing with paradoxes in complex organizations, rather than necessarily trying to eliminate them.

The *American Journal of Sociology* publishes a heated debate between the leading proponents and detractors of population ecology approaches to organization theory.

In the Age of the Smart Machine, by Shoshana Zuboff, examines the effects of information technology change on authority and hierarchy and thus on people and organizations.

1989   Rosabeth Moss Kanter's *When Giants Learn to Dance* explores how organizations can gain the advantages of smallness (flexibility) and size (staying power) at the same time.

1990   Sally Helgesen uses *diary studies* to explore how women leaders make decisions and gather and disperse information in organizations. In *The Female Advantage*, Helgesen suggests that "women may be the new Japanese" of management.

"In Praise of Hierarchy," by Elliott Jaques, argues that critics of hierarchy are misguided. Instead of needing new organizational forms, we need to learn how to manage hierarchies better.

In *Organizations, Uncertainties, and Risk*, Short and Clarke describe how organizational behavior is impacted by decision making under risk and uncertainty, and how, in turn, risk and uncertainty in the general society affect decision making in organizations.

Paul Goodman and Lee Sproull describe how organizational behavior is affected by new technologies. They argue in *Technology and Organizations* that technology's impacts are so profound that organizations must find new ways of conducting enterprise in order to survive.

Symbols and Artifacts: Views of the Corporate Landscape, by Pasquale Gagliardi, emphasizes corporate artifacts: buildings, objects, images, and forms that constitute corporate cultures. Gagliardi presents social-constructivist, phenomenological, and interpretive views of reality.

Peter Senge's highly influential management book *The Fifth Discipline* describes organizations with "learning disabilities" and how "learning organizations" defy the odds to overcome them.

David Ulrich and Dale Lake develop a theory of "inside competition" that emphasizes organizational capability. *Organizational Capability: Competing from the Inside Out* explains what "capability" is and how to develop competitiveness based on management action.

Lex Donaldson's *Academy of Management Review* article, "The Ethereal Hand: Organizational Economics and Management Theory," explains the potentialities and pitfalls of organizational economics.

Karl Weick's chapter "Technology as Equivoque: Sensemaking in New Technologies" examines cognitive processes that people use to adapt to work in environments where important events are unpredictable and often chaotic.

Publication of R. Roosevelt Thomas Jr.'s *Harvard Business Review* article, "From Affirmative Action to Affirming Diversity," introduces cultural diversity as an organizational concept and a definable goal.

Paul H. Rubin explains the costs of principal-agent relationships, how to minimize costs, and the effects of transaction costs on management decisions in *Managing Business Transactions*.

1991   Robert O. Lord and Karen J. Maher frame leadership in terms of how organizational "commandants" process information—rational, limited-capacity, expert, and cybernetic—and relate this to how other participants in the environment process information about commandants in *Information Processing: Linking Perceptions and Performance*.

Ryan and Oestreich's *Driving Fear Out of the Workplace: How to Overcome the Invisible Barriers to Quality, Productivity, and Innovation* explains the relationship between fear and workplace productivity. Management should take responsibility for fear in the workplace.

Manfred Kets de Vries demonstrates how individuals' rational and irrational behavior patterns influence organizations in *Organizations on the Couch*.

1992   Pauchant and Mitroff explore crisis-prone organizations and the psychological and emotional factors that enable managers to ignore the possibility of pending crises in *Transforming the Crisis-Prone Organization*.

Jeffrey Pfeffer's *Managing With Power* describes how to consolidate and use power for constructive organizational goals, urging managers to realize that if they do not use power, someone else will.

Barbara Czarniawska-Joerges explains sense making in organizational life—even when organizational behavior does not appear to make sense. *Exploring Complex Organizations: A Cultural Perspective* constitutes a cross-cultural and cross-contextual analysis of sense making in large organizations.

Organizational Architecture, by David Nadler, Marc Gerstein, and Robert Shaw, uses architecture as a metaphor to identify evolving forms and features of effective organizations, including autonomous work teams, high-performance work systems, spinouts, networks, self-designed organizations, and fuzzy boundaries.

In *Creating Corporate Culture: From Discord to Harmony*, Charles Hampden-Turner studies organizations facing challenges from evolving cultures, using the perspective of "core dilemmas." Dilemmas are two lemmas, or propositions, located on an axis with the organization located in between.

Joan Acker's "Gendering Organization Theory" argues that ordinary activities in organizations are not gender neutral. They perpetuate the "gendered substructure within the organization itself and within the wider society"—as well as in organization theory.

David Osborne and Ted Gaebler's best-selling book, *Reinventing Government: How the Entrepreneurial Spirit Is Transforming the Public Sector*, claims that public agencies are designed to protect against politicians and bureaucrats gaining too much power or misusing public money. Instead, we need "entrepreneurial government."

Ralph D. Stacey's book *Managing the Unknowable: Strategic Boundaries Between Order and Chaos* challenges the view that organizational success stems from stability, harmony, predictability, and stable equilibrium. Managers should embrace "unbounded instability" because disorder, chance, and irregularity can be beneficial.

Richard Beckhard and Wendy Pritchard's *Changing the Essence* discusses leadership behaviors that are necessary for initiating and managing fundamental organizational change.

1993   William Bergquist's *The Postmodern Organization* looks at premodern, modern, and postmodern views on five dimensions of organizational life: size and complexity, mission and boundaries, leadership, communication, and capital and worker values.

Cultural Diversity in Organizations, by Taylor Cox Jr., examines benefits and difficulties that may accrue to an organization from cultural diversity.

Ian Mitroff and Harold Linstone examine four ways of knowing, or "inquiry systems" for assisting decision making, in *The Unbounded Mind: Breaking the Chains of Traditional Business Thinking*.

Reengineering the Corporation, by Michael Hammer and James Champy, prescribes how to radically redesign a company's processes, organization, and culture to achieve quantum advances in performance.

In *The Corporate Culture*, James D. Woods and Jay H. Lucas explore what it is like to be gay in the corporate world and how to manage sexual identity in the workplace. They encourage openness in corporate practices, such as listing sexual preference along with gender and ethnicity in training, recruiting, and retention programs.

In "Nonlinear Dynamical Analysis: Assessing Systems Concepts in a Government Agency," Douglas Kiel suggests that nonlinear dynamics, or chaos theory, can be applied to public agencies because human organizations are indeed nonlinear systems.

Harrison M. Trice and Janice M. Beyer write a comprehensive treatise on organizational culture, *The Cultures of Work Organizations*.

Donald Kettl's *Sharing Power* adds to the growing debate about privatization of government goods and services, arguing that government must become a "smart buyer" when it contracts with the private sector.

Camilla Stivers's *Gender Images in Public Administration* examines the role that traditional public administrators — that is, professional experts, visionary leaders, guardians, and citizens — play in creating gender bias.

Michael Diamond's *The Unconscious Life of Organizations* provides a psychodynamic view of modern organizational complexities. Interactions from unconscious hierarchical dynamics and work relationships produce organizational values, rituals, emotions, and identities.

Christopher Pollitt's *Managerialism and the Public Services* applies managerialism to public administration.

Scott Cook and Dvora Yanow's *Culture and Organizational Learning* offers an explanation of organizational culture and organizational learning by suggesting that "the capacity of an organization to learn how to do what it does, where what it learns is possessed not by individual members of the organization but by the aggregate itself."

The Gore Report on Reinventing Government, Al Gore's "reinventing government" initiative, is published as the "National Performance Review."

1994   *Managing Chaos and Complexity in Government*, by Douglas Kiel, applies chaos theory to self-organization in public management. Kiel shows how the deep structures and processes of agency dynamics can foster learning and ability to cope with risk and uncertainty.

Bart Victor and Carroll Stephens sound a warning to those who advocate virtual offices, virtual occupations, and temporary working relationships without acknowledging the importance of "loyalty, dedication, and belonging" in "The Dark Side of the New Organizational Forms."

1995   Thierry C. Pauchant introduces the concept of "organizational existentialism" and urges the use of the existential tradition when examining managerial and organizational issues in *In Search of Meaning*.

Attribution theory—how people explain causes of their own and other's behavior—is explored through an organizational lens by Mark J. Martinko in *Attribution Theory: An Organizational Perspective*.

1996   *Organizational Communication: Theory and Behavior*'s editor, Peggy Yuhas Byers, presents a collection of essays on human communication in modern organizations.

Espejo, Schuhmann, Schwaninger, and Bilello address issues of organizational complexity and how organizational and managerial cybernetics can be useful in *Organizational Transformation and Learning: A Cybernetic Approach to Management*.

1997   In their book, *In Virtual Organizations and Beyond: Discover Imaginary Systems*, Hedberg, Dahlgren, Hansson, and Olve introduce "the imaginary organization," a new perspective on organizations where information technologies, alliances, and other networks inside and outside the organization are used to describe the entire system.

1998   "Technology as a Contingency Factor," by Richard M. Burton and Børge Obel, assesses technology's impacts on six dimensions of organization design: formalization, centralization, complexity, configuration, coordination and control, and incentives.

1999   David Thomas and John Gabarro compare experiences of successful minority and white executives and conclude that the paths to corporate success are distinctly different for people of color in *Breaking Through: The Making of Minority Executives in Corporate America*. They discuss the barriers that people of color have historically encountered but contend that minorities can overcome these barriers.

Shakespeare on Management: Wise Business Counsel from the Bard, by Jay M. Shafritz, offers a compelling twist to Shakespeare's literary contributions by exploring his thoughts on business and management.

In *Organizations Evolving* Howard Aldrich utilizes an evolutionary approach to explain the development of organizations and institutional change over time. Aldrich is concerned with interorganizational diversity and with the use of interdisciplinary perspectives for understanding why organizations persist and to identify factors that affect whether developing organizations accept or reject existing institutional forms.

Recommendation System: Decision Support for the Information Economy, by Edward A. Stohr and Sivakumar Viswanathan, examines the challenge of filtering out information in today's information-rich environment.

Janet Fulk and Gerardine DeSanctis's "Articulation of Communication Technology and Organizational Form" explores the connections between communication technology and organizational form in *Shaping Organization Form: Communication, Connection, and Community*.

2000   Glenn Carroll and Michael Hannan explore the theory, models, methods, and data used in demographic approaches to organizational studies in *Demography of Corporations and Industries*. They demonstrate how corporate populations change over time by exploring the processes of organizational founding, growth, decline, transformation, and mortality.

Scott Snook uses the 1994 shootdown of U.S. Blackhawk helicopters in Iraq as an example of organizational failure at the individual, group, and institutional levels in *Friendly Fire*. By examining these breakdowns individually and collectively, Snook offers insights as to how multiple factors cause system failures, not simply organizational shortcomings.

2001   Taylor Cox Jr. acknowledges the importance of organizational diversity, but asserts that "counting heads for the government" has failed to achieve and maintain multiculturalism in *Creating the Multicultural Organization: A Strategy for Capturing the Power of Diversity*. Cox introduces a proactive five-part model that includes strategies for creating a diverse and multicultural environment through leadership, research, and education.

Neil Fligstein's *The Architecture of Markets: An Economic Sociology of Twenty-First Century Capitalist Societies* uses a sociological and political-culture approach to explain the construction of American markets. His theory of "market institutionalism" offers insights into economic sociology that account for developments in globalization, American capitalism, and the role of government.

David Knoke employs a sociological perspective to assess intra- and interorganizational networks in *Changing Organizations: Business Networks in the New Political Economy*. Knoke considers ecology, institutionalism, power and resource dependence, transaction cost economics, organizational learning, and evolutionary theory as ways to understand a variety of contemporary corporate issues.

2002   In *Organizing America: Wealth, Power, and the Origins of Corporate Capitalism*, Charles Perrow asserts that the development of large bureaucratic organizations in America was both intentional and inevitable. Viewed from a sociological perspective, organizational entrepreneurs were able to take advantage of abundant resources and flourishing markets because many regulatory barriers that impede organizational development in other nations were eliminated by elected officials or legal decisions.

Although many students of organizational culture seek an integrated, shared set of cultural values, and the unity of cultural beliefs within an organization, Joanne Martin addresses the extent of diversity and the realities of differentiation in organizational culture—a fragmented culture—in *Organizational Culture: Mapping the Terrain*.

CHAPTER 1

Classical Organization Theory

No single date can be pinpointed as the beginning of serious thinking about how organizations work and how they should be structured and managed. One can trace writings about management and organizations as far back as the known origins of commerce. A lot can be learned from the early organizations of the Muslims, Hebrews, Greeks, and Romans. If we were to take the time, we could make the case that much of what we know about organization theory has its origins in ancient and medieval times. After all, it was Aristotle who first wrote of the importance of culture to management systems, ibn Taymiyyah who used the scientific method to outline the principles of administration within the framework of Islam, and Machiavelli who gave the world the definitive analysis of the use of power.

In order to provide an indication of organization theory's deep roots in earlier eras, we offer two examples of ancient wisdom on organization management. The first of our ancient examples is from the Book of Exodus, Chapter 18 (see the next page), in which Jethro, Moses' father-in-law, chastises Moses for failing to establish an organization through which he could delegate his responsibility for the administration of justice. In Verse 25, Moses accepts Jethro's advice; he "chose able men out of all Israel, and made them heads over the people, rulers of thousands, rulers of hundreds, rulers of fifties, and rulers of tens." Moses continued to judge the "hard cases," but his rulers judged "every small matter" themselves. Frederick Winslow Taylor would later develop this concept of "management by exception" for modern audiences.

In the second ancient example (the first selection in this chapter, "Socrates Discovers Generic Management"), Socrates anticipates the arguments for "generic management" and "principles of management" as he explains to Nicomachides that a leader who "knows what he needs, and is able to provide it, [can] be a good president, whether he have the direction of a chorus, a family, a city, or an army" (Xenophon, 1869). Socrates lists and discusses the duties of all good presidents of public and private institutions and emphasizes the similarities. This is the first known statement that organizations as entities are basically alike—and that a manager who could cope well with one would be equally adept at coping with others—even though their purposes and functions might be widely disparate.

Although it is great fun to delve into the wisdom of the ancients, most analysts of the origins of organization theory view the beginnings of the factory system in Great Britain in the eighteenth century as the birthplace of complex economic organizations and, consequently, of the field of organization theory. Classical organization theory, as its name implies, was the first theory of its kind, is considered traditional, and continues to be the base upon which other schools of organization theory have built. Thus, an understanding of classical organization theory is essential not only because of its historical interest but also, more importantly, because subsequent analyses and theories presume a knowledge of it.

Exodus Chapter 18

13 And it came to pass on the morrow, that Moses sat to judge the people: and the people stood by Moses from the morning unto the evening.

14 And when Moses' father-in-law saw all that he did to the people, he said, "What is this thing that thou doest to the people? why sittest thou thyself alone, and all the people stand by thee from morning unto even?"

15 And Moses said unto his father-in-law, "Because the people come unto me to inquire of God:

16 When they have a matter, they come unto me; and I judge between one and another, and I do make *them* know the statutes of God, and his laws."

17 And Moses' father-in-law said unto him, "The thing that thou doest is not good.

18 Thou wilt surely wear away, both thou, and this people that is with thee: for this thing is too heavy for thee: thou art not able to perform it thyself alone.

19 Hearken now unto my voice, I will give thee counsel, and God shall be with thee: Be thou for the people to God-ward, that thou mayest bring the causes unto God:

20 And thou shalt teach them ordinances and laws, and shalt shew them the way wherein they must walk, and the work that they must do.

21 Moreover thou shalt provide out of all the people able men, such as fear God, men of truth, hating covetousness; and place *such* over them, *to be* rulers of thousands, *and* rulers of hundreds, rulers of fifties, and rulers of tens:

22 And let them judge the people at all seasons and it shall be, *that* every great matter they shall bring unto thee, but every small matter they shall judge: so shall it be easier for thyself, and they shall bear *the burden* with thee.

23 If thou shalt do this thing, and God command thee so, then thou shalt be able to endure, and all this people shall also go to their place in peace."

24 So Moses hearkened to the voice of his father-in-law, and did all that he had said.

25 And Moses chose able men out of all Israel, and made them heads over the people, rulers of thousands, rulers of hundreds, rulers of fifties, and rulers of tens.

26 And they judged the people at all seasons: the hard cases they brought unto Moses, but every small matter they judged themselves.

27 And Moses let his father-in-law depart; and he went his way into his own land.

The classical school dominated organization theory into the 1930s and remains highly influential today (Merkle, 1980). Over the years, classical organization theory expanded and matured. Its basic tenets and assumptions, however, which were rooted in the industrial revolution of the 1700s and the professions of mechanical engineering, industrial engineering, and economics, have never been abandoned. They were only expanded upon, refined, adapted, and made more sophisticated. These fundamental tenets are:

1. Organizations exist to accomplish production-related and economic goals.
2. There is one best way to organize for production, and that way can be found through systematic, scientific inquiry.
3. Production is maximized through specialization and division of labor.
4. People and organizations act in accordance with rational economic principles.

The evolution of any theory must be viewed in context. The beliefs of early management theorists about how organizations worked or should work were a direct reflection of the societal values of their times—and the times were harsh. It was well into the twentieth century before the industrial workers of the United States and Europe began to enjoy even limited "rights" as organizational citizens. Workers were viewed not as individuals but as interchangeable parts in an industrial machine in which parts were made of flesh only when it was impractical to make them of steel.

The advent of power-driven machinery and hence of the modern factory system spawned our current concepts of economic organizations and organization for production. Power-driven equipment was expensive. Production workers could not purchase and use their own equipment as they had their own tools. Remember, the phrase for being fired, "get the sack," comes from the earliest days of the industrial revolution when a dismissed worker literally was given a sack in which to gather up his tools. Increasingly, workers without their own tools and often without any special skills had to gather for work where the equipment was—in factories. Expensive equipment had to produce enough output to justify its acquisition and maintenance costs.

The factory system presented managers of organizations with an unprecedented array of new problems. Managers had to arrange for heavy infusions of capital, plan and organize for reliable large-scale production, coordinate and control activities of large numbers of people and functions, contain costs (this was hardly a concern in "cottage industry" production), and maintain a trained and motivated work force.

Under the factory system, organizational success resulted from well-organized production systems that kept machines busy and costs under control. Industrial and mechanical engineers—and their machines—were the keys to production. Organizational structures and production systems were needed to take best advantage of the machines. Organizations, it was thought, should work like machines, using people, capital, and machines as their parts. Just as industrial engineers sought to design "the best" machines to keep factories productive, industrial and mechanical engineering–type thinking dominated theories about "the best way" to organize for production. Thus, the first theories of organizations were concerned primarily with the anatomy, or structure, of formal organizations. This was the milieu, or the environment, the mode of thinking, that shaped and influenced the tenets of classical organization theory.

Centralization of equipment and labor in factories, division of specialized labor, management of specialization, and economic paybacks on factory equipment all were concerns of the Scottish economist Adam Smith's work, *An Inquiry into the Nature and Causes of the Wealth of Nations* (1776). The historian Arnold Toynbee (1956) identified Adam Smith (1723–1790) and James Watt (1736–1819) as the two individuals who were most responsible for pushing the world into industrialization. Watt, of course, invented the steam engine.

Smith, who is considered the father of the academic discipline of economics, provided the intellectual foundation for laissez-faire capitalism. *The Wealth of Nations* devotes its first chapter, "Of the Division of Labour," to a discussion of the optimum organization of a pin factory. Why? Because specialization of labor was one of the pillars of Smith's "invisible hand" market mechanism in which the greatest rewards would go to those who were the most efficient in the competitive marketplace. Traditional pin makers could produce only a few dozen pins a day. When organized in a factory with each worker performing a limited operation, they could produce tens of thousands a day. Smith's "Of the Division of Labour" is reprinted here because, coming as it did at the dawn of the industrial revolution, it is the most famous and influential statement on the economic rationale of the factory system. Smith revolutionized thinking about economics and organizations. Thus we have operationally defined 1776, the year in which *Wealth of Nations* was published, as the beginning point of organization theory as an applied science and academic discipline. Besides, 1776 was a good year for other events as well.

In 1856, Daniel C. McCallum (1815–1878), the visionary general superintendent of the New York and Erie Railroad, elucidated general principles of organization that "may be regarded as settled and necessary." His principles included division of responsibilities, power commensurate with responsibilities, and a reporting system that allowed managers to know promptly if responsibilities were "faithfully executed" and to identify errors and "delinquent" subordinates. McCallum, who is also credited with creating the first modern organization chart, had an enormous influence on the managerial development of the American railroad industry.

In systematizing America's first big business before the Civil War, McCallum provided the model principles and procedures of management for the big businesses that would follow after the war. He became so much *the* authority on running railroads that, as a major general during the Civil War, he was chosen to run the Union's military rail system. Although McCallum was highly influential as a practitioner, he was no scholar, and the only coherent statement of his general principles comes from an annual report he wrote for the New York and Erie Railroad. Excerpts from his "Superintendent's Report" of March 25, 1856, are reprinted in this chapter.

During the 1800s, two practicing managers in the United States independently discovered that generally applicable principles of administration could be determined through systematic, scientific investigation—about thirty years before Frederick Winslow Taylor's *Principles of Scientific Management* or Henri Fayol's *General and Industrial Management*. The first, Captain Henry Metcalfe (1847–1917) of the United States Army's Frankford Arsenal in Philadelphia, urged managers to record production events and experiences systematically so that they could use the information to improve production processes. He published his propositions in *The Cost of Manufactures and the Administration of Workshops, Public and Private* (1885), which also pioneered in the application of "prescientific management" methods to the problems of managerial control and asserted that there is a "science of administration" based upon principles discoverable by diligent observation. Although Metcalfe's work is important historically, it is so similar to that of Taylor and others that it is not included here as a selection.

The second prescientific management advocate of the 1880s was Henry R. Towne (1844–1924), cofounder and president of the Yale & Towne Manufacturing Company. In 1886 Towne proposed that shop management was of equal importance to engineering management and that the American Society of Mechanical Engineers (ASME) should take a leadership role in establishing a multicompany, engineering/management "database" on shop practices or "the management of works." The information could then be shared among established and new enterprises. Several years later, ASME adopted his proposal. The paper he presented to the society, "The Engineer as Economist," was published in *Transactions of the American Society of Mechanical Engineers* (1886) and is reprinted here. Historians have often considered it the first call for scientific management.

Interestingly, Towne had several significant associations with Frederick Winslow Taylor. The two of them were fellow draftsmen at the Midvale Steel works during the 1880s. Towne gave Taylor one of his first true opportunities to succeed at applying scientific management principles at Yale & Towne in 1904. Towne also nominated Taylor for the presidency of ASME in 1906 and thus provided him with an international forum for advocating scientific management. Upon election, Taylor promptly reorganized the ASME according to scientific management principles.

While the ideas of Adam Smith, Frederick Winslow Taylor, and others are still dominant influences on the design and management of organizations, it was Henri Fayol (1841–1925), a French executive engineer, who developed the first comprehensive theory of management. While Taylor was tinkering with the technology employed by the individual worker, Fayol was theorizing about all of the elements necessary to organize and manage a major corporation. Fayol's major work, *Administration Industrielle et Générale* (published in France in 1916), was almost ignored in the United States until Constance Storr's English translation, *General and Industrial Management,* was published in 1949. Since that time, Fayol's theoretical contributions have been widely recognized, and his work is considered fully as significant as that of Taylor.

Fayol believed that his concept of management was universally applicable to every type of organization. Whereas he had six principles—technical (production of goods), commercial (buying, selling, and exchange activities), financial (raising and using capital), security (protection of property and people), accounting, and managerial (coordination, control, organization, planning, and command of people)—Fayol's primary interest and emphasis was on his final principle, managerial. It addressed such variables as division of work, authority and responsibility, discipline, unity of command, unity of direction, subordination of individual interest to general interest, remuneration of personnel, centralization, scalar chains, order, equity, stability of personnel tenure, initiative, and esprit de corps. Reprinted here is Fayol's "General Principles of Management," a chapter from his *General and Industrial Management.*

About 100 years after Adam Smith declared the factory to be the most appropriate means of mass production, Frederick Winslow Taylor and a group of his followers were "spreading the gospel" that factory workers could be much more productive if their work were designed scientifically. Taylor, the acknowledged father of the scientific management movement, pioneered the development of time and motion studies, originally under the name "Taylorism," or the "Taylor system." Taylorism, or its successor, "scientific management," was not a single invention but rather a series of methods and organizational arrangements designed by Taylor and his associates to increase the efficiency and speed of machine-shop production. Premised on the notion that there was "one best way" for accomplishing any given task, Taylor's scientific management sought to increase output by using scientific methods to discover the fastest, most efficient, and least fatiguing production methods.

The job of the scientific manager, once the "one best way" was found, was to impose this procedure on his or her organization. Classical organization theory derives from a corollary of this proposition. If there was one best way to accomplish any given production task, then correspondingly, there must also be one best way to accomplish any task of social organization—including organizing firms. Such principles of social organization were assumed to exist and to be waiting to be discovered by diligent scientific observation and analysis.

Scientific management, as espoused by Taylor, also contained a powerful puritanical social message. Taylor (1911) offered scientific management as the way for firms to increase profits, get rid of unions, "increase the thrift and virtue of the working classes," and raise productivity so that the broader society could enter a new era of harmony based on higher consumption of mass-produced goods by members of the laboring classes.

Scientific management emerged as a national movement during a series of events in 1910. The railroad companies in the eastern states of the United States filed for increased freight rates with the Interstate Commerce Commission. The railroads had been receiving poor press—they were being blamed for (among many other things) a cost-price squeeze that was bankrupting farmers—and the rate hearings received extensive media coverage. Louis D. Brandeis, a self-styled populist lawyer who would later be a distinguished Supreme Court justice, took the case against the railroads without pay. Brandeis called in Harrington Emerson, a consultant who had "systematized" the Santa Fe Railroad, to testify that the railroads did not need increased rates: they could "save a million dollars a day" by using what Brandeis initially called "scientific management" methods (Urwick, 1956). At first, Taylor was reluctant to use the phrase because it sounded too academic. But the ICC hearings meant that the national scientific management boom was underway, and Taylor was its leader.

Taylor had a profound—almost revolutionary—effect on the fields of business and public administration. He gained credence for the notion that organizational operations could be planned and controlled systematically by experts using scientific principles. Many of Taylor's concepts and precepts are still in use today. The legacy of scientific management is substantial. Taylor's best-known work is his 1911 book *The Principles of Scientific Management,* but he also wrote numerous other accounts on the subject. Reprinted here is an article, also entitled "The Principles of Scientific Management," which was the summary of an address Taylor gave on March 3, 1915, two weeks before his death.

Several of Taylor's associates subsequently built reputations for innovations that utilized principles of scientific management, including Frank Gilbreth (1868–1924) and Lillian Gilbreth (1878–1972), leaders in developing the tools and techniques of "time and motion study" including the "therblig" (Spriegel & Myers, 1953); Henry Laurence Gantt (1861–1919), who invented the Gantt chart for planning work output (Alford, 1932); and Carl O. Barth (1860–1939) who, among his other accomplishments, in 1908 convinced the dean of the new Harvard Business School to adopt *Taylorism* as the "foundation concept" of modern management (Urwick, 1956). Frank and Lillian Gilbreth also achieved wide public recognition for the book (1948) and movie, *Cheaper by the Dozen,* which described the couple's efforts to raise their twelve children using scientific management principles and practices.

In contrast with the fervent advocates of scientific management, Max Weber (1864–1920) was a brilliant analytical sociologist who happened to study bureaucratic organizations. It is hardly worth mentioning that bureaucracy has emerged as a dominant feature of the contemporary world. Virtually everywhere one looks in both developed and developing nations, economic, social, and political life is influenced extensively by bureaucratic organizations. *Bureaucracy* refers to a specific set of structural arrangements. It is also used to refer to specific patterns of behavior—patterns that are not restricted to formal bureaucracies. It is widely assumed that the structural characteristics of organizations properly defined as bureaucratic influence the behavior of individuals, whether clients or bureaucrats, who interact with them. Contemporary thinking along these lines began with the work of Max Weber. His analysis of bureaucracy, first published in 1922, remains the single most influential statement and the point of departure for all further analyses on the subject (including those of the "modern" structuralists in Chapter 4).

Drawing upon studies of ancient bureaucracies in Egypt, Rome, China, and the Byzantine Empire, as well as on the more modern ones emerging in Europe during the nineteenth and early part of the twentieth centuries, Weber used an "ideal-type" approach to extrapolate from the real world the central core of features characteristic of the most fully developed bureaucratic form of organization. Weber's "Bureaucracy," which is included here, is neither a description of reality nor a statement of normative preference. In fact, Weber feared the potential implications of bureaucracies. Rather, his ideal-type bureaucracy is merely an identification of the major variables or features that characterize this type of social institution.

Luther Gulick's "Notes on the Theory of Organization," which was influenced heavily by the work of Henri Fayol, is one of the best-known statements of the "principles" approach to managing the functions of organizations. It appeared in *Papers on the Science of Administration*, a collection that Gulick and Lyndall Urwick edited in 1937. Here Gulick introduced his famous mnemonic, POSDCORB, which stood for the seven major functions of executive management—planning, organizing, staffing, directing, coordinating, reporting, and budgeting. Gulick's principles of administration also included unity of command and span of control. Overall, *Papers on the Science of Administration* was a statement of the "state of the art" of organization theory. The study of organizations through analysis of management functions continues within the field of organization theory.

Daniel A. Wren (1972) observed that "the development of a body of knowledge about how to manage has . . . evolved within a framework of the economic, social, and political facets of various cultures. Management thought is both a process in and a product of its cultural environment." The selections we have chosen to represent the classical school of organization theory vividly demonstrate Wren's thesis. Looking through today's lenses, it is tempting to denigrate the contributions of the classicalists—to view them as narrow and simplistic. In the context of their times, however, they were brilliant pioneers. Their thinking provided invaluable foundations for the field of organization theory, and their influence upon organization theory and theorists continues today.

REFERENCES

Al-Buraey, M. A. (1985). *Administrative development: An Islamic perspective.* London: Kegan Paul International.

Alford, L. P. (1932). *Henry Laurence Gantt: Leader in industry.* New York: Harper & Row.

Babbage, C. (1832). *On the economy of machinery and manufactures.* Philadelphia, PA: Carey & Lea.

Fayol, H. (1949). *General and industrial management.* Trans. C. Storrs. London: Pitman. (Originally published in 1916.)

George, C. S., Jr. (1972). *The history of management thought.* 2d ed. Englewood Cliffs, NJ: Prentice Hall.

Gilbreth, F. B., Jr., & E. G. Carey (1948). *Cheaper by the dozen.* New York: Grosset & Dunlap.

Gulick, L. (1937). Notes on the theory of organization. In L. Gulick & L. Urwick, eds., *Papers on the science of administration* (pp. 3–34). New York: Institute of Public Administration.

McCallum, D. C. (1856). Superintendent's report, March 25, 1856. In *Annual report of the New York and Erie Railroad Company for 1855.* In A. D. Chandler Jr., ed., *The railroads* (pp. 101–108). New York: Harcourt Brace Jovanovich.

Merkle, J. A. (1980). *Management and ideology: The legacy of the international scientific management movement*. Berkeley, CA: University of California Press.

Metcalfe, H. (1885). *The cost of manufactures and the administration of workshops, public and private*. New York: Wiley.

Smith, A. (1776). Of the division of labour. In *An inquiry into the nature and causes of the wealth of nations* (chap. 1, pp. 5–15). Printed for W. Strahan and T. Cadell in the Strand, London, 1776.

Spriegel, W. R., & C. E. Myers, eds. (1953). *The writings of the Gilbreths*. Homewood, IL: Irwin.

Taylor, F. W. (1911). *The principles of scientific management*. New York: Norton.

Taylor, F. W. (1916, December). The principles of scientific management: *Bulletin of the Taylor Society*. An abstract of an address given by the late Dr. Taylor before the Cleveland Advertising Club, March 3, 1915.

Towne, H. R. (1886, May). The engineer as an economist. *Transactions of the American Society of Mechanical Engineers, 7*, 428–432. Paper presented at a meeting of the Society, Chicago, IL.

Toynbee, A. (1956). *The industrial revolution*. Boston: Beacon Press. (Originally published in 1884.)

Urwick, L. (1956). *The golden book of management*. London: Newman, Neame.

Weber, M. (1922). Bureaucracy. In H. Gerth & C. W. Mills, eds., *Max Weber: Essays in sociology*. Oxford, UK: Oxford University Press.

Wren, D. A. (1972). *The evolution of management thought*. New York: Ronald Press.

Xenophon (1869). *The memorabilia of Socrates*. Trans. Rev. J. S. Watson. New York: Harper & Row.

1

Socrates Discovers Generic Management

Xenophon

Seeing Nicomachides, one day, coming from the assembly for the election of magistrates, he asked him, "Who have been chosen generals, Nicomachides?"

"Are not the Athenians the same as ever, Socrates?" he replied; "for they have not chosen me, who am worn out with serving on the list, both as captain and centurion, and with having received so many wounds from the enemy (he then drew aside his robe, and showed the scars of the wounds), but have elected Antisthenes, who has never served in the heavy-armed infantry, nor done anything remarkable in the cavalry, and who indeed knows nothing, but how to get money."

"Is it not good, however, to know this," said Socrates, "since he will then be able to get necessaries for the troops?"

"But merchants," replied Nicomachides, "are able to collect money; and yet would not on that account, be capable of leading an army."

"Antisthenes, however," continued Socrates, "is given to emulation, a quality necessary in a general. Do you not know that whenever he has been chorus-manager he has gained the superiority in all his choruses?"

"But, by Jupiter," rejoined Nicomachides, "there is nothing similar in managing a chorus and an army."

"Yet Antisthenes," said Socrates, "though neither skilled in music nor in teaching a chorus, was able to find out the best masters in these departments."

"In the army, accordingly," exclaimed Nicomachides, "he will find others to range his troops for him, and others to fight for him!"

"Well, then," rejoined Socrates, "if he finds out and selects the best men in military affairs, as he has done in the conduct of his choruses, he will probably attain superiority in this respect also; and it is likely that he will be more willing to spend money for a victory in war on behalf of the whole state, than for a victory with a chorus in behalf of his single tribe."

"Do you say, then, Socrates," said he, "that it is in the power of the same man to manage a chorus well, and to manage an army well?"

"I say," said Socrates, "that over whatever a man may preside, he will, if he knows what he needs, and is able to provide it, to be a good president, whether he have the direction of a chorus, a family, a city, or an army."

"By Jupiter, Socrates," cried Nicomachides, "I should never have expected to hear from you that good managers of a family would also be good generals."

"Come, then," proceeded Socrates, "let us consider what are the duties of each of them, that we may understand whether they are the same, or are in any respect different."

"By all means."

"Is it not, then, the duty of both," asked Socrates, "to render those under their command obedient and submissive to them?"

"Unquestionably."

"Is it not also the duty of both to intrust various employments to such as are fitted to execute them?"

"That is also unquestionable."

"To punish the bad, and to honor the good, too, belongs, I think, to each of them."

Source: Xenophon, *The Anabasis or Expedition of Cyrus and the Memorabilia of Socrates,* trans. J. S. Watson (New York: Harper & Row, 1869), 430–433.

"Undoubtedly."

"And is it not honorable in both to render those under them well-disposed toward them?"

"That also is certain."

"And do you think it for the interest of both to gain for themselves allies and auxiliaries or not?"

"It assuredly is for their interest."

"Is it not proper for both also to be careful of their resources?"

"Assuredly."

"And is it not proper for both, therefore, to be attentive and industrious in their respective duties?"

"All these particulars," said Nicomachides, "are common alike to both; but it is not common to both to fight."

"Yet both have doubtless enemies," rejoined Socrates.

"That is probably the case," said the other.

"Is it not for the interest of both to gain the superiority over those enemies?"

"Certainly; but to say something on that point, what, I ask, will skill in managing a household avail, if it be necessary to fight?"

"It will doubtless in that case, be of the greatest avail," said Socrates; "for a good manager of a house, knowing that nothing is so advantageous or profitable as to get the better of your enemies when you contend with them, nothing so unprofitable and prejudicial as to be defeated, will zealously seek and provide every thing that may conduce to victory, will carefully watch and guard against whatever tends to defeat, will vigorously engage if he sees that his force is likely to conquer, and, what is not the least important point, will cautiously avoid engaging if he finds himself insufficiently prepared. Do not, therefore, Nicomachides," he added, "despise men skillful in managing a household; for the conduct of private affairs differs from that of public concerns only in magnitude; in other respects they are similar; but what is most to be observed, is, that neither of them are managed without men, and that private matters are not managed by one species of men, and public matters by another; for those who conduct public business make use of men not at all differing in nature from those whom the managers of private affairs employ; and those who know how to employ them conduct either public or private affairs judiciously, while those who do not know will err in the management of both."

2
Of the Division of Labour
Adam Smith

The greatest improvement in the productive powers of labour, and the greater part of the skill, dexterity, and judgment with which it is any where directed, or applied, seem to have been the effects of the division of labour.

The effects of the division of labour, in the general business of society, will be more easily understood, by considering in what manner it operates in some particular manufactures. It is commonly supposed to be carried furthest in some very trifling ones; not perhaps that it really is carried further in them than in others of more importance: but in those trifling manufactures which are destined to supply the small wants of but a small number of people, the whole number of workmen must necessarily be small; and those employed in every different branch of the work can often be collected into the same workhouse, and placed at once under the view of the spectator. In those great manufactures, on the contrary, which are destined to supply the great wants of the great body of the people, every different branch of the work employs so great a number of workmen, that it is impossible to collect them all into the same workhouse. We can seldom see more, at one time, than those employed in one single branch. Though in such manufactures, therefore, the work may really be divided into a much greater number of parts, than in those of a more trifling nature, the division is not near so obvious, and has accordingly been much less observed.

To take an example, therefore, from a very trifling manufacture; but one in which the division of labour has been very often taken notice of, the trade of the pin-maker; a workman not educated to this business (which the division of labour has rendered a distinct trade), nor acquainted with the use of the machinery employed in it (to the invention of which the same division of labour has probably given occasion), could scarce, perhaps, with his utmost industry, make one pin in a day, and certainly could not make twenty. But in the way in which this business is now carried on, not only the whole work is a peculiar trade, but it is divided into a number of branches, of which the greater part are likewise peculiar trades. One man draws out the wire, another straights it, a third cuts it, a fourth points it, a fifth grinds it at the top for receiving the head; to make the head requires two or three distinct operations; to put it on, is a peculiar business, to whiten the pins is another; it is even a trade by itself to put them into the paper; and the important business of making a pin is, in this manner, divided into about eighteen distinct operations, which, in some manufactories, are all performed by distinct hands, though in others the same man will sometimes perform two or three of them. I have seen a small manufactory of this kind where ten men only were employed, and where some of them consequently performed two or three distinct operations. But though they were very poor, and therefore but indifferently accommodated with the necessary machine, they could, when they exerted themselves, make among them about twelve pounds of pins in a day. There are in a pound upwards of four thousand pins of a middling size. Those ten persons, therefore, could make among them upwards of forty-eight thousand pins in a day. Each person,

Source: Adam Smith, An *inquiry into the nature and causes of the wealth of nations* (1776), chap. 1; footnotes omitted.

therefore, making a tenth part of forty-eight thousand pins, might be considered as making four thousand eight hundred pins in a day. But if they had all wrought separately and independently, and without any of them having been educated to this peculiar business, they certainly could not each of them have made twenty, perhaps not one pin in a day; that is, certainly, not the two hundred and fortieth, perhaps not the four thousand eight hundredth part of what they are at present capable of performing, in consequence of a proper division and combination of their different operations.

In every other art and manufacture, the effects of the division of labour are similar to what they are in this very trifling one; though, in many of them, the labour can neither be so much subdivided, nor reduced to so great a simplicity of operation. The division of labour, however, so far as it can be introduced, occasions, in every art, a proportionable increase of the productive powers of labour. The separation of different trades and employments from one another, seems to have taken place, in consequence of this advantage. This separation too is generally carried furthest in those countries which enjoy the highest degree of industry and improvement; what is the work of one man in a rude state of society, being generally that of several in an improved one. In every improved society, the farmer is generally nothing but a farmer; the manufacturer, nothing but a manufacturer. The labour too which is necessary to produce any one complete manufacture, is almost always divided among a great number of hands. How many different trades are employed in each branch of the linen and woollen manufactures, from the growers of the flax and the wool, to the bleachers and smoothers of the linen, or to the dyers and dressers of the cloth! The nature of agriculture, indeed, does not admit of so many subdivisions of labour, nor of so complete a separation of one business from another, as manufactures. It is impossible to separate so entirely, the business of the grazier from that of the corn-farmer, as the trade of the

carpenter is commonly separated from that of the smith. The spinner is almost always a distinct person from the weaver; but the ploughman, the harrower, the sower of the seed, and the reaper of the corn, are often the same. The occasions for those different sorts of labour returning with the different seasons of the year, it is impossible that one man should be constantly employed in any one of them. This impossibility of making so complete and entire a separation of all the different branches of labour employed in agriculture, is perhaps the reason why the improvement of the productive powers of labour in this art, does not always keep pace with their improvement in manufactures. The most opulent nations, indeed, generally excel all their neighbours in agriculture as well as in manufactures; but they are commonly more distinguished by their superiority in the latter than in the former. Their lands are in general better cultivated, and having more labour and expence bestowed upon them, produce more in proportion to the extent and natural fertility of the ground. But this superiority of produce is seldom much more than in proportion to the superiority of labour and expence. In agriculture, the labour of the rich country is not always much more productive than that of the poor; or, at least, it is never so much more productive, as it commonly is in manufactures. The corn of the rich country, therefore, will not always, in the same degree of goodness, come cheaper to market than that of the poor. The corn of Poland, in the same degree of goodness is as cheap as that of France, notwithstanding the superior opulence and improvement of the latter country. The corn of France is, in the corn provinces, fully as good, and most years nearly about the same price with the corn of England, though, in opulence and improvement, France is perhaps inferior to England. The corn lands of England, however, are better cultivated than those of France, and the corn lands of France are said to be much better cultivated than those of Poland. But though the poor country, notwithstanding the inferiority of its cultivation, can, in some measure, rival the rich in the cheapness and goodness of its corn, it can pretend to no such competition in its manufactures; at least if those manufactures suit the soil, climate, and situation of the rich country. The silks of France are better and cheaper than those of England, because the silk manufacture, at least under the present high duties upon the importation of raw silk, does not so well suit the climate of England as that of France. But the hardware and the coarse woollens of England are beyond all comparison superior to those of France, and much cheaper too in the same degree of goodness. In Poland there are said to be scarce any manufactures of any kind, a few of those coarser household manufactures excepted, without which no country can well subsist.

This great increase of the quantity of work, which, in consequence of the division of labour, the same number of people are capable of performing, is owing to three different circumstances; first, to the increase of dexterity in every particular workman; secondly, to the saving of the time which is commonly lost in passing from one species of work to another; and lastly, to the invention of a great number of machines which facilitate and abridge labour, and enable one man to do the work of many.

First, the improvement of the dexterity of the workman necessarily increases the quantity of the work he can perform; and the division of labour, by reducing every man's business to some one simple operation, and by making this operation the sole employment of his life, necessarily increases very much the dexterity of the workman. A common smith, who, though accustomed to handle the hammer, has never been used to make nails, if upon some particular occasion he is obliged to attempt it, will scarce, I am assured, be able to make above two or three hundred nails in a day, and those too very bad ones. A smith who has been accustomed to make nails, but whose sole or principal business has not been that of a nailer, can seldom with his utmost diligence make more than eight hundred or a

thousand nails in a day. I have seen several boys under twenty years of age who had never exercised any other trade but that of making nails, and who, when they exerted themselves, could make, each of them, upwards of two thousand three hundred nails in a day. The making of a nail, however, is by no means one of the simplest operations. The same person blows the bellows, stirs or mends the fire as there is occasion, heats the iron, and forges every part of the nail: In forging the head too he is obliged to change his tools. The different operations into which the making of a pin, or of a metal button, is subdivided, are all of them much more simple, and the dexterity of the person, of whose life it has been the sole business to perform them, is usually much greater. The rapidity with which some of the operations of those manufactures are performed, exceeds what the human hand could, by those who had never seen them, be supposed capable of acquiring.

Secondly, the advantage which is gained by saving the time commonly lost in passing from one sort of work to another, is much greater than we should at first view be apt to imagine it. It is impossible to pass very quickly from one kind of work to another, that is carried on in a different place, and with quite different tools. A country weaver, who cultivates a small farm, must lose a good deal of time in passing from his loom to his field, and from the field to his loom. When the two trades can be carried on in the same workhouse, the loss of time is no doubt much less. It is even in this case, however, very considerable. A man commonly saunters a little in turning his hand from one sort of employment to another. When he first begins the new work he is seldom very keen and hearty; his mind, as they say, does not go to it, and for some time he rather trifles than applies to good purpose. The habit of sauntering and of indolent careless application, which is naturally, or rather necessarily acquired by every country workman who is obliged to change his work and his tools every half hour, and to apply his hand in twenty different ways almost every day of his life, renders him almost always slothful and lazy, and incapable of any vigorous application even on the most pressing occasions. Independent, therefore, of his deficiency in point of dexterity, this cause alone must always reduce considerably the quantity of work which he is capable of performing.

Thirdly, and lastly, every body must be sensible how much labour is facilitated and abridged by the application of proper machinery. It is unnecessary to give any example. I shall only observe, therefore, that the invention of all those machines by which labour is so much facilitated and abridged, seems to have been originally owing to the division of labour. Men are much more likely to discover easier and readier methods of attaining any object, when the whole attention of their minds is directed towards that single object, than when it is dissipated among a great variety of things. But in consequence of the division of labour, the whole of every man's attention comes naturally to be directed towards some one very simple object. It is naturally to be expected, therefore, that some one or other of those who are employed in each particular branch of labour should soon find out easier and readier methods of performing their own particular work, wherever the nature of it admits of such improvement. A great part of the machines made use of in those manufactures in which labour is most subdivided, were originally the inventions of common workmen, who, being each of them employed in some very simple operation, naturally turned their thoughts towards finding out easier and readier methods of performing it. Whoever has been much accustomed to visit such manufactures, must frequently have been shewn very pretty machines, which were the inventions of such workmen, in order to facilitate and quicken their own particular part of the work. In the first fire-engines, a boy was constantly employed to open and shut alternately the communication between the boiler and the cylinder, according as the piston either ascended or descended. One of those boys, who loved to play with his companions, observed that, by

tying a string from the handle of the valve which opened this communication to another part of the machine, the valve would open and shut without his assistance, and leave him at liberty to divert himself with his playfellows. One of the greatest improvements that has been made upon this machine, since it was first invented, was in this manner the discovery of a boy who wanted to save his own labour.

All the improvements in machinery, however, have by no means been the inventions of those who had occasion to use the machines. Many improvements have been made by the ingenuity of the makers of the machines, when to make them become the business of a peculiar trade; and some by that of those who are called philosophers or men of speculation, whose trade it is not to do any thing, but to observe every thing; and who, upon that account, are often capable of combining together the powers of the most distant and dissimilar objects. In the progress of society, philosophy or speculation becomes, like every other employment, the principal or sole trade and occupation of a particular class of citizens. Like every other employment too, it is subdivided into a great number of different branches, each of which affords occupation to a peculiar tribe or class of philosophers; and this subdivision of employment in philosophy, as well as in every other business, improves dexterity, and saves time. Each individual becomes more expert in his own peculiar branch, more work is done upon the whole, and the quantity of science is considerably increased by it.

It is the great multiplication of the productions of all the different arts, in consequence of the division of labour, which occasions, in a well-governed society, that universal opulence which extends itself to the lowest ranks of the people. Every workman has a great quantity of his own work to dispose of beyond what he himself has occasion for; and every other workman being exactly in the same situation, he is enabled to exchange a great quantity of his own goods for a great quantity, or, what comes to the same thing, for the price of a great quantity of theirs. He supplies them abundantly with what they have occasion for, and they accommodate him as amply with what he has occasion for, and a general plenty diffuses itself through all the different ranks of the society.

Observe the accommodation of the most common artificer or day-labourer in a civilized and thriving country, and you will perceive that the number of people of whose industry a part, though but a small part, has been employed in procuring him his accommodation, exceeds all computation. The woollen coat, for example, which covers the day-labourer, as coarse and rough as it may appear, is the produce of the joint labour of a great multitude of workmen. The shepherd, the sorter of the wool, the woolcomber or carder, the dyer, the scribbler, the spinner, the weaver, the fuller, the dresser, with many others, must all join their different arts in order to complete even this homely production. How many merchants and carriers, besides, must have been employed in transporting the materials from some of those workmen to others who often live in a very distant part of the country! How much commerce and navigation in particular, how many ship-builders, sailors, sail-makers, rope-makers, must have been employed in order to bring together the different drugs made use of by the dyer, which often come from the remotest corners of the world! What a variety of labour too is necessary in order to produce the tools of the meanest of those workmen! To say nothing of such complicated machines as the ship of the sailor, the mill of the fuller, or even the loom of the weaver, let us consider only what a variety of labour is requisite in order to form that very simple machine, the shears with which the shepherd clips the wool. The miner, the builder of the furnace for smelting the ore, the feller of the timber, the burner of the charcoal to be made use of in the smelting-house, the brick-maker, the brick-layer, the work-men who attend the furnace, the mill-wright, the forger, the smith, must all of them join their different arts in order to produce them. Were we to examine, in the same manner, all the different parts of his dress and household furniture, the coarse linen shirt which he wears next his skin, the shoes which cover his feet, the bed which he lies on, and all the different parts which compose it, the kitchen grate at which he prepares his victuals, the coals which he makes use of for that purpose, dug from the bowels of the earth, and brought to him perhaps by a long sea and a long land carriage, all the other utensils of his kitchen, all the furniture of his table, the knives and forks, the earthen or pewter plates upon which he serves up and divides his victuals, the different hands employed in preparing his bread and his beer, the glass window which lets in the heat and the light, and keeps out the wind and the rain, with all the knowledge and art requisite for preparing that beautiful and happy invention, without which these northern parts of the world could scarce have afforded a very comfortable habitation, together with the tools of all the different workmen employed in producing those different conveniences; if we examine, I say, all these things, and consider what a variety of labour is employed about each of them, we shall be sensible that without the assistance and cooperation of many thousands, the very meanest person in a civilized country could not be provided, even according to, what we very falsely imagine, the easy and simple manner in which he is commonly accommodated. Compared, indeed, with the more extravagant luxury of the great, his accommodation must no doubt appear extremely simple and easy; and yet it may be true, perhaps, that the accommodation of an European prince does not always so much exceed that of an industrious and frugal peasant, as the accommodation of the latter exceeds that of many an African king. . . .

3

Superintendent's Report

Daniel C. McCallum

OFFICE GENERAL SUP'T N.Y. &
ERIE R. R.
NEW YORK, MARCH 25, 1856

HOMER RAMSDELL, ESQ.
PRESIDENT OF THE NEW YORK AND
ERIE RAILROAD COMPANY:

SIR:

The magnitude of the business of this road, its numerous and important connections, and the large number of employés engaged in operating it, have led many, whose opinions are entitled to respect, to the conclusion, that a proper regard to details, which enter so largely into the elements of success in the management of all railroads, cannot possibly be attained by any plan that contemplates its organization as a whole; and in proof of this position, the experience of shorter roads is referred to, the business operations of which have been conducted much more economically.

Theoretically, other things being equal, a long road should be operated for a less cost per mile than a short one. This position is so clearly evident and so generally admitted, that its truth may be assumed without offering any arguments in support of it; and, notwithstanding the reverse, so far as *practical* results are considered, has generally been the case, we must look to other causes than the mere difference in length of roads for a solution of the difficulty.

A Superintendent of a road fifty miles in length can give its business his personal attention, and may be almost constantly upon the line engaged in the direction of its details; each employé is familiarly known to him, and all questions in relation to its business are at once presented and acted upon; and any system, however imperfect, may under such circumstances prove comparatively successful.

In the government of a road five hundred miles in length a very different state of things exists. Any system which might be applicable to the business and extent of a short road, would be found entirely inadequate to the wants of a long one; and I am fully convinced, that in the want of a system perfect in its details, properly adapted and vigilantly enforced, lies the true secret of their failure; and that this disparity of cost per mile in operating long and short roads, is not produced by *a difference in length*, but is in proportion to the perfection of the system adopted.

Entertaining these views, I had the honor, more than a year since, to submit for your consideration and approval a plan for the more effective organization of this department. The system then proposed has to some extent been introduced, and experience, so far, affords the strongest assurances that when fully carried out, the most satisfactory results will be obtained.

In my opinion a system of operations, to be efficient and successful, should be such as to give to the principal and responsible head of the running department a complete daily history of details in all their minutiae. Without such supervision, the procurement of a satisfactory annual statement must be regarded as extremely problematical. The fact that dividends are earned without such control does not disprove the position, as in many cases the extraordinarily

Source: Daniel C. McCallum, "Superintendent's Report," March 25, 1856, in *Annual Report of the New York and Erie Railroad Company for 1855* (New York, 1856).

remunerative nature of an enterprise may ensure satisfactory returns under the most loose and inefficient management.

It may be proper here to remark that in consequence of that want of adaptation before alluded to, we cannot avail ourselves to any great extent of the plan of organization of shorter lines in framing one for this, nor have we any precedent or experience upon which we can fully rely in doing so. Under these circumstances, it will scarcely be expected that we can at once adopt any plan of operations which will not require amendment and a reasonable time to prove its worth. A few general principles, however, may be regarded as settled and necessary in its formation, amongst which are:

1. A proper division of responsibilities.
2. Sufficient power conferred to enable the same to be fully carried out, that such responsibilities may be real in their character.
3. The means of knowing whether such responsibilities are faithfully executed.
4. Great promptness in the report of all derelictions of duty, that evils may be at once corrected.
5. Such information, to be obtained through a system of daily reports and checks that will not embarrass principal officers, nor lessen their influence with their subordinates.
6. The adoption of a system, as a whole, which will not only enable the General Superintendent to detect errors immediately, but will also point out the delinquent.

4
The Engineer as Economist

Henry R. Towne

The monogram of our national initials, which is the symbol of our monetary unit, the dollar, is almost as frequently conjoined to the figures of an engineer's calculations as are the symbols indicating feet, minutes, pounds, or gallons. The final issue of his work, in probably a majority of cases, resolves itself into a question of dollars and cents, of relative or absolute values. This statement, while true in regard to the work of all engineers, applies particularly to that of the mechanical engineer, for the reason that his functions, more frequently than in the case of others, include the executive duties of organizing and superintending the operations of industrial establishments, and of directing the labor of the artisans whose organized efforts yield the fruition of his work.

To insure the best results, the organization of productive labor must be directed and controlled by persons having not only good executive ability, and possessing the practical familiarity of a mechanic or engineer with the goods produced and the processes employed, but having also, and equally, a practical knowledge of how to observe, record, analyze and compare essential facts in relation to wages, supplies, expense accounts, and all else that enters into or affects the economy of production and the cost of the product. There are many good mechanical engineers;—there are also many good "business men";—but the two are rarely combined in one person. But this combination of qualities, together with at least some skill as an accountant, either in one person or more, is essential to the successful management of industrial works, and has its highest effectiveness if united in

one person, who is thus qualified to supervise, either personally or through assistants, the operations of all departments of a business, and to subordinate each to the harmonious development of the whole.

Engineering has long been conceded a place as one of the modern arts, and has become a well-defined science, with a large and growing literature of its own, and of late years has subdivided itself into numerous and distinct divisions, one of which is that of mechanical engineering. It will probably not be disputed that the matter of shop management is of equal importance with that of engineering, as affecting the successful conduct of most, if not all, of our great industrial establishments, and that the *management of works* has become a matter of such great and far-reaching importance as perhaps to justify its classification also as one of the modern arts. The one is a well-defined science, with a distinct literature, with numerous journals and with many associations for the interchange of experience; the other is unorganized, is almost without literature, has no organ or medium for the interchange of experience, and is without association or organization of any kind. A vast amount of accumulated experience in the art of workshop management already exists, but there is no record of it available to the world in general, and each old enterprise is managed more or less in its own way, receiving little benefit from the parallel experience of other similar enterprises, and imparting as little of its own to them; while each new enterprise, starting *de novo* and with much labor, and usually at much cost for experience, gradually develops a more or less perfect system of

Source: Transactions of the American Society of Mechanical Engineers, vol. 7 (paper presented at May 1886 meeting of the society, Chicago), 428–432.

its own, according to the ability of its managers, receiving little benefit or aid from all that may have been done previously by others in precisely the same field of work.

Surely this condition of things is wrong and should be remedied. But the remedy must not be looked for from those who are "business men" or clerks and accountants only; it should come from those whose training and experience has given them an understanding of both sides (viz.: the mechanical and the clerical) of the important questions involved. It should originate, therefore, from those who are also engineers, and, for the reasons above indicated, particularly from mechanical engineers. Granting this, why should it not originate from, and be promoted by The American Society of Mechanical Engineers?

To consider this proposition more definitely, let us state the work which requires to be done. The questions to be considered, and which need recording and publication as conducing to discussion and the dissemination of useful knowledge in this specialty, group themselves under two principal heads, namely: Shop Management, and Shop Accounting. A third head may be named which is subordinate to, and partly included in each of these, namely: Shop Forms and Blanks. Under the head of Shop Management fall the questions of organization, responsibility, reports, systems of contract and piece work, and all that relates to the executive management of works, mills and factories. Under the head of Shop Accounting fall the questions of time and wages systems, determination of costs, whether by piece or day-work, the distribution of the various expense accounts, the ascertainment of profits, methods of bookkeeping, and all that enters into the system of accounts which relates to the manufacturing departments of a business, and to the determination and record of its results.

There already exists an enormous fund of information relating to such matters, based upon actual and most extensive experience. What is now needed is a medium for the interchange of this experience among those whom it interests and concerns. Probably no better way for this exists than that obtaining in other instances, namely, by the publication of papers and reports, and by meetings for the discussion of papers and interchange of opinions.

The subject thus outlined, however distinct and apart from the primary functions of this society, is, nevertheless, germane to the interests of most, if not all, of its members. Conceding this, why should not the function of the society be so enlarged as to embrace this new field of usefulness? This work, if undertaken, may be kept separate and distinct from the present work of the society by organizing a new "section" (which might be designated the "Economic Section"), the scope of which would embrace all papers and discussions relating to the topics herein referred to. The meetings of this section could be held either separately from, or immediately following the regular meetings of the society, and its papers could appear as a supplement to the regular transactions. In this way all interference would be avoided with the primary and chief business of the society, and the attendance at the meetings of the new section would naturally resolve itself into such portion of the membership as is interested in the objects for which it would be organized.

As a single illustration of the class of subjects to be covered by the discussions and papers of the proposed new section, and of the benefit to be derived therefrom, there may be cited the case of a manufacturing establishment in which there are now in use, in connection with the manufacturing accounts and exclusive of the ordinary commercial accounts, some twenty various forms of special record and account books, and more than one hundred printed forms and blanks. The primary object to which all of these contribute is the systematic recording of the operations of the different departments of the works, and the computation therefrom of such statistical information as is essential to the efficient management of the business, and especially to increased economy of production. All of these special

FIGURE 4.1 • THE ENGINEER AS ECONOMIST

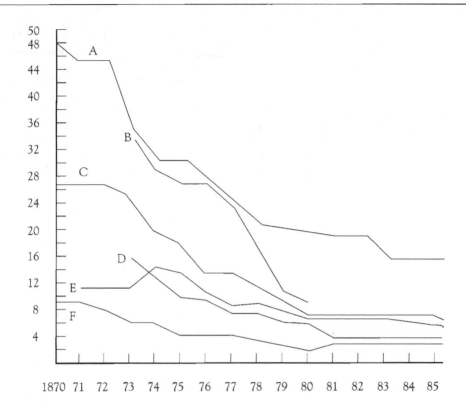

books and forms have been the outgrowth of experience extending over many years, and represent a large amount of thoughtful planning and intelligent effort at constant development and improvement. The methods thus arrived at would undoubtedly be of great value to others engaged in similar operations, and particularly to persons engaged in organizing and starting new enterprises. It is probable that much, if not all, of the information and experience referred to would be willingly made public through such a channel as is herein suggested, particularly if such action on the part of one firm or corporation would be responded to in like manner by others, so that each member could reasonably expect to receive some equivalent for his contributions by the benefit which he would derive from the experience of others.

In the case of the establishment above referred to, a special system of contract and piece-work has been in operation for some fifteen years, the results from which, in reducing the labor cost on certain products without encroaching upon the earnings of the men engaged, have been quite striking. A few of these results selected at random, are indicated by the accompanying diagram (Figure 4.1), the diagonal lines on which represent the fluctuations in the labor cost of certain special products during the time covered by the table, the vertical scale representing values.

Undoubtedly a portion of the reductions thus indicated resulted from improved appliances, larger product, and increased experience, but after making due allowance for all of these, there remains a large portion of the reduction which, to the writer's knowledge, is fairly attributable to the operation of the peculiar piece-work system adopted. The details and operations of this system would probably be placed before the society, in due time, through the channel of the proposed new section, should the latter take definite form. Other, and probably much more valuable, information and experience relating to systems of contract and piece-work would doubtless be contributed by other members, and in the aggregate a great amount of information of a most valuable character would thus be made available to the whole membership of the society.

In conclusion, it is suggested that if the plan herein proposed commends itself favorably to the members present at the meeting at which it is presented, the subject had best be referred to a special committee, by whom it can be carefully considered, and by whom, if it seems expedient to proceed further, the whole matter can be matured and formulated in an orderly manner, and thus be so presented at a future meeting as to enable the society then intelligently to act upon the question, and to decide whether or not to adopt the recommendations made by such committee.

5

General Principles of Management

Henri Fayol

The managerial function finds its only outlet through the members of the organization (body corporate). Whilst the other functions bring into play material and machines the managerial function operates only on the personnel. The soundness and good working order of the body corporate depend on a certain number of conditions termed indiscriminately principles, laws, rules. For preference I shall adopt the term principles whilst dissociating it from any suggestion of rigidity, for there is nothing rigid or absolute in management affairs, it is all a question of proportion. Seldom do we have to apply the same principle twice in identical conditions; allowance must be made for different changing circumstances, for men just as different and changing and for many other variable elements.

Therefore principles are flexible and capable of adaptation to every need; it is a matter of knowing how to make use of them, which is a difficult art requiring intelligence, experience, decision and proportion. Compounded of tact and experience, proportion is one of the foremost attributes of the manager. There is no limit to the number of principles of management, every rule or managerial procedure which strengthens the body corporate or facilitates its functioning has a place among the principles so long, at least, as experience confirms its worthiness. A change in the state of affairs can be responsible for change of rules which had been engendered by that state.

I am going to review some of the principles of management which I have most frequently had to apply; viz.—

1. Division of work.
2. Authority and responsibility.
3. Discipline.
4. Unity of command.
5. Unity of direction.
6. Subordination of individual interest to the general interest.
7. Remuneration of personnel.
8. Centralization.
9. Scalar chain (line of authority).
10. Order.
11. Equity.
12. Stability of tenure of personnel.
13. Initiative.
14. Esprit de corps.

1. DIVISION OF WORK

Specialization belongs to the natural order; it is observable in the animal world, where the more highly developed the creature the more highly differentiated its organs; it is observable in human societies where the more important the body corporate[1] the closer is the relationship between structure and function. As society grows, so new organs develop destined to replace the single one performing all functions in the primitive state.

The object of division of work is to produce more and better work with the same effort. The worker always on the same part, the manager concerned always with the same matters, acquire an ability, sureness, and accuracy which increase their output. Each change of work brings in its train an

Source: Henri Fayol, *General and Industrial Management*, trans. Constance Storrs (London: Pitman, 1949), 19–42; original work published 1916.

adaptation which reduces output. Division of work permits reduction in the number of objects to which attention and effort must be directed and has been recognized as the best means of making use of individuals and of groups of people. It is not merely applicable to technical work, but without exception to all work involving a more or less considerable number of people and demanding abilities of various types, and it results in specialization of functions and separation of powers. Although its advantages are universally recognized and although possibility of progress is inconceivable without the specialized work of learned men and artists, yet division of work has its limits which experience and a sense of proportion teach us may not be exceeded.

2. AUTHORITY AND RESPONSIBILITY

Authority is the right to give orders and the power to exact obedience. Distinction must be made between a manager's official authority deriving from office and personal authority, compounded of intelligence, experience, moral worth, ability to lead, past services, etc. In the make up of a good head personal authority is the indispensable complement of official authority. Authority is not to be conceived of apart from responsibility, that is apart from sanction— reward or penalty—which goes with the exercise of power. Responsibility is a corollary of authority, it is its natural consequence and essential counterpart, and wheresoever authority is exercised responsibility arises.

The need for sanction, which has its origin in a sense of justice, is strengthened and increased by this consideration, that in the general interest useful actions have to be encouraged and their opposite discouraged. Application of sanction to acts of authority forms part of the conditions essential for good management, but it is generally difficult to effect, especially in large concerns. First, the degree of responsibility must be established and then the weight of the sanction. Now, it is relatively easy to establish a workman's responsibility for his acts and a scale of corresponding sanctions; in the case of a foreman it is somewhat difficult, and proportionately as one goes up the scalar chain of businesses, as work grows more complex, as the number of workers involved increases, as the final result is more remote, it is increasingly difficult to isolate the share of the initial act of authority in the ultimate result and to establish the degree of responsibility of the manager. The measurement of this responsibility and its equivalent in material terms elude all calculation.

Sanction, then, is a question of kind, custom, convention, and judging it one must take into account the action itself, the attendant circumstances and potential repercussions. Judgment demands high moral character, impartiality and firmness. If all these conditions are not fulfilled there is a danger that the sense of responsibility may disappear from the concern.

Responsibility valiantly undertaken and borne merits some consideration; it is a kind of courage everywhere much appreciated. Tangible proof of this exists in the salary level of some industrial leaders, which is much higher than that of civil servants of comparable rank but carrying no responsibility. Nevertheless, generally speaking, responsibility is feared as much as authority is sought after, and fear of responsibility paralyses much initiative and destroys many good qualities. A good leader should possess and infuse into those around him courage to accept responsibility.

The best safeguard against abuse of authority and against weakness on the part of a higher manager is personal integrity and particularly high moral character of such a manager, and this integrity, it is well known, is conferred neither by election nor ownership.

3. DISCIPLINE

Discipline is in essence obedience, application, energy, behaviour, and outward marks of respect observed in accordance with the standing agreements between the firm and its employees, whether these agreements have been freely debated or accepted without prior discussion, whether they be written or implicit, whether they derive from the wish of the parties to them or from rules and customs, it is these agreements which determine the formalities of discipline.

Discipline, being the outcome of different varying agreements, naturally appears under the most diverse forms; obligations of obedience, application, energy, behavior, vary, in effect, from one firm to another, from one group of employees to another, from one time to another. Nevertheless, general opinion is deeply convinced that discipline is absolutely essential for the smooth running of business and that without discipline no enterprise could prosper.

This sentiment is very forcibly expressed in military hand-books, where it runs that "Discipline constitutes the chief strength of armies." I would approve unreservedly of this aphorism were it followed by this other, "Discipline is what leaders make it." The first one inspires respect for discipline, which is a good thing, but it tends to eclipse from view the responsibility of leaders, which is undesirable, for the state of discipline of any group of people depends essentially on the worthiness of its leaders.

When a defect in discipline is apparent or when relations between superiors and subordinates leave much to be desired, responsibility for this must not be cast heedlessly, and without going further afield, on the poor state of the team, because the ill mostly results from the ineptitude of the leaders. That, at all events, is what I have noted in various parts of France, for I have always found French workmen obedient and loyal provided they are ably led.

In the matter of influence upon discipline, agreements must set side by side with command. It is important that they be clear and, as far as possible, afford satisfaction to both

sides. This is not easy. Proof of that exists in the great strikes of miners, railwaymen, and civil servants which, in these latter years, have jeopardized national life at home and elsewhere and which arose out of agreements in dispute or inadequate legislation.

For half a century a considerable change has been effected in the mode of agreements between a concern and its employees. The agreements of former days fixed by the employer alone are being replaced, in ever increasing measure, by understandings arrived at by discussion between an owner or group of owners and workers' associations. Thus each individual owner's responsibility has been reduced and is further diminished by increasingly frequent state intervention in labour problems. Nevertheless, the setting up of agreements binding a firm and its employees from which disciplinary formalities emanate, should remain one of the chief preoccupations of industrial heads.

The well-being of the concern does not permit, in cases of offence against discipline, of the neglect of certain sanctions capable of preventing or minimizing their recurrence. Experience and tact on the part of a manager are put to the proof in the choice and degree of sanctions to be used, such as remonstrances, warning, fines, suspensions, demotion, dismissal. Individual people and attendant circumstances must be taken into account. In fine, discipline is respect for agreements which are directed at achieving obedience, application, energy, and the outward marks of respect. It is incumbent upon managers at high levels as much as upon humble employees, and the best means of establishing and maintaining it are—

1. Good superiors at all levels.
2. Agreements as clear and fair as possible.
3. Sanctions (penalties) judiciously applied.

4. UNITY OF COMMAND

For any action whatsoever, an employee should receive orders from one superior only. Such is the rule of unity of command, arising from general and ever-present necessity and wielding an influence on the conduct of affairs, which to my way of thinking, is at least equal to any other principle whatsoever. Should it be violated, authority is undermined, discipline is in jeopardy, order disturbed and stability threatened. This rule seems fundamental to me and so I have given it the rank of principle. As soon as two superiors wield their authority over the same person or department, uneasiness makes itself felt and should the cause persist, the disorder increases, the malady takes on the appearance of an animal organism troubled by a foreign body, and the following consequences are to be observed: either the dual command ends in disappearance or elimination of one of the superiors and organic wellbeing is restored, or else the organism continues to wither away. In no case is there adaptation of the social organism to dual command.

Now dual command is extremely common and wreaks havoc in all concerns, large or small, in home and in state. The evil is all the more to be feared in that it worms its way into the social organism on the most plausible pretexts. For instance —

(a) In the hope of being better understood or gaining time or to put a stop forthwith to an undesirable practice, a superior S^2 may give orders directly to an employee E without going via the superior S^1. If this mistake is repeated there is dual command with its consequences, *viz.*, hesitation on the part of the subordinate, irritation and dissatisfaction on the part of the superior set aside, and disorder in the work. It will be seen later that it is possible to bypass the scalar chain when necessary, whilst avoiding the drawbacks of dual command.

(b) The desire to get away from the immediate necessity of dividing up authority as between two colleagues, two friends, two members of one family, results at times in dual command reigning at the top of a concern right from the outset. Exercising the same powers and having the same authority over the same men, the two colleagues end up inevitably with dual command and its consequences. Despite harsh lessons, instances of this sort are still numerous. New

colleagues count on their mutual regard, common interest, and good sense to save them from every conflict, every serious disagreement and, save for rare exceptions, the illusion is short-lived. First an awkwardness makes itself felt, then a certain irritation and, in time, if dual command exists, even hatred. Men cannot bear dual command. A judicious assignment of duties would have reduced the danger without entirely banishing it, for between two superiors on the same footing there must always be some question ill-defined. But it is riding for a fall to set up a business organization with two superiors on equal footing without assigning duties and demarcating authority.

(c) Imperfect demarcation of departments also leads to dual command: two superiors issuing orders in a sphere which each thinks his own, constitutes dual command.

(d) Constant linking up as between different departments, natural intermeshing of functions, duties often badly defined, create an everpresent danger of dual command. If a knowledgeable superior does not put it in order, footholds are established which later upset and compromise the conduct of affairs.

In all human associations, in industry, commerce, army, home, state, dual command is a perpetual source of conflicts, very grave sometimes, which have special claim on the attention of superiors of all ranks.

5. UNITY OF DIRECTION

This principle is expressed as: one head and one plan for a group of activities having the same objective. It is the condition essential to unity of action, coordination of strength and focusing of effort. A body with two heads is in the social as in the animal sphere a monster, and has difficulty in surviving. Unity of direction (one head one plan) must not be confused with unity of command (one employee to have orders from one superior only). Unity of direction is provided for by sound organization of the body corporate, unity of command turns on the functioning of the personnel. Unity of command cannot exist without unity of direction, but does not flow from it.

6. SUBORDINATION OF INDIVIDUAL INTEREST TO GENERAL INTEREST

This principle calls to mind the fact that in a business the interest of one employee or group of employees should not prevail over that of the concern, that the interest of the home should come before that of its members and that the interest of the state should have pride of place over that of one citizen or group of citizens.

It seems that such an admonition should not need calling to mind. But ignorance, ambition, selfishness, laziness, weakness, and all human passions tend to cause the general interest to be lost sight of in favour of individual interest and a perpetual struggle has to be waged against them. Two interests of a different order, but claiming equal respect, confront each other and means must be found to reconcile them. That represents one of the great difficulties of management. Means of effecting it are —

1. Firmness and good example on the part of superiors.
2. Agreements as fair as is possible.
3. Constant supervision.

7. REMUNERATION OF PERSONNEL

Remuneration of personnel is the price of services rendered. It should be fair and, as far as is possible, afford satisfaction both to personnel and firm (employee and employer). The rate of remuneration depends, firstly, on circumstances independent of the employer's will and employee's worth, viz. cost of living, abundance or shortage of personnel, general business conditions, the economic position of the business, and after that it depends on the value of the employee and mode of payment adopted.

Appreciation of the factors dependent on the employer's will and on the value of employees, demands a fairly good knowledge of business, judgement, and impartiality. Later on in connection with selecting personnel we shall deal with assessing the value of employees; here only the mode of payment is under consideration as a factor operation on remuneration. The method of payment can exercise considerable influence on business progress, so the choice of this method is an important problem. It is also a thorny problem which in practice has been solved in widely different ways, of which so far none has proved satisfactory. What is generally looked for in the method of payment is that —

1. It shall assure fair remuneration.
2. It shall encourage keenness by rewarding well-directed effort.
3. It shall not lead to overpayment going beyond reasonable limits.

I am going to examine briefly the modes of payment in use for workers, junior managers, and higher managers.

Workers

The various modes of payment in use for workers are —

1. Time rates.
2. Job rates.
3. Piece rates.

These three modes of payment may be combined and give rise to important variations by the introduction of bonuses, profit-sharing schemes, payment in kind, and nonfinancial incentives.

1. Time rates. Under this system the workman sells the employer, in return for a predetermined sum, a day's work under definite conditions. This system has the disadvantage of conducing to negligence and of demanding constant supervision. It is inevitable where the work done is not susceptible to measurement and in effect it is very common.

2. Job rates. Here payment made turns upon the execution of a definite job set in advance and may be independent of the length of the job. When payment is due only on condition that the job be completed during the normal work spell, this method merges into time rate. Payment by daily job does not require as close a supervision as payment by the day, but it has the drawback of levelling the output of good workers down to that of mediocre ones. The good ones are not satisfied, because they feel that they could earn more; the mediocre ones find the task set too heavy.

3. Piece rates. Here payment is related to work done and there is no limit. This system is often used in workshops where a large number of similar articles have to be made, and is found where the product can be measured by weight, length, or cubic capacity, and in general is used wherever possible. It is criticized on the grounds of emphasizing quantity at the expense of quality and of provoking disagreements when rates have to be revised in the light of manufacturing improvements. Piece-work becomes contract work when applied to an important unit of work. To reduce the contractor's risk, sometimes there is added to the contract price a payment for each day's work done.

Generally, piece rates give rise to increased earnings which act for some time as a stimulus, then finally a system prevails in which this mode of payment gradually approximates to time rates for a prearranged sum.

The above three modes of payment are found in all large concerns; sometimes time rates prevail, sometimes one of the other two. In a workshop the same workman may be seen working now on piece rates, not on time rates. Each one of these methods had its advantages and drawbacks, and their effectiveness depends on circumstances and the ability of superiors. Neither method nor rate of payment absolves management from competence and tact, and keenness of workers and peaceful atmosphere of the workshop depend largely upon it.

Bonuses

To arouse the worker's interest in the smooth running of the business, sometimes an increment in the nature of a bonus is added to the time-, job- or piece-rate: for good time keeping, hard work, freedom from machine breakdown output, cleanliness, etc. The relative importance, nature and qualifying conditions of these bonuses are very varied. There are to be found the small daily supplement, the monthly sum, the annual award, shares or portions of shares distributed to the most meritorious, and also even profit-sharing schemes such as, for example certain monetary allocations distributed annually among workers in some large firms. Several French collieries started some years back the granting of a bonus proportional to profits distributed or to extra profits. No contract is required from the workers save that the earning of the bonus is subject to certain conditions, for instance, that there shall be no strike during the year, or that absenteeism shall not have exceeded a given number of days. This type of bonus introduced an element of profit-sharing into miners' wages without any prior discussion as between workers and employer. The workman did not refuse a gift, largely gratuitous, on the part of the employer, that is, the contract was a unilateral one. Thanks to a successful trading period the yearly wages have been appreciably increased by the operation of the bonus. But what is to happen in lean times? This interesting procedure is as yet too new to be judged, but obviously it is no general solution of the problem. . . .

Profit-Sharing

1. Workers. The idea of making workers share in profits is a very attractive one and it would seem that it is from there that harmony as between Capital and Labour should come. But the practical formula for such sharing has not yet been found. Workers' profit-sharing has hitherto come up against insurmountable difficulties of application in the case of large concerns. Firstly, let us note that it cannot exist in enterprises having no monetary objective (State services, religion, philanthropic, scientific societies) and also that it is not possible in the case of businesses running at a loss. Thus profit-sharing is excluded from a great number of concerns. There remain the prosperous business concerns and of these latter the desire to reconcile and harmonize workers' and employers' interests is nowhere so great as in French mining and metallurgical industries. Now, in these industries I know of no clear application of workers' profitsharing, whence it may be concluded forthwith that the matter is difficult, if not impossible. It is very difficult indeed. Whether a business is making a profit or not the worker must have an immediate wage assured him, and a system which would make workers' payment depend entirely on eventual future profit is unworkable. But perhaps a part of wages might come from business profits. Let us see. Viewing all contingent factors, the workers' greater or lesser share of activity or ability in the final outcome of a large concern is impossible to assess and is, moreover, quite insignificant. The portion accruing to him of distributed dividend would at the most be a few centimes on a wage of five francs for instance, that is to say the smallest extra effort, the stroke of a pick or of a file operating directly on his wage, would prove of greater advantage to him. Hence the worker has no interest in being rewarded by a share in profits proportionate to the effect he has upon profits. It is worthy of note that, in most large concerns, wages increases, operative now for some twenty years, represent a total sum greater than the amount of capital shared out. In effect, unmodified real profit-sharing by workers of large concerns has not yet entered the sphere of practical business politics.

2. Junior Managers. Profit-sharing for foremen, superintendents, engineers, is scarcely more advanced than for workers. Nevertheless the influence of these employees on the results of a business is quite considerable, and if they are not consistently interested in profits the only reason is that the basis for participation is difficult to establish. Doubtless managers have no need of monetary incentive to carry out their duties, but they are not indifferent to material satisfactions and it must be acknowledged that the hope of extra profit is capable of arousing their enthusiasm. So employees at middle levels should, where possible, be induced to have an interest in profits. It is relatively easy in businesses which are starting out or on trial, where exceptional effort can yield outstanding results. Sharing may then be applied to overall business profits or merely to the running of the particular department of the employee in question. When the business is of long standing and well run the zeal of a junior manager is scarcely apparent in the general outcome, and it is very hard to establish a useful basis on which he may participate. In fact, profit-sharing among junior managers in France is very rare in large concerns. Production or workshop output bonuses — not to be confused with profit-sharing — are much more common.

3. Higher Managers. It is necessary to go right up to top management to find a class of employee with frequent interest in the profits of large-scale French concerns. The head of the business, in view of his knowledge, ideas, and actions, exerts considerable influence on general results, so it is quite natural to try and provide him with an interest in them. Sometimes it is possible to establish a close connection between his personal activity and its effects. Nevertheless, generally speaking, there exist other influences quite independent of the personal capability of the manager which can influence results to a greater extent than can his personal activity. If the manager's salary were exclusively dependent upon profits, it might at times be reduced to nothing. There are besides, businesses being built up, wound up, or merely passing through temporary crisis, wherein management depends no less on talent than in the case of prosperous ones, and wherein profit-sharing cannot be a basis for remuneration for the manager. In fine, senior civil servants cannot be paid on a profit-sharing basis. Profit-sharing, then, for either higher managers or workers is not a general rule of remuneration. To sum up, then: profit-sharing is a mode of payment capable of giving excellent results in certain cases, but is not a general rule. It does not seem to me possible, at least for the present, to count on this mode of payment for appeasing conflict between Capital and Labour. Fortunately, there are other means which hitherto have been sufficient to maintain relative social quiet. Such methods have not lost their power and it is up to managers to study them, apply them, and make them work well.

Payment in Kind, Welfare Work, Non-Financial Incentives

Whether wages are made up of money only or whether they include various additions such as heating, light, housing, food, is of little consequence provided that the employee be satisfied.

From another point of view, there is no doubt that a business will be better served in proportion as its employees are more energetic, better educated, more conscientious and more permanent. The employer should have regard, if merely in the interests of the business, for the health, strength, education, morale, and stability of his personnel. These elements of smooth running are not acquired in the workshop alone, they are formed and developed as well, and particularly, outside it, in the home and school, in civil and religious life. Therefore, the employer comes to be concerned with his employees outside the works and here the question of proportion comes up again. Opinion is greatly divided on this point. Certain unfortunate experiments have resulted in some employers stopping short their interest, at the works gate and at the regulation of wages. The majority consider that the employer's activity may be used to good purpose outside the factory confines provided that there be discretion and prudence, that it be sought after rather than

imposed, be in keeping with the general level of education and taste of those concerned and that it have absolute respect for their liberty. It must be benevolent collaboration, not tyrannical stewardship, and therein lies an indispensable condition of success. . . .

8. CENTRALIZATION

Like division of work, centralization belongs to the natural order; this turns on the fact that in every organism, animal or social, sensations converge towards the brain or directive part, and from the brain or directive part orders are sent out which set all parts of the organism in movement. Centralization is not a system of management good or bad of itself, capable of being adopted or discarded at the whim of managers or of circumstances; it is always present to a greater or less extent. The question of centralization or decentralization, is a simple question of proportion, it is a matter of finding the optimum degree for the particular concern. In small firms, where the manager's orders go directly to subordinates there is absolute centralization; in large concerns, where a long scalar chain is interposed between manager and lower grades, orders and counterinformation too, have to go through a series of intermediaries. Each employee, intentionally or unintentionally, puts something of himself into the transmission and execution of orders and of information received too. He does not operate merely as a cog in a machine. What appropriate share of initiative may be left to intermediaries depends on the personal character of the manager, on his moral worth, on the reliability of his subordinates, and also on the condition of the business. The degree of centralization must vary according to different cases. The objective to pursue is the optimum utilization of all faculties of the personnel.

If the moral worth of the manager, his strength, intelligence, experience, and swiftness of thought allow him to have a wide span of activities he will be able to carry centralization quite far and reduce his seconds in command to mere executive agents. If, conversely, he prefers to have greater recourse to the experience, opinions, and counsel of his colleagues whilst reserving to himself the privilege of giving general directives, he can effect considerable decentralization.

Seeing that both absolute and relative value of manager and employees are constantly changing, it is understandable that the degree of centralization or decentralization may itself vary constantly. It is a problem to be solved according to circumstances, to the best satisfaction of the interests involved. It arises, not only in the case of higher authority, but for superiors at all levels and not one but can extend or confine, to some extent, his subordinates' initiative.

The finding of the measure which shall give the best overall yield: that is the problem of centralization or decentralization. Everything which goes to increase the importance of the subordinate's role is decentralization, everything which goes to reduce it is centralization.

9. SCALAR CHAIN

The scalar chain is the chain of superiors ranging from the ultimate authority to the lowest ranks. The line of authority is the route followed—via every link in the chain—by all communications which start from or go to the ultimate authority. This path is dictated both by the need for some transmission and by the principle of unity of command, but it is not always the swiftest. It is even at times disastrously lengthy in large concerns, notably in governmental ones. Now, there are many activities whose success turns on speedy execution, hence respect for the line of authority must be reconciled with the need for swift action.

Let us imagine that section F has to be put into contact with section P in a business

whose scalar chain is represented by the double ladder G-A-Q thus—

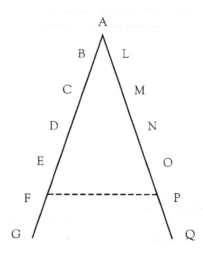

By following the line of authority the ladder must be climbed from F to A and then descended from A to P, stopping at each rung, then ascended again from P to A, and descended once more from A to F, in order to get back to the starting point. Evidently it is much simpler and quicker to go directly from F to P by making use of FP as a "gang plank" and that is what is most often done. The scalar principle will be safeguarded if managers E and O have authorized their respective subordinates F and P to treat directly, and the position will be fully regularized if F and P inform their respective superiors forthwith of what they have agreed upon. So long as F and P remain in agreement, and so long as their actions are approved by their immediate superiors, direct contact may be maintained, but from the instant that agreement ceases or there is no approval from the superiors direct contact comes to an end, and the scalar chain is straightway resumed. Such is the actual procedure to be observed in the great majority of businesses. It provides for the usual exercise of some measure of initiative at all levels of authority. In the small concern, the general interest, viz. that of the concern proper, is easy to grasp, and the employer is present to recall this interest to those tempted to lose sight of it. In government enterprise the general interest is such a complex, vast, remote thing, that it is not easy to get a clear idea of it, and for the majority of civil servants the employer is somewhat mythical and unless the sentiment of general interest be constantly revived by higher authority, it becomes blurred and weakened and each section tends to regard itself as its own aim and end and forgets that it is only a cog in a big machine, all of whose parts must work in concert. It becomes isolated, cloistered, aware only of the line of authority.

The use of the "gang plank" is simple, swift, sure. It allows the two employees F and P to deal at one sitting, and in a few hours, with some question or other which via the scalar chain would pass through twenty transmissions, inconvenience many people, involve masses of paper, lose weeks or months to get to a conclusion less satisfactory generally than the one which could have been obtained via direct contact as between F and P.

Is it possible that such practices, as ridiculous as they are devastating, could be in current use? Unfortunately there can be little doubt of it in government department affairs. It is usually acknowledged that the chief cause is fear of responsibility. I am rather of the opinion that it is insufficient executive capacity on the part of those in charge. If supreme authority A insisted that his assistants B and L made use of the "gang plank" themselves and made its use incumbent upon their subordinates C and M, the habit and courage of taking responsibility would be established and at the same time the custom of using the shortest path.

It is an error to depart needlessly from the line of authority, but it is an even greater one to keep to it when detriment to the business ensues. The latter may attain extreme gravity in certain conditions. When an employee is obliged to choose between the two practices, and it is impossible for him to take advice from his superior, he should be courageous enough and feel free enough to adopt the line dictated by the general interest. But

for him to be in this frame of mind there must have been previous precedent, and his superiors must have set him the example — for example must always come from above.

10. ORDER

The formula is known in the case of material things "A place for everything and everything in its place." The formula is the same for human order. "A place for everyone and everyone in his place."

Material Order

In accordance with the preceding definition, so that material order shall prevail, there must be a place appointed for each thing and each thing must be in its appointed place. Is that enough? Is it not also necessary that the place shall have been well chosen? The object of order must be avoidance of loss of material, and for this object to be completely realized not only must things be in their place suitably arranged but also the place must have been chosen so as to facilitate all activities as much as possible. If this last condition be unfulfilled, there is merely the appearance of order. Appearance of order may cover over real disorder. I have seen a works yard used as a store for steel ingots in which the material was well stacked, evenly arranged and clean and which gave a pleasing impression of orderliness. On close inspection it could be noted that the same heap included five or six types of steel intended for different manufacture all mixed up together. Whence useless handling, lost time, risk of mistakes because each thing was not in its place. It happens, on the other hand, that the appearance of disorder may actually be true order. Such is the case with papers scattered about at a master's whim which a well-meaning but incompetent servant re-arranges and sticks in neat piles. The master can no longer find his way about them. Perfect order presupposes a judiciously chosen place and the appearance of order is merely a false or imperfect image of real order. Cleanliness is a corollary of orderliness, there is no appointed place for dirt. A diagram representing the entire premises divided up into as many sections as there are employees responsible facilitates considerably the establishing and control of order.

Social Order

For social order to prevail in a concern there must, in accordance with the definition, be an appointed place for every employee and every employee be in his appointed place. Perfect order requires, further, that the place be suitable for the employee and the employee for the place—in English idiom, "The right man in the right place."

Thus understood, social order presupposes the successful execution of the two most difficult managerial activities: good organization and good selection. Once the posts essential to the smooth running of the business have been decided upon and those to fill such posts have been selected, each employee occupies that post wherein he can render most service. Such is perfect social order "A place for each one and each one in his place." That appears simple, and naturally we are so anxious for it to be so that when we hear for the twentieth time a government departmental head assert this principle, we conjure up straightway a concept of perfect administration. This is a mirage.

Social order demands precise knowledge of the human requirements and resources of the concern and a constant balance between these requirements and resources. Now this balance is most difficult to establish and maintain and all the more difficult the bigger the business, and when it has been upset and individual interests resulted in neglect or sacrifice of the general interest, when ambition, nepotism, favouritism, or merely ignorance, has multiplied positions without good reason or filled them with incompetent employees, much talent and strength of will and more persistence

than current instability of ministerial appointments presupposes, are required in order to sweep away abuses and restore order. . . .

11. EQUITY

Why equity and not justice? Justice is putting into execution established conventions, but conventions cannot foresee everything, they need to be interpreted or their inadequacy supplemented. For the personnel to be encouraged to carry out its duties with all the devotion and loyalty of which it is capable it must be treated with kindliness, and equity results from the combination of kindliness and justice. Equity excludes neither forcefulness nor sternness and the application of it requires much good sense, experience, and good nature.

Desire for equity and equality of treatment are aspirations to be taken into account in dealing with employees. In order to satisfy these requirements as much as possible without neglecting any principle or losing sight of the general interest, the head of the business must frequently summon up his highest faculties. He should strive to instil a sense of equity throughout all levels of the scalar chain.

12. STABILITY OF TENURE OF PERSONNEL

Time is required for an employee to get used to new work and succeed in doing it well, always assuming that he possesses the requisite abilities. If when he has got used to it, or before then, he is removed, he will not have had time to render worthwhile service. If this be repeated indefinitely the work will never be properly done. The undesirable consequences of such insecurity of tenure are especially to be feared in large concerns, where the settling in of managers is generally a lengthy matter. Much time is needed indeed to get to know men and things in a large concern in order to be in a position to decide on a plan of action, to gain confidence in oneself, and inspire it in others. Hence it has often been recorded that a mediocre manager who stays is infinitely preferable to outstanding managers who merely come and go.

Generally the managerial personnel of prosperous concerns is stable, that of unsuccessful ones is unstable. Instability of tenure is at one and the same time cause and effect of bad running. The apprenticeship of a higher manager is generally a costly matter. Nevertheless, changes of personnel are inevitable; age, illness, retirement, death, disturb the human make-up of the firm, certain employees are no longer capable of carrying out their duties, whilst others become fit to assume greater responsibilities. In common with all the other principles, therefore, stability of tenure and personnel is also a question of proportion.

13. INITIATIVE

Thinking out a plan and ensuring its success is one of the keenest satisfactions for an intelligent man to experience. It is also one of the most powerful stimulants of human endeavour. This power of thinking out and executing is what is called initiative, and freedom to propose and to execute belongs too, each in its way, to initiative. At all levels of the organizational ladder zeal and energy on the part of employees are augmented by initiative. The initiative of all, added to that of the manager, and supplementing it if need be, represents a great source of strength for businesses. This is particularly apparent at difficult times; hence it is essential to encourage and develop this capacity to the full.

Much tact and some integrity are required to inspire and maintain everyone's initiative, within the limits imposed, by respect for authority and for discipline. The manager must be able to sacrifice some personal vanity in order to grant this sort of satisfaction to subordinates. Other things being equal, moreover, a manager able to

permit the exercise of initiative on the part of subordinates is infinitely superior to one who cannot do so.

14. ESPRIT DE CORPS

"Union is strength." Business heads would do well to ponder on this proverb. Harmony, union among the personnel of a concern, is great strength in that concern. Effort, then, should be made to establish it. Among the countless methods in use I will single out specially one principle to be observed and two pitfalls to be avoided. The principle to be observed is unity of command; the dangers to be avoided are *(a)* a misguided interpretation of the motto "divide and rule," *(b)* the abuse of written communications.

(a) Personnel must not be split up. Dividing enemy forces to weaken them is clever, but dividing one's own team is a grave sin against the business. Whether this error results from inadequate managerial capacity or imperfect grasp of things, or from egoism which sacrifices general interest to personal interest, it is always reprehensible because harmful to the business. There is no merit in sowing dissension among subordinates; any beginner can do it. On the contrary, real talent is needed to coordinate effort, encourage keenness, use each man's abilities, and reward each one's merit without arousing possible jealousies and disturbing harmonious relations.

(b) Abuse of written communications. In dealing with a business matter or giving an order which requires explanation to complete it, usually it is simpler and quicker to do so verbally than in writing. Besides, it is well known that differences and misunderstandings which a conversation could clear up, grow more bitter in writing. Thence it follows that, wherever possible, contacts should be verbal; there is a gain in speed, clarity and harmony. Nevertheless, it happens in some firms that employees of neighbouring departments with numerous points of contact, or even employees within a department, who could quite easily meet, only communicate with each other in writing. Hence arise increased work and complications and delays harmful to the business. At the same time, there is to be observed a certain animosity prevailing between different departments or different employees within a department. The system of written communications usually brings this result. There is a way of putting an end to this deplorable system and that is to forbid all communications in writing which could easily and advantageously be replaced by verbal ones. There again, we come up against a question of proportion. . . .

There I bring to an end this review of principles, not because the list is exhausted—this list has no precise limits—but because to me it seems at the moment especially useful to endow management theory with a dozen or so well-established principles, on which it is appropriate to concentrate general discussion. The foregoing principles are those to which I have most often had recourse. I have simply expressed my personal opinion in connection with them. Are they to have a place in the management code which is to be built up? General discussion will show.

This code is indispensable. Be it a case of commerce, industry, politics, religion, war, or philanthropy, in every concern there is a management function to be performed, and for its performance there must be principles, that is to say acknowledged truths regarded as proven on which to rely. And it is the code which represents the sum total of these truths at any given moment.

Surprise might be expressed at the outset that the eternal moral principles, the laws of the Decalogue and Commandments of the Church are not sufficient guide for the manager, and that a special code is needed. The explanation is this: the higher laws of religious or moral order envisage the individual only, or else interests which are not of this world, whereas management principles aim at the success of associations of individuals and at the satisfying of economic interests. Given that the aim is different, it is not surprising that the means are not the same. There is no identity, so there is no contradiction. Without principles one is in darkness and chaos; interest, experience, and proportion are still very handicapped, even with the best principles. The principle is the lighthouse fixing the bearings, but it can only serve those who already know the way into port.

NOTE

1. *"Body corporate."* Fayol's term "corps social," meaning all those engaged in a given corporate activity in any sphere, is best rendered by this somewhat unusual term because (*a*) it retains his implied biological metaphor; (*b*) it represents the structure as distinct from the process of organization. The term will be retained in all contexts where these two requirements have to be met. (Translator's note.)

6
The Principles of Scientific Management

Frederick Winslow Taylor

By far the most important fact which faces the industries of our country, the industries, in fact, of the civilized world, is that not only the average worker, but nineteen out of twenty workmen throughout the civilized world firmly believe that it is for their best interests to go slow instead of to go fast. They firmly believe that it is for their interest to give as little work in return for the money that they get as is practical. The reasons for this belief are twofold, and I do not believe that the workingmen are to blame for holding these fallacious views.

If you will take any set of workmen in your own town and suggest to those men that it would be a good thing for them in their trade if they were to double their output in the coming year, each man turn out twice as much work and become twice as efficient, they would say, "I don't know anything about other people's trades; what you are saying about increasing efficiency being a good thing may be good for other trades, but I know that the only result if you come to our trade would be that half of us would be out of a job before the year was out." That to the average workingman is an axiom; it is not a matter subject to debate at all. And even among the average business men of this country that opinion is almost universal. They firmly believe that that would be the result of a great increase in efficiency, and yet directly the opposite is true.

THE EFFECT OF LABOR-SAVING DEVICES

Whenever any labor-saving device of any kind has been introduced into any trade—go back into the history of any trade and see it—even though that labor-saving device may turn out ten, twenty, thirty times that output that was originally turned out by men in that trade, the result has universally been to make work for more men in that trade, not work for less men.

Let me give you one illustration. Let us take one of the staple businesses, the cotton industry. About 1840 the power loom succeeded the old hand loom in the cotton industry. It was invented many years before, somewhere about 1780 or 1790, but it came in very slowly. About 1840 the weavers of Manchester, England, saw that the power loom was coming, and they knew it would turn out three times the yardage of cloth in a day that the hand loom turned out. And what did they do, these five thousand weavers of Manchester, England, who saw starvation staring them in the face? They broke into the establishments into which those machines were being introduced, they smashed them, they did everything possible to stop the introduction of the power loom. And the same result followed that follows every attempt to interfere with the introduction of any labor-saving device, if it is really a labor-saving device. Instead of stopping the introduction of the power loom, their opposition apparently accelerated it, just as opposition to scientific management all over the country, bitter labor opposition today, is accelerating the introduction of it instead of retarding it. History repeats itself in that respect. The power loom came right straight along.

And let us see the result in Manchester. Just what follows in every industry when

Source: Bulletin of the Taylor Society (December 1916). An abstract of an address given by Taylor before the Cleveland Advertising Club, March 3, 1915, two weeks before his death, and repeated the following day at Youngstown, Ohio (this presentation was Taylor's last public appearance).

any labor-saving device is introduced. Less than a century has gone by since 1840. The population of England in that time has now more than doubled. Each man in the cotton industry in Manchester, England, now turns out, at a restricted estimate ten yards of cloth for every yard of cloth that was turned out in 1840. In 1840 there were 5,000 weavers in Manchester. Now there are 265,000. Has that thrown men out of work? Has the introduction of labor-saving machinery, which has multiplied the output per man by tenfold, thrown men out of work?

What is the real meaning of this? All that you have to do is to bring wealth into this world and the world uses it. That is the real meaning. The meaning is that where in 1840 cotton goods were a luxury to be worn only by rich people when they were hardly ever seen on the street, now every man, woman, and child all over the world wears cotton goods as a daily necessity.

Nineteen-twentieths of the real wealth of this world is used by the poor people, and not the rich, so that the workingman who sets out as a steady principle to restrict output is merely robbing his own kind. That group of manufacturers which adopts as a permanent principle restriction of output, in order to hold up prices, is robbing the world. The one great thing that marks the improvement of this world is measured by the enormous increase in output of the individuals in this world. There is fully twenty times the output per man now than there was three hundred years ago. That marks the increase in the real wealth of the world; that marks the increase of the happiness of the world, that gives us the opportunity for shorter hours, for better education, for amusement, for art, for music, for everything that is worthwhile in this world — goes right straight back to this increase in the output of the individual. The workingmen of today live better than the king did three hundred years ago. From what does the progress the world has made come? Simply from the increase in the output of the individual all over the world.

THE DEVELOPMENT OF SOLDIERING

The second reason why the workmen of this country and of Europe deliberately restrict output is a very simple one. They, for this reason, are even less to blame than they are for the other. If, for example, you are manufacturing a pen, let us assume for simplicity that a pen can be made by a single man. Let us say that the workman is turning out ten pens per day, and that he is receiving $2.50 a day for his wages. He has a progressive foreman who is up to date, and that foreman goes to the workman and suggests, "Here, John, you are getting $2.50 a day, and you are turning out ten pens. I would suggest that I pay you 25 cents for making that pen." The man takes the job, and through the help of his foreman, through his own ingenuity, through his increased work, through his interest in his business, through the help of his friends, at the end of the year he finds himself turning out twenty pens instead of ten. He is happy, he is making $5, instead of $2.50 a day. His foreman is happy because, with the same room, with the same men he had before, he has doubled the output of his department, and the manufacturer himself is sometimes happy, but not often. Then someone on the board of directors asks to see the payroll, and he finds that we are paying $5 a day where other similar mechanics are only getting $2.50, and in no uncertain terms he announces that we must stop ruining the labor market. We cannot pay $5 a day when the standard rate of wages is $2.50; how can we hope to compete with surrounding towns? What is the result? Mr. Foreman is sent for, and he is told that he has got to stop ruining the labor market of Cleveland. And the foreman goes back to his workman in sadness, in depression, and tells his workman, "I am sorry, John, but I have got to cut the price down for that pen; I cannot let you earn $5 a day; the board of directors has got on to it, and it is ruining the labor market; you ought to be willing to have the price reduced. You cannot earn more than $3 or

$2.75 a day, and I will have to cut your wages so that you will only get $3 a day." John, of necessity accepts the cut, but he sees to it that he never makes enough pens to get another cut.

CHARACTERISTICS OF THE UNION WORKMAN

There seem to be two divergent opinions about the workmen of this country. One is that a lot of the trade unions' workmen, particularly in this country, have become brutal, have become dominating, careless of any interests but their own, and are a pretty poor lot. And the other opinion which those same trade unionists hold of themselves is that they are pretty close to little gods. Whichever view you may hold of the workingmen of this country, and my personal view of them is that they are a pretty fine lot of fellows, they are just about the same as you and I. But whether you hold the bad opinion or the good opinion, it makes no difference. Whatever the workingmen of this country are or whatever they are not, they are not fools. And all that is necessary is for a workingman to have but one object lesson, like that I have told you, and he soldiers for the rest of his life.

There are a few exceptional employers who treat their workmen differently, but I am talking about the rule of the country. Soldiering is the absolute rule with all workmen who know their business. I am not saying it is for their interest to soldier. You cannot blame them for it. You cannot expect them to be large enough minded men to look at the proper view of the matter. Nor is the man who cuts the wages necessarily to blame. It is simply a misfortune in industry.

THE DEVELOPMENT OF SCIENTIFIC MANAGEMENT

There has been, until comparatively recently, no scheme promulgated by which the evils of rate cutting could be properly avoided, so soldiering has been the rule.

Now the first step that was taken toward the development of those methods, of those principles, which rightly or wrongly have come to be known under the name of scientific management—the first step that was taken in an earnest endeavor to remedy the evils of soldiering; an earnest endeavor to make it unnecessary for workmen to be hypocritical in this way, to deceive themselves, to deceive their employers, to live day in and day out a life of deceit, forced upon them conditions—the very first step that was taken toward the development was to overcome that evil. I want to emphasize that, because I wish to emphasize the one great fact relating to scientific management, the greatest factor: namely, that scientific management is no new set of theories that has been tried on by any one at every step. Scientific management at every step has been an evolution, not a theory. In all cases the practice has preceded the theory, not succeeded it. In every case one measure after another has been tried out, until the proper remedy has been found. That series of proper eliminations, that evolution, is what is called scientific management. Every element of it has had to fight its way against the elements that preceded it, and prove itself better or it would not be there tomorrow.

All the men that I know of who are in any way connected with scientific management are ready to abandon any scheme, and theory in favor of anything else that could be found that is better. There is nothing in scientific management that is fixed. There is no one man, or group of men, who have invented scientific management.

What I want to emphasize is that all of the elements of scientific management are an evolution, not an invention. Scientific management is in use in an immense range and variety of industries. Almost every type of industry in this country has scientific management working successfully. I think I can safely say that on the average in those establishments in which scientific management has been introduced, the average workman is turning out double the output he was before. I think that is a conservative statement.

THE WORKMEN: THE CHIEF BENEFICIARIES

Three or four years ago I could have said there were about fifty thousand men working under scientific management, but now I know there are many more. Company after company is coming under it, many of which I know nothing about. Almost universally they are working successfully. This increasing of the output per individual in the trade, results, of course, in cheapening the product; it results, therefore, in larger profit usually to the owners of the business; it results also, in many cases, in a lowering of the selling price, although that has not come to the extent it will later. In the end the public gets the good. Without any question, the large good which so far has come from scientific management has come to the worker. To the workmen has come, practically right off as soon as scientific management is introduced, an increase in wages amounting from 33 to 100 percent, and yet that is not the greatest good that comes to the workmen from scientific management. The great good comes from the fact that, under scientific management, they look upon their employers as the best friends they have in the world; the suspicious watchfulness which characterizes the old type management, the semi-antagonism, or the complete antagonism between workmen and employers is entirely superseded, and in its place comes genuine friendship between both sides. That is the greatest good that has come under scientific management. As a proof of this in the many businesses in which scientific management has been introduced, I know of not one single strike of workmen working under it after it had been introduced, and only two or three while it was in process of introduction. In this connection I must speak of the

fakers, those who have said they can introduce scientific management into a business in six months or a year. That is pure nonsense. There have been many strikes stirred up by that type of man. Not one strike has ever come, and I do not believe ever will come, under scientific management.

WHAT SCIENTIFIC MANAGEMENT IS

What is scientific management? It is no efficiency device, nor is it any group of efficiency devices. Scientific management is no new scheme for paying men, it is no bonus system, no piecework system, no premium system of payment; it is no new method of figuring costs. It is no one of the various elements by which it is commonly known, by which people refer to it. It is not time study nor man study. It is not the printing of a ton or two of blanks and unloading them on a company and saying, "There is your system, go ahead and use it." Scientific management does not exist and cannot exist until there has been a complete mental revolution on the part of the workmen working under it, as to their duties toward themselves and toward their employers, and a complete mental revolution in the outlook for the employers, toward their duties, toward themselves, and toward their workmen. And until this great mental change takes place, scientific management does not exist. Do you think you can make a great mental revolution in a large group of workmen in a year, or do you think you can make it in a large group of foremen and superintendents in a year? If you do, you are very much mistaken. All of us hold mighty close to our ideas and principles in life, and we change very slowly toward the new, and very properly too.

Let me give you an idea of what I mean by this change in mental outlook. If you are manufacturing a hammer or a mallet, into the cost of that mallet goes a certain amount of raw materials, a certain amount of wood and metal. If you will take the cost of the raw materials and then add to it that cost which is frequently called by various names—overhead expenses, general expense, indirect expense; that is, the proper share of taxes, insurance, light, heat, salaries of officers and advertising—and you have a sum of money. Subtract that sum from the selling price, and what is left over is called the surplus. It is over this surplus that all of the labor disputes in the past have occurred. The workman naturally wants all he can get. His wages come out of that surplus. The manufacturer wants all he can get in the shape of profits, and it is from the division of this surplus that all the labor disputes have come in the past—the equitable division.

The new outlook that comes under scientific management is this: The workmen, after many object lessons, come to see and the management come to see that this surplus can be made so great, providing both sides will stop their pulling apart, will stop their fighting and will push as hard as they can to get as cheap an output as possible, that there is no occasion to quarrel. Each side can get more than ever before. The acknowledgement of this fact represents a complete mental revolution. . . .

WHAT SCIENTIFIC MANAGEMENT WILL DO

I am going to try to prove to you that the old style of management has not a ghost of a chance in competition with the principles of scientific management. Why? In the first place, under scientific management, the initiative of the workmen, their hard work, their goodwill, their best endeavors are obtained with absolute regularity. There are cases all the time where men will soldier, but they become the exception, as a rule, and they give their true initiative under scientific management. That is the least of the two sources of gain. The greatest source of gain under scientific management comes from the new and almost unheard-of duties and burdens which are voluntarily assumed,

not by the workmen, but by the men on the management side. These are the things which make scientific management a success. These new duties, these new burdens undertaken by the management have rightly or wrongly been divided into four groups, and have been called the principles of scientific management.

The first of the great principles of scientific management, the first of the new burdens which are voluntarily undertaken by those on the management side is the deliberate gathering together of the great mass of traditional knowledge which, in the past, has been in the heads of the workmen, recording it, tabulating it, reducing it in most cases to rules, laws, and in many cases to mathematical formulae, which, with these new laws, are applied to the cooperation of the management to the work of the workmen. This results in an immense increase in the output, we may say, of the two. The gathering in of this great mass of traditional knowledge, which is done by the means of motion study, time study, can be truly called the science.

Let me make a prediction. I have before me the first book, so far as I know, that has been published on motion study and on time study. That is, the motion study and time study of the cement and concrete trades. It contains everything relating to concrete work. It is of about seven hundred pages and embodies the motions of men, the time and the best way of doing that sort of work. It is the first case in which a trade has been reduced to the same condition that engineering data of all kinds have been reduced, and it is this sort of data that is bound to sweep the world.

I have before me something which has been gathering for about fourteen years, the time or motion study of the machine shop. It will take probably four or five years more before the first book will be ready to publish on that subject. There is a collection of sixty or seventy thousand elements affecting machine-shop work. After a few years, say three, four or five years more, someone will be ready to publish the first book giving the laws of the movements of men in the machine shop—all the laws, not only a few of them. Let me predict, just as sure as the sun shines, that is going to come in every trade. Why? Because it pays, for no other reason. That results in doubling the output in any shop. Any device which results in an increased output is bound to come in spite of all opposition, whether we want it or not. It comes automatically.

THE SELECTION OF THE WORKMAN

The next of the four principles of scientific management is the scientific selection of the workman, and then his progressive development. It becomes the duty under scientific management of not one, but of a group of men on the management side, to deliberately study the workmen who are under them; study them in the most careful, thorough and painstaking way; and not just leave it to the poor, overworked foreman to go out and say, "Come on, what do you want? If you are cheap enough I will give you a trial."

That is the old way. The new way is to take a great deal of trouble in selecting the workmen. The selection proceeds year after year. And it becomes the duty of those engaged in scientific management to know something about the workmen under them. It becomes their duty to set out deliberately to train the workmen in their employ to be able to do a better and still better class of work than ever before, and to then pay them higher wages than ever before. This deliberate selection of the workmen is the second of the great duties that devolve on the management under scientific management.

BRINGING TOGETHER THE SCIENCE AND THE MAN

The third principle is the bringing together of this science of which I have spoken and the trained workmen. I say bringing because

they don't come together unless someone brings them. Select and train your workmen all you may, but unless there is someone who will make the men and the science come together, they will stay apart. The "make" involves a great many elements. They are not all disagreeable elements. The most important and largest way of "making" is to do something nice for the man whom you wish to make come together with the science. Offer him a plum, something that is worthwhile. There are many plums offered to those who come under scientific management—better treatment, more kindly treatment, more consideration for their wishes, and an opportunity for them to express their wants freely. That is one side of the "make." An equally important side is, whenever a man will not do what he ought, to either make him do it or stop it. If he will not do it, let him get out. I am not talking of any mollycoddle. Let me disabuse your minds of any opinion that scientific management is a mollycoddle scheme. . . .

THE PRINCIPLE OF THE DIVISION OF WORK

The fourth principle is the plainest of all. It involves a complete re-division of the work of the establishment. Under the old scheme of management, almost all of the work was done by the workmen. Under the new, the work of the establishment is divided into two large parts. All of that work which formerly was done by the workmen alone is divided into two large sections, and one of those sections is handed over to the management. They do a whole division of the work formerly done by the workmen. It is this real cooperation, this genuine division of the work between the two sides, more than any other element which accounts for the fact that there never will be strikes under scientific management. When the workman realizes that there is hardly a thing he does that does not have to be preceded by some act of preparation on the part of management, and when that workman realizes when the management falls down and does not do its part, that he is not only entitled to a kick, but that he can register that kick in the most forcible possible way, he cannot quarrel with the men over him. It is teamwork. There are more complaints made every day on the part of the workmen that the men on the management side fail to do their duties than are made by the management that the men fail. Every one of the complaints of the men have to be heeded, just as much as the complaints from the management that the workmen do not do their share. That is characteristic of scientific management. It represents a democracy, co-operation, a genuine division of work which never existed before in this world.

THE PROOF OF THE THEORY

I am through now with the theory. I will try to convince you of the value of these four principles by giving you some practical illustrations. I hope that you will look for these four elements in the illustrations. I shall begin by trying to show the power of these four elements when applied to the greatest kind of work I know of that is done by man. The reason I have heretofore chosen pig-iron for an illustration is that it is the lowest form of work that is known.

A pig of iron weighs about ninety-two pounds on an average. A man stoops down and, with no other implement than his hands, picks up a pig of iron, walks a few yards with it, and drops it on a pile. A large part of the community has the impression that scientific management is chiefly handling pig-iron. The reason I first chose pig-iron for an illustration is that, if you can prove to any one the strength, the effect, of those four principles when applied to such rudimentary work as handling pig-iron, the presumption is that it can be applied to something better. The only way to prove it is to start at the bottom and show those four principles all along the line. I am sorry

I cannot, because of the lack of time, give you the illustration of handling pig-iron. Many of you doubt whether there is much of any science in it. I am going to try to prove later with a high class mechanic that the workman who is fit to work at any type of work is almost universally incapable of understanding the principles without the help of some one else. I will use shoveling because it is a shorter illustration, and I will try to show what I mean by the science of shoveling, and the power which comes to the man who knows the science of shoveling. It is a high art compared with pig-iron handling.

THE SCIENCE OF SHOVELING

When I went to the Bethlehem Steel Works, the first thing I saw was a gang of men unloading rice coal. They were a splendid set of fellows, and they shoveled fast. There was no loafing at all. They shoveled as hard as you could ask any man to work. I looked with the greatest of interest for a long time, and finally they moved off rapidly down into the yard to another part of the yard and went right at handling iron ore. One of the main facts connected with that shoveling was that the work those men were doing was that, in handling the rice coal, they had on their shovels a load of 3¾ pounds, and when the same men went to handling ore with the same shovel, they had over 38 pounds on their shovels. Is it asking too much of anyone to inquire whether 3¾ pounds is the right load for a shovel, or whether 38 pounds is the right load for a shovel? Surely if one is right the other must be wrong. I think that is a self-evident fact, and yet I am willing to bet that that is what workmen are doing right now in Cleveland.

That is the old way. Suppose we notice that fact. Most of us do not notice it because it is left to the foreman. At the Midvale works, we had to find out these facts. What is the old way of finding them out? The old way was to sit down and write one's friends and ask them the questions.

They got answers from contractors about what they thought it ought to be, and then they averaged them up, or took the most reliable man, and said, "That is all right; now we have a shovel load of so much." The more common way is to say, "I want a good shovel foreman." They will send for the foreman of the shovelers and put the job up to him to find what is the proper load to put on a shovel. He will tell you right off the bat. I want to show you the difference under scientific management.

Under scientific management you ask no one. Every little trifle,—here is nothing too small,—becomes the subject of experiment. The experiments develop into a law; they save money; they increase the output of the individual and make the thing worthwhile. How is this done? What we did in shoveling experiments was to deliberately select two first class shovelers, the best we knew how to get. We brought them into the office and said, "Jim and Mike, you two fellows are both good shovelers. I have a proposition to make to you. I am going to pay you double wages if you fellows will go out and do what I want you to do. There will be a young chap go along with you with a pencil and a piece of paper, and he will tell you to do a lot of fool things, and you will do them, and he will write down a lot of fool things, and you will think it is a joke, but it is nothing of the kind. Let me tell you one thing: if you fellows think that you can fool that chap you are very much mistaken, you cannot fool him at all. Don't get it through your heads you can fool him. If you take this double wages, you will be straight and do what you are told." They both promised and did exactly what they were told. What we told them was this: "We want you to start in and do whatever shoveling you are told to do and work at just the pace, all day long, that when it comes night you are going to be good and tired, but not tired out. I do not want you exhausted or anything like that, but properly tired. You know what a good day's work is. In other words, I do not want any loafing business or any overwork business. If you find yourself overworked and

getting too tired, slow down." Those men did that and did it in the most splendid kind of way day in and day out. We proved their cooperation because they were in different parts of the yard, and they both got near enough the same results. Our results were duplicated.

I have found that there are a lot of schemes among my working friends, but no more among them than among us. They are good, straight fellows if you only treat them right, and put the matter up squarely to them. We started in at a pile of material, with a very large shovel. We kept innumerable accurate records of all kinds, some of them useless. Thirty or forty different items were carefully observed about the work of those two men. We counted the number of shovelfuls thrown in a day. We found with a weight of between thirty-eight and thirty-nine pounds on the shovel, the man made a pile of material of a certain height. We then cut off the shovel, and he shoveled again and with a thirty-four pound load his pile went up and he shoveled more in a day. We again cut off the shovel to thirty pounds, and the pile went up again. With twenty-six pounds on the shovel, the pile again went up, and at twenty-one and one-half pounds the men could do their best. At twenty pounds the pile went down, at eighteen it went down, at fourteen it went down, so that they were at the peak of twenty-one and one-half pounds. There is a scientific fact. A first class shoveler ought to take twenty-one and one-half pounds on his shovel in order to work to the best possible advantage. You are not giving that man a chance unless you give him a shovel which will hold twenty-one pounds.

The men in the yard were run by the old fashioned foreman. He simply walked about with them. We at once took their shovels away from them. We built a large labor tool room which held ten to fifteen different kinds of shoveling implements so that for each kind of material that was handled in that yard, all the way from rice coals, ashes, coke, all the way up to ore, we would have a shovel that would just hold twenty-one pounds, or average twenty-one. One time it would hold eighteen, the next twenty-four, but it will average twenty-one.

When you have six hundred men laboring in the yard, as we had there, it becomes a matter of quite considerable difficulty to get, each day, for each one of those six hundred men, engaged in a line one and one-half to two miles long and a half mile wide, just the right shovel for shoveling material. That requires organization to lay out and plan for those men in advance. We had to lay out the work each day. We had to have large maps on which the movements of the men were plotted out a day in advance. When each workman came in the morning, he took out two pieces of paper. One of the blanks gave them a statement of the implements which they had to use, and the part of the yard in which they had to work. That required organization planning in advance.

One of the first principles we adopted was that no man in that labor gang could work on the new way unless he earned sixty percent higher wages than under the old plan. It is only just to the workman that he shall know right off whether he is doing his work right or not. He must not be told a week or month after, that he fell down. He must know it the next morning. So the next slip that came out of the pigeon hole was either a white or yellow slip. We used the two colors because some of the men could not read. The yellow slip meant that he had not earned his sixty per cent higher wages. He knew that he could not stay in that gang and keep on getting yellow slips.

TEACHING THE MEN

I want to show you again the totally different outlook there is under scientific management by illustrating what happened when that man got his yellow slips. Under the old scheme, the foreman could say to him, "You are no good, get out of this; no time for you, you cannot earn sixty percent higher wages; get out of this! Go!" It was not done politely, but the foreman had no

time to palaver. Under the new scheme what happened? A teacher of shoveling went down to see that man. A teacher of shoveling is a man who is handy with a shovel, who has made his mark in life with a shovel, and yet who is a kindly fellow and knows how to show the other fellow what he ought to do. When that teacher went there he said, "See here, Jim, you have a lot of those yellow slips, what is the matter with you? What is up? Have you been drunk? Are you tired? Are you sick? Anything wrong with you? Because if you are tired or sick we will give you a show somewhere else." "Well, no, I am all right." "Then if you are not sick, or there is nothing wrong with you, you have forgotten how to shovel. I showed you how to shovel. You have forgotten something, now go ahead and shovel and I will show you what is the matter with you." Shoveling is a pretty big science, it is not a little thing.

If you are going to use the shovel right you should always shovel off an iron bottom; if not an iron bottom, a wooden bottom; and if not a wooden bottom a hard dirt bottom. Time and again the conditions are such that you have to go right into the pile. When that is the case, with nine out of ten materials it takes more trouble and more time and more effort to get the shovel into the pile than to do all the rest of the shoveling. That is where the effort comes. Those of you again who have taught the art of shoveling will have taught your workmen to do this. There is only one way to do it right. Put your forearm down onto the upper part of your leg, and when you push into the pile, throw your weight against it. That relieves your arm of work. You then have an automatic push, we will say, about eighty pounds, the weight of your body thrown on to it. Time and again we would find men whom we had taught to shovel right were going at it in the same old way, and of course, they could not do a day's work. The teacher would simply stand over that fellow and say, "There is what is the matter with you, Jim, you have forgotten to shovel into the pile."

You are not interested in shoveling, you are not interested in whether one way or the other is right, but I do hope to interest you in the difference of the mental attitude of the men who are teaching under the new system. Under the new system, if a man falls down, the presumption is that it is our fault at first, that we probably have not taught the man right, have not given him a fair show, have not spent time enough in showing him how to do his work.

Let me tell you another thing that is characteristic of scientific management. In my day, we were smart enough to know when the boss was coming, and when he came up we were apparently really working. Under scientific management, there is none of that pretense. I cannot say that in the old days we were delighted to see the boss coming around. We always expected some kind of roast if he came too close. Under the new, the teacher is welcomed; he is not an enemy, but a friend. He comes there to try to help the man get bigger wages, to show him how to do something. It is the great mental change, the change in the outlook that comes, rather than the details of it.

DOES SCIENTIFIC MANAGEMENT PAY?

It took the time of a number of men for about three years to study the art of shoveling in that yard at the Bethlehem Steel Works alone. They were carefully trained college men, and they were busy all the time. That costs money, the tool room costs money, the clerks we had to keep there all night figuring up how much the men did the day before cost money, the office in which the men laid out and planned the work cost money. The very fair and proper question, the only question to ask is "Does it pay?" because if scientific management does not pay in dollars and cents, it is the rankest kind of nonsense. There is nothing philanthropic about it. It has got to pay, because business which cannot be done on a profitable basis, ought not to be done on a

philanthropic basis, for it will not last. At the end of three and one-half years we had a very good chance to know whether or not it paid.

Fortunately in the Bethlehem Steel Works they had records of how much it cost to handle the materials under the old system, where the single foreman led a group of men around the works. It costs them between seven and eight cents a ton to handle materials, on an average throughout the year. After paying for all this extra work I have told you about, it cost between three and four cents a ton to handle materials, and there was a profit of between seventy-five and eighty thousand dollars a year in that yard by handling those materials in the new way. What the men got out of it was this: Under the old system there were between four and six hundred men handling the material in that yard, and when we got through there were about one hundred and forty. Each one was earning a great deal more money. We made careful investigation and found they were almost all saving money, living better, happier; they are the most contented set of laborers to be seen anywhere. It is only by this kind of justification, justification of a profit for both sides, an advantage to both sides, that scientific management can exist.

I would like to give you one more illustration. I want to try to prove to you that even the highest class mechanic cannot possibly understand the philosophy of his work, cannot possibly understand the laws under which he has to operate. There is a man who has had a high school education, an ingenious fellow who courts variety in life, to whom it is pleasant to change from one kind of work to another. He is not a cheap man, he is rather a high grade man among the machinists of this country. The case of which I am going to tell you is one in which my friend Barth went to introduce scientific management in the works of an owner, who, at between 65 and 70 years of age, had built up his business from nothing to almost five thousand men. They had a squabble, and after they got through,

Mr. Barth made the proposition, "I will take any machine that you use in your shop, and I will show you that I can double the output of that machine." A very fair machine was selected. It was a lathe on which the workman had been working about twelve years. The product of that shop is a patented machine with a good many parts, 350 men working making those parts year in and year out. Each man had ten or a dozen parts a year.

The first thing that was done was in the presence of the foreman, the superintendent and the owner of the establishment. Mr. Barth laid down the way in which all of the parts were to be machined on that machine by the workman. Then Mr. Barth, with one of his small slide rules, proceeded to analyze the machine. With the aid of this analysis, which embodies the laws of cutting metals, Mr. Barth was able to take his turn at the machine; his gain was from two and one-half times to three times the amount of work turned out by the other man. This is what can be done by science as against the old rule of thumb knowledge. That is not exaggeration; the gain is as great as that in many cases.

Let me tell you something. The machines of this country, almost universally in the machine shops of our country, are speeded two or three hundred percent wrong. I made that assertion before the tool builders in Atlantic City. I said, "Gentlemen, in your own shops, many of your machines are two and three hundred percent wrong in speeds. Why? Because you have guessed at it." I am trying to show you what are the losses under the old opinions, the difference between knowledge on the one hand and guesswork on the other.

In 1882, at the end of a long fight with the machinists of the Midvale Steel Works, I went there as a laborer, and finally became a machinist after serving my apprenticeship outside. I finally got into the shop, and worked up to the place of a clerk who had something wrong with him. I then did a little bit more work than the others were doing, not too much. They came to me and said, "See here, Fred, you are not going to be a piecework hog." I said, "You fellows mean that you think I am not going to try to get any more work off these machines? I certainly am. Now I am on the other side, and I am going to be straight with you, and I will tell you so in advance." They said, "All right then, we will give you fair notice you will be outside the fence inside of six weeks." Let me tell you gentlemen, if any of you have been through a fight like that, trying to get workmen to do what they do not want to do, you will know the meanness of it, and you will never want to go into another one. I never would have gone into it if I had known what was ahead of me. After the meanest kind of a bitter fight, at the end of three years, we fairly won out and got a big increase in output. I had no illusion at the end of that time as to my great ability or anything else. I knew that those workmen knew about ten times as much as I did about doing the work. I set out deliberately to get on our side some of that knowledge that those workmen had.

Mr. William Sellers was the president, and he was a man away beyond his generation in progress. I went to him and said, "I want to spend quite a good deal of money trying to educate ourselves on the management side of our works. I do not know much of anything, and I am just about in the same condition as all the rest of the foremen around here." Very reluctantly, I may say, he allowed us to start to spend money. That started the study of the art of cutting metals. At the end of six months, from the standpoint of how to cut the metal off faster, the study did not amount to anything, but we unearthed a gold mine of information. Mr. Sellers laughed at me, but when I was able to show him the possibilities that lay ahead of us, the number of things we could find out, he said, "Go ahead." So until 1889, that experiment went straight ahead day in and day out. That was done because it paid in dollars and cents.

After I left the Midvale Steel Works, we had no means of figuring those experiments except the information which we had already gotten. Ten different machines were built to develop the art of cutting metals, so that almost continuously from 1882 for twenty-six years, all sorts of experiments went on to determine the twelve great elements that go to make up the art of cutting metals. I am trying to show you just what is going to take place in every industry throughout this world. You must know those facts if you are going to manufacture cheaply, and the only way to know them is to pay for them. . . .

THE EFFECT ON THE WORKMAN

Almost every one says, "Why, yes, that may be a good thing for the manufacturer, but how about the workmen? You are taking all the initiative away from that workman, you are making a machine out of him; what are you doing for him? He becomes merely a part of the machine." That is the almost universal impression. Again let me try to sweep aside the fallacy of that view by an illustration. The modern surgeon without a doubt is the finest mechanic in the world. He combines the greatest manual dexterity with the greatest knowledge of implements and the greatest knowledge of materials on which he is working. He is a true scientist, and he is a very highly skilled mechanic.

How does the surgeon teach his trade to the young men who come to the medical school? Does he say to them, "Now, young men, we belong to an older generation than you do, but the new generation is going to far outstrip anything that has been done in our generation; therefore, what we want of you is your initiative. We must have your brains, your thought, with your initiative.

Of course, you know we old fellows have certain prejudices. For example, if we were going to amputate a leg, when we come down to the bone we are accustomed to take a saw, and we use it in that way and saw the bone off. But, gentlemen, do not let that fact one minute interfere with your originality, with your initiative, if you prefer an axe or a hatchet." Does the surgeon say this? He does not. He says, "You young men are going to outstrip us, but we will show you how. You shall not use a single implement in a single way until you know just which one to use, and we will tell you which one to use, and until you know how to use it, we will tell you how to use that implement, and after you have learned to use that implement our way, if you then see any defects in the implements, any defects in the method, then invent; but, invent so that you can invent upwards. Do not go inventing things which we discarded years ago."

That is just what we say to our young men in the shops. Scientific management makes no pretense that there is any finality in it. We merely say that the collective work of thirty or forty men in this trade through eight or ten years has gathered together a large amount of data. Every man in the establishment must start that way, must start our way, then if he can show us any better way, I do not care what it is, we will make an experiment to see if it is better. It will be named after him, and he will get a prize for having improved on one of our standards. There is the way we make progress under scientific management. There is your justification for all this. It does not dwarf initiative, it makes true initiative. Most of our progress comes through our workmen, but comes in a legitimate way.

7
Bureaucracy
Max Weber Fixed + official Jurisdiction

1. CHARACTERISTICS OF BUREAUCRACY

Modern officialdom functions in the following specific manner:

I. There is the principle of fixed and official jurisdictional areas, which are generally ordered by rules, that is, by laws or administrative regulations.

1. The regular activities required for the purposes of the bureaucratically governed structure are distributed in a fixed way as official duties.

2. The authority to give the commands required for the discharge of these duties is distributed in a stable way and is strictly delimited by rules concerning the coercive means, physical, sacerdotal, or otherwise, which may be placed at the disposal of officials.

3. Methodical provision is made for the regular and continuous fulfillment of these duties and for the execution of the corresponding rights; only persons who have the generally regulated qualifications to serve are employed.

In public and lawful government these three elements constitute "bureaucratic authority." In private economic domination, they constitute bureaucratic "management." Bureaucracy, thus understood, is fully developed in political and ecclesiastical communities only in the modern state, and, in the private economy, only in the most advanced institutions of capitalism. Permanent and public office authority, with fixed jurisdiction, is not the historical rule but rather the exception. This is so even in large political structures such as those of the ancient Orient, the Germanic and Mongolian empires of conquest, or of many feudal structures of state. In all these cases, the ruler executes the most important measures through personal trustees, table-companions, or courtservants. Their commissions and authority are not precisely delimited and are temporarily called into being for each case.

II. The principles of office hierarchy and of levels of graded authority mean a firmly ordered system of super- and subordination in which there is a supervision of the lower offices by the higher ones. Such a system offers the governed the possibility of appealing the decision of a lower office to its higher authority, in a definitely regulated manner. With the full development of the bureaucratic type, the office hierarchy is monocratically organized. The principle of hierarchical office authority is found in all bureaucratic structures: in state and ecclesiastical structures as well as in large party organizations and private enterprises. It does not matter for the character of bureaucracy whether its authority is called "private" or "public."

When the principle of jurisdictional "competency" is fully carried through, hierarchical subordination—at least in public office—does not mean that the "higher" authority is simply authorized to take over the business of the "lower." Indeed, the opposite is the rule. Once established and having fulfilled its task, an office tends to

Source: From Max Weber: Essays in Sociology, ed. and trans., H. H. Gerth and C. Wright Mills (New York: Oxford University Press, 1964); footnotes omitted. © 1946, 1958, 1973 by Hans H. Gerth and C. Wright Mills. Used by permission of Oxford University Press, Inc.

continue in existence and be held by another incumbent.

III. The management of the modern office is based upon written documents ("the files"), which are preserved in their original or draught form. There is, therefore, a staff or subaltern officials and scribes of all sorts. The body of officials actively engaged in a "public" office, along with the respective apparatus of material implements and the files, make up a "bureau." In private enterprise, "the bureau" is often called "the office."

In principle, the modern organization of the civil service separates the bureau from the private domicile of the official, and, in general, bureaucracy segregates official activity as something distinct from the sphere of private life. Public monies and equipment are divorced from the private property of the official. This condition is everywhere the product of a long development. Nowadays, it is found in public as well as in private enterprises; in the latter, the principle extends even to the leading entrepreneur. In principle, the executive office is separated from the household, business from private correspondence, and business assets from private fortunes. The more consistently the modern type of business management has been carried through the more are these separations the case. The beginnings of this process are to be found as early as the Middle Ages.

It is the peculiarity of the modern entrepreneur that he conducts himself as the "first official" of his enterprise, in the very same way in which the ruler of a specifically modern bureaucratic state spoke of himself as "the first servant" of the state. The idea that the bureau activities of the state are intrinsically different in character from the management of private economic offices is a continental European notion and, by way of contrast, is totally foreign to the American way.

IV. Office management, at least all specialized office management—and such management is distinctly modern—usually presupposes thorough and expert training. This increasingly holds for the modern executive and employee of private enterprises, in the same manner as it holds for the state official.

V. When the office is fully developed, official activity demands the full working capacity of the official, irrespective of the fact that his obligatory time in the bureau may be firmly delimited. In the normal case, this is only the product of a long development, in the public as well as in the private office. Formerly, in all cases, the normal state of affairs was reversed: official business was discharged as a secondary activity.

VI. The management of the office follows general rules, which are more or less stable, more or less exhaustive, and which can be learned. Knowledge of these rules represents a special technical learning which the officials possess. It involves jurisprudence, or administrative or business management.

The reduction of modern office management to rules is deeply embedded in its very nature. The theory of modern public administration, for instance, assumes that the authority to order certain matters by decree—which has been legally granted to public authorities—does not entitle the bureau to regulate the matter by commands given for each case, but only to regulate the matter abstractly. This stands in extreme contrast to the regulation of all relationships through individual privileges and bestowals of favor, which is absolutely dominant in patrimonialism, at least in so far as such relationships are not fixed by sacred tradition.

2. THE POSITION OF THE OFFICIAL

All this results in the following for the internal and external position of the official:

I. Office holding is a "vocation." This is shown, first, in the requirement of a firmly prescribed course of training, which demands the entire capacity for work for a long period of time, and in the generally prescribed and special examinations which are prerequisites of employment. Furthermore, the position of the official is in the nature of a duty. This determines the internal structure of his relations, in the following manner: Legally and actually, office holding is not considered a source to be exploited for rents or emoluments, as was normally the case during the Middle Ages and frequently up to the threshold of recent times. Nor is office holding considered a usual exchange of services for equivalents, as is the case with free labor contracts. Entrance into an office, including one in the private economy, is considered an acceptance of a specific obligation of faithful management in return for a secure existence. It is decisive for the specific nature of modern loyalty to an office that, in the pure type, it does not establish a relationship to a *person*, like the vassal's or disciple's faith in feudal or in patrimonial relations of authority. Modern loyalty is devoted to impersonal and functional purposes. Behind the functional purposes, of course, "ideas of culture-values" usually stand. These are *ersatz* for the earthly or supra-mundane personal master: ideas such as "state," "church," "community," "party," or "enterprise" are thought of as being realized in a community; they provide an ideological halo for the master.

The political official—at least in the fully developed modern state—is not considered the personal servant of a ruler. Today, the bishop, the priest, and the preacher are in fact no longer, as in early Christian times, holders of purely personal charisma. The supra-mundane and sacred values which they offer are given to everybody who seems to be worthy of them and who asks for them. In former times, such leaders acted upon the personal command of their master; in principle, they were responsible only to him. Nowadays, in spite of the partial survival of the old theory, such religious leaders are officials in the service of a functional purpose, which in the present-day "church" has become routinized and, in turn, ideologically hallowed.

II. The personal position of the official is patterned in the following way:

1. Whether he is in a private office or a public bureau, the modern official always strives and usually enjoys a distinct *social esteem* as compared with the governed. His social position is guaranteed by the prescriptive rules of rank order and, for the political official, by special definitions of the criminal code against "insults of officials" and "contempt" of state and church authorities.

The actual social position of the official is normally highest where, as in old civilized countries, the following conditions prevail: a strong demand for administration by trained experts; a strong and stable social differentiation, where the official predominantly derives from socially and economically privileged strata because of the social distribution of power; or where the costliness of the required training and status conventions are binding upon him. The possession of educational certificates—to be discussed elsewhere—are usually linked with qualification for office. Naturally, such certificates or patents enhance the "status element" in the social position of the official. For the rest this status factor in individual cases is explicitly and impassively acknowledged; for example, in the prescription that the acceptance or rejection of an aspirant to an official career depends upon the consent ("election") of the members of the official body. This is the case in the German army with the officer corps. Similar phenomena, which promote this guild-like closure of officialdom, are typically found in patrimonial and, particularly, in prebendal officialdoms of the past. The desire to resurrect such phenomena in changed forms is by no means infrequent among modern bureaucrats. For instance, they have played a role among the demands of the quite proletarian and expert officials (the *tretyj* element) during the Russian revolution.

Usually the social esteem of the officials as such is especially low where the demand for expert administration and the dominance of status conventions are weak. This is especially the case in the United States; it is often the case in new settlements by virtue of their wide fields for profitmaking and the great instability of their social stratification.

2. The pure type of bureaucratic official is *appointed* by a superior authority. An official elected by the governed is not a purely bureaucratic figure. Of course, the formal existence of an election does not by itself mean that no appointment hides behind the election—in the state, especially, appointment by party chiefs. Whether or not this is the case does not depend upon legal statutes but upon the way in which the party mechanism functions. Once firmly organized, the parties can turn a formally free election into the mere acclamation of a candidate designated by the party chief. As a rule, however, a formally free election is turned into a fight, conducted according to definite rules, for votes in favor of one of two designated candidates.

In all circumstances, the designation of officials by means of an election among the governed modifies the strictness of hierarchical subordination. In principle, an official who is so elected has an autonomous position opposite the superordinate official. The elected official does not derive his position "from above" but "from below," or at least not from a superior authority of the official hierarchy but from powerful party men ("bosses"), who also determine his further career. The career of the elected official is not, or at least not primarily, dependent upon his chief in the administration. The official who is not elected but appointed by a chief normally functions more exactly, from a technical point of view, because, all other circumstances being equal, it is more likely that purely functional points of consideration and qualities will determine his selection and career. As laymen, the governed can become acquainted with the extent to which a candidate is expertly qualified for office only in terms of experience, and hence only after his service. Moreover, in every sort of selection of officials by election, parties quite naturally give decisive weight not to expert considerations but to the services a follower renders

to the party boss. This holds for all kinds of procurement of officials by elections, for the designation of formally free, elected officials by party bosses when they determine the slate of candidates, or the free appointment by a chief who has himself been elected. The contrast, however, is relative: substantially similar conditions hold where legitimate monarchs and their subordinates appoint officials, except that the influence of the followings is then less controllable.

Where the demand for administration by trained experts is considerable, and the party followings have to recognize an intellectually developed, educated, and freely moving "public opinion," the use of unqualified officials falls back upon the party in power at the next election. Naturally, this is more likely to happen when the officials are appointed by the chief. The demand for a trained administration now exists in the United States, but in the large cities, where immigrant votes are "corralled," there is, of course, no educated public opinion. Therefore, popular elections of the administrative chief and also of his subordinate officials usually endanger the expert qualification of the official as well as the precise functioning of the bureaucratic mechanism. It also weakens the dependence of the officials upon the hierarchy. This holds at least for the large administrative bodies that are difficult to supervise. The superior qualification and integrity of federal judges, appointed by the President, as over against elected judges in the United States is well known, although both types of officials have been selected primarily in terms of party considerations. The great changes in American metropolitan administrations demanded by reformers have proceeded essentially from elected mayors working with an apparatus of officials who were appointed by them. These reforms have thus come about in a "Caesarist" fashion. Viewed technically, as an organized form of authority, the efficiency of "Caesarism," which often grows out of democracy, rests in general upon the position of the "Caesar" as a free trustee of the masses (of the army or of the citizenry), who is un-fettered by tradition. The "Caesar" is thus the unrestrained master of a body of highly qualified military officers and officials whom he selects freely and personally without regard to tradition or to any other consider-ations. This "rule of the personal genius," however, stands in contradiction to the for-mally "democratic" principle of a univer-sally elected officialdom.

3. Normally, the position of the official is held for life, at least in public bureaucracies; and this is increasingly the case for all sim-ilar structures. As a factual rule, *tenure for life* is presupposed, even where the giving of notice or periodic reappointment occurs. In contrast to the worker in a private enter-prise, the official normally holds tenure. Le-gal or actual life-tenure, however, is not recognized as the official's right to the pos-session of office, as was the case with many structures of authority in the past. Where legal guarantees against arbitrary dismissal or transfer are developed, they merely serve to guarantee a strictly objective discharge of specific office duties free from all personal considerations. In Germany, this is the case for all juridical and, increasingly, for all administrative officials.

Within the bureaucracy, therefore, the measure of "independence," legally guaran-teed by tenure, is not always a source of in-creased status for the official whose position is thus secured. Indeed, often the reverse holds, especially in old cultures and com-munities that are highly differentiated. In such communities, the stricter the subordi-nation under the arbitrary rule of the mas-ter, the more it guarantees the maintenance of the conventional seigneurial style of liv-ing for the official. Because of the very ab-sence of these legal guarantees of tenure, the conventional esteem for the official may rise in the same way as, during the Middle Ages, the esteem of the nobility of office rose at the expense of esteem for the freemen, and as the king's judge surpassed that of the people's judge. In Germany, the military officer or the administrative official can be removed from office at any time, or at least

far more readily than the "independent judge," who never pays with loss of his office for even the grossest offense against the "code of honor" or against social conven-tions of the salon. For this very reason, if other things are equal, in the eyes of the master stratum the judge is considered less qualified for social intercourse than are officers and administrative officials, whose greater dependence on the master is a greater guarantee of their conformity with status conventions. Of course, the average official strives for a civil-service law, which would materially secure his old age and pro-vide increased guarantees against his arbi-trary removal from office. This striving, however, has its limits. A very strong de-velopment of the "right to the office" natu-rally makes it more difficult to staff them with regard to technical efficiency, for such a development decreases the career oppor-tunities of ambitious candidates for office. This makes for the fact that officials, on the whole, do not feel their dependency upon those at the top. This lack of a feeling of de-pendency, however, rests primarily upon the inclination to depend upon one's equals rather than upon the socially inferior and governed strata. The present conservative movement among the Badenia clergy, occa-sioned by the anxiety of a presumably threatening separation of church and state, has been expressly determined by the desire not to be turned "from a master into a ser-vant of the parish."

4. The official receives the regular *pecu-niary* compensation of a normally fixed *salary* and the old age security provided by a pension. The salary is not measured like a wage in terms of work done, but according to "status," that is, according to the kind of function (the "rank") and, in addition, pos-sibly, according to the length of service. The relatively great security of the official's income, as well as the rewards of social es-teem, make the office a sought-after posi-tion, especially in countries which no longer provide opportunities for colonial profits. In such countries, this situation per-mits relatively low salaries for officials.

5. The official is set for a "*career*" within the hierarchical order of the public service. He moves from the lower, less important, and lower paid to the higher positions. The average official naturally desires a mechanical fixing of the conditions of promotion: if not of the offices, at least of the salary levels. He wants these conditions fixed in terms of "seniority," or possibly according to grades achieved in a developed system of expert examinations. Here and there, such examinations actually form a character *indelebilis* of the official and have lifelong effects on his career. To this is joined the desire to qualify the right to office and the increasing tendency toward status group closure and economic security. All of this makes for a tendency to consider the offices as "prebends" of those who are qualified by educational certificates. The necessity of taking general personal and intellectual qualifications into consideration, irrespective of the often subaltern character of the education certificate, has led to a condition in which the highest political offices, especially the positions of "ministers," are principally filled without reference to such certificates.

8

Notes on the Theory of Organization

Luther Gulick

Every large-scale or complicated enterprise requires many men to carry it forward. Wherever many men are thus working together the best results are secured when there is a division of work among these men. The theory of organization, therefore, has to do with the structure of co-ordination imposed upon the work-division units of an enterprise. Hence it is not possible to determine how an activity is to be organized without, at the same time, considering how the work in question is to be divided. Work division is the foundation of organization; indeed, the reason for organization.

1. THE DIVISION OF WORK

It is appropriate at the outset of this discussion to consider the reasons for and the effect of the division of work. It is sufficient for our purpose to note the following factors.

Why Divide Work?

Because men differ in nature, capacity and skill, and gain greatly in dexterity by specialization; Because the same man cannot be at two places at the same time; Because the range of knowledge and skill is so great that a man cannot within his life-span know more than a small fraction of it. In other words, it is a question of human nature, time, and space.

In a shoe factory it would be possible to have 1,000 men each assigned to making complete pairs of shoes. Each man would cut his leather, stamp in the eyelets, sew up the tops, sew on the bottoms, nail on the heels, put in the laces, and pack each pair in a box. It might take two days to do the job. One thousand men would make 500 pairs of shoes a day. It would also be possible to divide the work among these same men, using the identical hand methods, in an entirely different way. One group of men would be assigned to cut the leather, another to putting in the eyelets, another to stitching up the tops, another to sewing on the soles, another to nailing on the heels, another to inserting the laces and packing the pairs of shoes. We know from common sense and experience that there are two great gains in this latter process: first, it makes possible the better utilization of the varying skills and aptitudes of the different workmen, and encourages the development of specialization; and second, it eliminates the time that is lost when a workman turns from a knife, to a punch, to a needle and awl, to a hammer, and moves from table to bench, to anvil, to stool. Without any pressure on the workers, they could probably turn out twice as many shoes in a single day. There would be additional economies, because inserting laces and packing could be assigned to unskilled and low-paid workers. Moreover, in the cutting of the leather there would be less spoilage because the less skillful pattern cutters would be eliminated and assigned to other work. It would also be possible to cut a dozen shoe tops at the same time from same pattern with little additional effort. All of these advances would follow, without the introduction of new labor saving machinery.

Source: Papers on the Science of Administration, ed. Luther Gulick and Lyndall Urwick (New York: Institute of Public Administration, 1937), 3–13. Reprinted with permission.

The introduction of machinery accentuates the division of work. Even such a simple thing as a saw, a typewriter, or a transit requires increased specialization, and serves to divide workers into those who can and those who cannot use the particular instrument effectively. Division of work on the basis of the tools and machines used in work rests no doubt in part on aptitude, but primarily upon the development and maintenance of skill through continued manipulation.

Specialized skills are developed not alone in connection with machines and tools. They evolve naturally from the materials handled, like wood, or cattle, or paint, or cement. They arise similarly in activities which center in a complicated series of interrelated concepts, principles, and techniques. These are most clearly recognized in the professions, particularly those based on the application of scientific knowledge, as in engineering, medicine, and chemistry. They are none the less equally present in law, ministry, teaching, accountancy, navigation, aviation, and other fields.

The nature of these subdivisions is essentially pragmatic, in spite of the fact that there is an element of logic underlying them. They are therefore subject to a gradual evolution with the advance of science, the invention of new machines, the progress of technology and the change of the social system. In the last analysis, however, they appear to be based upon differences in individual human beings. But it is not to be concluded that the apparent stability of "human nature," whatever that may be, limits the probable development of specialization. The situation is quite the reverse. As each field of knowledge and work is advanced, constituting a continually larger and more complicated nexus of related principles, practices and skills, any individual will be less and less able to encompass it and maintain intimate knowledge and facility over the entire area, and there will thus arise a more minute specialization because knowledge and skill advance while man stands still. Division of work and in-

tegrated organization are the bootstraps by which mankind lifts itself in the process of civilization.

The Limits of Division

There are three clear limitations beyond which the division of work cannot to advantage go. The first is practical and arises from the volume of work involved in man-hours. Nothing is gained by subdividing work if that further subdivision results in setting up a task which requires less than the full time of one man. This is too obvious to need demonstration. The only exception arises where space interferes, and in such cases the part-time expert must fill in his spare time at other tasks, so that as a matter of fact a new combination is introduced.

The second limitation arises from technology and custom at a given time and place. In some areas nothing would be gained by separating undertaking from the custody and cleaning of churches, because by custom the sexton is the undertaker; in building construction it is extraordinarily difficult to redivide certain aspects of electrical and plumbing work and to combine them in a more effective way, because of the jurisdictional conflicts of craft unions; and it is clearly impracticable to establish a division of cost accounting in a field in which no technique of costing has yet been developed.

This second limitation is obviously elastic. It may be changed by invention and by education. If this were not the fact, we should face a static division of labor. It should be noted, however, that a marked change has two dangers. It greatly restricts the labor market from which workers may be drawn and greatly lessens the opportunities open to those who are trained for the particular specialization.

The third limitation is that the subdivision of work must not pass beyond physical division into organic division. It might seem far more efficient to have the front half of the cow in the pasture grazing and the rear half in the barn being milked all of the time, but this organic division would fail. Similarly there is no gain from splitting a single movement or gesture like licking an envelope, or tearing apart a series of intimately and intricately related activities.

It may be said that there is in this an element of reasoning in a circle; that the test here applied as to whether an activity is organic or not is whether it is divisible or not—which is what we set out to define. This charge is true. It must be a pragmatic test. Does the division work out? Is something vital destroyed and lost? Does it bleed?

The Whole and the Parts

It is axiomatic that the whole is equal to the sum of its parts. But in dividing up any "whole," one must be certain that every part, including unseen elements and relationships, is accounted for. The marble sand to which the Venus de Milo may be reduced by a vandal does not equal the statue, though every last grain be preserved; nor is a thrush just so much feathers, bones, flesh and blood; nor a typewriter merely so much steel, glass, paint, and rubber. Similarly a piece of work to be done cannot be subdivided into the obvious component parts without great danger that the central design, the operating relationships, the imprisoned idea, will be lost. . . .

When one man builds a house alone he plans as he works; he decides what to do first and what next, that is, he "co-ordinates the work." When many men work together to build a house this part of the work, the co-ordinating, must not be lost sight of.

In the "division of the work" among the various skilled specialists, a specialist in planning and coordination must be sought as well. Otherwise, a great deal of time may be lost, workers may get in each other's way, material may not be on hand when needed, things may be done in the wrong order, and there may even be a difference of opinion as to where the various doors and windows are to go. It is self-evident that the more the

work is subdivided, the greater is the danger of confusion, and the greater is the need of overall supervision and coordination. Co-ordination is not something that develops by accident. It must be won by intelligent, vigorous, persistent, and organized effort.

2. THE CO-ORDINATION OF WORK

If subdivision of work is inescapable, co-ordination becomes mandatory. There is, however, no one way to co-ordination. Experience shows that it may be achieved in two primary ways. These are:

1. By organization, that is, by interrelating the subdivisions of work by allotting them to men who are placed in a structure of authority, so that the work may be co-ordinated by orders of superiors to subordinates, reaching from the top to the bottom of the entire enterprise.
2. By the dominance of an idea, that is, the development of intelligent singleness of purpose in the minds and wills of those who are working together as a group, so that each worker will of his own accord fit his task into the whole with skill and enthusiasm.

These two principles of co-ordination are not mutually exclusive, in fact, no enterprise is really effective without the extensive utilization of both.

Size and time are the great limiting factors in the development of coordination. In a small project, the problem is not difficult; the structure of authority is simple, and the central purpose is real to every worker. In a large complicated enterprise, the organization becomes involved, the lines of authority tangled, and there is danger that the workers will forget that there is any central purpose, and so devote their best energies only to their own individual advancement and advantage.

The interrelated elements of time and habit are extraordinarily important in coordination. Man is a creature of habit. When an enterprise is built up gradually from small beginnings the staff can be "broken in" step by step. And when difficulties develop, they can be ironed out, and the new method followed from that point on as a matter of habit, with the knowledge that that particular difficulty will not develop again. Routines may even be mastered by drill as they are in the army. When, however, a large new enterprise must be set up or altered overnight, then the real difficulties of co-ordination make their appearance. The factor of habit, which is thus an important foundation of co-ordination when time is available, becomes a serious handicap when time is not available, that is, when rules change. The question of co-ordination therefore must be approached with different emphasis in small and in large enterprises; in simple and in complex situations; in stable and in new or changing organizations.

Coordination through Organization

Organization as a way of coordination requires the establishment of a system of authority whereby the central purpose or objective of an enterprise is translated into reality through the combined efforts of many specialists, each working in his own field at a particular time and place.

It is clear from long experience in human affairs that such a structure of authority requires not only many men at work in many places at selected times, but also a single directing executive authority.[1] The problem of organization thus becomes the problem of building up between the executive at the center and the subdivisions of work on the periphery of an effective network of communication and control.

The following outline may serve further to define the problem:

  I. First Step: Define the job to be done, such as the furnishing of pure water to all of the people and industries within a given area at the lowest possible cost;
 II. Second Step: Provide a director to see that the objective is realized;
III. Third Step: Determine the nature and number of individualized and specialized work units into which the job will have to be divided. As has been seen above, this subdivision depends partly upon the size of the job (no ultimate subdivision can generally be so small as to require less than the full time of one worker) and upon the status of technological and social development at a given time;
 IV. Fourth Step: Establish and perfect the structure of authority between the director and the ultimate work subdivisions.

It is this fourth step which is the central concern of the theory of organization. It is the function of this organization (IV) to enable the director (II) to co-ordinate and energize all of the subdivisions of work (III) so that the major objective (I) may be achieved efficiently.

The Span of Control

In this undertaking we are confronted at the start by the inexorable limits of human nature. Just as the hand of man can span only a limited number of notes on the piano, so the mind and will of man can span but a limited number of immediate managerial contacts. The problem has been discussed brilliantly by Graicunas in his paper included in this collection. The limit of control is partly a matter of the limits of knowledge, but even more is it a matter of the limits of time and of energy. As a result the executive of any enterprise can personally direct only a few persons. He must depend upon these to direct others, and upon them in turn to direct still others, until the last man in the organization is reached. . . .

But when we seek to determine how many immediate subordinates the director of an enterprise can effectively supervise, we enter a realm of experience which has not been brought under sufficient scientific study to furnish a final answer. Sir Ian Hamilton says, "The nearer we approach the supreme head of the whole organization, the more we ought to work towards groups of three; the closer we get to the foot of the whole organization (the Infantry of the Line), the more we work towards groups of six."[2]

The British Machinery of Government Committee of 1918 arrived at the conclusions that "The Cabinet should be small in number—preferably ten or, at most, twelve."[3]

Henri Fayol said "[In France] a minister has twenty assistants, where the Administrative Theory says that a manager at the head of a big undertaking should not have more than five or six."[4]

Graham Wallas expressed the opinion that the cabinet should not be increased "beyond the number of ten or twelve at which organized oral discussion is most efficient."[5]

Léon Blum recommended for France a prime minister with a technical cabinet modelled after the British War Cabinet, which was composed of five members.[6]

It is not difficult to understand why there is this divergence of statement among authorities who are agreed on the fundamentals. It arises in part from the differences in the capacities and work habits of individual executives observed, and in part from the noncomparable character of the work covered. It would seem that insufficient attention has been devoted to three factors: first, the element of diversification of function; second, the element of time; and third, the element of space. A chief of public works can deal effectively with more direct subordinates than can the general of the army, because all of his immediate subordinates in the department of public works will be in the general field of engineering, while in the army there will be many different elements, such as communications, chemistry, aviation, ordinance, motorized service, engineering, supply, transportation, etc., each with its own technology. The element of time is also of great significance as has been indicated above. In a stable organization the chief executive can deal with more immediate subordinates than in a new or changing organization. Similarly, space influences the span of control. An organization located in one building can be supervised through more immediate subordinates than can the same organization if scattered in several cities. When scattered there is not only need for more supervision, and therefore more supervisory personnel, but also for a fewer number of contacts with the chief executive because of the increased difficulty faced by the chief executive in learning sufficient details about a far-flung organization to do an intelligent job. The failure to attach sufficient importance to these variables has served to limit the scientific validity of the statements which have been made that one man can supervise but three, or five, or eight, or twelve immediate subordinates.

These considerations do not, however, dispose of the problem. They indicate rather the need for further research. But without further research we may conclude that the chief executive of an organization can deal with only a few immediate subordinates; that this number is determined not only by the nature of the work, but also by the nature of the executive; and that the number of immediate subordinates in a large, diversified and dispersed organization must be even less than in a homogeneous and unified organization to achieve the same measure of coordination.

One Master

From the earliest times it has been recognized that nothing but confusion arises under multiple command. "A man cannot serve two masters" was adduced as a theological argument because it was already accepted as a principle of human relation in everyday life. In administration this is known as the principle of "unity of command."[7] The principle may be stated as follows: A workman subject to orders from several superiors will be confused, inefficient, and irresponsible; a workman subject to orders from but one superior may be methodical, efficient, and responsible. Unity of command thus refers to those who are commanded, not to those who issue the commands.[8]

The significance of this principle in the process of co-ordination and organization must not be lost sight of. In building a structure of co-ordination, it is often tempting to set up more than one boss for a man who is doing work which has more than one relationship. Even as great a philosopher of management as Taylor fell into this error in setting up separate foremen to deal with machinery, with materials, with speed, etc., each with the power of giving orders directly to the individual workman.[9] The rigid adherence to the principle of unity of command may have its absurdities; these are, however, unimportant in comparison with the certainty of confusion, inefficiency and irresponsibility which arise from the violation of the principle.

Technical Efficiency

There are many aspects of the problem of securing technical efficiency. Most of these do not concern us here directly. They have been treated extensively by such authorities as Taylor, Dennison, and Kimball, and their implications for general organization by Fayol, Urwick, Mooney, and Reiley. There is, however, one efficiency concept which concerns us deeply in approaching the theory of organization. It is the principle of homogeneity.

It has been observed by authorities in many fields that the efficiency of a group working together is directly related to the homogeneity of the work they are performing, of the processes they are utilizing, and of the purposes which actuate them. From top to bottom, the group must be unified. It must work together.

It follows from this (1) that any organizational structure which brings together in a single unit work divisions which are non-homogeneous in work, in technology, or in purpose will encounter the danger of friction and inefficiency; and (2) that a unit based on a given specialization cannot be given technical direction by a layman.

In the realm of government it is not difficult to find many illustrations of the unsatisfactory results of non-homogeneous administrative combinations. It is generally agreed that agricultural development and education cannot be administered by the same men who enforce pest and disease control, because the success of the former rests upon friendly co-operation and trust of the farmers, while the latter engenders resentment and suspicion. Similarly, activities like drug control established in protection of the consumer do not find appropriate homes in departments dominated by the interests of the producer. In the larger cities and in states it has been found that hospitals cannot be so well administered by the health department directly as they can be when set up independently in a separate department, or at least in a bureau with an extensive autonomy, and it is generally agreed that public welfare administration and police administration require separation, as do public health administration and welfare administration, though both of these combinations may be found in successful operation under special conditions. No one would think of combining water supply and public education, or tax administration and public recreation. In every one of these cases, it will be seen that there is some element either of work to be done, or of the technology used, or of the end sought which is non-homogeneous.

Another phase of the combination of incompatible functions in the same office may be found in the common American practice of appointing unqualified laymen and politicians to technical positions or to give technical direction to highly specialized services. As Dr. Frank J. Goodnow pointed out a generation ago, we are faced here by two heterogeneous functions, "politics" and "administration," the combination of which cannot be undertaken within the structure of the administration without producing inefficiency.

Caveamus Expertum

At this point a word of caution is necessary. The application of the principle of homogeneity has its pitfalls. Every highly trained technician, particularly in the learned professions, has a profound sense of omniscience and a great desire for complete independence in the service of society. When employed by government he knows exactly what the people need better than they do themselves, and he knows how to render this service. He tends to be utterly oblivious of all other needs, because, after all, is not his particular technology the road to salvation? Any restraint applied to him is "limitation of freedom," and any criticism "springs from ignorance and jealousy." Every budget increase he secures is "in the public interest," while every increase secured elsewhere is "a sheer waste." His efforts and maneuvers to expand are "public education" and "civic organization," while similar efforts by others are "propaganda" and "politics."

Another trait of the expert is his tendency to assume knowledge and authority in fields in which he has no competence. In this particular, educators, lawyers, priests, admirals, doctors, scientists, engineers, accountants, merchants and bankers are all the same—having achieved technical competence or "success" in one field, they come to think this competence is a general quality detachable from the field and inherent in themselves. They step without embarrassment into other areas. They do not remember that the robes of authority of one kingdom confer no sovereignty in another; but that there they are merely a masquerade.

The expert knows his "stuff." Society needs him, and must have him more and more as man's technical knowledge becomes more and more extensive. But history shows us that the common man is a better judge of his own needs in the long run than any cult of experts. Kings and ruling classes, priests and prophets, soldiers and lawyers, when permitted to rule rather than serve mankind, have in the end done more to check the advance of human welfare than they have to advance it. The true place of the expert is, as A. E. said so well, "on tap, not on top." The essential validity of democracy rests upon this philosophy, for democracy is a way of government in which the common man is the final judge of what is good for him.

Efficiency is one of the things that is good for him because it makes life richer and safer. That efficiency is to be secured more and more through the use of technical specialists. These specialists have no right to ask for, and must not be given freedom from supervisory control, but in establishing that control, a government which ignores the conditions of efficiency cannot expect to achieve efficiency.

3. ORGANIZATIONAL PATTERNS

Organization Up or Down?

One of the great sources of confusion in the discussion of the theory of organization is that some authorities work and think primarily from the top down, while others work and think from the bottom up. This is perfectly natural because some authorities are interested primarily in the executive and in the problems of central management, while others are interested primarily in individual services and activities. Those who work from the top down regard the organization as a system of subdividing the enterprise under the chief executive, while those who work from the bottom up, look upon organization as a system of combining the individual units of work into aggregates which are in turn subordinated to the chief executive. It may be argued that either approach leads to a consideration of the entire problem, so that it is of no great significance which way the organization is viewed. Certainly it makes this very important practical difference: those who work from the top down must guard themselves from the danger of sacrificing the effectiveness of the individual services in their zeal to achieve a model structure at the top, while those who start from the bottom, must guard themselves from the danger of thwarting coordination in their eagerness to develop effective individual services.

In any practical situation the problem of organization must be approached from both top and bottom. This is particularly true in the reorganization of a going concern. May it not be that this practical necessity is likewise the sound process theoretically? In that case one would develop the plan of an organization or reorganization both from the top downward and from the bottom upward, and would reconcile the two at the center. In planning the first subdivisions under the chief executive, the principle of the limitation of the span of control must apply; in building up the first aggregates of specialized functions, the principle of homogeneity must apply. If any enterprise has such an array of functions that the first subdivisions from the top down do not readily meet the first aggregations from the bottom up, then additional divisions and additional aggregates must be introduced, but at each further step there must be a less and less rigorous adherence to the two conflicting principles until their juncture is effected. . . .

Organizing the Executive

The effect of the suggestion presented above is to organize and institutionalize the executive function as such so that it may be more adequate in a complicated situation. This is in reality not a new idea. We do not, for example, expect the chief executive to write his own letters. We give him a private secretary, who is part of his office and assists him to do this part of his job. This secretary is not a part of any department, he is a subdivision of the executive himself. In just this way, though on a different plane, other phases of the job of the chief executive may be organized.

Before doing this, however, it is necessary to have a clear picture of the job itself. This brings us directly to the question, "What is the work of the chief executive? What does he do?"

The answer is POSDCORB.

POSDCORB is, of course, a made-up word designed to call attention to the various functional elements of the work of a chief executive because "administration"

and "management" have lost all specific content.[10] POSDCORB is made up of the initials and stands for the following activities:

Planning, that is working out in broad outline the things that need to be done and the methods for doing them to accomplish the purpose set for the enterprise;

Organizing, that is the establishment of the formal structure of authority through which work subdivisions are arranged, defined and co-ordinated for the defined objective;

Staffing, that is the whole personnel function of bringing in and training the staff and maintaining favorable conditions of work;

Directing, that is the continuous task of making decisions and embodying them in specific and general orders and instructions and serving as the leader of the enterprise;

Co-ordinating, that is the all important duty of interrelating the various parts of the work;

Reporting, that is keeping those to whom the executive is responsible informed as to what is going on, which thus includes keeping himself and his subordinates informed through records, research, and inspection;

Budgeting, with all that goes with budgeting in the form of fiscal planning, accounting, and control.

This statement of the work of a chief executive is adapted from the functional analysis elaborated by Henri Fayol in his "Industrial and General Administration." It is believed that those who know administration intimately will find in this analysis a valid and helpful pattern, into which can be fitted each of the major activities and duties of any chief executive.

If these seven elements may be accepted as the major duties of the chief executive, it follows that they *may* be separately organized as subdivisions of the executive. The need for such subdivision depends entirely on the size and complexity of the enterprise. In the largest enterprises, particularly where the chief executive is as a matter of fact unable to do the work that is thrown upon him, it may be presumed that one or more par   f POSDCORB should be suborganize

NOTES

1. I.e., when *organization is the basis of coordination*. Wherever the central executive authority is composed of several who exercise their functions jointly by majority vote, as on a board, this is from the standpoint of organization still a "single authority"; where the central executive is in reality composed of several men acting freely and independently, then organization cannot be said to be the basis of co-ordination; it is rather the dominance of an idea and falls under the second principle stated above.

2. Sir Ian Hamilton, "The Soul and Body of an Army." Arnold, London, 1921, p. 230.

3. Great Britain. Ministry of Reconstruction. Report of the Machinery of Government Committee. H. M. Stationery Office, London, 1918, p. 5.

4. Henri Fayol, "The Administrative Theory in the State." Address before the Second International Congress of Administrative Science at Brussels, September 13, 1923.

5. Graham Wallas, "The Great Society." Macmillan, London and New York, 1919, p. 264.

6. Léon Blum, "La Réforme Gouvernementale." Grasset, Paris, 1918. Reprinted in 1936, p. 59.

7. Henri Fayol, "Industrial and General Administration." English translation by J. A. Coubrough. International Management Association, Geneva, 1930.

8. Fayol terms the latter "unity of direction."

9. Frederick Winslow Taylor, "Shop Management." Harper and Brothers, New York and London, 1911, p. 99.

10. See Minutes of the Princeton Conference on Training for the Public Service, 1935, p. 35. See also criticism of this analysis in Lewis Meriam, "Public Service and Special Training." University of Chicago Press, 1936, pp. 1, 2, 10 and 15, where this functional analysis is misinterpreted as a statement of qualifications for appointment.

CHAPTER 2

Neoclassical Organization Theory

There is no precise definition of *neoclassical* in the context of organization theory. The general connotation is that of a theoretical perspective that revises and/or is critical of classical organization theory—particularly for minimizing issues related to the humanness of organizational members, the coordination needs among administrative units, the operation of internal-external organizational relations, and the processes used in decision making. The major writers of the classical school did their most significant work before World War II. The neoclassical writers gained their reputations as organization theorists by attacking the classical writers from the end of the war through the 1950s. Because classical theories were, to a large measure, derived intellectually rather than empirically, their artificial assumptions left them vulnerable to attack. Theorists of the classical period thought that organizations should be based on universally applicable scientific principles.

In spite of their frequent and vigorous attacks upon the classicalists, the neoclassicalists did not develop a body of theory that could adequately replace the classical school. The neoclassical school modified, added to, and somewhat extended classical theory. It attempted to blend assumptions of classical theory with concepts that subsequently were used by later organization theorists from all schools. The neoclassical school attempted to save classical theory by introducing modifications based upon research findings in the behavioral sciences. It did not have a bona fide theory of its own. To a great extent, it was an "antischool."

Despite its limitations, the neoclassical school was very important in the historical development of organization theory. But, like a rebellious teenager, neoclassical theory could not permanently stand on its own. It was a transitional, somewhat reactionary school. Why, then, was the neoclassical school so important? First, because it initiated the theoretical movement away from the overly simplistic mechanistic views of the classical school. The neoclassicalists challenged some of the basic tenets of the classical school *head on*. And remember, the classical school was the only school at that time. Organization theory and classical organization theory were virtually synonymous.

Second, in the process of challenging the classical school, the neoclassicalists raised issues and initiated theories that became central to the foundations of most of the schools that have followed. The neoclassical school was a critically important forerunner. Most serious post-1960 articles from *any* school of organization cite neoclassical theorists. All of the neoclassical selections that we include in this chapter are important precursors of the human relations, "modern" structural, systems, power and politics, and organizational culture perspectives of organization theory.

In the Introduction, we noted that most groupings of theories into schools or frames are based on two variables: shared perspectives on organizations *and* the period in time during which the most important works were written. Thus, the giants of the neoclassical era include, for example, James March, Philip Selznick, and Herbert Simon. This does not mean, however, that their significance ended with their neoclassical-era work. These three theorists in particular have continued to make major contributions into the turn of the century—contributions that have extended beyond the limits of both the neoclassical era and the perspective.

Chester Barnard's purposes in writing *The Functions of the Executive* were ambitious. He sought to create a comprehensive theory of behavior in organizations that was centered on the need for people in organizations to cooperate—to enlist others to help accomplish tasks that individuals could not accomplish alone. In Barnard's view, cooperation holds an organization together. Thus, the responsibility of an executive is (1) to create and maintain a sense of purpose and a *moral code* for the organization—a set of ethical visions that established "*right* or *wrong* in a moral sense, of deep feeling, of innate conviction, not arguable; emotional, not intellectual in character" (1938, p. 266); (2) to establish systems of formal and informal communication; and (3) to ensure the willingness of people to cooperate.

In "The Economy of Incentives," the chapter reprinted here from *The Functions of the Executive,* Barnard argues that individuals must be induced to cooperate, since to do otherwise will result in dissolution of the organization or, at the least, in changes of organizational purpose. The executive needs to employ different strategies for inducing cooperation: to find and use objective positive incentives and reduce negative incentives, but also to "change the state of mind, or attitudes, or motives so that the available objective incentives can become effective." This approach Barnard refers to as "persuasion," and he claims that "in every type of organization, for whatever purpose, several incentives are necessary, and some degree of persuasion likewise, in order to secure and maintain the contributions to organization that are required."

In a 1940 issue of the journal *Social Forces*, Robert Merton, one of the most influential of the mid-century sociologists, published an article titled "Bureaucratic Structure and Personality," which proclaimed that the "ideal-type" bureaucracy as described by Max Weber had inhibiting dysfunctions—characteristics that prevented it from being optimally efficient—and negative effects on the people who worked in it. These critical themes have been echoed both in subsequent empirical studies and in the polemics of politicians. In the 1950s, Merton revised this article slightly for inclusion in his collection of essays *Social Theory and Social Structure*. The revision is reprinted here.

Herbert A. Simon was one of the first neoclassicalists to raise serious challenges to classical organization theory. Simon didn't just criticize classical theory, he attacked it. In his widely quoted 1946 *Public Administration Review* article "The Proverbs of Administration," Simon is devastating in his criticism of the classical approach to "general principles of management," such as those proposed by Fayol, Gulick, and others, as being inconsistent, conflicting, and inapplicable to many of the administrative situations facing managers. He suggests that such "principles" as "span of control" and "unity of command" can, with equal logic, be applied in diametrically opposed ways to the same set of circumstances. Simon concludes that the so-called principles of administration are instead proverbs of administration. The basic themes of the article were incorporated later in his landmark book *Administrative Behavior,* which is now in its fourth edition.

One of the major themes of the neoclassical organization theorists was that organizations did not and could not exist as self-contained islands isolated from their environments. As might be expected, the first significant efforts to "open up" organizations (theoretically speaking) came from analysts whose professional identities required them to take a broad view of things: sociologists. One such sociologist, Philip Selznick, in his 1948 *American Sociological Review* article "Foundations of the Theory of Organization" (which is reprinted here), asserts that while it is possible to describe and design organizations in a purely rational manner, such efforts can never hope to cope with the nonrational aspects of organizational behavior. In contrast with the classical theorists, Selznick maintains that organizations consist not simply of a number of positions for management to control, but of individuals, whose goals and aspirations might not necessarily coincide with the formal goals of the organization. Selznick is perhaps best known for his concept of "cooptation," which describes the process of an organization bringing and subsuming new elements into its policy-making process in order to prevent such elements from becoming a threat to the organization or its mission. The fullest account of Selznick's "cooptation" is found in *TVA and the Grass Roots*, his 1949 case study of how the Tennessee Valley Authority first gained local support for its programs. Selznick's approach to studying organizations and his intellectual distinction between the concepts of "organization" and "institution" have been lauded as models of organizational theory's insightfulness and usefulness by such writers on organizational culture as Ott (1989), Pedersen and Sorensen (1989), Siehl and Martin (1984), Walker (1986), and Wilkins (1983; 1989).

We have focused on Philip Selznick here, but many other sociologists made important contributions to the neoclassical school and to the general development of the field of organization theory. For example:

- Melville Dalton (1950; 1959) focused on structural frictions between line and staff units and between the central office of an organization and geographically dispersed facilities. His work drew attention to some of the universal ingredients of conflict within organizations and to problems of educating and socializing managers.
- Talcott Parsons introduced an approach to the analysis of formal organizations using the general theory of social systems. In his 1956 article "Suggestions for a Sociological Approach to the Theory of Organizations," Parsons defined an organization as a social system that focuses on the attainment of specific goals and contributes, in turn, to the accomplishment of goals of a more comprehensive system, such as the larger organization or even society itself.
- William F. Whyte (1948) studied human relations in the restaurant business in order to understand and describe stresses that result from interrelations and status differences in the workplace.

As we mentioned earlier, Herbert Simon and his associates at the Carnegie Institute of Technology (now Carnegie-Mellon University) also were major developers of theories of organizational decision making. Simon was a firm believer that decision making should be the focus of a new "administrative science." For example, he asserted (1947) that organizational theory is, in fact, the theory of the bounded rationality of human beings who "satisfice" because they do not have the intellectual capacity to maximize. Simon (1960) also drew a distinction between "programmed" and "unprogrammed" organizational decisions and highlighted the importance of the distinction for management information systems. His work on administrative science and decision making went in two major directions. First, he was a pioneer in developing the "science" of improved organizational decision making through quantitative methods, such as operations research and computer technology. Second, and perhaps even more important, he was a leader in studying the processes by which administrative organizations make decisions. Herbert Simon's extensive contributions continue to influence the field of organization theory.

Two of Simon's colleagues at Carnegie Tech during the early 1960s, R. M. Cyert and James G. March, analyze the impact of power and politics on the establishment of organizational goals in "A Behavioral Theory of Organizational Objectives," reprinted here. This was a perspective that did not receive serious attention from organizational theorists until the mid-1970s. Cyert and March discuss the formation and activation of coalitions, as well as negotiations to impose coalitions' demands on the organization. The article subsequently was merged into their widely cited 1963 book *A Behavioral Theory of the Firm*, which postulated that corporations tended to "satisfice" rather than engage in economically rational profit-maximizing behavior.

The neoclassical school played a very important role in the evolution of organization theory. Its writers provided the intellectual and empirical impetus to break the classicalists' simplistic, mechanically oriented, monopolistic dominance of the field. Neoclassicalists also paved the way— opened the door —for the soon-to-follow explosions of thinking from the human relations, "modern" structural, systems, power and politics, and organizational culture perspectives of organizations.

REFERENCES

Barnard, C. I. (1938, 1968). *The functions of the executive*. Cambridge, MA: Harvard University Press.

Cyert, R. M., & J. G. March (1959). Behavioral theory of organizational objectives. In M. Haire, ed., *Modern organization theory* (pp. 76–90). New York: Wiley.

Cyert, R. M., & J. G. March (1963). *A behavioral theory of the firm*. Englewood Cliffs, NJ: Prentice Hall.

Dalton, M. (1950, June). Conflicts between staff and line managerial officers. *American Sociological Review, 15*(3), 342–351.

Dalton, M. (1959). *Men who manage*. New York: Wiley.

Durkheim, E. (1947). *The division of labor in society*. Trans. George Simpson. New York: Free Press. (Originally published in 1893.)

Etzioni, A. (1961). *A comparative analysis of complex organizations*. New York: Free Press.

Gordon, C. W., & N. Babchuk (1959). A typology of voluntary associations. *American Sociological Review, 24*, 22–29.

Merton, R. K. (1957). "Bureaucratic Structure and Personality." In R. K. Merton, *Social Theory and Social Structure*, rev. and enl. ed. New York: Free Press. (A revised version of an article of the same title that appeared in *Social Forces, 18* [1940]).

Ott, J. S. (1989). *The organizational culture perspective*. Ft. Worth, TX: Harcourt Brace.

Parsons, T. (1956, June). Suggestions for a sociological approach to the theory of organizations. *Administrative Science Quarterly, 1*, 63–85.

Pedersen, J. S., & J. S. Sorensen (1989). *Organisational cultures in theory and practice*. Aldershot, UK: Gower.

Selznick, P. (1948). Foundations of the theory of organization. *American Sociological Review, 13*, 25–35.

Siehl, C., & J. Martin (1984). The role of symbolic management: How can managers effectively transmit organizational culture? In J. G. Hunt, D. M. Hosking, C. A. Schriesheim, & R. Stewart, eds., *Leaders and managers* (pp. 227–269). New York: Pergamon Press.

Simon, H. A. (1946, Winter). The proverbs of administration. *Public Administration Review, 6*, 53–67.

Simon, H. A. (1947). *Administrative behavior*. New York: Macmillan.

Simon, H. A. (1960). *The new science of management decisions*. New York: Harper & Row.

Simon, H. A. (1997). *Administrative behavior*, 4th ed. New York: Free Press.

Walker, W. E. (1986). *Changing organizational culture: Strategy, structure, and professionalism in the U.S. General Accounting Office*. Knoxville, TN: University of Tennessee Press.

Whyte, W. F. (1948). *Human relations in the restaurant business*. New York: McGraw-Hill.

Wilkins, A. A. (1983). Organizational stories as symbols which control the organization. In L. R. Pondy, P. J. Frost, G. Morgan, & T. C. Dandridge, eds., *Organizational symbolism* (pp. 93–107). Greenwich, CT: JAI Press.

Wilkins, A. A. (1989). *Developing corporate character*. San Francisco: Jossey-Bass.

9

The Economy of Incentives

Chester I. Barnard

[An] essential element of organizations is the willingness of persons to contribute their individual efforts to the coöperative system. The power of coöperation, which is often spectacularly great when contrasted with that even of large numbers of individuals unorganized, is nevertheless dependent upon the willingness of individuals to coöperate and to contribute their efforts to the coöperative system. The contributions of personal efforts which constitute the energies of organizations are yielded by individuals because of incentives. The egotistical motives of self-preservation and of self-satisfaction are dominating forces; on the whole, organizations can exist only when consistent with the satisfaction of these motives, unless, alternatively, they can change these motives. The individual is always the basic strategic factor in organization. Regardless of his history or his obligations he must be induced to coöperate, or there can be no coöperation.

It needs no further introduction to suggest that the subject of incentives is fundamental in formal organizations and in conscious efforts to organize. Inadequate incentives mean dissolution, or changes of organization purpose, or failure of coöperation. Hence, in all sorts of organizations the affording of adequate incentives becomes the most definitely emphasized task in their existence. It is probably in this aspect of executive work that failure is most pronounced, though the causes may be due either to inadequate understanding or to the breakdown of the effectiveness of organization.

I

The net satisfactions which induce a man to contribute his efforts to an organization result from the positive advantages as against the disadvantages which are entailed.[1] It follows that a net advantage may be increased or a negative advantage made positive either by increasing the number or the strength of the positive inducements or by reducing the number or the strength of the disadvantages. It often occurs that the positive advantages are few and meager, but the burdens involved are also negligible, so that there is a strong net advantage. Many "social" organizations are able to exist under such a state of affairs. Conversely, when the burdens involved are numerous or heavy, the offsetting positive advantages must be either numerous or powerful.

Hence, from the viewpoint of the organization requiring or seeking contributions from individuals, the problem of effective incentives may be either one of finding positive incentives or of reducing or eliminating negative incentives or burdens. For example, employment may be made attractive either by reducing the work required — say, by shortening hours or supplying tools or power, that is, by making conditions of employment less onerous — or by increasing positive inducement, such as wages.

In practice, although there are many cases where it is clear which side of the "equation" is being adjusted, on the whole specific practices and conditions affect both sides simultaneously or it is impossible to determine which they affect. Most specific factors in

Source: Chester I. Barnard, *Functions of the Executive* (Cambridge, MA.: Harvard University Press, 1938). © 1938, 1968 by the President and Fellows of Harvard College. Reprinted by permission of the publisher.

so-called working conditions may be viewed either as making employment positively attractive or as making work less onerous. We shall, therefore, make no attempt to treat specific inducements as increasing advantages or as decreasing disadvantages; but this underlying aspect is to be kept in mind.

More important than this is the distinction between the objective and the subjective aspects of incentives. Certain common positive incentives, such as material goods and in some senses money, clearly have an objective existence; and this is true also of negative incentives like working hours, conditions of work. Given a man of a certain state of mind, of certain attitudes, or governed by certain motives, he can be induced to contribute to an organization by a given combination of these objective incentives, positive or negative. It often is the case, however, that the organization is unable to offer objective incentives that will serve as an inducement to that state of mind, or to those attitudes, or to one governed by those motives. The only alternative then available is to change the state of mind, or attitudes, or motives, so that the available objective incentives can become effective.

An organization can secure the efforts necessary to its existence, then, either by the objective inducements it provides or by changing states of mind. It seems to me improbable that any organization can exist as a practical matter which does not employ both methods in combination. In some organizations the emphasis is on the offering of objective incentives—this is true of most industrial organizations. In others the preponderance is on the state of mind—this is true of most patriotic and religious organizations.

We shall call the processes of offering objective incentives "the method of incentives"; and the processes of changing subjective attitudes "the method of persuasion." Using these new terms, let us repeat what we have said: In commercial organizations the professed emphasis is apparently almost wholly on the side of the method of incentives. In religious and political organizations

the professed emphasis is apparently almost wholly on the side of persuasion. But in fact, especially if account be taken of the different kinds of contributions required from different individuals, both methods are used in all types of organizations. Moreover, the centrifugal forces of individualism and the competition between organizations for individual contributions result in both methods being ineffective, with few exceptions, for more than short periods or a few years.

I. THE METHOD OF INCENTIVES

We shall first discuss the method of incentives. It will facilitate our consideration of the subject if at the outset we distinguish two classes of incentives: first those that are specific and can be specifically offered to an individual; and second, those that are general, not personal, that cannot be specifically offered. We shall call the first class specific inducements, the second general incentives.

The specific inducements that may be offered are of several classes, for example: (a) material inducements; (b) personal nonmaterial opportunities; (c) desirable physical conditions; (d) ideal benefactions. General incentives afforded are, for example: (e) associational attractiveness; (f) adaptation of conditions to habitual methods and attitudes; (g) the opportunity of enlarged participation; (h) the condition of communion. Each of these classes of incentives is known under various names, and the list does not purport to be complete, since our purpose now is illustrative. But to accomplish this purpose it is necessary briefly to discuss the incentives named.

(a) Material inducements are money, things, or physical conditions that are offered to the individual as inducements to accepting employment, compensation for service, reward for contribution. Under a money economy and the highly specialized production of material goods, the range and profusion of material inducements are very great. The complexity of schedules of money compensation, the difficulty of securing the monetary means of compensation, and the power of exchange which money gives in organized markets, have served to exaggerate the importance of money in particular and material inducements in general as incentives to personal contributions to organized effort. It goes without elaboration that where a large part of the time of an individual is devoted to one organization, the physiological necessities—food, shelter, clothing—require that material inducements should be present in most cases; but these requirements are so limited that they are satisfied with small quantities. The unaided power of material incentives, when the minimum necessities are satisfied, in my opinion is exceedingly limited as to most men, depending almost entirely for its development upon persuasion. Notwithstanding the great emphasis upon material incentives in modern times and especially in current affairs, there is no doubt in my mind that, unaided by other motives, they constitute weak incentives beyond the level of the bare physiological necessities.

To many this view will not be readily acceptable. The emphasis upon material rewards has been a natural result of the success of technological developments—relative to other incentives it is the material things which have been progressively easier to produce, and therefore to offer. Hence there has been a forced cultivation of the love of material things among those above the level of subsistence. Since existing incentives seem always inadequate to the degree of coöperation and of social integration theoretically possible and ideally desirable, the success of the sciences and the arts of material production would have been partly ineffective, and in turn would have been partly impossible, without inculcating the desire of the material. The most significant result of this situation has been the expansion of population, most of which has been necessarily at the bare subsistence level, at which level material inducements are, on the whole, powerful incentives. This has perpetuated the illusion that beyond

this subsistence level material incentives are also the most effective.[2]

A concurrent result has been the creation of sentiments in individuals that they *ought* to want material things. The inculcation of "proper" ambitions in youth have greatly stressed material possessions as an evidence of good citizenship, social adequacy, etc. Hence, when underlying and governing motives have not been satisfied, there has been strong influence to rationalize the default as one of material compensation, and not to be conscious of the controlling motives or at least not to admit them.

Yet it seems to me to be a matter of common experience that material rewards are ineffective beyond the subsistence level excepting to a very limited proportion of men; that most men neither work harder for more material things, nor can be induced thereby to devote more than a fraction of their possible contribution to organized effort. It is likewise a matter of both present experience and past history that many of the most effective and powerful organizations are built up on incentives in which the materialistic elements, above bare subsistence, are either relatively lacking or absolutely absent. Military organizations have been relatively lacking in material incentives. The greater part of the work of political organizations is without material incentive. Religious organizations are characterized on the whole by material sacrifice. It seems to me to be definitely a general fact that even in purely commercial organizations material incentives are so weak as to be almost negligible except when reinforced by other incentives, and then only because of wholesale general persuasion in the form of salesmanship and advertising.

It will be noted that the reference has been to material incentives rather than to money. What has been said requires some, but not great, qualification with reference to money as an incentive—solely for the reason that money in our economy may be used as the indirect means of satisfying non-materialistic motives—philanthropic, artistic, intellectual, and religious motives for example—and because money income becomes an index of social status, personal development, etc.

(b) Inducements of a personal, non-materialistic character are of great importance to secure coöperative effort above the minimum material rewards essential to subsistence. The opportunities for distinction, prestige, personal power,[3] and the attainment of dominating position are much more important than material rewards in the development of all sorts of organizations, including commercial organizations. In various ways this fact applies to many types of human beings, including those of limited ability and children. Even in strictly commercial organizations, where it is least supposed to be true, money without distinction, prestige, position, is so utterly ineffective that it is rare that greater income can be made to serve even temporarily as an inducement if accompanied by suppression of prestige. At least for short periods inferior material rewards are often accepted if assurance of distinction is present; and usually the presumption is that material rewards ought to follow or arise from or even are made necessary by the attainment of distinction and prestige. There is unlimited experience to show that among many men, and especially among women, the real value of differences of money rewards lies in the recognition or distinction assumed to be conferred thereby, or to be procured therewith—one of the reasons why differentials either in money income or in material possessions are a source of jealousy and disruption if not accompanied by other factors of distinction.

(c) Desirable physical conditions of work are often important conscious, and more often important unconscious, inducements to coöperation.

(d) Ideal benefactions as inducements to coöperation are among the most powerful and the most neglected. By ideal benefaction I mean the capacity of organizations to satisfy personal ideals usually relating to non-material, future, or altruistic relations. They include pride of workmanship, sense of adequacy, altruistic service for family or others, loyalty to organization in patriotism, etc., aesthetic and religious feeling. They also include the opportunities for the satisfaction of the motives of hate and revenge, often the controlling factor in adherence to and intensity of effort in some organizations.

All of these inducements—material rewards, personal nonmaterial opportunities, desirable physical conditions, and ideal benefactions—may be and frequently are definitely offered as inducements to contribute to organizations. But there are other conditions which cannot usually be definitely offered, and which are known or recognized by their absence in particular cases. Of these I consider associational attractiveness as exceedingly, and often critically, important.

(e) By associational attractiveness I mean social compatibility. It is in many cases obvious that racial hostility, class antagonism, and national enmities absolutely prevent coöperation, in others decrease its effectiveness, and in still others make it impossible to secure coöperation except by great strengthening of other incentives. But it seems clear that the question of personal compatibility or incompatibility is much more far-reaching in limiting coöperative effort than is recognized, because an intimate knowledge of particular organizations is usually necessary to understand its precise character. When such an intimate knowledge exists, personal compatibility or incompatibility is so thoroughly sensed, and the related problems are so difficult to deal with, that only in special or critical cases is conscious attention given to them. But they can be neglected only at peril of disruption. Men often will not work at all, and will rarely work well, under other incentives if the social situation *from their point of view* is unsatisfactory. Thus often men of inferior education cannot work well with those of superior education, and vice versa. Differences not merely of race, nation, religion, but of customs, morals, social status, education, ambition, are frequently controlling.

Hence, a powerful incentive to the effort of almost all men is favorable associational conditions from their viewpoint. . . .

(*f*) Another incentive of the general type is that of customary working conditions and conformity to habitual practices and attitudes. This is made obvious by the universal practice, in all kinds of organizations, of rejecting recruits trained in different methods or possessing "foreign" attitudes. It is taken for granted that men will not or cannot do well by strange methods or under strange conditions. What is not so obvious is that men will frequently not attempt to coöperate if they recognize that such methods or conditions are to be accepted.

(*g*) Another indirect incentive that we may regard as of general and often of controlling importance is the opportunity for the feeling of enlarged participation in the course of events. It affects all classes of men under some conditions. It is sometimes, though not necessarily, related to love of personal distinction and prestige. Its realization is the feeling of importance of result of effort because of the importance of the coöperative effort as a whole. Thus, *other things being equal,* many men prefer association with large organizations, organizations which they regard as useful, or organizations they regard as effective, as against those they consider small, useless, ineffective.

(*h*) The most intangible and subtle of incentives is that which I have called the condition of communion. It is related to social compatibility, but is essentially different. It is the feeling of personal comfort in social relations that is sometimes called solidarity, social integration, the gregarious instinct, or social security (in the original, not in its present debased economic, sense). It is the opportunity for comradeship, for mutual support in personal attitudes. The need for communion is a basis of informal organization that is essential to the operation of every formal organization. It is likewise the basis for informal organization within but hostile to formal organization.[4]

It is unnecessary for our purpose to exhaust the list of inducements and incentives

to coöperative contributions of individuals to organization. Enough has been said to suggest that the subject of incentives is important and complex when viewed in its objective aspects. One fact of interest now is that different men are moved by different incentives or combinations of incentives, and by different incentives or combinations at different times. Men are unstable in their desires, a fact partly reflecting the instability of their environments. A second fact is that organizations are probably never able to offer all the incentives that move men to coöperative effort, and are usually unable to offer adequate incentives. To the reasons for this fact we shall advert later; but a result of it to which we shall turn our attention now is the necessity of persuasion.

II. THE METHOD OF PERSUASION

If an organization is unable to afford incentives adequate to the personal contributions it requires it will perish unless it can by persuasion so change the desires of enough men that the incentives it can offer will be adequate, Persuasion in the broad sense in which I am here using the word includes: (*a*) the creation of coercive conditions; (*b*) the rationalization of opportunity; (*c*) the inculcation of motives.

(*a*) Coercion is employed both to exclude and to secure the contribution of individuals to an organization. Exclusion is often intended to be exclusion permanently and nothing more. It is an aspect of competition or hostility between organizations or between organizations and individuals. . . . I suppose it is generally accepted that no superior permanent or very complex system of coöperation can be supported to a great extent merely by coercion.

(*b*) The rationalization of opportunity is a method of persuasion of much greater importance in most modern activities. Even under political and economic regimes in which coercion of individuals is at least temporarily and in some degree the basic process of persuasion, as in Russia, Germany, and Italy, it is observed that the processes of rationalization of other incentives, that is, propaganda, are carried on more extensively than anywhere else.

The rationalization of incentives occurs in two degrees; the general rationalization that is an expression of social organization as a whole and has chiefly occurred in connection with religious and political organizations, and the specific rationalization that consists in attempting to convince individuals or groups that they "ought," "it is to their interest," to perform services or conform to requirements of specific organizations.

The general rationalization of incentives on a noteworthy scale has occurred many times. The rationalization of religious motives as a basis of the Crusades is one of the most striking. The rationalization of communist doctrine in Russia is another. The rationalization of hate as a means of increasing organization (national) "solidarity" is well known. One of the most interesting of these general rationalizations is that of materialistic progress, to which we have already referred. It is an important basis of the characteristic forms of modern western organization. In its most general form it consists in the cult of science as a means to material ends, the glorification of inventions and inventive talent, including patent legislation; and the exaltation of the exploitation of land, forests, mineral resources, and of the means of transportation. In its more obvious current forms it consists in extensive and intensive salesmanship, advertising, and propaganda concerning the satisfactions to be had from the use of material products. . . .

Specific rationalization of incentives is the process of personal appeal to "join" an organization, to accept a job or position, to undertake a service, to contribute to a cause. It is the process of proselyting or recruiting that is commonly observed in connection with industrial, military, political, and religious organizations. It consists in emphasizing opportunities for satisfaction that are

offered, usually in contrast with those available otherwise; and in attempting to elicit interest in those incentives which are most easily or most outstandingly afforded.

The background of the individual to whom incentives are rationalized consists of his physiological requirements, his geographical and social location, and the general rationalization and especially the social influences to which he has previously been subjected by his society, his government, and his church. . . .

This brief[5] discussion of the incentives has been a necessary introduction to the considerations that are important to our study of the subject of organization and the executive functions. The processes concerned are each of them difficult in themselves, and are subject to highly developed techniques and skills. Their importance as a whole arises from the inherent difficulty that organizations experience either in supplying incentives or in exercising persuasion. The most appropriate phrase to apply to this inherent difficulty is "economy of incentives"; but it should be understood that "economy" is used in a broad sense and refers not merely to material or monetary economy.

II

In the economy of incentives we are concerned with the net effects of the income and outgo of things resulting from the production of objective incentives and the exercise of persuasion. An organization which makes material things the principal incentive will be unable long to offer this kind of incentive if it is unable to secure at least as much material or money as it pays out. This is the ordinary economic aspect which is well understood. But the same principle applies to other incentives. The possibilities of offering non-material opportunities, desirable conditions, ideal benefactions, desirable associations, stability of practice, enlarged participation, or communion advantages are limited and usually insufficient, so that the utmost economy is ordinarily essential not only in the material sense but in the broader sense as well. The limitations are due not alone to the relationship of the organization to the external physical environment, but also to its relationship to the social environment, and to its internal efficiency.

A complete exposition of the economy of incentives would among other things involve some duplication of the theories of general economics, rewritten from the point of view of organization. This is not the place to attempt such an exposition; but as the economy of incentives as a whole in terms of organization is not usually stressed in economic theory[6] and is certainly not well understood, I shall attempt to indicate the outlines of the theory. It will be convenient to do this with reference to organizations of three radically different purposes: (*a*) an industrial organization; (*b*) a political organization; and (*c*) a religious organization.

(*a*) In an industrial organization the purpose[7] is the production of material goods, or services. For the sake of simplicity we may assume that it requires no capital. It secures material production by applying the energies of men to the physical environment. These energies will result in a gross production; but if the inducements offered to secure these energies are themselves material, and are sufficient, then it will pay out of its production something on this account. If the amount paid out is no more than the production the organization can survive; but if the amount paid out is more than the production, it must cease, since it cannot then continue to offer inducements.

Whether this occurs depends upon the combined effect of four factors: the difficulties of the environment, the effectiveness of organization effort, the internal efficiency of organization, and the amount of inducements paid. Obviously many coöperative efforts fail because the environment is too resistant, others because the organization is ineffective, others because internal losses are large, others because the price paid for services is too large. Within the range of ordinary experience, these are mutually

dependent variables, or mutually interacting factors. Under very favorable environmental conditions, relative ineffectiveness and relative internal inefficiency with high outgo for inducements are possible. Under unfavorable conditions, effectiveness, efficiency, and low inducements are necessary.

In most cases the limitations of conditions, of effectiveness, and of efficiency permit only limited material inducements; and both effectiveness and efficiency require an output of individual energies that cannot be elicited from most men by material inducements in any event. Hence, in practice other inducements also must be offered. But in such an organization such inducements in some degree, and usually to a considerable degree, require again material inducements. Thus, satisfactory physical conditions of work mean material inducements to factors not directly productive; satisfactory social conditions mean the rejection of some of those best able to contribute the material production and acceptance of some less able. Almost every type of incentive that can be, or is, necessary will itself in some degree call for material outgo, so that the question is one of choice of methods and degree of emphasis upon different incentives to find the most efficient combination of incentives determined from the material viewpoint. Hence, the various incentives are in competition with each other even from the material point of view.

But the economy of incentives in an industrial organization only begins with the analysis of incentives from the standpoint of material; that is, dollars and cents, costs. The non-material incentives often conflict with each other or are incompatible. Thus opportunity for personal prestige as an incentive for one person necessarily involves a relative depression of others; so that if this incentive is emphasized as to one person, it must be in conjunction with other persons to whom personal prestige is relatively an unimportant inducement.

The difficulties of finding the workable balance of incentives is so great that recourse must be had to persuasion. But persuasion in connection with an industrial effort itself involves material outgo. Thus if coercion is the available method of persuasion, the maintenance of force for this purpose is involved; and if the contribution that can be secured by coercion is limited, as it usually is, except for short periods, the cost of coercion exceeds its effect. The limited efficiencies of slavery systems is an example.

If the method of persuasion is rationalization, either in the form of general propaganda[8] or that of specific argument to individuals (including processes of "selection"), again the overhead cost is usually not negligible. When the general social conditioning is favorable, of course, it is a windfall like favorable physical environment.

(b) A political organization is not ordinarily productive in the materialistic sense. The motives which lie at its roots are ideal benefactions and community satisfactions. Such organizations appear not to survive long unless they can afford these incentives; yet it is obvious that every extensive political organization requires the use of "inferior" incentives. Of these, opportunity for personal prestige and material rewards are most prominent. Hence the necessity, under all forms of political organization, for obtaining great supplies of material inducements for use either in the form of direct payments or of "paying jobs." Accordingly, a striking characteristic of political organizations has been the necessity for securing material contributions from "members" either to capture the opportunities to secure additional material (through taxation) or for direct payment (as in campaigns). But here again the balancing of incentives is necessary. For the limitations of material resources, the impossibility of giving more than is received, the discrimination between recipients as respects either material benefits or prestige granted, all tend either to destroy the vital idealism upon which political organization is based or to minimize the *general* material advantages which are perhaps an alternative basis of political organization in many cases.

It is hardly necessary to add that persuasion in its many forms is an important aspect of political recruiting—and that much of the material expenditure goes for this purpose; but this thereby decreases the material available as an incentive to intensive efforts of the "faithful."

(c) In religious organizations the predominant incentives[9] appear to be ideal benefactions and the communion of "kindred spirits," although inferior incentives no doubt often are effective. The fundamental contributions required of members are intensity of faith and loyalty to organization. A most important effort of religious organizations has been persuasion, known as missionary or proselyting effort. But both the maintenance of organization and missionary effort (and coercion when this is used) require material means, so that superficially, and often primarily, members are required by various methods to make material contributions to permit great material expenditures. . . .

It will be evident, perhaps, without more elaborate illustration, that in every type of organization, for whatever purpose, several incentives are necessary, and some degree of persuasion likewise, in order to secure and maintain the contributions to organization that are required. It will also be clear that, excepting in rare instances, the difficulties of securing the means of offering incentives, of avoiding conflict of incentives, and of making effective persuasive efforts, are inherently great; and that the determination of the precise combination of incentives and of persuasion that will be both effective and feasible is a matter of great delicacy. Indeed, it is so delicate and complex that rarely, if ever, is the scheme of incentives determinable in advance of application. It can only evolve; and the questions relating to it become chiefly those of strategic factors from time to time in the course of the life of the organization. It is also true, of course, that the scheme of incentives is probably the most unstable of the elements of the coöperative system, since invariably external conditions affect the possibilities of material incentives; and human motives are likewise highly variable. Thus incentives represent the final residual of all the conflicting forces involved in organization, a very slight change in underlying forces often making a great change in the power of incentives; and yet it is only by the incentives that the effective balancing of these forces is to be secured, if it can be secured at all. . . . Since all incentives are costly to organization, and the costs tend to prevent its survival, and since the balancing of organization outgo and income is initially to be regarded as impossible without the utmost economy, the distribution of incentives must be proportioned to the value and effectiveness of the various contributions sought.

This is only too much accepted as respects material incentives, that is, material things or money payment. No enduring or complex formal organization of any kind seems to have existed without differential material payments, though material compensation may be indirect to a considerable extent. This seems true up to the present even though contrary to the expressed attitude of the organization or not in harmony with its major purpose, as often in the case of churches and socialistic states.

The same doctrine applies in principle and practice even more to non-material incentives. The hierarchy of positions, with gradation of honors and privileges, which is the universal accompaniment of all complex organization, is essential to the adjustment of non-material incentives to induce the services of the most able individuals or the most valuable potential contributors to organization, and it is likewise necessary to the maintenance of pride of organization, community sense, etc., which are important general incentives to all classes of contributors.

NOTES

1. The method of statement convenient for this exposition should not be allowed to mislead. Only occasionally as to most persons and perhaps as to all persons is the determination of satisfactions and dissatisfactions a matter of logical thought.

2. It has been suggested to me that the illusion is also a result of the neglect of motives and the excessive imputation of logical processes in men by the earlier economists, and in purely theoretical economics. This was associated with the deterministic and especially the utilitarian doctrines of the greater part of the nineteenth century, and with the materialistic philosophies of Marx and others.

3. Largely an illusion, but a very dear one to some.

4. Referring to this paragraph, one of my valued correspondents, an army officer of long experience in active service, writes to the effect that I do not relatively emphasize this incentive sufficiently. Speaking of comradeship he says: "I was impressed, somewhat to my innocent surprise, during 1918, by the influence of this factor. I came out of the war with the definite impression that it was perhaps the strongest constructive moral factor, stronger than patriotism, and in many cases stronger than religion." He quotes Professor Joergensenson of Denmark, in his treatise appearing (with other contributions) in the Interparliamentary Union's book *What Would Be the Character of a New War?* as saying: "In the opinion of many experts these feelings [of brotherhood and comradeship among the troops] constituted the most important source of inner strength from a psychological point of view, and helped the soldiers to bear the sufferings and perils of the battlefield."

5. Among other matters it has not been necessary to develop here are those of fraud, trickery, and "economic compulsion," as related either to force or social pressures. At periods or in specific situations all have been important, and in the aggregate at any time no doubt are substantial. In principle, however, it is usually evident that, like direct coercion, they all involve disadvantages or sacrifices that offset their advantages; and it is doubtful if they often are the dominant factors in coöperation. On the contrary they arise from and are chiefly evidence of non-coöperation. They are disruptive, not integrating, methods.

6. I think it doubtful that many of the aspects of the economy of incentives have any place in theoretical economics.

7. The purpose is *not* profit, notwithstanding that business men, economists, ecclesiastics, politicians, labor unions, persistently misstate the purpose. Profit may be essential to having a supply of inducements to satisfy the motives of that class of contributors usually called owners or investors whose contributions in turn were essential to the supply of inducements to other classes of contributors. The possibilities of profit and their realization in some degree are necessary in some economies as conditions under which a continuing supply of incentives is possible; but the objective purpose of no organization is profit, but services. Among industrialists this has been most emphasized by Mr. Ford and some utility organizations.

8. General propaganda of industrial concerns usually relates to that class of contributors to organizations known as consumers.

9. That is, without taking into account supernatural benefactions.

10

Bureaucratic Structure and Personality

Robert K. Merton

A formal, rationally organized social structure involves clearly defined patterns of activity in which, ideally, every series of actions is functionally related to the purposes of the organization.[1] In such an organization there is integrated a series of offices, of hierarchized statuses, in which inhere a number of obligations and privileges closely defined by limited and specific rules. Each of these offices contains an area of imputed competence and responsibility. Authority, the power of control which derives from an acknowledged status, inheres in the office and not in the particular person who performs the official role. Official action ordinarily occurs within the framework of preexisting rules of the organization. The system of prescribed relations between the various offices involves a considerable degree of formality and clearly defined social distance between the occupants of these positions. Formality is manifested by means of a more or less complicated social ritual which symbolizes and supports the pecking order of the various offices. Such formality, which is integrated with the distribution of authority within the system, serves to minimize friction by largely restricting (official) contact to modes which are previously defined by the rules of the organization. Ready calculability of others' behavior and a stable set of mutual expectations are thus built up. Moreover, formality facilitates the interaction of the occupants of offices despite their (possibly hostile) private attitudes toward one another. In this way, the subordinate is protected from the arbitrary action of his superior, since the actions of both are constrained by a mutually recognized set of rules. Specific procedural devices foster objectivity and restrain the "quick passage of impulse into action."[2]

THE STRUCTURE OF BUREAUCRACY

The ideal type of such formal organization is bureaucracy and, in many respects, the classical analysis of bureaucracy is that by Max Weber.[3] As Weber indicates, bureaucracy involves a clear-cut division of integrated activities which are regarded as duties inherent in the office. A system of differentiated controls and sanctions is stated in the regulations. The assignment of roles occurs on the basis of technical qualifications which are ascertained through formalized, impersonal procedures (*e.g.*, examinations). Within the structure of hierarchically arranged authority, the activities of "trained and salaried experts" are governed by general, abstract, and clearly defined rules which preclude the necessity for the issuance of specific instructions for each specific case. The generality of the rules requires the constant use of *categorization*, whereby individual problems and cases are classified on the basis of designated criteria and are treated accordingly. The pure type of bureaucratic official is appointed, either by a superior or through the exercise of impersonal competition; he is not elected. A measure of flexibility in the bureaucracy is attained by electing higher functionaries who presumably express the will of the elector-

Source: Robert K. Merton, *Social Theory and Social Structure* (New York: Free Press, 1957). © 1957 by The Free Press; © renewed 1985 by Robert K. Merton. Reprinted with the permission of The Free Press, a division of Simon & Schuster Adult Publishing Group. All rights reserved.

ate (*e.g.*, a body of citizens or a board of directors). The election of higher officials is designed to affect the purposes of the organization, but the technical procedures for attaining these ends are carried out by continuing bureaucratic personnel.[4]

Most bureaucratic offices involve the expectation of life-long tenure, in the absence of disturbing factors which may decrease the size of the organization. Bureaucracy maximizes vocational security.[5] The function of security of tenure, pensions, incremental salaries and regularized procedures for promotion is to ensure the devoted performance of official duties, without regard for extraneous pressures.[6] The chief merit of bureaucracy is its technical efficiency, with a premium placed on precision, speed, expert control, continuity, discretion, and optimal returns on input. The structure is one which approaches the complete elimination of personalized relationships and nonrational considerations (hostility, anxiety, affectual involvements, etc.).

With increasing bureaucratization, it becomes plain to all who would see that man is to a very important degree controlled by his social relations to the instruments of production. This can no longer seem only a tenet of Marxism, but a stubborn fact to be acknowledged by all, quite apart from their ideological persuasion. Bureaucratization makes readily visible what was previously dim and obscure. More and more people discover that to work, they must be employed. For to work, one must have tools and equipment. And the tools and equipment are increasingly available only in bureaucracies, private or public. Consequently, one must be employed by the bureaucracies in order to have access to tools in order to work in order to live. It is in this sense that bureaucratization entails separation of individuals from the instruments of production, as in modern capitalistic enterprise or in state communistic enterprise (of the midcentury variety), just as in the postfeudal army, bureaucratization entailed complete separation from the instruments of destruction. Typically, the worker no longer owns his

tools nor the soldier, his weapons. And in this special sense, more and more people become workers, either blue collar or white collar or stiff shirt. So develops, for example, the new type of scientific worker, as the scientist is "separated" from his technical equipment—after all, the physicist does not ordinarily own his cyclotron. To work at his research, he must be employed by a bureaucracy with laboratory resources.

Bureaucracy is administration which almost completely avoids public discussion of its techniques, although there may occur public discussion of its policies.[7] This secrecy is confined neither to public nor to private bureaucracies. It is held to be necessary to keep valuable information from private economic competitors or from foreign and potentially hostile political groups. And though it is not often so called, espionage among competitors is perhaps as common, if not as intricately organized, in systems of private economic enterprise as in systems of national states. Cost figures, lists of clients, new technical processes, plans for production—all these are typically regarded as essential secrets of private economic bureaucracies which might be revealed if the bases of all decisions and policies had to be publicly defended.

THE DYSFUNCTIONS OF BUREAUCRACY

In these bold outlines, the positive attainments and functions of bureaucratic organization are emphasized and the internal stresses and strains of such structures are almost wholly neglected. The community at large, however, evidently emphasizes the imperfections of bureaucracy, as is suggested by the fact that the "horrid hybrid," bureaucrat, has become an epithet, a *Schimpfwort*.

The transition to a study of the negative aspects of bureaucracy is afforded by the application of Veblen's concept of "trained incapacity," Dewey's notion of "occupational psychosis" or Warnotte's view of "professional deformation." Trained incapacity refers to that state of affairs in which one's abilities function as inadequacies or blind spots. Actions based upon training and skills which have been successfully applied in the past may result in inappropriate responses *under changed conditions*. An inadequate flexibility in the application of skills, will, in a changing milieu, result in more or less serious maladjustments.[8] Thus, to adopt a barnyard illustration used in this connection by Burke, chickens may be readily conditioned to interpret the sound of a bell as a signal for food. The same bell may now be used to summon the trained chickens to their doom as they are assembled to suffer decapitation. In general, one adopts measures in keeping with one's past training and, under new conditions which are not recognized as *significantly* different, the very soundness of this training may lead to the adoption of the wrong procedures. Again, in Burke's almost echolalic phrase, "people may be unfitted by being fit in an unfit fitness"; their training may become an incapacity.

Dewey's concept of occupational psychosis rests upon much the same observations. As a result of their day to day routines, people develop special preferences, antipathies, discriminations and emphases.[9] (The term psychosis is used by Dewey to denote a "pronounced character of the mind.") These psychoses develop through demands put upon the individual by the particular organization of his occupational role.

The concepts of both Veblen and Dewey refer to a fundamental ambivalence. Any action can be considered in terms of what it attains or what it fails to attain. "A way of seeing is also a way of not seeing—a focus upon object A involves a neglect of object B."[10] In his discussion, Weber is almost exclusively concerned with what the bureaucratic structure attains: precision, reliability, efficiency. This same structure may be examined from another perspective provided by the ambivalence. What are the limitations of the organizations designed to attain these goals?

For reasons which we have already noted, the bureaucratic structure exerts a constant pressure upon the official to be "methodical, prudent, disciplined." If the bureaucracy is to operate successfully, it must attain a high degree of reliability of behavior, an unusual degree of conformity with prescribed patterns of action. Hence, the fundamental importance of discipline which may be as highly developed in a religious or economic bureaucracy as in the army. Discipline can be effective only if the ideal patterns are buttressed by strong sentiments which entail devotion to ones duties, a keen sense of the limitation of one's authority and competence, and methodical performance of routine activities. The efficacy of social structure depends ultimately upon infusing group participants with appropriate attitudes and sentiments. As we shall see, there are definite arrangements in the bureaucracy for inculcating and reinforcing these sentiments.

At the moment, it suffices to observe that in order to ensure discipline (the necessary reliability of response), these sentiments are often more intense than is technically necessary. There is a margin of safety, so to speak, in the pressure exerted by these sentiments upon the bureaucrat to conform to his patterned obligations, in much the same sense that added allowances (precautionary overestimations) are made by the engineer in designing the supports for a bridge. But this very emphasis leads to a transference of the sentiments from the *aims* of the organization onto the particular details of behavior required by the rules. Adherence to the rules, originally conceived as a means, becomes transformed into an end-in-itself; there occurs the familiar process of *displacement of goals* whereby "an instrumental value becomes a terminal value."[11] Discipline, readily interpreted as conformance with regulations, whatever the situation, is seen not as a measure designed for specific purposes but becomes an immediate value in the life-organization of the bureaucrat. This emphasis, resulting from the displacement of the original goals, develops into rigidities and an inability to adjust readily. Formalism, even ritualism, ensues with an unchallenged insistence upon punctilious adherence to formalized procedures.[12] This may be exaggerated to the point where primary concern with conformity to the rules interferes with the achievement of the purposes of the organization, in which case we have the familiar phenomenon of the technicism or red tape of the official. An extreme product of this process of displacement of goals is the bureaucratic virtuoso, who never forgets a single rule binding his action and hence is unable to assist many of his clients.[13] A case in point, where strict recognition of the limits of authority and literal adherence to rules produced this result, is the pathetic plight of Bernt Balchen, Admiral Byrd's pilot in the flight over the South Pole.

> According to a ruling of the department of labor Bernt Balchen . . . cannot receive his citizenship papers. Balchen, a native of Norway, declared his intention in 1927. It is held that he has failed to meet the condition of five years' continuous residence in the United States. The Byrd antarctic voyage took him out of the country, although he was on a ship carrying the American flag, was an invaluable member of the American expedition, and in a region to which there is an American claim because of the exploration and occupation of it by Americans, this region being Little America.
>
> The bureau of naturalization explains that it cannot proceed on the assumption that Little America is American soil. That would be *trespass on international questions* where it has no sanction. So far as the bureau is concerned, Balchen was out of the country and *technically* has not complied with the law of naturalization.[14]

STRUCTURAL SOURCES OF OVERCONFORMITY

Such inadequacies in orientation which involve trained incapacity clearly derive from structural sources. The process may be briefly recapitulated. (1) An effective bureaucracy demands reliability of response and strict devotion to regulations. (2) Such devotion to the rules leads to their transformation into absolutes; they are no longer conceived as relative to a set of purposes. (3) This interferes with ready adaptation under special conditions not clearly envisaged by those who drew up the general rules. (4) Thus, the very elements which conduce toward efficiency in general produce inefficiency in specific instances. Full realization of the inadequacy is seldom attained by members of the group who have not divorced themselves from the meanings which the rules have for them. These rules in time become symbolic in cast, rather than strictly utilitarian.

Thus far, we have treated the ingrained sentiments making for rigorous discipline simply as data, as given. However, definite features of the bureaucratic structure may be seen to conduce to these sentiments. The bureaucrat's official life is planned for him in terms of a graded career, through the organizational devices of promotion by seniority, pensions, incremental salaries, etc., all of which are designed to provide incentives for disciplined action and conformity to the official regulations.[15] The official is tacitly expected to and largely does adapt his thoughts, feelings and actions to the prospect of this career. But *these very devices* which increase the probability of conformance also lead to an over-concern with strict adherence to regulations which induces timidity, conservatism, and technicism. Displacement of sentiments from goals onto means is fostered by the tremendous symbolic significance of the means (rules).

Another feature of the bureaucratic structure tends to produce much the same result. Functionaries have the sense of a common destiny for all those who work together. They share the same interests, especially since there is relatively little competition in so far as promotion is in terms of seniority. In-group aggression is thus minimized and this arrangement is therefore conceived to be positively functional for the bureaucracy. However, the *esprit de corps* and informal social organization which typically develops in such situations often leads the personnel to defend their entrenched interests rather than to assist their clientele and elected higher officials. As President Lowell reports, if the bureaucrats believe that their status is not adequately recognized by an incoming elected official, detailed information will be withheld from him, leading him to errors for which he is held responsible. Or, if he seeks to dominate fully, and thus violates the sentiment of self-integrity of the bureaucrats, he may have documents brought to him in such numbers that he cannot manage to sign them all, let alone read them.[16] This illustrates the defensive informal organization which tends to arise whenever there is an apparent threat to the integrity of the group.[17]

It would be much too facile and partly erroneous to attribute such resistance by bureaucrats simply to vested interests. Vested interests oppose any new order which either eliminates or at least makes uncertain their differential advantage deriving from the current arrangements. This is undoubtedly involved in part in bureaucratic resistance to change but another process is perhaps more significant. As we have seen, bureaucratic officials affectively identify themselves with their way of life. They have a pride of craft which leads them to resist change in established routines; at least, those changes which are felt to be imposed by others. This nonlogical pride of craft is a familiar pattern found even, to judge from Sutherland's *Professional Thief*, among pickpockets who, despite the risk, delight in mastering the prestige-bearing feat of "beating a left breech" (picking the left front trousers pocket).

In a stimulating paper, Hughes has applied the concepts of "secular" and "sacred" to various types of division of labor; "the sacredness" of caste and *Stände* prerogatives contrasts sharply with the increasing secularism of occupational differentiation in our society.[18] However, as our discussion suggests, there may ensue, in particular vocations and in particular types of organization, the *process of sanctification* (viewed as the counterpart of the process of seculariza-

tion). This is to say that through sentiment-formation, emotional dependence upon bureaucratic symbols and status, and affective involvement in spheres of competence and authority, there develop prerogatives involving attitudes of moral legitimacy which are established as values in their own right, and are no longer viewed as merely technical means for expediting administration. One may note a tendency for certain bureaucratic norms, originally introduced for technical reasons, to become rigidified and sacred, although, as Durkheim would say, they are *laïque en apparence*.[19] Durkheim has touched on this general process in his description of the attitudes and values which persist in the organic solidarity of a highly differentiated society.

PRIMARY VERSUS SECONDARY RELATIONS

Another feature of the bureaucratic structure, the stress on depersonalization of relationships, also plays its part in the bureaucrat's trained incapacity. The personality pattern of the bureaucrat is nucleated about this norm of impersonality. Both this and the categorizing tendency, which develops from the dominant role of general, abstract rules, tend to produce conflict in the bureaucrat's contacts with the public or clientele. Since functionaries minimize personal relations and resort to categorization, the peculiarities of individual cases are often ignored. But the client who, quite understandably, is convinced of the special features of *his* own problem often objects to such categorical treatment. Stereotyped behavior is not adapted to the exigencies of individual problems. The impersonal treatment of affairs which are at times of great personal significance to the client gives rise to the charge of "arrogance" and "haughtiness" of the bureaucrat. Thus, at the Greenwich Employment Exchange, the unemployed worker who is securing his insurance payment resents what he deems to be "the impersonality and, at times, the apparent abruptness and even harshness of his treatment by the clerks. . . . Some men complain of the superior attitude which the clerks have."[20]

Still another source of conflict with the public derives from the bureaucratic structure. The bureaucrat, in part irrespective of his position within the hierarchy, acts as a representative of the power and prestige of the entire structure. In his official role he is vested with definite authority. This often leads to an actually or apparently domineering attitude, which may only be exaggerated by a discrepancy between his position within the hierarchy and his position with reference to the public.[21] Protest and recourse to other officials on the part of the client are often ineffective or largely precluded by the previously mentioned *esprit de corps* which joins the officials into a more or less solidary in-group. This source of conflict *may* be minimized in private enterprise since the client can register an effective protest by transferring his trade to another organization within the competitive system. But with the monopolistic nature of the public organization, no such alternative is possible. Moreover, in this case, tension is increased because of a discrepancy between ideology and fact: the governmental personnel are held to be "servants of the people," but in fact they are often superordinate, and release of tension can seldom be afforded by turning to other agencies for the necessary service.[22] This tension is in part attributable to the confusion of the status of bureaucrat and client; the client may consider himself socially superior to the official who is at the moment dominant.[23]

Thus, with respect to the relations between officials and clientele, one structural source of conflict is the pressure for formal and impersonal treatment when individual, personalized consideration is desired by the client. The conflict may be viewed, then, deriving from the introduction of inappropriate attitudes and relationships. Conflict within the bureaucratic structure arises from the converse situation, namely, when personalized relationships are substituted

for the structurally required impersonal relationships. This type of conflict may be characterized as follows.

The bureaucracy, as we have seen, is organized as a secondary, formal group. The normal responses involved in this organized network of social expectations are supported by affective attitudes of members of the group. Since the group is oriented toward secondary norms of impersonality, any failure to conform to these norms will arouse antagonism from those who have identified themselves with the legitimacy of these rules. Hence, the substitution of personal for impersonal treatment within the structure is met with widespread disapproval and is characterized by such epithets as graft, favoritism, nepotism, apple-polishing, etc. These epithets are clearly manifestations of injured sentiments.[24] The function of such virtually automatic resentment can be clearly seen in terms of the requirements of bureaucratic structure.

Bureaucracy is a secondary group structure designed to carry on certain activities which cannot be satisfactorily performed on the basis of primary group criteria.[25] Hence behavior which runs counter to these formalized norms becomes the object of emotionalized disapproval. This constitutes a functionally significant defence set up against tendencies which jeopardize the performance of socially necessary activities. To be sure, these reactions are not rationally determined practices explicitly designed for the fulfillment of this function. Rather, viewed in terms of the individual's interpretation of the situation, such resentment is simply an immediate response opposing the "dishonesty" of those who violate the rules of the game. However, this subjective frame of reference notwithstanding, these reactions serve the latent function of maintaining the essential structural elements of bureaucracy by reaffirming the necessity for formalized, secondary relations and by helping to prevent the disintegration of the bureaucratic structure which would occur should these be supplanted by personalized relations. This type of conflict may be generically described as the intrusion of primary group attitudes when secondary group attitudes are institutionally demanded, just as the bureaucrat-client conflict often derives from interaction on impersonal terms when personal treatment is individually demanded.[26]

PROBLEMS FOR RESEARCH

The trend towards increasing bureaucratization in Western Society, which Weber had long since foreseen, is not the sole reason for sociologists to turn their attention to this field. Empirical studies of the interaction of bureaucracy and personality should especially increase our understanding of social structure. A large number of specific questions invite our attention. To what extent are particular personality types selected and modified by the various bureaucracies (private enterprise, public service, the quasi-legal political machine, religious orders)? Inasmuch as ascendancy and submission are held to be traits of personality, despite their variability in different stimulus-situations, do bureaucracies select personalities of particularly submissive or ascendant tendencies? And since various studies have shown that these traits can be modified, does participation in bureaucratic office tend to increase ascendant tendencies? Do various systems of recruitment (*e.g.*, patronage, open competition involving specialized knowledge or general mental capacity, practical experience) select different personality types?[27] Does promotion through seniority lessen competitive anxieties and enhance administrative efficiency? A detailed examination of mechanisms for imbuing the bureaucratic codes with affect would be instructive both sociologically and psychologically. Does the general anonymity of civil service decisions tend to restrict the area of prestige-symbols to a narrowly defined inner circle? Is there a tendency for differential association to be especially marked among bureaucrats?

The range of theoretically significant and practically important questions would seem to be limited only by the accessibility of the concrete data. Studies of religious, educational, military, economic, and political bureaucracies dealing with the interdependence of social organization and personality formation should constitute an avenue for fruitful research. On that avenue, the functional analysis of concrete structures may yet build a Solomon's House for sociologists.

NOTES

1. For a development of the concept of "rational organization," see Karl Mannheim, *Mensch und Gesellschaft im Zeitalter des Umbaus* (Leiden: A. W. Sijthoff, 1935), esp. 28 ff.

2. H. D. Lasswell, *Politics* (New York: McGraw-Hill, 1936), 120–121.

3. Max Weber, *Wirtschaft und Gesellschaft* (Tübingen: J. C. B. Mohr, 1922), pt. 3, chap. 6; 650–678. For a brief summary of Weber's discussion, see Talcott Parsons, *The Structure of Social Action*, esp. 506 ff. For a description, which is not a caricature, of the bureaucrat as a personality type, see C. Rabany, "Les types sociaux: le fonctionnaire," *Revue générale d'administration* 88 (1907), 5–28.

4. Karl Mannheim, *Ideology and Utopia* (New York: Harcourt Brace Jovanovich, 1936), 18n., 105 ff. See also Ramsay Muir, *Peers and Bureaucrats* (London: Constable, 1910), 12–13.

5. E. G. Cahen-Salvador suggests that the personnel of bureaucracies is largely constituted by those who value security above all else. See his "La situation matérielle et morale des fonctionnaires," *Revue politique et parlementaire* (1926), 319.

6. H. J. Laski, "Bureaucracy," *Encyclopedia of the Social Sciences*. This article is written primarily from the standpoint of the political scientist rather than that of the sociologist.

7. Weber, *op. cit.*, 671.

8. For a stimulating discussion and application of these concepts, see Kenneth Burke, *Permanence and Change* (New York: New

Republic, 1935), pp. 50 ff.; Daniel Warnotte, "Bureaucratie et Fonctionnarisme," *Revue de l'Institut de Sociologie* 17 (1937), 245.

9. *Ibid.*, 58–59.

10. *Ibid.*, 70.

11. This process has often been observed in various connections. Wundt's *heterogony of ends* is a case in point; Max Weber's *Paradoxie der Folgen* is another. See also MacIver's observations on the transformation of civilization into culture and Lasswell's remark that "the human animal distinguishes himself by his infinite capacity for making ends of his means." See Merton, "The unanticipated consequences of purposive social action," *American Sociological Review* 1 (1936), 894–904. In terms of the psychological mechanisms involved, this process has been analyzed most fully by Gordon W. Allport, in his discussion of what he calls "the functional autonomy of motives." Allport emends the earlier formulations of Woodworth, Tolman, and William Stern, and arrives at a statement of the process from the standpoint of individual motivation. He does not consider those phases of the social structure which conduce toward the "transformation of motives." The formulation adopted in this paper is thus complementary to Allport's analysis; the one stressing the psychological mechanisms involved, the other considering the constraints of the social structure. The convergence of psychology and sociology toward this central concept suggests that it may well constitute one of the conceptual bridges between the two disciplines. See Gordon W. Allport, *Personality* (New York: Henry Holt & Co., 1937), chap. 7.

12. See E. C. Hughes. "Institutional office and the person," *American Journal of Sociology*, 43 (1937), 404–413; E. T. Hiller, "Social structure in relation to the person," *Social Forces* 16 (1937).

13. Mannheim, *Ideology and Utopia*, 106.

14. Quoted from the *Chicago Tribune* (June 24, 1931, p. 10) by Thurman Arnold, *The Symbols of Government* (New Haven: Yale University Press, 1935), 201–202. (My italics.)

15. Mannheim, *Mensch und Gesellschaft*, 32–33. Mannheim stresses the importance

of the "Lebensplan" and the "Amtskarriere." See the comments by Hughes, *op. cit.*, 413.

16. A. L. Lowell, *The Government of England* (New York, 1908), I, 189 ff.

17. For an instructive description of the development of such a defensive organization in a group of workers, see F. J. Roethlisberger and W. J. Dickson, *Management and the Worker* (Boston: Harvard School of Business Administration, 1934).

18. E. C. Hughes. "Personality types and the division of labor," *American Journal of Sociology* 33 (1928), 754–768. Much the same distinction is drawn by Leopold von Wiese and Howard Becker, *Systematic Sociology* (New York: John Wiley & Sons, 1932), 222–225 *et passim*.

19. Hughes recognizes one phase of this process of sanctification when he writes that professional training "carries with it as a by-product assimilation of the candidate into a set of professional attitudes and controls, *a professional conscience and solidarity. The profession claims and aims to become a moral unit.*" Hughes, *op. cit.*, 762 (italics inserted). In this same connection, Sumner's concept of *pathos*, as the halo of sentiment which protects a social value from criticism, is particularly relevant, inasmuch as it affords a clue to the mechanism involved in the process of sanctification. See his *Folkways*, 180–181.

20. "'They treat you like a lump of dirt they do. I see a navvy reach across the counter and shake one of them by the collar the other day. The rest of us felt like cheering. Of course he lost his benefit over it. . . . But the clerk deserved it for his sassy way.'" (E. W. Bakke, *The Unemployed Man*, 79–80). Note that the domineering attitude was *imputed* by the unemployed client who is in a state of tension due to his loss of status and self-esteem in a society where the ideology is still current that an "able man" can always find a job. That the imputation of arrogance stems largely from the client's state of mind is seen from Bakke's own observation that "the clerks were rushed, and had no time for pleasantries, but there was little sign of harshness or a superiority feeling in their treatment of the men." In so far as there is an objective basis for the imputation of arrogant behavior

to bureaucrats, it may possibly be explained by the following juxtaposed statements. "Auch der moderne, sei es öffentliche, sei es private, Beamte erstrebt immer and geniesst meist den Beherrschten gegenüber eine spezifisch gehobene, 'ständische' soziale Schätzung." (Weber, *op. cit.*, 652.) "In persons in whom the craving for prestige is uppermost, hostility usually takes the form of a desire to humiliate others." K. Horney, *The Neurotic Personality of Our Time*, 178–179.

21. In this connection, note the relevance of Koffka's comments on certain features of the pecking-order of birds. "If one compares the behavior of the bird at the top of the pecking list, the despot, with that of one very far down, the second or third from the last, then one finds the latter much more cruel to the few others over whom he lords it than the former in his treatment of all members. As soon as one removes from the group all members above the penultimate, his behavior becomes milder and may even become very friendly. . . . It is not difficult to find analogies to this in human societies, and therefore one side of such behavior must be primarily the effects of the social groupings, and not of individual characteristics." K. Koffka, *Principles of Gestalt Psychology* (New York: Harcourt Brace Jovanovich, 1935), 668–669.

22. At this point the political machine often becomes functionally significant. As Steffens and others have shown, highly personalized relations and the abrogation of formal rules (red tape) by the machine often satisfy the needs of individual "clients" more fully than the formalized mechanism of governmental bureaucracy.

23. As one of the unemployed men remarked about the clerks at the Greenwich Employment Exchange: "'And the bloody blokes wouldn't have their jobs if it wasn't for us men out of a job either. That's what gets me about their holding their noses up.'" Bakke, *op. cit.*, 80. See also H. D. Lasswell and G. Almond, "Aggressive behavior by clients towards public relief administrators," *American Political Science Review* 28 (1934), 643–655.

24. The diagnostic significance of such linguistic indices as epithets has scarcely been explored by the sociologist. Sumner properly observes that epithets produce "summary criticisms" and definitions of social situations. Dollard also notes that "epithets frequently define the central issues in a society," and Sapir has rightly emphasized the importance of context of situations in appraising the significance of epithets. Of equal relevance is Linton's observation that "in case histories the way in which the community felt about a particular episode is, if anything, more important to our study than the actual behavior. . . ." A sociological study of "vocabularies of encomium and opprobrium" should lead to valuable findings.

25. *Cf.* Ellsworth Faris, *The Nature of Human Nature* (New York: McGraw-Hill, 1937), 41 ff.

26. Community disapproval of many forms of behavior may be analyzed in terms of one or the other of these patterns of substitution of culturally inappropriate types of relationship. Thus, prostitution constitutes a type-case where coitus, a form of intimacy which is institutionally defined as symbolic of the most "sacred" primary group relationship, is placed within a contractual contest, symbolized by the exchange of that most impersonal of all symbols, money. See Kingsley Davis, "The sociology of prostitution." *American Sociological Review* 2 (1937), 744–755.

27. Among recent studies of recruitment to bureaucracy are: Reinhard Bendix, *Higher Civil Servants in American Society* (Boulder: University of Colorado Press, 1949); Dwaine Marwick, *Career Perspectives in a Bureaucratic Setting* (Ann Arbor: University of Michigan Press, 1954); R. K. Kelsall, *Higher Civil Servants in Britain* (London: Routledge & Kegan Paul, 1955); W. L. Warner and J. C. Abegglen, *Occupational Mobility in American Business and Industry* (Minneapolis: University of Minnesota Press, 1955).

11

The Proverbs of Administration

Herbert A. Simon

A fact about proverbs that greatly enhances their quotability is that they almost always occur in mutually contradictory pairs. "Look before you leap!"—but "He who hesitates is lost."

This is both a great convenience and a serious defect—depending on the use to which one wishes to put the proverbs in question. If it is a matter of rationalizing behavior that has already taken place or justifying action that has already been decided upon, proverbs are ideal. Since one is never at a loss to find one that will prove his point or the precisely contradictory point, for that matter—they are a great help in persuasion, political debate, and all forms of rhetoric.

But when one seeks to use proverbs as the basis of a scientific theory, the situation is less happy. It is not that the propositions expressed by the proverbs are insufficient; it is rather that they prove too much. A scientific theory should tell what is true but also what is false. If Newton had announced to the world that particles of matter exert either an attraction or a repulsion on each other, he would not have added much to scientific knowledge. His contribution consisted in showing that an attraction was exercised and in announcing the precise law governing its operation.

Most of the propositions that make up the body of administrative theory today share, unfortunately, this defect of proverbs. For almost every principle one can find an equally plausible and acceptable contradictory principle. Although the two principles of the pair will lead to exactly opposite organizational recommendations, there is nothing in the theory to indicate which is the proper one to apply.[1]

It is the purpose of this paper to substantiate this sweeping criticism of administrative theory, and to present some suggestions—perhaps less concrete than they should be—as to how the existing dilemma can be solved.

SOME ACCEPTED ADMINISTRATIVE PRINCIPLES

Among the more common "principles" that occur in the literature of administration are these:

1. Administrative efficiency is increased by a specialization of the task among the group.
2. Administrative efficiency is increased by arranging the members of the group in a determinate hierarchy of authority.
3. Administrative efficiency is increased by limiting the span of control at any point in the hierarchy to a small number.
4. Administrative efficiency is increased by grouping the workers, for purposes of control, according to (a) purpose, (b) process, (c) clientele, or (d) place. (This is really an elaboration of the first principle but deserves separate discussion.)

Since these principles appear relatively simple and clear, it would seem that their application to concrete problems of administrative organization would be unambiguous and that their validity would be easily submitted to empirical test. Such, however, seems not to be the case. To show why it is not, each of the four principles just listed will be considered in turn.

Source: Public Administration Review (winter 1946): 6, 53–67. © 1946 by the American Society for Public Administration (ASPA), 1120 G Street NW, Suite 700, Washington, DC 20005. Reprinted with permission. All rights reserved.

Specialization. Administrative efficiency is supposed to increase with an increase in specialization. But is this intended to mean that *any* increase in specialization will increase efficiency? If so, which of the following alternatives is the correct application of the principle in a particular case?

1. A plan of nursing should be put into effect by which nurses will be assigned to districts and do all nursing within that district, including school examinations, visits to homes of school children, and tuberculosis nursing.
2. A functional plan of nursing should be put into effect by which different nurses will be assigned to school examinations, visits to homes of school children, and tuberculosis nursing. The present method of generalized nursing by districts impedes the development of specialized skills in the three very diverse programs.

Both of these administrative arrangements satisfy the requirement of specialization—the first provides specialization by place; the second, specialization by function. The principle of specialization is of no help at all in choosing between the two alternatives.

It appears that the simplicity of the principle of specialization is a deceptive simplicity—a simplicity which conceals fundamental ambiguities. For "specialization" is not a condition of efficient administration; it is an inevitable characteristic of all group effort, however efficient or inefficient that effort may be. Specialization merely means that different persons are doing different things—and since it is physically impossible for two persons to be doing the same thing in the same place at the same time, two persons are always doing different things.

The real problem of administration, then, is not to "specialize," but to specialize in that particular manner and along those particular lines which will lead to administrative efficiency. But, in thus rephrasing this "principle" of administration, there has been brought clearly into the open its fundamental ambiguity: "Administrative efficiency is increased by a specialization of the task

among the group in the direction which will lead to greater efficiency."

Further discussion of the choice between competing bases of specialization will be undertaken after two other principles of administration have been examined.

Unity of Command. Administrative efficiency is supposed to be enhanced by arranging the members of the organization in a determinate hierarchy of authority in order to preserve "unity of command."

Analysis of this "principle" requires a clear understanding of what is meant by the term "authority." A subordinate may be said to accept authority whenever he permits his behavior to be guided by a decision reached by another, irrespective of his own judgment as to the merits of that decision.

In one sense the principle of unity of command, like the principle of specialization, cannot be violated; for it is physically impossible for a man to obey two contradictory commands—that is what is meant by "contradictory commands." Presumably, if unity of command is a principle of administration, it must assert something more than this physical impossibility. Perhaps it asserts this: that it is undesirable to place a member of an organization in a position where he receives orders from more than one superior. This is evidently the meaning that Gulick attaches to the principle when he says,

The significance of this principle in the process of co-ordination and organization must not be lost sight of. In building a structure of co-ordination, it is often tempting to set up more than one boss for a man who is doing work which has more than one relationship. Even as great a philosopher of management as Taylor fell into this error in setting up separate foremen to deal with machinery, with materials, with speed, etc., each with the power of giving orders directly to the individual workman. The rigid adherence to the principle of unity of command may have its absurdities; these are, however, unimportant in comparison with the certainty of confusion, inefficiency and irresponsibility which arise from the violation of the principle.[2]

Certainly the principle of unity of command, thus interpreted, cannot be criticized for any lack of clarity or any ambiguity. The definition of authority given above should provide a clear test whether, in any concrete situation, the principle is observed. The real fault that must be found with this principle is that it is incompatible with the principle of specialization. One of the most important uses to which authority is put in organization is to bring about specialization in the work of making decisions, so that each decision is made at a point in the organization where it can be made most expertly. As a result, the use of authority permits a greater degree of expertness to be achieved in decision making than would be possible if each operative employee had himself to make all the decisions upon which his activity is predicated. The individual fireman does not decide whether to use a two-inch hose or a fire extinguisher; that is decided for him by his officers, and the decision is communicated to him in the form of a command.

However, if unity of command, in Gulick's sense, is observed, the decisions of a person at any point in the administrative hierarchy are subject to influence through only one channel of authority; and if his decisions are of a kind that require expertise in more than one field of knowledge, then advisory and informational services must be relied upon to supply those premises which lie in a field not recognized by the mode of specialization in the organization. For example, if an accountant in a school department is subordinate to an educator, and if unity of command is observed, then the finance department cannot issue direct orders to him regarding the technical, accounting aspects of his work. Similarly, the director of motor vehicles in the public works department will be unable to issue direct orders on care of motor equipment to the fire-truck driver.[3]

Gulick, in the statement quoted above, clearly indicates the difficulties to be faced if unity of command is not observed. A certain amount of irresponsibility and confusion are almost certain to ensue. But perhaps this is not too great a price to pay for the increased expertise that can be applied to decisions. What is needed to decide the issue is a principle of administration that would enable one to weigh the relative advantages of the two courses of action. But neither the principle of unity of command nor the principle of specialization is helpful in adjudicating the controversy. They merely contradict each other without indicating any procedure for resolving the contradiction. . . .

The principle of unity of command is perhaps more defensible if narrowed down to the following: In case two authoritative commands conflict, there should be a single determinate person whom the subordinate is expected to obey; and the sanctions of authority should be applied against the subordinate only to enforce his obedience to that one person.

If the principle of unity of command is more defensible when stated in this limited form, it also solves fewer problems. In the first place, it no longer requires, except for settling conflicts of authority, a single hierarchy of authority. Consequently, it leaves unsettled the very important question of how authority should be zoned in a particular organization (i.e., the modes of specialization) and through what channels it should be exercised. Finally, even this narrower concept of unity of command conflicts with the principle of specialization, for whenever disagreement does occur and the organization members revert to the formal lines of authority, then only those types of specialization which are represented in the hierarchy of authority can impress themselves on decisions. If the training officer of a city exercises only functional supervisions over the police training officer, then in case of disagreement with the police chief, specialized knowledge of training problems will be subordinated or ignored. That this actually occurs is shown by the frustration so commonly expressed by functional supervisors at their lack of authority to apply sanctions.

Span of Control. Administrative efficiency is supposed to be enhanced by limiting the number of subordinates who re-port directly to any one administrator to a small number — say six. This notion that the "span of control" should be narrow is confidently asserted as a third incontrovert-ible principle of administration. The usual common-sense arguments for restricting the span of control are familiar and need not be repeated here. What is not so gener-ally recognized is that a contradictory prov-erb of administration can be stated which, though it is not so familiar as the principle of span of control, can be supported by ar-guments of equal plausibility. The proverb in question is the following: Administrative efficiency is enhanced by keeping at a min-imum the number of organizational levels through which a matter must pass before it is acted upon.

This latter proverb is one of the funda-mental criteria that guide administrative analysis in procedures simplification work. Yet in many situations the results to which this principle leads are in direct contradic-tion to the requirements of the principle of span of control, the principle of unity of command, and the principle of specializa-tion. The present discussion is concerned with the first of these conflicts. To illustrate the difficulty, two alternative proposals for the organization of a small health depart-ment will be presented — one based on the restriction of span of control, the other on the limitation of number of organization levels:

1. The present organization of the depart-ment places an administrative overload on the health officer by reason of the fact that all eleven employees of the department re-port directly to him and the further fact that some of the staff lack adequate tech-nical training. Consequently, venereal dis-ease clinic treatments and other details re-quire an undue amount of the health officer's personal attention.

   It has previously been recommended that the proposed medical officer be placed in charge of the venereal disease and chest clinics and all child hygiene work. It is further recommended that one of the inspectors be designated chief in-spector and placed in charge of all the de-partment's inspectional activities and that one of the nurses be designated as head nurse. This will relieve the health com-missioner of considerable detail and will leave him greater freedom to plan and su-pervise the health program as a whole, to conduct health education, and to coordi-nate the work of the department with that of other community agencies. If the de-partment were thus organized, the effec-tiveness of all employees could be substan-tially increased.

2. The present organization of the depart-ment leads to inefficiency and excessive red tape by reason of the fact that an unnecessary supervisory level intervenes between the health officer and the op-erative employees, and that those four of the twelve employees who are best trained technically are engaged largely in "overhead" administrative duties. Con-sequently, unnecessary delays occur in securing the approval of the health offi-cer on matters requiring his attention, and too many matters require review and re-review.

   The medical officer should be left in charge of the venereal disease and chest clinics and child hygiene work. It is rec-ommended, however, that the position of chief inspector and head nurse be abol-ished and that the employees now filling these positions perform regular inspec-tional and nursing duties. The details of work scheduling now handled by these two employees can be taken care of more economically by the secretary to the health officer, and, since broader matters of policy have, in any event, always re-quired the personal attention of the health officer, the abolition of these two positions will eliminate a wholly unneces-sary step in review, will allow an expan-sion of inspectional and nursing services, and will permit at least a beginning to be made in the recommended program of health education. The number of persons reporting directly to the health officer will be increased to nine, but since there are few matters requiring the coordination of these employees, other than the work schedules and policy questions referred to above, this change will not materially increase his work load.

The dilemma is this: in a large organization with complex interrelations between members, a restricted span of control inevitably produces excessive red tape, for each contact between organization members must be carried upward until a common superior is found. If the organization is at all large, this will involve carrying all such matters upward through several levels of officials for decision and then downward again in the form of orders and instructions — a cumbersome and time-consuming process.

The alternative is to increase the number of persons who are under the command of each officer, so that the pyramid will come more rapidly to a peak, with fewer intervening levels. But this, too, leads to difficulty, for if an officer is required to supervise too many employees, his control over them is weakened.

If it is granted, then, that both the increase and the decrease in span of control has some undesirable consequences, what is the optimum point? Proponents of a restricted span of control have suggested three, five, even eleven, as suitable numbers, but nowhere have they explained the reasoning which led them to the particular number they selected. The principle as stated casts no light on this very crucial question. One is reminded of current arguments about the proper size of the national debt.

Organization by Purpose, Process, Clientele, Place. Administrative efficiency is supposed to be increased by grouping workers according to (a) purpose, (b) process, (c) clientele, or (d) place. But from the discussion of specialization it is clear that this principle is internally inconsistent; for purpose, process, clientele, and place are competing bases of organization, and at any given point of division the advantages of three must be sacrificed to secure the advantages of the fourth. If the major departments of a city, for example, are organized on the basis of major purpose, then it follows that all the physicians, all the lawyers, all the engineers, all the statisticians will

not be located in a single department exclusively composed of members of their profession but will be distributed among the various city departments needing their services. The advantages of organization by process will thereby be partly lost.

Some of these advantages can be regained by organizing on the basis of process *within* the major departments. Thus there may be an engineering bureau within the public works department, or the board of education may have a school health service as a major division of its work. Similarly, within small units there may be division by area or by clientele: e.g., a fire department will have separate companies located throughout the city, while a welfare department may have intake and case work agencies in various locations. Again, however, these major types of specialization cannot be simultaneously achieved, for at any point in the organization it must be decided whether specialization at the next level will be accomplished by distinction of major purpose, major process, clientele, or area.

The conflict may be illustrated by showing how the principle of specialization according to purpose would lead to a different result from specialization according to clientele in the organization of a health department.

1. Public health administration consists of the following activities for the prevention of disease and the maintenance of healthful conditions: (1) vital statistics; (2) child hygiene — prenatal, maternity, postnatal, infant, preschool, and school health programs; (3) communicable disease control; (4) inspection of milk, foods, and drugs; (5) sanitary inspection; (6) laboratory service; (7) health education.

   One of the handicaps under which the health department labors is the fact that the department has no control over school health, that being an activity of the county board of education, and there is little or no coordination between that highly important part of the community health program and the balance of the program which is conducted by the city-county health unit. It is recommended that the city and county open negotiations with the board of education for the transfer of all school health work and the appropriation therefore to the joint health unit. . . .

2. To the modern school department is entrusted the care of children during almost the entire period that they are absent from the parental home. It has three principal responsibilities toward them: (1) to provide for their education in useful skills and knowledge and in character; (2) to provide them with wholesome play activities outside school hours; (3) to care for their health and to assure the attainment of minimum standards of nutrition.

One of the handicaps under which the school board labors is the fact that, except for school lunches, the board has no control over child health and nutrition, and there is little or no coordination between that highly important part of the child development program and the balance of the program which is conducted by the board of education. It is recommended that the city and county open negotiations for the transfer of all health work for children of school age to the board of education.

Here again is posed the dilemma of choosing between alternative, equally plausible, administrative principles. But this is not the only difficulty in the present case, for a closer study of the situation shows there are fundamental ambiguities in the meanings of the key terms—"purpose," "process," "clientele," and "place."

"Purpose" may be roughly defined as the objective or end for which an activity is carried on; "process" as a means for accomplishing a purpose. Processes, then, are carried on in order to achieve purposes. But purposes themselves may generally be arranged in some sort of hierarchy. A typist moves her fingers in order to type; types in order to reproduce a letter, reproduces a letter in order that an inquiry may be answered. Writing a letter is then the purpose for which the typing is performed; while writing a letter is also the process whereby the purpose of replying to an inquiry is achieved. It follows that the same activity may be described as purpose or as process.

This ambiguity is easily illustrated for the case of an administrative organization. A health department conceived as a unit whose task it is to care for the health of the community is a purpose organization; the same department conceived as a unit which makes use of the medical arts to carry on its work is a process organization. In the same way, an education department may be viewed as a purpose (to educate) organization, or a clientele (children) organization; the forest service as a purpose (forest conservation), process (forest management), clientele (lumbermen and cattlemen utilizing public forests), or area (publicly owned forest lands) organization. When concrete illustrations of this sort are selected, the lines of demarcation between these categories become very hazy and unclear indeed.

"Organization by major purpose," says Gulick, ". . . serves to bring together in a single large department all of those who are at work endeavoring to render a particular service."[4] But what is a particular service? Is fire protection a single purpose, or is it merely a part of the purpose of public safety?—or is it a combination of purposes including fire prevention and fire fighting? It must be concluded that there is no such thing as a purpose, or a unifunctional (single-purpose) organization. What is to be considered a single function depends entirely on language and techniques.[5] If the English language has a comprehensive term which covers both of two subpurposes it is natural to think of the two together as a single purpose. If such a term is lacking, the two subpurposes become purposes in their own right. On the other hand, a single activity may contribute to several objectives, but since they are technically (procedurally) inseparable, the activity is considered a single function or purpose.

The fact, mentioned previously, that purposes form a hierarchy, each subpurpose contributing to some more final and comprehensive end, helps to make clear the relation between purpose and process. "Organization by major process," says Gulick,

". . . tends to bring together in a single department all of those who are at work making use of a given special skill or technology, or are members of a given profession."[6] Consider a simple skill of this kind—typing. Typing is a skill which brings about a means-end coordination of muscular movements, but a very low level in the means-end hierarchy. The content of the typewritten letter is indifferent to the skill that produces it. The skill consists merely in the ability to hit the letter "t" quickly whenever the letter "t" is required by the content and to hit the letter "a" whenever the letter "a" is required by the content.

There is, then, no essential difference between a "purpose" and a "process," but only a distinction of degree. A "process" is an activity whose immediate purpose is at a low level in the hierarchy of means and ends, while a "purpose" is a collection of activities whose orienting value or aim is at a high level in the means-end hierarchy.

Next consider "clientele" and "place" as bases of organization. These categories are really not separate from purpose, but a part of it. A complete statement of the purpose of a fire department would have to include the area served by it: "to reduce fire losses on property in the city of X." Objectives of an administrative organization are phrased in terms of a service to be provided and an area for which it is provided. Usually, the term "purpose" is meant to refer only to the first element, but the second is just as legitimately an aspect of purpose. Area of service, of course, may be a specified clientele quite as well as a geographical area. In the case of an agency which works on "shifts," time will be a third dimension of purpose—to provide a given service in a given area (or to a given clientele) during a given time period.

With this clarification of terminology, the next task is to reconsider the problem of specializing the work of an organization. It is no longer legitimate to speak of a "purpose" organization, a "process" organization, a "clientele" organization, or an "area" organization. The same unit might fall into any one of these four categories, depending on the nature of the larger organizational unit of which it was a part. A unit providing public health and medical services for school-age children in Multnomah County might be considered (1) an "area" organization if it were part of a unit providing the same service for the state of Oregon; (2) a "clientele" organization if it were part of a unit providing similar services for children of all ages; (3) a "purpose" or a "process" organization (it would be impossible to say which) if it were part of an education department.

It is incorrect to say that Bureau A is a process bureau; the correct statement is that Bureau A is a process bureau *within* Department X.[7] This latter statement would mean that Bureau A incorporates all the processes of a certain kind in Department X, without reference to any special subpurposes, subareas, or subclientele of Department X. Now it is conceivable that a particular unit might incorporate all processes of a certain kind but that these processes might relate to only certain particular subpurposes of the department purpose. In this case, which corresponds to the health unit in an education department mentioned above, the unit would be specialized by both purpose and process. The health unit would be the only one in the education department using the medical art (process) and concerned with health (subpurpose).

Even when the problem is solved of proper usage for the terms "purpose," "process," "clientele," and "area," the principles of administration give no guide as to which of these four competing bases of specialization is applicable in any particular situation. The British Machinery of Government Committee had no doubts about the matter. It considered purpose and clientele as the two possible bases of organization and put its faith entirely in the former. Others have had equal assurance in choosing between purpose and process. The reasoning which leads to these unequivocal conclusions leaves something to be desired. The

Machinery of Government Committee gives this sole argument for its choice:

> Now the inevitable outcome of this method of organization [by clientele] is a tendency to Lilliputian administration. It is impossible that the specialized service which each Department has to render to the community can be of as high a standard when its work is at the same time limited to a particular class of persons and extended to every variety of provision for them, as when the Department concentrates itself on the provision of the particular service only by whomsoever required, and looks beyond the interest of comparatively small classes.[8]

The faults in this analysis are obvious. First, there is no attempt to determine how a service is to be recognized. Second, there is a bald assumption, absolutely without proof, that a child health unit, for example, in a department of child welfare could not offer services of "as high a standard" as the same unit if it were located in a department of health. Just how the shifting of the unit from one department to another would improve or damage the quality of its work is not explained. Third, no basis is set forth for adjudicating the competing claims of purpose and process—the two are merged in the ambiguous term "service." It is not necessary here to decide whether the committee was right or wrong in its recommendation; the important point is that the recommendation represented a choice, without any apparent logical or empirical grounds, between contradictory principles of administration. . . .

These contradictions and competitions have received increasing attention from students of administration during the past few years. For example, Gulick, Wallace, and Benson have stated certain advantages and disadvantages of the several modes of specialization, and have considered the conditions under which one or the other mode might best be adopted.[9] All this analysis has been at a theoretical level—in the sense that data have not been employed to demonstrate the superior effectiveness claimed for the different modes. But though

theoretical, the analysis has lacked a theory. Since no comprehensive framework has been constructed within which the discussion could take place, the analysis has tended either to the logical one-sidedness which characterizes the examples quoted above or to inconclusiveness.

The Impasse of Administrative Theory. The four "principles of administration" that were set forth at the beginning of this paper have now been subjected to critical analysis. None of the four survived in very good shape, for in each case there was found, instead of an unequivocal principle, a set of two or more mutually incompatible principles apparently equally applicable to the administrative situation.

Moreover, the reader will see that the very same objections can be urged against the customary discussions of "centralization" versus "decentralization," which usually conclude, in effect, that "on the one hand, centralization of decision-making functions is desirable; on the other hand, there are definite advantages in decentralization."

Can anything be salvaged which will be useful in the construction of an administrative theory? As a matter of fact, almost everything can be salvaged. The difficulty has arisen from treating as "principles of administration" what are really only criteria for describing and diagnosing administrative situations. Closet space is certainly an important item in the design of a successful house; yet a house designed entirely with a view to securing a maximum of closet space—all other considerations being forgotten—would be considered, to say the least, somewhat unbalanced. Similarly, unity of command, specialization by purpose, and decentralization are all items to be considered in the design of an efficient administrative organization. No single one of these items is of sufficient importance to suffice as a guiding principle for the administrative analyst. In the design of administrative organizations, as in their operation, overall efficiency must be the guiding criterion. Mutually incompatible advantages must be balanced against each other, just as an architect weighs the advantages of additional closet space against the advantages of a larger living room.

This position, if it is a valid one, constitutes an indictment of much current writing about administrative matters. As the examples cited in this chapter amply demonstrate, much administrative analysis proceeds by selecting a single criterion and applying it to an administrative situation to reach a recommendation; while the fact that equally valid, but contradictory, criteria exist which could be applied with equal reason, but with a different result, is conveniently ignored. A valid approach to the study of administration requires that *all* the relevant diagnostic criteria be identified; that each administrative situation be analyzed in terms of the entire set of criteria; and that research be instituted to determine how weights can be assigned to the several criteria when they are, as they usually will be, mutually incompatible.

AN APPROACH TO ADMINISTRATIVE THEORY

This program needs to be considered step by step. First, what is included in the description of administrative situations for purposes of such an analysis? Second, how can weights be assigned to the various criteria to give them their proper place in the total picture?

The Description of Administrative Situations. Before a science can develop principles, it must possess concepts. Before a law of gravitation could be formulated, it was necessary to have the notions of "acceleration" and "weight." The first task of administrative theory is to develop a set of concepts that will permit the description in terms relevant to the theory of administrative situations. These concepts, to be scientifically useful, must be operational; that is, their meanings must correspond to empirically observable facts or situations. The definition of *authority* given earlier in this paper is an example of an operational definition.

What is a scientifically relevant description of an organization? It is a description that, so far as possible, designates for each person in the organization what decisions that person makes and the influences to which he is subject in making each of these decisions. Current descriptions of administrative organizations fall far short of this standard. For the most part, they confine themselves to the allocation of *functions* and the formal structure of *authority*. They give little attention to the other types of organizational influence or to the system of communications. . . .[10]

Consider the term "centralization." How is it determined whether the operations of a particular organization are "centralized" or "decentralized"? Does the fact that field offices exist prove anything about decentralization? Might not the same decentralization take place in the bureaus of a centrally located office? A realistic analysis of centralization must include a study of the allocation of decisions in the organization and the methods of influence that are employed by the higher levels to affect the decisions at the lower levels. Such an analysis would reveal a much more complex picture of the decision-making process than any enumeration of the geographical locations of organizational units at the different levels.

Administrative description suffers currently from superficiality, oversimplification, lack of realism. It had confined itself too closely to the mechanism of authority and has failed to bring within its orbit the other, equally important, modes of influence on organizational behavior. It has refused to undertake the tiresome task of studying the actual allocation of decision-making functions. It has been satisfied to speak of "authority," "centralization," "span of control," "function," without seeking operational definitions of these terms. Until administrative description reaches a higher level of sophistication, there is little reason to hope that rapid progress will be made toward the identification and verification of valid administrative principles.

Does this mean that a purely formal description of an administrative organization is impossible — that a relevant description must include an account of the content of the organization's decisions? This is a question that is almost impossible to answer in the present state of knowledge of administrative theory. One thing seems certain: content plays a greater role in the application of administrative principles than is allowed for in the formal administrative theory of the present time. This is a fact that is beginning to be recognized in the literature of administration. If one examines the chain of publications extending from Mooney and Reilley, through Gulick and the President's Committee controversy, to Schuyler Wallace and Benson, he sees a steady shift of emphasis from the "principles of administration" themselves to a study of the *conditions* under which competing principles are respectively applicable. Recent publications seldom say that "organization should be by purpose," but rather that "under such and such conditions purpose organization is desirable." It is to these conditions which underlie the application of the proverbs of administration that administrative theory and analysis must turn in their search for really valid principles to replace the proverbs.

The Diagnosis of Administrative Situations. Before any positive suggestions can be made, it is necessary to digress a bit and to consider more closely the exact nature of the propositions of administrative theory. The theory of administration is concerned with how an organization should be constructed and operated in order to accomplish its work efficiently. A fundamental principle of administration, which follows almost immediately from the rational character of "good" administration, is that among several alternatives involving the same expenditure that one should always be selected which leads to the greatest accomplishment of administrative objectives; and

among several alternatives that lead to the same accomplishment that one should be selected which involves the least expenditure. Since this "principle of efficiency" is characteristic of any activity that attempts rationally to maximize the attainment of certain ends with the use of scarce means, it is as characteristic of economic theory as it is of administrative theory. The "administrative man" takes his place alongside the classical "economic man."[11]

Actually, the "principle" of efficiency should be considered a definition rather than a principle: it is a definition of what is meant by "good" or "correct" administrative behavior. It does not tell *how* accomplishments are to be maximized, but merely states that this maximization is the aim of administrative activity, and that administrative theory must disclose under what conditions the maximization takes place.

Now what are the factors that determine the level of efficiency which is achieved by an administrative organization? It is not possible to make an exhaustive list of these but the principal categories can be enumerated. Perhaps the simplest method of approach is to consider the single member of the administrative organization and ask what the limits are to the quantity and quality of his output. These limits include (*a*) limits on his ability to perform and (*b*) limits on his ability to make correct decisions. To the extent that these limits are removed, the administrative organization approaches its goal of high efficiency. Two persons, given the same skills, the same objectives and values, the same knowledge and information, can rationally decide only upon the same course of action. Hence, administrative theory must be interested in the factory that will determine with what skills, values, and knowledge the organization member undertakes his work. These are the "limits" to rationality with which the principles of administration must deal.

On one side, the individual is limited by those skills, habits, and reflexes which are no longer in the realm of the conscious. His performance, for example, may be limited by his manual dexterity or his reaction time or his strength. His decision-making processes may be limited by the speed of his mental processes, his skill in elementary arithmetic, and so forth. In this area, the principles of administration must be concerned with the physiology of the human body and with the laws of skill-training and of habit. This is the field that has been most successfully cultivated by the followers of Taylor and in which has been developed time-and-motion study and the therblig.

On a second side, the individual is limited by his values and those conceptions of purpose which influence him in making decisions. If his loyalty to the organization is high, his decisions may evidence sincere acceptance of the objectives set for the organization; if that loyalty is lacking, personal motives may interfere with his administrative efficiency. If his loyalties are attached to the bureau by which he is employed, he may sometimes make decisions that are inimical to the larger unit of which the bureau is a part. In this area the principles of administration must be concerned with the determinants of loyalty and morale, with leadership and initiative, and with the influences that determine where the individual's organizational loyalties will be attached.

On a third side, the individual is limited by the extent of his knowledge of things relevant to his job. This applies both to the basic knowledge required in decision-making—a bridge designer must know the fundamentals of mechanics—and to the information that is required to make his decisions appropriate to the given situation. In this area, administrative theory is concerned with such fundamental questions as these: What are the limits on the mass of knowledge that human minds can accumulate and apply? How rapidly can knowledge be assimilated? How is specialization in the administrative organization to be related to the specializations of knowledge that are prevalent in the community's occupational structure? How is the system of communication to channel knowledge and information to the appropriate decision-points?

What types of knowledge can, and what types cannot, be easily transmitted? How is the need for intercommunication of information affected by the modes of specialization in the organization? This is perhaps the *terra incognita* of administrative theory, and undoubtedly its careful exploration will cast great light on the proper application of the proverbs of administration.

Perhaps this triangle of limits does not completely bound the area of rationality, and other sides need to be added to the figure. In any case, this enumeration will serve to indicate the kinds of considerations that must go into the construction of valid and noncontradictory principles of administration.

An important fact to be kept in mind is that the limits of rationality are variable limits. Most important of all, consciousness of the limits may in itself alter them. Suppose it were discovered in a particular organization, for example, that organizational loyalties attached to small units had frequently led to a harmful degree of intraorganizational competition. Then, a program which trained members of the organization to be conscious of their loyalties, and to subordinate loyalties to the smaller group to those of the large, might lead to a very considerable alteration of the limits in that organization.[12]

A related point is that the term "rational behavior" as employed here, refers to rationality when that behavior is evaluated in terms of the objectives of the larger organization; for, as just pointed out, the difference in direction of the individual's aims from those of the larger organization is just one of those elements of nonrationality with which the theory must deal.

A final observation is that, since administrative theory is concerned with the nonrational limits of the rational, it follows that the larger the area in which rationality has been achieved the less important is the exact form of the administrative organization. For example, the function of plan preparation, or design, if it results in a written plan that can be communicated interpersonally without difficulty, can be located almost anywhere in the organization without affecting results. All that is needed is a procedure whereby the plan can be given authoritative status, and this can be provided in a number of ways. A discussion, then, of the proper location for a planning or designing unit is apt to be highly inconclusive and is apt to hinge on the personalities in the organization and their relative enthusiasm, or lack of it, toward the planning function rather than upon any abstract principles of good administration.[13]

On the other hand, when factors of communication or faiths or loyalty are crucial to the making of a decision, the location of the decision in the organization is of great importance. The method of allocating decisions in the army, for instance, automatically provides (at least in the period prior to the actual battle) that each decision will be made where the knowledge is available for coordinating it with other decisions.

Assigning Weights to the Criteria. A first step, then, in the overhauling of the proverbs of administration is to develop a vocabulary, along the lines just suggested, for the description of administrative organization. A second step, which has also been outlined, is to study the limits of rationality in order to develop a complete and comprehensive enumeration of the criteria that must be weighed in evaluating an administrative organization. The current proverbs represent only a fragmentary and unsystematized portion of these criteria.

When these two tasks have been carried out, it remains to assign weights to the criteria. Since the criteria, or "proverbs," are often mutually competitive or contradictory, it is not sufficient merely to identify them. Merely to know, for example, that a specified change in organization will reduce the span of control is not enough to justify the change. This gain must be balanced against the possible resulting loss of contact between the higher and lower ranks of the hierarchy.

Hence, administrative theory must also be concerned with the question of the weights that are to be applied to these criteria — to the problems of their relative importance in any concrete situation. This question is not one that can be solved in a vacuum. Arm-chair philosophizing about administration — of which the present paper is an example — has gone about as far as it can profitably go in this particular direction. What is needed now is empirical research and experimentation to determine the relative desirability of alternative administrative arrangements.

The methodological framework for this research is already at hand in the principle of efficiency. If an administrative organization whose activities are susceptible to objective evaluation be subjected to study, then the actual change in accomplishment that results from modifying administrative arrangements in these organizations can be observed and analyzed.

There are two indispensable conditions to successful research along these lines. First, it is necessary that the objectives of the administrative organization under study be defined in concrete terms so that results, expressed in terms of these objectives, can be accurately measured. Second, it is necessary that sufficient experimental control be exercised to make possible the isolation of the particular effect under study from other disturbing factors that might be operating on the organization at the same time.

These two conditions have seldom been even partially fulfilled in so-called "administrative experiments." The mere fact that a legislature passes a law creating an administrative agency, that the agency operates for five years, that the agency is finally abolished, and that a historical study is then made of the agency's operations is not sufficient to make of that agency's history an "administrative experiment." Modern American legislation is full of such "experiments" which furnish orators in neighboring states with abundant ammunition when similar issues arise in their bailiwicks, but which provide the scientific investigator with little or nothing in the way of objective evidence, one way or the other. . . .

Perhaps the program outlined here will appear an ambitious or even a quixotic one. There should certainly be no illusions, in undertaking it, as to the length and deviousness of the path. It is hard to see, however, what alternative remains open. Certainly neither the practitioner of administration nor the theoretician can be satisfied with the poor analytic tools that the proverbs provide him. Nor is there any reason to believe that a less drastic reconversion than that outlined here will rebuild those tools to usefulness.

It may be objected that administration cannot aspire to be a "science"; that by the nature of its subject it cannot be more than an "art." Whether true or false, this objection is irrelevant to the present discussion. The question of how "exact" the principles of administration can be made is one that only experience can answer. But as to whether they should be logical or illogical there can be no debate. Even an "art" cannot be founded on proverbs.

NOTES

1. Lest it be thought that this deficiency is peculiar to the science — or "art"— of administration, it should be pointed out that the same trouble is shared by most Freudian psychological theories, as well as by some sociological theories.

2. Luther Gulick, "Notes on the Theory of Organization," in Luther Gulick and L. Urwick (eds.), *Papers on the Science of Administration* (Institute of Public Administration, Columbia University, 1937), p. 9.

3. This point is discussed in Herbert A. Simon, "Decision-Making and Administrative Organization," 4 *Public Administration Review* 20–21 (Winter, 1944).

4. Gulick and Urwick (eds.), *op. cit.*, p. 21.

5. If this is correct, then any attempt to prove that certain activities belong in a single department because they relate to a single purpose is doomed to fail. See, for example, John M. Gaus and Leon Wolcott, *Public Administration and the U.S. Department of Agriculture* (Public Administration Service, 1940).

6. *Op. cit.*, p. 23.

7. This distinction is implicit in most of Gulick's analysis of specialization. However, since he cites as examples single departments within a city, and since he usually speaks of "grouping activities" rather than "dividing work," the relative character of these categories is not always apparent in this discussion (*op. cit.*, pp. 15–30).

8. *Report of the Machinery of Government Committee* (H. M. Stationery Office, 1918).

9. Gulick, "Notes on the Theory of Organization," pp. 21–30; Schuyler Wallace, *Federal Departmentalization* (Columbia University Press, 1941); George C. S. Benson, "International Administrative Organization," 1 *Public Administration Review* 473–486 (Autumn, 1941).

10. The monograph by Macmahon, Millett, and Ogden, *op. cit.*, perhaps approaches nearer than any other published administrative study to the sophistication required in administrative description. See, for example, the discussion on pp. 233–236 of headquarters-field relationships.

11. For an elaboration of the principle of efficiency and its place in administrative theory see Clarence E. Ridley and Herbert A. Simon, *Measuring Municipal Activities* (International City Managers' Association, 2nd ed., 1943), particularly Chapter 1 and the preface to the second edition.

12. For an example of the use of such training, see Herbert A. Simon and William Divine, "Controlling Human Factors in an Administrative Experiment," 1 *Public Administration Review* 487–492 (Autumn, 1941).

13. See, for instance, Robert A. Walker, *The Planning Function in Urban Government* (University of Chicago Press, 1941), pp. 166–175. Walker makes out a strong case for attaching the planning agency to the chief executive. But he rests his entire case on the rather slender reed that "as long as the planning agency is outside the governmental structure . . . planning will tend to encounter resistance from public officials as an invasion of their responsibility and jurisdiction." This "resistance" is precisely the type of nonrational loyalty which has been referred to previously, and which is certainly a variable.

12

Foundations of the Theory of Organization

Philip Selznick

Trades unions, governments, business corporations, political parties, and the like are formal structures in the sense that they represent rationally ordered instruments for the achievement of stated goals. "Organization," we are told, "is the arrangement of personnel for facilitating the accomplishment of some agreed purpose through the allocation of functions and responsibilities."[1] Or, defined more generally, formal organization is "a system of consciously coordinated activities or forces of two or more persons."[2] Viewed in this light, formal organization is the structural expression of rational action. The mobilization of technical and managerial skills requires a pattern of coordination, a systematic ordering of positions and duties which defines a chain of command and makes possible the administrative integration of specialized functions. In this context *delegation* is the primordial organization act, a precarious venture which requires the continuous elaboration of formal mechanisms of coordination and control. The security of all participants, and of the system as a whole, generates a persistent pressure for the institutionalization of relationships, which are thus removed from the uncertainties of individual fealty or sentiment. Moreover, it is necessary for the relations within the structure to be determined in such a way that individuals will be interchangeable and the organization will thus be free of dependence upon personal qualities.[3] In this way, the formal structure becomes subject to calculable manipulation, an instrument of rational action.

But as we inspect these formal structures we begin to see that they never succeed in conquering the nonrational dimensions of organizational behavior. The latter remain at once indispensable to the continued existence of the system of coordination and at the same time the source of friction, dilemma, doubt, and ruin. This fundamental paradox arises from the fact that rational action systems are inescapably imbedded in an institutional matrix, in two significant senses: (1) the action system — or the formal structure of delegation and control which is its organizational expression — is itself only an aspect of a concrete social structure made up of individuals who may interact as *wholes*, not simply in terms of their formal roles within the system; (2) the formal system, and the social structure within which it finds concrete existence, are alike subject to the pressure of an institutional environment to which some overall adjustment must be made. The formal administrative design can never adequately or fully reflect the concrete organization to which it refers, for the obvious reason that no abstract plan or pattern can — or may, if it is to be useful — exhaustively describe an empirical totality. At the same time, that which is not included in the abstract design (as reflected, for example, in a staff-and-line organization chart) is vitally relevant to the maintenance and development of the formal system itself.

Organization may be viewed from two standpoints which are analytically distinct but which are empirically united in a context of reciprocal consequences. On the one hand, any concrete organizational system is an economy; at the same time, it is an adaptive social structure. Considered as an

Source: American Sociological Review 13 (1948): 25–35.

economy, organization is a system of relationships which define the availability of scarce resources *and* which may be manipulated in terms of efficiency and effectiveness. It is the economic aspect of organization which commands the attention of management technicians and, for the most part, students of public as well as private administration.[4] Such problems as the span of executive control, the role of staff or auxiliary agencies, the relation of headquarters to field offices, and the relative merits of single or multiple executive boards are typical concerns of the science of administration. The coordinative scalar, and functional principles, as elements of the theory of organization, are products of the attempt to explicate the most general features of organization as a "technical problem" or, in our terms, as an economy.

Organization as an economy is, however, necessarily conditioned by the organic states of the concrete structure, outside of the systematics of delegation and control. This becomes especially evident as the attention of leadership is directed toward such problems as the legitimacy of authority and the dynamics of persuasion. It is recognized implicitly in action and explicitly in the work of a number of students that the possibility of manipulating the system of coordination depends on the extent to which that system is operating within an environment of effective inducement to individual participants and of conditions in which the stability of authority is assured. This is in a sense the fundamental thesis of Barnard's remarkable study, *The Functions of the Executive*. It is also the underlying hypothesis which makes it possible for Urwick to suggest that "proper" or formal channels in fact function to "confirm and record" decisions arrived at by more personal means.[5] We meet it again in the concept of administration as a process of education, in which the winning of consent and support is conceived to be a basic function of leadership.[6] In short, it is recognized that control and consent cannot be divorced even within formally authoritarian structures.

The indivisibility of control and consent makes it necessary to view formal organizations as *cooperative* systems, widening the frame of reference of those concerned with the manipulation of organizational resources. At the point of action, of executive decision, the economic aspect of organization provides inadequate tools for control over the concrete structure. This idea may be readily grasped if attention is directed to the role of the individual within the organizational economy. From the standpoint of organization as a formal system, persons are viewed functionally, in respect to their *roles*, as participants in assigned segments of the cooperative system. But in fact individuals have a propensity to resist depersonalization, to spill over the boundaries of their segmentary roles, to participate as *wholes*. The formal systems (at an extreme, the disposition of "rifles" at a military perimeter) cannot take account of the deviations thus introduced, and consequently break down as instruments of control when relied upon alone. The whole individual raises new problems for the organization, partly because of the needs of his own personality, partly because he brings with him a set of established habits as well, perhaps, as commitments to special groups outside of the organization.

Unfortunately for the adequacy of formal systems of coordination, the needs of individuals do not permit a singleminded attention to the stated goals of the system within which they have been assigned. The hazard inherent in the act of delegation derives essentially from this fact. Delegation is an organizational act, having to do with formal assignments to functions and powers. Theoretically, these assignments are made to roles or official positions, not to individuals as such. In fact, however, delegation necessarily involves concrete individuals who have interests and goals which do not always coincide with the goals of the formal system. As a consequence, individual personalities may offer resistance to the demands made upon them by the official conditions of delegation. These resistances are not accounted for within the categories of coordination and delegation, so that when they occur they must be considered as unpredictable and accidental. Observations of this type of situation within formal structures are sufficiently commonplace. A familiar example is that of delegation to a subordinate who is also required to train his own replacement. The subordinate may resist this demand in order to maintain unique access to the "mysteries" of the job, and thus insure his indispensability to the organization.

In large organizations, deviations from the formal system tend to become institutionalized, so that "unwritten laws" and informal associations are established. Institutionalization removes such deviations from the realm of personality differences, transforming them into a persistent structural aspect of formal organizations.[7] These institutionalized rules and modes of informal cooperation are normally attempts by participants in the formal organization to control the group relations which form the environment of organizational decisions. The informal patterns (such as cliques) arise spontaneously, are based on personal relationships, and are usually directed to the control of some specific situation. They may be generated anywhere within a hierarchy, often with deleterious consequences for the formal goals of the organization, but they may also function to widen the available resources of executive control and thus contribute to rather than hinder the achievement of the stated objectives of the organization. The deviations tend to force a shift away from the purely formal system as the effective determinant of behavior to (1) a condition in which informal patterns buttress the formal, as through the manipulation of sentiment within the organization in favor of established authority; or (2) a condition wherein the informal controls effect a consistent modification of formal goals, as in the case of some bureaucratic patterns.[8] This trend will eventually result in the formalization of erstwhile informal activities, with the cycle of deviation and transformation beginning again on a new level.

The relevance of informal structures to organizational analysis underlines the significance of conceiving of formal organizations as cooperative systems. When the totality of interacting groups and individuals becomes the object of inquiry, the latter is not restricted by formal, legal, or procedural dimensions. The *state of the system* emerges as a significant point of analysis, as when an internal situation charged with conflict qualifies and informs actions ostensibly determined by formal relations and objectives. A proper understanding of the organizational process must make it possible to interpret changes in the formal system — new appointments or rules or reorganizations — in their relation to the informal and unavowed ties of friendship, class loyalty, power cliques, or external commitment. This is what it means "to know the score." . . .

To recognize the sociological relevance of formal structures is not, however, to have constructed a theory of organization. It is important to set the framework of analysis, and much is accomplished along this line when, for example, the nature of authority in formal organizations is reinterpreted to emphasize the factors of cohesion and persuasion as against legal or coercive sources.[9] This redefinition is logically the same as that which introduced the conception of the self as social. The latter helps make possible, but does not of itself fulfill, the requirements for a dynamic theory of personality. In the same way, the definition of authority as conditioned by sociological factors of sentiment and cohesion — or more generally the definition of formal organizations as cooperative systems — only sets the stage, as an initial requirement, for the formulation of a theory of organization.

STRUCTURAL-FUNCTIONAL ANALYSIS

Cooperative systems are constituted of individuals interacting as wholes in relation to a formal system of coordination. The concrete structure is therefore a resultant of the reciprocal influences of the formal and informal aspects of organization. Furthermore, this structure is itself a totality, an adaptive "organism" reacting to influences upon it from an external environment. These considerations help to define the objects of inquiry; but to progress to a system of predicates *about* these objects it is necessary to set forth an analytical method which seems to be fruitful and significant. The method must have a relevance to empirical materials, which is to say, it must be more specific in its reference than discussions of the logic or methodology of social science.

The organon which may be suggested as peculiarly helpful in the analysis of adaptive structures has been referred to as "structural-functional analysis."[10] This method may be characterized in a sentence: *Structural-functional analysis relates contemporary and variable behavior to a presumptively stable system of needs and mechanisms.* This means that a given empirical system is deemed to have basic needs, essentially related to self-maintenance; the system develops repetitive means of self-defense; and day-to-day activity is interpreted in terms of the function served by that activity for the maintenance and defense of the system. Put thus generally, the approach is applicable on any level in which the determinate "states" of empirically isolable systems undergo self-impelled and repetitive transformations when impinged upon by external conditions. This self-impulsion suggests the relevance of the term "dynamic," which is often used in referring to physiological, psychological, or social systems to which this type of analysis has been applied.[11]

It is a postulate of the structural-functional approach that the basic need of all empirical systems is the maintenance of the integrity and continuity of the system itself. Of course, such a postulate is primarily useful in directing attention to a set of "derived imperatives" or needs which are sufficiently concrete to characterize the system at hand.[12] It is perhaps rash to attempt a catalogue of these imperatives for formal

organizations, but some suggestive formulation is needed in the interests of setting forth the type of analysis under discussion. In formal organizations, the "maintenance of the system" as a generic need may be specified in terms of the following imperatives:

1. *The security of the organization as a whole in relation to social forces in its environment.* This imperative requires continuous attention to the possibilities of encroachment and to the forestalling of threatened aggressions or deleterious (though perhaps unintended) consequences from the actions of others.

2. *The stability of the lines of authority and communication.* One of the persistent reference-points of administrative decision is the weighing of consequences for the continued capacity of leadership to control and to have access to the personnel or ranks.

3. *The stability of informal relations within the organization.* Ties of sentiment and self-interest are evolved as unacknowledged but effective mechanisms of adjustment of individuals and subgroups to the conditions of life within the organization. These ties represent a cementing of relationships which sustains the formal authority in day-to-day operations and widens opportunities for effective communication.[13] Consequently, attempts to "upset" the informal structure, either frontally or as an indirect consequence of formal reorganization, will normally be met with considerable resistance.

4. *The continuity of policy and of the sources of its determination.* For each level within the organization, and for the organization as a whole, it is necessary that there be a sense that action taken in the light of a given policy will not be placed in continuous jeopardy. Arbitrary or unpredictable changes in policy undermine the significance of (and therefore the attention to) day-to-day action by injecting a note of capriciousness. At the same time, the organization will seek stable roots (or firm statutory authority or popular mandate) so that a sense of the permanency and legitimacy of its acts will be achieved.

5. *A homogeneity of outlook with respect to the meaning and role of the organization.* The minimization of disaffection requires a

unity derived from a common understanding of what the character of the organization is meant to be. When this homogeneity breaks down, as in situations of internal conflict over basic issues, the continued existence of the organization is endangered. On the other hand, one of the signs of "healthy" organization is the ability to effectively orient new members and readily slough off those who cannot be adapted to the established outlook.

This catalogue of needs cannot be thought of as final, but it approximates the stable system generally characteristic of formal organizations. These imperatives are derived, in the sense that they represent the conditions for survival or self-maintenance of cooperative systems of organized action. An inspection of these needs suggests that organizational survival is intimately connected with the struggle for relative prestige, both for the organization and for elements and individuals within it. It may therefore be useful to refer to a *prestige-survival motif* in organizational behavior as a shorthand way of relating behavior needs, especially when the exact nature of the needs remains in doubt. However, it must be emphasized that prestige-survival in organizations does not derive simply from like motives in individuals. Loyalty and self-sacrifice may be individual expressions of organizational or group egotism and self-consciousness.

The concept of organizational need directs analysis to the *internal relevance* of organizational behavior. This is especially pertinent with respect to discretionary action undertaken by agents manifestly in pursuit of formal goals. The question then becomes one of relating the specific act of discretion to some presumptively stable organizational need. In other words, it is not simply action plainly oriented internally (such as in-service training) but also action presumably oriented externally which must be inspected for its relevance to internal conditions. This is of prime importance for the understanding of bureaucratic behavior, for it is of the essence of the latter that action formally undertaken for substantive

goals be weighed and transformed in terms of its consequences for the position of the officialdom. . . .

The setting of structural-functional analysis as applied to organizations requires some qualification, however. Let us entertain the suggestion that the interesting problem in social science is not so much why men act the way they do as why men in certain circumstances *must* act the way they do. This emphasis upon constraint, if accepted, releases us from an ubiquitous attention to behavior in general, and especially from any undue fixation upon statistics. On the other hand, it has what would seem to be a salutary consequence of focusing inquiry upon certain necessary relationships of the type "if . . . then," for example: If the cultural level of the rank and file members of a formally democratic organization is below that necessary for participation in the formulation of policy, then there will be pressure upon the leaders to use the tools of demagogy.

Is such a statement universal in its applicability? Surely not in the sense that one can predict without remainder the nature of all or even most political groups in a democracy. Concrete behavior is a resultant, a complex vector, shaped by the operation of a number of such general constraints. But there is a test of general applicability: it is that of noting whether the relation made explicit must be *taken into account* in action. This criterion represents an empirical test of the significance of social generalizations. If a theory is significant it will state a relation which will either (1) be taken into account as an element of achieving control; or (2) be ignored only at the risk of losing control and will evidence itself in a ramification of objective or unintended consequences.[14] It is a corollary of this principle of significance that investigation must search out the underlying factors in organizational action, which requires a kind of intensive analysis of the same order as psychoanalytic probing.

A frame of reference which invites attention to the constraints upon behavior will tend to highlight tensions and dilemmas, the characteristic paradoxes generated in the course of action. The dilemma may be said to be the handmaiden of structural-functional analysis, for it introduces the concept of *commitment* or *involvement* as fundamental to organizational analysis. A dilemma in human behavior is represented by an inescapable commitment which cannot be reconciled with the needs of the organism or the social system. There are many spurious dilemmas which have to do with verbal contradictions, but inherent dilemmas to which we refer are of a more profound sort, for they reflect the basic nature of the empirical system in question. An economic order committed to profit as its sustaining incentive may, in Marxist terms, sow the seed of its own destruction. Again, the anguish of man, torn between finitude and pride, is not a matter of arbitrary and replaceable assumptions but is a reflection of the psychological needs of the human organism, and is concretized in his commitment to the institutions which command his life; he is in the world and of it, inescapably involved in its goals and demands; at the same time, the needs of the spirit are compelling, proposing modes of salvation which have continously disquieting consequences for worldly involvements. In still another context, the need of the human organism for affection and response necessitates a commitment to elements of the culture which can provide them; but the rule of the super-ego is uncertain since it cannot be completely reconciled with the need for libidinal satisfaction. . . .

Organizational analysis, too, must find its selective principle; otherwise the indiscriminate attempts to relate activity functionally to needs will produce little in the way of significant theory. Such a principle might read as follows: *Our frame of reference is to select out those needs which cannot be fulfilled within approved avenues of expression and thus must have recourse to such adaptive mechanisms as ideology and to the manipulation of formal processes and structures in terms of informal goals.* This formulation has many difficulties, and is not presented as conclusive, but it suggests the kind of principle

which is likely to separate the quick and the dead, the meaningful and the trite, in the study of cooperative systems in organized action.[15]

The frame of reference outlined here for the theory of organization may now be identified as involving the following major ideas: (1) the concept of organizations as cooperative systems, adaptive social structures, made up of interacting individuals, subgroups, and informal plus formal relationships; (2) structural-functional analysis, which relates variable aspects of organization (such as goals) to stable needs and self-defensive mechanisms; (3) the concept of recalcitrance as a quality of the tools of social action, involving a break in the continuum of adjustment and defining an environment of constraint, commitment, and tension. This frame of reference is suggested as providing a specifiable *area of relations* within which predicates in the theory of organization will be sought, and at the same time setting forth principles of selection and relevance in our approach to the data of organization.

It will be noted that we have set forth this frame of reference within the overall context of social action. The significance of events may be defined by their place and operational role in a means-end scheme. If functional analysis searches out the elements important for the maintenance of a given structure, and that structure is one of the materials to be manipulated in action, then that which is functional in respect to the structure is also functional in respect to the action system. This provides a ground for the significance of functionally derived theories. At the same time, relevance to control in action is the empirical test of their applicability or truth.

CO-OPTATION AS A MECHANISM OF ADJUSTMENT

The frame of reference stated above is in fact an amalgam of definition, resolution, and substantive theory. There is an element of *definition* on conceiving of formal organizations as cooperative systems, though of course the interaction of informal and formal patterns is a question of fact; in a sense, we are *resolving* to employ structural-functional analysis on the assumption that it will be fruitful to do so, though here, too, the specification of needs or derived imperatives is a matter for empirical inquiry; and our predication of recalcitrance as a quality of the tools of action is itself a *substantive theory*, perhaps fundamental to a general understanding of the nature of social action.

A theory of organization requires more than a general frame of reference, though the latter is indispensable to inform the approach of inquiry to any given set of materials. What is necessary is the construction of generalizations concerning transformations within and among cooperative systems. These generalizations represent, from the standpoint of particular cases, possible predicates which are relevant to the materials as we know them in general, but which are not necessarily controlling in all circumstances. A theory of transformations in organization would specify those states of the system which resulted typically in predictable, or at least understandable, changes in such aspects of organization as goals, leadership, doctrine, efficiency, effectiveness, and size. These empirical generalizations would be systematized as they were related to the stable needs of the cooperative system.

Changes in the characteristics of organizations may occur as a result of many different conditions, not always or necessarily related to the processes of organization as such. But the theory of organization must be selective, so that explanations of transformations will be sought within its own assumptions or frame of reference. Consider the question of size. Organizations may expand for many reasons — the availability of markets, legislative delegations, the swing of opinion — which may be accidental from the point of view of the organizational process. To explore changes in size (as of, say, a trades union) as related to

changes in nonorganizational conditions may be necessitated by the historical events to be described, but it will not of itself advance the frontiers of the theory of organization. However, if "the innate propensity of all organizations to expand" is asserted as a function of "the inherent instability of incentives"[16] then transformations have been stated within the terms of the theory of organization itself. It is likely that in many cases the generalization in question may represent only a minor aspect of the empirical changes, but these organizational relations must be made explicit if the theory is to receive development.

In a frame of reference which specifies needs and anticipates the formulation of a set of self-defensive responses or mechanisms, the latter appear to constitute one kind of empirical generalization or "possible predicate" within the general theory. The needs of organizations (whatever investigation may determine them to be) are posited as attributes of all organizations, but the responses to disequilibrium will be varied. The mechanisms used by the system in fulfillment of its needs will be repetitive and thus may be described as a specifiable set of assertions within the theory of organization, but any given organization may or may not have recourse to the characteristic modes of response. Certainly no given organization will employ all of the possible mechanisms which are theoretically available. When Barnard speaks of an "innate propensity of organization to expand," he is in fact formulating one of the general mechanisms, namely, expansion, which is a characteristic mode of response available to an organization under pressure from within. These responses necessarily involve a transformation (in this case, size) of some structural aspect of the organization.

Other examples of the self-defensive mechanisms available to organizations may derive primarily from the response of these organizations to the institutional environments in which they live. The tendency to construct ideologies, reflecting the need to come to terms with major social forces, is one such mechanism. Less well understood as a mechanism of organizational adjustment is what we may term *co-optation*. Some statement of the meaning of this concept may aid in clarifying the foregoing analysis.

Co-optation is the process of absorbing new elements into the leadership or policy-determining structure of an organization as a means of averting threats to its stability or existence. This is a defensive mechanism, formulated as one of a number of possible predicates available for the interpretation of organizational behavior. Co-optation tells us something about the process by which an institutional environment impinges itself upon an organization and effects changes in its leadership and policy. Formal authority may resort to co-optation under the following general conditions:

1. When there exists a hiatus between consent and control, so that the legitimacy of the formal authority is called into question. The "indivisibility" of consent and control refers, of course, to an optimum situation. Where control lacks an adequate measure of consent, it may revert to coercive measures or attempt somehow to win the consent of the governed. One means of winning consent is to co-opt elements into the leadership or organization, usually elements which in some way reflect the sentiment, or possess the confidence of the relevant public or mass. As a result, it is expected that the new elements will lend respectability or legitimacy to the organs of control and thus reestablish the stability of formal authority. This process is widely used, and in many different contexts. It is met in colonial countries, where the organs of alien control reaffirm their legitimacy by co-opting native leaders into the colonial administration. We find it in the phenomenon of "crisis-patriotism" wherein formally disfranchised groups are temporarily given representation in the councils of government in order to win their solidarity in a time of national stress. Co-optation is presently being considered by the United States Army in its study of proposals to give enlisted personnel

representation in the court-martial machinery—a clearly adaptive response to stresses made explicit during the war, the lack of confidence in the administration of army justice. The "unity" parties of totalitarian states are another form of co-optation; company unions or some employee representation plans in industry are still another. In each of these cases, the response of formal authority (private or public, in a large organization or a small one) is an attempt to correct a state of imbalance by *formal* measures. It will be noted, moreover, that what is shared is the *responsibility* for power rather than power itself. These conditions define what we shall refer to as *formal co-optation*.

2. Co-optation may be a response to the pressure of specific centers of power. This is not necessarily a matter of legitimacy or of a general and diffuse lack of confidence. These may be well established; and yet organized forces which are able to threaten the formal authority may effectively shape its structure and policy. The organization in respect to its institutional environment— or the leadership in respect to its ranks—must take these forces into account. As a consequence, the outside elements may be brought into the leadership or policy-determining structure, may be given a place as a recognition of and concession to the resources they can independently command. The representation of interests through administrative constituencies is a typical example of this process. Or, within an organization, individuals upon whom the group is dependent for funds or other resources may insist upon and receive a share in the determination of policy. This form of cooperation is typically expressed in informal terms, for the problem is not one of responding to a state of imbalance with respect to the "people as a whole" but rather one of meeting the pressure of specific individuals or interest-groups which are in a position to enforce demands. The latter are interested in the substance of power and not its forms. Moreover, an open acknowledgement of capitulation to specific interests may itself undermine the sense of legitimacy of the formal authority within the community. Consequently, there is a positive pressure to refrain from explicit recognition of the

relationship established. This form of the co-optative mechanism, having to do with the sharing of power as a response to specific pressures, may be termed *informal co-optation*.

Co-optation reflects a state of tension between formal authority and social power. The former is embodied in a particular structure and leadership, but the latter has to do with subjective and objective factors which control the loyalties and potential manipulability of the community. Where the formal authority is an expression of social power, its stability is assured. On the other hand, when it becomes divorced from the sources of social power its continued existence is threatened. This threat may arise from the sheer alienation of sentiment or from the fact that other leaderships have control over the sources of social power. Where a formal authority has been accustomed to the assumption that its constituents respond to it as individuals, there may be a rude awakening when organization of those constituents on a nongovernmental basis creates nuclei of power which are able effectively to demand a sharing of power.[17]

The significance of co-optation for organizational analysis is not simply that there is a change in or a broadening of leadership, and that this is an adaptive response, but also that *this change is consequential for the character and role of the organization*. Co-optation involves commitment, so that the groups to which adaptation has been made constrain the field of choice available to the organization or leadership in question. The character of the co-opted elements will necessarily shape (inhibit or broaden) the modes of action available to the leadership which has won adaptation and security at the price of commitment. The concept of co-optation thus implicitly sets forth the major points of the frame of reference outlined above: it is an adaptive response of a cooperative system to a stable need, generating transformations which reflect constraints enforced by the recalcitrant tools of action.

NOTES

1. John M. Gaus, "A Theory of Organization in Public Administration," in *The Frontiers of Public Administration* (Chicago: University of Chicago Press, 1936), p. 66.

2. Chester I. Barnard, *The Functions of the Executive* (Cambridge: Harvard University Press, 1938), p. 73.

3. Cf. Talcott Parsons' generalization (after Max Weber) of the "law of the increasing rationality of action systems," in *The Structure of Social Action* (New York: McGraw-Hill, 1937), p. 752.

4. See Luther Gulick and Lydall Urwick (eds.), *Papers on the Science of Administration* (New York: Institute of Public Administration, Columbia University, 1937); Lydall Urwick, *The Elements of Administration* (New York, Harper, 1943); James D. Mooney and Alan C. Reiley, *The Principles of Organization* (New York: Harper, 1939); H. S. Dennison, *Organization Engineering* (New York: McGraw-Hill, 1931).

5. Urwick, *The Elements of Administration, op. cit.*, p. 47.

6. See Gaus, *op. cit.* Studies of the problem of morale are instances of the same orientation, having received considerable impetus in recent years from the work of the Harvard Business School group.

7. The creation of informal structures within various types of organizations has received explicit recognition in recent years. See F. J. Roethlisberger and W. J. Dickson, *Management and the Worker* (Cambridge: Harvard University Press, 1941), p. 524; also Barnard, *op. cit.*, c. ix; and Wilbert E. Moore, *Industrial Relations and the Social Order* (New York: Macmillan, 1946), chap. xv.

8. For an analysis of the latter in these terms, see Philip Selznick, "An Approach to a Theory of Bureaucracy," *American Sociological Review* 8 (February, 1943).

9. Robert Michels, "Authority," *Encyclopedia of the Social Sciences* (New York: Macmillan, 1931), pp. 319ff.; also Barnard, *op. cit.*, c. xii.

10. For a presentation of this approach having a more general reference than the study of formal organizations, see Talcott Parsons,

"The Present Position and Prospects of Systematic Theory in Sociology," in Georges Gurvitch and Wilbert E. Moore (ed.), *Twentieth Century Sociology* (New York: The Philosophical Library, 1945).

11. "Structure" refers to both the relationships within the system (formal plus informal patterns in organization) and the set of needs and modes of satisfaction which characterize the given type of empirical system. As the utilization of this type of analysis proceeds, the concept of "need" will require further clarification. In particular, the imputation of a "stable set of needs" to organizational systems must not function as a new instinct theory. At the same time, we cannot avoid using these inductions as to generic needs, for they help us to stake out our area of inquiry. The author is indebted to Robert K. Merton who has, in correspondence, raised some important objections to the use of the term "need" in this context.

12. For "derived imperative" see Bronislaw Malinowski, *The Dynamics of Culture Change* (New Haven: Yale University Press, 1945), pp. 44ff. For the use of "need" in place of "motive" see the same author's *A Scientific Theory of Culture* (Chapel Hill: University of North Carolina Press, 1944), pp. 89–90.

13. They may also *destroy* those relationships, as noted above, but the need remains, generating one of the persistent dilemmas of leadership.

14. See R. M. MacIver's discussion of the "dynamic assessment" which "brings the external world selectively into the subjective realm, conferring on it subjective significance for the ends of action." *Social Causation* (Boston: Ginn, 1942), chaps. 11, 12. The analysis of this assessment within the context of organized action yields the implicit knowledge which guides the choice among alternatives. See also Robert K. Merton, "The Unanticipated Consequences of Purposive Social Action," *American Sociological Review* 1 (December, 1936).

15. This is not meant to deprecate the study of organizations as *economies* or formal systems. The latter represent an independent level, abstracted from organizational structures as cooperative or adaptive systems ("organisms").

16. Barnard, *op. cit.*, pp. 158–159.

17. It is perhaps useful to restrict the concept of co-optation to formal organizations, but in fact it probably reflects a process characteristic of all group leaderships. This has received some recognition in the analysis of class structure, wherein the ruling class is interpreted as protecting its own stability by absorbing new elements. Thus Michels made the point that "an aristocracy cannot maintain an enduring stability by sealing itself off hermetically." See Robert Michels, *Umschichtungen in den herrschenden Klassen nach dem Kriege* (Stuttgart: Kohlhammer, 1934), p. 39; also Gaetano Mosca, *The Ruling Class* (New York: McGraw-Hill, 1939), p. 413ff. The alliance or amalgamation of classes in the face of a common threat may be reflected in formal and informal co-optative responses among formal organizations sensitive to class pressures. In a forthcoming volume, *TVA and the Grass Roots*, the author has made extensive use of the concept of co-optation in analyzing some aspects of the organizational behavior of a government agency.

13
A Behavioral Theory of Organizational Objectives

Richard M. Cyert & James G. March

Organizations make decisions. They make decisions in the same sense in which individuals make decisions: The organization as a whole behaves as though there existed a central coordination and control system capable of directing the behavior of the members of the organization sufficiently to allow the meaningful imputation of purpose to the total system. Because the central nervous system of most organizations appears to be somewhat different from that of the individual system, we are understandably cautious about viewing organization decision-making in quite the same terms as those applied to individual choice. Nevertheless, organizational choice is a legitimate and important focus of research attention.

As in theories of individual choice, theories of organizational decision-making fall into two broad classes. Normative theorists—particularly economic theorists of the firm—have been dedicated to the improvement of the rationality of organizational choice. Recent developments in the application of mathematics to the solution of economic decision-problems are fully and effectively in such a tradition (Cooper, Hitch, Baumol, Shubik, Schelling, Valavanis, and Ellsberg, 1958). The empirical theory of organizational decision-making has a much more checkered tradition and is considerably less well-developed (March and Simon, 1958).

The present efforts to develop a behavioral theory of organizational decision-making represent attempts to overcome the disparity between the importance of decision-making in organizations and our understanding of how, in fact, such decisions are made. The research as a whole, as well as that part of it discussed below, is based on three initial commitments. The first of these is to develop an explicitly empirical theory rather than a normative one. Our interest is in understanding how complex organizations make decisions, not how they ought to do so. Without denying the importance of normative theory, we are convinced that the major current needs are for empirical knowledge.

The second commitment is to focus on the classic problems long explored in economic theory—pricing, resource allocation, and capital investment. This commitment is intended to overcome some difficulties with existing organization theory. By introducing organizational propositions into models of rather complex systems, we are driven to increase the precision of the propositions considerably. At present, anyone taking existing organization theory as a base for predicting behavior within organizations finds that he can make a number of rather important predictions of the general form: If x varies, y will vary. Only rarely will he find either the parameters of the functions or more elaborate predictions for situations in which the *ceteris paribus* assumptions are not met.

The third commitment is to approximate in the theory the process by which decisions are made by organizations. This commitment to a process-oriented theory is not

Source: Modern Organization Theory, ed. Mason Haire (New York: Wiley, 1959), 76–90. Reprinted by permission of James G. March.

new. It has typified many organization theorists in the past (Marshall, 1919; Weber, 1947). The sentiment that one should substitute observation for assumption whenever possible seems, a priori, reasonable. Traditionally, the major dilemma in organization theory has been between putting into the theory all the features of organizations we think are relevant and thereby making the theory unmanageable, or pruning the model down to a simple system, thereby making it unrealistic. So long as we had to deal primarily with classical mathematics, there was, in fact, little we could do. With the advent of the computer and use of simulation, we have a methodology that will permit us to expand considerably the emphasis on actual process without losing the predictive precision essential to testing (Cyert and March, 1959).

In models currently being developed there are four major subsystems. Since they operate more or less independently, it is possible to conceive them as the four basic subtheories required for a behavioral theory of organizational decision-making; first, the theory of organizational objectives; second, the theory of organizational expectations; third, the theory of organizational choice; fourth, the theory of organizational implementation. In this paper we discuss the first of these only, the theory of organizational objectives.

THE ORGANIZATION AS A COALITION

Let us conceive the organization as a coalition. It is a coalition of individuals, some of them organized into subcoalitions. In the business organization, one immediately thinks of such coalition members as managers, workers, stockholders, suppliers, customers, lawyers, tax collectors, etc. In the governmental organization, one thinks of such members as administrators, workers, appointive officials, elective officials, legislators, judges, clientele, etc. In the voluntary charitable organization, one thinks of paid functionaries, volunteers, donors, donees, etc.

This view of an organization as a coalition suggests, of course, several different recent treatments of organization theory in which a similar basic position is adopted. In particular, inducements-contributions theory (Barnard, 1938; Simon, 1947), theory of games (von Neumann and Morgenstern, 1947), and theory of teams (Marschak, in this volume). Each of these theories is substantially equivalent on this score. Each specifies:

1. That organizations include individual participants with (at least potentially) widely varying preference orderings.
2. That through bargaining and side payments the participants in the organization enter into a coalition agreement for purposes of the game. This agreement specifies a joint preference-ordering (or organizational objective) for the coalition.
3. That thereafter the coalition can be treated as a single strategist, entrepreneur, or what have you.

Such a formulation permits us to move immediately to modern decision theory, which has been an important part of recent developments in normative organization theory. In our view, however, a joint preference ordering is not a particularly good description of actual organization goals. Studies of organizational objectives suggest that to the extent to which there is agreement on objectives, it is agreement on highly ambiguous goals (Truman, 1951; Kaplan, Dirlam, and Lanzillotti, 1958). Such agreement is undoubtedly important to choice within the organization, but it is a far cry from a clear preference ordering. The studies suggest further that behind this agreement on rather vague objectives there is considerable disagreement and uncertainty about subgoals; that organizations appear to be pursuing one goal at one time and another (partially inconsistent) goal at another; and that different parts of the organization appear to be pursuing different goals at the same time (Kaplan, Dirlam, and Lanzillotti, 1958; Selznick, 1949). Finally, the studies suggest that most organization objectives take the form of an aspiration level rather than an imperative to "maximize" or "minimize," and that the aspiration level changes in response to experience (Blau, 1955; Alt, 1949).

In the theory to be outlined here, we consider three major ways in which the objectives of a coalition are determined. The first of these is the bargaining process by which the composition and general terms of the coalition are fixed. The second is the internal organizational process of control by which objectives are stabilized and elaborated. The third is the process of adjustment to experience, by which coalition agreements are altered in response to environmental changes. Each of these processes is considered, in turn, in the next three sections of the paper.

FORMATION OF COALITION OBJECTIVES THROUGH BARGAINING

A basic problem in developing a theory of coalition formation is the problem of handling side payments. No matter how we try we simply cannot imagine that the side payments by which organizational coalitions are formed even remotely satisfy the requirements of unrestricted transferability of utility. Side payments are made in many forms: money, personal treatment, authority, organization policy, etc. A winning coalition does not have a fixed booty which it then divides among its members. Quite to the contrary, the total value of side payments available for division among coalition members is a function of the composition of the coalition; and the total utility of the actual side payments depends on the distribution made within the coalition. There is no conservation of utility.

For example, if we can imagine a situation in which any dyad is a viable coalition (e.g., a partnership to exploit the proposition that two can live more cheaply in coalition than separately), we would predict a greater total utility for those dyads in which needs were complementary than for those in which they were competitive. Generally speaking, therefore, the partitioning of the adult population into male-female dyads is probably more efficient from the point of view of total utility accruing to the coalition than is a partition into sexually homogeneous pairs.

Such a situation makes game theory as it currently exists virtually irrelevant for a treatment of organizational side payments (Luce and Raiffa, 1957). But the problem is in part even deeper than that. The second requirement of such theories as game theory, theory of teams, and inducements-contributions theory, is that after the side payments are made, a joint preference ordering is defined. All conflict is settled by the side-payment bargaining. The employment-contract form of these theories, for example, assumes that the entrepreneur has an objective. He then purchases whatever services he needs to achieve the objective. In return for such payments, employees contract to perform whatever is required of them — at least within the range of permissible requirements. For a price, the employee adopts the "organization" goal.

One strange feature of such a conception is that it describes a coalition asymmetrically. To what extent is it arbitrary that we call wage payments "costs" and dividend payments "profits"—rather than the other way around? Why is it that in our quasi-genetic moments we are inclined to say that in the beginning there was a manager and he recruited workers and capital? For the development of our own theory we make two major arguments. First, the emphasis on the asymmetry has seriously confused our understanding of organizational goals. The confusion arises because ultimately it makes only slightly more sense to say that the goal of a business organization is to maximize profit than it does to say that its goal is to maximize the salary of Sam Smith, Assistant to the Janitor.

Second, despite this there are important reasons for viewing some coalition members as quite different from others. For example, it is clear that employees and management make somewhat different demands on the organization. In their bargaining, side payments appear traditionally to have performed the classical function of specifying a joint preference ordering. In addition, some coalition members (e.g., many stockholders) devote substantially less time to the particular coalition under consideration than do others. It is this characteristic that has usually been used to draw organizational boundaries between "external" and "internal" members of the coalition. Thus, there are important classes of coalition members who are passive most of the time. A condition of such passivity must be that the payment demands they make are of such a character that most of the time they can be met rather easily.

Although we thereby reduce substantially the size and complexity of the coalition relevant for most goal-setting, we are still left with something more complicated than an individual entrepreneur. It is primarily through bargaining within this active group that what we call organizational objectives arise. Side payments, far from being incidental distribution of a fixed, transferable booty, represent the central process of goal specification. That is, a significant number of these payments are in the form of policy commitments.

The distinction between demands for monetary side payments and demands for policy commitments seems to underlie management-oriented treatments of organizations. It is clear that in many organizations this distinction has important ideological and therefore affective connotations. Indeed, the breakdown of the distinction in our generation has been quite consistently violent. Political party-machines in this country have changed drastically the ratio of direct monetary side payments (e.g., patronage, charity) to policy commitments (e.g., economic legislation). Labor unions are conspicuously entering into what has been viewed traditionally as the management prerogatives of policy-making, and

demanding payments in that area. Military forces have long since given up the substance—if not entirely the pretense—of being simply hired agents of the regime. The phenomenon is especially obvious in public (Dahl and Lindblom, 1953; Simon, Smithburg, and Thompson, 1950) and voluntary (Sills, 1957; Messinger, 1955) organizations; but all organizations use policy side payments. The marginal cost to other coalition members is typically quite small.

This trend toward policy side payments is particularly observable in contemporary organizations, but the important point is that we have never come close to maintenance of a sharp distinction in the kinds of payments made and demanded. Policy commitments have (one is tempted to say always) been an important part of the method by which coalitions are formed. In fact, an organization that does not use such devices can exist in only a rather special environment.

To illustrate coalition formation under conditions where the problem is not scarce resources for side payments, but varying complementarities of policy demands, imagine a nine-man committee appointed to commission a painting for the village hall. The nine members make individually the following demands:

Committeeman A: The painting must be an abstract monotone.
Committeeman B: The painting must be an impressionistic oil.
Committeeman C: The painting must be small and oval in shape.
Committeeman D: The painting must be small and in oil.
Committeeman E: The painting must be square in shape and multicolored.
Committeeman F: The painting must be an impressionistic square.
Committeeman G: The painting must be a monotone and in oil.
Committeeman H: The painting must be multicolored and impressionistic.
Committeeman I: The painting must be small and oval.

In this case, each potential coalition member makes two simple demands. Assuming that five members are all that are required to make the decision, there are three feasible coalitions. A, C, D, G, and I can form a coalition and commission a small, oval, monotone, oil abstract. B, C, D, H, and I can form a coalition and commission a small, oval, multicolored, impressionistic oil. B, D, E, F, and H can form a coalition and commission a small, square, multicolored, impressionistic oil.

Committeeman D, it will be noted, is in the admirable position of being included in every possible coalition. The reason is clear; his demands are completely consistent with the demands of everyone else.

Obviously at some level of generality the distinction between money and policy payments disappears because any side payment can be viewed as a policy constraint. When we agree to pay someone $35,000 a year, we are constrained to that set of policy decisions that will allow such a payment. Any allocation of scarce resources (such as money) limits the alternatives for the organization. But the scarcity of resources is not the only kind of problem. Some policy demands are strictly inconsistent with other demands. Others are completely complementary. If I demand of the organization that John Jones be shot and you demand that he be sainted, it will be difficult for us both to stay in the organization. This is not because either bullets or haloes are in short supply or because we don't have enough money for both.

To be sure, the problems of policy consistency are in *principle* amenable to explicit optimizing behavior. But they add to the computational difficulties facing the coalition members and make it even more obvious why the bargaining leading to side payment and policy agreements is only slightly related to the bargaining anticipated in a theory of omniscient rationality. The tests of short-run feasibility that they represent lead to the familiar complications of conflict, disagreement, and rebargaining.

In the process of bargaining over side payments many of the organizational objectives are defined. Because of the form the

bargaining takes, the objectives tend to have several important attributes. First, they are imperfectly rationalized. Depending on the skill of the leaders involved, the sequence of demands leading to the new bargaining, the aggressiveness of various parts of the organization, and the scarcity of resources, the new demands will be tested for consistency with existing policy. But this testing is normally far from complete. Second, some objectives are stated in the form of aspiration-level constraints. Objectives arise in this form when demands which are consistent with the coalition are stated in this form. For example, the demand, "We must allocate ten percent of our total budget to research." Third, some objectives are stated in a nonoperational form. In our formulation such objectives arise when potential coalition members have demands which are nonoperational or demands which can be made nonoperational. The prevalence of objectives in this form can be explained by the fact that nonoperational objectives are consistent with virtually any set of objectives.

STABILIZATION AND ELABORATION OF OBJECTIVES

The bargaining process goes on more or less continuously, turning out a long series of commitments. But a description of goal formation simply in such terms is not adequate. Organizational objectives are, first of all, much more stable than would be suggested by such a model, and secondly, such a model does not handle very well the elaboration and clarification of goals through day-to-day bargaining.

Central to an understanding of these phenomena is again an appreciation for the limitations of human capacities and time to devote to any particular aspect of the organizational system. Let us return to our conception of a coalition having monetary and policy side payments. These side-payment agreements are incomplete. They do not anticipate effectively all possible future situations, and they do not identify all considerations that might be viewed as important by the coalition members at some future time. Nevertheless, the coalition members are motivated to operate under the agreements and to develop some mutual control-systems for enforcing them.

One such mutual control-system in many organizations is the budget. A budget is a highly explicit elaboration of previous commitments. Although it is usually viewed as an asymmetric control-device (i.e., a means for superiors to control subordinates), it is clear that it represents a form of mutual control. Just as there are usually severe costs to the department in exceeding the budget, so also are there severe costs to other members of the coalition if the budget is not paid in full. As a result, budgets in every organization tend to be self-confirming.

A second major, mutual control-system is the allocation of functions. Division of labor and specialization are commonly treated in management textbooks simply as techniques of rational organization. If, however, we consider the allocation of functions in much the way we would normally view the allocation of resources during budgeting, a somewhat different picture emerges. When we define the limits of discretion, we constrain the individual or subgroup from acting outside those limits. But at the same time, we constrain any other members of the coalition from prohibiting action within those limits. Like the allocation of resources in a budget, the allocation of discretion in an organization chart is largely self-confirming.

The secondary bargaining involved in such mutual control-systems serves to elaborate and revise the coalition agreements made on entry (Thompson and McEwen, 1958). In the early life of an organization, or after some exceptionally drastic organizational upheaval, this elaboration occurs in a context where very little is taken as given. Relatively deliberate action must be taken on everything from pricing policy to paperclip policy. Reports from individuals who have lived through such early stages emphasize the lack of structure that typifies settings for day-to-day decisions (Simon, 1953).

In most organizations most of the time, however, the elaboration of objectives occurs within much tighter constraints. Much of the situation is taken as given. This is true primarily because organizations have memories in the form of precedents, and individuals in the coalition are strongly motivated to accept the precedents as binding. Whether precedents are formalized in the shape of an official standard-operating-procedure or are less formally stored, they remove from conscious consideration many agreements, decisions, and commitments that might well be subject to renegotiation in an organization without a memory (Cyert and March, 1960). Past bargains become precedents for present situations. A budget becomes a precedent for future budgets. An allocation of functions becomes a precedent for future allocations. Through all the well-known mechanisms, the coalition agreements of today are institutionalized into semipermanent arrangements. A number of administrative aphorisms come to mind: an unfilled position disappears; see an empty office and fill it up; there is nothing temporary under the sun. As a result of organizational precedents, objectives exhibit much greater stability than would typify a pure bargaining situation. The "accidents" of organizational genealogy tend to be perpetuated.

CHANGES IN OBJECTIVES THROUGH EXPERIENCE

Although considerably stabilized by memory and institutionalization-phenomena, the demands made on the coalition by individual members do change with experience. Both the nature of the demands and their quantitative level vary over time.

Since many of the requirements specified by individual participants are in the form of attainable goals rather than general maximizing constraints, objectives are subject to the usual phenomena associated with aspiration levels. As an approximation to the aspiration-level model, we can take the following set of propositions:

1. In the steady state, aspiration level exceeds achievement by a small amount.
2. Where achievement increases at an increasing rate, aspiration level will exhibit short-run lags behind achievement.
3. Where achievement decreases, aspiration level will be substantially above achievement.

These propositions derive from simpler assumptions requiring that current aspiration be an optimistic extrapolation of past achievement and past aspiration. Although such assumptions are sometimes inappropriate, the model seems to be consistent with a wide range of human goal-setting behavior (Lewin, Dembo, Festinger, and Sears, 1944). Two kinds of achievement are, of course, important. The first is the achievement of the participant himself. The second is the achievement of others in his reference group (Festinger, 1954).

Because of these phenomena, our theory of organizational objectives must allow for drift in the demands of members of the organization. No one doubts that aspirations with respect to monetary compensation vary substantially as a function of payments received. So also do aspirations regarding advertising budget, quality of product, volume of sales, product mix, and capital investment. Obviously, until we know a great deal more than we do about the parameters of the relation between achievement and aspiration we can make only relatively weak predictions. But some of these predictions are quite useful, particularly in conjunction with search theory (Cyert, Dill, and March, 1958).

For example, two situations are particularly intriguing. What happens when the rate of improvement in the environment is great enough so that it outruns the upward adjustment of aspiration? Second, what happens when the environment becomes less favorable? The general answer to both of these questions involves the concept of organizational slack (Cyert and March, 1956). When the environment outruns aspiration-level adjustment, the organization secures, or at least has the potentiality of securing, resources in excess of its demands. Some of these resources are simply not obtained—although they are available. Others are used to meet the revised demands of those members of the coalition whose demands adjust most rapidly—usually those most deeply involved in the organization. The excess resources would not be subject to very general bargaining because they do not involve allocation in the face of scarcity. Coincidentally perhaps, the absorption of excess resources also serves to delay aspiration-level adjustment by passive members of the coalition.

When the environment becomes less favorable, organizational slack represents a cushion. Resource scarcity brings on renewed bargaining and tends to cut heavily into the excess payments introduced during plusher times. It does not necessarily mean that precisely those demands that grew abnormally during better days are pruned abnormally during poorer ones; but in general we would expect this to be approximately the case.

Some attempts have been made to use these very simple propositions to generate some meaningful empirical predictions. Thus, we predict that, discounting for the economies of scale, relatively successful firms will have higher unit-costs than relatively unsuccessful ones. We predict that advertising expenditures will be a function of sales in the previous time period at least as much as the reverse will be true.

The nature of the demands also changes with experience in another way. We do not conceive that individual members of the coalition will have a simple listing of demands, with only the quantitative values changing over time. Instead we imagine each member as having a rather disorganized file case full of demands. At any point in time, the member attends to only a rather small subset of his demands, the number and variety depending again on the extent of his involvement in the organization and on the demands of his other commitments on his attention.

Since not all demands are attended to at the same time, one important part of the theory of organizational objectives is to predict when particular units in the organization will attend to particular goals. Consider the safety goal in a large corporation. For the safety engineers, this is a very important goal most of the time. Other parts of the organization rarely even consider it. If, however, the organization has some drastic experience (e.g., a multiple fatality), attention to a safety goal is much more widespread and safety action quite probable.

Whatever the experience, it shifts the attention-focus. In some (as in the safety example), adverse experience suggests a problem area to be attacked. In others, solutions to problems stimulate attention to a particular goal. An organization with an active personnel-research department will devote substantial attention to personnel goals not because it is necessarily a particularly pressing problem but because the subunit keeps generating solutions that remind other members of the organization of a particular set of objectives they profess.

The notion of attention-focus suggests one reason why organizations are successful in surviving with a large set of unrationalized goals. They rarely see the conflicting objectives simultaneously. For example, let us reconsider the case of the pair of demands that John Jones be either (a) shot or (b) sainted. Quite naturally, these were described as inconsistent demands. Jones cannot be simultaneously shot and sainted. But the emphasis should be on *simultaneously*. It is quite feasible for him to be first shot and then sainted, or vice versa. It is logically feasible because a halo can be attached as firmly to a dead man as to a live one and a saint is as susceptible to bullets as a sinner. It is organizationally feasible because the probability is low that both of these demands will be attended to simultaneously.

The sequential attention to goals is a simple mechanism. A consequence of the mechanism is that organizations ignore many conditions that outside observers see as direct contradictions. They are contradictions only if we imagine a well-established, joint preference ordering or omniscient bargaining. Neither condition exists in an organization. If we assume that attention to goals is limited, we can explain the absence of any strong pressure to resolve apparent internal inconsistencies. This is not to argue that all conflicts involving objectives can be resolved in this way, but it is one important mechanism that deserves much more intensive study.

CONSTRUCTING A PREDICTIVE THEORY

Before the general considerations outlined above can be transformed into a useful predictive theory, a considerable amount of precision must be added. The introduction of precision depends, in turn, on the future success of research into the process of coalition formation. Nevertheless, some steps can be taken now to develop the theory. In particular, we can specify a general framework for a theory and indicate its needs for further development.

We assume a set of coalition members, actual or potential. Whether these members are individuals or groups of individuals is unimportant. Some of the possible subsets drawn from this set are viable coalitions. That is, we will identify a class of combinations of members such that any of these combinations meet the minimal standards imposed by the external environment on the organization. Patently, therefore, the composition of the viable set of coalitions will depend on environmental conditions.

For each of the potential coalition members we require a set of demands. Each such individual set is partitioned into an active part currently attended to and an inactive part currently ignored. Each demand can be characterized by two factors; first, its marginal resource requirements, given the demands of all possible other combinations of demands from potential coalition members; second, its marginal consistency with all possible combinations of demands from potential coalition members.

For each potential coalition member we also require a set of problems, partitioned similarly into an active and an inactive part.

This provides us with the framework of the theory. In addition, we need five basic mechanisms. First, we need a mechanism that changes the quantitative value of the demands over time. In our formulation, this becomes a version of the basic aspiration-level and mutual control theory outlined earlier.

Second, we need an attention-focus mechanism that transfers demands among the three possible states; active set, inactive set, not-considered set. We have said that some organizational participants will attend to more demands than other participants and that for all participants some demands will be considered at one time and others at other times. But we know rather little about the actual mechanisms that control this attention factor.

Third, we need a similar attention-focus mechanism for problems. As we have noted, there is a major interaction between what problems are attended to and what demands are attended to, but research is also badly needed in this area.

Fourth, we need a demand-evaluation procedure that is consistent with the limited capacities of human beings. Such a procedure must specify how demands are checked for consistency and for their resource demands. Presumably, such a mechanism will depend heavily on a rule that much of the problem is taken as given and only incremental changes are considered.

Fifth, we need a mechanism for choosing among the potentially viable coalitions. In our judgment, this mechanism will probably look much like the recent suggestions of game theorists that only small changes are evaluated at a time (Luce and Raiffa, 1957).

Given these five mechanisms and some way of expressing environmental resources, we can describe a process for the determination of objectives in an organization that will exhibit the important attributes of organizational goal-determination. At the moment, we can approximate some of the required functions. For example, it has been possible to introduce into a complete model a substantial part of the first mechanism, and some elements of the second, third, and fourth (Cyert, Feigenbaum, and March, 1959). Before the theory can develop further, however, and particularly before it can focus intensively on the formation of objectives through bargaining and coalition formation (rather than on the revision of such objectives and the selective attention to them), we require greater empirical clarification of the phenomena involved.

REFERENCES

Alt, R. M. (1949). The internal organization of the firm and price formation: An illustrative case. *Quarterly J. of Econ.*, 63, 92–110.

Barnard, C. I. (1938). *The functions of the executive*. Cambridge: Harvard University Press.

Blau, P. M. (1955). *The dynamics of bureaucracy*. Chicago: University of Chicago Press.

Cooper, W. W., Hitch, C., Baumol, W. J., Shubik, M., Schelling, T. C., Valavanis, S., & Ellsberg, D. (1958). Economics and operations research: A symposium. *The Rev. of Econ. and Stat.*, 40, 195–229.

Cyert, R. M., Dill, W. R., & March, J. G. (1958). The role of expectations in business decision making. *Adm. Sci. Quarterly*, 3, 307–340.

Cyert, R. M., Feigenbaum, E. A., & March, J. G. (1959). Models in a behavioral theory of the firm. *Behavioral Sci.*, 4, 81–95.

Cyert, R. M., & March, J. G. (1956). Organizational factors in the theory of oligopoly. *Quarterly J. of Econ.*, 70, 44–64.

Cyert, R. M., & March, J. G. (1959). Research on a behavioral theory of the firm. *Management Rev.*

Cyert, R. M., & March, J. G. (1960). Business operating procedure. In B. von H. Gilmer (ed.), *Industrial psychology*. New York: McGraw-Hill.

Dahl, R. A., & Lindblom, C. E. (1953). *Politics, economics, and welfare*. New York: Harper.

Festinger, L. (1954). A theory of social comparison processes. *Human Relations, 7,* 117–140.

Kaplan, A. D. H., Dirlam, J. B., & Lanzillotti, R. F. (1958). *Pricing in big business*. Washington: Brookings Institution.

Lewin, L., Dembo, T., Festinger, L., & Sears, P. (1944). Level of aspiration. In J. M. Hunt (ed.), *Personality and the behavior disorders*, vol. 1. New York: Ronald Press.

Luce, R. D., & Raiffa, H. (1957). *Games and decisions*. New York: Wiley.

March, J. G., & Simon, H. A. (1958). *Organizations*. New York: Wiley.

Marshall, A. (1919). *Industry and trade*. London: Macmillan.

Messinger, S. L. (1955). Organizational transformation: A case study of a declining social movement. *Amer. Sociol. Rev., 20,* 3–10.

Selznick, P. (1949). *TVA and the grass roots*. Berkeley: University of California Press.

Sills, D. L. (1957). *The volunteers*. Glencoe, IL: Free Press.

Simon, H. A. (1947). *Administrative behavior*. New York: Macmillan.

Simon, H. A. (1953). Birth of an organization: The economic cooperation administration. *Public Adm. Rev., 13,* 227–236.

Simon, H. A., Smithburg, D. W., & Thompson, V. A. (1950). *Public administration*. New York: Knopf.

Thompson, J. D., & McEwen, W. J. (1958). Organizational goals and environment: Goal setting as an interaction process. *Amer. Sociol. Rev., 23,* 23–31.

Truman, D. B. (1951). *The governmental process*. New York: Knopf.

Von Neumann, J., & Morgenstern, O. (1947). *Theory of games and economic behavior,* 2nd ed. Princeton, NJ: Princeton University Press.

Weber, M. (1947). *The theory of social and economic organization* (A. M. Henderson & T. Parsons, trans.). New York: Oxford University Press.

CHAPTER 3

Human Resource Theory, or the Organizational Behavior Perspective

Students and practitioners of management have always been interested in and concerned with the behavior of people in organizations. But fundamental assumptions about the behavior of people at work did not change dramatically from the beginnings of humankind's attempts to organize until only a few decades ago. Using the traditional "the boss knows best" mindset (set of assumptions), Hugo Münsterberg (1863–1916), the German-born psychologist whose later work at Harvard would earn him the title "father of industrial or applied psychology," pioneered the application of psychological findings from laboratory experiments to practical matters. He sought to match the abilities of new hires with a company's work demands, to positively influence employee attitudes toward their work and their company, and to understand the impact of psychological conditions on employee productivity (H. Münsterberg, 1913; M. Münsterberg, 1922). Münsterberg's approach characterized how the behavioral sciences tended to be applied in organizations well into the 1950s. During and following World War II, the armed services were particularly active in conducting and sponsoring research into how the military could best *find and shape people to fit its needs.*

In contrast to the Münsterberg-type perspective on organizational behavior, the "modern breed" of applied behavioral scientists has focused attention on seeking to answer questions such as how organizations could and should allow and encourage their people to grow and develop. From this perspective, it is *assumed* that organizational creativity, flexibility, and prosperity flow naturally from employee growth and development. The essence of the relationship between organizations and people is redefined from dependence to codependence. People are considered to be as important as or more important than the organization itself. The organizational behavior methods and techniques of the 1960s, 1970s, and 1980s could not have been used in Münsterberg's days *because we didn't believe (assume) that codependence was the "right" relationship between an organization and its employees.*

Although practitioners and researchers have been interested in the behavior of people inside organizations for a very long time, it has only been since about 1957—when our basic assumptions about the relationship between organizations and people truly began to change—that the organizational behavior perspective, or human resource theory, came into being. Those who see organizations through the "lenses" of the organizational behavior perspective focus on people, groups, and the relationships among them and the organizational environment. Because the organizational behavior perspective places a very high value on humans as individuals, things typically are done very openly and honestly, providing employees with maximum amounts of accurate information so they can make informed decisions with free will about their future (Argyris, 1970).

145

Human resource theory draws on a body of research and theory built around the following assumptions:

1. Organizations exist to serve human needs (rather than the reverse).
2. Organizations and people need each other. (Organizations need ideas, energy, and talent; people need careers, salaries, and work opportunities.)
3. When the fit between the individual and the organization is poor, one or both will suffer: individuals will be exploited, or will seek to exploit the organization, or both.
4. A good fit between individual and organization benefits both: human beings find meaningful and satisfying work, and organizations get the human talent and energy that they need (Bolman & Deal, 1997, pp. 102, 103).

No other perspective of organizations has ever had such a wealth of research findings and methods at its disposal.

The single most significant set of events that preceded and presaged a conscious theory (and field) of organizational behavior was the multiyear work done by the Elton Mayo team at the Hawthorne plant of the Western Electric Company beginning in 1927 (Mayo, 1933; Roethlisberger & Dickson, 1939). It is important to note that the Mayo team began its work trying to fit into the mold of classical organization theory thinking. The team phrased its questions in the language and concepts industry was accustomed to using in order to see and explain problems such as productivity in relation to such factors as the amount of light, the rate of flow of materials, and alternative wage payment plans. The Mayo team succeeded in making significant breakthroughs in understanding only after it redefined the Hawthorne problems as social psychological problems—problems conceptualized in such terms as interpersonal relations in groups, group norms, control over one's own environment, and personal recognition. It was only after the Mayo team achieved this breakthrough that it became the "grandfather"—the direct precursor—of the field of organizational behavior and human resource theory. The Hawthorne studies laid the foundation for a set of assumptions that would be fully articulated and would displace the assumptions of classical organization theory twenty years later. The experiments were the emotional and intellectual wellspring of the organizational behavior perspective and modern theories of motivation; they showed that complex, interacting variables make the difference in motivating people—things like attention paid to workers as individuals, workers' control over their own work, differences between individuals' needs, management's willingness to listen, group norms, and direct feedback.

According to human resource theory, the organization is not the independent variable to be manipulated in order to change behavior (as a dependent variable), even though organizations pay employees to help them achieve organizational goals. Instead, the organization must be seen as the context in which behavior occurs. It is both an independent and a dependent variable. The organization influences human behavior just as behavior shapes the organization. The interactions shape conceptualizations of jobs, human communication and interaction in work groups, the impact of participation in decisions about one's own work in general, and the roles of leaders in particular.

It should be evident that human resource organization theory is an enormous field of study supported by a large body of literature both because it addresses numerous subfields and because it has so much research available for use. In this chapter, we can only introduce a few of its most important ideas and best-known authors. For a more thorough presentation, we suggest the third edition of the anthology compiled by Ott, Parkes, and Simpson (2003), *Classic Readings in Organizational Behavior.* Ott, Parkes, and Simpson group the literature of human resource theory by its most pervasive themes:

- leadership;
- motivation;
- individuals in teams and groups;
- effects of the work environment on individuals;
- power and influence; and
- organizational change.

In this chapter, we have limited the selections to a few classic readings on leadership, motivation, and group dynamics. The first article reprinted here is a truly pioneering treatise on the situational or contingency approach to leadership, "The Giving of Orders," by Mary Parker Follett. Follett discusses how orders should be given in any organization: they should be depersonalized "to unite all concerned in a study of the situation, to discover the law of the situation and obey that." Follett thus argues for a participatory leadership style, whereby employees and employers cooperate to assess the situation and decide what should be done at that moment in that situation. Once the "law" of the situation is discovered, "the employee can issue it to the employer as well as employer to employee." This manner of giving orders facilitates better attitudes within an organization because nobody is necessarily under another person; rather, all take their cues from the situation.

In 1924, a team of researchers under the aegis of the National Academy of Sciences' National Research Council went to the Hawthorne plant of the Western Electric Company, near Chicago, to study ways for improving productivity. The research team began its work from the perspective of scientific management. Scientific investigative procedures were used to find and identify environmental changes that would increase worker productivity. The investigations focused on room temperature, humidity, and illumination levels. By 1927, the results were so snarled that Western Electric and the National Research Council were ready to abandon the entire endeavor. In that year, though, George Pennock, Western Electric's superintendent of inspection, heard Harvard professor Elton Mayo speak at a meeting and invited him to take a team to Hawthorne. Team members eventually included Frederick (Fritz) Roethlisberger, George Homans, and T. N. Whitehead. The results were the legendary "Hawthorne studies." Roethlisberger became the best-known chronicler of the studies and, with William J. Dickson of the Western Electric Company, wrote the most comprehensive account of them, *Management and the Worker* (1939). Roethlisberger's chapter, "The Hawthorne Experiments," which is reprinted here, is from his shorter 1941 book, *Management and Morale.*

All discussions of motivation start with Abraham Maslow. His hierarchy of needs stands alongside the Hawthorne experiments and Douglas McGregor's Theory X and Theory Y as the points of departure for studying motivation in organizations. An overview of Maslow's basic theory of needs is presented here from his 1943 *Psychological Review* article, "A Theory of Human Motivation." Maslow's theoretical premises can be summarized in a few phrases:

- All humans have needs that underlie their motivational structure.
- As lower levels of needs are satisfied, they no longer "drive" behavior.

- Satisfied needs are not motivators.
- As lower-level needs of workers become satisfied, higher-order needs take over as the motivating forces.

Maslow's theory has been attacked frequently. Few empirical studies have supported it, and it oversimplifies the complex structure of human needs and motivations. Several modified needs hierarchies have been proposed over the years that reportedly are better able to withstand empirical testing (for example, Alderfer, 1969). Despite the criticisms and the continuing advances across the spectrum of applied behavioral sciences, Abraham Maslow's theory continues to occupy a most honored and prominent place in organizational behavior and management textbooks.

Between 1957 and 1960, the organizational behavior perspective exploded onto the organization scene. On April 9, 1957, Douglas M. McGregor delivered the fifth anniversary convocation address to the School of Industrial Management at the Massachusetts Institute of Technology. He titled his address "The Human Side of Enterprise." McGregor expanded his talk into some of the most influential articles and books in the history of organizational behavior and organization theory. In "The Human Side of Enterprise," McGregor explained how managerial assumptions about employees become self-fulfilling prophecies. He labeled his two sets of contrasting assumptions Theory X and Theory Y, but they are more than just theories. McGregor had articulated the basic assumptions of the organizational behavior perspective.

"The Human Side of Enterprise" is a cogent statement of the basic assumptions of the organizational behavior perspective. Theory X and Theory Y are contrasting basic managerial assumptions about employees that, in McGregor's words, become self-fulfilling prophecies. Managerial assumptions cause employee behavior. Theory X and Theory Y are ways of seeing and thinking about people that, in turn, affect their behavior. Thus, "The Human Side of Enterprise" (1957b), which is reprinted in this chapter, is a landmark theory of motivation.

Theory X assumptions represent a restatement of the tenets of the scientific management movement. For example, Theory X holds that human beings inherently dislike work and will avoid it if possible. Most people must be coerced, controlled, directed, or threatened with punishment to get them to work toward the achievement of organizational objectives; in addition, humans prefer to be directed and to avoid responsibility, and will seek security above all else. These assumptions serve as polar opposites to McGregor's Theory Y.

Theory Y assumptions postulate, for example, that people do not inherently dislike work; work can be a source of satisfaction. People will exercise self-direction and self-control if they are committed to organization objectives. People are willing to seek and to accept responsibility; avoidance of responsibility is not natural, it is a consequence of experiences. The intellectual potential of most humans is only partially utilized at work.

Irving Janis' 1971 article "Groupthink" is a study of pressures for conformance — the reasons that social conformity is encountered so frequently in groups. Janis examines high-level decision makers and decision making during times of major fiascoes: the 1962 Bay of Pigs, the Johnson administration's decision to escalate the Vietnam War, and the 1941 failure to prepare for the attack on Pearl Harbor. Groupthink is "the mode of thinking that persons engage in when *concurrence seeking* becomes so dominant in a cohesive in-group that it tends to override realistic appraisal of alternative courses of action . . . the desperate drive for consensus at any cost that suppresses dissent among the mighty in the corridors of power." Janis identifies eight symptoms of groupthink that are relatively easy to observe:

- an illusion of invulnerability;
- collective construction of rationalizations that permit group members to ignore warnings or other forms of negative feedback;
- unquestioning belief in the morality of the in-group;
- strong, negative, stereotyped views about the leaders of enemy groups;
- rapid application of pressure against group members who express even momentary doubts about virtually any illusions the group shares;
- careful, conscious, personal avoidance of deviation from what appears to be a group consensus;
- shared illusions of unanimity of opinion; and
- establishment of *mindguards*—people who "protect the leader and fellow members from adverse information that might break the complacency they shared about the effectiveness and morality of past decisions."

Janis concludes with an assessment of the negative influence of groupthink on executive decision making (including overestimation of the group's capability and self-imposed isolation from new or opposing information and points of view), as well as preventive and remedial steps for dealing with groupthink.

The organizational behavior perspective is the most optimistic of all perspectives or schools of organization theory. Building from Douglas McGregor's Theory X and Theory Y assumptions, organizational behavior has assumed that under the right circumstances, people and organizations will grow and prosper together. The ultimate worth of people is an overarching value of the human relations movement, a worthy end in and of itself— not simply a means or process for achieving a higher-order organizational end. Individuals and organizations are not necessarily antagonists. Managers can learn to unleash previously stifled energies and creativity. The beliefs, values, and tenets of organizational behavior are noble, uplifting, and exciting. They hold a promise for humankind, especially those who will spend their lives working in organizations.

As one would expect of a very optimistic and humanistic set of assumptions and values, they (and the strategies of organizational behavior) became strongly normative (prescriptive). For many organizational behavior practitioners of the 1960s, 1970s, and 1980s, this perspective's assumptions and methods became a cause. Hopefully, through the choice of articles and the introductions to each chapter, this volume communicates these optimistic tenets and values and articulates the logical and emotional reasons why the organizational behavior perspective developed into a virtual movement. This is the true essence of *organizational behavior*.

REFERENCES

Alderfer, J. S. (1969). An empirical test of a new theory of human needs. *Organizational Behavior and Human Performance, 4*, 142–175.

Argyris, C. (1962). *Interpersonal competence and organizational effectiveness*. Homewood, IL: Dorsey Press and Richard D. Irwin.

Argyris, C. (1970). *Intervention theory and method*. Reading, MA: Addison-Wesley.

Argyris, C. (1990). *Overcoming organizational defenses: Facilitating organizational learning.* Boston: Allyn & Bacon.

Bennis, W. G. (1989). *Why leaders can't lead: The unconscious conspiracy continues.* San Francisco: Jossey-Bass.

Bennis, W. G. (2000). *Managing the dream: Reflections on leadership and change.* Cambridge, MA: Perseus.

Blanchard, K., & T. Waghorn (1997). *Mission possible: Becoming a world-class organization while there's still time.* New York: McGraw-Hill.

Bolman, L. G., & T. E. Deal (1997). *Reframing organizations: Artistry, choice, and leadership.* 2d ed. San Francisco: Jossey-Bass.

Chemers, M. M. (2002). Efficacy and effectiveness: Integrating models of leadership and intelligence. In R. E. Riggio, S. E. Murphy, & F. J. Pirozzlo, eds., *Multiple intelligences and leadership.* Mahwah, NJ: Lawrence Erlbaum.

Cox, T. H., Jr. (1993). *Cultural diversity in organizations: Theory, research, and practice.* San Francisco: Berrett-Koehler.

Follett, M. P. (1926). The giving of orders. In H. C. Metcalf, ed., *Scientific foundations of business administration.* Baltimore, MD: Williams & Wilkins.

French, W. L., & C. H. Bell Jr. (1995). *Organization development: Behavioral science interventions for organization improvement.* 5th ed. Englewood Cliffs, NJ: Prentice Hall.

Haire, M. (1954). Industrial social psychology. In G. Lindzey, ed., *Handbook of social psychology,* vol. 2: *Special fields and applications* (pp. 1104–1123). Reading, MA: Addison-Wesley.

Hersey, P., & K. H. Blanchard (1982). *Management of organizational behavior: Utilizing human resources.* 4th ed. Englewood Cliffs, NJ: Prentice Hall.

Janis, I. L. (1971, November). Groupthink. *Psychology Today,* 44–76.

Kearney, R. C., & S. W. Hays (1998, Fall). Reinventing government, the new public management and civil service systems in international perspective: The danger of throwing the baby out with the bathwater. *Review of Public Personnel Administration, 18*(4), 38–54.

Lewin, K. (1947). Frontiers in group dynamics: Concept, method and reality in social science: Social equilibrium and social change. *Human Relations, 1,* 5–41.

Lewin, K. (1948). *Resolving social conflicts.* New York: Harper.

Lipnack, J., & J. Stamps (1999). Virtual teams: The new way to work. *Strategy & Leadership, 27*(1), 14–19.

Locke, E. A. (2001). Self-set goals and self-efficacy as mediators of incentives and personality. In M. Erez, U. Kleinbeck, & H. Thierry, eds., *Work motivation in the context of a globalizing economy.* Mahway, NJ: Lawrence Erlbaum.

Maslow, A. H. (1943). A theory of human motivation. *Psychological Review, 50*(4), 370–396.

Mayo, G. E. (1933). *The human problems of an industrial civilization.* Boston, MA: Harvard Business School, Division of Research.

McGregor, D. M. (1957a, April). The human side of enterprise. Address to the fifth anniversary convocation of the School of Industrial Management, Massachusetts Institute of Technology. In *Adventure in thought and action.* Cambridge, MA: MIT School of Industrial Management, 1957. Reprinted in W. G. Bennis, E. H. Schein, & C. McGregor, eds. (1966), *Leadership and motivation: Essays of Douglas McGregor* (pp. 3–20). Cambridge, MA: MIT Press.

McGregor, D. M. (1957b, November). The human side of enterprise. *Management Review, 46,* 22–28, 88–92.

McGregor, D. M. (1960). *The human side of enterprise.* New York: McGraw-Hill.

Münsterberg, H. (1913). *Psychology and industrial efficiency.* Boston: Houghton Mifflin.

Münsterberg, M. (1922). *Hugo Münsterberg: His life and work.* New York: Appleton.

Northouse, P. G. (1997). *Leadership: Theory and practice.* Thousand Oaks, CA: Sage.

Ott, J. S., S. J. Parkes, & R. B. Simpson, eds. (2003). *Classic readings in organizational behavior*. 3d ed. Belmont, CA: Wadsworth/Thomson.

Pascale, R. T. (2001). Laws of the jungle and the new laws of business. *Leader to Leader, 20*, 21–35.

Porter, L. W., E. E. Lawler III, & J. R. Hackman (1975). *Behavior in organizations* (pp. 403–422). New York: McGraw-Hill.

Roethlisberger, F. J. (1941). *Management and morale*. Cambridge, MA: Harvard University Press.

Roethlisberger, F. J., & W. J. Dickson (1939). *Management and the worker*. Cambridge, MA: Harvard University Press.

Victor, B., & C. Stephens (1994, November). The dark side of the new organizational forms. *Organization Science, 5*(4), 479–482.

Wheatley, M. (2000). *Leadership and the new science*. San Francisco: Jossey-Bass.

Wren, D. A. (1972). *The evolution of management thought*. New York: Ronald Press.

14
The Giving of Orders
Mary Parker Follett

To some men the matter of giving orders seems a very simple affair; they expect to issue their own orders and have them obeyed without question. Yet, on the other hand, the shrewd common sense of many a business executive has shown him that the issuing of orders is surrounded by many difficulties; that to demand an unquestioning obedience to orders not approved, not perhaps even understood, is bad business policy. Moreover, psychology, as well as our own observation, shows us not only that you cannot get people to do things most satisfactorily by ordering them or exhorting them; but also that even reasoning with them, even convincing them intellectually, may not be enough. Even the "consent of the governed" will not do all the work it is supposed to do, an important consideration for those who are advocating employee representation. For all our past life, our early training, our later experience, all our emotions, beliefs, prejudices, every desire that we have, have formed certain habits of mind that the psychologists call habit-patterns, action-patterns, motor-sets.

Therefore it will do little good merely to get intellectual agreement; unless you change the habit-patterns of people, you have not really changed your people. . . .

If we analyse this matter a little further we shall see that we have to do three things. I am now going to use psychological language: (1) build up certain attitudes; (2) provide for the release of these attitudes; (3) augment the released response as it is being carried out. What does this mean in the language of business? A psychologist has given us the example of the salesman.

The salesman first creates in you the attitude that you want his article; then, at just the "psychological" moment, he produces his contract blank which you may sign and thus release that attitude; then if, as you're preparing to sign, some one comes in and tells you how pleased he has been with his purchase of this article, that augments the response which is being released.

If we apply this to the subject of orders and obedience, we see that people can obey an order only if previous habit patterns are appealed to or new ones created. . . .

This is an important consideration for us, for from one point of view business success depends largely on this — namely, whether our business is so organized and administered that it tends to form certain habits, certain mental attitudes. It has been hard for many old-fashioned employers to understand that *orders will not take the place of training.* I want to italicize that. Many a time an employer has been angry because, as he expressed it, a workman "wouldn't" do so and so, when the truth of the matter was that the workman couldn't, actually couldn't, do as ordered because he could not go contrary to life-long habits. This whole subject might be taken up under the heading of education, for there we could give many instances of the attempt to make arbitrary authority take the place of training. In history, the aftermath of all revolutions shows us the results of the lack of training.

. . . A boy may respond differently to the same suggestion when made by his teacher and when made by his schoolmate. Moreover, he may respond differently to the same suggestion made by the teacher in the

Source: Scientific Foundations of Business Administration, ed. Henry C. Metcalf (Baltimore: Williams & Wilkins, 1926); footnotes omitted. © 1926 by The Williams & Wilkins Co. Reprinted by permission.

schoolroom and made by the teacher when they are taking a walk together. Applying this to the giving of orders, we see that the place in which orders are given, the circumstances under which they are given, may make all the difference in the world as to the response which we get. Hand them down a long way from President or Works Manager and the effect is weakened. One might say that the strength of favourable response to an order is in inverse ratio to the distance the order travels. Production efficiency is always in danger of being affected whenever the long-distance order is substituted for the face-to-face suggestion. There is, however, another reason for that which I shall consider in a moment.

. . . I should say that the giving of orders and the receiving of orders ought to be a matter of integration through circular behaviour, and that we should seek methods to bring this about.

Psychology has another important contribution to make on this subject of issuing orders or giving directions: before the integration can be made between order-giver and order-receiver, there is often an integration to be made within one or both of the individuals concerned. There are often two dissociated paths in the individual; if you are clever enough to recognize these, you can sometimes forestall a Freudian conflict, make the integration appear before there is an acute stage. . . .

Business administration has often to consider how to deal with the dissociated paths in individuals or groups, but the methods of doing this successfully have been developed much further in some departments than in others. We have as yet hardly recognized this as part of the technique of dealing with employees, yet the clever salesman knows that it is the chief part of his job. The prospective buyer wants the article and does not want it. The able salesman does not suppress the arguments in the mind of the purchaser against buying, for then the purchaser might be sorry afterwards for his purchase, and that would not be good salesmanship. Unless he can unite, integrate, in the purchaser's mind, the reasons for buying and the reasons for not buying, his future sales will be imperilled, he will not be the highest grade salesman.

Please note that this goes beyond what the psychologist whom I quoted at the beginning of this section told us. He said, "The salesman must create in you the attitude that you want his article." Yes, but only if he creates this attitude by integration, not by suppression.

Apply all this to orders. An order often leaves the individual to whom it is given with two dissociated paths; an order should seek to unite, to integrate, dissociated paths. Court decisions often settle arbitrarily which of two ways is to be followed without showing a possible integration of the two, that is, the individual is often left with an internal conflict on his hands. This is what both courts and business administration should try to prevent, the internal conflicts of individuals or groups.

. . . Probably more industrial trouble has been caused by the manner in which orders are given than in any other way. In the *Report on Strikes and Lockout*, a British Government publication, the cause of a number of strikes is given as "alleged harassing conduct of the foreman," "alleged tyrannical conduct of an under-foreman," "alleged overbearing conduct of officials." The explicit statement, however, of the tyranny of superior officers as the direct cause of strikes is I should say, unusual, yet resentment smoulders and breaks out in other issues. And the demand for better treatment is often explicit enough. We find it made by the metal and wood-working trades in an aircraft factory, who declared that any treatment of men without regard to their feelings of self-respect would be answered by a stoppage of work. We find it put in certain agreements with employers that "the men must be treated with proper respect, and threats and abusive language must not be used."

What happens to [a] man, *in* a man, when an order is given in a disagreeable manner by his foreman, head of department, his immediate superior in store, bank or factory? The man addressed feels that his self-respect is attacked, that one of his most inner sanctuaries is invaded. He loses his temper or becomes sullen or is on the defensive; he begins thinking of his "rights"—a fatal attitude for any of us. In the language we have been using, the wrong behaviour pattern is aroused, the wrong motor-set; that is, he is now "set" to act in a way which is not going to benefit the enterprise in which he is engaged.

There is a more subtle psychological point here, too; the more you are "bossed" the more your activity of thought will take place within the bossing-pattern, and your part in that pattern seems usually to be opposition to the bossing.

This complaint of the abusive language and the tyrannical treatment of the one just above the worker is an old story to us all, but there is an opposite extreme which is far too little considered. The immediate superior officer is often so close to the worker that he does not exercise the proper duties of his position. Far from taking on himself an aggressive authority, he has often evaded one of the chief problems of his job: how to do what is implied in the fact that he has been put in a position over others. . . .

Now what is our problem here? How can we avoid the two extremes: too great bossism in giving orders, and practically no orders given? I am going to ask how *you* are avoiding these extremes. My solution is to depersonalize the giving of orders, to unite all concerned in a study of the situation, to discover the law of the situation and obey that. Until we do this I do not think we shall have the most successful business administration. This is what does take place, what has to take place, when there is a question between two men in positions of equal authority. The head of the sales departments does not give orders to the head of the production department, or vice versa. Each studies the market and the final decision is made as the market demands. This is, ideally, what should take place between foremen and the rank and file, between any head and his subordinates. One *person*

should not give orders to another *person*, but both should agree to take their orders from the situation. If orders are simply part of the situation, the question of someone giving and someone receiving does not come up. Both accept the orders given by the situation. Employers accept the orders given by the situation; employees accept the orders given by the situation. This gives, does it not, a slightly different aspect to the whole of business administration through the entire plant?

We have here, I think, one of the largest contributions of scientific management: it tends to depersonalize orders. From one point of view, one might call the essence of scientific management the attempt to find the law of the situation. With scientific management the managers are as much under orders as the workers, for both obey the law of the situation. Our job is not how to get people to obey orders, but how to devise methods by which we can best *discover* the order integral to a particular situation. When that is found, the employee can issue it to the employer, as well as employer to employee. This often happens easily and naturally. My cook or my stenographer point out the law of the situation, and I, if I recognize it as such, accept it, even although it may reverse some "order" I have given.

If those in supervisory positions should depersonalize orders, then there would be no overbearing authority on the one hand, nor on the other that dangerous *laissez-aller* which comes from the fear of exercising authority. Of course we should exercise authority, but always the authority of the situation. I do not say that we have found the way to a frictionless existence, far from it, but we now understand the place which we mean to give to friction. We intend to set it to work for us as the engineer does when he puts the belt over the pulley. There will be just as much, probably more, room for disagreement in the method I am advocating. The situation will often be seen differently, often be interpreted differently. But we shall know what to do with it, we shall have found a method of dealing with it.

I call it depersonalizing because there is no time to go any further into the matter. I think it really is a matter of *repersonalizing*. We, persons, have relations with each other, but we should find them in and through the whole situation. We cannot have any sound relations with each other as long as we take them out of that setting which gives them their meaning and value. This divorcing of persons and the situation does a great deal of harm. I have just said that scientific management depersonalizes; the deeper philosophy of scientific management shows us personal relations within the whole setting of that thing of which they are a part. . . .

I said above that we should substitute for the long-distance order the face-to-face suggestion. I think we can now see a more cogent reason for this than the one then given. It is not the face-to-face suggestion that we want so much as the joint study of the problem, and such joint study can be made best by the employee and his immediate superior or employee and special expert on that question.

I began this talk by emphasizing the advisability of preparing in advance the attitude necessary for the carrying out of orders, and in the previous paper we considered preparing the attitude for integration; but we have now, in our consideration of the joint study of situations, in our emphasis on obeying the law of the situation, perhaps got a little beyond that, or rather we have now to consider in what sense we wish to take the psychologist's doctrine of prepared-in-advance attitudes. . . .

We should not try to create the attitude we *want*, although that is the usual phrase, but the attitude required for cooperative study and decision. This holds good even for the salesman. We said above that when the salesman is told that he should create in the prospective buyer the attitude that he wants the article, he ought also to be told that he should do this by integration rather than by suppression. We have now a hint of *how* he is to attain this integration.

I have spoken of the importance of changing some of the language of business personnel relations. We considered whether the words "grievances," "complaints," or Ford's "trouble specialists" did not arouse the wrong behaviour-patterns. I think "order" certainly does. If that word is not to mean any longer external authority, arbitrary authority, but the law of the situation, then we need a new word for it. It is often the order that people resent as much as the thing ordered. People do not like to be ordered even to take a holiday. I have often seen instances of this. The wish to govern one's own life is, of course, one of the most fundamental feelings in every human being. To call this "the instinct of self-assertion," "the instinct of initiative," does not express it wholly. I think it is told in the life of some famous American that when he was a boy and his mother said, "Go get a pail of water," he always replied, "I won't," before taking up the pail and fetching the water. This is significant; he resented the command, the command of a person; but he went and got the water, not, I believe, because he had to, but because he recognized the demand of the situation. *That*, he knew he had to obey; *that*, he was willing to obey. And this kind of obedience is not opposed to the wish to govern one's self, but each is involved in the other; both are part of the same fundamental urge at the root of one's being. We have here something far more profound than "the egoistic impulse" or "the instinct of self-assertion." We have the very essence of the human being.

This subject of orders has led us into the heart of the whole question of authority and consent. When we conceive of authority and consent as parts of an inclusive situation, does that not throw a flood of light on this question? The point of view here presented gets rid of several dilemmas which have seemed to puzzle people in dealing with consent. The feeling of being "under" someone, of "subordination," of "servility," of being "at the will of another," comes out again and again in the shop stewards movement and in the testimony before the Coal Commission. One man said before the Coal Commission, "It is all right to work with anyone; what is disagreeable is to feel too distinctly that you are working *under* anyone." *With* is a pretty good preposition, not because it connotes democracy, but because it connotes functional unity, a much more profound conception than that of democracy as usually held. The study of the situation involves the *with* preposition. Then Sadie is not left alone by the head of the cloak department, nor does she have to obey her. The head of the department says, "Let's see how such cases had better be handled, then we'll abide by that." Sadie is not under the head of the department, but both are *under* the situation.

Twice I have had a servant applying for a place ask me if she would be treated as a menial. When the first woman asked me that, I had no idea what she meant, I thought perhaps she did not want to do the roughest work, but later I came to the conclusion that to be treated as a menial meant to be obliged to be under someone, to follow orders without using one's own judgment. If we believe that what heightens self-respect increases efficiency, we shall be on our guard here.

Very closely connected with this is the matter of pride in one's work. If an order goes against what the craftsman or the clerk thinks is the way of doing his work which will bring the best results, he is justified in not wishing to obey that order. Could not that difficulty be met by a joint study of the situation? It is said that it is characteristic of the British workman to feel, "I know my job and won't be told how." The peculiarities of the British workman might be met by a joint study of the situation, it being understood that he probably has more to contribute to that study than anyone else. . . .

There is another dilemma which has to be met by everyone who is in what is called a position of authority: how can you expect people merely to obey orders and at the same time to take that degree of responsibility which they should take? Indeed, in my experience, the people who enjoy following orders blindly, without any thought on their own part, are those who like thus to get rid of responsibility. But the taking of responsibility, each according to his capacity, each according to his function in the whole . . ., this taking of responsibility is usually the most vital matter in the life of every human being, just as the allotting of responsibility is the most important part of business administration.

A young trade unionist said to me, "how much dignity can I have as a mere employee?" He can have all the dignity in the world if he is allowed to make his fullest contribution to the plant *and to assume definitely the responsibility therefor*.

I think one of the gravest problems before us is how to make the reconciliation between receiving orders and taking responsibility. And I think the reconciliation can be made through our conception of the law of the situation. . . .

We have considered the subject of symbols. It is often very apparent that an order is a symbol. The referee in the game stands watch in hand and says, "Go." It is an order, but order only as symbol. I may say to an employee, "Do so and so," but I should say it only because we have both agreed, openly or tacitly, that that which I am ordering done is the best thing to be done. The order is then a symbol. And if it is a philosophical and psychological truth that we owe obedience only to a functional unity to which we are contributing, we should remember that a more accurate way of stating that would be to say that our obligation is to a unifying, to a process.

This brings us now to one of our most serious problems in this matter of orders. It is important, but we can touch on it only briefly; it is what we spoke of . . . as the evolving situation. I am trying to show here that the order must be integral to the situation and must be recognized as such. But we saw that the situation was always developing. If the situation is never stationary, then the order should never be stationary, so to speak; how to prevent it from being so is our problem. The situation is changing while orders are being carried out. How is the order to keep up with the situation? External orders never can, only those drawn fresh from the situation.

Moreover, if taking a *responsible* attitude toward experience involves recognizing the evolving situation, a *conscious* attitude toward experience means that we note the change which the developing situation makes in ourselves; the situation does not change without changing us.

. . . When I asked a very intelligent girl what she thought would be the result of profit sharing and employee representation in the factory where she worked, she replied joyfully, "We shan't need foremen any more." While her entire ignoring of the fact that the foreman has other duties than keeping workers on their jobs was amusing, one wants to go beyond one's amusement and find out what this objection to being watched really means. . . .

I have seen similar instances cited. Many workmen feel that being watched is unbearable. What can we do about it? How can we get proper supervision without this watching which a worker resents? Supervision is necessary; supervision is resented—how are we going to make the integration there? Some say, "Let the workers elect the supervisors." I do not believe in that.

There are three other points closely connected with the subject of this paper which I should like merely to point out. First, when and how do you point out mistakes, misconduct? One principle can surely guide us here: don't blame for the sake of blaming, make what you have to say accomplish something; say it in that form, at that time, under those circumstances, which will make it a real education to your subordinate. Secondly, since it is recognized that the one who gives the orders is not as a rule a very popular person, the management sometimes tries to offset this by allowing the person who has this onus upon him to give any pleasant news to the workers, to have the credit of any innovation which the workers very much desire. One manager told me that he always tried to do this. I suppose that this is good behaviouristic psychology, and yet I am not sure that it is a method I wholly like. It is quite different, however, in the case of a mistaken order having been given; then I think the one who made the mistake should certainly be the one to rectify it, not as a matter of strategy, but because it is better for him too. It is better for all of us not only to acknowledge our mistakes, but to do something about them. If a foreman discharges someone and it is decided to reinstate the man, it is obviously not only good tactics but a square deal to the foreman to allow him to do the reinstating.

There is, of course, a great deal more to this matter of giving orders than we have been able to touch on; far from exhausting the subject, I feel that I have only given hints. I have been told that the artillery men suffered more mentally in the war than others, and the reason assigned for this was that their work was directed from a distance. The combination of numbers by which they focused their fire was telephoned to them. The result was also at a distance. Their activity was not closely enough connected with the actual situation at either end.

15

The Hawthorne Experiments

Fritz J. Roethlisberger

There seems to be an assumption today that we need a complex set of ideas to handle the complex problems of this complex world in which we live. We assume that a big problem needs a big idea; a complex problem needs a complex idea for its solution. As a result, our thinking tends to become more and more tortuous and muddled. Nowhere is this more true than in matters of human behavior. It seems to me that the road back to sanity—and here is where my title comes in—lies

(1) In having a few simple and clear ideas about the world in which we live.

(2) In complicating our ideas, not in a vacuum, but only in reference to things we can observe, see, feel, hear, and touch. Let us not generalize from verbal definitions; let us know in fact what we are talking about.

(3) In having a very simple method by means of which we can explore our complex world. We need a tool which will allow us to get the data from which our generalizations are to be drawn. We need a simple skill to keep us in touch with what is sometimes referred to as "reality."

(4) In being "tough-minded," i.e. in not letting ourselves be too disappointed because the complex world never quite fulfills our most cherished expectations of it. Let us remember that the concrete phenomena will always elude any set of abstractions that we can make of them.

(5) In knowing very clearly the class of phenomena to which our ideas and methods relate. Now, this is merely a way of saying, "Do not use a saw as a hammer." A saw is a useful tool precisely because it is limited and designed for a certain purpose. Do not criticize the usefulness of a saw because it does not make a good hammer.

It is my simple thesis that a human problem requires a human solution. First, we have to learn to recognize a human problem when we see one; and, second, upon recognizing it, we have to learn to deal with it as such and not as if it were something else. Too often at the verbal level we talk glibly about the importance of the human factor; and too seldom at the concrete level of behavior do we recognize a human problem for what it is and deal with it as such. *A human problem to be brought to a human solution requires human data and human tools.* It is my purpose to use the Western Electric researches as an illustration of what I mean by this statement, because, if they deserve the publicity and acclaim which they have received, it is because, in my opinion, they have so conclusively demonstrated this point. In this sense they are the road back to sanity in management-employee relations.

EXPERIMENTS IN ILLUMINATION

The Western Electric researches started about sixteen years ago, in the Hawthorne plant, with a series of experiments on illumination. The purpose was to find out the relation of the quality and quantity of illumination to the efficiency of industrial workers. These studies lasted several years, and I shall not describe them in detail. It will suffice to point out that the results were quite different from what had been expected.

In one experiment the workers were divided into two groups. One group, called

Source: Management and Morale, ed. F. J. Roethlisberger (Cambridge, MA: Harvard University Press, 1941), pp. 7–26. © 1941 by the President and Fellows of Harvard College; © renewed 1969 by F. J. Roethlisberger. Reprinted with permission.

the "test group," was to work under different illumination intensities. The other group, called the "control group," was to work under an intensity of illumination as nearly constant as possible. During the first experiment, the test group was submitted to three different intensities of illumination of increasing magnitude, 24, 46, and 70 foot candles. What were the results of this early experiment? Production increased in both rooms—in both the test group and the control group—and the rise in output was roughly of the same magnitude in both cases.

In another experiment, the light under which the test group worked was decreased from 10 to 3 foot candles, while the control group worked, as before, under a constant level of illumination intensity. In this case the output rate in the test group went up instead of down. It also went up in the control group.

In still another experiment, the workers were allowed to believe that the illumination was being increased, although, in fact, no change in intensity was made. The workers commented favorably on the improved lighting condition, but there was no appreciable change in output. At another time, the workers were allowed to believe that the intensity of illumination was being decreased, although again, in fact, no actual change was made. The workers complained somewhat about the poorer lighting, but again there was no appreciable effect on output.

And finally, in another experiment, the intensity of illumination was decreased to .06 of a foot candle, which is the intensity of illumination approximately equivalent to that of ordinary moonlight. Not until this point was reached was there any appreciable decline in the output rate.

What did the experimenters learn? Obviously, as Stuart Chase said, there was something "screwy," but the experimenters were not quite sure who or what was screwy—they themselves, the subjects, or the results. One thing was clear: the results were negative. Nothing of a positive nature had been learned about the relation of illumination to industrial efficiency. If the results were to be taken at their face value, it would appear that there was no relation between illumination and industrial efficiency. However, the investigators were not yet quite willing to draw this conclusion. They realized the difficulty of testing for the effect of a single variable in a situation where there were many uncontrolled variables. It was thought therefore that another experiment should be devised in which other variables affecting the output of workers could be better controlled.

A few of the tough-minded experimenters already were beginning to suspect their basic ideas and assumptions with regard to human motivation. It occurred to them that the trouble was not so much with the results or with the subjects as it was with their notion regarding the way their subjects were supposed to behave—the notion of a simple cause-and-effect, direct relationship between certain physical changes in the workers' environment and the responses of the workers to these changes. Such a notion completely ignored the human meaning of these changes to the people who were subjected to them.

In the illumination experiments, therefore, we have a classic example of trying to deal with a human situation in nonhuman terms. The experimenters had obtained no human data; they had been handling electric-light bulbs and plotting average output curves. Hence their results had no human significance. That is why they seemed screwy. Let me suggest here, however, that the results were not screwy, but the experimenters were—a "screwy" person being by definition one who is not acting in accordance with the customary human values of the situation in which he finds himself.

THE RELAY ASSEMBLY TEST ROOM

Another experiment was framed, in which it was planned to submit a segregated group of workers to different kinds of working conditions. The idea was very simple: A group of five girls were placed in a separate room where their conditions of work could be carefully controlled, where their output could be measured, and where they could be closely observed. It was decided to introduce at specified intervals different changes in working conditions and to see what effect these innovations had on output. . . . Under these conditions of close observation the girls were studied for a period of five years. Literally tons of material were collected. Probably nowhere in the world has so much material been collected about a small group of workers for such a long period of time.

But what about the results? They can be stated very briefly. When all is said and done, they amount roughly to this: A skillful statistician spent several years trying to relate variations in output with variations in the physical circumstances of these five operators. . . . The attempt to relate changes in physical circumstances to variations in output resulted in not a single correlation of enough statistical significance to be recognized by any competent statistician as having any meaning.

Now, of course, it would be misleading to say that this negative result was the only conclusion reached. There were positive conclusions, and it did not take the experimenters more than two years to find out that they had missed the boat. After two years of work, certain things happened which made them sit up and take notice. Different experimental conditions of work, in the nature of changes in the number and duration of rest pauses and differences in the length of the working day and week, had been introduced in this Relay Assembly Test Room. For example, the investigators first introduced two five-minute rests, one in the morning and one in the afternoon. Then they increased the length of these rests, and after that they introduced the rests at different times of the day. During one experimental period they served the operators a specially prepared lunch during the rest. In the later periods, they decreased the length of the working day by one-half hour and then by one hour. They gave the operators Saturday morning off for

a while. Altogether, thirteen such periods of different working conditions were introduced in the first two years.

During the first year and a half of the experiment, everybody was happy, both the investigators and the operators. The investigators were happy because as conditions of work improved the output rate rose steadily. Here, it appeared, was strong evidence in favor of their preconceived hypothesis that fatigue was the major factor limiting output. The operators were happy because their conditions of work were being improved, they were earning more money, and they were objects of considerable attention from top management. But then one investigator — one of those tough-minded fellows — suggested that they restore the original conditions of work, that is, go back to a full forty-eight-hour week without rests, lunches and what not. This was Period XII. Then the happy state of affairs, when everything was going along as it theoretically should, went sour. Output, instead of taking the expected nose dive, maintained its high level.

Again the investigators were forcibly reminded that human situations are likely to be complex. In any human situation, whenever a simple change is introduced — a rest pause, for example — other changes, unwanted and unanticipated, may also be brought about. What I am saying here is very simple. If one experiments on a stone, the stone does not know it is being experimented upon — all of which makes it simple for people experimenting on stones. But if a human being is being experimented upon, he is likely to know it. Therefore, his attitudes toward the experiment and toward the experimenters become very important factors in determining his responses to the situation.

Now that is what happened in the Relay Assembly Test Room. To the investigators, it was essential that the workers give their full and whole-hearted coöperation to the experiment. They did not want the operators to work harder or easier depending upon their attitude toward the conditions that were imposed. They wanted them to work as they felt, so that they could be sure that the different physical conditions of work were solely responsible for the variations in output. For each of the experimental changes, they wanted subjects whose responses would be uninfluenced by so-called "psychological factors."

In order to bring this about, the investigators did everything in their power to secure the complete coöperation of their subjects, with the result that almost all the practices common to the shop were altered. The operators were consulted about the changes to be made, and, indeed, several plans were abandoned because they met with the disapproval of the girls. They were questioned sympathetically about their reactions to the conditions imposed, and many of these conferences took place in the office of the superintendent. The girls were allowed to talk at work; their "bogey" was eliminated. Their physical health and well-being became matters of great concern. Their opinions, hopes, and fears were eagerly sought. What happened was that in the very process of setting the conditions for the test—a so-called "controlled" experiment—the experimenters had completely altered the social situation of the room. Inadvertently a change had been introduced which was far more important than the planned experimental innovations: the customary supervision in the room had been revolutionized. This accounted for the better attitudes of the girls and their improved rate of work.

THE DEVELOPMENT OF A NEW AND MORE FRUITFUL POINT OF VIEW

After Period XII in the Relay Assembly Test Room, the investigators decided to change their ideas radically. What all their experiments had dramatically and conclusively demonstrated was the importance of employee attitudes and sentiments. It was clear that the responses of workers to what was happening about them were dependent upon the significance these events had for them. In most work situations the meaning of a change is likely to be as important, if not more so, than the change itself. This was the great *éclaircissement*, the new illumination, that came from the research. It was an illumination quite different from what they had expected from the illumination studies. Curiously enough, this discovery is nothing very new or startling. It is something which anyone who has had some concrete experience in handling other people intuitively recognizes and practices. Whether or not a person is going to give his services whole-heartedly to a group depends, in good part, on the way he feels about his job, his fellow workers, and supervisors—the meaning for him of what is happening about him.

However, when the experimenters began to tackle the problem of employee attitudes and the factors determining such attitudes—when they began to tackle the problem of "meaning"—they entered a sort of twilight zone where things are never quite what they seem. Moreover, overnight, as it were, they were robbed of all the tools they had so carefully forged; for all their previous tools were nonhuman tools concerned with the measurement of output, temperature, humidity, etc., and these were no longer useful for the human data that they now wanted to obtain. What the experimenters now wanted to know was how a person felt, what his intimate thinking, reflections, and preoccupations were, and what he liked and disliked about his work environment. In short, what did the whole blooming business—his job, his supervision, his working conditions—mean to him? Now this was human stuff, and there were no tools, or at least the experimenters knew of none, for obtaining and evaluating this kind of material.

Fortunately, there were a few courageous souls among the experimenters. These men were not metaphysicians, psychologists, academicians, professors, intellectuals, or what have you. They were men of common sense and of practical affairs. They were not driven by any great heroic desire to change the world. They were true experimenters, that is, men compelled to follow the implications of their own monkey business. All the evidence of their studies was pointing in one direction. Would they take the jump? They did.

EXPERIMENTS IN INTERVIEWING WORKERS

A few tough-minded experimenters decided to go into the shops and—completely disarmed and denuded of their elaborate logical equipment and in all humility—to see if they could learn how to get the workers to talk about things that were important to them and could learn to understand what the workers were trying to tell them. This was a revolutionary idea in the year 1928, when this interviewing program started— the idea of getting a worker to talk to you and to listen sympathetically, but intelligently, to what he had to say. In that year a new era of personnel relations began. It was the first real attempt to get human data and to forge human tools to get them. In that year a novel idea was born; dimly the experimenters perceived a new method of human control. In that year the Rubicon was crossed from which there could be no return to the "good old days." Not that the experimenters ever wanted to return, because they now entered a world so exciting, so intriguing, and so full of promise that it made the "good old days" seem like the prattle and play of children.

When these experimenters decided to enter the world of "meaning," with very few tools, but with a strong sense of curiosity and a willingness to learn, they had many interesting adventures. It would be too long a story to tell all of them, or even a small part of them. They made plenty of mistakes, but they were not afraid to learn.

At first, they found it difficult to learn to give full and complete attention to what a person had to say without interrupting him before he was through. They found it difficult to learn not to give advice, not to make or imply moral judgments about the speaker, not to argue, not to be too clever, not to dominate the conversation, not to ask leading questions. They found it difficult to get the person to talk about matters which were important to him and not to the interviewer. But, most important of all, they found it difficult to learn that perhaps the thing most significant to a person was not something in his immediate work situation.

Gradually, however, they learned these things. They discovered that sooner or later a person tends to talk about what is uppermost in his mind to a sympathetic and skillful listener, and they became more proficient in interpreting what a person is saying or trying to say. Of course they protected the confidences given to them and made absolutely sure that nothing an employee said could ever be used against him. Slowly they began to forge a simple human tool—imperfect, to be sure—to get the kind of data they wanted. They called this method "interviewing." I would hesitate to say the number of man-hours of labor which went into the forging of this tool. There followed from studies made through its use a gradually changing conception of the worker and his behavior.

A NEW WAY OF VIEWING EMPLOYEE SATISFACTION AND DISSATISFACTION

When the experimenters started to study employee likes and dislikes, they assumed, at first, that they would find a simple and logical relation between a person's likes or dislikes and certain items and events in his immediate work situation. They expected to find a simple connection, for example, between a person's complaint and the object about which he was complaining. Hence, the solution would be easy: correct the object of the complaint, if possible, and presto! the complaint would disappear. Unfortunately, however, the world of human behavior is not so simple as this conception of it; and it took the investigators several arduous and painful years to find this out. I will mention only a few interesting experiences they had.

Several times they changed the objects of the complaint only to find that the attitudes of the complainants remained unchanged. In these cases, correcting the object of the complaint did not remedy the complaint or the attitude of the person expressing it. A certain complaint might disappear, to be sure, only to have another one arise. Here the investigators were running into so-called "chronic kickers," people whose dissatisfactions were more deeply rooted in factors relating to their personal histories. . . .

Several times they did absolutely nothing about the object of the complaint, but after the interview, curiously enough, the complaint disappeared. A typical example of this was that of a woman who complained at great length and with considerable feeling about the poor food being served in the company restaurant. When, a few days later, she chanced to meet the interviewer, she commented with great enthusiasm upon the improved food and thanked the interviewer for communicating her grievance to management and for securing such prompt action. Here no change had been made in the thing criticized; yet the employee felt that something had been done.

Many times they found that people did not really want anything done about the things of which they were complaining. What they did want was an opportunity to talk about their troubles to a sympathetic listener. It was astonishing to find the number of instances in which workers complained about things which had happened many, many years ago, but which they described as vividly as if they had happened just a day before.

Here again, something was "screwy," but

this time the experimenters realized that it was their assumptions which were screwy. They were assuming that the meanings which people assign to their experience are essentially logical. They were carrying in their heads the notion of the "economic man," a man primarily motivated by economic interest, whose logical capacities were being used in the service of this self-interest.

Gradually and painfully in the light of the evidence, which was overwhelming, the experimenters had been forced to abandon this conception of the worker and his behavior. Only with a new working hypothesis could they make sense of the data they had collected. The conception of the worker which they developed is actually nothing very new or startling; it is one which any effective administrator intuitively recognizes and practices in handling human beings.

First, they found that the behavior of workers could not be understood apart from their feelings or sentiments. I shall use the word "sentiment" hereafter to refer not only to such things as feelings and emotions, but also to a much wider range of phenomena which may not be expressed in violent feelings or emotions—phenomena that are referred to by such words as "loyalty," "integrity," "solidarity."

Secondly, they found that sentiments are easily disguised, and hence are difficult to recognize and to study. Manifestations of sentiment take a number of different forms. Feelings of personal integrity, for example, can be expressed by a handshake; they can also be expressed, when violated, by a sitdown strike. Moreover, people like to rationalize their sentiments and to objectify them. We are not so likely to say "I feel bad," as to say "The world is bad." In other words, we like to endow the world with those attributes and qualities which will justify and account for the feelings and sentiments we have toward it; we tend to project our sentiments on the outside world.

Thirdly, they found that manifestations of sentiment could not be understood as things in and by themselves, but only in terms of the total situation of the person. To comprehend why a person felt the way he did, a wider range of phenomena had to be explored. The following three diagrams illustrate roughly the development of this point of view.

It will be remembered that at first the investigators assumed a simple and direct relation between certain physical changes in the worker's environment and his responses to them. This simple state of mind is illustrated in diagram I of Figure 15.1. But all the evidence of the early experiments showed that the responses of employees to changes in their immediate working environment can be understood only in terms of their attitudes—the "meaning" these changes have for them. This point of view is represented in diagram II of Figure 15.1. However, the "meaning" which these changes have for the worker is not strictly and primarily logical, for they are fraught with human feelings and values. The "meaning," therefore, which any individual worker assigns to a particular change depends upon (1) his social "conditioning," or what sentiments (values, hopes, fears, expectations, etc.) he is bringing to the work situation because of his previous family and group associations, and hence the relation

of the change to these sentiments; and (2) the kind of human satisfactions he is deriving from his social participation with other workers and supervisors in the immediate work group of which he is a member, and hence the effect of the change on his customary interpersonal relations. This way of regarding the responses of workers (both verbal and overt) is represented in diagram III of Figure 15.1. It says briefly: Sentiments do not appear in a vacuum; they do not come out of the blue; they appear in a social context. They have to be considered in terms of that context, and apart from it they are likely to be misunderstood.

One further point should be made about that aspect of the worker's environment designated "Social Situation at Work" in diagram III (Figure 15.1). What is meant is that the worker is not an isolated, atomic individual; he is a member of a group, or of groups. Within each of these groups the individuals have feelings and sentiments toward each other, which bind them together in collaborative effort. Moreover, these collective sentiments can, and do, become attached to every item and object in the industrial environment—even to output. Material goods, output, wages, hours of work, and so on, cannot be treated as things in themselves. Instead, they must be interpreted as carriers of social value.

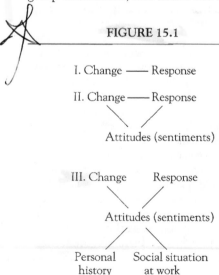

FIGURE 15.1

I. Change —— Response

II. Change —— Response

Attitudes (sentiments)

III. Change   Response

Attitudes (sentiments)

Personal   Social situation
history   at work

OUTPUT AS A FORM OF SOCIAL BEHAVIOR

That output is a form of social behavior was well illustrated in a study made by the Hawthorne experimenters, called the Bank Wiring Observation Room. This room contained fourteen workmen representing three occupational groups—wiremen, soldermen, and inspectors. These men were on group piecework, where the more they turned out the more they earned. In such a situation one might have expected that they would have been interested in maintaining total output and that the faster workers would have put pressure on the slower workers to improve their efficiency. But this was not the case. Operating within this group were four basic sentiments, which can be expressed briefly as follows: (1) You should not turn out too much work; if you do, you are a "rate buster." (2) You should not turn out too little work; if you do, you are a "chiseler." (3) You should not say anything to a supervisor which would react to the detriment of one of your associates; if you do, you are a "squealer." (4) You should not be too officious; that is, if you are an inspector you should not act like one.

To be an accepted member of the group a man had to act in accordance with these social standards. One man in this group exceeded the group standard of what constituted a fair day's work. Social pressure was put on him to conform, but without avail, since he enjoyed doing things the others disliked. The best-liked person in the group was the one who kept his output exactly where the group agreed it should be.

Inasmuch as the operators were agreed as to what constituted a day's work, one might have expected rate of output to be about the same for each member of the group. This was by no means the case; there were marked differences. At first the experimenters thought that the differences in individual performance were related to differences in ability, so they compared each worker's relative rank in output with his relative rank in intelligence and dexterity as measured by certain tests. The results were interesting: the lowest producer in the room ranked first in intelligence and third in dexterity; the highest producer in the room was seventh in dexterity and lowest in intelligence. Here surely was a situation in which the native capacities of the men were not finding expression. From the viewpoint of logical, economic behavior, this room did not make sense. Only in terms of powerful sentiments could these individual differences in output level be explained. Each worker's level of output reflected his position in the informal organization of the group.

WHAT MAKES THE WORKER NOT WANT TO COÖPERATE

As a result of the Bank Wiring Observation Room, the Hawthorne researchers became more and more interested in the informal employee groups which tend to form within the formal organization of the company, and which are not likely to be represented in the organization chart. They became interested in the beliefs and creeds which have the effect of making each individual feel an integral part of the group and which make the group appear as a single unit, in the social codes and norms of behavior by means of which employees automatically work together in a group without any conscious choice as to whether they will or will not coöperate. They studied the important social functions these groups perform for their members, the histories of these informal work groups, how they spontaneously appear, how they tend to perpetuate themselves, multiply, and disappear, how they are in constant jeopardy from technical change, and hence how they tend to resist innovation. In particular, they became interested in those groups whose norms and codes of behavior are at variance with the technical and economic objectives of the company as a whole. They examined the social conditions under which it is more likely for the employee group to separate itself out in opposition to the remainder of the groups which make up the total organization. In such phenomena they felt that they had at last arrived at the heart of the problem of effective collaboration. They obtained a new enlightenment of the present industrial scene; from this point of view, many perplexing problems became more intelligible.

Some people claim, for example, that the size of the pay envelope is the major demand which the employee is making of his job. All the worker wants is to be told what to do and to get paid for doing it. If we look at him and his job in terms of sentiments, this is far from being as generally true as we would like to believe. Most of us want the satisfaction that comes from being accepted and recognized as people of worth by our friends and work associates. Money is only a small part of this social recognition. The way we are greeted by our boss, being asked to help a newcomer, being asked to keep an eye on a difficult operation, being given a job requiring special skill—all of these are acts of social recognition. They tell us how we stand in our work group. We all want tangible evidence of our social importance. We want to have a skill that is socially recognized as useful. We want the feeling of security that comes not so much from the amount of money we have in the bank as from being an accepted member of a group. A man whose job is without social function is like a man without a country; the activity to which he has to give the major portion of his life is robbed of all human meaning and significance. . . .

In summary, therefore, the Western Electric researches seem to me like a beginning on the road back to sanity in employee relations because (1) they offer a fruitful working hypothesis, a few simple and relatively clear ideas for the study and understanding of human situations in business; (2) they offer a simple method by means of which we can explore and deal with the complex human problems in a business organization—this method is a human method: it deals with things which are important to people; and (3) they throw a new light on the precondition for effective collaboration. Too often we think of collaboration as something which can be logically or legally contrived. The Western Electric studies indicate that it is far more a matter of sentiment than a matter of logic. Workers are not isolated, unrelated individuals; they are social animals and should be treated as such.

This statement—the worker is a social animal and should be treated as such—is simple, but the systematic and consistent practice of this point of view is not. If it were systematically practiced, it would revolutionize present-day personnel work. Our technological development in the past hundred years has been tremendous. Our methods of handling people are still archaic. If this civilization is to survive, we must obtain a new understanding of human motivation and behavior in business organizations—an understanding which can be simply but effectively practiced. The Western Electric researches contribute a first step in this direction.

16

A Theory of Human Motivation

Abraham H. Maslow

I. INTRODUCTION

In a previous paper [13] various propositions were presented which would have to
be included in any theory of human motivation that could lay claim to being definitive. These conclusions may be briefly summarized as follows:

1. The integrated wholeness of the organism
    must be one of the foundation stones of
    motivation theory.
2. The hunger drive (or any other physiolog-
    ical drive) was rejected as a centering point
    or model for a definitive theory of motiva-
    tion. Any drive that is somatically based
    and localizable was shown to be atypical
    rather than typical in human motivation.
3. Such a theory should stress and center it-
    self upon ultimate or basic goals rather
    than partial or superficial ones, upon
    ends rather than means to these ends.
    Such a stress would imply a more central
    place for unconscious than for conscious
    motivations.
4. There are usually available various cultural
    paths to the same goal. Therefore con-
    scious, specific, local-cultural desires are
    not as fundamental in motivation theory
    as the more basic, unconscious goals.
5. Any motivated behavior, either prepara-
    tory or consummatory, must be understood
    to be a channel through which many basic
    needs may be simultaneously expressed or
    satisfied. Typically an act has *more* than
    one motivation.
6. Practically all organismic states are to
    be understood as motivated and as
    motivating.
7. Human needs arrange themselves in hier-
    archies of prepotency. That is to say, the
    appearance of one need usually rests on
    the prior satisfaction of another, more

pre-potent need. Man is a perpetually
wanting animal. Also no need or drive can
be treated as if it were isolated or discrete;
every drive is related to the state of satisfaction or dissatisfaction of other drives.

8. Lists of drives will get us nowhere for var-
    ious theoretical and practical reasons.
    Furthermore any classification of motiva-
    tions must deal with the problem of lev-
    els of specificity or generalization of the
    motives to be classified.
9. Classifications of motivations must be
    based upon goals rather than upon insti-
    gating drives or motivated behavior.
10. Motivation theory should be human-
    centered rather than animal-centered.
11. The situation or the field in which the or-
    ganism reacts must be taken into account
    but the field alone can rarely serve as an
    exclusive explanation for behavior. Fur-
    thermore the field itself must be inter-
    preted in terms of the organism. Field
    theory cannot be a substitute for motiva-
    tion theory.
12. Not only the integration of the organism
    must be taken into account, but also the
    possibility of isolated, specific, partial or
    segmental reactions.

It has since become necessary to add to
these another affirmation.

13. Motivation theory is not synonymous
    with behavior theory. The motivations
    are only one class of determinants of be-
    havior. While behavior is almost always
    motivated, it is also almost always bio-
    logically, culturally and situationally
    determined as well.

The present paper is an attempt to formulate a positive theory of motivation
which will satisfy these theoretical demands
and at the same time conform to the known

Source: *Psychological Review* 50 (1943): 370–396.

facts, clinical and observational as well as experimental. It derives most directly, however, from clinical experience. This theory is, I think, in the functionalist tradition of James and Dewey, and is fused with the holism of Wertheimer [19], Goldstein [6], and Gestalt Psychology, and with the dynamicism of Freud [4] and Adler [1]. This fusion or synthesis may arbitrarily be called a "general-dynamic" theory.

It is far easier to perceive and to criticize the aspects in motivation theory than to remedy them. Mostly this is because of the very serious lack of sound data in this area. I conceive this lack of sound facts to be due primarily to the absence of a valid theory of motivation. The present theory then must be considered to be a suggested program or framework for future research and must stand or fall, not so much on facts available or evidence presented, as upon researches yet to be done, researches suggested perhaps, by the questions raised in this paper.

II. THE BASIC NEEDS

The "Physiological" Needs. The needs that are usually taken as the starting point for motivation theory are the so-called physiological drives. Two recent lines of research make it necessary to revise our customary notions about these needs, first, the development of the concept of homeostasis, and second, the finding that appetites (preferential choices among foods) are a fairly efficient indication of actual needs or lacks in the body.

Homeostasis refers to the body's automatic efforts to maintain a constant, normal state of the blood stream. Cannon [2] has described this process for (1) the water content of the blood, (2) salt content, (3) sugar content, (4) protein content, (5) fat content, (6) calcium content, (7) oxygen content, (8) constant hydrogen-ion level (acid-base balance) and (9) constant temperature of the blood. Obviously this list can be extended to include other minerals, the hormones, vitamins, etc.

Young in a recent article [21] has summarized the work on appetite in its relation to body needs. If the body lacks some chemical, the individual will tend to develop a specific appetite or partial hunger for that food element. . . .

It should be pointed out again that any of the physiological needs and the consummatory behavior involved with them serve as channels for all sorts of other needs as well. That is to say, the person who thinks he is hungry may actually be seeking more for comfort, or dependence, than for vitamins or proteins. Conversely, it is possible to satisfy the hunger need in part by other activities such as drinking water or smoking cigarettes. In other words, relatively isolable as these physiological needs are, they are not completely so.

Undoubtedly these physiological needs are the most prepotent of all needs. What this means specifically is that, in the human being who is missing everything in life in an extreme fashion, it is most likely that the major motivation would be the physiological needs rather than any others. A person who is lacking food, safety, love, and esteem would most probably hunger for food more strongly than for anything else.

If all the needs are unsatisfied, and the organism is then dominated by the physiological needs, all other needs may become simply nonexistent or be pushed into the background. . . . For the man who is extremely and dangerously hungry, no other interests exist but food. He dreams food, he remembers food, he thinks about food, he emotes only about food, he perceives only food and he wants only food. The more subtle determinants that ordinarily fuse with the physiological drives in organizing even feeding, drinking or sexual behavior, may not be so completely overwhelmed as to allow us to speak at this time (but *only* at this time) of pure hunger drive and behavior, with the one unqualified aim of relief.

Another peculiar characteristic of the human organism when it is dominated by a certain need is that the whole philosophy of the future tends also to change. For our chronically and extremely hungry man, Utopia can be defined very simply as a place where there is plenty of food. He tends to think that, if only he is guaranteed food for the rest of his life, he will be perfectly happy and will never want anything more. Life itself tends to be defined in terms of eating. Anything else will be defined as unimportant. Freedom, love, community feeling, respect, philosophy, may all be waved aside as fripperies which are useless since they fail to fill the stomach. Such a man may fairly be said to live by bread alone.

It cannot possibly be denied that such things are true but their *generality* can be denied. Emergency conditions are, almost by definition, rare in the normally functioning peaceful society. . . .

At once other (and "higher") needs emerge and these, rather than physiological hungers, dominate the organism. And when these in turn are satisfied, again new (and still "higher") needs emerge and so on. This is what we mean by saying that the basic human needs are organized into a hierarchy of relative prepotency.

One main implication of this phrasing is that gratification becomes as important a concept as deprivation in motivation theory, for it releases the organism from the domination of a relatively more physiological need, permitting thereby the emergence of other more social goals. The physiological needs, along with their partial goals, when chronically gratified cease to exist as active determinants or organizers of behavior. They now exist only in a potential fashion in the sense that they may emerge again to dominate the organism if they are thwarted. But a want that is satisfied is no longer a want. The organism is dominated and its behavior organized only by unsatisfied needs. If hunger is satisfied, it becomes unimportant in the current dynamics of the individual. . . .

The Safety Needs. If the physiological needs are relatively well gratified, there then emerges a new set of needs, which we may categorize roughly as the safety needs.

All that has been said of the physiological needs is equally true, although in lesser degree, of these desires. The organism may equally well be wholly dominated by them. They may serve as the almost exclusive organizers of behavior, recruiting all the capacities of the organism in their service, and we may then fairly describe the whole organism as a safety-seeking mechanism. Again we may say of the receptors, the effectors, of the intellect and the other capacities that they are primarily safety-seeking tools. Again, as in the hungry man, we find that the dominating goal is a strong determinant not only of his current world-outlook and philosophy but also of his philosophy of the future. Practically everything looks less important than safety (even sometimes the physiological needs which being satisfied, are now underestimated). A man, in this state, if it is extreme enough and chronic enough, may be characterized as living almost for safety alone.

Although in this paper we are interested primarily in the needs of the adult, we can approach an understanding of his safety needs perhaps more efficiently by observation of infants and children, in whom these needs are much more simple and obvious. One reason for the clearer appearance of the threat or danger reaction in infants, is that they do not inhibit this reaction at all, whereas adults in our society have been taught to inhibit it at all costs. Thus even when adults do feel their safety threatened we may not be able to see this on the surface. Infants will react in a total fashion and as if they were endangered, if they are disturbed or dropped suddenly, startled by loud noises, flashing light, or other unusual sensory stimulation, by rough handling, by general loss of support in the mother's arms, or by inadequate support.[1]

In infants we can also see a much more direct reaction to bodily illnesses of various kinds. Sometimes these illnesses seem to be immediately and *per se* threatening and seem to make the child feel unsafe. For instance, vomiting, colic or other sharp pains seem to make the child look at the whole world in a different way. At such a moment of pain, it may be postulated that, for the child, the appearance of the whole world suddenly changes from sunniness to darkness, so to speak, and becomes a place in which anything at all might happen, in which previously stable things have suddenly become unstable. Thus a child who because of some bad food is taken ill may, for a day or two, develop fear, nightmares, and a need for protection and reassurance never seen in him before his illness.

Another indication of the child's need for safety is his preference for some kind of undisrupted routine or rhythm. He seems to want a predictable, orderly world. For instance, injustice, unfairness, or inconsistency in the parents seems to make a child feel anxious and unsafe. This attitude may be not so much because of the injustice *per se* or any particular pains involved, but rather because this treatment threatens to make the world look unreliable, or unsafe, or unpredictable. Young children seem to thrive better under a system which has at least a skeletal outline of rigidity, in which there is a schedule of a kind, some sort of routine, something that can be counted upon, not only for the present but also far into the future. Perhaps one could express this more accurately by saying that the child needs an organized world rather than an unorganized or unstructured one. . . .

From these and similar observations, we may generalize and say that the average child in our society generally prefers a safe, orderly, predictable, organized world, which he can count on, and in which unexpected, unmanageable or other dangerous things do not happen, and in which, in any case, he has all-powerful parents who protect and shield him from harm.

That these reactions may so easily be observed in children is in a way a proof of the fact that children in our society, feel too unsafe (or, in a word, are badly brought up). Children who are reared in an unthreatening, loving family do *not* ordinarily react as we have described above [17]. In such children the danger reactions are apt to come

mostly to objects or situations that adults too would consider dangerous.[2]

The healthy, normal, fortunate adult in our culture is largely satisfied in his safety needs. The peaceful, smoothly running, "good" society ordinarily makes its members feel safe enough from wild animals, extremes of temperature, criminals, assault and murder, tyranny, etc. Therefore, in a very real sense, he no longer has any safety needs as active motivators. Just as a sated man no longer feels hungry, a safe man no longer feels endangered. If we wish to see these needs directly and clearly we must turn to neurotic or near-neurotic individuals, and to the economic and social underdogs. In between these extremes, we can perceive the expressions of safety needs only in such phenomena as, for instance, the common preference for a job with tenure and protection, the desire for a savings account, and for insurance of various kinds (medical, dental, unemployment, disability, old age).

Other broader aspects of the attempt to seek safety and stability in the world are seen in the very common preference for familiar rather than unfamiliar things, or for the known rather than the unknown. The tendency to have some religion or world-philosophy that organizes the universe and the men in it into some sort of satisfactorily coherent, meaningful whole is also in part motivated by safety-seeking. Here too we may list science and philosophy in general as partially motivated by the safety needs (we shall see later that there are also other motivations to scientific, philosophical or religious endeavor).

Otherwise the need for safety is seen as an active and dominant mobilizer of the organism's resources only in emergencies, *e.g.*, war, disease, natural catastrophes, crime waves, societal disorganization, neurosis, brain injury, chronically bad situation. . . .

The neurosis in which the search for safety takes its clearest form is in the compulsive-obsessive neurosis. Compulsive-obsessives try frantically to order and stabilize the world so that no unmanageable, unexpected or unfamiliar dangers will ever appear [14]. They hedge themselves about with all sorts of ceremonials, rules and formulas so that every possible contingency may be provided for and so that no new contingencies may appear. They are much like the brain injured cases, described by Goldstein [6], who manage to maintain their equilibrium by avoiding everything unfamiliar and strange and by ordering their restricted world in such a neat, disciplined, orderly fashion that everything in the world can be counted upon. . . .

The Love Needs. If both the physiological and the safety needs are fairly well gratified, then there will emerge the love and affection and belongingness needs, and the whole cycle already described will repeat itself with this new center. Now the person will feel keenly, as never before, the absence of friends, or a sweetheart, or a wife, or children. He will hunger for affectionate relations with people in general, namely, for a place in his group, and he will strive with great intensity to achieve this goal. He will want to attain such a place more than anything else in the world and may even forget that once, when he was hungry, he sneered at love. . . .

One thing that must be stressed at this point is that love is not synonymous with sex. Sex may be studied as a purely physiological need. Ordinarily sexual behavior is multi-determined, that is to say, determined not only by sexual but also by other needs chief among which are the love and affection needs. Also not to be overlooked is the fact that the love needs involve both giving *and* receiving love.[3]

The Esteem Needs. All people in our society (with a few pathological exceptions) have a need or desire for a stable, firmly based, (usually) high evaluation of themselves, for self-respect, or self-esteem, and for the esteem of others. By firmly based self-esteem, we mean that which is soundly based upon real capacity, achievement and respect from others. These needs may be classified into two subsidiary sets. These are,

first, the desire for strength, for achievement, for adequacy, for confidence in the face of the world, and for independence and freedom.[4] Secondly, we have what we may call the desire for reputation or prestige (defining it as respect or esteem from other people), recognition, attention, importance or appreciation.[5] These needs have been relatively stressed by Alfred Adler and his followers, and have been relatively neglected by Freud and the psychoanalysts. More and more today however there is appearing widespread appreciation of their central importance.

Satisfaction of the self-esteem need leads to feelings of self-confidence, worth, strength, capability and adequacy of being useful and necessary in the world. But thwarting of these needs produces feelings of inferiority, of weakness and of helplessness. These feelings in turn give rise to either basic discouragement or else compensatory or neurotic trends. An appreciation of the necessity of basic self-confidence and an understanding of how helpless people are without it, can be easily gained from a study of severe traumatic neurosis [8].[6]

The Need for Self-Actualization. Even if all these needs are satisfied, we may still often (if not always) expect that a new discontent and restlessness will soon develop, unless the individual is doing what he is fitted for. A musician must make music, an artist must paint, a poet must write, if he is to be ultimately happy. What a man can be, he must be. This need we may call self-actualization.

This term, first coined by Kurt Goldstein, is being used in this paper in a much more specific and limited fashion. It refers to the desire for self-fulfillment, namely, to the tendency for him to become actualized in what he is potentially. This tendency might be phrased as the desire to become more and more what one is, to become everything that one is capable of becoming.

The specific form that these needs will take will of course vary greatly from person to person. In one individual it may take the form of the desire to be an ideal mother, in another it may be expressed athletically, and in still another it may be expressed in painting pictures or in inventions. It is not necessarily a creative urge although in people who have any capacities for creation it will take this form.

The clear emergence of these needs rests upon prior satisfaction of the physiological, safety, love and esteem needs. We shall call people who are satisfied in these needs, basically satisfied people, and it is from these that we may expect the fullest (and healthiest) creativeness.[7] Since, in our society, basically satisfied people are the exception, we do not know much about self-actualization, either experimentally or clinically. It remains a challenging problem for research.

The Preconditions for the Basic Need Satisfactions. There are certain conditions which are immediate prerequisites for the basic need satisfactions. Danger to these is reacted to almost as if it were a direct danger to the basic needs themselves. Such conditions as freedom to speak, freedom to do what one wishes so long as no harm is done to others, freedom to express one's self, freedom to investigate and seek for information, freedom to defend one's self, justice, fairness, honesty, orderliness in the group are examples of such preconditions for basic need satisfactions. Thwarting in these freedoms will be reacted to with a threat or emergency response. These conditions are not ends in themselves but they are *almost* so since they are so closely related to the basic needs, which are apparently the only ends in themselves. These conditions are defended because without them the basic satisfactions are quite impossible, or at least, very severely endangered.

If we remember that the cognitive capacities (perceptual, intellectual, learning) are a set of adjustive tools, which have, among other functions, that of satisfaction of our basic needs, then it is clear that any danger to them, any deprivation or blocking of their free use, must also be indirectly threatening to the basic needs themselves. Such a state-

ment is a partial solution of the general problems of curiosity, the search for knowledge, truth and wisdom, and the ever-persistent urge to solve the cosmic mysteries.

We must therefore introduce another hypothesis and speak of degrees of closeness to the basic needs, for we have already pointed out that *any* conscious desires (partial goals) are more or less important as they are more or less close to the basic needs. The same statement may be made for various behavior acts. An act is psychologically important if it contributes directly to satisfaction of basic needs. The less directly it so contributes, or the weaker this contribution is, the less important this act must be conceived to be from the point of view of dynamic psychology. A similar statement may be made for the various defense or coping mechanisms. Some are very directly related to the protection or attainment of the basic needs, others are only weakly and distantly related. Indeed if we wished, we could speak of more basic and less basic defense mechanisms, and then affirm that danger to the more basic defenses is more threatening than danger to less basic defenses (always remembering that this is so only because of their relationship to the basic needs). . . .

III. FURTHER CHARACTERISTICS OF THE BASIC NEEDS

The Degree of Fixity of the Hierarchy of Basic Needs. We have spoken so far as if this hierarchy were a fixed order but actually it is not nearly as rigid as we may have implied. It is true that most of the people with whom we have worked have seemed to have these basic needs in about the order that has been indicated. However, there have been a number of exceptions.

(1) There are some people in whom, for instance, self-esteem seems to be more important than love. This most common reversal in the hierarchy is usually due to the development of the notion that the person who is most likely to be loved is a strong or powerful person, one who inspires respect

or fear, and who is self-confident or aggressive. Therefore such people who lack love and seek it, may try hard to put on a front of aggressive, confident behavior. But essentially they seek high self-esteem and its behavior expressions more as a means-to-an-end than for its own sake; they seek selfassertion for the sake of love rather than for self-esteem itself.

(2) There are other, apparently innately creative people in whom the drive to creativeness seems to be more important than any other counter-determinant. Their creativeness might appear not as self-actualization released by basic satisfaction, but in spite of lack of basic satisfaction.

(3) In certain people the level of aspiration may be permanently deadened or lowered. That is to say, the less prepotent goals may simply be lost, and may disappear forever, so that the person who has experienced life at a very low level, i.e., chronic unemployment, may continue to be satisfied for the rest of his life if only he can get enough food.

(4) The so-called "psychopathic personality" is another example of permanent loss of the love needs. These are people who, according to the best data available [9], have been starved for love in the earliest months of their lives and have simply lost forever the desire and the ability to give and to receive affection (as animals lose sucking or pecking reflexes that are not exercised soon enough after birth).

(5) Another cause of reversal of the hierarchy is that when a need has been satisfied for a long time, this need may be underevaluated. . . .

(6) Another partial explanation of *apparent* reversals is seen in the fact that we have been talking about the hierarchy of prepotency in terms of consciously felt wants or desires rather than behavior. Looking at behavior itself may give us the wrong impression. What we have claimed is that the person will *want* the more basic of two needs when deprived in both. There is no necessary implication here that he will act upon his desires. Let us say again that there

are many determinants of behavior other than the needs and desires.

(7) Perhaps more important than all these exceptions are the ones that involve ideals, high social standards, high values and the like. With such values people become martyrs; they will give up everything for the sake of a particular ideal, or value. These people may be understood, at least in part, by reference to one basic concept (or hypothesis) which may be called "increased frustration-tolerance through early gratification." People who have been satisfied in their basic needs throughout their lives, particularly in their earlier years, seem to develop exceptional power to withstand present or future thwarting of these needs simply because they have strong, healthy character structure as a result of basic satisfaction. They are the "strong" people who can easily weather disagreement or opposition, who can swim against the stream of public opinion and who can stand up for the truth at great personal cost. It is just the ones who have loved and been well loved, and who have had many deep friendships who can hold out against hatred, rejection or persecution.

I say all this in spite of the fact that there is a certain amount of sheer habituation which is also involved in any full discussion of frustration-tolerance. For instance, it is likely that those persons who have been accustomed to relative starvation for a long time, are partially enabled thereby to withstand food deprivation. What sort of balance must be made between these two tendencies, of habituation on the one hand, and of past satisfaction breeding present frustration-tolerance on the other hand, remains to be worked out by further research. Meanwhile we may assume that they are both operative, side by side, since they do not contradict each other. In respect to this phenomenon of increased frustration-tolerance, it seems probable that the most important gratifications come in the first two years of life. That is to say, people who have been made secure and strong in the earliest years, tend to remain secure and strong thereafter in the face of whatever threatens.

Degrees of Relative Satisfaction. So far, our theoretical discussion may have given the impression that these five sets of needs are somehow in a step-wise, all-or-none relationship to each other. We have spoken in such terms as the following: "If one need is satisfied, then another emerges." This statement might give the false impression that a need must be satisfied 100 per cent before the next need emerges. In actual fact, most members of our society who are normal, are partially satisfied in all their basic needs and partially unsatisfied in all their basic needs at the same time. A more realistic description of the hierarchy would be in terms of decreasing percentages of satisfaction as we go upon the hierarchy of prepotency. For instance, if I may assign arbitrary figures for the sake of illustration, it is as if the average citizen is satisfied perhaps 85 per cent in his physiological needs, 70 per cent in his safety needs, 50 per cent in his love needs, 40 per cent in his self-esteem needs, and 10 per cent in his self-actualization needs.

As for the concept of emergence of a new need after satisfaction of the prepotent need, this emergence is not a sudden, saltatory phenomenon but rather a gradual emergence by slow degrees from nothingness. For instance, if prepotent need A is satisfied only 10 per cent then need B may not be visible at all. However, as this need A becomes satisfied 25 per cent, need B may emerge 5 per cent, as need A becomes satisfied 75 per cent need B may emerge 90 per cent, and so on.

Unconscious Character of Needs. These needs are neither necessarily conscious nor unconscious. On the whole, however, in the average person, they are more often unconscious rather than conscious. . . .

Cultural Specificity and Generality of Needs. This classification of basic needs makes some attempt to take account of the relative unity behind the superficial differences in specific desires from one culture to another. Certainly in any particular culture an individual's conscious motivational content will usually be extremely different from the conscious motivational content of an individual in another society. However, it is the common experience of anthropologists that people, even in different societies, are much more alike than we would think from our first contact with them, and that as we know them better we seem to find more and more of this commonness. . . .

Multiple Motivations of Behavior. These needs must be understood *not* to be *exclusive* or single determiners of certain kinds of behavior. An example may be found in any behavior that seems to be physiologically motivated, such as eating, or sexual play or the like. The clinical psychologists have long since found that any behavior may be a channel through which flow various determinants. Or to say it in another way, most behavior is multi-motivated. Within the sphere of motivational determinants any behavior tends to be determined by several or *all* of the basic needs simultaneously rather than by only one of them. The latter would be more an exception than the former. Eating may be partially for the sake of filling the stomach, and partially for the sake of comfort and amelioration of other needs. One may make love not only for pure sexual release, but also to convince one's self of one's masculinity, or to make a conquest, to feel powerful, or to win more basic affection. As an illustration, I may point out that it would be possible (theoretically if not practically) to analyze a single act of an individual and see in it the expression of his physiological needs, his safety needs, his love needs, his esteem needs and self-actualization. This contrasts sharply with the more naive brand of trait psychology in which one trait or one motive accounts for a certain kind of act, *i.e.*, an aggressive act is traced solely to a trait of aggressiveness.

Multiple Determinants of Behavior.
Not all behavior is determined by the basic needs. We might even say that not all behavior is motivated. There are many determinants of behavior other than motives.[8] For instance, one other important class of determinants is the so-called "field" determinants. Theoretically, at least, behavior may be determined completely by the field, or even by specific isolated external stimuli, as in association of ideas, or certain conditioned reflexes. If in response to the stimulus word "table," I immediately perceive a memory image of a table, this response certainly has nothing to do with my basic needs.

Secondly, we may call attention again to the concept of "degree of closeness to the basic needs" or "degree of motivation." Some behavior is highly motivated, other behavior is only weakly motivated. Some is not motivated at all (but all behavior is determined).

Another important point[9] is that there is a basic difference between expressive behavior and coping behavior (functional striving, purposive goal seeking). An expressive behavior does not try to do anything; it is simply a reflection of the personality. A stupid man behaves stupidly, not because he wants to, or tries to, or is motivated to, but simply because he *is* what he is. The same is true when I speak in a bass voice rather than tenor or soprano. The random movements of a healthy child, the smile on the face of a happy man even when he is alone, the springiness of the healthy man's walk, and the erectness of his carriage are other examples of expressive, non-functional behavior. Also the *style* in which a man carries out almost all his behavior, motivated as well as unmotivated, is often expressive.

We may then ask, is *all* behavior expressive or reflective of the character structure? The answer is "No." Rote, habitual, automatized, or conventional behavior may or may not be expressive. The same is true for most "stimulus-bound" behaviors.

It is finally necessary to stress that expressiveness of behavior, and goal-directedness of behavior are not mutually exclusive categories. Average behavior is usually both.

Goals as Centering Principle in Motivation Theory. It will be observed that the basic principle in our classification has been neither the instigation nor the motivated behavior but rather the functions, effects, purposes, or goals of the behavior. It has been proven sufficiently by various people that this is the most suitable point for centering any motivation theory.[10]

Animal- and Human-Centering. This theory starts with the human being rather than any lower and presumably "simpler" animal. Too many of the findings that have been made in animals have been proven to be true for animals but not for the human being. There is no reason whatsoever why we should start with animals in order to study human motivation. . . .

Motivation and the Theory of Psychopathogenesis. The conscious motivational content of everyday life has, according to the foregoing, been conceived to be relatively important or unimportant accordingly as it is more or less closely related to the basic goals. A desire for an ice cream cone might actually be an indirect expression of a desire for love. If it is, then this desire for the ice cream cone becomes extremely important motivation. If however the ice cream is simply something to cool the mouth with, or a casual appetitive reaction, then the desire is relatively unimportant. Everyday conscious desires are to be regarded as symptoms, as *surface indicators of more basic needs*. If we were to take these superficial desires at their face value we would find ourselves in a state of complete confusion which could never be resolved, since we would be dealing seriously with symptoms rather than with what lay behind the symptoms.

Thwarting of unimportant desires produces no psychopathological results; thwarting of a basically important need does produce such results. Any theory of psychopathogenesis must then be based on a sound theory of motivation. A conflict or a frustration is not necessarily pathogenic. It becomes so only when it threatens or thwarts the basic needs, or partial needs that are closely related to the basic needs [10].

The Role of Gratified Needs. It has been pointed out above several times that our needs usually emerge only when more prepotent needs have been gratified. Thus gratification has an important role in motivation theory. Apart from this, however, needs cease to play an active determining or organizing role as soon as they are gratified.

What this means is that, *e.g.*, a basically satisfied person no longer has the needs for esteem, love, safety, etc. . . .

It is such considerations as these that suggest the bold postulation that a man who is thwarted in any of his basic needs may fairly be envisaged simply as a sick man. This is a fair parallel to our designation as "sick" of the man who lacks vitamins or minerals. Who is to say that a lack of love is less important than a lack of vitamins? Since we know the pathogenic effects of love starvation, who is to say that we are invoking value-questions in an unscientific or illegitimate way, any more than the physician does who diagnoses and treats pellagra or scurvy? If I were permitted this usage, I should then say simply that a healthy man is primarily motivated by his needs to develop and actualize his fullest potentialities and capacities. If a man has any other basic needs in any active, chronic sense, then he is simply an unhealthy man. He is as surely sick as if he had suddenly developed a strong salt-hunger or calcium hunger.[11]

If this statement seems unusual or paradoxical the reader may be assured that this is only one among many such paradoxes that will appear as we revise our ways of looking at man's deeper motivations. When we ask what man wants of life, we deal with his very essence.

IV. SUMMARY

(1) There are at least five sets of goals, which we may call basic needs. These are briefly physiological, safety, love, esteem, and self-actualization. In addition, we are motivated by the desire to achieve or maintain the various conditions upon which these basic satisfactions rest and by certain more intellectual desires.

(2) These basic goals are related to each other, being arranged in a hierarchy of prepotency. This means that the most prepotent goal will monopolize consciousness and will tend of itself to organize the recruitment of the various capacities of the organism. The less prepotent needs are minimized, even forgotten or denied. But when a need is fairly well satisfied, the next prepotent ("higher") need emerges, in turn to dominate the conscious life and to serve as the center of organization of behavior, since gratified needs are not active motivators.

Thus man is a perpetually wanting animal. Ordinarily the satisfaction of these wants is not altogether mutually exclusive, but only tends to be. The average member of our society is most often partially satisfied and partially unsatisfied in all of his wants. The hierarchy principle is usually empirically observed in terms of increasing percentages of nonsatisfaction as we go up the hierarchy. Reversals of the average order of the hierarchy are sometimes observed. Also it has been observed that an individual may permanently lose the higher wants in the hierarchy under special conditions. There are not only ordinarily multiple motivations for usual behavior, but in addition many determinants other than motives.

(3) Any thwarting or possibility of thwarting of these basic human goals, or danger to the defenses which protect them, or to the conditions upon which they rest, is considered to be a psychological threat. With a few exceptions, all psychopathology may be partially traced to such threats. A basically thwarted man may actually be defined as a "sick" man, if we wish.

(4) It is such basic threats which bring about the general emergency reactions. . . .

NOTES

1. As the child grows up, sheer knowledge and familiarity as well as better motor development make these "dangers" less and less dangerous and more and more manageable. Throughout life it may be said that one of the main conative functions of education is this neutralizing of apparent dangers through knowledge, e.g., I am not afraid of thunder because I know something about it.

2. A "test battery" for safety might be confronting the child with a small exploding firecracker, or with a bewhiskered face, having the mother leave the room, putting him upon a high ladder, a hypodermic injection, having a mouse crawl up to him, etc. Of course I cannot seriously recommend the deliberate use of such "tests" for they might very well harm the child being tested. But these and similar situations come up by the score in the child's ordinary day-to-day living and may be observed. There is no reason why these stimuli should not be used with, for example, young chimpanzees.

3. For further details see [12].

4. Whether or not this particular desire is universal we do not know. The crucial question, especially important today, is "Will men who are enslaved and dominated, inevitably feel dissatisfied and rebellious?" We may assume on the basis of commonly known clinical data that a man who has known true freedom (not paid for by giving up safety and security but rather built on the basis of adequate safety and security) will not willingly or easily allow his freedom to be taken away from him. But we do not know that this is true for the person born into slavery. The events of the next decade should give us our answer. See discussion of this problem in [5].

5. Perhaps the desire for prestige and respect from others is subsidiary to the desire for self-esteem or confidence in oneself. Observation of children seems to indicate that this is so, but clinical data give no clear support for such a conclusion.

6. For more extensive discussion of normal self-esteem, as well as for reports of various researchers, see [11].

7. Clearly creative behavior, like painting, is like any other behavior in having multiple determinants. It may be seen in "innately creative" people whether they are satisfied or not, happy or unhappy, hungry or sated. Also it is clear that creative activity may be compensatory, ameliorative or purely economic. It is my impression (as yet unconfirmed) that it is possible to distinguish the artistic and intellectual products of basically satisfied people from those of basically unsatisfied people by inspection alone. In any case, here too we must distinguish, in a dynamic fashion, the overt behavior itself from its various motivations or purposes.

8. I am aware that many psychologists and psychoanalysts use the term "motivated" and "determined" synonymously, e.g., Freud. But I consider this an obfuscating usage. Sharp distinctions are necessary for clarity of thought, and precision in experimentation.

9. To be discussed fully in a subsequent publication.

10. The interested reader is referred to the very excellent discussion of this point in Murray's *Explorations in Personality* [15].

11. If we were to use the word "sick" in this way, we should then also have to face squarely the relations of man to his society. One clear implication of our definition would be that (1) since a man is to be called sick who is basically thwarted, and (2) since such basic thwarting is made possible ultimately only by forces outside the individual, then (3) sickness in the individual must come ultimately from a sickness in the society. The "good" or healthy society would then be defined as one that permitted man's highest purposes to emerge by satisfying all his prepotent basic needs.

REFERENCES

1. Adler, A. *Social interest*. London: Faber & Faber, 1938.

2. Cannon, W. B. *Wisdom of the body*. New York: Norton, 1932.

3. Freud, A. *The ego and the mechanisms of defense*. London: Hogarth, 1937.

4. Freud, S. *New introductory lectures on psychoanalysis*. New York: Norton, 1933.

5. Fromm, E. *Escape from freedom*. New York: Farrar and Rinehart, 1941.

6. Goldstein, K. *The organism*. New York: American Book Co., 1939.

7. Horney, K. *The neurotic personality of our time*. New York: Norton, 1937.

8. Kardiner, A. *The traumatic neuroses of war*. New York: Hoeber, 1941.

9. Levy, D. M. Primary effect of hunger. *Amer. J. Psychiat.*, 1937, 94, 643–652.

10. Maslow, A. H. Conflict, frustration, and the theory of threat. *J. abnorm. (soc.) Psychol.*, 1943, 38, 81–86.

11. ———. Dominance, personality and social behavior in women. *J. soc. Psychol.*, 1939, 10, 3–39.

12. ———. The dynamics of psychological security-insecurity. *Character & Pers.*, 1942, 10, 331–344.

13. ———. A preface to motivation theory. *Psychosomatic Med.*, 1943, 5, 85–92.

14. ———, & Mittlemann, B. *Principles of abnormal psychology*. New York: Harper & Bros., 1941.

15. Murray, H. A., *et al. Explorations in personality*. New York: Oxford University Press, 1938.

16. Plant, J. *Personality and the cultural pattern*. New York: Commonwealth Fund, 1937.

17. Shirley, M. Children's adjustments to a strange situation. *J. abnorm. (soc.) Psychol.*, 1942, 37, 201–217.

18. Tolman, E. C. *Purposive behavior in animals and men*. New York: Century, 1932.

19. Wertheimer, M. Unpublished lectures at the New School for Social Research.

20. Young, P. T. *Motivation of behavior*. New York: Wiley, 1936.

21. ———. The experimental analysis of appetite. *Psychol. Bull.*, 1941, 38, 129–164.

17

The Human Side of Enterprise

Douglas Murray McGregor

It has become trite to say that industry has the fundamental know-how to utilize physical science and technology for the material benefit of mankind, and that we must now learn how to utilize the social sciences to make our human organizations truly effective.

To a degree, the social sciences today are in a position like that of the physical sciences with respect to atomic energy in the thirties. We know that past conceptions of the nature of man are inadequate and, in many ways, incorrect. We are becoming quite certain that, under proper conditions, unimagined resources of creative human energy could become available within the organizational setting. . . .

MANAGEMENT'S TASK: THE CONVENTIONAL VIEW

The conventional conception of management's task in harnessing human energy to organizational requirements can be stated broadly in terms of three propositions. In order to avoid the complications introduced by a label, let us call this set of propositions "Theory X":

1. Management is responsible for organizing the elements of productive enterprise—money, materials, equipment, people—in the interest of economic ends.
2. With respect to people, this is a process of directing their efforts, motivating them, controlling their actions, modifying their behavior to fit the needs of the organization.
3. Without this active intervention by management, people would be passive—even resistant—to organizational needs. They must therefore be persuaded, rewarded, punished, controlled—their activities must be directed. This is management's task. We often sum it up by saying that management consists of getting things done through other people.

Behind this conventional theory there are several additional beliefs—less explicit, but widespread:

4. The average man is by nature indolent—he works as little as possible.
5. He lacks ambition, dislikes responsibility, prefers to be led.
6. He is inherently self-centered, indifferent to organizational needs.
7. He is by nature resistant to change.
8. He is gullible, not very bright, the ready dupe of the charlatan and the demagogue.

The human side of economic enterprise today is fashioned from propositions and beliefs such as these. Conventional organization structures and managerial policies, practices, and programs reflect these assumptions.

In accomplishing its task—with these assumptions as guides—management has conceived of a range of possibilities.

At one extreme, management can be "hard" or "strong." The methods for directing behavior involve coercion and threat (usually disguised), close supervision, tight controls over behavior. At the other extreme, management can be "soft" or "weak." The methods for directing behavior involve being permissive, satisfying people's

Source: Management Review (November 1957). © 1957 by the American Management Association, New York. Reprinted by permission. All rights reserved.
Note: This article is based on an address by Dr. McGregor before the Fifth Anniversary Convocation of the MIT School of Industrial Management.

demands, achieving harmony. Then they will be tractable, accept direction.

This range has been fairly completely explored during the past half century, and management has learned some things from the exploration. There are difficulties in the "hard" approach. Force breeds counterforces: restriction of output, antagonism, militant unionism, subtle but effective sabotage of management objectives. This "hard" approach is especially difficult during times of full employment.

There are also difficulties in the "soft" approach. It leads frequently to the abdication of management — to harmony, perhaps, but to indifferent performance. People take advantage of the soft approach. They continually expect more but they give less and less.

Currently, the popular theme is "firm but fair." This is an attempt to gain the advantages of both the hard and the soft approaches. It is reminiscent of Teddy Roosevelt's "speak softly and carry a big stick."

IS THE CONVENTIONAL VIEW CORRECT?

. . . The social scientist does not deny that human behavior in industrial organization today is approximately what management perceives it to be. He has, in fact, observed it and studied it fairly extensively. But he is pretty sure that this behavior is *not* a consequence of man's inherent nature. It is a consequence rather of the nature of industrial organizations, of management philosophy, policy, and practice. The conventional approach of Theory X is based on mistaken notions of what is cause and what is effect.

Perhaps the best way to indicate why the conventional approach of management is inadequate is to consider the subject of motivation.

PHYSIOLOGICAL NEEDS

Man is a wanting animal — as soon as one of his needs is satisfied, another appears in

its place. This process is unending. It continues from birth to death. . . .

A *satisfied need is not a motivator of behavior!* This is a fact of profound significance that is regularly ignored in the conventional approach to the management of people. Consider your own need for air: Except as you are deprived of it, it has no appreciable motivating effect upon your behavior.

SAFETY NEEDS

When the physiological needs are reasonably satisfied, needs at the next higher level begin to dominate man's behavior — to motivate him. These are called *safety needs*. They are needs for protection against danger, threat, deprivation. Some people mistakenly refer to these as needs for security. However, unless man is in a dependent relationship where he fears arbitrary deprivation, he does not demand security. The need is for the "fairest possible break." When he is confident of this, he is more than willing to take risks. But when he feels threatened or dependent, his greatest need is for guarantees, for protection, for security.

The fact needs little emphasis that, since every industrial employee is in a dependent relationship, safety needs may assume considerable importance. Arbitrary management actions, behavior which arouses uncertainty with respect to continued employment or which reflects favoritism or discrimination, unpredictable administration of policy — these can be powerful motivators of the safety needs in the employment relationship *at every level*, from worker to vice president.

SOCIAL NEEDS

When man's physiological needs are satisfied and he is no longer fearful about his physical welfare, his *social needs* become important motivators of his behavior — needs for belonging, for association, for acceptance by his fellows, for giving and receiving friendship and love.

Management knows today of the existence of these needs, but it often assumes quite wrongly that they represent a threat to the organization. Many studies have demonstrated that the tightly knit, cohesive work group may, under proper conditions, be far more effective than an equal number of separate individuals in achieving organization goals.

Yet management, fearing group hostility to its own objectives, often goes to considerable lengths to control and direct human efforts in ways that are inimical to the natural "groupiness" of human beings. When man's social needs—and perhaps his safety needs, too—are thus thwarted, he behaves in ways which tend to defeat organizational objectives. He becomes resistant, antagonistic, uncooperative. But this behavior is a consequence, not a cause.

EGO NEEDS

Above the social needs—in the sense that they do not become motivators until lower needs are reasonably satisfied—are the needs of greatest significance to management and to man himself. They are the *egoistic needs,* and they are of two kinds:

1. Those needs that relate to one's self-esteem—needs for self-confidence, for independence, for achievement, for competence, for knowledge.
2. Those needs that relate to one's reputation—needs for status, for recognition, for appreciation, for the deserved respect of one's fellows.

Unlike the lower needs, these are rarely satisfied: man seeks indefinitely for more satisfaction of these needs once they have become important to him. But they do not appear in any significant way until physiological, safety, and social needs are all reasonably satisfied.

The typical industrial organization offers few opportunities for the satisfaction of these egoistic needs to people at lower

levels in the hierarchy. The conventional methods of organizing work, particularly in mass-production industries, give little heed to these aspects of human motivation. If the practices of scientific management were deliberately calculated to thwart these needs, they could hardly accomplish this purpose better than they do.

SELF-FULFILLMENT NEEDS

Finally—a capstone, as it were, on the hierarchy of man's needs—there are what we may call the *needs for self-fulfillment.* These are the needs for realizing one's own potentialities, for continued self-development, for being creative in the broadest sense of that term.

It is clear that the conditions of modern life give only limited opportunity for these relatively weak needs to obtain expression. The deprivation most people experience with respect to other lower-level needs diverts their energies into the struggle to satisfy *those* needs, and the needs for self-fulfillment remain dormant.

MANAGEMENT AND MOTIVATION

We recognize readily enough that a man suffering from a severe-dietary deficiency is sick. The deprivation of physiological needs has behavioral consequences. The same is true—although less well recognized—of deprivations of higher-level needs. The man whose needs for safety, association, independence, or status are thwarted is sick just as surely as the man who has rickets. And his sickness will have behavioral consequences. We will be mistaken if we attribute his resultant passivity, his hostility, his refusal to accept responsibility to his inherent "human nature." These forms of behavior are *symptoms* of illness—of deprivation of his social and egoistic needs.

The man whose lower-level needs are satisfied is not motivated to satisfy those needs any longer. For practical purposes they exist no longer. Management often asks, "Why aren't people more productive? We pay good wages, provide good working conditions, have excellent fringe benefits and steady employment. Yet people do not seem to be willing to put forth more than minimum effort."

The fact that management has provided for these physiological and safety needs has shifted the motivational emphasis to the social and perhaps to the egoistic needs. Unless there are opportunities *at work* to satisfy these higher-level needs, people will be deprived; and their behavior will reflect this deprivation. Under such conditions, if management continues to focus its attention on physiological needs, its efforts are bound to be ineffective.

People *will* make insistent demands for more money under these conditions. It becomes more important than ever to buy the material goods and services which can provide limited satisfaction of the thwarted needs. Although money has only limited value in satisfying many higher-level needs, it can become the focus of interest if it is the *only* means available.

THE CARROT-AND-STICK APPROACH

The carrot-and-stick theory of motivation (like Newtonian physical theory) works reasonably well under certain circumstances. The *means* for satisfying man's physiological and (within limits) his safety needs can be provided or withheld by management. Employment itself is such a means, and so are wages, working conditions, and benefits. By these means the individual can be controlled so long as he is struggling for subsistence.

But the carrot-and-stick theory does not work at all once man has reached an adequate subsistence level and is motivated primarily by higher needs. Management cannot provide a man with self-respect, or with the respect of his fellows, or with the satisfaction of needs for self-fulfillment. It

can create such conditions that he is encouraged and enabled to seek such satisfactions for *himself,* or it can thwart him by failing to create those conditions.

But this creation of conditions is not "control." It is not a good device for directing behavior. And so management finds itself in an odd position. The high standard of living created by our modern technological know-how provides quite adequately for the satisfaction of physiological and safety needs. The only significant exception is where management practices have not created confidence in a "fair break"—and thus where safety needs are thwarted. But by making possible the satisfaction of low-level needs, management has deprived itself of the ability to use as motivators the devices on which conventional theory has taught it to rely—rewards, promises, incentives, or threats and other coercive devices.

The philosophy of management by direction and control—*regardless of whether it is hard or soft*—is inadequate to motivate because the human needs on which this approach relies are today unimportant motivators of behavior. Direction and control are essentially useless in motivating people whose important needs are social and egoistic. Both the hard and the soft approach fail today because they are simply irrelevant to the situation.

People, deprived of opportunities to satisfy at work the needs which are now important to them, behave exactly as we might predict—with indolence, passivity, resistance to change, lack of responsibility, willingness to follow the demagogue, unreasonable demands for economic benefits. It would seem that we are caught in a web of our own weaving.

A NEW THEORY OF MANAGEMENT

For these and many other reasons, we require a different theory of the task of managing people based on more adequate assumptions about human nature and human motivation. I am going to be so bold as to suggest the broad dimensions of such a theory. Call it "Theory Y," if you will.

1. Management is responsible for organizing the elements of productive enterprise — money, materials, equipment, people — in the interest of economic ends.
2. People are *not* by nature passive or resistant to organizational needs. They have become so as a result of experience in organizations.
3. The motivation, the potential for development, the capacity for assuming responsibility, the readiness to direct behavior toward organizational goals are all present in people. Management does not put them there. It is a responsibility of management to make it possible for people to recognize and develop these human characteristics for themselves.
4. The essential task of management is to arrange organizational conditions and methods of operation so that people can achieve their own goals *best* by directing *their own* efforts toward organizational objectives.

This is a process primarily of creating opportunities, releasing potential, removing obstacles, encouraging growth, providing guidance. It is what Peter Drucker has called "management by objectives" in contrast to "management by control." It does *not* involve the abdication of management, the absence of leadership, the lowering of standards, or the other characteristics usually associated with the "soft" approach under Theory X.

SOME DIFFICULTIES

It is no more possible to create an organization today which will be a full, effective application of this theory than it was to build an atomic power plant in 1945. There are many formidable obstacles to overcome.

The conditions imposed by conventional organization theory and by the approach of scientific management for the past half century have tied men to limited jobs which do not utilize their capabilities, have discouraged the acceptance of responsibility,

have encouraged passivity, have eliminated meaning from work. Man's habits, attitudes, expectations — his whole conception of membership in an industrial organization — have been conditioned by his experience under these circumstances.

People today are accustomed to being directed, manipulated, controlled in industrial organizations and to finding satisfaction for their social, egoistic, and self-fulfillment needs away from the job. This is true of much of management as well as of workers. Genuine "industrial citizenship" — to borrow again a term from Drucker — is a remote and unrealistic idea, the meaning of which has not even been considered by most members of industrial organizations.

Another way of saying this is that Theory X places exclusive reliance upon external control of human behavior, while Theory Y relies heavily on self-control and self-direction. It is worth noting that this difference is the difference between treating people as children and treating them as mature adults. After generations of the former, we cannot expect to shift to the latter overnight.

STEPS IN THE RIGHT DIRECTION

Before we are overwhelmed by the obstacles, let us remember that the application of theory is always slow. Progress is usually achieved in small steps. Some innovative ideas which are entirely consistent with Theory Y are today being applied with some success.

Decentralization and Delegation
These are ways of freeing people from the too-close control of conventional organization, giving them a degree of freedom to direct their own activities, to assume responsibility, and, importantly, to satisfy their egoistic needs. In this connection, the flat organization of Sears, Roebuck and Company provides an interesting example. It forces "management by objectives," since it

enlarges the number of people reporting to a manager until he cannot direct and control them in the conventional manner.

Job Enlargement

This concept, pioneered by I.B.M. and Detroit Edison, is quite consistent with Theory Y. It encourages the acceptance of responsibility at the bottom of the organization; it provides opportunities for satisfying social and egoistic needs. In fact, the reorganization of work at the factory level offers one of the more challenging opportunities for innovation consistent with Theory Y.

Participation and Consultative Management

Under proper conditions, participation and consultative management provide encouragement to people to direct their creative energies toward organizational objectives, give them some voice in decisions that affect them, provide significant opportunities for the satisfaction of social and egoistic needs. . . .

Performance Appraisal

Even a cursory examination of conventional programs of performance appraisal within the ranks of management will reveal how completely consistent they are with Theory X. In fact, most such programs tend to treat the individual as though he were a product under inspection on the assembly line.

A few companies—among them General Mills, Ansul Chemical, and General Electric—have been experimenting with approaches which involve the individual in setting "targets" or objectives *for himself* and in a *self*-evaluation of performance semiannually or annually. Of course, the superior plays an important leadership role in this process — one, in fact, which demands substantially more competence than the conventional approach. The role is, however, considerably more congenial to many managers than the role of "judge" or "inspector" which is usually forced upon them. Above all, the individual is encouraged to take a greater responsibility for planning and appraising his own contribution to organizational objectives; and the accompanying effects on egoistic and self-fulfillment needs are substantial.

APPLYING THE IDEAS

The not infrequent failure of such ideas as these to work as well as expected is often attributable to the fact that a management has "bought the idea" but applied it within the framework of Theory X and its assumptions.

Delegation is not an effective way of exercising management by control. Participation becomes a farce when it is applied as a sales gimmick or a device for kidding people into thinking they are important. Only the management that has confidence in human capacities and is itself directed toward organizational objectives rather than toward the preservation of personal power can grasp the implications of this emerging theory. Such management will find and apply successfully other innovative ideas as we move slowly toward the full implementation of a theory like Y.

THE HUMAN SIDE OF ENTERPRISE

. . . The ingenuity and the perseverance of industrial management in the pursuit of economic ends have changed many scientific and technological dreams into commonplace realities. It is now becoming clear that the application of these same talents to the human side of enterprise will not only enhance substantially these materialistic achievements, but will bring us one step closer to "the good society."

18

Groupthink: The Desperate Drive for Consensus at Any Cost

Irving L. Janis

"How could we have been so stupid?" President John F. Kennedy asked after he and a close group of advisers had blundered into the Bay of Pigs invasion. For the last two years I have been studying that question, as it applies not only to the Bay of Pigs decision-makers but also to those who led the United States into such other major fiascoes as the failure to be prepared for the attack on Pearl Harbor, the Korean War stalemate and the escalation of the Vietnam War.

Stupidity certainly is not the explanation. The men who participated in making the Bay of Pigs decision, for instance, comprised one of the greatest arrays of intellectual talent in the history of American Government—Dean Rusk, Robert McNamara, Douglas Dillon, Robert Kennedy, McGeorge Bundy, Arthur Schlesinger Jr., Allen Dulles and others.

It also seemed to me that explanations were incomplete if they concentrated only on disturbances in the behavior of each individual within a decision-making body: temporary emotional states of elation, fear, or anger that reduce a man's mental efficiency, for example, or chronic blind spots arising from a man's social prejudices or idiosyncratic biases.

I preferred to broaden the picture by looking at the fiascoes from the standpoint of group dynamics as it has been explored over the past three decades, first by the great social psychologist Kurt Lewin and later in many experimental situations by myself and other behavioral scientists. My conclusion after poring over hundreds of relevant documents—historical reports about formal group meetings and informal conversations among the members—is that the groups that committed the fiascoes were victims of what I call "groupthink."

"Groupy." In each case study, I was surprised to discover the extent to which each group displayed the typical phenomena of social conformity that are regularly encountered in studies of group dynamics among ordinary citizens. For example, some of the phenomena appear to be completely in line with findings from social-psychological experiments showing that powerful social pressures are brought to bear by the members of a cohesive group whenever a dissident begins to voice his objections to a group consensus. Other phenomena are reminiscent of the shared illusions observed in encounter groups and friendship cliques when the members simultaneously reach a peak of "groupy" feelings.

Above all, there are numerous indications pointing to the development of group norms that bolster morale at the expense of critical thinking. One of the most common norms appears to be that of remaining loyal to the group by sticking with the policies to which the group has already committed itself, even when those policies are obviously working out badly and have unintended consequences that disturb the conscience

Source: Psychology Today 5 (November 1971): 43–44, 46, 74–76. © 1971 Sussex Publishers, Inc. Reprinted with permission of *Psychology Today*.

of each member. This is one of the key characteristics of groupthink.

1984. I use the term groupthink as a quick and easy way to refer to the mode of thinking that persons engage in when *concurrence-seeking* becomes so dominant in a cohesive ingroup that it tends to override realistic appraisal of alternative courses of action. Groupthink is a term of the same order as the words in the newspeak vocabulary George Orwell used in his dismaying world of 1984. In that context, groupthink takes on an invidious connotation. Exactly such a connotation is intended, since the term refers to a deterioration in mental efficiency, reality testing and moral judgments as a result of group pressures.

The symptoms of groupthink arise when the members of decision-making groups become motivated to avoid being too harsh in their judgments of their leaders' or their colleagues' ideas. They adopt a soft line of criticism, even in their own thinking. At their meetings, all the members are amiable and seek complete concurrence on every important issue, with no bickering or conflict to spoil the cozy, "we-feeling" atmosphere.

Kill. Paradoxically, soft-headed groups are often hard-hearted when it comes to dealing with outgroups or enemies. They find it relatively easy to resort to dehumanizing solutions — they will readily authorize bombing attacks that kill large numbers of civilians in the name of the noble cause of persuading an unfriendly government to negotiate at the peace table. They are unlikely to pursue the more difficult and controversial issues that arise when alternatives to a harsh military solution come up for discussion. Nor are they inclined to raise ethical issues that carry the implication that *this fine group of ours, with its humanitarianism and its high-minded principles, might be capable of adopting a course of action that is inhumane and immoral.*

Norms. There is evidence from a number of social-psychological studies that as the members of a group feel more accepted by the others, which is a central feature of increased group cohesiveness, they display less overt conformity to group norms. Thus we would expect that the more cohesive a group becomes, the less the members will feel constrained to censor what they say out of fear of being socially punished for antagonizing the leader or any of their fellow members.

In contrast, the groupthink type of conformity tends to increase as group cohesiveness increases. Groupthink involves nondeliberate suppression of critical thoughts as a result of internalization of the group's norms, which is quite different from deliberate suppression on the basis of external threats of social punishment. The more cohesive the group, the greater the inner compulsion on the part of each member to avoid creating disunity, which inclines him to believe in the soundness of whatever proposals are promoted by the leader or by a majority of the group's members.

In a cohesive group, the danger is not so much that each individual will fail to reveal his objections to what the others propose but that he will think the proposal is a good one, without attempting to carry out a careful, critical scrutiny of the pros and cons of the alternatives. When groupthink becomes dominant, there also is considerable suppression of deviant thoughts, but it takes the form of each person's deciding that his misgivings are not relevant and should be set aside, that the benefit of the doubt regarding any lingering uncertainties should be given to the group consensus.

Stress. I do not mean to imply that all cohesive groups necessarily suffer from groupthink. All ingroups may have a mild tendency toward groupthink, displaying one or another of the symptoms from time to time, but it need not be so dominant as to influence the quality of the group's final decision. Neither do I mean to imply that there is anything necessarily inefficient or harmful about group decisions in general. On the contrary, a group whose members have properly defined roles, with traditions concerning the procedures to follow in pursuing a critical inquiry, probably is capable of making better decisions than any individual group member working alone.

The problem is that the advantages of having decisions made by groups are often lost because of powerful psychological pressures that arise when the members work closely together, share the same set of values and, above all, face a crisis situation that puts everyone under intense stress.

The main principle of groupthink, which I offer in the spirit of Parkinson's Law, is this: *The more amiability and esprit de corps there is among the members of a policy-making ingroup, the greater the danger that independent critical thinking will be replaced by groupthink, which is likely to result in irrational and dehumanizing actions directed against outgroups.*

Symptoms. In my studies of high-level governmental decision-makers, both civilian and military, I have found eight main symptoms of groupthink.

1. *Invulnerability.* Most or all of the members of the ingroup share an illusion of invulnerability that provides for them some degree of reassurance about obvious dangers and leads them to become over-optimistic and willing to take extraordinary risks. It also causes them to fail to respond to clear warnings of danger.

The Kennedy ingroup, which uncritically accepted the Central Intelligence Agency's disastrous Bay of Pigs plan, operated on the false assumption that they could keep secret the fact that the United States was responsible for the invasion of Cuba. Even after news of the plan began to leak out, their belief remained unshaken. They failed even to consider the danger that awaited them: a worldwide revulsion against the U.S.

A similar attitude appeared among the members of President Lyndon B. Johnson's ingroup, the "Tuesday Cabinet," which kept escalating the Vietnam War despite repeated setbacks and failures. "There was a belief," Bill Moyers commented after he resigned, "that if we indicated a willingness to use our power, they [the North Vietnamese] would get the message and back away from an all-out confrontation. . . . There was a confidence — it was never bragged about, it was just there — that when the chips were really down, the other people would fold."

A most poignant example of an illusion of invulnerability involves the ingroup around Admiral H. E. Kimmel, which failed to prepare for the possibility of a Japanese attack on Pearl Harbor despite repeated warnings. Informed by his intelligence chief that radio contact with Japanese aircraft carriers had been lost, Kimmel joked about it: "What, you don't know where the carriers are? Do you mean to say that they could be rounding Diamond Head (at Honolulu) and you wouldn't know it?" The carriers were in fact moving full-steam toward Kimmel's command post at the time. Laughing together about a danger signal, which labels it as a purely laughing matter, is a characteristic manifestation of groupthink.

2. *Rationale.* As we see, victims of groupthink ignore warnings; they also collectively construct rationalizations in order to discount warnings and other forms of negative feedback that, taken seriously, might lead the group members to reconsider their assumptions each time they recommit themselves to past decisions. Why did the Johnson ingroup avoid reconsidering its escalation policy when time and again the expectations on which they based their decisions turned out to be wrong? James C. Thomson, Jr., a Harvard historian who spent five years as an observing participant in both the State Department and the White House, tells us that the policymakers avoided critical discussion of their prior decisions and continually invented new rationalizations so that they could sincerely recommit themselves to defeating the North Vietnamese.

In the fall of 1964, before the bombing of North Vietnam began, some of the policymakers predicted that six weeks of air strikes would induce the North Vietnamese to seek peace talks. When someone asked, "What if they don't?" the answer was that another four weeks certainly would do the trick. . . .

3. *Morality.* Victims of groupthink believe unquestioningly in the inherent morality of their ingroup; this belief inclines the members to ignore the ethical or moral consequences of their decisions.

Evidence that this symptom is at work usually is of a negative kind—the things that are left unsaid in group meetings. At least two influential persons had doubts about the morality of the Bay of Pigs adventure. One of them, Arthur Schlesinger, Jr., presented his strong objections in a memorandum to President Kennedy and Secretary of State Rusk but suppressed them when he attended meetings of the Kennedy team. The other, Senator J. William Fulbright, was not a member of the group, but the President invited him to express his misgivings in a speech to the policymakers. However, when Fulbright finished speaking the President moved on to other agenda items without asking for reactions of the group.

David Kraslow and Stuart H. Loory, in *The Secret Search for Peace in Vietnam*, report that during 1966 President Johnson's ingroup was concerned primarily with selecting bomb targets in North Vietnam. They based their selections on four factors—the military advantage, the risk to American aircraft and pilots, the danger of forcing other countries into the fighting, and the danger of heavy civilian casualties. At their regular Tuesday luncheons, they weighed these factors the way school teachers grade examination papers, averaging them out. Though evidence on this point is scant, I suspect that the group's ritualistic adherence to a standardized procedure induced the members to feel morally justified in their destructive way of dealing with the Vietnamese people—after all, the danger of heavy civilian casualties from U.S. air strikes was taken into account on their checklists.

4. *Stereotypes.* Victims of groupthink hold stereotyped views of the leaders of enemy groups: they are so evil that genuine attempts at negotiating differences with them are unwarranted, or they are too weak or too stupid to deal effectively with whatever attempts the ingroup makes to defeat their purposes, no matter how risky the attempts are.

Kennedy's groupthinkers believed that Premier Fidel Castro's air force was so ineffectual that obsolete B-26's could knock it out completely in a surprise attack before the invasion began. They also believed that Castro's army was so weak that a small Cuban-exile brigade could establish a well-protected beachhead at the Bay of Pigs. In addition, they believed that Castro was not smart enough to put down any possible internal uprisings in support of the exiles. They were wrong on all three assumptions. Though much of the blame was attributable to faulty intelligence, the point is that none of Kennedy's advisers even questioned the CIA planners about these assumptions.

The Johnson advisers' sloganistic thinking about "the Communist apparatus" that was "working all around the world" (as Dean Rusk put it) led them to overlook the powerful nationalistic strivings of the North Vietnamese government and its efforts to ward off Chinese domination. The crudest of all stereotypes used by Johnson's inner circle to justify their policies was the domino theory ("If we don't stop the Reds in South Vietnam, tomorrow they will be in Hawaii and next week they will be in San Francisco," Johnson once said). The group so firmly accepted this stereotype that it became almost impossible for any adviser to introduce a more sophisticated viewpoint.

In the documents on Pearl Harbor, it is clear to see that the Navy commanders stationed in Hawaii had a naive image of Japan as a midget that would not dare to strike a blow against a powerful giant.

5. *Pressure.* Victims of groupthink apply direct pressure to any individual who momentarily expresses doubts about any

of the group's shared illusions or who questions the validity of the arguments supporting a policy alternative favored by the majority. This gambit reinforces the concurrence-seeking norm that loyal members are expected to maintain.

President Kennedy probably was more active than anyone else in raising skeptical questions during the Bay of Pigs meetings, and yet he seems to have encouraged the group's docile, uncritical acceptance of defective arguments in favor of the CIA's plan. At every meeting, he allowed the CIA representatives to dominate the discussion. He permitted them to give their immediate refutations in response to each tentative doubt that one of the others expressed, instead of asking whether anyone shared the doubt or wanted to pursue the implications of the new worrisome issue that had just been raised. And at the most crucial meeting, when he was calling on each member to give his vote for or against the plan, he did not call on Arthur Schlesinger, the one man there who was known by the President to have serious misgivings.

Historian Thomson informs us that whenever a member of Johnson's ingroup began to express doubts, the group used subtle social pressures to "domesticate" him. To start with, the dissenter was made to feel at home provided that he lived up to two restrictions: 1) that he did not voice his doubts to outsiders, which would play into the hands of the opposition; and 2) that he kept his criticisms within the bounds of acceptable deviation, which meant not challenging any of the fundamental assumptions that went into the group's prior commitments. One such "domesticated dissenter" was Bill Moyers. When Moyers arrived at a meeting, Thomson tells us, the President greeted him with, "Well, here comes Mr. Stop-the-Bombing."

6. *Self-Censorship.* Victims of groupthink avoid deviating from what appears to be group consensus; they keep silent about their misgivings and even minimize to themselves the importance of their doubts.

As we have seen, Schlesinger was not at all hesitant about presenting his strong objections to the Bay of Pigs plan in a memorandum to the President and the Secretary of State. But he became keenly aware of his tendency to suppress objections at the White House meetings. "In the months after the Bay of Pigs, I bitterly reproached myself for having kept so silent during those crucial discussions in the cabinet room," Schlesinger writes in *A Thousand Days*, "I can only explain my failure to do more than raise a few timid questions by reporting that one's impulse to blow the whistle on this nonsense was simply undone by the circumstances of the discussion."

7. *Unanimity.* Victims of groupthink share an illusion of unanimity within the group concerning almost all judgments expressed by members who speak in favor of the majority view. This symptom results partly from the preceding one, whose effects are augmented by the false assumption that any individual who remains silent during any part of the discussion is in full accord with what the others are saying.

When a group of persons who respect each other's opinions arrives at a unanimous view, each member is likely to feel that the belief must be true. This reliance on consensual validation within the group tends to replace individual critical thinking and reality testing, unless there are clearcut disagreements among the members. In contemplating a course of action such as the invasion of Cuba, it is painful for the members to confront disagreements within their group, particularly if it becomes apparent that there are widely divergent views about whether the preferred course of action is too risky to undertake at all. Such disagreements are likely to arouse anxieties about making a serious error. Once the sense of unanimity is shattered, the members no longer can feel complacently confident about the decision they are inclined to make. Each man must then face the annoying realization that there are troublesome uncertainties and he must diligently seek out the best information he can get in order to decide for himself exactly how serious the risks might be. This is one of the unpleasant consequences of being in a group of hardheaded, critical thinkers.

To avoid such an unpleasant state, the members often become inclined, without quite realizing it, to prevent latent disagreements from surfacing when they are about to initiate a risky course of action. The group leader and the members support each other in playing up the areas of convergence in their thinking, at the expense of fully exploring divergencies that might reveal unsettled issues. . . .

8. *Mindguards.* Victims of groupthink sometimes appoint themselves as mindguards to protect the leader and fellow members from adverse information that might break the complacency they shared about the effectiveness and morality of past decisions. At a large birthday party for his wife, Attorney General Robert F. Kennedy, who had been constantly informed about the Cuban invasion plan, took Schlesinger aside and asked him why he was opposed. Kennedy listened coldly and said, "You may be right or you may be wrong, but the President has made his mind up. Don't push it any further. Now is the time for everyone to help him all they can."

Rusk also functioned as a highly effective mindguard by failing to transmit to the group the strong objections of three "outsiders" who had learned of the invasion plan—Undersecretary of State Chester Bowles, USIA Director Edward R. Murrow, and Rusk's intelligence chief, Roger Hilsman. Had Rusk done so, their warnings might have reinforced Schlesinger's memorandum and jolted some of Kennedy's ingroup, if not the President himself, into reconsidering the decision.

Products. When a group of executives frequently displays most or all of these interrelated symptoms, a detailed study of their deliberations is likely to reveal a number of immediate consequences. These consequences are, in effect, products of poor

decision-making practices because they lead to inadequate solutions to the problems under discussion.

First, the group limits its discussions to a few alternative courses of action (often only two) without an initial survey of all the alternatives that might be worthy of consideration.

Second, the group fails to reexamine the course of action initially preferred by the majority after they learn of risks and drawbacks they had not considered originally.

Third, the members spend little or no time discussing whether there are nonobvious gains they may have overlooked or ways of reducing the seemingly prohibitive costs that made rejected alternatives appear undesirable to them.

Fourth, members make little or no attempt to obtain information from experts within their own organizations who might be able to supply more precise estimates of potential losses and gains.

Fifth, members show positive interest in facts and opinions that support their preferred policy, and they tend to ignore facts and opinions that do not.

Sixth, members spend little time deliberating about how the chosen policy might be hindered by bureaucratic inertia, sabotaged by political opponents, or temporarily derailed by common accidents. Consequently, they fail to work out contingency plans to cope with foreseeable setbacks that could endanger the overall success of their chosen course.

Support. The search for an explanation of why groupthink occurs has led me through a quagmire of complicated theoretical issues in the murky area of human motivation. My belief, based on recent social psychological research, is that we can best understand the various symptoms of groupthink as a mutual effort among the group members to maintain self-esteem and emotional equanimity by providing social support to each other, especially at times when they share responsibility for making vital decisions.

Even when no important decision is pending, the typical administrator will begin to doubt the wisdom and morality of his past decisions each time he receives information about setbacks, particularly if the information is accompanied by negative feedback from prominent men who originally had been his supporters. It should not be surprising, therefore, to find that individual members strive to develop unanimity and esprit de corps that will help bolster each other's morale, to create an optimistic outlook about the success of pending decisions, and to reaffirm the positive value of past policies to which all of them are committed.

Pride. Shared illusions of invulnerability, for example, can reduce anxiety about taking risks. Rationalizations help members believe that the risks are really not so bad after all. The assumption of inherent morality helps the members to avoid feelings of shame or guilt. Negative stereotypes function as stress-reducing devices to enhance a sense of moral righteousness as well as pride in a lofty mission.

The mutual enhancement of self-esteem and morale may have functional value in enabling the members to maintain their capacity to take action, but it has maladaptive consequences insofar as concurrence-seeking tendencies interfere with critical, rational capacities and lead to serious errors of judgment.

While I have limited my study to decision-making bodies in government, groupthink symptoms appear in business, industry and any other field where small, cohesive groups make the decisions. It is vital, then, for all sorts of people—and especially group leaders—to know what steps they can take to prevent groupthink.

Remedies. To counterpoint my case studies of the major fiascoes, I have also investigated two highly successful group enterprises, the formulation of the Marshall Plan in the Truman Administration and the handling of the Cuban missile crisis by President Kennedy and his advisers. I have

found it instructive to examine the steps Kennedy took to change his group's decision-making processes. These changes ensured that the mistakes made by his Bay of Pigs ingroup were not repeated by the missile-crisis ingroup, even though the membership of both groups was essentially the same.

The following recommendations for preventing groupthink incorporate many of the good practices I discovered to be characteristic of the Marshall Plan and missile crisis groups:

1. The leader of a policy-forming group should assign the role of critical evaluator to each member, encouraging the group to give high priority to open airing of objections and doubts. This practice needs to be reinforced by the leader's acceptance of criticism of his own judgments in order to discourage members from soft-pedaling their disagreements and from allowing their striving for concurrence to inhibit critical thinking.

2. When the key members of a hierarchy assign a policy-planning mission to any group within their organization, they should adopt an impartial stance instead of stating preferences and expectations at the beginning. This will encourage open inquiry and impartial probing of a wide range of policy alternatives.

3. The organization routinely should set up several outside policy-planning and evaluation groups to work on the same policy question, each deliberating under a different leader. This can prevent the insulation of an ingroup.

4. At intervals before the group reaches a final consensus, the leader should require each member to discuss the group's deliberations with associates in his own unit of the organization—assuming that those associates can be trusted to adhere to the same security regulations that govern the policy-makers—and then to report back their reactions to the group.

5. The group should invite one or more outside experts to each meeting on a staggered basis and encourage the experts to challenge the views of the core members.

6. At every general meeting of the group, whenever the agenda calls for an evaluation of policy alternatives, at least one member should play devil's advocate, functioning as a good lawyer in challenging the testimony of those who advocate the majority position.

7. Whenever the policy issue involves relations with a rival nation or organization, the group should devote a sizable block of time, perhaps an entire session, to a survey of all warning signals from the rivals and should write alternative scenarios on the rivals' intentions.

8. When the group is surveying policy alternatives for feasibility and effectiveness, it should from time to time divide into two or more subgroups to meet separately, under different chairmen, and then come back together to hammer out differences.

9. After reaching a preliminary consensus about what seems to be the best policy, the group should hold a "second-chance" meeting at which every member expresses as vividly as he can all his residual doubts, and rethinks the entire issue before making a definitive choice.

How. These recommendations have their disadvantages. To encourage the open airing of objections, for instance, might lead to prolonged and costly debates when a rapidly growing crisis requires immediate solution. It also could cause rejection, depression and anger. A leader's failure to set a norm might create cleavage between leader and members that could develop into a disruptive power struggle if the leader looks on the emerging consensus as anathema. Setting up outside evaluation groups might increase the risk of security leakage. Still, inventive executives who know their way around the organizational maze probably can figure out how to apply one or another of the prescriptions successfully, without harmful side effects.

They also could benefit from the advice of outside experts in the administrative and behavioral sciences. Though these experts have much to offer, they have had few chances to work on policy-making machinery within large organizations. As matters now stand, executives innovate only when they need new procedures to avoid repeating serious errors that have deflated their self-images.

In this era of atomic warheads, urban disorganization and ecocatastrophes, it seems to me that policymakers should collaborate with behavioral scientists and give top priority to preventing groupthink and its attendant fiascoes.

CHAPTER 4

"Modern" Structural Organization Theory

Usually when someone refers to the structure of an organization, that person is talking about the relatively stable relationships among the positions, groups of positions (units), and work processes that make up the organization. Structural organization theory is concerned with vertical differentiations—hierarchical levels of organizational authority and coordination, and horizontal differentiations between organizational units—such as those between product or service lines, geographical areas, or skills. The organization chart is the ever-present tool of a structural organization theorist.

Why do we use the label "modern" to modify structural organization theory? Most organizational theorists from the classical school also were structuralists. They focused their attention on the structure—or design—of organizations and their production processes. Some examples that are reprinted in Chapter 1 include works by Adam Smith, Henri Fayol, Daniel McCallum, Frederick Winslow Taylor, and Max Weber. Thus we use the word "modern" (always in quotation marks) merely to differentiate between the structural organization theorists who wrote in the second half of the twentieth century and the pre–World War II classical school structuralists.

The "modern" structuralists are concerned with many of the same issues that the classical structuralists were, but their theories have been influenced by and benefited greatly from advancements in organization theory since World War II. "Modern" structuralists' roots are in the thinking of Fayol, Taylor, Gulick, and Weber, and their underlying tenets are quite similar: organizational efficiency is the essence of organizational rationality, and the goal of rationality is to increase the production of wealth in terms of real goods and services. However, "modern" structural theories also have been influenced substantially by the more recent schools of organization theorists.

Bolman and Deal (1997) identify the basic assumptions of the structural perspective:

1. Organizations are rational institutions whose primary purpose is to accomplish established objectives; rational organizational behavior is achieved best through systems of defined rules and formal authority. Organizational control and coordination are key for maintaining organizational rationality.

2. There is a "best" structure for any organization, or at least a most appropriate structure in light of its given objectives, the environmental conditions surrounding it (for example, its markets, the competition, and the extent of government regulation), the nature of its products and/or services (the "best" structure for a management consulting firm probably differs substantially from that for a certified public accounting firm), and the technology of the production processes (a coal mining company has a different "best structure" than the high-tech manufacturer of computer microcomponents).

3. Specialization and the division of labor increase the quality and quantity of production, particularly in highly skilled operations and professions.

4. Most problems in an organization result from structural flaws and can be solved by changing the structure.

What sorts of practical issues are best addressed by "modern" structural organization theory? Is it useful? The most immediate issue in the design of any organization is the question of structure. What should it look like? How should it work? How will it deal with the most common structural questions of specialization, departmentalization, span of control, and the coordination and control of specialized units?

Tom Burns and G. M. Stalker, of the Tavistock Institute in London—which is widely acknowledged as the birthplace of the "sociotechnical approach" to organizations—developed their widely cited theory of "mechanistic and organic systems" of organization while examining rapid technological change in the British and Scottish electronics industry in the post–World War II years. Their account, "Mechanistic and Organic Systems," from their 1961 book *The Management of Innovation*, is reprinted here. Burns and Stalker found that stable conditions may suggest the use of a mechanistic form of organization where a traditional pattern of hierarchy, reliance on formal rules and regulations, vertical communications, and structured decision making is possible. However, more dynamic conditions—situations in which the environment changes rapidly—require the use of an organic form of organization where there is less rigidity, more participation, and more reliance on workers to define and redefine their positions and relationships. For example, technological creativity, an essential ingredient in an organic system, requires an organizational climate and management systems that are supportive of innovation. The impacts of these two organizational forms on individuals are substantially different. Supervisors and managers find that the mechanistic form provides them with a greater sense of security in dealing with their environment than the organic form, which introduces much greater uncertainty. Burns and Stalker conclude that either form of organization may be appropriate in particular situations.

In "The Concept of Formal Organization," a chapter from their 1962 book *Formal Organizations: A Comparative Approach*, Peter M. Blau and W. Richard Scott assert that all organizations include both a formal and an informal element. The informal organization by its nature is rooted in the formal structure and supports its formal organization by establishing norms for the operation of the organization that cannot always be spelled out by rules and policies. For these reasons, Blau and Scott maintain that it is impossible to know and understand the true structure of a formal organization without a similar understanding of its parallel informal organization. Clearly, Blau and Scott were influenced by the "classical philosopher" Chester Barnard's 1938 book *The Functions of the Executive*, which held that

> informal organization, although comprising the processes of society which are unconscious as contrasted with those of formal organizations which are conscious, has two important classes of effects: (a) it establishes certain attitudes, understandings, customs, habits, [and] institutions, and (b) it creates the condition under which formal organization may arise.

In their 1968 *Harvard Business Review* article, "Organizational Choice: Product vs. Function," Arthur H. Walker and Jay W. Lorsch grapple with one of the perennial questions facing those who would design organizations: should an organization be structured according to product or function? "Should all specialists in a given function be grouped under a common boss, regardless of differences in products they are involved in, or should the various functional specialists working on a single product be grouped together under the same superior?" Walker and Lorsch tackle this problem by examining two firms in the same industry—one organized by product and the other by function. They conclude that either structural arrangement can be appropriate, depending upon the organization's environment and the nature of the organization itself.

In 1776, Adam Smith advocated the division of labor to increase the effectiveness of the factory system of production. In 1922, Max Weber described two strong and opposing forces that have an impact on all organizations: the need for division of labor and specialization, and the need for centralizing authority. Division of labor is an inevitable consequence of specialization by skills, products, or processes. Most "modern" structuralists use the word *differentiation*, which means essentially the same thing as specialization but also reflects increased appreciation of the myriad and rapidly changing external environmental forces with which organizations interact (for example, different markets, sociopolitical cultures, regulatory environments, technologies, competition, and the economy). Thus, complex differentiation also is essential for organizational effectiveness as well as efficiency. However, differentiation means diverse forces that "pull organizations apart." Differentiation increases the need for organizational coordination and control that, in the language of "modern" structuralists, is labeled "integration."

Henry Mintzberg emerged as one of the most widely respected management and organizational theorists during the second half of the twentieth century. Mintzberg began compiling a theory of management policy in the 1960s—a field of management and organization theory that had been largely overlooked. He has been highly influential in part because he has synthesized many schools of organization and management theory—and has done so with coherence. His 1979 book *The Structuring of Organizations* addresses the first component of the model. His 1983 book *Power in and Around Organizations* addresses the second component of the model. A chapter from it is reprinted in our Chapter 6. In his chapter "The Five Basic Parts of the Organization," which is reprinted here, Mintzberg uses James D. Thompson's (1967) concepts of "pooled, sequential, and reciprocal organizational coupling" to create a model of organizations with five interdependent parts: the strategic apex, the middle line, the operating core, the technostructure, and the support staff. His model is a creative and useful departure from traditional views of formal organization structure.

Since the mid-1960s, the attacks against the bureaucratic form of organization have expanded and become more heated. Is the bureaucratic form of organization on an inevitable road to extinction? Is it being replaced by systems of temporary democratic networks or structures without hierarchical layers of authority, responsibility, and accountability? Over the past ten or fifteen years, the answer has changed from "if so, the trend isn't apparent yet" to "yes, the change is widely evident." Despite the rapid movement toward "donut organizations" (Handy, 1990), organizational networks, and "virtual organizations" (Fulk & DeSanctis, 1999), however, bureaucracy continues to hold its own quite well in practice—albeit often in forms that Max Weber would not recognize. Indeed, a small body of literature exists in the field of public administration that justifies the bureaucratic form of organization because of its ability to provide continuity, consistency, and efficiency and its promotion of equity and representativeness (Kaufman, 1977; Krislov & Rosenbloom, 1981; Goodsell, 1994).

Elliott Jaques, whose studies of organizations and structure spanned more than fifty years, from the Tavistock Institute's sociotechnical systems "Glacier Project" in 1950 to the turn of the century, remains as a rather lonely defender of the hierarchical-bureaucratic form of organization. Jaques contends that those who argue against hierarchy are "simply wrong, and all their proposals are based on an inadequate understanding of not only hierarchy but also human nature." Hierarchical layers enable organizations to cope with discontinuities in mental and physical complexities, thereby separating tasks into manageable series of steps: "What we need is not some new kind of organization. What we need is managerial hierarchy that understands its own nature and purpose." According to Jaques, hierarchy is *the* best alternative for large organizations: "We need to stop casting about fruitlessly for organizational Holy Grails and settle down to the hard work of putting our managerial hierarchies in order."

"Technology as a Contingency Factor," by Richard M. Burton and Børge Obel, focuses on an important set of issues: the effects that various dimensions of technology have on organizational design. Burton and Obel structure their findings using a series of propositions that incorporate theories from Woodward (1965), Perrow (1967), Galbraith (1974), and Scott (1998). The effects of technology are assessed on six dimensions of organization: formalization, centralization, complexity, configuration, coordination and control, and incentives. A subchapter within Burton and Obel's chapter also provides a comprehensive discussion of information technology, the interdependence between organizational form and information technology, organizations as information processing entities, the effects of media richness on design, and design criteria for fitting information technology to decentralized organizations.

REFERENCES

Barnard, C. I. (1938). *The functions of the executive*. Cambridge, MA: Harvard University Press.

Bennis, W. G. (1966). *Changing organizations*. New York: McGraw-Hill.

Bennis, W. G., & P. E. Slater (1968). *The temporary society*. New York: Harper & Row.

Blau, P. M., & W. R. Scott (1962). *Formal organizations: A comparative approach*. San Francisco: Jossey-Bass.

Bolman, L. G., & T. E. Deal (1997). *Reframing organizations: Artistry, choice, and leadership*. 2d ed. San Francisco: Jossey-Bass.

Burns, T., & G. M. Stalker (1961). *The management of innovation*. London: Tavistock Publications.

Burton, R. M., & B. Obel. (1998). *Strategic organizational diagnosis and design: Developing theory for application*. 2d ed. Boston: Kluwer Academic.

Crozier, M. (1964). *The bureaucratic phenomenon*. Chicago: University of Chicago Press.

Davis, S. M., & P. R. Lawrence (1977). *Matrix*. Reading, MA: Addison-Wesley.

Drucker, P. F. (1988, January–February). The coming of the new organization. *Harvard Business Review*, 66(1), 45–53.

Etzioni, A. (1961). *A comparative analysis of complex organizations*. Englewood Cliffs, NJ: Prentice Hall.

Fulk, J., & DeSanctis, G. (1999). Articulation of communication technology and organizational form. In G. DeSanctis and J. Fulk (Eds.), *Shaping organization form: Communication, connection, and community* (pp. 5–32). Thousand Oaks, CA: Sage.

Goodsell, C. T. (1994). *The case for bureaucracy: A public administration polemic*. 3d ed. Chatham, NJ: Chatham House.

Handy, C. (1990). *The Age of Unreason*. Boston, MA: Harvard Business School Press.

Jaques, E. (1990, January–February). In praise of hierarchy. *Harvard Business Review*, 68(1), 127–133.

Kaufman, H. (1977). *Red tape*. Washington, DC: Brookings Institution.

Krislov, S., & D. H. Rosenbloom (1981). *Representative bureaucracy and the American political system*. New York: Praeger.

Lawrence, P. R., & J. W. Lorsch (1969). *Developing organizations*. Reading, MA: Addison-Wesley.

Mintzberg, H. (1979). *The structuring of organizations*. Englewood Cliffs, NJ: Prentice Hall.

Mintzberg, H. (1983). *Power in and around organizations*. Englewood Cliffs, NJ: Prentice Hall.

Schein, E. H. (1989, Winter). Reassessing the "divine rights" of managers. *Sloan Management Review*, 30(2), 63–68.

Thompson, J. D. (1967). *Organizations in action*. New York: McGraw-Hill.

Thompson, V. A. (1961). *Modern organization*. New York: Knopf.

Walker, A. H., & J. W. Lorsch (1968, November–December). Organizational choice: Product vs. function. *Harvard Business Review*, 46, 129–138.

19

Mechanistic and Organic Systems

Tom Burns & G. M. Stalker

We are now at the point at which we may set down the outline of the two management systems which represent for us the two polar extremities of the forms which such systems can take when they are adapted to a specific rate of technical and commercial change. The cases we have tried to establish from the literature, as from our research experience . . . , is that the different forms assumed by a working organization do exist objectively and are not merely interpretations offered by observers of different schools.

Both types represent a "rational" form of organization, in that they may both, in our experience, be explicitly and deliberately created and maintained to exploit the human resources of a concern in the most efficient manner feasible in the circumstances of the concern. Not surprisingly, however, each exhibits characteristics which have been hitherto associated with different kinds of interpretation. For it is our contention that empirical findings have usually been classified according to sociological ideology rather than according to the functional specificity of the working organization to its task and the conditions confronting it.

We have tried to argue that these are two formally contrasted forms of management system. These we shall call the mechanistic and organic forms.

A *mechanistic* management system is appropriate to stable conditions. It is characterized by:

(a) the specialized differentiation of functional tasks into which the problems and tasks facing the concern as a whole are broken down;

(b) the abstract nature of each individual task, which is pursued with techniques and purposes more or less distinct from those of the concern as a whole; *i.e.*, the functionaries tend to pursue the technical improvement of means, rather than the accomplishment of the ends of the concern;

(c) the reconciliation, for each level in the hierarchy, of these distinct performances by the immediate superiors, who are also, in turn, responsible for seeing that each is relevant in his own special part of the main task.

(d) the precise definition of rights and obligations and technical methods attached to each functional role;

(e) the translation of rights and obligations and methods into the responsibilities of a functional position;

(f) hierarchic structure of control, authority, and communication;

(g) a reinforcement of the hierarchic structure by the location of knowledge of actualities exclusively at the top of the hierarchy, where the final reconciliation of distinct tasks and assessment of relevance is made.[1]

(h) a tendency for interaction between members of the concern to be vertical, *i.e.*, between superior and subordinate;

(i) a tendency for operations and working behavior to be governed by the instructions and decisions issued by superiors;

(j) insistence on loyalty to the concern and obedience to superiors as a condition of membership;

(k) a greater importance and prestige attaching to internal (local) than to general (cosmopolitan) knowledge, experience, and skill.

Source: Tom Burns and G. M. Stalker, *The Management of Innovation*, rev. ed. (1961; Oxford: Oxford University Press, 1994), 119–125; references omitted, notes retained. © 1961 Tom Burns and G. M. Stalker. Reprinted by permission of the publisher.

The *organic* form is appropriate to changing conditions, which give rise constantly to fresh problems and unforeseen requirements for action which cannot be broken down or distributed automatically arising from the functional roles defined within a hierarchic structure. It is characterized by:

(a) the contributive nature of special knowledge and experience to the common task of the concern;

(b) the "realistic" nature of the individual task, which is seen as set by the total situation of the concern;

(c) the adjustment and continual redefinition of individual tasks through interaction with others;

(d) the shedding of "responsibility" as a limited field of rights, obligations and methods (problems may not be posted upwards, downwards or sideways as being someone else's responsibility);

(e) the spread of commitment to the concern beyond any technical definition;

(f) a network structure of control, authority, and communication. The sanctions which apply to the individual's conduct in his working role derive more from presumed community of interest with the rest of the working organization in the survival and growth of the firm, and less from a contractual relationship between himself and a nonpersonal corporation, represented for him by an immediate superior;

(g) omniscience no longer imputed to the head of the concern; knowledge about the technical or commercial nature of the here and now task may be located anywhere in the network; this location becoming the ad hoc centre of control authority and communication;

(h) a lateral rather than a vertical direction of communication through the organization, communication between people of different rank, also, resembling consultation rather than command;

(i) a content of communication which consists of information and advice rather than instructions and decisions;

(j) commitment to the concern's task and to the "technological ethos" of material progress and expansion is more highly valued than loyalty and obedience;

(k) importance and prestige attach to affiliations and expertise valid in the industrial and technical and commercial milieux external to the firm.

One important corollary to be attached to this account is that while organic systems are not hierarchic in the same sense as they are mechanistic, they remain stratified. Positions are differentiated according to seniority—*i.e.*, greater expertise. The lead in joint decisions is frequently taken by seniors, but it is an essential presumption of the organic system that the lead, *i.e.*, "authority," is taken by whoever shows himself most informed and capable, *i.e.*, the "best authority." The location of authority is settled by consensus.

A second observation is that the area of commitment to the concern—the extent to which the individual yields himself as a resource to be used by the working organization—is far more extensive in organic than in mechanistic systems. Commitment, in fact, is expected to approach that of the professional scientist to his work, and frequently does. One further consequence of this is that it becomes far less feasible to distinguish "informal" from "formal" organization.

Thirdly, the emptying out of significance from the hierarchic command system, by which co-operation is ensured and which serves to monitor the working organization under a mechanistic system, is countered by the development of shared beliefs about the values and goals of the concern. The growth and accretion of institutionalized values, beliefs, and conduct, in the form of commitments, ideology, and manners, around an image of the concern in its industrial and commercial setting make good the loss of formal structure.

Finally, the two forms of systems represent a polarity, not a dichotomy; there are, as we have tried to show, intermediate stages between the extremities empirically known to us. Also, the relation of one form to the other is elastic, so that a concern oscillating between relative stability and relative change may also oscillate between the two forms. A concern may (and frequently does) operate with a management system which includes both types.

The organic form, by departing from the familiar clarity and fixity of the hierarchic structure, is often experienced by the individual manager as an uneasy, embarrassed, or chronically anxious quest for knowledge about what he should be doing, or what is expected of him, and similar apprehensiveness about what others are doing. Indeed, as we shall see later, this kind of response is necessary if the organic form of organization is to work effectively. Understandably, such anxiety finds expression in resentment when the apparent confusion besetting him is not explained. In these situations, all managers some of the time, and many managers all of the time, yearn for more definition and structure.

On the other hand, some managers recognize a rationale of nondefinition, a reasoned basis for the practice of those successful firms in which designation of status, function, and line of responsibility and authority has been vague or even avoided.

The desire for more definition is often in effect a wish to have the limits of one's task more neatly defined — to know what and when one doesn't have to bother about as much as to know what one does have to. It follows that the more definition is given, the more omniscient the management must be, so that no functions are left whole or partly undischarged, no person is overburdened with undelegated responsibility, or left without the authority to do his job properly. To do this, to have all the separate functions attached to individual roles fitting together and comprehensively, to have communication between persons constantly maintained on a level adequate to the needs of each functional role, requires rules or traditions of behavior proved over a long time and an equally fixed, stable task. The omniscience which may then be credited to the head of the concern is expressed throughout its body through the lines of command, extending in a clear, explicitly titled hierarchy of officers and subordinates.

The whole mechanistic form is instinct with this twofold principle of definition and dependence which acts as the frame within which action is conceived and carried out. It works, unconsciously, almost in the smallest minutiae of daily activity. "How late is late?" The answer to this question is not to be found in the rule book, but in the superior. Late is when the boss thinks it is late. Is he the kind of man who thinks 8:00 is the time, and 8:01 is late? Does he think that 8:15 is all right occasionally if it is not a regular thing? Does he think that everyone should be allowed a 5-minute grace after 8:00 but after that they are late?

Settling questions about how a person's job is to be done in this way is nevertheless simple, direct, and economical of effort. We shall, in a later chapter, examine more fully the nature of the protection and freedom (in other respects than his job) which this affords the individual.

One other feature of mechanistic organization needs emphasis. It is a necessary condition of its operation that the individual "works on his own," functionally isolated; he "knows his job," he is "responsible for seeing it's done." He works at a job which is in a sense artificially abstracted from the realities of the situation the concern is dealing with, the accountant "dealing with the costs side," the works manager "pushing production," and so on. As this works out in practice, the rest of the organization becomes part of the problem situation the individual has to deal with in order to perform successfully; *i.e.*, difficulties and problems arising from work or information which has been handed over the "responsibility barrier" between two jobs or departments are regarded as "really" the responsibility of the person from whom they were received. As a design engineer put it,

When you get designers handing over designs completely to production, it's "their responsibility" now. And you get tennis games played with the responsibility for anything that goes wrong. What happens is that you're constantly getting unsuspected faults arising from characteristics which you didn't think important in the design. If you get to hear of these through a sales person, or a production person, or somebody to whom the design was handed over to in the dim past, then, instead of being a design problem, it's an annoyance caused by that particular person, who can't do his own job—because you'd thought you were finished with that one, and you're on to something else now.

When the assumptions of the form of organization make for preoccupation with specialized tasks, the chances of career success, or of greater influence, depend rather on the relative importance which may be attached to each special function by the superior whose task it is to reconcile and control a number of them. And, indeed, to press the claims of one's job or department for a bigger share of the firm's resources is in many cases regarded as a mark of initiative, of effectiveness, and even of "loyalty to the firm's interests." The state of affairs thus engendered squares with the role of the superior, the man who can see the wood instead of just the trees, and gives it the reinforcement of the aloof detachment belonging to a court of appeal. The ordinary relationship prevailing between individual managers "in charge of" different functions is one of rivalry, a rivalry which may be rendered innocuous to the persons involved by personal friendship or the norms of sociability, but which turns discussion about the situations which constitute the real problems of the concern— how to make the products more cheaply, how to sell more, how to allocate resources, whether to curtail activity in one sector, whether to risk expansion in another and so on—into an arena of conflicting interests.

The distinctive feature of the second, organic system is the pervasiveness of the working organization as an institution. In concrete terms, this makes itself felt in a preparedness to combine with others in serving the general aims of the concern. Proportionately to the rate and extent of change, the less can the omniscience appropriate to command organizations be ascribed to the head of the organization; for executives, and even operatives, in a chang-

ing firm it is always theirs to reason why. Furthermore, the less definition can be given to status roles, and modes of communication, the more do the activities of each member of the organization become determined by the real tasks of the firm as he sees them than by instruction and routine. The individual's job ceases to be self-contained; the only way in which "his" job can be done is by his participating continually with others in the solution of problems which are real to the firm, and put in a language of requirements and activities meaningful to them all. Such methods of working put much heavier demands on the individual. . . .

We have endeavored to stress the appropriateness of each system to its own specific set of conditions. Equally, we desire to avoid the suggestion that either system is superior under all circumstances to the other. In particular, nothing in our experience justifies the assumption that mechanistic systems should be superseded by organic, in conditions of stability.[2] The beginning of administrative wisdom is the awareness that there is no one optimum type of management system.

NOTES

1. This functional attribute to the head of a concern often takes on a clearly expressive aspect. It is common enough for concerns to instruct all people with whom they deal to address correspondence to the firm (*i.e.*, to its formal head) and for all outgoing letters and orders to be signed by the head of the concern. Similarly, the printed letter heading used by Government departments carries instructions for the replies to be addressed to the Secretary, etc. These instructions are not always taken seriously, either by members of the organization or their correspondents, but in one company this practice was insisted upon and was taken to somewhat unusual lengths; *all* correspondence was delivered to the managing director, who would thereafter distribute excerpts to members of the staff, synthesizing their replies into the letter of reply which he eventually sent. Telephone

communication was also controlled by limiting the number of extensions, and by monitoring incoming and outgoing calls.

2. A recent instance of this assumption is contained in H. A. Shepard's paper addressed to the Symposium on the Direction of Research Establishments, 1956. "There is much evidence to suggest that the optimal use of human resources in industrial organizations requires a different set of conditions, assumptions, and skills from those traditionally present in industry. Over the past twenty-five years, some new orientations have emerged from organizational experiments, observations, and inventions. The new orientations depart radically from doctrines associated with 'Scientific Management' and traditional bureaucratic patterns. The central emphases in this development are as follows:

1. Wide participation in decision-making, rather than centralized decision-making.

2. The face-to-face group, rather than the individual, as the basic unit of organization.

3. Mutual confidence, rather than authority, the integrative force in organization.

4. The supervisor as the agent for maintaining intragroup and intergroup communication, rather than as the agent of higher authority.

5. Growth of members of the organization to greater responsibility, rather than external control of the member's performance or their tasks."

20

The Concept of Formal Organization

Peter M. Blau & W. Richard Scott

SOCIAL ORGANIZATION AND FORMAL ORGANIZATIONS

Although a wide variety of organizations exists, when we speak of an organization it is generally quite clear what we mean and what we do not mean by this term. We may refer to the American Medical Association as an organization, or to a college fraternity; to the Bureau of Internal Revenue, or to a union; to General Motors, or to a church; to the Daughters of the American Revolution, or to an army. But we would not call a family an organization, nor would we so designate a friendship clique, or a community, or an economic market, or the political institutions of a society. What is the specific and differentiating criterion implicit in our intuitive distinction of organizations from other kinds of social groupings or institutions? It has something to do with how human conduct becomes socially organized, but it is not, as one might first suspect, whether or not social controls order and organize the conduct of individuals, since such social controls operate in both types of circumstances.

Before specifying what is meant by formal organization, let us clarify the general concept of social organization. "Social organization" refers to the ways in which human conduct becomes socially organized, that is, to the observed regularities in the behavior of people that are due to the social conditions in which they find themselves rather than to their physiological or psychological characteristics as individuals. The many social conditions that influence the conduct of people can be divided into two main types, which constitute the two basic aspects of social organizations: (1) the structure of social relations in a group or larger collectivity of people, and (2) the shared beliefs and orientations that unite the members of the collectivity and guide their conduct.

The conception of structure or system implies that the component units stand in some relation to one another and, as the popular expression "The whole is greater than the sum of its parts" suggests, that the relations between units add new elements to the situation.[1] This aphorism, like so many others, is a half-truth. The sum of fifteen apples, for example, is no more than fifteen times one apple. But a block of ice is more than the sum of the atoms of hydrogen and oxygen that compose it. In the case of the apples, there exist no linkages or relations between the units comprising the whole. In the case of the ice, however, specific connections have been formed between H and O atoms and among H_2O molecules that distinguish ice from hydrogen and oxygen, on the one hand, and from water, on the other. Similarly, a busload of passengers does not constitute a group, since no social relations unify individuals into a common structure.[2] But a busload of club members on a Sunday outing is a group, because a network of social relations links the members into a social structure, a structure which is an emergent characteristic of the collectivity that cannot be reduced to the attributes of its individual members. In short, a network of social relations transforms an aggregate of individuals into a group (or an aggregate of groups into a larger social structure), and the group is

Source: Peter M. Blau and W. Richard Scott, *Formal Organizations: A Comparative Approach* (San Francisco: Chandler, 1962), 2–8. © 1962 Chandler Publishing. © 2003 by the Board of Trustees of the Leland Stanford Jr. University new material. Used by permission of Stanford University Press.

more than the sum of the individuals composing it since the structure of social relations is an emergent element that influences the conduct of individuals.

To indicate the nature of social relations, we can briefly dissect this concept. Social relations involve, first, patterns of social interaction: the frequency and duration of the contacts between people, the tendency to initiate these contacts, the direction of influence between persons, the degree of cooperation, and so forth. Second, social relations entail people's sentiments to one another, such as feelings of attraction, respect, and hostility. The differential distribution of social relations in a group, finally, defines its status structure. Each member's status in the group depends on his relations with the others — their sentiments toward and interaction with him. As a result, integrated members become differentiated from isolates, those who are widely respected from those who are not highly regarded, and leaders from followers. In addition to these relations between individuals within groups, relations also develop between groups, relations that are a source of still another aspect of social status, since the standing of the group in the larger social system becomes part of the status of any of its members. An obvious example is the significance that membership in an ethnic minority, say, Puerto Rican, has for an individual's social status.

The networks of social relations between individuals and groups, and the status structure defined by them, constitute the core of the social organization to a collectivity, but not the whole of it. The other main dimension of social organization is a system of shared beliefs and orientations, which serve as standards for human conduct. In the course of social interaction common notions arise as to how people should act and interact and what objectives are worthy of attainment. First, common values crystallize, values that govern the goals for which men strive — their ideals and their ideas of what is desirable — such as our belief in democracy or the importance financial success

assumes in our thinking. Second, social norms develop — that is, common expectations concerning how people ought to behave — and social sanctions are used to discourage violations of these norms. These socially sanctioned rules of conduct vary in significance from moral principles or mores, as Sumner calls them, to mere customs or folkways. If values define the ends of human conduct, norms distinguish behavior that is a legitimate means for achieving these ends from behavior that is illegitimate. Finally, aside from the norms to which everybody is expected to conform, differential role expectations also emerge, expectations that become associated with various social positions. Only women in our society are expected to wear skirts, for example. Or, the respected leader of a group is expected to make suggestions, and the other members will turn to him in times of difficulties, whereas group members who have not earned the respect of others are expected to refrain from making suggestions and generally to participate little in group discussions.

These two dimensions of social organization — the networks of social relations and the shared orientations — are often referred to as the social structure and the culture, respectively.[3] Every society has a complex social structure and a complex culture, and every community within a society can be characterized by these two dimensions of social organization, and so can every group within a community (except that the specific term "culture" is reserved for the largest social systems). The prevailing cultural standards and the structure of social relations serve to organize human conduct in the collectivity. As people conform more or less closely to the expectations of their fellows, and as the degree of their conformity in turn influences their relations with others and their social status, and as their status in further turn affects their inclinations to adhere to social norms and their chances to achieve valued objectives, their patterns of behavior become socially organized.

In contrast to the social organization that emerges whenever men are living together, there are organizations that have been deliberately established for a certain purpose.[4] If the accomplishment of an objective requires collective effort, men set up an organization designed to coordinate the activities of many persons and to furnish incentives for others to join them for this purpose. For example, business concerns are established in order to produce goods that can be sold for a profit, and workers organize unions in order to increase their bargaining power with employers. In these cases, the goals to be achieved, the rules the members of the organization are expected to follow, and the status structure that defines the relations between them (the organizational chart) have not spontaneously emerged in the course of social interaction but have been consciously designed a priori to anticipate and guide interaction and activities. Since the distinctive characteristic of these organizations is that they have been formally established for the explicit purpose of achieving certain goals, the term "formal organization" is used to designate them. And this formal establishment for an explicit purpose is the criterion that distinguishes our subject matter from the study of social organization in general.

FORMAL ORGANIZATION AND INFORMAL ORGANIZATION

The fact that an organization has been formally established, however, does not mean that all activities and interactions of its members conform strictly to the official blueprint. Regardless of the time and effort devoted by management to designing a rational organization chart and elaborate procedure manuals, this official plan can never completely determine the conduct and social relations of the organization's members. Stephen Vincent Benét illustrates this limitation when he contrasts the military blueprint with military action:

If you take a flat map
And move wooden blocks upon it strategically,

The thing looks well, the blocks behave as they should.
The science of war is moving live men like blocks.
And getting the blocks into place at a fixed moment.
But it takes time to mold your men into blocks
And flat maps turn into country where creeks and gullies
Hamper your wooden squares. They stick in the brush,
They are tired and rest, they straggle after ripe blackberries.
And you cannot lift them up in your hand and move them.[5]

In every formal organization there arise informal organizations. The constituent groups of the organization, like all groups, develop their own practices, values, norms, and social relations as their members live and work together. The roots of these informal systems are embedded in the formal organization itself and nurtured by the very formality of its arrangements. Official rules must be general to have sufficient scope to cover the multitude of situations that may arise. But the application of these general rules to particular cases often poses problems of judgment, and informal practices tend to emerge that provide solutions for these problems. Decisions not anticipated by official regulations must frequently be made, particularly in times of change, and here again unofficial practices are likely to furnish guides for decisions long before the formal rules have been adapted to the changing circumstances. Moreover, unofficial norms are apt to develop that regulate performance and productivity. Finally, complex networks of social relations and informal status structures emerge, within groups and between them, which are influenced by many factors besides the organizational chart, for example by the background characteristics of various persons, their abilities, their willingness to help others, and their conformity to group norms. But to say that these informal structures are not completely determined by the formal institutions is not to say that they are entirely independent of it. For informal organizations develop in response to the opportunities created and the problems posed by their environment, and the formal organization constitutes the immediate environment of the groups within it.

When we speak of formal organizations in this book, we do not mean to imply that attention is confined to formally instituted patterns; quite the contrary. It is impossible to understand the nature of a formal organization without investigating the networks of informal relations and the unofficial norms as well as the formal hierarchy of authority and the official body of rules, since the formally instituted and the informally emerging patterns are inextricably intertwined. The distinction between the formal and the informal aspects of organizational life is only an analytical one and should not be reified; there is only one actual organization. Note also that one does not speak of the informal organization of a family or of a community. The term "informal organization" does not refer to all types of emergent patterns of social life but only to those that evolve within the framework of a formally established organization. Excluded from our purview are social institutions that have evolved without explicit design; included are the informally emerging as well as the formally instituted patterns within formally established organizations.

The decision of the members of a group to formalize their endeavors and relations by setting up a specific organization, say, a social and athletic club, is not fortuitous. If a group is small enough for all members to be in direct social contact, and if it has no objectives that require coordination of activities, there is little need for explicit procedures or a formal division of labor. But the larger the group and the more complex the task it seeks to accomplish, the greater are the pressures to become explicitly organized.[6] Once a group of boys who merely used to hang around a drugstore decide to participate in the local baseball league, they must organize a team. And the complex coordination of millions of soldiers with thousands of specialized duties in a modern army requires extensive formalized procedures and a clear-cut authority structure.

Since formal organizations are often very large and complex, some authors refer to them as "large-scale" or as "complex" organizations. But we have eschewed these terms as misleading in two respects. First, organizations vary in size and complexity, and using these variables as defining criteria would result in such odd expressions as "a small large-scale organization" or "a very complex complex organization." Second, although formal organizations often become very large and complex, their size and complexity do not rival those of the social organization of a modern society, which includes such organizations and their relations with one another in addition to other nonorganizational patterns. (Perhaps the complexity of formal organizations is so much emphasized because it is man-made whereas the complexity of societal organization has slowly emerged, just as the complexity of modern computers is more impressive than that of the human brain. Complexity by design may be more conspicuous than complexity by growth or evolution.)

The term "bureaucratic organization" which also is often used, calls attention to the fact that organizations generally possess some sort of administrative machinery. In an organization that has been formally established, a specialized administrative staff usually exists that is responsible for maintaining the organization as a going concern and for coordinating the activities of its members. Large and complex organizations require an especially elaborate administrative apparatus. In a large factory, for example, there is not only an industrial work force directly engaged in production but also an administration composed of executive, supervisory, clerical, and other staff personnel. The case of a government agency is more complicated, because such an agency is part of the administrative arm of the nation. The entire personnel of, say, a law-enforcement agency is engaged in administration, but administration of different kinds; whereas operating officials administer the law and thereby help maintain social order in the society, their superiors and the auxiliary staff administer agency procedures and help maintain the organization itself.

One aspect of bureaucratization that has received much attention is the elaboration of detailed rules and regulations that the members of the organization are expected to faithfully follow. Rigid enforcement of the minutiae of extensive official procedures often impedes effective operations. Colloquially, the term "bureaucracy" connotes such rule-encumbered inefficiency. In sociology, however, the term is used neutrally to refer to the administrative aspects of organizations. If bureaucratization is defined as the amount of effort devoted to maintaining the organization rather than to directly achieving its objectives, all formal organizations have at least a minimum of bureaucracy—even if this bureaucracy involves no more than a secretary-treasurer who collects dues. But wide variations have been found in the degree of bureaucratization in organizations, as indicated by the amount of effort devoted to administrative problems, the proportion of administrative personnel, the hierarchical character of the organization, or the strict enforcement of administrative procedures and rigid compliance with them.

NOTES

1. For a discussion of some of the issues raised by this assertion, see Ernest Nagel, "On the Statement 'The Whole Is More Than the Sum of Its Parts'," Paul F. Lazarsfeld and Morris Rosenberg (eds.), *The Language of Social Research* (Glencoe, IL: Free Press, 1955), pp. 519–527.

2. A purist may, concededly, point out that all individuals share the role of passenger and so are subject to certain generalized norms, courtesy for example.

3. See the recent discussion of these concepts by Kroeber and Parsons, who conclude by defining culture as "transmitted and created content and patterns of values, ideas, and other symbolic meaningful systems" and social structure or system as "the specifically relational system of interaction among individuals and collectivities." A. L. Kroeber and Talcott Parsons, "The Concepts of Culture and of Social System," *American Sociological Review*, 23 (1958), p. 583.

4. Sumner makes this distinction between, in his terms, *crescive* and *enacted* social institutions. William Graham Sumner, *Folkways* (Boston: Ginn, 1907), p. 54.

5. From *John Brown's Body*. Holt, Rinehart & Winston, Inc. Copyright, 1927, 1928, by Stephen Vincent Benét. Copyright renewed, 1955, 1956, by Rosemary Carr Benét.

6. For a discussion of size and its varied effects on the characteristics of social organization, see Theodore Caplow, "Organizational Size," *Administrative Science Quarterly*, 1 (1957), pp. 484–505.

21

Organizational Choice:
Product versus Function

Arthur H. Walker & Jay W. Lorsch

Of all the issues facing a manager as he thinks about the form of his organization, one of the thorniest is the question of whether to group activities primarily by product or by function. Should all specialists in a given function be grouped under a common boss, regardless of differences in products they are involved in, or should the various functional specialists working on a single product be grouped together under the same superior?

In talks with managers we have repeatedly heard them anguishing over this choice. For example, recently a divisional vice president of a major U.S. corporation was contemplating a major organizational change. After long study, he made this revealing observation to his subordinate managers:

> We still don't know which choice will be the best one. Should the research, engineering, marketing, and production people be grouped separately in departments for each function? Or would it be better to have them grouped together in product departments, each department dealing with a particular product group?
>
> We were organized by product up until a few years ago. Then we consolidated our organization into specialized functional departments, each dealing with all of our products. Now I'm wondering if we wouldn't be better off to divide our operations again into product units. Either way I can see advantages and disadvantages, trade-offs. What criteria should I use? How can we predict what the outcomes will be if we change?

Companies that have made a choice often feel confident that they have resolved this dilemma. Consider the case of a large advertising agency that consolidated its copy, art, and television personnel into a "total creative department." Previously they had reported to group heads in their areas of specialization. In a memo to employees the company explained the move:

> Formation of the "total creative" department completely tears down the walls between art, copy, and television people. Behind this move is the realization that for best results all creative people, regardless of their particular specialty, must work together under the most intimate relationship as total advertising people, trying to solve creative problems together from start to finish.
>
> The new department will be broken into five groups reporting to the senior vice president and creative director, each under the direction of an associate creative director. Each group will be responsible for art, television, and copy in their accounts.

But our experience is that such reorganizations often are only temporary. The issues involved are so complex that many managements oscillate between these two choices or try to effect some compromise between them.

In this article we shall explore—from the viewpoint of the behavioral scientist—some of the criteria that have been used in the past to make these choices, and present ideas from recent studies that suggest more relevant criteria for making the decision. We hope to provide a way of thinking about these problems that will lead to the most sensible decisions for the accomplishment of organizational goals.

Source: *Harvard Business Review* (November–December 1968). © 1968 by the President and Fellows of Harvard College. Reprinted by permission of *Harvard Business Review*. All rights reserved.

The dilemma of products versus function is by no means new; managers have been facing the same basic question for decades. As large corporations like Du Pont and General Motors grew, they found it necessary to divide their activities among product divisions.[1] Following World War II, as companies expanded their sales of existing products and added new products and businesses, many of them implemented a transition from functional organizations handling a number of different products to independently managed product divisions. These changes raised problems concerning divisionalization, decentralization, corporate staff activities, and the like.

As the product divisions grew and prospered, many companies extended the idea of product organization further down in their organizations under such labels as "the unit management concept." Today most of the attention is still being directed to these changes and innovations *within* product or market areas below the divisional level.

We are focusing therefore on these organizational issues at the middle and lower echelons of management, particularly on the crucial questions being faced by managers today within product divisions. The reader should note, however, that a discussion of these issues is immensely complicated by the fact that a choice at one level of the corporate structure affects the choices and criteria for choice at other levels. Nonetheless, the ideas we suggest in this article are directly relevant to organizational choice at any level.

ELEMENTS TO CONSIDER

To understand more fully the factors that make these issues so difficult, it is useful to review the criteria often relied on in making this decision. Typically, managers have used technical and economic criteria. They ask themselves, for instance, "Which choice will minimize payroll costs?" Or, "Which will best utilize equipment and specialists?" This approach not only makes real sense in

the traditional logic of management, but it has strong support from the classical school of organization theorists. Luther Gulick, for example, used it in arguing for organization by function:

> It guarantees the maximum utilization of up-to-date technical skill and . . . makes it possible in each case to make use of the most effective divisions of work and specialization. . . . [It] makes possible also the economies of the maximum use of labor-saving machinery and mass production. . . . [It] encourages coordination in all of the technical and skilled work of the enterprise. . . . [It] furnishes an excellent approach to the development of central coordination and control.[2]

In pointing to the advantages of the product basis of organization, two other classical theorists used the same approach:

> Product or product line is an important basis for departmentalizing, because it permits the maximum use of personal skills and specialized knowledge, facilitates the employment of specialized capital and makes easier a certain type of coordination.[3]

In sum, these writers on organization suggested that the manager should make the choice based on three criteria:

1. Which approach permits maximum use of special technical knowledge?
2. Which provides the most efficient utilization of machinery and equipment?
3. Which provides the best hope of obtaining the required control and coordination?

There is nothing fundamentally wrong with these criteria as far as they go, and, of course, managers have been using them. But they fail to recognize the complex set of trade-offs involved in these decisions. As a consequence, managers make changes that produce unanticipated results and may even reduce the effectiveness of their organization. For example:

> A major manufacturer of corrugated containers a few years ago shifted from a product basis to a functional basis. The rationale for the decision was that it would lead to improved control of production costs and efficiencies in production and marketing. While the organi-

zation did accomplish these aims, it found it-self less able to obtain coordination among its local sales and production units. The functional specialists now reported to the top officers in charge of production and sales, and there was no mechanism for one person to coordinate their work below the level of division management. As a result, the company encountered numerous problems and unresolved conflicts among functions and later returned to the product form.

This example pinpoints the major trade-off that the traditional criteria omit. Developing highly specialized functional units makes it difficult to achieve coordination or integration among these units. On the other hand, having product units as the basis for organization promotes collaboration between specialists, but the functional specialists feel less identification with functional goals.

BEHAVIORISTS' FINDINGS

We now turn to some new behavioral science approaches to designing organization structure. . . . Studies[4] have highlighted three other important factors about specialization and coordination:

- As we have suggested, the classical theorists saw specialization in terms of grouping similar activities, skills, or even equipment. They did not look at its psychological and social consequences. . . . Behavioral scientists (including the authors) have found that there is an important relationship between a unit's or individual's assigned activities and the unit members' patterns of thought and behavior. Functional specialists tend to develop patterns of behavior and thought that are in tune with the demands of their jobs and their prior training, and as a result these specialists (*e.g.*, industrial engineers and production supervisors) have different ideas and orientation about what is important in getting the job done. This is called *differentiation,* which simply means the differences in behavior and thought patterns that develop among different specialists in relation to their respective tasks. Differentiation is

necessary for functional specialists to perform their jobs effectively.

- Differentiation is closely related to achievement of coordination, or what behavioral scientists call *integration*. This means collaboration between specialized units or individuals. Recent studies have demonstrated that there is an inverse relationship between differentiation and integration: the more two functional specialists (or their units) differ in their patterns of behavior and thought, the more difficult it is to bring about integration between them. Nevertheless, this research has indicated, achievement of both differentiation and integration is essential if organizations are to perform effectively.
- While achievement of both differentiation and integration is possible, it can occur only when well-developed means of communication among specialists exist in the organization and when the specialists are effective in resolving the inevitable cross-functional conflicts.

These recent studies, then, point to certain related questions that managers must consider when they choose between a product or functional basis of organization.

1. How will the choice affect differentiation among specialists? Will it allow the necessary differences in viewpoint to develop so that specialized tasks can be performed effectively?
2. How does the decision affect the prospects of accomplishing integration? Will it lead, for instance, to greater differentiation, which will increase the problems of achieving integration?
3. How will the decision affect the ability of organization members to communicate with each other, resolve conflicts, and reach the necessary joint decisions?

There appears to be a connection between the appropriate extent of differentiation and integration and the organization's effectiveness in accomplishing its economic goals. What the appropriate pattern is depends on the nature of external factors—markets, technology, and so on—facing the organization, as well as the goals themselves. The question of how the organizational pattern will affect individual members is equally complex. Management must consider how much stress will be associated with a certain pattern and whether such stress should be a serious concern.

To explore in more detail the significance of modern approaches to organizational structuring, we shall describe one recent study conducted in two manufacturing plants—one organized by *product*, the other on a *functional* basis.[5]

PLANT F AND PLANT P

The two plants where this study was conducted were selected because they were closely matched in several ways. They were making the same product; their markets, technology, and even raw materials were identical. The parent companies were also similar: both were large, national corporations that developed, manufactured, and marketed many consumer products. In each case divisional and corporate headquarters were located more than 100 miles from the facilities studied. The plants were separated from other structures at the same site, where other company products were made.

Both plants had very similar managment styles. They stressed their desire to foster employees' initiative and autonomy and placed great reliance on selection of well-qualified department heads. They also identified explicitly the same two objectives.

FIGURE 21.1 • ORGANIZATIONAL CHART AT PLANT F

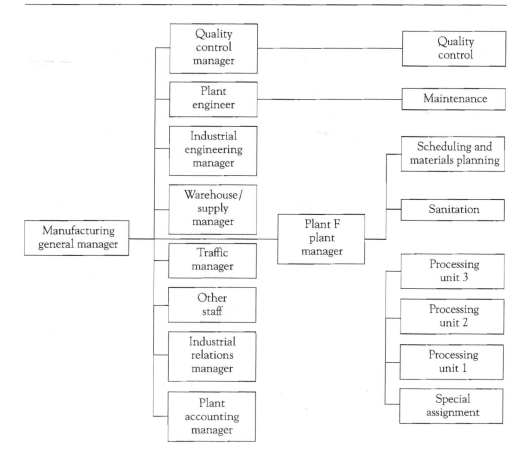

FIGURE 21.2 • ORGANIZATIONAL CHART AT PLANT P

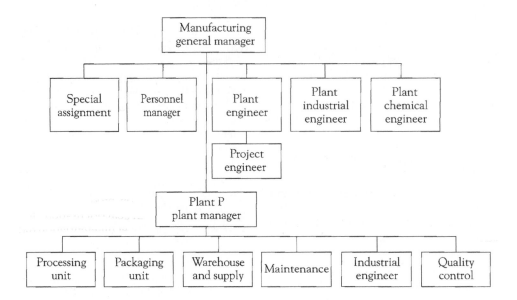

The first was to formulate, package, and ship the products in minimum time at specified levels of quality and at minimum costs — that is, within existing capabilities. The second was to improve the capabilities of the plant.

In each plant there were identical functional specialists involved with the manufacturing units and packing unit, as well as quality control, planning and scheduling, warehousing, industrial engineering, and plant engineering. In Plant F (with the *functional* basis of organization), only the manufacturing departments and the planning and scheduling function reported to the plant manager responsible for the product (see Figure 21.1). All other functional specialists reported to the staff of the divisional manufacturing manager, who was also responsible for plants manufacturing other products. At Plant P (with the *product* basis of organization), all functional specialists with the exception of plant engineering reported to the plant manager (see Figure 21.2).

State of Differentiation

In studying differentiation, it is useful to focus on the functional specialists' differences in outlook in terms of: orientation toward goals, orientation toward time, and perception of the formality of organization.

Goal Orientation. The bases of organization in the two plants had a marked effect on the specialists' differentiated goal orientations. In Plant F they focused sharply on their specialized goals and objectives. For example, quality control specialists were concerned almost exclusively with meeting quality standards, industrial engineers with methods improvements and cost reduction, and scheduling specialists with how to meet requirements. An industrial engineer in Plant F indicated this intensive interest in his own activity:

We have 150 projects worth close to a million dollars in annual savings. I guess I've completed some that save as much as $90,000 a year. Right now I'm working on cutting departmental costs. You need a hard shell in this work. No one likes to have his costs cut, but that is my job.

That these intense concerns with specialized objectives were expected is illustrated by the apologetic tone of a comment on production goals by an engineering supervisor at Plant F:

> At times we become too much involved in production. It causes a change in heart. We are interested in production, but not at the expense of our own standards of performance. If we get too much involved, then we may become compromised.

A final illustration is when production employees stood watching while members of the maintenance department worked to start a new production line, and a production supervisor remarked:

> I hope that they get that line going soon. Right now, however, my hands are tied. Maintenance has the job. I can only wait. My people have to wait, too.

This intense concern with one set of goals is analogous to a rifle shot; in a manner of speaking, each specialist took aim at one set of goals and fired at it. Moreover, the specialists identified closely with their counterparts in other plants and at divisional headquarters. As one engineer put it:

> We carry the ball for them (the central office). We carry a project through and get it working right.

At Plant P the functional specialists' goals were more diffuse—like buckshot. Each specialist was concerned not only with his own goals, but also with the operation of the entire plant. For example, in contrast to the Plant F production supervisor's attitude about maintenance, a Plant P maintenance manager said, under similar circumstances:

> We're all interested in the same thing. If I can help, I'm willing. If I have a mechanical problem, there is no member of the operating department who wouldn't go out of his way to solve it.

Additional evidence of this more diffuse orientation toward goals is provided by comments such as these which came from Plant P engineers and managers:

> We are here for a reason—to run this place the best way we know how. There is no reluctance to be open and frank despite various backgrounds and ages.
>
> The changeovers tell the story. Everyone shows willingness to dig in. The whole plant turns out to do cleaning up.

Because the functional specialists at Plant F focused on their individual goals, they had relatively wide differences in goals and objectives. Plant P's structure, on the other hand, seemed to make functional specialists more aware of common product goals and reduced differences in goal orientation. Yet, as we shall see, this lesser differentiation did not hamper their performance.

Time Orientation. The two organizational bases had the opposite effect, however, on the time orientation of functional managers. At Plant F, the specialists shared a concern with short-term issues (mostly daily problems). The time orientation of specialists at Plant P was more differentiated. For example, its production managers concentrated on routine matters, while planning and industrial engineering focused on issues that needed solution within a week, and quality control specialists worried about even longer-term problems.

The reason is not difficult to find. Since Plant P's organization led its managers to identify with product goals, those who could contribute to the solution of longer-term problems became involved in these activities. In Plant F, where each unit focused on its own goals, there was more of a tendency to worry about getting daily progress. On the average, employees of Plant P reported devoting 30 percent of their time to daily problems, while at Plant F this figure was 49 percent. We shall have more to say shortly about how these factors influenced the results achieved in the two plants.

Organizational Formality. In the study, the formality of organizational structure in each functional activity was measured by three criteria: clarity of definition of job responsibilities, clarity of dividing lines between jobs, and importance of rules and procedures.

It was found that at Plant F there were fewer differences among functional activities in the formality of organization structure than at Plant P. Plant F employees reported that a uniform degree of structure existed across functional specialities; job responsibilities were well defined, and the distinctions between jobs were clear. Similarly, rules and procedures were extensively relied on. At Plant P, on the other hand, substantial differences in the formality of organization existed. Plant engineers and industrial engineers, for example, were rather vague about their responsibilities and about the dividing line between their jobs and other jobs. Similarly, they reported relatively low reliance on rules and procedures. Production managers, on the other hand, noted that their jobs were well defined and that rules and procedures were more important to them.

The effects of these two bases of organization on differentiation along these three dimensions are summarized in Table 21.1. Overall, differentiation was greater between functional specialists at Plant P than at Plant F.

Integration Achieved

While the study found that both plants experienced some problems in accomplishing integration, these difficulties were more noticeable at Plant F. Collaboration between maintenance and production personnel and between production and scheduling was a problem there. In Plant P the only relationship where integration was unsatisfactory was that between production and quality control specialists. Thus Plant P seemed to be getting slightly better integration in spite of the greater differentiation among specialists in that organization. Since differentiation and integration are basically antagonistic, the only way managers at Plant P could get both was by being effective at communication and conflict resolution. They were better at this than were managers at Plant F.

Communication Patterns. In Plant P, communication among employees was more frequent, less formal, and more often of a face-to-face nature than was the case with Plant F personnel. One Plant P employee volunteered:

> Communications are no problem around here. You can say it. You can get an answer.

Members of Plant F did not reflect such positive feelings. They were heard to say:

> Why didn't they tell me this was going to happen? Now they've shut down the line.
> When we get the information, it is usually too late to do any real planning. We just do our best.

The formal boundaries outlining positions that were more prevalent at Plant F appeared to act as a damper on communi-

TABLE 21.1 • DIFFERENTIATION IN PLANTS F AND P

Dimensions of Differentiation	Plant F	Plant P
Goal orientation	More differentiated and focused	Less differentiated and more diffuse
Time orientation	Less differentiated and shorter term	More differentiated and longer term
Formality of structure	Less differentiated, with more formality	More differentiated, with less formality

cation. The encounters observed were often a succession of two-man conversations, even though more than two may have been involved in a problem. The telephone and written memoranda were more often employed than at Plant P, where spontaneous meetings involving several persons were frequent, usually in the cafeteria.

Dealing with Conflict. In both plants, *confrontation* of conflict was reported to be more typical than either the use of power to force one's own position or an attempt to *smooth* conflict by "agreeing to disagree." There was strong evidence, nevertheless, that in Plant P managers were coming to grips with conflicts more directly than in Plant F. Managers at Plant F reported that more conflicts were being smoothed over. They worried that issues were often not getting settled. As they put it:

> We have too many nice guys here.
>
> If you can't resolve an issue, you go to the plant manager. But we don't like to bother him often with small matters. We should be able to settle them ourselves. The trouble is we don't. So it dies.

Thus, by ignoring conflict in the hope it would go away, or by passing it to a higher level, managers at Plant F often tried to smooth over their differences. While use of the management hierarchy is one acceptable way to resolve conflict, so many disagreements at Plant F were pushed upstairs that the hierarchy became overloaded and could not handle all the problems facing it. So it responded by dealing with only the more immediate and pressing ones.

At Plant P the managers uniformly reported that they resolved conflicts themselves. There was no evidence that conflicts were being avoided or smoothed over. As one manager said:

> We don't let problems wait very long. There's no sense to it. And besides, we get together frequently and have plenty of chances to discuss differences over a cup of coffee.

As this remark suggests, the quicker resolution of conflict was closely related to the

open and informal communication pattern prevailing at Plant P. In spite of greater differentiation in time and orientation and structure, then, Plant P managers were able to achieve more satisfactory integration because they could communicate and resolve conflict effectively.

Performance and Attitudes

Before drawing some conclusions from the study of these two plants, it is important to make two more relevant comparisons between them—their effectiveness in terms of the goals set for them and the attitudes of employees.

Plant Performance. As we noted before, the managements of the two plants were aiming at the same two objectives: maximizing current output within existing capabilities and improving the capabilities of the plant. Of the two facilities, Plant F met the first objective more effectively; it was achieving a higher production rate with greater efficiency and at less cost than was Plant P. In terms of the second objective, however, Plant P was clearly superior to Plant F; the former's productivity had increased by 23 percent from 1963 to 1966 compared with the latter's increment of only 3 percent. One key manager at Plant F commented:

> There has been a three- or four-year effort to improve our capability. Our expectations have simply not been achieved. The improvement in performance is just not there. We are still where we were three years ago. But our targets for improvements are realistic.

By contrast, a key manager at Plant P observed:

> Our crews have held steady, yet our volume is up. Our quality is consistently better too.

Another said:

> We are continuing to look for and find ways to improve and consolidate jobs.

Employee Attitudes. Here, too, the two organizations offer a contrast, but the contrast presents a paradoxical situation. Key personnel at Plant P appeared to be more deeply involved in their work than did managers at Plant F, and they admitted more often to feeling stress and pressure than did their opposite numbers at Plant F. But Plant F managers expressed more satisfaction with their work than did those at Plant P; they liked the company and their jobs more than did managers at Plant P.

Why Plant P managers felt more involved and had a higher level of stress, but were less satisfied than Plant F managers, can be best explained by linking these findings with the others we have reported.

Study Summary

The characteristics of these two organizations are summarized in Table 21.2. The nature of the organization at Plant F seemed to suit its stable but high rate of efficiency. Its specialists concentrated on their own goals and performed well, on the whole. The jobs were well defined and managers worked within procedures and rules. The managers were concerned primarily with short-term matters. They were not particularly effective in communicating with each

other and in resolving conflict. But this was not very important to achieve steady, good performance, since the coordination necessary to meet this objective could be achieved through plans and procedures and through the manufacturing technology itself.

As long as top management did not exert much pressure to improve performance dramatically, the plant's managerial hierarchy was able to resolve the few conflicts arising from daily operations. And as long as the organization avoided extensive problem solving, a great deal of personal contact was not very important. It is not surprising therefore that the managers were satisfied and felt relatively little pressure. They attended strictly to their own duties, remained uninvolved, and got the job done. For them, this combination was satisfying. And higher management was pleased with the facility's production efficiency.

The atmosphere at Plant P, in contrast, was well suited to the goal of improving plant capabilities, which it did very well. There was less differentiation between goals, since the functional specialists to a degree shared the product goals. Obviously, one danger in this form of organization is the potential attraction of specialist man-

TABLE 21.2 • OBSERVED CHARACTERISTICS OF
THE TWO ORGANIZATIONS

Characteristics	Plant F	Plant P
Differentiation	Less differentiation except in goal orientation	Greater differentiation in structure and time orientation
Integration	Somewhat less effective	More effective
Conflict management	Confrontation, but also "smoothing over" and avoidance; rather restricted communication pattern	Confrontation of conflict; open, face-to-face communication
Effectiveness	Efficient, stable production; but less successful in improving plant capabilities	Successful in improving plant capabilities, but less effective in stable production
Employee attitudes	Prevalent feeling of satisfaction, but less feeling of stress and involvement	Prevalent feeling of stress and involvement, but less satisfaction

agers to total goals to the extent that they lose sight of their particular goals and become less effective in their jobs. But this was not a serious problem at Plant P.

Moreover, there was considerable differentiation in time orientation and structure; some specialists worked at the routine and programmed tasks in operating the plant, while others concentrated on longer-term problems to improve manufacturing capability. The latter group was less constrained by formal procedures and job definitions, and this atmosphere was conducive to problem solving. The longer time orientation of some specialists, however, appeared to divert their attention from maintaining schedules and productivity. This was a contributing factor to Plant P's less effective current performance.

In spite of the higher degree of differentiation in these dimensions, Plant P managers were able to achieve the integration necessary to solve problems that hindered plant capability. Their shared goals and a common boss encouraged them to deal directly with each other and confront their conflicts. Given this pattern, it is not surprising that they felt very involved in their jobs. Also they were under stress because of their great involvement in their jobs. This stress could lead to dissatisfaction with their situation. Satisfaction for its own sake, however, may not be very important; there was no evidence of higher turnover of managers at Plant P.

Obviously, in comparing the performance of these two plants operating with similar technologies and in the same market, we might predict that, because of its greater ability to improve plant capabilities, Plant P eventually will reach a performance level at least as high as Plant F's. While this might occur in time, it should not obscure one important point: the functional organization seems to lead to better results in a situation where stable performance of a routine task is desired, while the product organization leads to better results in situations where the task is less predictable and requires innovative problem solving.

CLUES FOR MANAGERS

How can the manager concerned with the function versus product decision use these ideas to guide him in making the appropriate choice? The essential step is identifying the demands of the task confronting the organization.

Is it a routine, repetitive task? Is it one where integration can be achieved by plan and conflict managed through the hierarchy? This was the way the task was implicitly defined at Plant F. If this is the nature of the task, or, to put it another way, if management is satisfied with this definition of the task, then the functional organization is quite appropriate. While it allows less differentiation in time orientation and structure, it does encourage differentiation in goal orientation. This combination is important for specialists to work effectively in their jobs.

Perhaps even more important, the functional structure also seems to permit a degree of integration sufficient to get the organization's work done. Much of this can be accomplished through paper systems and through the hardware of the production line itself. Conflict that comes up can more safely be dealt with through the management hierarchy, since the difficulties of resolving conflict are less acute. This is so because the tasks provide less opportunity for conflict and because the specialists have less differentiated viewpoints to overcome. This form of organization is less psychologically demanding for the individuals involved.

On the other hand, if the task is of a problem-solving nature, or if management defines it this way, the product organization seems to be more appropriate. This is especially true where there is a need for tight integration among specialists. As illustrated at Plant P, the product organization form allows the greater differentiation in time orientation and structure that specialists need to attack problems. While encouraging identification with superordinate goals, this organizational form does allow enough differentiation in goals for specialists to make their contributions.

Even more important, to identify with product ends and have a common boss encourages employees to deal constructively with conflict, communicate directly and openly with each other, and confront their differences, so they can collaborate effectively. Greater stress and less satisfaction for the individual may be unavoidable, but it is a small price to pay for the involvement that accompanies it.

The manager's problem in choosing between product and functional forms is complicated by the fact that in each organization there are routine tasks and tasks requiring problem solving, jobs requiring little interdependence among specialists and jobs requiring a great deal. Faced with these mixtures, many companies have adopted various compromises between product and functional bases. They include (in ascending order of structural complexity):

1. *The use of cross-functional teams to facilitate integration.* These teams provide some opportunity for communication and conflict resolution and also a degree of the common identification with product goals that characterizes the product organization. At the same time, they retain the differentiation provided by the functional organization.
2. *The appointment of full-time integrators or coordinators around a product.* These product managers or project managers encourage the functional specialists to become committed to product goals and help resolve conflicts between them. The specialists still retain their primary identification with their functions.[6]
3. *The "matrix" or grid organization, which combines the product and functional forms by overlaying them.* Some managers wear functional hats and are involved in the day-to-day, more routine activities. Naturally, they identify with functional goals. Others, wearing product or project hats, identify with total product goals and are more involved in the problem-solving activity required to cope with long-range issues and to achieve cross-functional coordination.

These compromises are becoming popular because they enable companies to deal with multiple tasks simultaneously. But we do not propose them as a panacea, because they make sense only for those situations where the differentiation and integration required by the sum of all the tasks make a middle approach necessary. Further, the complexity of interpersonal plus organizational relationships in these forms and the ambiguity associated with them make them difficult to administer effectively and psychologically demanding on the persons involved.

In our view, the only solution to the product versus function dilemma lies in analysis of the multiple tasks that must be performed, the differences between specialists, the integration that must be achieved, and the mechanisms and behavior required to resolve conflict and arrive at these states of differentiation and integration. This analysis provides the best hope of making a correct product or function choice or of arriving at some appropriate compromise solution.

NOTES

1. For a historical study of the organizational structure of U.S. corporations, see Alfred D. Chandler, Jr., *Strategy and Structure* (Cambridge: The M.I.T. Press, 1962).
2. Luther Gulick, "Notes on the Theory of Organization," in *Papers on the Science of Administration*, edited by Luther Gulick and Lyndall F. Urwick (New York Institute of Public Administration, 1917), pp. 23–24.
3. Harold D. Koontz, and C. J. O'Donnell, *Principles of Management* (New York, McGraw-Hill, 2nd ed. 1959), p. 111.
4. See Paul R. Lawrence and Jay W. Lorsch, *Organization and Environment* (Boston, Division of Research, Harvard Business School, 1967); and Eric J. Miller and A. K. Rice, *Systems of Organization* (London, Tavistock Publications, 1967).
5. Arthur H. Walker, *Behavioral Consequences of Contrasting Patterns of Organization* (Boston, Harvard Business School, unpublished doctoral dissertation, 1967).
6. See Paul R. Lawrence and Jay W. Lorsch, "New Management Job: The Integrator," *HBR* November-December 1967, p. 142.

22

The Five Basic Parts of the Organization

Henry Mintzberg

[Previously] organizations were described in terms of their use of the coordinating mechanisms. We noted that, in theory, the simplest organization can rely on mutual adjustment to coordinate its basic work of producing a product or service. Its *operators*—those who do this basic work—are largely self-sufficient.

As the organization grows, however, and adopts a more complex division of labor among its operators, the need is increasingly felt for direct supervision. Another brain— that of a *manager*—is needed to help coordinate the work of the operators. So, whereas the division of labor up to this point has been between the operators themselves, the introduction of a manager introduces a first *administrative* division of labor in the structure—between those who do the work and those who supervise it. And as the organization further elaborates itself, more managers are added—not only managers of operators but also managers of managers. An administrative *hierarchy* of authority is built.

As the process of elaboration continues, the organization turns increasingly to standardization as a means of coordinating the work of its operators. The responsibility for much of this standardization falls on a third group, composed of *analysts*. Some, such as work study analysts and industrial engineers, concern themselves with the standardization of work processes; others, such as quality control engineers, accountants, planners, and production schedulers, focus on the standardization of outputs; while a few, such as personnel trainers, are charged with the standardization of skills (although most

of this standardization takes place outside the organization, before the operators are hired). The introduction of these analysts brings a second kind of administrative division of labor to the organization, between those who do and who supervise the work, and those who standardize it. Whereas in the first case managers assume responsibility from the operators for some of the coordination of their work by substituting direct supervision for mutual adjustment, the analysts assumed responsibility from the managers (and the operators) by substituting standardization for direct supervision (and mutual adjustment). Earlier, some of the control over the work was removed from the operator; now it begins to be removed from the manager as well, as the systems designed by the analysts take increasing responsibility for coordination. The analyst "institutionalizes" the manager's job.

We end up with an organization that consists of a core of operators, who do the basic work of producing the products and services, and an *administrative* component of managers and analysts, who take some of the responsibility for coordinating their work. This leads us to the conceptual description of the organization shown in Figure 22.1. This figure will be used repeatedly throughout the book, sometimes overlaid to show flows, sometimes distorted to illustrate special structures. It emerges, in effect, as the "logo," or symbol, of the book.

At the base of the logo is the *operating* core, wherein the operators carry out the basic work of the organization—the input, processing, output, and direct support tasks

Source: Henry Mintzberg, *The Structure of Organizations: A Synthesis of Research* (Upper Saddle River, NJ: Prentice Hall, 1979), 18–34 © 1979 Prentice-Hall, Inc. Adapted by permission of Pearson Education, Inc., Upper Saddle River, NJ.

FIGURE 22.1 • THE FIVE BASIC PARTS OF ORGANIZATIONS

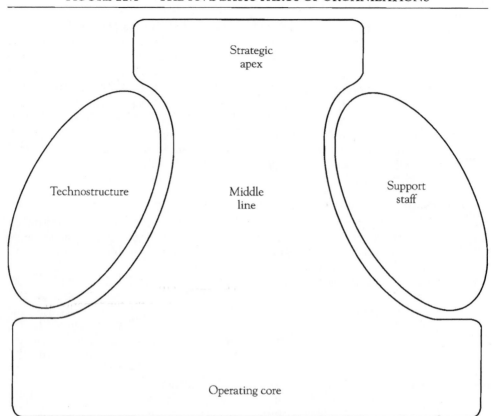

associated with producing the products or services. Above them sits the administrative component, which is shown in three parts. First, are the managers, divided into two groups. Those at the very top of the hierarchy, together with their own personal staff, form the *strategic apex*. And those below, who join the strategic apex to the operating core through the chain of command (such as it exists), make up the *middle line*. To their left stands the *technostructure*, wherein the analysts carry out their work of standardizing the work of others, in addition to applying their analytical techniques to help the organization adapt to its environment. Finally, we add a fifth group, the *support staff*, shown to the right of the middle line. This staff supports the functioning of the operating core indirectly, that is, outside the basic flow of operating work. The support staff goes largely unrecognized in the literature of organizational structuring, yet a quick glance at the chart of virtually any large organization indicates that it is a major segment, one that should not be confused with the other four. Examples of support groups in a typical manufacturing firm are research and development, cafeteria, legal council, payroll, public relations, and mailroom.

Figure 22.1 shows a small strategic apex connected by a flaring middle line to a large, flat operating core. These three parts of the organization are shown in one uninterrupted sequence to indicate that they are typically connected through a single line of formal authority. The technostructure and the support staff are shown off to either side to indicate that they are separate from this main line of authority, and influence the operating core only indirectly.

It might be useful at this point to relate this scheme to some terms commonly used in organizations. The term "middle management," although seldom carefully defined, generally seems to include all members of the organization not at the strategic apex or in the operating core. In our scheme, therefore, "middle management" would comprise three distinct groups — the middle-line managers, the analysts, and the support staff. To avoid confusion, however, the term *middle level* will be used here to describe these three groups together, the term "management" being reserved for the managers of the strategic apex and the middle line.

The word "staff" should also be put into this context. In the early literature, the term was used in contrast to "line": in theory, line positions had formal authority to make decisions, while staff positions did not; they merely advised those who did. (This has sometimes been referred to as "functional" authority, in contrast to the line's formal or "hierarchical" authority.) Allen (1955), for example, delineates the staff's major activities as (1) providing advice, counsel, suggestions, and guidance on planning objectives, policies, and procedures to govern the operations of the line departments on how best to put decisions into practice; and (2) performing specific service activities for the line, for example, installing budgeting systems and recruiting line personnel, "which may include making decisions that the line has asked it to make" (p. 348). As we shall see later, this distinction between line and staff holds up in some kinds of structures and breaks down in others. Nevertheless, the distinction between line and staff is of some use to us, and we shall retain the terms here though in somewhat modified form. *Staff* will be used to refer to the technostructure *and* the support staff, those groups shown on either side in Figure 22.1. *Line* will refer to the central part of Figure 22.1, those managers in the flow of formal authority from the strategic to the operating core. Note that this definition

does not mention the power to decide or advise. As we shall see, the support staff does not primarily advise; it has distinct functions to perform and decisions to make, although these relate only indirectly to the functions of the operating core. The chef in the plant cafeteria may be engaged in a production process, but it has nothing to do with the basic manufacturing process. Similarly, the technostructure's power to advise sometimes amounts to the power to decide, but that is outside the flow of formal authority that oversees the operating core.[1]

Some conceptual ideas of James D. Thompson. Before proceeding with a more detailed description of each of the five basic parts of the organization, it will be helpful to introduce at this point some of the important conceptual ideas of James D. Thompson (1967). To Thompson, "Uncertainty appears as the fundamental problem for complex organizations, and coping with uncertainty, as the essence of the administrative process" (p. 159). Thompson describes the organization in terms of a "technical core," equivalent to our operating core, and a group of "boundary spanning units." In his terms, the organization reduces uncertainty by sealing off this core from the environment so that the operating activities can be protected. The boundary spanning units face the environment directly and deal with its uncertainties. For example, the research department interprets the confusing scientific environment for the organization, while the public relations department placates a hostile social environment. . . .

Thompson also introduces a conceptual scheme to explain the *interdependencies* among organizational members. He distinguishes three ways in which the work can be coupled, shown in Figure 22.2. First is *pooled coupling,* where members share common resources but are otherwise independent. Figure 22.2(a) could represent teachers in a school who share common facilities and budgets but work alone with their pupils. In *sequential coupling,* members work

FIGURE 22.2 • POOLED, SEQUENTIAL, AND RECIPROCAL COUPLING OF WORK

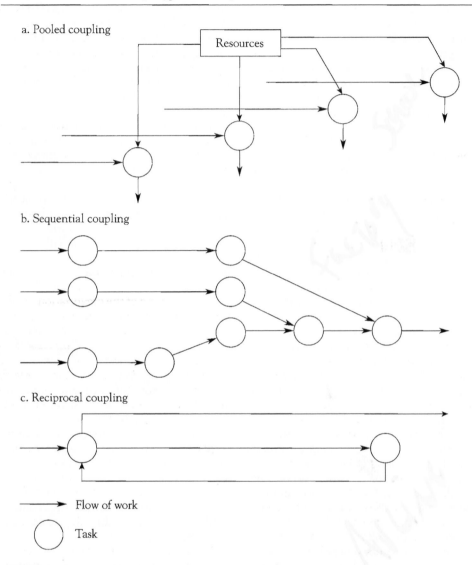

a. Pooled coupling

Resources

b. Sequential coupling

c. Reciprocal coupling

⟶ Flow of work

◯ Task

in series, as in a relay race where the baton passes from runner to runner. Figure 22.2(b) could represent a mass production factory, where raw materials enter at one end, are sequentially fabricated and machined, then fed into an assembly line at various points, and finally emerge at the other end as finished products. In *reciprocal coupling*, the members feed their work back and forth among themselves; in effect each receives inputs from and provides outputs to the others. "This is illustrated by the airline which contains both operations and maintenance units. The production of the maintenance unit is an input for operations, in the form of a serviceable aircraft; and the product (or by-product) of operations is an input for maintenance, in the form of an aircraft needing maintenance" (Thompson, 1967, p. 55). Figure 22.2(c) could be taken to represent this example, or one in a hospital in which the nurse "preps" the patient, the surgeon operates, and the nurse then takes care of the post-operative care.

Clearly, pooled coupling involves the least amount of interdependence among members. Anyone can be plucked out; and, as long as there is no great change in the resources available, the others can continue to work uninterrupted. Pulling out a member of a sequentially coupled organization, however, is like breaking a link in a chain—the whole activity must cease to function. Reciprocal coupling is, of course, more interdependent still, since a change in one task affects not only those farther along but also those behind.

Now let us take a look at each of the five parts of the organization.

THE OPERATING CORE

The operating core of the organization encompasses those members—the operators—who perform the basic work related directly to the production of products and services. The operators perform four prime functions: (1) They *secure the inputs* for production. For example, in a manufacturing firm, the purchasing department buys the raw materials and the receiving department takes it in the door. (2) They *transform the inputs into outputs*. Some organizations transform raw materials, for example, by chopping down trees and converting them to pulp and then paper. Others transform individual parts into complete units, for example, by assembling typewriters, while still others transform information or people, by writing consulting reports, educating students, cutting hair, or curing illness. (3) They *distribute the outputs*, for example, by selling and physically distributing what comes out of the transformation process. (4) They *provide direct support* to the input, transformation, and output functions, for example, by performing maintenance on the operating machines and inventorying the raw materials.

Since it is the operating core that the other parts of the organization seek to protect, standardization is generally carried furthest here. How far, of course, depends on the work being done: assemblers in automobile factories and professors in universities are both operators, although the work of the former is far more standardized than that of the latter.

The operating core is the heart of every organization, the part that produces the essential outputs that keep it alive. But except for the very smallest one, organizations need to build *administrative* components. The administrative component comprises the strategic apex, middle line, and technostructure.

THE STRATEGIC APEX

At the other end of the organization lies the strategic apex. Here are found those people charged with overall responsibility for the organization—the chief executive officer (whether called president, superintendent, Pope, or whatever), and any other top-level managers whose concerns are global. Included here as well are those who provide direct support to the top managers—their secretaries, assistants, and so on.[2] In some organizations, the strategic apex includes the executive committee (because its mandate is global even if its members represent specific interests); in others, it includes what is known as the chief executive office—two or three individuals who share the job of chief executive.

The strategic apex is charged with ensuring that the organization serves its mission in an effective way, and also that it serves the needs of those people who control or otherwise have power over the organization (such as owners, government agencies, unions of the employees, pressure groups). This entails three sets of duties. One already discussed is that of direct supervision. To the extent that the organization relies on this mechanism of coordination, it is the managers of the strategic apex and middle line who effect it. Among the managerial roles (Mintzberg, 1973) associated with direct supervision are resource allocator, including the design of the structure itself, the assignment of people and resources to tasks, the issuing of work orders, and the authorization of major decisions made by the employees; disturbance handler, involving the resolution of conflicts, exceptions, and disturbances sent up the hierarchy for resolution; monitor, involving the review of employees' activities; disseminator, involving the transmission of information to employees; and leader, involving the staffing of the organization and the motivating and rewarding of them. In its essence, direct supervision at the strategic apex means ensuring that the whole organization function smoothly as a single integrated unit.

But there is more to managing an organization than direct supervision. That is why even organizations with a minimal need for direct supervision, for example the very smallest that can rely on mutual adjustment, or professional ones that rely on formal training, still need managers. The second set of duties of the strategic apex involves the management of the organization's boundary conditions—its relationships with its environment. The managers of the strategic apex must spend a good deal of their time acting in the roles of spokesman, in informing influential people in the environment about the organization's activities; liaison, to develop high-level contact for the organization, and monitor, to tap these for information and to serve as the contact point for those who wish to influence the organization's goals; negotiator, when major agreements must be reached with outside parties; and sometimes even figurehead, in carrying out ceremonial duties, such as greeting important customers. (Someone once defined the manager, only half in jest, as that person who sees the visitors so that everyone else can get their work done.)

The third set of duties relates to the development of the organization's strategy. Strategy may be viewed as a mediating force between the organization and its environment. Strategy formulation therefore involves the interpretation of the environment and the development of consistent patterns in streams of organizational decisions ("strategies") to deal with it. Thus, in managing the boundary conditions of the organization, the managers of the strategic apex develop an understanding of its environment; and in carrying out the duties of direct supervision, they seek to tailor a strategy to its strengths and its needs, trying to maintain a pace of change that is responsive to the environment without being disruptive to the organization. Specifically, in the entrepreneur role, the top managers search for effective ways to carry out the organization's "mission" (i.e., its production of basic products and services), and sometimes even seek to change that mission. . . .

In general, the strategic apex takes the widest, and as a result the most abstract, perspective of the organization. Work at this level is generally characterized by a minimum of repetition and standardization, considerable discretion, and relatively long decision-making cycles. Mutual adjustment is the favored mechanism for coordination among the managers of the strategic apex itself.

THE MIDDLE LINE

The strategic apex is joined to the operating core by the chain of middle-line managers with formal authority. This chain runs from the senior managers just below the strategic apex to the *first-line supervisors* (e.g., the shop foremen), who have direct authority over the operators, and embodies the coordinating mechanism that we have called direct supervision. Figure 22.3 shows one famous chain of authority, that of the U.S. Army, from four-star general at the strategic apex to sergeant as first-line supervisor. This particular chain of authority is *scalar*, that is, it runs in a single line from top to bottom. But as we shall see later, not all need be: some divide and rejoin; a "subordinate" can have more than one "superior."

FIGURE 22.3 • THE SCALAR CHAIN OF COMMAND IN THE U.S. ARMY

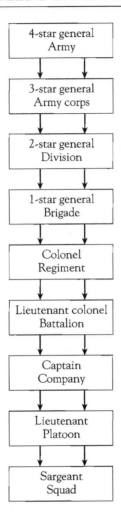

What do all these levels of managers do? If the strategic apex provides overall direction and the operating core produces the products or services, why does the organization need this whole chain of middle-line managers? One answer seems evident. To the extent that the organization is large and reliant on direct supervision for coordination, it requires middle-line managers. In theory, one manager—the chief executive at the strategic apex—can supervise all the operators. In practice, however, direct

supervision requires close personal contact between manager and operator, with the result that there is some limit to the number of operators any one manager can supervise—his so-called span of control. Small organizations can get along with one manager (at the strategic apex); bigger ones require more (in the middle-line). As Moses was told in the desert:

> Thou shalt provide out of all the people able men, such as fear God, men of truth, hating covetousness; and place such over them, to be rulers of thousands, and rulers of hundreds, rulers of fifties, and rulers of tens: and let them judge the people at all seasons: and it shall be, that every great matter they shall bring unto thee, but every small matter they shall judge: so shall it be easier for thyself, and they shall bear the burden with thee. If thou shalt do this thing, and God command thee so, then thou shalt be able to endure, and all this people shall also go to their place in peace (Exodus 18:21–24).

Thus, an organizational *hierarchy* is built as a first-line supervisor is put in charge of a number of operators to form a basic organizational unit, another manager is put in charge of a number of these units to form a higher level unit, and so on until all the remaining units can come under a single manager at the strategic apex—designated the "chief executive officer"—to form the whole organization.

In this hierarchy, the middle-line manager performs a number of tasks in the flow of direct supervision above and below him. He collects "feedback" information on the performance of his own unit and passes some of this up to the managers above him, often aggregating it in the process. The sales manager of the machinery firm may receive information on every sale, but he reports to the district sales manager only a monthly total. He also intervenes in the flow of decisions. Flowing up are disturbances in the unit, proposals for change, decisions requiring authorization. Some the middle-line manager handles himself, while others he passes on up for action at a higher level in the hierarchy. Flowing down are resources that he must allocate in his unit, rules and plans that he must elaborate and projects that he must implement there. For example, the strategic apex in the Postal Service may decide to implement a project to sell "domestograms." Each regional manager and, in turn, each district manager must elaborate the plan as it applies to his geographical area.

But like the top manager, the middle manager is required to do more than simply engage in direct supervision. He, too, has boundary conditions to manage, horizontal ones related to the environment of his own unit. That environment may include other units within the larger organization as well as groups outside the organization. The sales manager must coordinate by mutual adjustment with the managers of production and of research, and he must visit some of the organization's customers. The foreman must spend a good deal of time with the industrial engineers who standardize the work processes of the operators and with the supplier installing a new machine in his shop, while the plant manager may spend his time with the production scheduler and the architect designing a new factory. In effect, each middle-line manager maintains liaison contacts with the other managers, analysts, support staffers, and outsiders whose work is interdependent with that of his own unit. Furthermore, the middle-line manager, like

the top manager, is concerned with formulating the strategy for his unit, although this strategy is, of course, significantly affected by the strategy of the overall organization.

In general, the middle-line manager performs all the managerial roles of the chief executive, but in the context of managing his own unit (Mintzberg, 1973). He must serve as a figurehead for his unit and lead its members; develop a network of liaison contacts; monitor the environment and his unit's activities and transmit some of the information he receives into his own unit, up the hierarchy, and outside the chain of command; allocate resources within his unit; negotiate with outsiders; initiate strategic change; and handle exceptions and conflicts.

Managerial jobs do, however, shift in orientation as they descend in the chain of authority. There is clear evidence that the job becomes more detailed and elaborated, less abstract and aggregated, more focused on the work flow itself. Thus, the "real-time" roles of the manager—in particular, negotiation and the handling of disturbances—become especially important at lower levels in the hierarchy (Mintzberg, 1973, pp. 110–113). Martin (1956) studied the decisions made by four levels of production managers in the chain of authority and concluded that at each successively lower level, the decisions were more frequent, of shorter

FIGURE 22.4 • THE LINE MANAGER IN THE MIDDLE

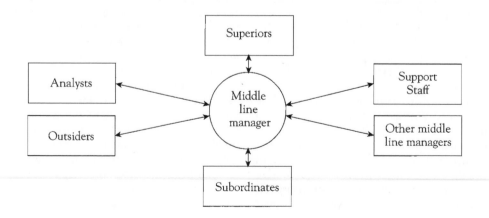

duration, and less elastic, ambiguous, and abstract; solutions tended to be more pat or predetermined; the significance of events and interrelationships was more clear; in general, lower-level decision making was more structured.

Figure 22.4 shows the line manager in the middle of a field of forces. Sometimes these forces become so great—especially those of the analysts to institutionalize his job by the imposition of rules on the unit— that the individual in the job can hardly be called a "manager" at all, in the sense of really being "in charge" of an organizational unit. This is common at the level of first-line supervisor—for example, the foreman in some mass production manufacturing firms and branch managers in some large banking systems.

THE TECHNOSTRUCTURE

In the technostructure we find the analysts (and their supporting clerical staff) who serve the organization by affecting the work of others. These analysts are removed from the operating work flow—they may design it, plan it, change it, or train the people who do it, but they do not do it themselves. Thus, the technostructure is effective only when it can use its analytical techniques to make the work of others more effective.[3]

Who makes up the technostructure? There are the analysts concerned with adaptation, with changing the organization to meet environmental change, and those concerned with control, with stabilizing and standardizing patterns of activity in the organization (Katz and Kahn, 1966). In this book we are concerned largely with the control analysts, those who focus their attention directly on the design and functioning of structure. The control analysts of the technostructure serve to effect standardization in the organization. This is not to say that operators cannot standardize their own work, just as everyone establishes his or her own procedure for getting dressed in the morning, or that managers cannot do

it for them. But in general, the more standardization an organization uses, the more it relies on its technostructure. Such standardization reduces the need for direct supervision, in effect enabling clerks to do what managers once did.

We can distinguish three types of control analysts who correspond to the three forms of standardization: work study analysts (such as industrial engineers), who standardize work processes; planning and control analysts (such as long-range planners, budget analysts, and accountants), who standardize outputs; and personnel analysts (including trainers and recruiters), who standardize skills.

In a fully developed organization, the technostructure may perform at all levels of the hierarchy. At the lowest levels of the manufacturing firm, analysts standardize the operating work flow by scheduling production, carrying out time-and-method studies of the operator's work, and instituting systems of quality control. At middle levels, they seek to standardize the intellectual work of the organization (e.g., by training middle managers) and carry out operations research studies of informational tasks. On behalf of the strategic apex, they design strategic planning systems and develop financial systems to control the goals of major units.

While the analysts exist to standardize the work of others, their own work would appear to be coordinated with others largely through mutual adjustment. (Standardization of skills does play a part in this coordination, however, because analysts are typically highly trained specialists.) Thus, analysts spend a good deal of their time in informal communication. Guetzkow (1965, p. 537), for example, notes that staff people typically have wider communication contacts than line people, and my review of the literature on managerial work (Mintzberg, 1973, pp. 116–118) showed some evidence that staff managers pay more attention to the information processing roles—monitor, disseminator, spokesman—than do line managers.

SUPPORT STAFF

A glance at the chart of almost any large contemporary organization reveals a great number of units, all specialized, that exist to provide support to the organization outside the operating work flow. Those comprise the *support staff*. For example, in a university, we find the alma mater fund, building and grounds department, museum, university press, bookstore, printing service, payroll department, janitorial service, endowment office, mailroom, real estate office, security department, switchboard, athletics department, student placement office, student residence, faculty club, guidance service, and chaplainery. None is a part of the operating core, that is, none engages in teaching or research, or even supports it directly (as does,

say, the computing center or the library), yet each exists to provide indirect support to these basic missions. In the manufacturing firm, these units run the gamut from legal counsel to plant cafeteria. . . .

The support units can be found at various levels of the hierarchy, depending on the receivers of their service. In most manufacturing firms, public relations and legal counsel are located near the top, since they tend to serve the strategic apex directly. At middle levels are found the units that support the decisions made there, such as industrial relations, pricing, and research and development. And at the lower levels are found the units with more standardized work, that akin to the work of the operating core—cafeteria, mailroom, reception, payroll. Figure 22.5 shows all these support

FIGURE 22.5 • SOME MEMBERS AND UNITS OF THE PARTS OF THE MANUFACTURING FIRM

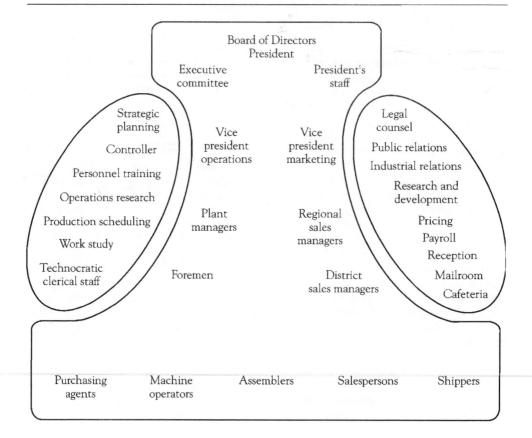

groups overlaid on our logo, together with typical groups from the other four parts of the organization, again using the manufacturing firm as our example.

Because of the wide variations in the types of support units, we cannot draw a single definitive conclusion about the favored coordinating mechanism for all of them. Each unit relies on whatever mechanism is most appropriate for itself—standardization of skills in the office of legal counsel, mutual adjustment in the research laboratory, standardization of work processes in the cafeteria. However, because many of the support units are highly specialized and rely on professional staff, standardization of skills may be the single most important coordinating mechanism. . . .

The most dramatic growth in organizations in recent decades has been in these staff groups, both the technostructure and the support staff. For example, Litterer (1973, pp. 584–585), in a study of thirty companies, noted the creation of 292 new staff units between 1920 and 1960, nearly ten units per company. More than half these units were in fact created between 1950 and 1960.

Organizations have always had operators and top managers, people to do the basic work and people to hold the whole system together. As they grew, typically they first elaborated their middle-line component, on the assumption in the early literature that coordination had to be effected by direct supervision. But as standardization became an accepted coordinating mechanism, the technostructure began to emerge. The work of Frederick Taylor gave rise to the "scientific management" movement of the 1920s, which saw the hiring of many work study analysts. Just after World War II, the establishing of operations research and the advent of the computer pushed the influence of the technostructure well into the middle levels of the organization, and with the more recent popularity of techniques such as strategic planning and sophisticated financial controls, the technostructure has entrenched itself firmly at the highest levels of the organization as well.

And the growth of the support staff has perhaps been even more dramatic, as all kinds of specializations developed during this century—scientific research in a wide number of fields, industrial relations, public relations and many more. Organizations have sought increasingly to bring these as well as the more traditional support functions such as maintenance and cafeteria within their boundaries. Thus, the ellipses to the left and right in the logo have become great bulges in many organizations. Joan Woodward (1965, p. 60) found in her research that firms in the modern process industries (such as oil refining) averaged one staff member for less than three operators, and in some cases the staff people actually outnumbered the operators by wide margins.[4]

NOTES

1. There are other, completely different, uses of the term "staff" that we are avoiding here. The military "chiefs of staff" are really managers of the strategic apex; the hospital "staff" physicians are really operators. Also, the introduction of the line/staff distinction here is not meant to sweep all of its problems under the rug, only to distinguish those involved directly from those involved peripherally with the operating work of organizations. By our definition, the production and sales functions in the typical manufacturing firm are clearly line activities, marketing research and public relations clearly staff. To debate whether engineering is line or staff—does it serve the operating core indirectly or is it an integral part of it?—depends on the importance one imputes to engineering in a particular firm. There is a gray area between line and staff: where it is narrow, for many organizations, we retain the distinction; where it is wide, we shall explicitly discard it.

2. Our subsequent discussion will focus only on the managers of the strategic apex, the work of the latter group being considered an integral part of their own.

3. This raises an interesting point: that the technostructure has a built-in commitment to change, to perpetual improvement. The modern organization's obsession with

change probably derives in part at least from large and ambitious technostructures seeking to ensure their own survival. The perfectly stable organization has no need for a technostructure.

4. Woodward's tables and text here are very confusing, owing in part at least to some line errors in the page makeup. The data cited above are based on Figure 18, page 60, which seems to have the title that belongs to Figure 17 and which seems to relate back to Figure 7 on page 28, not to Figure 8 as Woodward claims.

REFERENCES

Allen, L. A. (1955, September). The line-staff relationship. *Management Record*, 346–349, 374–376.

Guetzkow, H. (1965). Communications in organizations. In J. G. March (Ed.), *Handbook of organizations* (Chap. 12). Chicago: Rand McNally.

Katz, D., & Kahn, R. L. (1966). *The social psychology of organizations*. New York: Wiley.

Kaufman, H., & Seidman, D. (1970). The morphology of organization. *Administrative Science Quarterly*, 439–445.

Litterer, J. A. (1973). *The analysis of organizations* (2nd ed.). New York: Wiley. Used with permission.

Martin, N. H. (1956). Differential decisions in the management of an industrial plant. *The Journal of Business*, 249–260.

Mintzberg, H. (1973). *The nature of managerial work*. New York: Harper & Row.

———. (1978). Patterns in strategy formation. *Management Science*, 934–948.

Thompson, J. D. (1967). *Organizations in action*. New York: McGraw-Hill.

Woodward, J. (1965). *Industrial organization: Theory and practice*. New York: Oxford University Press. Used with permission.

23

In Praise of Hierarchy

Elliott Jaques

At first glance, hierarchy may seem difficult to praise. Bureaucracy is a dirty word even among bureaucrats, and in business there is a widespread view that managerial hierarchy kills initiative, crushes creativity, and has therefore seen its day. Yet 35 years of research have convinced me that managerial hierarchy is the most efficient, the hardiest, and in fact the most natural structure ever devised for large organizations. Properly structured, hierarchy can release energy and creativity, rationalize productivity, and actually improve morale. Moreover, I think most managers know this intuitively and have only lacked a workable structure and a decent intellectual justification for what they have always known could work and work well.

As presently practiced, hierarchy undeniably has its drawbacks. One of business's great contemporary problems is how to release and sustain among the people who work in corporate hierarchies the thrust, initiative, and adaptability of the entrepreneur. This problem is so great that it has become fashionable to call for a new kind of organization to put in place of managerial hierarchy, an organization that will better meet the requirements of what is variously called the Information Age, the Services Age, or the Post-Industrial Age.

As vague as the description of the age is the definition of the kind of new organization required to suit it. Theorists tell us it ought to look more like a symphony orchestra or a hospital or perhaps the British raj. It ought to function by means of primus groups or semiautonomous work teams or matrix overlap groups. It should be organic or entrepreneurial or tight-loose. It should hinge on skunk works or on management by walking around or perhaps on our old friend, management by objective.

All these approaches are efforts to overcome the perceived faults of hierarchy and find better ways to improve morale and harness human creativity. But the theorists' belief that our changing world requires an alternative to hierarchical organization is simply wrong, and all their proposals are based on an inadequate understanding of not only hierarchy but also human nature.

Hierarchy is not to blame for our problems. Encouraged by gimmicks and fads masquerading as insights, we have burdened our managerial systems with a makeshift scaffolding of inept structures and attitudes. What we need is not simply a new, flatter organization but an understanding of how managerial hierarchy functions—how it relates to the complexity of work and how we can use it to achieve a more effective deployment of talent and energy.

The reason we have a hierarchical organization of work is not only that tasks occur in lower and higher degrees of complexity—which is obvious—but also that there are sharp discontinuities in complexity that separate tasks into a series of steps or categories—which is not so obvious. The same discontinuities occur with respect to mental work and to the breadth and duration of accountability. The hierarchical kind of organization we call bureaucracy did not emerge accidentally. It is the only form of organization that can enable a company to employ large numbers of people and yet preserve unambiguous accountability for

Source: Harvard Business Review (January–February 1990). © 1990 by the President and Fellows of Harvard College. Reprinted by permission of *Harvard Business Review*. All rights reserved.

the work they do. And that is why, despite its problems, it has so doggedly persisted.

Hierarchy has not had its day. Hierarchy never did have its day. As an organizational system, managerial hierarchy has never been adequately described and has just as certainly never been adequately used. The problem is not to find an alternative to a system that once worked well but no longer does; the problem is to make it work efficiently for the first time in its 3,000-year history.

WHAT WENT WRONG . . .

There is no denying that hierarchical structure has been the source of a great deal of trouble and inefficiency. Its misuse has hampered effective management and stifled leadership, while its track record as a support for entrepreneurial energy has not been exemplary. We might almost say that successful businesses have had to succeed despite hierarchical organization rather than because of it.

One common complaint is excessive layering—too many rungs on the ladder. Information passes through too many people, decisions through too many levels, and managers and subordinates are too close together in experience and ability, which smothers effective leadership, cramps accountability, and promotes buck passing. Relationships grow stressful when managers and subordinates bump elbows, so to speak, within the same frame of reference.

Another frequent complaint is that few managers seem to add real value to the work of their subordinates. The fact that the breakup value of many large corporations is greater than their share value shows pretty clearly how much value corporate managers can *subtract* from their subsidiary businesses, but in fact few of us know exactly what managerial added value would look like as it was occurring.

Many people also complain that our present hierarchies bring out the nastier aspects of human behavior, like greed, insensitivity,

careerism, and self-importance. These are the qualities that have sent many behavioral scientists in search of cooperative, group-oriented, nonhierarchical organizational forms. But are they the inevitable companions of hierarchy, or perhaps a product of the misuse of hierarchy that would disappear if hierarchy were properly understood and structured?

. . . AND WHAT CONTINUES TO GO WRONG

The fact that so many of hierarchy's problems show up in the form of individual misbehavior has led to one of the most widespread illusions in business, namely, that a company's managerial leadership can be significantly improved solely by doing psychotherapeutic work on the personalities and attitudes of its managers. Such methods can help individuals gain greater personal insight, but I doubt that individual insight, personality matching, or even exercises in group dynamics can produce much in the way of organizational change or an overall improvement in leadership effectiveness. The problem is that our managerial hierarchies are so badly designed as to defeat the best effort even of psychologically insightful individuals.

Solutions that concentrate on groups, on the other hand, fail to take into account the real nature of employment systems. People are not employed in groups. They are employed individually, and their employment contracts—real or implied—are individual. Group members may insist in moments of great esprit de corps that the group as such is the author of some particular accomplishment, but once the work is completed, the members of the group look for individual recognition and individual progression in their careers. And it is not groups but individuals whom the company will hold accountable. The only true group is the board of directors, with its corporate liability.

None of the group-oriented panaceas face this issue of accountability. All the theorists refer to group authority, group decisions, and group concensus, none of them to group accountability. Indeed, they avoid the issue of accountability altogether, for to hold a group accountable, the employment contract would have to be with the group, not with the individuals, and companies simply do not employ groups as such.

To understand hierarchy, you must first understand employment. To be employed is to have an ongoing contract that holds you accountable for doing work of a given type for a specified number of hours per week in exchange for payment. Your specific tasks within that given work are assigned to you by a person called your manager (or boss or supervisor), who *ought to be held accountable* for the work you do.

If we are to make our hierarchies function properly, it is essential to place the emphasis on *accountability for getting work done*. This is what hierarchical systems ought to be about. Authority is a secondary issue and flows from accountability in the sense that there should be just that amount of authority needed to discharge the accountability. So if a group is to be given authority, its members must be held accountable as a group, and unless this is done, it is very hard to take so-called group decisions seriously. If the CEO or the manager of the group is held accountable for outcomes, then in the final analysis, he or she will have to agree with group decisions or have the authority to block them, which means that the group never really had decision-making power to begin with. Alternatively, if groups are allowed to make decisions without their manager's seal of approval, then accountability as such will suffer, for if a group does badly, the group is never fired. (And it would be shocking if it were.)

In the long run, therefore, group authority *without* group accountability is dysfunctional, and group authority *with* group accountability is unacceptable. So images of organizations that are more like symphony orchestras or hospitals or the British raj are surely nothing more than metaphors to express a desired feeling of togetherness — the togetherness produced by a conductor's baton, the shared concern of doctors and nurses for their patients, or the apparent unity of the British civil service in India.

In employment systems, after all, people are not mustered to play together as their manager beats time. As for hospitals, they are the essence of everything bad about bureaucratic organization. They function in spite of the system, only because of the enormous professional devotion of their staffs. The Indian civil service was in many ways like a hospital, its people bound together by the struggle to survive in a hostile environment. Managers do need authority, but authority based appropriately on the accountabilities they must discharge.

WHY HIERARCHY?

The bodies that govern companies, unions, clubs, and nations all employ people to do work, and they all organize these employees in managerial hierarchies, systems that allow organizations to hold people accountable for getting assigned work done. Unfortunately, we often lose sight of this goal and set up the organizational layers in our managerial hierarchies to accommodate pay brackets and facilitate career development instead. If work happens to get done as well, we consider that a useful bonus.

But if our managerial hierarchical organizations tend to choke so readily on debilitating bureaucratic practices, how do we explain the persistence and continued spread of this form of organization for more than 3,000 years? And why has the determined search for alternatives proved so fruitless?

The answer is that managerial hierarchy is and will remain the *only* way to structure unified working systems with hundreds, thousands, or tens of thousands of employees, for the very good reason that managerial hierarchy is the expression of two fundamental characteristics of real work. First, the tasks we carry out are not only more or less complex but they also become more complex as they separate out into discrete categories or types of complexity. Second, the same is true of the mental work that people do on the job, for as this work grows more complex, it too separates out into distinct categories or types of mental activity. In turn, these two characteristics permit hierarchy to meet four of any organization's fundamental needs: to add real value to work as it moves through the organization, to identify and nail down accountability at each stage of the value-adding process, to place people with the necessary competence at each organizational layer, and to build a general consensus and acceptance of the managerial structure that achieves these ends.

HIERARCHICAL LAYERS

The complexity of the problems encountered in a particular task, project, or strategy is a function of the variables involved— their number, their clarity or ambiguity, the rate at which they change, and, overall, the extent to which they are distinct or tangled. Obviously, as you move higher in a managerial hierarchy the most difficult problems you have to contend with become increasingly complex. The biggest problems faced by the CEO of a large corporation are vastly more complex than those encountered on the shop floor. The CEO must cope not only with a huge array of often amorphous and constantly changing data but also with variables so tightly interwoven that they must be disentangled before they will yield useful information. Such variables might include the cost of capital, the interplay of corporate cash flow, the structure of the international competitive market, the uncertainties of Europe after 1992, the future of Pacific Rim development, social developments with respect to labor, political developments in Eastern Europe, the Middle East, and the Third World, and technological research and change.

That the CEO's and the lathe operator's problems are different in quality as well as

quantity will come as no surprise to anyone. The question is—and always has been— where does the change in quality occur? On a continuum of complexity from the bottom of the structure to the top, where are the discontinuities that will allow us to identify layers of hierarchy that are distinct and separable, as different as ice is from water and water from steam? I spent years looking for the answer, and what I found was somewhat unexpected.

My first step was to recognize the obvious, that the layers have to do with manager-subordinate relationships. The manager's position is in one layer and the subordinate's is in the next layer below. What then sets the necessary distance between? This question cannot be answered without knowing just what it is that a manager does.

The managerial role has three critical features. First, and *most* critical, every manager must be held accountable not only for the work of subordinates but also for adding value to their work. Second, every manager must be held accountable for sustaining a team of subordinates capable of doing this work. Third, every manager must be held accountable for setting direction and getting subordinates to follow willingly, indeed enthusiastically. In brief, every manager is accountable for work and leadership.

In order to make accountability possible, managers must have enough authority to ensure that their subordinates can do the work assigned to them. This authority must include at least these four elements: (1) the right to veto any applicant who, in the manager's opinion, falls below the minimum standards of ability; (2) the power to make work assignments; (3) the power to carry out performance appraisals and, within the limits of company policy, to make decisions—not recommendations— about raises and merit rewards; and (4) the authority to initiate removal—at least from the manager's own team— of anyone who seems incapable of doing the work.

But defining the basic nature of the managerial role reveals only part of what a managerial layer means. It cannot tell us how wide a managerial layer should be, what the difference in responsibility should be between a manager and a subordinate, or, most important, where the break should come between one managerial layer and another. Fortunately, the next step in the research process supplied the missing piece of the puzzle.

RESPONSIBILITY AND TIME

This second step was the unexpected and startling discovery that the level of responsibility in any organizational role — whether a manager's or an individual contributor's — can be objectively measured in terms of the target completion time of the *longest* task, project, or program assigned to that role. The more distant the target completion date of the longest task or program, the heavier the weight of responsibility is felt to be. I call this measure the responsibility time span of the role. For example, a supervisor whose principal job is to plan tomorrow's production assignments and next week's work schedule but who also has ongoing responsibility for uninterrupted production supplies for the month ahead has a responsibility time span of one month. A foreman who spends most of his time riding herd on this week's production quotas but who must also develop a program to deal with the labor requirements of next year's retooling has a responsibility time span of a year or a little more. The advertising vice president who stays late every night working on next week's layouts but who also has to begin making contingency plans for the expected launch of two new local advertising media campaigns three years hence has a responsibility time span of three years.

To my great surprise, I found that in all types of managerial organizations in many different countries over 35 years, people in roles at the same time span experience the same weight of responsibility and declare the same level of pay to be fair, regardless of their occupation or actual pay. The time-span range runs from a day at the bottom of

a large corporation to more than 20 years at the top, while the felt-fair pay ranges from $15,000 to $1 million and more.

Armed with my definition of a manager and my time-span measuring instrument, I then bumped into the second surprising finding — repeatedly confirmed — about layering in managerial hierarchies: the boundaries between successive managerial layers occur at certain specific time-span increments, just as ice changes to water and water to steam at certain specific temperatures. And the fact that everyone in the hierarchy, regardless of status, seems to see these boundaries in the same places suggests that the boundaries reflect some universal truth about human nature.

Figure 23.1 shows the hierarchical structure of part of a department at one company I studied, along with the approximate responsibility time span for each position. The longest task for manager A was more than five years, while for B, C, and D, the longest task fell between two and five years. Note also that according to the organization chart, A is the designated manager of B, B of C, and C of D.

In reality, the situation was quite different. Despite the managerial roles specified by the company, B, C, and D all described

FIGURE 23.1 • MANAGERIAL
HIERARCHY IN FICTION
AND IN FACT

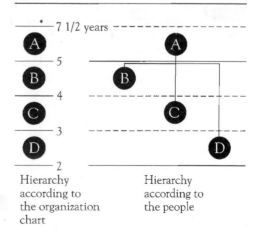

Hierarchy according to the organization chart

Hierarchy according to the people

A as their "real" boss. C complained that B was "far too close" and "breathing down my neck." D had the same complaint about C. B and C also admitted to finding it very difficult to manage their immediate subordinates, C and D respectively, who seemed to do better if treated as colleagues and left alone.

In short, there appeared to be a cutoff at five years, such that those with responsibility time spans of less than five years felt they needed a manager with a responsibility time span of more than five years. Manager D, with a time span of two to three years, did not feel that C, with a time span of three to four, was distant enough hierarchically to take order from. D felt the same way about B. Only A filled the bill for any of the other three.

As the responsibility time span increased in the example from two years to three to four and approached five, no one seemed to perceive a qualitative difference in the nature of the responsibility that a manager discharged. Then, suddenly, when a manager had responsibility for tasks and projects that exceeded five years in scope, everyone seemed to perceive a difference not only in the scope of responsibility but also in its quality and in the kind of work and worker required to discharge it.

I found several such discontinuities that appeared consistently in more than 100 studies. Real managerial and hierarchical boundaries occur at time spans of three months, one year, two years, five years, ten years, and twenty years.

These natural discontinuities in our perception of the responsibility time span create hierarchical strata that people in different companies, countries, and circumstances all seem to regard as genuine and acceptable. The existence of such boundaries has important implications in nearly every sphere of organizational management. One of these is performance appraisal. Another is the capacity of managers to add value to the work of their subordinates.

The only person with the perspective and authority to judge and communicate personal effectiveness is an employee's accountable manager, who, in most cases, is also the only person from whom an employee will accept evaluation and coaching. This accountable manager must be the supervisor one real layer higher in the hierarchy, not merely the next higher employee on the pay scale.

As I suggested earlier, part of the secret to making hierarchy work is to distinguish carefully between hierarchical layers and pay grades. The trouble is that companies need two to three times as many pay grades as they do working layers, and once they've established the pay grades, which are easy to describe and set up, they fail to take the next step and set up a different managerial hierarchy based on responsibility rather than salary. The result is too many layers.

My experience with organizations of all kinds in many different countries has convinced me that effective value-adding managerial leadership of subordinates can come only from an individual one category higher in cognitive capacity, working one category higher in problem complexity. By contrast, wherever managers and subordinates are in the same layer—separated only by pay grade—subordinates see the boss as too close, breathing down their necks, and they identify their "real" boss as the next manager at a genuinely higher level of cognitive and task complexity. This kind of overlayering is what produces the typical symptoms of bureaucracy in its worst form—too much passing problems up and down the system, bypassing, poor task setting, frustrated subordinates, anxious managers, wholly inadequate performance appraisals, "personality problems" everywhere, and so forth.

LAYERING AT COMPANY X

Companies need more than seven pay grades—as a rule, many more. But seven hierarchical layers is enough or more than enough for all but the largest corporations.

Let me illustrate this pattern of hierarchical layering with the case of two divisions of

FIGURE 23.2 • TWO DIVISIONS OF CORPORATION X

	Layer	Time Span	Felt-Fair Pay*
CEO	VII	20 years	$1,040
EVP — EVP — EVP — EVP	VI	10 years	520
President — President — President	V	5 years	260
General manager — General editor — General manager — General manager	IV	2 years	130
Unit managers — Editors	III	1 year	68
First-line managers	II	3 months	38
Technicians and operators — Typists	I	1 day	20

*(In thousands of dollars)

Company X, a corporation with 32,000 employees and annual sales of $7 billion. As shown in Figure 23.2 the CEO sets strategic goals that look ahead as far as 25 years and manages executive vice presidents with responsibility for 12- to 15-year development programs. One vice president is accountable for several strategic business units, each with a president who works with critical tasks of up to 7 years duration.

One of these units (Y Products) employs 2,800 people, has annual sales of $250 million, and is engaged in the manufacture and sale of engineering products, with traditional semiskilled shop-floor production at Layer I. The other unit (Z Press) publishes books and employs only 88 people. Its funding and negotiations with authors are in the hands of a general editor at Layer IV, assisted by a small group of editors at Layer III, each working on projects that may take up to 18 months to complete.

So the president of Y Products manages more people, governs a greater share of corporate resources, and earns a lot more money for the parent company than does the president of Z Press. Yet the two presidents occupy the same hierarchical layer, have similar authority, and take home comparable salaries. This is neither coincidental nor unfair. It is natural, correct, and efficient.

It is the level of responsibility, *measured in terms of time span*, that tells you how many layers you need in an enterprise—not the number of subordinates or the magnitude of sales or profits. These factors may have a marginal influence on salary; they have no bearing at all on hierarchical layers.

CHANGES IN THE QUALITY OF WORK

The widespread and striking consistency of this underlying pattern of true managerial layers leads naturally to the question of why it occurs. Why do people perceive a sudden leap in status from, say, four-and-a-half years to five and from nine to ten?

The answer goes back to the earlier discussion of complexity. As we go higher in a managerial hierarchy, the most difficult problems that arise grow increasingly complex, and, as the complexity of a task increases, so does the complexity of the mental work required to handle it. What I found when I looked at this problem over the course of ten years was that this complexity, like responsibility time span, also occurs in leaps or jumps. In other words, the most difficult tasks found within any given layer are all characterized by the same type or category of complexity, just as water remains in the same liquid state from 0° to 100° Celsius, even though it ranges from very cold to very hot. (A few degrees cooler or hotter and water changes in state, to ice or steam.)

It is this suddenly increased level of necessary mental capacity, experience, knowledge, and mental stamina that allows managers to add value to the work of their subordinates. What they add is a new perspective, one that is broader, more experienced, and, most important, one that extends further in time. If, at Z Press, the editors at Layer III find and develop manuscripts into books with market potential,

it is their general editor at Layer IV who fits those books into the press's overall list, who thinks ahead to their position on next year's list and later allocates resources to their production and marketing, and who makes projections about the publishing and book-buying trends of the next two to five years.

It is also this sudden change in the quality, not just the quantity, of managerial work that subordinates accept as a natural and appropriate break in the continuum of hierarchy. It is why they accept the boss's authority and not just the boss's power.

So the whole picture comes together. Managerial hierarchy or layering is the only effective organizational form for deploying people and tasks at complementary levels, where people can do the tasks assigned to them, where the people in any given layer can add value to the work of those in the layer below them, and, finally, where this stratification of management strikes everyone as necessary and welcome.

What we need is not some new kind of organization. What we need is managerial hierarchy that understands its own nature and purpose. Hierarchy is the best structure for getting work done in big organizations. Trying to raise efficiency and morale without first setting this structure to rights is like trying to lay bricks without mortar. No amount of exhortation, attitudinal engineering, incentive planning, or even leadership will have any permanent effect unless we understand what hierarchy is and why and how it works. We need to stop casting about fruitlessly for organizational Holy Grails and settle down to the hard work of putting our managerial hierarchies in order.

24

Technology as a Contingency Factor

Richard M. Burton & Børge Obel

The various dimensions of technology have an effect on the organizational design. We consider technology's effect on formalization, centralization, complexity, configuration, coordination and control, and incentives.

TECHNOLOGY EFFECTS ON FORMALIZATION

In Table 24.1, Propositions 1 and 2 relate technology routineness to formalization. The more routine the technology, the more the activities are predictable. Exceptions are few and easy to resolve. Less information needs to be processed. With a high routineness, it is advantageous and efficient to establish rules and a program to regulate and coordinate the work (Perrow, 1967, pp. 199–200). When routineness is low, such rules and programs are likely to be incorrect much of the time. Thus, a good deal of information will need to be processed to schedule and coordinate processes. The re-

lationship has been questioned (Robbins, 1990) but it has obtained empirical support by many including the metaanalysis by Miller, Glick, Wang, and Huber (1991).

Miller, Glick, Wang, and Huber (1991) also found that the strength of the relationship was modified by two factors. These are incorporated into Propositions 3 and 4. First, an organization with many professionals has a mitigating effect on routineness and formalization. The argument is that professionalization and formalization are alternative forms for coordination and control so that when one is in place, the effect of the other vanishes. The important factor is standardized behavior for the organization. There are more means to obtain such behavior.

Second, Miller, Glick, Wang, and Huber (1991) found that the type of industry influenced the strength of Propositions 1 and 2. They argued that one would expect that routineness of the technology was more positively related to centralization, formalization, and specialization in manufacturing

---

TABLE 24.1 • TECHNOLOGY EFFECTS ON FORMALIZATION, PROPOSITIONS 1–6

---

1. If technology routineness is low, then formalization should be low.
2. If technology routineness is high, then formalization should be high.
3. If the organization employs many professionals, then Proposition 2 is not so strong.
4. If the organization is in the service industry, then the strength of Propositions 1 and 2 is greater than if it is in the manufacturing industry. Retail and wholesale organizations can be expected to fall in between.
5. If the technology type is process (i.e., high automation), then formalization should be higher than it would be otherwise.
6. If the organization uses modern information technology, then formalization should be high.

Source: Richard M. Burton and Børge Obel, sec. 7.3.2 from "Technology," chap. 7 in Burton and Obel, *Strategic organizational diagnosis and design: Developing theory for application,* 2d ed. (Boston: Kluwer Academic, 1998), 224–234. Reprinted by permission.

organizations than in service organizations. However, their metaanalysis showed exactly the opposite. Jackson and Morgan (1978, p. 196) argue that the reason for such findings may be that in manufacturing the production process is linked to machines and their performance, and these machines indirectly introduce standardization. In service organizations more rules and procedures are needed to obtain the same level of standardized behavior. Additionally, in manufacturing the quality control related to the process may secure high quality of the products while rules are needed to obtain high quality in service organizations. This implies a higher reliance on formalization and centralization. This also fits the view expressed in Mills and Moberg (1982) on the differences between manufacturing and service technologies.

This kind of analysis leads to Proposition 5, which indicates that highly automated technology should have a greater formalization than otherwise suggested. This proposition is also supported by Child (1973, p. 183), who states that automation leads to higher formalization. However, it is directly opposed to Woodward's original results. She found that process production had low formalization. The difference may be attributed to the difference in size of mass production firms and process production firms (Hickson, Pugh, and Pheysey, 1979). The mass production firms were generally larger than the process production firms; therefore, from a size argument, formalization was higher in the mass production firms than in the process production firms.

Automation is related to the use of computers and information technology. Zeffane

(1989) found that such use would increase formalization. We posit that if the introduction of modern information technology is not followed by standard rules on how to use it, the likelihood of inefficient operations is high. We therefore suggest Proposition 6. Such standardization also may have negative side effects. We all have received letters from companies urging us to pay their bills when we have done so some days before. If the company's computer has a standard procedure writing letters to all those who have not paid within a given deadline, then it may not be possible to alter procedures.

TECHNOLOGY EFFECTS ON CENTRALIZATION

In Table 24.2 the relationship between technology routineness and centralization is not as simple as that given in Propositions 7 and 8. These incorporate issues of size as well as technology. If the organization is small and has a technology that is very routine, then the manager can more easily assess the operations than if the routineness was low. A manager can handle the required information. Therefore, the argument that for small organizations the centralization should be high is further strengthened.

When the organization is large and has a technology that is routine, then it is very likely both from the size paradigm and from Proposition 2 that formalization should be high. A control and coordination mechanism, therefore, is in place (Zeffane, 1989). . . . Propositions 7 and 8 are supported by the metaanalysis by Miller, Glick, Wang, and Huber (1991).

TABLE 24.2 • TECHNOLOGY EFFECTS ON CENTRALIZATION,
PROPOSITIONS 7–8

7. If technology routineness is high and the size of the organization is small, then centralization should be high.

8. If the organization is large and technology routineness is high, then centralization should be medium.

TECHNOLOGY EFFECTS ON ORGANIZATIONAL COMPLEXITY

The relationship between technology and complexity is not simple either, as given in Propositions 9 and 10 (see Table 24.3). Size is a moderator again. Generally, the larger organization with a routine technology is more complex.

The argument is that large organizations can better specialize and, therefore, use the routine technology to create experts for each specialty; horizontal differentiation increases. Propositions 9 and 10 are partly supported by Miller, Glick, Wang, and Huber (1991). However, a reverse argument also can be made. If the technology is nonroutine, then the work is very complex, and it is likely that the appropriate span of control is low. Therefore complexity increases vertical differentiation particularly. We therefore state in Proposition 11 that for a large organization with a nonroutine technology, complexity should be high — particularly vertical differentiation.

Both Propositions 10 and 11 were based on a span-of-control argument; because supervision has limited information-processing capacity and can deal with a limited number of issues or exceptions, a nonroutine technology will yield. These arguments are formalized in Propositions 12 and 13.

The argument is that the more complex the work, the less people a manager can supervise and control. This is a bounded-rationality argument and is widely supported (Robbins, 1990). That both non-routine and routine technology may lead to high complexity, but for different reasons, may explain why Miller, Glick, Wang, and Huber, (1991), in their metaanalysis using averages, did not find a significant relationship between routineness and specialization. There may be other technology-based reasons than routineness that may lead to structural conclusions.

Since process organizations use more automation and more skilled personnel, the span-of-control argument suggests that process organizations are more complex than other types. This is Proposition 14. However, Woodward (1965) . . . found the opposite in her research on manufacturing firms. This contrast also may be related to the discussion about the effect of size. Woodward's results have been criticized because it was argued that when controlled for size her results disappeared (Hickson, Pugh, and Pheysey, 1979). Because organizations that use a process technology are less labor intensive, they tend to be of smaller size. In most cases . . . Proposition 14 does not take the size of the organization into consideration. The balancing of the two propositions will result in the correct recommendation for the particular organization. . . .

TECHNOLOGY EFFECTS ON CONFIGURATION

Technology also affects the configuration in many ways (see Table 24.4). Proposition 15 indicates that a unit technology is more

TABLE 24.3 • TECHNOLOGY EFFECTS ON ORGANIZATIONAL COMPLEXITY, PROPOSITIONS 9–14

9. If the size of the organization is large and the organization has a technology that is routine, then complexity should be high — particularly horizontal differentiation.

10. If the size of the organization is small and the organization has a technology that is routine, then complexity should be medium.

11. If the size of the organization is large and has a nonroutine technology, then complexity should be high — particularly vertical differentiation.

12. If the organization has a nonroutine technology, then the span of control should be narrow.

13. If the organization has a routine technology, then the span of control should be wide.

14. If the technology type is process (high automation), then complexity is high.

TABLE 24.4 • EFFECTS ON CONFIGURATION, PROPOSITIONS 15–20

15. If the technology type is unit, then it is more likely that the organization has a matrix configuration.
16. If the organization has a nonroutine technology, then the functional configuration is not likely to be an efficient configuration.
17. If the technology is not divisible, then the configuration cannot be divisional.
18. If the technology is divisible, then it is not very likely that the configuration should be a matrix configuration.
19. If the organization has a nonroutine technology, then it is not likely that a machine or professional bureaucracy is an efficient configuration.
20. If the technology is not nonroutine, then the configuration cannot be an ad hoc configuration.

likely to require a matrix organization. One reason for this is that it may be needed to assign experienced and skilled personnel from one production unit to the next. This sharing of valued and limited resources requires on-line coordination, which can be realized in a matrix structure.

We now turn to a number of mismatches between technology and some configurations. Proposition 16 indicates that a functional configuration for a nonroutine technology is not likely to be efficient because a functional structure requires high horizontal differentiation, which may be unlikely for a nonroutine technology. And it certainly will require a lot of cross-function coordination, which the functional configuration will not do in a timely fashion.

A different limitation is given in Proposition 17; a divisional configuration and a nondivisible technology is a mismatch. Divisional organizations require that the task be divided and placed in each division. Since these divisions are relatively autonomous, a high degree of interrelationship between them is costly to coordinate. On the other hand, a matrix structure is not needed for a divisible technology, as given in Proposition 18. The argument is as follows. If the technology is divisible, then the work can be separated into units that are not dependent. A high level of coordination is, therefore, not required due to technological reasons. A matrix structure with its lateral relations for coordination is too costly, and there is little to coordinate.

A bureaucracy requires standard behavior either through the use of rules or the use of professionals. Rules are very likely to obstruct needed adjustments for a nonroutine technology. This is expressed in Proposition 19.

Finally, adhocracies are costly to coordinate and can operate only where the uncertainty related to the tasks is relatively high. Therefore, an ad hoc configuration cannot operate if the technology is very routine and will not operate efficiently.

TECHNOLOGY EFFECTS ON COORDINATION AND CONTROL MECHANISMS

Propositions 21 and 22 relate the technology routineness to the recommendations on coordination, media richness, and incentives (Table 24.5). Generally, the propositions state that with more routine technology, more rule-oriented coordination, and less rich media, the incentives can be procedure based. In contrast, less routine technology calls for coordination by integrators and group meetings using richer media and results-based incentives. The supporting arguments are fundamentally information processing in nature. . . . A routine technology does not change much. Activities are largely known and can be planned. There is little new, detailed, or current need for information. The information is well defined, known for some time, and likely to

TABLE 24.5   TECHNOLOGY EFFECTS ON COORDINATION AND CONTROL
MECHANISMS, PROPOSITIONS 21–23

21. If the size of the organization is not small and if the technology is routine, then coordination and control should be obtained via rules and planning, and a media with low richness and a small amount of information can be used. Incentives should be based on procedures.

22. If the technology is nonroutine, then coordination should be obtained via group meetings, and media with high richness and a large amount of information should be used. Incentives should be based on results.

23. If the organization does not have a dominant technology, then the technology-structure recommendation should be discounted relative to other contingency factors.

Information Technology[1]

Information technology includes computers, e-mail, voice mail, video-conferencing, databases, expert systems, and other electronic means to store, analyze, move or communicate information in an organization. Information technology is then a means for an organization to process information. The organization itself is an information processing entity and thus, information technology is a means for the organization to accomplish its fundamental work. Of course, there are many other nonelectronic means for the organization to process information: pencil and paper calculations, face-to-face conversations, paper memoranda, etc. Here, we want to explore the implications that the organizational design has for the choice of the information technology.

The connection between the organizational confirmation and properties and the organization's information technology has a long tradition and vast literature. As Hunter (1998) suggests, most of the research and studies have focused on the influence of information technology, computers, e-mail, etc., on the structure, properties, behavior and performance of the organization, i.e., the information technology is the independent variable and its effect is the dependent variable (Huber, 1990, Malone and Rockart, 1990). More recent research has taken a new approach of advanced structuration theory (DeSanctis & Poole, 1994) which focuses on the complex interactions between the organizational actors and the information technology.

The emergent behavior is uncertain and difficult to predict; the research goal is to describe and understand the interplay between the organization and the information technology without resorting to an independent variable, dependent variable approach. Here, we want to focus on the information technology design or choice question, i.e., what information technology should be adopted by the organization to be compatible with the organizational configuration and the organizational properties. This switches the independent and dependent variables so that the organizational design is the independent variable and the information system is the dependent variable.

The organizational design question more directly addresses the managerial question of "What kind of information system do I need to fit with my organization?" Consequently, we want to consider what the information technology should be. This seems reasonable, but most research questions have not been posited in this manner and thus the empirical evidence is wanting. There is a good deal of research on the effect of decentralization when an advanced e-mail system is introduced; however, it is not conclusive.

. . . The organization is an information processing entity, i.e., the organizational task is accomplished by processing information: gathering data, analyzing information, deciding what to do, communicating information, implementing and controlling events, measuring events and results. Individuals talk to each other in the hallway, they write e-mails, they go to meetings, etc. Some organizations have lots of meetings, but discourage hallway conversations. The list of possibilities is long. The organizational design then helps rationalize and organize how the information will be processed, e.g., a decentralized organization processes information differently than a centralized organization to accomplish the same organizational task. We suggest that a decentralized organization will use e-mail differently than a centralized organization. "Who makes what decision when" is different and we suggest that the content and frequency of the e-mail would be different. But the e-mail is only a small part of the organization, and indeed, the information, i.e., the electronic information system is only a small part of the organizational information processing. Yet, the electronic information system is an important part of the total organization and it should fit with the rest of the organization.

[Previously] we introduced the concept of media richness: a high media richness requires that information come from many sources, many formats, and probably in large amounts. A low media richness requires much less information from the environment. For high media richness, the information system is most likely to have many elements: e-mail, listservers, the web, news services, trade services, telephones with voice mails and ready access to the outside, multiple formats to receive information and then internally, some information processing capability to make sense of the diverse and large amount of information. In brief, the information system should support the gathering of vast and diverse information and also support its interpretation and meaning for the organization.

A low media richness need can be met with a focused single information system, e.g., in a low complexity environment, low uncertainty and low equivocality, it may be sufficient to look only at last year's sales. However, this would be very inadequate for a high media richness need.

As we suggested above, the centralization of the organization also affects the choice of the information technology. Most of the studies consider the opposite question of what is the effect of a given information element, e.g., e-mail on the centralization. Huber (1990, p. 57) suggests that the greater use of information technology will be mediating: highly centralized organizations will become more decentralized, and highly decentralized organizations will become more centralized. This is insightful and summarizes what we know; yet, we can not say definitively what the effect of the information technology will be on centralization of the organization.

But let us consider the design question, if we want to obtain a decentralized organization, what kind of information technology do we need? A decentralized organization means that the decision making is at a low level in the organization. If the relevant information is local and nearby, the decentralized organization would not require an advanced information system; the individuals can look at the situation and talk among themselves to make the decisions. Here a centralized organization would require the gathering and transmission of the same information up the hierarchy to make the same decision and hence an advanced information system could be quite helpful. On the other hand, if the relevant information for decision making is external and widely dispersed, then an advanced information system would support decentralized decision making. So, the centralization, advanced information system question requires information about the source of the relevant information as well.

The organizational design question can be stated: for the organizational configuration and organizational properties, what is an appropriate information technology? Here we want to explore some plausible responses to this design question. We will state a few propositions and then [assess them] for their reasonableness. The supporting arguments do have some research support, but their validity rests primarily upon their reasonableness.

A highly formalized organization has a large number of rules and standardized routines. What kind of information technology is appropriate? Without an electronic information technology, the formalization was contained in written documents and the rules were realized through the expertise of the employees who followed the rules. With an electronic information technology, it is possible to incorporate the rules directly into the operations of the organization through quick reference or actual control. Many airline reservation systems incorporate detailed rules and many airline personnel are permitted less discretion than in older paper systems. A highly formalized organization can use information technology to operationalize the rules and control implementation.

A low formalization has few rules. What is an appropriate information technology here? With few rules, information about the environment, customers, competitors, technology, scheduling, etc., becomes information for decision making and coordination. Would electronic technology such as e-mail, voice mail, bulletin boards, shared databases, etc., be helpful? Yes, it seems reasonable. Here too, an electronic information technology could be helpful.

So we conclude that an electronic information technology can be appropriate for both high or low formalization. However, there is a difference in detail in what the information technology does: for a high formalization, the rules are incorporated; for a low formalization, information is widely made available throughout the organization. Electronic information technology is a mediating technology; it supports the information processing demands of the organization. In the above discussion, the discriminating variable is the content of the information technology and what we want it to do. So, we must conclude that the information technology is not the primary concern, but what it does is the main issue: how does it help (or, hinder) the organizational demand for information processing capability.

We can now state design propositions:

If the organizational formalization is high, then the information technology should incorporate the rules and routines.

If the organizational formalization is low, then the information technology should augment the availability of information through e-mail, voice mail and shared databases.

Whether a given organizational design increases or decreases the need for information technology is not the issue. The question is: what kinds of information technology support the organizational design? Let us explore some other propositions.

If the organizational configuration is matrix, then the information technology should be e-mail, voice mail, video-conferencing, and shared databases.

A matrix organization requires a good deal of give-and-take and adaptation to circumstances. The information processing demands are high, both in quantity and type. In addition to face-to-face meetings, telephone calls, etc., these information technologies can augment the availability and communication of information to support the matrix design.

Equally, an information technology which is locked in rules and restricted format may well hinder the matrix design.

If the organizational complexity is low and particularly the vertical differentiation is low, then the information technology should facilitate quick hierarchical flow and the aggregation of information.

A low vertical differentiation means that there are few levels in the hierarchy—top to bottom. There is no large middle management or the organization is "delayered." In information terms, middle management aggregated information as they passed it up, and disaggregated information as they passed it down. And frequently, they simply passed the information on without modification. With low vertical differentiation, the information technology should respond to this information requirement. The specific information technology would also depend upon the organizational degree of centralization as discussed above.

We could add a number of other propositions on other organizational design configurations and properties. The supporting arguments must emerge from the information demands of the organization and how the information technology will aid the particular information needs. It is too easy to say that we need more information technology. It begs the question: to do what? Different information technologies are required for different organizational designs.

---

[1] Starling Hunter contributed greatly to this discussion.

---

be numerical: production quantities, product dimensions, and so on. Incentives can be procedure based as procedures are known and well defined and the challenge is to follow them correctly.

The nonroutine technology, in contrast, calls for a large amount of information. There are many issues to decide, implement,

and control. The products and the procedures themselves are likely to change often. Galbraith (1974), in his information processing framework, suggested that the information processing requirements are large for this situation. Integrators and frequent group meetings are appropriate organizational strategies to obtain the required coordination. Daft (1992, p. 290) and Daft and Lengel (1986) argue that relatively rich media will be required to deal with an ambiguous situation when much is unknown and is to be discovered during the decision-making phase. A nonroutine technology could also be described as equivocal and uncertain. . . . The need for rich media can be realized in a number of ways. Face-to-face is the richest, which is the medium of integrators and group meetings. That is, integrators and group meetings are rich media provided there is truly discussion, joint problem solving, and a give-and-take atmosphere. Integrators who simply tell and meetings that only inform will not work. Finally, incentives must fit the routineness of the technology and the other organizational design recommendations. A routine technology indicates that we know what to do; the incentive is to do it—that is, a procedural-based incentive to follow the rules and implement the plans. The nonroutine technology creates the opposite requirements. The goal is to obtain results in the face of the nonroutine technology. The goal is a working product or a satisfied customer. This result is important, and the procedure is to be developed. Kerr (1975) argues that the best incentive is to reward what the organization wants, and here the organization wants results. Many organizations use many different technologies—some routine and some nonroutine. The various technologies may push the organization in different directions. If that is the situation, technology is not a strong contingency on the overall recommendation relative to other contingencies. Each technology, of course, will be an important factor for the micro design. This is expressed in Proposition 23.

REFERENCES

Burton, Richard M., and Børge Obel. 1984. *Designing Efficient Organizations: Modelling and Experimentation*. Amsterdam: North-Holland.

Child, John. 1973. "Predicting and Understanding Organization Structure." *Administrative Science Quarterly*, 18, 168–185.

Daft, Richard L. 1992. *Organization Theory and Design* (4th ed.). St. Paul, MN: West. (2nd ed. 1986, 3rd ed. 1989.)

Daft, Richard, and Robert H. Lengel. 1986. "Organizational Information Requirements, Media Richness and Structural Design." *Management Science*, 32(5), 554–571.

DeSanctis, Geradine and Marshall Scott Poole. 1994. "Capturing the Complexity in Advanced Technology Use: Adaptive Structuration Theory," *Organization Science*, 5(2), 121–146.

Galbraith, Jay R. 1974. "Organization Design: An Information Processing View." *Interfaces*, 4(3), 28–36.

Giffi, Craig, Aleda V. Roth, and Gregory M. Seal. 1990. *Competing in World-Class Manufacturing: America's Twentyfirst Century Challenge*. Homewood, IL: Irwin, Inc. http://www.sas.se/sas/aboutsas/inbrief.html

Hickson, David J., D. S. Pugh, and Diana C. Pheysey. 1979. "Operations Technology and Organization Structure: An Empirical Reappraisal." *Administrative Science Quarterly*, 24, 375–397.

Huber, George P. 1990. "A Theory of the Effects of Advanced Information Technologies on Organizational Design, Intelligence, and Decision Making." *Academy of Management Review*, 15(1), 47–71.

Hunter, Starling. 1998. *Information Technology & New Organization Forms*. Unpublished Doctoral Dissertation, Duke University.

Jackson, John H., and Cyril P. Morgan. 1978. *Organization Theory: A Macro Perspective for Management*. Englewood Cliffs, NJ: Prentice-Hall.

Kerr, Steve. 1975. "On the Folly of Rewarding A While Hoping for B." *Academy of Management Journal*, 18, 769–793.

Malone, Thomas, and J. Rockart. 1990. "Computers, Networks, and the Corporation," *Scientific American*, 128–136.

Miller, Chet, William H. Glick, Yau-de Wang, and George P. Huber. 1991. "Understanding Technology-Structure Relationships: Theory Development and Meta-Analytic

Theory Testing." *Academy of Management Journal*, 34(2), 370–399.

Mills, Peter K., and Dennis J. Moberg. 1982. "Perspectives on the Technology of Service Operations." *Academy of Management Review*, 7(3), 467–478.

Mintzberg, Henry. 1979. *The Structuring of Organizations*. Englewood Cliffs, NJ: Prentice-Hall.

Perrow, Charles. 1967. "A Framework for the Comparative Analysis of Organization." *American Sociological Review*, 32(2), 144–208.

Robbins, Stephen P. 1990. *Organization Theory: Structure, Design and Application*. Englewood Cliffs, NJ: Prentice-Hall.

SAS. 1982–1990. *SAS Annual Reports*. Stockholm: SAS.

SAS. 1994. SAS *Annual Reports*. Stockholm: SAS.

SAS. 1995. *Annual Report*. Stockholm: SAS.

SAS. 1996. *Miljøregnskab*. Stockholm: SAS.

SAS. 1996. *Annual Report*. Stockholm: SAS.

SAS. 1996. *De første 50 år*. Stockholm: SAS.

SAS. 1996. *Scandination Airlines 1946–1996*. Stockholm: SAS.

SAS. 1997. *Delårsrapport 1: 1997*. Stockholm: SAS.

Scott, W. Richard. 1998. *Organizations: Rational, Natural and Open Systems*. Englewood Cliffs, NJ: Prentice-Hall.

Thompson, J. D. 1967. *Organizations in Action*. New York: McGraw-Hill.

Woodward, Joan. 1965. *Industrial Organization Theory and Practice*. Oxford: Oxford University Press.

Zeffane, Rachid. 1989. "Computer Use and Structural Control: A Study of Australian Enterprises." *Journal of Management Studies*, 26(6), 621–648.

CHAPTER 5

Organizational Economics Theory

Organizational economists use concepts and tools from the field of economics to study the internal processes and structures of the firm. They ask questions such as "Why do organizations exist?" "What determines the size, scope, and structure of a firm?" "Why are some workers paid hourly rates while others receive salaries?" and "What factors determine organizational survival and growth?" Most of the serious developments in this field occurred in the second half of the 20th century, including the introduction of important ideas associated with, for example, agency theory, behavioral theory, incomplete contract theory, theory of teams, transaction cost economics, and game theory (Augier, Kreiner, and March, 2000).

The recognized field of organizational economics originated with a 1937 article by Ronald H. Coase, "The Nature of the Firm." Coase asked a framing question: "Why would firms exist if market and price systems worked perfectly?" His answer was that in some situations, the cost of using market and price mechanisms exceeded the cost of using a firm. Thus, establishing a firm—creating a hierarchy—was more profitable. Therefore, the discipline of economics could not rely on price theory alone to explain behavior in and of firms. Although price theory often could adequately explain some resource allocation decisions, a second coordinating mechanism—hierarchy—also had to be considered.

The interests and concerns of organizational economics have expanded greatly since 1937. Some of the key questions organizational economists have addressed over the past seventy years have included: the contractual nature of firms, bounded rationality, the significance of investment in specific assets, the distinction between specific rights and residual rights, and the effects of imperfect information. These different approaches to organizational economics share a common attention to explaining the emergence and expansion of organizations—hierarchies—given the existence of costs associated with uncertainties, information asymmetries, bounded rationality, and cognitive barriers.

Four articles are reprinted here that introduce the essence of organizational economics and its core theory components: transaction cost theory, agency theory, and the theory of property rights: "Market and Hierarchies: Understanding the Employment Relation" by Oliver E. Williamson (1975); "Theory of the Firm: Managerial Behavior, Agency Costs, and Ownership Structure," by Michael Jensen and William Meckling (1976); "Learning from Organizational Economics," by Jay Barney and William Ouchi (1986); and "Managing Business Transactions," by Paul Rubin (1990). Barney and Ouchi's "Learning from Organizational Economics" provides a particularly informative integrative overview of these three central themes that organizational economists have contributed to organization theory.

"Understanding the Employment Relation" from Williamson's book, *Markets and Hierarchies*, assesses organizational decisions to produce goods and services internally versus externally by analyzing the applicability of various types of economic contracts and market models to employment relations. Williamson conceives of the decision process leading to an employer-employee relationship as being analogous to a market transaction, and uses economic market analysis to assess the viability of alternative internal labor market and contract models. Then, "Understanding the Employment Relation" turns to earlier work by Herbert Simon (1957) to examine implications of models for organizational authority and "the transaction rationale for internal labor markets (in terms mainly of economizing on bounded rationality and attenuating opportunism)."

Agency theory defines managers and other employees as "agents" of owners ("principals"), who out of necessity must delegate some authority to agents. Price theory has been concerned with how to structure organizations for the free interplay of markets among agents and principals. As Donaldson (1990, p. 370) queries, "Why should not all economic activity be arranged as free contracts [including the pricing structure needed to keep agents working in the best interests of principals]?" However, price theory falls short: "Since the interests of the principal and agent are inclined to diverge, the delegation of authority from the principal to the agent allows a degree of under-fulfillment of the wishes of the principal by the agent" (p. 369).

There is good reason to believe that agents will not always act in the best interests of principals. Like everyone else, agents are utility maximizers who tend to act in their *own* best interests. Agency theory thus examines the combined use of price theory mechanisms (for example, incentives) and hierarchy mechanisms (for example, monitoring) that principals can use "to limit the aberrant activities of the agent" (Jensen & Meckling, 1976, p. 308).

The *theory of property rights* addresses the allocation of costs and rewards among the participants in an organization and, for example, how "claims on the assets and cash flows of the organization . . . can generally be sold without permission of the other contracting individuals" (p. 311). An organization is a form of legal fiction, a "multitude of complex relationships (i.e., contracts) between the legal fiction (the firm) and the owners of labor, material and capital inputs and the consumers of output" (Jensen & Meckling, 1976, p. 311). The intellectual heritage of property rights theory can be traced to John Locke's *Two Treatises of Government* (1967) and, to a lesser extent, Jean-Jacques Rousseau's "The Social Contract" (1947). And, in this century, Richard Cyert and James March's seminal (1963) book *A Behavioral Theory of the Firm* describes organizations as coalitions of self-interested participants.

Once again, the core element of organizational economics, *transaction cost theory*, is the topic of Paul Rubin's chapter, "Managing Business Transactions." Rubin's focus is the cost of maintaining the principal-agent relationship, how to minimize the costs, and the effects of transaction costs on management decisions. Rubin's underlying principles of business transactions are: "First, people are self-interested and opportunistic. Second, it is impossible to write complete contracts which take account of any and all possible events and which eliminate all forms of opportunism or cheating." Thus, "other mechanisms must be used to minimize agency costs." Rubin suggests several such precontractual and postcontractual mechanisms, including adverse selection, the market, the "use of hostages and credible commitments to support exchange," strategically selected payment schemes, reputation, and ethics (the role of which he downplays).

In sum, organizational economics deals with a fundamental and universal problem of organizations: how to induce managers and other employees to act in the best interests of those who control ownership or, in the case of government agencies and nonprofit organizations, those who have the authority to control policy and resource allocation decisions. The current wave of management theorists who advocate devolution, outsourcing, and employee and group empowerment approaches must address the types of issues that the organizational economists have been wrestling with since 1937.

REFERENCES

Augier, M., K. Kreiner, & J. G. March (2000). Introduction: Some roots and branches of organizational economics. *Industrial and Corporate Change* 9(4), 555–565.

Barney, J. B., & W. G. Ouchi (1986). *Organizational economics.* San Francisco: Jossey-Bass.

Coase, R. H. (1937). The nature of the firm. *Economica [new series], 4,* 386–405.

Cyert, R. M., & J. G. March (1963). *A behavioral theory of the firm.* Englewood Cliffs, NJ: Prentice Hall.

Donaldson, L. (1990). The ethereal hand: Organizational economics and management theory. *Academy of Management Review, 15*(3), 369–381.

Jensen, M. C., & W. H. Meckling (1976). Theory of the firm: Managerial behavior, agency costs, and ownership structure. *Journal of Financial Economics, 3,* 305–360.

Locke, J. (1967). *Two treatises of government.* 2d ed. P. Lastett, ed. London: Cambridge University Press. (Originally published in 1690.)

Rousseau, J. J. (1947). The social contract. In E. Barker, ed., *Social contract* (pp. 167–307). London: Oxford University Press. (Originally published in 1762.)

Rubin, P. H. (1990). *Managing business transactions.* New York: Free Press.

Simon, H. A. (1957). *Models of man.* New York: Wiley.

Williamson, O. E. (1975). *Markets and hierarchies.* New York: Free Press.

25

Markets and Hierarchies: Understanding the Employment Relation

Oliver E. Williamson

This chapter is concerned with the implications of an extreme form of nonhomogeneity—namely, job idiosyncracy—for understanding the employment relation. Although it refers largely to production workers, the argument can be extended, with appropriate modifications, to cover nonproduction workers as well. The purpose is to better assess the employment relation in circumstances where workers *acquire*, during the course of their employment, *significant job-specific skills and related task-specific knowledge*. What Hayek referred to as knowledge of "particular circumstances of time and place" (1945, p. 521) and what was referred to as first-mover advantages . . . thus play a prominent role in the analysis. . . .

This is not to suggest, however that extra-economic considerations are thought to be unimportant. To the contrary, the proposition . . . that supplying a satisfying exchange relation is part of the economic problem, broadly construed, has special relevance where an employment relation is involved. Indeed, some of the ways in which internal labor markets bear on this proposition are developed in Section 2.3, below. But placing primary reliance on atmosphere to explain internal labor markets poses the following dilemma: Assuming that the same considerations of contractual satisfaction with respect to the nature of the exchange relationship applies to production jobs of all kinds, how is the coexistence of structured (internal) and structureless (recurrent spot) labor markets to be explained? By contrast, rationalizing the absence of structure, where

jobs are fungible, and the conscious creation of structure, for idiosyncratic jobs, is relatively straightforward if an efficiency orientation is adopted. Accordingly, the argument runs throughout principally in efficiency terms.

Four alternative labor contracting modes are examined. Two of these, recurrent spot contracting and contingent claims contracting, rely entirely on market-mediated transactions. The other two modes involve a mixture of market-mediated exchange and hierarchy (internal organization). What is commonly referred to as the "authority relation" and the internal labor market mode are of this second kind. These several alternative contracting modes are assessed in cost-economizing terms, where costs include both production and transaction cost elements. Considering that the focus throughout is on contracting, transaction costs naturally receive primary attention.

My purposes, briefly, are as follows:

1. To demonstrate that the interesting problems of labor organization involve the study of transactions and contracting and, except in a rather special idiosyncratic sense, do not turn mainly on technology.
2. To isolate and assess the idiosyncratic job features which characterize internal labor markets with the help of the organizational failures framework.
3. To set out the transactional detail that would attend complex contingent claims contracting in idiosyncratic job circumstances, thereby to disclose why such contracts are prohibitively costly or infeasible.
4. To demonstrate that sequential spot contracting is unsuited to the idiosyncratic

Source: The Bell Journal of Economics 6 (1975). © 1975. Reprinted by permission of RAND.

tasks in question, whence Alchian and Demsetz' (1972) discussion of the employ ment relation requires qualification.

5. To examine the authority relation and in dicate the limitations associated with Si mon's (1957) evaluation of alternative contracting modes.

6. To develop the transactional rationale for internal labor markets (in terms mainly of economizing on bounded rationality and attenuating opportunism) where jobs are idiosyncratic in nontrivial degree. . . .

1. TECHNOLOGY: CONVENTIONAL AND IDIOSYNCRATIC CONSIDERATIONS

It is widely felt that technology has an im portant, if not fully determinative, influ ence on the employment relationship. I agree, but take exception with the usual view in several respects. First, . . . indivisi bilities (of the usual kinds) are neither nec essary nor sufficient for market contracting to be supplanted by internal organization. Second, I contend that nonseparabilities at most explain small-group organization. Third, and most important, I argue that the leading reason why an internal labor mar ket supplants spot contracting is because of small-numbers exchange relations. This last turns on task idiosyncrasies as these appear in a moving equilibrium context.

1.1 Conventional Treatments

1.1.1 Indivisibilities. . . . It is entirely feasible, as a technological matter, for phys ical assets and informational services for which indivisibilities are significant to be monopoly owned and sold for hire. What impedes such ownership and exchange ar rangements are the transactional difficulties which attend small-numbers trades. I raise the issue at this time merely to restate my po sition that conventional arguments which rely on indivisibilities to explain the em ployment relation do not, without more, go through. Recourse to transactional consid erations is ultimately necessary.

1.1.2 Nonseparabilities. More relevant to our purposes here is the allegation

that technological nonseparabilities consti tute the principal reason for the employ ment relation, whence hierarchy, to appear (Alchian and Demsetz, 1972). But for such technological conditions, a "normal sales relationship" would purportedly govern the terms under which labor would be made available for hire.

. . . It is the joining of nonseparability with opportunism and a condition of infor mation impactedness, rather than nonsepa rability by itself, that occasions the substi tution of hierarchy for market exchange. Absent opportunism, free riding problems, of which shirking is one, would never ap pear. Absent information impactedness, op portunistic inclinations could be checked by paying the appropriate discriminating wage.

Regarded in transactional terms, techno logical nonseparability represents a case where information impactedness is particu larly severe; but I emphasize that this is merely a matter of degree. Lesser degrees of information impactedness plainly exist that do not have these same technological ori gins but which can and often do occasion the supplanting of markets by hierarchies. (As urged in the preceding chapter, most tasks appear to be separable in a buffer inventory sense — often as between indi vidual workers and almost invariably be tween small groups of workers —yet hierar chy commonly appears.) Our assessment of the technological nonseparability argu ment thus comes down to this: Such condi tions are *merely symptomatic* of a set of un derlying transactional factors which, both here and elsewhere, ultimately explain the organization of economic activity as be tween markets and hierarchies.

1.2 Small Numbers and Task Idiosyncracies

It is generally agreed that small-numbers exchange conditions are attended by seri ous market exchange problems. . . . The frequency of and manner in which small numbers labor exchange conditions de velop, however, is less widely appreciated. It is [our] thesis . . . that task idiosyn cracies are common, that these give rise to small-numbers exchange conditions, and that market contracting is supplanted by an employment relation principally for this reason.

1.2.1 General. Doeringer and Piore describe idiosyncratic tasks in the following way (1971, pp. 15–16):

> Almost every job involves some specific skills. Even the simplest custodial tasks are facilitated by familiarity with the physical environment specific to the workplace in which they are being performed. The apparently routine operation of standard machines can be importantly aided by familiarity with the particular piece of operating equipment. . . . In some cases workers are able to anticipate trouble and diagnose its source by subtle changes in the sound or smell of the equipment. Moreover, performance in some production or managerial jobs involves a team element, and a critical skill is the ability to operate effectively with the given members of the team. This ability is dependent upon the interaction skills of the personalities of the members, and the individual's work "skills" are specific in the sense that skills necessary to work on one team are never quite the same as those required on another.

More generally, task idiosyncracies can arise in at least four ways: (1) equipment idiosyncracies, due to incompletely standardized, albeit common, equipment, the unique characteristics of which become known through experience; (2) process idiosyncracies, which are fashioned or "adopted" by the worker and his associates in specific operating contexts; (3) informal team accommodations, attributable to mutual adaptation among parties engaged in recurrent contact but which are upset, to the possible detriment of group performance, when the membership is altered; and (4) communication idiosyncracies with respect to information channels and codes that are of value only within the firm. Because "technology is [partly] unwritten and that part of the specificity derives from improvements which the work force itself introduces, workers are in a position to perfect their monopoly over the knowledge of the technology should there be an incentive to do so" (Doeringer and Piore, 1971, p. 84).

Training for idiosyncratic jobs ordinarily takes place in an on-the-job context. Classroom training is unsuitable both because the unique attributes associated with particular operations, machines, the work group, and, more generally, the atmosphere of the workplace may be impossible to duplicate in the classroom, and because job incumbents, who are in possession of the requisite skills and knowledge with which the new recruit or candidate must become familiar, may be unable to describe, demonstrate, or otherwise impart this information except in an operational context (Doeringer and Piore, 1971, p. 20). Teaching-by-doing thus facilitates the learning-by-doing process. Where such uniqueness and teaching attributes are at all important, specific exposure in the workplace at some stage becomes essential. Outsiders who lack specific experience can thus achieve parity with insiders only by being hired and incurring the necessary startup costs.

The success of on-the-job training is plainly conditional on the information disclosure attitudes of incumbent employees. Both individually and as a group, incumbents are in possession of a valuable resource (knowledge) and can be expected to fully and candidly reveal it only in exchange for value. The way the employment relation is structured turns out to be important in this connection. The danger is that incumbent employees will hoard information to their personal advantage and engage in a series of bilateral monopolistic exchanges with the management — to the detriment of both the firm and other employees as well.

An additional feature of these tasks not described above but nevertheless important to an understanding of the contractual problems associated with the employment relation is that the activity in question is subject to periodic disturbance by environmental changes. Shifts in demand due to changes in the prices of complements or substitutes or to changes in consumer incomes or tastes occur; relative factor price changes appear; and technological changes of both product design and production technique types take place. Successive adaptations to changes of each of these kinds is typically needed if efficient production performance is to be realized. In addition, life cycle changes in the work force occur which occasion turnover, upgrading, and continuous training. The tasks in question are thus to be regarded in moving equilibrium terms. Put differently, they are not tasks for which a once-for-all adaptation by workers is sufficient, thereafter to remain unchanged.

1.2.2 Interpretation. The production tasks that are of transactional interest in this chapter are ones that are either themselves rather complex or are embedded in a complex set of technological and organizational circumstances. Furthermore, successive adaptations are required to realize efficiency in the face of changing internal and environmental events. A nontrivial degree of uncertainty/complexity may thus be said to characterize the tasks. Training for such tasks occurs in an on-the-job context because of the impossibility, or great cost, of disclosing job nuances in a classroom situation. The relevant job details simply cannot be identified, accurately described, and effectively communicated in a classroom context on account of information processing limitations of both originators (teachers) and receivers (trainees). Sometimes, indeed, the requisite language will not even exist. The pairing of bounded rationality with an uncertainty/complexity condition thus gives rise to the job-specific training situation. *Teaching-by-doing and learning-by-doing both economize on bounded rationality in these idiosyncratic job circumstances.*[1]

Specialized skills and knowledge accrue to individuals and small groups as a result of their specific training and experience. But while such skills and information accrue naturally, they can be disclosed strategically—in an incomplete or distorted fashion—if the affected parties should choose to. Whether this will obtain depends on the structure of the bargaining relationship. Where job incumbents acquire nontrivial first-mover advantages over outsiders, and, in addition, are opportunistically inclined,

what was once a large-numbers bidding situation, at the time original job assignments were made, is converted into a small-numbers bargaining situation if adaptations to unplanned (and perhaps unforeseeable) internal and market changes are subsequently proposed. The reasons for and consequences of this shift from a large-numbers bargaining relationship at the outset to bilateral bargaining subsequently are further developed below.

2. INDIVIDUALISTIC BARGAINING MODELS[2]

Four types of individualistic contracting modes can be distinguished: (1) contract now for the specific performance of x in the future; (2) contract now for the delivery of x_i contingent on event e_i obtaining in the future; (3) wait until the future materializes and contract for the appropriate (specific) x at the time; and (4) contract now for the right to select a specific x from within an admissable set X, the determination of the particular x to be deferred until the future. Simon's study of the employment relation (1957, pp. 183–195) treats contracts of the first type, which he characterizes as sales contracts, to be the main alternative to the so-called authority relation (type 4). This, however, is unfortunate because type 1 contracts, being rigid, are singularly unsuited to permit adaptation in response to changing internal and market circumstances. By contrast, contingent claims contracts (type 2) and sequential spot sales contracts (type 3) both permit adaptation. If complexity/uncertainty is held to be a central feature of the environment with which we are concerned, which it is, the deck is plainly stacked against contracts of type 1 from the outset. Accordingly, type 1 contracts will hereafter be disregarded.

2.1 Contingent Claims Contracts
Suppose that the efficient choice of x on each date depends on how the future unfolds. Suppose, furthermore, that the parties are instructed to negotiate a once-for-all

labor contract in which the obligations of both employer and employee are fully stipulated at the outset. A complex contingent claims contract would then presumably result. The employer would agree to pay a particular wage now in return for which the employee agrees to deliver stipulated future services of a contingent kind, the particular services being dependent upon the circumstances which eventuate.

Contracting problems of several kinds can be anticipated. First, can the complex contract be written? Second, even if it can, is a meaningful agreement between the parties feasible? Third, can such agreements be implemented in a low cost fashion? The issues posed can all usefully be considered in the context of the framework sketched out above.

The feasibility of writing complex contingent claims contracts reduces fundamentally to a bounded rationality issue.

Recall in this connection the conclusion reached by Feldman and Kanter in their assessment of complex decision trees, to wit, "The comprehensive decision model is not feasible for most interesting decision problems" (1965, p. 615). Plainly, the complex labor agreements needed for comprehensive description of the idiosyncratic tasks in question are of this kind. Not only are changing market circumstances (product demand, rivalry, factor prices, technological conditions, and the like) impossibly complex to enumerate, but the appropriate adaptations thereto cannot be established with any degree of confidence *ex ante*. Changing life cycle conditions with respect to the internal labor force compound the complexities.

The enumeration problems referred to are acknowledged by Meade in his discussion of contingent claims contracts. "When environmental uncertainties are so numerous that they cannot all be considered . . . or, what comes perhaps to much the same thing, when any particular environmental risks are so hard to define and to distinguish from each other that it is impossible to base a firm betting or insurance contract upon the occurrence or non-occurrence of any of

them, then for this reason alone it is impossible to have a system of contingency . . . markets" (1971, p. 183). Except for bounded rationality, Meade's concerns with excessive numbers, undefinable risks, and indistinguishable events would vanish.

But suppose, *arguendo*, that exhaustive complex contracts could be written at reasonable expense. Would such contracts be acceptable to the parties? I submit that a problem of incomprehensibility will frequently arise and impede reaching agreement. At least one of the parties, probably the worker, will be unable to meaningfully assess the implications of the complex agreement to which he is being asked to accede. Sequential contracting, in which experience permits the implications of various contingent commitments to be better understood, is thus apt to be favored instead.

Assume, however, that *ex ante* understanding poses no bar to contracting. *Ex post* enforcement issues then need to be addressed. First, there is the problem of declaring what state of the world has obtained. Meade's remarks that contingent claims contracts are infeasible in circumstances where it is impossible, on the contract execution date, "to decide precisely enough for the purposes of a firm legal contract" what state of the world has eventuated (1971, p. 183) bear on this. While it is easy to agree with Meade's contentions, I think it noteworthy to observe that, were it not for opportunism and information impactedness, the impediments to contracting which he refers to vanish. Absent these conditions, the responsibility for declaring what state of the world had obtained could simply be assigned to the best informed party. Once he has made the determination, the appropriate choice of *x* is found by consulting the contract. Execution then follows directly.

It is hazardous, however, to permit the best informed party unilaterally to make state of the world declarations where opportunism can be anticipated. If the worker is not indifferent between supplying services of type x_j rather than x_k, and if the declaration of the state of the world were to be left to him, he will be inclined, when circumstances permit, to represent the state of the world in terms most favorable to him. Similar problems are to be expected for those events for which the employer is thought to be the best informed party and unilaterally declares, from among a plausible set, which e_i has eventuated.[3] Moreover, mediation by a third party is no answer since, by assumption, an information impactedness condition prevails with respect to the observations in question.

Finally, even were it that state of the world issues could be settled conclusively at low cost, there is still the problem of execution. Did the worker really supply x_i in response to condition e_i, as he should, or did he (opportunistically) supply x_j instead? If the latter, how does the employer show this in a way that entitles him to a remedy? These are likewise information impactedness issues. Problems akin to moral hazard are posed.

Ordinarily, bounded rationality renders the description of once-for-all contingent claims employment contracts strictly infeasible. Occasions to examine the negotiability and enforcement properties of such contracts thus rarely develop. It is sufficient for our purposes here, however, merely to establish that problems of any of these kinds impair contingent claims contracting. In consideration of these difficulties, alternatives to the once-for-all supply relations ought presumably to be examined.

2.2 Sequential Spot Contracts
Alchian and Demsetz take the position that it is a delusion to characterize the relation between employer and employee by reference to fiat, authority, or the like. Rather, it is their contention that the relation between an employer and his employee is identical to that which exists between a shopper and his grocer in fiat and authority respects (1972, p. 777):

> The single consumer can assign his grocer to the task of obtaining whatever the customer can induce the grocer to provide at a price acceptable to both parties. That is precisely all that an employer can do to an employee. To speak of managing, directing, or assigning

workers to various tasks is a deceptive way of noting that the employer continually is involved in renegotiation of contracts on terms that must be acceptable to both parties. . . . Long term contracts between employer and employee are not the essence of the organization we call a firm.

Implicit in their argument, I take it, is an assumption that the transition costs associated with employee turnover are negligible. Employers, therefore, are able easily to adapt to changing market circumstances by filling jobs on a spot market basis. Although job incumbents may continue to hold jobs for a considerable period of time and may claim to be subject to an authority relationship, all that they are essentially doing is continuously meeting bids for their jobs in the spot market. This is option number three, among the contracting alternatives described at the beginning of this section, done repeatedly.

That adaptive, sequential decision-making can be effectively implemented in sequential spot labor markets which satisfy the low transition cost assumption (as some apparently do, for example, migrant farm labor)[4] without posing issues that differ in kind from the usual grocer-customer relationship seems uncontestable. I submit, however, that many jobs do not satisfy this assumption. In particular, the tasks of interest here are not of this primitive variety. Where tasks are idiosyncratic, in nontrivial degree, the worker-employer relationship is no longer contractually equivalent to the usual grocer-customer relationship and the feasibility of sequential spot market contracting breaks down.

Whereas the problems of contingent claims contracts were attributed to bounded rationality and opportunism conditions, sequential spot contracts are principally impaired only by the latter. (Bounded rationality poses a less severe problem because no effort is made to describe the complex decision tree from the outset. Instead, adaptations to uncertainty are devised as events unfold.) Wherein does opportunism arise and how is sequential spot contracting impaired?

. . . Opportunism pose[s] a contractual problem only to the extent that it appears in a small-numbers bargaining context. Otherwise, large-numbers bidding effectively checks opportunistic inclinations and competitive outcomes result. The problem with the tasks in question is that while large-numbers bidding conditions obtain at the outset, before jobs are first assigned and the work begun, the idiosyncratic nature of the work experience effectively destroys parity at the contract renewal interval. Incumbents who enjoy nontrivial advantages over similarly qualified but inexperienced bidders are well-situated to demand some fraction of the cost savings which their idiosyncratic experience has generated.

One possible adaptation is for employers to avoid idiosyncratic technologies and techniques in favor of more well-standardized operations. Although least-cost production *technologies* are sacrificed in the process, pecuniary gains may nevertheless result since incumbents realize little strategic advantage over otherwise qualified but inexperienced outsiders. Structuring the initial bidding in such a way as to permit the least-cost technology and techniques to be employed without risking untoward contract renewal outcomes is, however, plainly to be preferred. Two possibilities warrant consideration: (1) extract a promise from each willing bidder at the outset that he will not use his idiosyncratic knowledge and experience in a monopolistic way at the contract renewal interval; or (2) require incumbents to capitalize the prospective monopoly gains that each will accrue and extract corresponding lump sum payments from winning bidders at the outset.

The first of these can be dismissed as utopian. It assumes that promises not to behave opportunistically are either self-enforcing or can be enforced in the courts. Self-enforcement is tantamount to denying that human agents are prone to be opportunists, and fails for want of reality testing. Enforcement of such promises by the courts is likewise unrealistic. Neither case by case litigation nor simple rule-making disposition of the issues is feasible. Litigation on the merits of each case is prohibitively costly, while rules to the effect that "all workers shall receive only competitive wages" fail because courts cannot, for information impactedness reasons, determine whether workers put their energies and inventiveness into the job in a way which permits task-specific cost savings to be fully realized—in which case disaffected workers can counter such rules by withholding effort.

The distinction between consummate and perfunctory cooperation is important in this connection. Consummate cooperation is an affirmative job attitude—to include the use of judgment, filling gaps, and taking initiative in an instrumental way.[5] Perfunctory cooperation, by contrast, involves job performance of a minimally acceptable sort—where minimally acceptable means that incumbents, who through experience have acquired task-specific skills, need merely to maintain a slight margin over the best available inexperienced candidate (whose job attitude, of necessity, is an unknown quantity). The upshot is that workers, by shifting to a perfunctory performance mode, are in a position to "destroy" idiosyncratic efficiency gains. Reliance on pre-employment promises as a means by which to deny workers from participating in such gains is accordingly self-defeating.

Consider, therefore, the second alternative in which, though worker participation in realized cost savings is assumed to be normal, workers are required to submit lump sum bids for jobs at the outset. Assuming that large numbers of applicants are qualified to bid for these jobs at the outset, will such a scheme permit employers to fully appropriate the expected, discounted value of future cost savings by awarding the job to whichever worker offers to make the highest lump sum payment?

Such a contracting scheme amounts to long-term contracting in which many of the details of the agreement are left unspecified. As might be anticipated, numerous problems are posed. For one thing, it assumes that workers are capable of assessing complex future circumstances in a sophisticated way and making a determination of what the prospective gains are. Plainly, a serious bounded rationality issue is raised. Second, even if workers had the competence to complete such an exercise, it is seriously to be doubted that they could raise the funds, if their personal assets were deficient, to make the implied full valuation bids. As Malmgren has observed, in a somewhat different but nevertheless related context: ". . . some [individuals] will see opportunities, but be unable to communicate their own information and expectations favorably to bankers, and thus be unable to acquire finance, or need to pay a higher charge for the capital borrowed" (1961, p. 416). The communication difficulties referred to are due to language limitations (attributable to bounded rationality) that the parties experience. That bankers are unwilling to accept the representations of loan-seekers at face value is because of the risks of opportunism.

Third, and crucially, the magnitude of the estimated future gains to be realized by workers often depends not merely on exogenous events and/or activities that each worker fully controls but also on the posture of coworkers and the posture of the employer. Problems with coworkers arise if, despite steady state task separability, the consent or active cooperation of workers who interface with the task in question must be secured each time an adaptation is proposed. This effectively means that related sets of workers must enter bids as teams, which complicates the bidding scheme greatly and offers opportunities for free riding. Problems also arise if gains cannot be realized independently of the decisions taken by management with respect, for example, to the organization of production, complementary new asset acquisitions, equipment repair policy, and so forth. Lump sum bidding is plainly hazardous where workers are entering bids on life cycle earnings streams that are repeatedly exposed to rebargaining.[6]

Finally, but surely of negligible importance in relation to the issues already raised, there is the question of efficient risk-bearing: which party is best situated to bear the risks of future uncertainties — the individ-

ual workers or the firm? That individual workers may be poorly suited to bear such risks and, as a group, can pool risks only with difficulty seems evident and further argues against the bidding scheme proposed.

Transactional difficulties thus beset both contingent claims and sequential spot market contracting for the idiosyncratic tasks of interest in this chapter. Consider, therefore, the so-called authority relation as the solution to the contracting problems in question.

2.3 The Authority Relation

Simon has made one of the few attempts to formally assess the employment relation. Letting B designate the employer (or boss), W be the employee (or worker), and x be an element in the set of possible behavior patterns of W, he defines an authority relation as follows (1957, p. 184):

> We will say that B exercises *authority* over W if W permits B to select x. That is, W accepts authority when his behavior is determined by B's decision. In general, W will accept authority only if x_0 the x chosen by B, is restricted to some subset (W's "area of acceptance") of all the possible values.

An employment contract is then said to exist whenever W agrees to accept the authority of B in return for which B agrees to pay W a stated wage (1957, p. 184).

Simon then asks when will such an employment relationship be preferred to a sales contract, and offers the following two conjectures (1957, p. 185):

1. W will be willing to enter into an employment contract with B only if it does not matter to him "very much" which x (within the agreed upon area of acceptance) B will choose, or if W is compensated in some way for the possibility that B will choose x that is not desired by W (i.e., that B will ask W to perform an unpleasant task).
2. It will be advantageous to B to offer W added compensation for entering into an employment contract if B is unable to predict with certainty, at the time the contract is made, which x will be the optimum one, from his stand-point. That is, B will pay for the privilege of postponing, until some time after the contract is made, the selection of x.

He then goes on to develop a formal model in which he demonstrates that the employment contract commonly has attractive properties, under conditions of uncertainty, *provided that the alternatives are* (1) the promise of a particular *x* in exchange for a given wage *w* (what he considers to be the sales contract option), or (2) a set of *X* from which a particular *x* will subsequently be chosen in exchange for a given wage *w'* (the employment contract option).

Put differently, the deterministic sales contract is shown to be inferior to an incompletely specified employment relation in which *W* and *B* do not agree on all terms *ex ante*, but "agree to agree later"— or better, "agree to tell and be told." But plainly the terms are rigged from the outset. As noted previously, the particular type of sales contract to which Simon refers in attempting to establish the rationale for an authority relation is the only one of the three types of sales contracts described at the beginning of this section that lacks adaptability in response to changing market circumstances. Since employment contracts of both the contingent claims and sequential spot marketing kinds are not similarly flawed, a better test of the authority relation would be to compare it with either of these instead.

Simon's modeling apparatus, unfortunately, does not lend itself to such purposes. It is simply silent with respect to the efficiency properties of alternative contracts in which adaptability is featured. Not only is it unable to discriminate between the authority relation, contingent claims contract, and spot market contracting in adaptability respects, but Simon's model fails to raise transaction cost issues of the types described here.

This is not, however, to suggest that the authority relation has nothing to commend it. To the contrary, such a relation does not require that the complex decision tree be generated in advance, and thus does not pose the severe bounded rationality problems that the contingent claims contracting model is subject to. The authority relation also, presumably, reduces the frequency with which contracts must be negotiated in comparison with the sequential spot contracting mode. Adaptations in the small can be costlessly accomplished under an authority relation because such changes, to the worker, do not matter very much.

Assuming, however, that the parties are prospectively joined in a long-term association and the jobs in question are of the idiosyncratic kind, most of the problems of sequential spot contracting still need to be faced. Thus, how are wage and related terms of employment to be adjusted through time in response to either small, but cumulative, or large, discrete changes in the data? What happens when hitherto unforeseen and unforeseeable contingencies eventuate? How are differences between parties regarding state of the world determinations, the definition of the task, and job performance to be reconciled? Substantially all of the problems that are posed by idiosyncratic tasks in the sequential spot contracting mode appear, I submit, under the authority relation as well.

3. THE EFFICIENCY IMPLICATIONS OF INTERNAL LABOR MARKET STRUCTURES

The upshot is that none of the above contracting schemes has acceptable properties for tasks of the idiosyncratic variety. Contingent claims contracting (Meade, 1971, Chap. 10) fails principally because of bounded rationality. Spot market contracting (Alchian and Demetz, 1972, p. 777) is impaired by first-mover advantages and problems of opportunism. The authority relation (Simon, 1957, pp. 183–195) is excessively vague and, ultimately, is confronted with the same types of problems as is spot market contracting. Faced with this result, the question of alternative contracting schemes naturally arises. Can more effective schemes be designed? Do more efficient contracting modes exist?

The analysis here is restricted to the latter of these questions, which is answered in the affirmative. Although it cannot be said that internal labor market structures are optimally efficient with respect to idiosyncratic tasks, it is nevertheless significant that their efficiency properties have been little noted or understated by predominantly non-neoclassical interpretations of these markets in the past.

My assessment of the efficiency implications of internal labor market structures is in three parts. The occasion for and purposes of collective organization are sketched first. The salient structural attributes of internal labor markets are then described and the efficiency implications of each, expressed in terms of the language of the organizational failures framework, is indicated. Several caveats, including a brief discussion of atmosphere, follow.

3.1 Collective Organization

To observe that the pursuit of perceived individual interests can sometimes lead to defective collective outcomes is scarcely novel. Schelling has treated the issue extensively in the context of the "ecology of micromotives" (1971). The individual in each of his examples is both small in relation to the system—and thus his behavior, by itself, has no decisive influence on the system—and is unable to appropriate the collective gains that would obtain were he voluntarily to forego individual self-interest seeking. Schelling then observes that the remedy involves collective action. An enforceable social contract which imposes a cooperative solution on the system is needed (1971, p. 69).

Although it is common to think of collective action as action by the state, this is plainly too narrow. As Arrow (1969, p. 62) and Schelling (1971, p. 68) emphasize, both private collective action (of which the firm, with its hierarchical controls, is an example) and norms of socialization are also devices for realizing cooperative solutions. The internal labor market is usefully interpreted in this same spirit.

Although it is in the interest of each worker, bargaining individually or as a part of a small team, to acquire and exploit monopoly positions, it is plainly not in the interest of the *system* that employees should behave in this way. Opportunistic bargaining not only in itself absorbs real resources, but efficient adaptations are delayed and

possibly foregone altogether. Accordingly, what this suggests is that the employment relation be transformed in such a way that systems concerns are made more fully to prevail and the following objectives are realized: (1) bargaining costs are much lower; (2) the internal wage structure is rationalized in terms of objective task characteristics; (3) consummate rather than perfunctory cooperation is encouraged; and (4) investments of idiosyncratic types, which constitute a potential source of monopoly, are undertaken without risk of exploitation. For the reasons and in the ways developed below, internal labor markets can have, and some do have, the requisite properties to satisfy this prescription.[7]

3.2 Structural Attributes and their Efficiency Consequences

3.2.1 Wage Bargaining. A leading difficulty with individual contracting schemes where jobs are idiosyncratic is that workers are strategically situated to bargain opportunistically. The internal labor market achieves a fundamental transformation by shifting to a system where wage rates are attached mainly to jobs rather than to workers. Not only is individual wage bargaining thereby discouraged, but it may even be legally foreclosed (Summers, 1969, p. 531). Once wages are expressly removed from individual bargaining, there is really no occasion for the worker to haggle over the incremental gains that are realized when adaptations of degree are proposed by the management. The incentives to behave opportunistically, which infect individual bargaining schemes, are correspondingly attenuated.

Moreover, not only are affirmative incentives lacking, but there are disincentives, of group disciplinary and promotion ladder types, which augur against resistance to authority on matters that come within the range customarily covered by the authority relation.[8] Promotion ladder issues are taken up in conjunction with the discussion of ports of entry in section 3.2.4, below; consider, therefore, group disciplinary effects.

In this connection Barnard observes (1962, p. 169):

> Since the efficiency of organization is affected by the degree to which individuals assent to orders, denying the authority of an organization communication is a threat to the interests of all individuals who derive a net advantage from their connection with the organization, unless the orders are unacceptable to them also. Accordingly, at any given time there is among most of the contributors an active personal interest in the maintenance of the authority of all orders which to them are within the zone of indifference. The maintenance of this interest is largely a function of informal organization.

The application of group pressures thus combines with promotional incentives to facilitate adaptations in the small.[9] Even individuals who have exhausted their promotional prospects can thereby be induced to comply. System interests are made more fully to prevail. This concern with viability possibly explains the position taken in labor law that orders which are ambiguous with respect to, and perhaps even exceed, the scope of authority, are to be fulfilled first and disputed later (Summers, 1969, pp. 538, 573).

3.2.2 Contractual Incompleteness/Arbitration. Internal labor market agreements are commonly reached through collective bargaining. Cox observes in this connection that the collective bargaining agreement should be understood as an instrument of government as well as an instrument of exchange. "The collective agreement governs complex, many-sided relations between large-numbers of people in a going concern for very substantial periods of time" (1958, p. 22). Provision for unforeseeable contingencies is made by writing the contract in general and flexible terms and supplying the parties with a special arbitration machinery. "One simply cannot spell out every detail of life in an industrial establishment, or even of that portion which both management and labor agree is a matter of mutual concern" (Cox, 1958, p. 23). Such contractual incompleteness is an implicit concession to bounded rationality. Rather than attempt

to anticipate all bridges that might conceivably be faced, which is impossibly ambitious and excessively costly, bridges are crossed as they appear.

However attractive, in bounded rationality respects, adaptive, sequential decision-making is, admitting gaps into the contract also poses hazards. Where parties are not indifferent with respect to the manner in which gaps are to be filled, fractious bargaining or litigation commonly result. It is for the purpose of forestalling the worst outcomes of this kind that the special arbitration apparatus is devised.

Important differences between commercial and labor arbitration are to be noted in this connection. For one thing, ". . . the commercial arbitrator finds facts—did the cloth meet the sample—while the labor arbitrator necessarily pours meaning into the general phrases and interstices of a document" (Cox, 1958, p. 23). In addition, the idiosyncratic practices of the firm and its employees also constitute "shop law" and, to the labor arbitrator, are essential background for purposes of understanding a collective agreement and interpreting its intent (Cox, 1958, p. 24).

In the language of the organizational failures framework, the creation of such a special arbitration apparatus serves to overcome information impactedness because the arbitrator is able to explore the facts in greater depth and with greater sensitivity to idiosyncratic attributes of the enterprise than could normal judicial proceedings. Furthermore, once it becomes recognized that the arbitrator is able to apprise himself of the facts in a discerning and low cost way, opportunistic misrepresentations of the data are discouraged as well.

3.2.3 Grievances. Also of interest in relation to the above is the matter of who is entitled to activate the arbitration machinery when an individual dispute arises. Cox takes the position that (1958, p. 24)[10]

> . . . giving the union control over all claims arising under the collective agreement comports so much better with the functional nature of a collective bargaining agreement. . . .

Allowing an individual to carry a claim to arbitration whenever he is dissatisfied with the adjustment worked out by the company and the union . . . discourages the kind of day-to-day cooperation between company and union which is normally the mark of sound industrial relations—a relationship in which grievances are treated as problems to be solved and contracts are only guideposts in a dynamic human relationship. When . . . the individual's claim endangers group interests, the union's function is to resolve the competition by reaching an accommodation or striking a balance.

The practice described by Cox of giving the union control over arbitration claims plainly permits group interests, whence the concern for system viability, to supercede individual interests, thereby curbing small numbers opportunism.

3.2.4 Internal Promotion/Ports of Entry.
Acceding to authority on matters that fall within the zone of acceptance[11] merely requires that employees respond in a minimally acceptable, even perfunctory way. This may be sufficient for tasks that are reasonably well-structured. In such circumstances, the zeal with which an instruction is discharged may have little effect on the outcome. As indicated, however, consummate cooperation is valued for the tasks of interest here. But how is cooperation of this more extensive sort to be realized?

A simple answer is to reward cooperative behavior by awarding incentive payments on a transaction-specific basis. The employment relation would then revert to a series of haggling encounters over the nature of the *quid pro quo*, however, and would hardly be distinguishable from a sequential spot contract. Moreover, such payments would plainly violate the nonindividualistic wage bargaining attributes of internal labor markets described in Section 3.2.1, above.

The internal promotion practices in internal labor markets are of special interest in this connection. Access to higher-level positions on internal promotion ladders are not open to all comers on an unrestricted basis. Rather, as part of the internal incentive system, higher-level positions (of the

prescribed kinds)[12] are filled by promotion from within whenever this is feasible. This practice, particularly if it is followed by other enterprises to which the workers might otherwise turn for upgrading opportunities, ties the interests of the workers to the firm in a continuing way.[13] Given these ties, the worker looks to internal promotion as the principal means of improving his position.

The practice of restricting entry to lower-level jobs and promoting from within has interesting experience-rating implications. It permits firms to protect themselves against low productivity types, who might otherwise successfully represent themselves to be high productivity applicants, by bringing employees in at low level positions and then upgrading them as experience warrants. Furthermore, employees who may have been incorrectly upgraded but later have been "found out," and hence barred from additional internal promotions, are unable to move to a new organization without penalty.[14] Were unpenalized lateral moves possible, workers might, considering the problems of accurately transmitting productivity valuations between firms, be able to disguise their true productivity attributes from their new employers long enough to achieve some additional promotions. Restricting access to low level positions serves to protect the firm against exploitation by opportunistic types who would, if they could, change jobs strategically for the purpose of compounding evaluation errors between successive independent organizations.

Were it, however, that markets could perform equally well these experience-rating functions, the port of entry restrictions described would be unnecessary. The (comparative) limitations of markets in experience-rating respects . . . warrant elaboration. The principal impediment to effective interfirm experience-rating is one of communication.[15] By comparison with the firm, markets lack a rich and common rating language. The language problem is particularly severe where the judgments to be made are highly subjective. The advantages of hierarchy in these circumstances are especially great if those persons who are the most familiar with a worker's characteristics, usually his immediate supervisor, also do the experience-rating. The need to rationalize subjective assessments that are confidently held but, by reason of bounded rationality, difficult to articulate is reduced. Put differently, interfirm experience-rating is impeded in information impactedness respects.

Reliance on internal promotion has affirmative incentive properties because workers can anticipate that differential talent and degrees of co-operativeness will be rewarded. Consequently, although the attachment of wages to jobs rather than to individuals may result in an imperfect correspondence between wages and marginal productivity at ports of entry, productivity differentials will be recognized over a time and a more perfect correspondence can be expected for higher-level assignments in the internal labor market job hierarchy.

4. CONCLUDING REMARKS

Organizational failure and systems considerations appear repeatedly in the foregoing assessment of the properties of alternative contracting modes in relation to idiosyncratic tasks. These highlights are briefly recapitulated here, after which some qualifications are offered.

4.1 Application of the Organizational Failures Framework

But for uncertainty, adaptive sequential decision-making problems would never be posed. Accordingly, the occasion to devise flexible contracts would never develop.

But for bounded rationality, complex contingent claims contracts could be written, and there would be no occasion to investigate other forms of contracting.

But for opportunism, individuals would honestly disclose all information pertinent to the bargain and would self-enforce promises to forego the monopoly powers which accrue to incumbents. Alternatively,

were it not for task idiosyncracies, information impactedness conditions would never develop and outsiders would be on a parity with incumbents in bidding for jobs. In either event, the distortions associated with monopoly advantage would vanish and spot market contracting would suffice. In circumstances, however, where incumbents realize idiosyncratic knowledge and skill advantages over otherwise qualified outsiders, small-numbers conditions evolve. If, additionally, incumbents behave opportunistically, spot market contracting is hazardous.

4.2 The Collective Agreement as a Systems Solution

Frequently more important than the question of whether workers accept authority in the limited sense of "do this" or "do that," at the appointed time and place and in some highly prescribed manner, is their attitude toward cooperation. We have accordingly distinguished between perfunctory and consummate cooperation and have argued that collective organization, in the form of an internal labor market, is well-suited to promote consummate cooperation.

In this respect and others, internal labor markets serve to promote efficiency. Job evaluation attaches wages to jobs, rather than to individuals, thereby foreclosing individual bargaining. The resulting wage structure reflects objective long-term job values rather than current bargaining exigencies. Internal promotion ladders encourage a positive worker attitude toward on-the-job training and enable the firm to reward cooperative behavior. A grievance procedure, with impartial arbitration as the usual final step, allows the firm and the workers to deal with continually changing conditions in a relatively nonlitigious manner. Contract revision and renewal take place in an atmosphere of mutual restraint in which the parties are committed to continuing accommodation. Unionization commonly facilitates the orderly achievement of these results, though it is not strictly necessary, especially in small organizations. . . .

NOTES

1. Doing-while-learning also contributes to the output of the firm. Classroom training is typically at a disadvantage in this respect.

2. Lest the ensuing discussion of autonomous bargaining modes be thought to be contrived and/or unnecessary, since "everyone knows" such bargaining modes are inapposite, I make the following observations: First, though it is widely recognized that complex contingent claims contracting is infeasible [for example, Radner notes that the Arrow-Debreu contracting model "requires that the economic agents possess capabilities of imagination and calculation that exceed reality by many orders of magnitude" (1970, p. 457)], the reasons for this are rarely fully spelled out—either in general or, even less, with respect to labor market contracting. I attempt to rectify this condition in Section 2.1. . . .
Second, as our discussion of Alchian and Demsetz in Section 2.2 reveals, it is plainly not the case that everyone appreciates that idiosyncratic tasks need to be distinguished from tasks in general and that sequential spot contracting is singularly unsuited for jobs of the idiosyncratic kind. Third, so as to correct the widely held belief that the authority relation represents a well-defined alternative to "normal" market contracting (as recently illustrated by Arrow's (1974, pp. 25, 63–65) reliance on Simon's treatment of the authority relation), I think it important that the ambiguities of the authority relation be exposed.

3. The issue here is somewhat more subtle, however. The employer, when he assumes the role of the best informed party, will not wish to declare a false state of the world *unless*, at the time he got the worker to agree to a wage w, he represented to the worker that services of type x_i would be called for when event e_i obtained when in fact x_i' services, which the worker dislikes, yield a greater e_i gain. The worker, being assured that he would be called on to perform x_i' services only when the unlikely event e_i' occurred, agreed to a lower wage than he would have if he realized that an x_i' response would be called for in both e_i and e_i' situations—because the employer will falsely declare e_i to be e_i' so as to get x_i' performed.

4. See Doeringer and Piore (1971, pp. 4–5); also Kerr (1954, p. 95).

5. Consummate cooperation involves working in a fully functional, undistorted mode. Efforts are not purposefully withheld; neither is behavior of a knowingly inapt kind undertaken. Blau and Scott are plainly concerned with the difference between perfunctory and consummate cooperation in the following passage (1962, p. 140):

> the contract obligates employees to perform only a set of duties in accordance with minimum standards and does not assure their striving to achieve optimum performance. . . . [L]egal authority does not and cannot command the employee's willingness to devote his ingenuity and energy to performing his tasks to the best of his ability. . . . It promotes compliance with directives and discipline, but does not encourage employees to exert effort, to accept responsibilities, or to exercise initiative.

6. There is the related problem of comparing the bids of workers who have different age, health, and other characteristics. Possibly this could be handled by stipulating that winners have claims to jobs in perpetuity, so that a job can be put up for rebidding by the estate of a worker who dies or retires. Such rebidding, however, is hazardous if the new worker must secure anew the cooperation of his colleagues. Established workers are then in a position strategically to appropriate some of the gains. (This assumes that coalition asymmetries exist which favor old workers in relation to the new.)

7. Common's discussion with Sidney Hillman concerning the transformation of membership attitudes among the Amalgamated Clothing Workers illustrates some of the systems attributes of collective agreements (1970, p. 130):

> Ten years after World War I, I asked Sidney Hillman . . . why his members were less revolutionary than they had been when I knew them twenty-five years before in the sweatshop. . . . Hillman replied. "They know now that they are citizens of the industry. They know that they must make the corporation a success on account of their own jobs." They were citizens because

they had an arbitration system which gave them security against arbitrary foremen. They had an unemployment system by agreement with the firm which gave them security of earnings. This is an illustration of the meaning of part-whole relations.

8. Authority relation is used here in the qualified short run sense suggested in our discussion of Simon in Section 2.3. . . .

9. Of course, informal organization does not operate exclusively in the context of a collectivized wage bargain. Autonomous bargainers, however, are ordinarily expected to behave in autonomous ways. The extent to which group powers serve as a check on challenges to authority is accordingly much weaker where the individual bargaining mode prevails (March and Simon, 1958, pp. 59, 66). By contrast, the individual in the collectivized system who refuses to accede to orders on matters that fall within the customarily defined zone of acceptance is apt to be regarded as cantankerous or malevolent, since there is no private pecuniary gain to be appropriated, and will be ostracized by his peers.

10. I am informed that his practice is changing and offer three comments in this regard. First, institutional change does not always promote efficiency outcomes; backward steps will sometimes occur—possibly because the efficiency implications are not understood. Second, relegating control to the union on whether a grievance is to be submitted to arbitration can sometimes lead to capricious results. Disfavored workers can be unfairly disadvantaged by those who control the union decision-making machinery. Some form of appeal may therefore be a necessary corrective. Third, that workers are given rights to bring grievances on their own motion does not imply that this will happen frequently. Grievances that fail to secure the support of peers are unlikely to be brought unless they represent egregious conditions on which the grievant feels confidently he will prevail. The bringing of trivial grievances not only elicits the resentment of peers but impairs the grievant's standing when more serious matters are posed.

11. The zone of acceptance is discussed in the quotation from Barnard in Section 3.2.1. . . .

12. For a discussion, see Doeringer and Piore (1971, pp. 42–47).

13. Since access to idiosyncratic types of jobs is limited by requiring new employees to accept lower-level jobs at the bottom of promotion ladders, individuals can usually not shift laterally between firms without cost: "Employees in nonentry jobs in one enterprise often have access only to entry-level jobs in other enterprises. The latter will often pay less than those which the employees currently hold" (Doeringer and Piore, 1971, p. 78).

14. Agents seeking transfer may have gotten ahead in an organization by error. Experience-rating, after all, is a statistical inference process and is vulnerable to "Type II" error. When a mistake has been discovered and additional promotions are not forthcoming, the agent might seek transfer in the hope that he can successfully disguise his true characteristics in the new organization and thereby secure further promotions. Alternatively, the agent may have been promoted correctly, but changed his work attitudes subsequently— in which case further promotion is denied. Again, he might seek transfer in the hope of securing additional promotion in an organization that, because of the difficulty of interfirm communication about agent characteristics, is less able to ascertain his true characteristics initially.

15. Interfirm experience-rating may also suffer in veracity respects, since firms may choose deliberately to mislead rivals. The major impediment, however, is one of communication.

REFERENCES

Alchian, A. A., "Uncertainty, Evolution and Economic Theory," *Journal of Political Economy*, 58: 211–221, June 1950.

———, "Costs and Outputs," in M. Abramovitz et al., *The Allocation of Economic Resources: Essays in Honor of Bernard Francis Haley*. Stanford: Stanford University Press, 1959, pp. 23–40.

———, "Corporate Management and Property Rights," In H. G. Manne, ed., *Economic Policy and Regulation of Corporate Securities*. Washington: American Enterprise Institute for Public Policy Research, 1969, pp. 337–360.

——— and H. Demsetz, "Production, Information Costs, and Economic Organization," *American Economic Review*, 62: 777–795, December 1972.

Arrow, K. J., "Economic Welfare and the Allocation of Resources for Invention," in *The Rate and Direction of Inventive Activity*. Princeton: Princeton University Press, 1962, pp. 609–625.

———, "Comment," The Rate and Direction of Inventive Activity. Princeton: Princeton University Press, 1962, pp. 353–358.

———, *Aspects of the Theory of Risk Bearing*. Helsinki: Yrjo Jahnssonin Saatio, 1965.

———, "The Organization of Economic Activity," *The Analysis and Evaluation of Public Expenditure: The PPB System*. Joint Economic Committee, 91st Cong., 1st Sess., 1969, pp. 59–73.

———, *Essays in the Theory of Risk-Bearing*. Chicago: Markham, 1971.

———, "Gifts and Exchanges," *Philosophy and Public Affairs*, Summer 1972, 343–362.

———, *Limits of Organization*. New York: W. W. Norton & Company, Inc., 1974.

Barnard, C. L., *The Functions of the Executive*, 2d ed., Cambridge: Harvard University Press, 1962.

———, "Functions and Pathology of Status Systems in Formal Organizations," in W. F. Whyte, ed., *Industry and Society*. New York: McGraw-Hill Book Company, Inc., 1946, pp. 46–83.

Blau, P. M., & R. W. Scott, *Formal Organizations*. San Francisco: Chandler Publishing Company, 1962.

Commons, John R., *Institutional Economics*. Madison: University of Wisconsin Press, 1934.

———, *The Economics of Collective Action*. Madison: University of Wisconsin Press, 1970.

Cox, A., "The Legal Nature of Collective Bargaining Agreements," *Michigan Law Review*, 57: 1–36, November 1958.

Doeringer, P., & M. Piore, *Internal Labor Markets and Manpower Analysis*. Boston: D. C. Heath and Company, 1971.

Feldman, J., & H. Kanter, "Organizational Decision Making," in J. March, ed., *Handbook of Organizations*. Chicago: Rand McNally & Company, 1965, pp. 614–649.

Hayek, F., "The Use of Knowledge in Society," *American Economic Review*, 35: 519–530, September 1945.

Kerr, C., "The Balkanization of Labor Markets," in E. Wight Bakke et. al., *Labor Mobility and Economic Opportunity*. Cambridge and New York: The Technology Press of the Massachusetts Institute of Technology, and John Wiley & Sons, Inc., 1954, pp. 92–110.

Malmgren, H., "Information, Expectations and the Theory of the Firm," *Quarterly Journal of Economics*, 75: 399–421, August 1961.

March, J. G., & H. A. Simon, *Organizations*. New York: John Wiley & Sons, Inc., 1958.

Meade, J. E., *The Controlled Economy*. London: George Allen & Unwin, Ltd., 1971.

Radner, R., "Competitive Equilibrium Under Uncertainty," *Econometrica*, 36: 31–58, January 1968.

———, "Problems in the Theory of Markets Under Uncertainty," *American Economic Review*, 60: 454–460, May 1970.

———. "Existence of Equilibrium of Plans, Prices, and Price Expectations in a Sequence of Markets," *Econometrica*, 40: 289–304, March 1972.

Shelling, T. C., *The Strategy of Conflict*. Cambridge: Harvard University Press, 1960.

———, "On the Ecology of Micromotives," *Public Interest*, 25: 61–98, Fall 1971.

Simon, H. A., *Models of Man*. New York: John Wiley & Sons, Inc., 1957.

———, *Administrative Behavior*. 2d ed., New York: The Macmillan Company, 1961.

———, "The Architecture of Complexity," *Proceedings of the American Philosophical Society*, 106: 467–482, December 1962.

———, *The Sciences of the Artificial*. Cambridge: Massachusetts Institute of Technology Press, 1969.

———, "Theories of Bounded Rationality," in C. McGuire and R. Radner, eds., *Decision and Organization*. Amsterdam: North-Holland Publishing Company, 1972, pp. 161–176.

Summers, C., "Collective Agreements and the Law of Contracts." *Yale Law Journal*, 78: 527–575, March 1969.

26

Theory of the Firm: Managerial Behavior, Agency Costs and Ownership Structure

Michael C. Jensen & William H. Meckling

1. INTRODUCTION AND SUMMARY

1.1. Motivation of the Paper: In this paper we draw on recent progress in the theory of (1) property rights, (2) agency, and (3) finance to develop a theory of ownership structure[1] for the firm. In addition to tying together elements of the theory of each of these three areas, our analysis casts new light on and has implications for a variety of issues in the professional and popular literature such as the definition of the firm, the "separation of ownership and control," the "social responsibility" of business, the definition of a "corporate objective function," the determination of an optimal capital structure, the specification of the content of credit agreements, the theory of organizations, and the supply side of the completeness of markets problem.

Our theory helps explain:

1. why an entrepreneur or manager in a firm which has a mixed financial structure (containing both debt and outside equity claims) will choose a set of activities for the firm such that the total value of the firm is less than it would be if he were the sole owner and why this result is independent of whether the firm operates in monopolistic or competitive product or factor markets;
2. why his failure to maximize the value of the firm is perfectly consistent with efficiency;
3. why the sale of common stock is a viable source of capital even though managers do not literally maximize the value of the firm;

4. why debt was relied upon as a source of capital before debt financing offered any tax advantage relative to equity;
5. why preferred stock would be issued;
6. why accounting reports would be provided voluntarily to creditors and stockholders, and why independent auditors would be engaged by management to testify to the accuracy and correctness of such reports;
7. why lenders often place restrictions on the activities of firms to whom they lend, and why firms would themselves be led to suggest the imposition of such restrictions;
8. why some industries are characterized by owner-operated firms whose sole outside source of capital is borrowing;
9. why highly regulated industries such as public utilities or banks will have higher debt equity ratios for equivalent levels of risk than the average non-regulated firm;
10. why security analysis can be socially productive even if it does not increase portfolio returns to investors.

1.2. Theory of the Firm: An Empty Box? While the literature of economics is replete with references to the "theory of the firm," the material generally subsumed under that heading is not a theory of the firm but actually a theory of markets in which firms are important actors. The firm is a "black box" operated so as to meet the relevant marginal conditions with respect to inputs and outputs, thereby maximizing profits, or more accurately, present value. Except for a few recent and tentative steps, however, we have no theory which explains how the conflicting objectives of the individual participants are brought into equilibrium so

Source: Journal of Financial Economics 3 (1976): 305–360. Reprinted by permission of Oxford University Press.

as to yield this result. The limitations of this black box view of the firm have been cited by Adam Smith and Alfred Marshall, among others. More recently, popular and professional debates over the "social responsibility" of corporations, the separation of ownership and control, and the rash of reviews of the literature on the "theory of the firm" have evidenced continuing concern with these issues.[2]

A number of major attempts have been made during recent years to construct a theory of the firm by substituting other models for profit or value maximization; each attempt motivated by a conviction that the latter is inadequate to explain managerial behavior in large corporations.[3] Some of these reformulation attempts have rejected the fundamental principle of maximizing behavior as well as rejecting the more specific profit maximizing model. We retain the notion of maximizing behavior on the part of all individuals in the analysis to follow.[4]

1.3. Property Rights. An independent stream of research with important implications for the theory of the firm has been stimulated by the pioneering work of Coase, and extended by Alchian, Demsetz and others.[5] A comprehensive survey of this literature is given by Furubotn and Pejovich (1972). While the focus of this research has been "property rights,"[6] the subject matter encompassed is far broader than that term suggests. What is important for the problems addressed here is that specification of individual rights determines how costs and rewards will be allocated among the participants in any organization. Since the specification of rights is generally effected through contracting (implicit as well as explicit), individual behavior in organizations, including the behavior of managers, will depend upon the nature of these contracts. We focus in this paper on the behavioral implications of the property rights specified in the contracts between the owners and managers of the firm.

1.4. Agency Costs. Many problems associated with the inadequacy of the current

theory of the firm can also be viewed as special cases of the theory of agency relationships in which there is a growing literature.[7] This literature has developed independently of the property rights literature even though the problems with which it is concerned are similar; the approaches are in fact highly complementary to each other.

We define an agency relationship as a contract under which one or more persons (the principal(s)) engage another person (the agent) to perform some service on their behalf which involves delegating some decision-making authority to the agent. If both parties to the relationship are utility maximizers there is good reason to believe that the agent will not always act in the best interests of the principal. The *principal* can limit divergences from his interest by establishing appropriate incentives for the agent and by incurring monitoring costs designed to limit the aberrant activities of the agent. In addition in some situations it will pay the *agent* to expend resources (bonding costs) to guarantee that he will not take certain actions which would harm the principal or to ensure that the principal will be compensated if he does take such actions. However, it is generally impossible for the principal or the agent at zero cost to ensure that the agent will make optimal decisions from the principal's viewpoint. In most agency relationships the principal and the agent will incur positive monitoring and bonding costs (nonpecuniary as well as pecuniary), and in addition there will be some divergence between the agent's decisions[8] and those decisions which would maximize the welfare of the principal. The dollar equivalent of the reduction in welfare experienced by the principal due to this divergence is also a cost of the agency relationship, and we refer to this latter cost as the "residual loss." We define *agency costs* as the sum of:

1. the monitoring expenditures by the principal,[9]
2. the bonding expenditures by the agent,
3. the residual loss.

Note also that agency costs arise in any situation involving cooperative effort (such as the co-authoring of this paper) by two or more people even though there is no clear cut principal–agent relationship. Viewed in this light it is clear that our definition of agency costs and their importance to the theory of the firm bears a close relationship to the problem of shirking and monitoring of team production which Alchian and Demsetz (1972) raise in their paper on the theory of the firm.

Since the relationship between the stockholders and manager of a corporation fits the definition of a pure agency relationship it should be no surprise to discover that the issues associated with the "separation of ownership and control" in the modern diffuse ownership corporation are intimately associated with the general problem of agency. We show below that an explanation of why and how the agency costs generated by the corporate form are born leads to a theory of the ownership (or capital) structure of the firm.

Before moving on, however, it is worthwhile to point out the generality of the agency problem. The problem of inducing an "agent" to behave as if he were maximizing the "principal's" welfare is quite general. It exists in all organizations and in all cooperative efforts—at every level of management in firms,[10] in universities, in mutual companies, in cooperatives, in governmental authorities and bureaus, in unions, and in relationships normally classified as agency relationships such as are common in the performing arts and the market for real estate. The development of theories to explain the form which agency costs take in each of these situations (where the contractual relations differ significantly), and how and why they are born will lead to a rich theory of organizations which is now lacking in economics and the social sciences generally. We confine our attention in this paper to only a small part of this general problem—the analysis of agency costs generated by the contractual arrangements between the owners and top management of the corporation.

Our approach to the agency problem here differs fundamentally from most of the existing literature. That literature focuses almost exclusively on the normative aspects of the agency relationship; that is how to structure the contractual relation (including compensation incentives) between the principal and agent to provide appropriate incentives for the agent to make choices which will maximize the principal's welfare given that uncertainty and imperfect monitoring exist. We focus almost entirely on the positive aspects of the theory. That is, we assume individuals solve these normative problems and given that only stocks and bonds can be issued as claims, we investigate the incentives faced by each of the parties and the elements entering into the determination of the equilibrium contractual form characterizing the relationship between the manager (i.e., agent) of the firm and the outside equity and debt holders (i.e., principals).

1.5. Some General Comments on the Definition of the Firm. Ronald Coase (1937) in his seminal paper on "The Nature of the Firm" pointed out that economics had no positive theory to determine the bounds of the firm. He characterized the bounds of the firm as that range of exchanges over which the market system was suppressed and resource allocation was accomplished instead by authority and direction. He focused on the cost of using markets to effect contracts and exchanges and argued that activities would be included within the firm whenever the costs of using markets were greater than the costs of using direct authority. Alchian and Demsetz (1972) object to the notion that activities within the firm are governed by authority, and correctly emphasize the role of contracts as a vehicle for voluntary exchange. They emphasize the role of monitoring in situations in which there is joint input or team production.[11] We sympathize with the importance they attach to monitoring, but we believe the emphasis which Alchian–Demsetz place on joint input production is too narrow and therefore misleading. Contractual relations are the essence of the firm, not only with employees but with suppliers, customers, creditors, etc. The problem of agency costs and monitoring exists for all of these contracts, independent of whether there is joint production in their sense; i.e., joint production can explain only a small fraction of the behavior of individuals associated with a firm. A detailed examination of these issues is left to another paper.

It is important to recognize that most organizations are simply *legal fictions*[12] *which serve as a nexus for a set of contracting relationships among individuals*. This includes firms, non-profit institutions such as universities, hospitals and foundations, mutual organizations such as mutual savings banks and insurance companies and co-operatives, some private clubs, and even governmental bodies such as cities, states and the Federal government, government enterprises such as TVA, the Post Office, transit systems, etc.

The private corporation or firm is simply one form of *legal fiction which serves as a nexus for contracting relationships and which is also characterized by the existence of divisible residual claims on the assets and cash flows of the organization which can generally be sold without permission of the other contracting individuals*. While this definition of the firm has little substantive content, emphasizing the essential contractual nature of firms and other organizations focuses attention on a crucial set of questions—why particular sets of contractual relations arise for various types of organizations, what the consequences of these contractual relations are, and how they are affected by changes exogenous to the organization. Viewed this way, it makes little or no sense to try to distinguish those things which are "inside" the firm (or any other organization) from those things that are "outside" of it. There is in a very real sense only a multitude of complex relationships (i.e., contracts) between the legal fiction (the firm) and the owners of labor, material and capital inputs and the consumers of output.[13]

Viewing the firm as the nexus of a set of contracting relationships among individuals also serves to make it clear that the personalization of the firm implied by asking questions such as "what should be the objective function of the firm," or "does the firm have a social responsibility" is seriously misleading. *The firm is not an individual.* It is a legal fiction which serves as a focus for a complex process in which the conflicting objectives of individuals (some of whom may "represent" other organizations) are brought into equilibrium within a framework of contractual relations. In this sense the "behavior" of the firm is like the behavior of a market; i.e., the outcome of a complex equilibrium process. We seldom fall into the trap of characterizing the wheat or stock market as an individual, but we often make this error by thinking about organizations as if they were persons with motivations and intentions.[14]. . .

2. THE AGENCY COSTS OF OUTSIDE EQUITY

2.1. Overview. . . . If a wholly owned firm is managed by the owner, he will make operating decisions which maximize his utility. These decisions will involve not only the benefits he derives from pecuniary returns but also the utility generated by various non-pecuniary aspects of his entrepreneurial activities such as the physical appointments of the office, the attractiveness of the secretarial staff, the level of employee discipline, the kind and amount of charitable contributions, personal relations ("love," "respect," etc.) with employees, a larger than optimal computer to play with, purchase of production inputs from friends, etc. The optimum mix (in the absence of taxes) of the various pecuniary and non-pecuniary benefits is achieved when the marginal utility derived from an additional dollar of expenditure (measured net of any productive effects) is equal for each non-pecuniary item and equal to the marginal utility derived from an additional dollar of after tax purchasing power (wealth).

If the owner-manager sells equity claims on the corporation which are identical to his (i.e., share proportionately in the profits of the firm and have limited liability) agency costs will be generated by the divergence between his interest and those of the outside shareholders, since he will then bear only a fraction of the costs of any nonpecuniary benefits he takes out in maximizing his own utility. If the manager owns only 95 percent of the stock, he will expend resources to the point where the marginal utility derived from a dollar's expenditure of the firm's resources on such items equals the marginal utility of an additional 95 cents in general purchasing power (i.e., *his* share of the wealth reduction) and not one dollar. Such activities, on his part, can be limited (but probably not eliminated) by the expenditure of resources on monitoring activities by the outside stockholders. But as we show below, the owner will bear the entire wealth effects of these expected costs so long as the equity market anticipates these effects. Prospective minority shareholders will realize that the owner-manager's interests will diverge somewhat from theirs, hence the price which they will pay for shares will reflect the monitoring costs and the effect of the divergence between the manager's interest and theirs. Nevertheless, ignoring for the moment the possibility of borrowing against his wealth, the owner will find it desirable to bear these costs as long as the welfare increment he experiences from converting his claims on the firm into general purchasing power[15] is large enough to offset them.

As the owner-manager's fraction of the equity falls, his fractional claim on the outcomes falls and this will tend to encourage him to appropriate larger amounts of the corporate resources in the form of perquisites. This also makes it desirable for the minority shareholders to expend more resources in monitoring his behavior. Thus, the wealth costs to the owner of obtaining additional cash in the equity markets rise as his fractional ownership falls.

We shall continue to characterize the agency conflict between the owner-manager and outside shareholders as deriving from the manager's tendency to appropriate perquisites out of the firm's resources for his own consumption. However, we do not mean to leave the impression that this is the only or even the most important source of conflict. Indeed, it is likely that the most important conflict arises from the fact that as the manager's ownership claim falls, his incentive to devote significant effort to creative activities such as searching out new profitable ventures falls. He may in fact avoid such ventures simply because it requires too much trouble or effort on his part to manage or to learn about new technologies. Avoidance of these personal costs and the anxieties that go with them also represent a source of on-the-job utility to him and it can result in the value of the firm being substantially lower than it otherwise could be. . . .

7. CONCLUSIONS

The publicly held business corporation is an awesome social invention. Millions of individuals voluntarily entrust billions of dollars, francs, pesos, etc., of personal wealth to the care of managers on the basis of a complex set of contracting relationships which delineate the rights of the parties involved. The growth in the use of the corporate form as well as the growth in market value of established corporations suggests that at least, up to the present, creditors and investors have by and large not been disappointed with the results, despite the agency costs inherent in the corporate form.

Agency costs are as real as any other costs. The level of agency costs depends among other things on statutory and common law and human ingenuity in devising contracts. Both the law and the sophistication of contracts relevant to the modern corporation are the products of a historical process in which there were strong incentives for individuals to minimize agency costs. Moreover, there were alternative organizational forms available, and opportunities to invent new ones. Whatever its shortcomings, the corporation has thus far survived the market test against potential alternatives.

NOTES

1. We do not use the term "capital structure" because that term usually denotes the relative quantities of bonds, equity, warrants, trade credit, etc., which represent the liabilities of a firm. Our theory implies there is another important dimension to this problem—namely the relative amounts of ownership claims held by insiders (management) and outsiders (investors with no direct role in the management of the firm).

2. Reviews of this literature are given by Peterson (1965), Alchian (1965, 1968), Machlup (1967), Shubik (1970), Cyert and Hedrick (1972), Branch (1973), Preston (1975).

3. See Williamson (1964, 1970, 1975), Marris (1964), Baumol (1959), Penrose (1958), and Cyert and March (1963). Thorough reviews of these and other contributions are given by Machlup (1961) and Alchian (1965).

   Simon (1955) developed a model of human choice incorporating information (search) and computational costs which also has important implications for the behavior of managers. Unfortunately, Simon's work has often been misinterpreted as a denial of maximizing behavior, and misused, especially in the marketing and behavioral science literature. His later use of the term "satisficing" [Simon (1959)] has undoubtedly contributed to this confusion because it suggests rejection of maximizing behavior rather than maximization subject to costs of information and of decision making.

4. See Meckling (1976) for a discussion of the fundamental importance of the assumption of resourceful, evaluative, maximizing behavior on the part of individuals in the development of theory.

Klein (1976) takes an approach similar to the one we embark on in this paper in his review of the theory of the firm and the law.

5. See Coase (1937, 1959, 1960), Alchian (1965, 1968), Alchian and Kessel (1962), Demsetz (1967), Alchian and Demsetz (1972), Monsen and Downs (1965), Silver and Auster (1969), and McManus (1975).

6. Property rights are of course human rights, i.e., rights which are possessed by human beings. The introduction of the wholly false distinction between property rights and human rights in many policy discussions is surely one of the all time great semantic flim flams.

7. Cf. Berhold (1971), Ross (1973, 1974a), Wilson (1968, 1969), and Heckerman (1975).

8. Given the optimal monitoring and bonding activities by the principal and agent.

9. As it is used in this paper the term monitoring includes more than just measuring or observing the behavior of the agent. It includes efforts on the part of the principal to "control" the behavior of the agent through budget restrictions, compensation policies, operating rules etc.

10. As we show below, the existence of positive monitoring and bonding costs will result in the manager of a corporation possessing control over some resources which he can allocate (within certain constraints) to satisfy his own preferences. However, to the extent that he must obtain the cooperation of others in order to carry out his tasks (such as divisional vice presidents) and to the extent that he cannot control their behavior perfectly and costlessly they will be able to appropriate some of these resources for their own ends. In short, there are agency costs generated at every level of the organization. Unfortunately, the analysis of these more general oganizational issues is even more difficult than that of the "ownership and control" issue because the nature of the contractual obligations and rights of the parties are much more varied and generally not as well specified in explicit contractual arrangements. Nevertheless, they exist and we believe that extensions of our analysis in these directions show promise of producing insights into a viable theory of organization.

11. They define the classical capitalist firm as a contractual organization of inputs in which there is "(a) joint input production, (b) several input owners, (c) one party who is common to all the contracts of the joint inputs, (d) who has rights to renegotiate any input's contract independently of contracts with other input owners, (e) who holds the residual claim, and (f) who has the right to sell his contractual residual status."

12. By legal fiction we mean the artificial construct under the law which allows certain organizations to be treated as individuals.

13. For example, we ordinarily think of a product as leaving the firm at the time it is sold, but implicitly or explicitly such sales generally carry with them continuing contracts between the firm and the buyer. If the product does not perform as expected the buyer often can and does have a right to satisfaction. Explicit evidence that such implicit contracts do exist is the practice we occasionally observe of specific provision that all sales are final.

14. This view of the firm points up the important role which the legal system and the law play in social organizations, especially, the organization of economic activity. Statutory laws set bounds on the kinds of contracts into which individuals and organizations may enter without risking criminal prosecution. The police powers of the state are available and used to enforce performance of contacts or to enforce the collection of damages for non-performance. The courts adjudicate conflicts between contracting parties and establish precedents which form the body of common law. All of these government activities affect both the kinds of contracts executed and the extent to which contracting is relied upon. This in turn determines the usefulness, productivity, profitability and viability of various forms of organization. Moreover, new laws as well as court decisions often can and do change the rights of contracting parties ex post, and they can and do serve as a vehicle for redistribution of wealth. An analysis of some of the implications of these facts is contained in Jensen and Meckling (1976) and we shall not pursue them here.

15. For use in consumption, for the diversification of his wealth, or more importantly, for the financing of "profitable" projects which he could not otherwise finance out of his personal wealth. We deal with these issues below after having developed some of the elementary analytical tools necessary to their solution.

REFERENCES

Alchian, A. A., 1965, The basis of some recent advances in the theory of management of the firm, *Journal of Industrial Economics*, Nov., 30–44.

Alchian, A. A., 1968, Corporate management and property rights, in: *Economic policy and the regulation of securities* (American Enterprise Institute, Washington, DC).

Alchian, A. A., and H. Demsetz, 1972, Production, information costs, and economic organization, *American Economic Review* LXII, no. 5, 777–795.

Alchian, A. A., and R. A. Kessel, 1962, Competition, monopoly and the pursuit of pecuniary gain, in: *Aspects of labor economics* (National Bureau of Economic Research, Princeton, NJ).

Baumol, W. J., 1959, *Business behavior, value and growth* (Macmillan, New York).

Berhold, M., 1971, A theory of linear profit sharing incentives, *Quarterly Journal of Economics* LXXXV, Aug., 460–482.

Branch, B., 1973, Corporate objectives and market performance, *Financial Management*, Summer, 24–29.

Coase, R. H., 1937, The nature of the firm, *Economica, New Series*, IV, 386–405. Reprinted in: *Readings in price theory* (Irwin, Homewood, IL) 331–351.

Coase, R. H., 1959, The Federal Communications Commission, *Journal of Law and Economics II*, Oct., 1–40.

Coase, R. H., 1960, The problem of social cost, *Journal of Law and Economics III*, Oct., 1–44.

Coase, R. H., 1964, Discussion, *American Economic Review LIV*, no. 3, 194–197.

Cyert, R. M., and C. L. Hedrick, 1972, Theory of the firm: Past, present and future; An interpretation, *Journal of Economic Literature X*, June, 398–412.

Cyert, R. M., and J. G. March, 1963, *A behavioral theory of the firm* (Prentice Hall, Englewood Cliffs, NJ).

Demsetz, H., 1967, Toward a theory of property rights, *American Economic Review LVII*, May, 347–359.

Furubotn, E. G. and S. Pejovich, 1972, Property rights and economic theory: A survey of recent literature, *Journal of Economic Literature X*, Dec., 1137–1162.

Heckerman, D. G., 1975, Motivating managers to make investment decisions, *Journal of Financial Economics 2*, no. 3, 273–292.

Jensen, M. C. and W. H. Meckling, 1976, Can the corporation survive? Center for Research in Government Policy and Business Working Paper no. PPS 76-4 (University of Rochester, Rochester, NY).

Klein, W. A., 1976, Legal and economic perspectives on the firm, unpublished manuscript (University of California, Los Angeles, CA).

Machlup, F., 1967, Theories of the firm: Marginalist, behavioral, managerial, *American Economic Review*, March, 1–33.

Marris, R., 1964, *The economic theory of managerial capitalism* (Free Press of Glencoe, Glencoe, IL).

Mason, E. S., 1959, *The corporation in modern society* (Harvard University Press, Cambridge MA).

McManus, J. C., 1975, The costs of alternative economic organizations, *Canadian Journal of Economics VIII*, Aug., 334–350.

Meckling, W. H., 1976, Values and the choice of the model of the individual in the social sciences, *Schweizerische Zeitschrift für Volkswirtschaft und Statistik*, Dec.

Monsen, R. J. and A. Downs, 1965, A theory of large managerial firms, *Journal of Political Economy*, June, 221–236.

Penrose, E., 1958, *The theory of the growth of the firm* (Wiley, New York).

Preston, L. E., 1975, Corporation and society: The search for a paradigm, *Journal of Economic Literature XIII*, June, 434–453.

Ross, S. A., 1973, The economic theory of agency: The principals problems, *American Economic Review LXII*, May, 134–139.

Ross, S. A., 1974a, The economic theory of agency and the principle of similarity, in: M. D. Balch et al., eds., *Essays on economic behavior under uncertainty* (North-Holland, Amsterdam).

Shubik, M., 1970, A curmudgeon's guide to microeconomics, *Journal of Economic Literature VIII*, June, 405–434.

Silver, M. and R. Auster, 1969, Entrepreneurship, profit and limits on firm size, *Journal of Business 42*, July, 277–281.

Simon, H. A., 1955, A behavioral model of rational choice, *Quarterly Journal of Economics 69*, 99–118.

Simon, H. A., 1959, Theories of decision making in economics and behavioral science, *American Economic Review*, June, 253–283.

Williamson, O. E., 1964, *The economics of discretionary behavior: Managerial objectives in a theory of the firm* (Prentice-Hall, Englewood Cliffs, NJ).

Williamson, O. E., 1970, *Corporate control and business behavior* (Prentice-Hall, Englewood Cliffs, NJ).

Williamson, O. E., 1975, *Markets and hierarchies: Analysis and antitrust implications* (The Free Press, New York).

Wilson, R., 1968, On the theory of syndicates, *Econometrica 36*, Jan., 119–132.

Wilson, R., 1969, La decision: Agregation et dynamique des orders de preference, Extrait (Editions du Centre National de la Recherche Scientifique, Paris) 288–307.

27

Learning from Organizational Economics

Jay B. Barney & William G. Ouchi

... Much of what organization theorists can learn from organizational economics has less to do with specific applications of concepts or models, and more to do with a way of thinking about organizations and about organizational phenomena. Incorporating these ways of thinking into organization theory is likely to have as important an impact on organization theory as would incorporating any particular model or concept taken from organizational economics. We next consider three specific aspects of this economic way of thinking and their implications for organization theory.

Equilibrium Analysis

... Equilibrium reasoning has a soiled reputation among many organization theorists, because this form of reasoning is often associated with the abstractions of neoclassical price theory. Organization theorists might question spending so much time and energy attempting to characterize intra- and interorganizational equilibria when it is obvious that real organizations are never in such states.

But, in many ways, this question misses the point about equilibrium reasoning. First, equilibrium reasoning is not the same as neoclassical price theory. One does not need to assume perfect information, zero transaction costs, homogeneous products and firms, and so on in order to use equilibrium reasoning. Rather, the focus is on underlying processes within and between organizations and on the stable state to which those processes will evolve if left alone. ...

Second, the criticism that equilibrium arguments waste intellectual energy describing results that will never exist misses the importance of such arguments in suggesting why these states never develop. In fact, the strength of the equilibrium form of reasoning rests in its ability to highlight the reasons why equilibrium states do not actually develop. ...

A final strength of equilibrium analyses lies in their inherently dynamic form. Equilibrium analysis does not stop at: the actions of firm A engender the actions of firm B. Rather, it tells us that the actions of A lead to the actions of B, which in turn lead to more responses by A (and by other firms, C and D), and so on. This multistage dynamic stands in contrast to what is seen in most organization theory models, where behavior A leads to behavior B, and that is the end of it. This limitation in the reasoning used by most organization theorists has already been pointed out in the case of resource dependence theory (Pfeffer and Salancik, 1978), where an equilibrium analysis of resource dependence logic suggests that industries characterized by any uncertainty will be dominated by a small number of large, vertically integrated firms. Since this is not the case in most industries, the question that resource dependence theory should ask but has yet to is: why not? What constraints face firms seeking to reduce their dependence to zero? What constraints prevent the equilibrium that is the result of following resource dependence logic to its conclusion?

Source: Jay B. Barney and William G. Ouchi, *Organizational Economics* (San Francisco: Jossey-Bass, 1986). Used by permission of John Wiley & Sons, Inc.

The Transaction as the Unit of Analysis

In organization theory and organizational behavior, there is a widespread belief that research on organization needs to go forward on multiple levels of analysis simultaneously. The levels of analysis cited most commonly are the individual, the group, intergroup relations, the organization, interorganizational relations, and, finally, organization-environment relations. The discipline bases of these units of analysis also increase in scope from psychology to social psychology to sociology and political science. Recently, anthropology has begun to reemerge as an important discipline in understanding intergroup and organizational phenomena.

While research conducted at multiple levels of analysis is not unknown, it is nevertheless relatively rare. The reasons for this are clear. Each level of analysis has associated with it different disciplines, although they overlap to some extent. The theoretical content of these disciplines is typically based on different sets of assumptions and beliefs. Developing single frameworks to deal with multilevel phenomena requires at least a partial integration of theories based on different disciplines. Such "general social theories" tend to be very abstract indeed, often divorced from the empirical reality. Perhaps the best example of the pitfalls of such multilevel general social theories can be found in the highly abstract, and no longer influential, work of Talcott Parsons (1951). Thus, rather than fall subject to these abstractions, research in organization theory has tended to retreat to single levels of analysis, only rarely venturing forth to multiple levels and then only in a tentative way.

Much of the theory of organizational economics overcomes the liabilities of multiple levels of analysis by positing the existence of only one appropriate level: the transaction. A transaction, as defined by Williamson (1981), is simply an exchange between technologically separable entities. In this way, the definition of a transaction is closely related to exchange theory as it has been developed in sociology and social psychology (Blau, 1964; Homans, 1958). And even though the language is not used universally among organizational economists, such concepts as "the nexus of contracts" and "interspecific human capital" as used by property rights, agency, and transaction-costs theorists all build on this single unit of analysis.

Organizational sociologists, in particular, are likely to find the abandonment of multiple levels of analysis particularly troubling, since they often see in this abandonment the destruction of their discipline. Ever since Durkheim (1966), sociologists have specialized in arguing that there is something distinctly different about sociological phenomena, that it requires a separate unit of analysis for explanation.

Adoption of the transaction as the single unit of analysis in organization theory would have important implications for research and teaching in the field. Many old and familiar concepts suddenly disappear. For example, there is no such thing as an "organizational boundary," at least as it has been defined; that is, there is no longer a clear inside and outside to a firm. Some economic exchanges occur between separate legal entities but are longlasting and cooperative. What meaning does the concept of a boundary have for these exchanges?

By implication, then, there is no such thing as an "organizational environment." Rather, firms face hundreds of microenvironments for each of the different transactions in which they engage. Some of these may be uncertain and complex, while others may be certain and simple. Overall characterizations of environments as uncertain or turbulent or complex or simple become meaningless in this context. Also, there is no such thing as an "organization's structure," at least as this concept traditionally has been used. Rather, exchanges are governed in a wide variety of ways, using competition or cooperation, rules or trust, and bureaucracies or clans, all simultaneously. Obviously, characterizing a structure as centralized or decentralized when it might be both simultaneously is misleading.

All this is not to suggest that macro-organizational analyses are impossible when using the transaction as the unit of analysis. Indeed, Williamson's (1975) M-form hypothesis is just such an analysis. However, by adopting the transaction as the unit of analysis, careful attention must be focused on important questions about: the process of aggregating individual transactions into bundles of transactions to discuss groups; aggregating groups to discuss intergroup relations (that is, transactions between groups); aggregating even further to focus on firms and firm structure; and, finally, aggregating transactions to the point where interfirm relations can be discussed. In other words, adopting the transaction as the unity of analysis, and then proceeding to conduct a macroanalysis of organizations necessitates multiple levels of analysis and cross-discipline research.

The Concept of Organization

Finally, organizational economists have been able to point to a fundamental ambiguity at the heart of organization theory. This ambiguity lies in what does and does not constitute organization. For organizational economists, an event or process is organized if it exhibits regular patterns and structures. Thus, market exchanges, because they exhibit such regular patterns, are organized social events, subject to study and analysis (Hirshleifer, 1980). Also, the structure of events inside firms can be organized and is subject to similar forms of analysis (Hoenack, 1983).

For organization theorists, on the other hand, organization is typically meant to include activities within and between what might be called firms (both for profit and nonprofit) and within and between government bureaucracies. This concept of organization is much more narrow and restrictive than what would be accepted by organizational economists.

One of the liabilities of adopting this narrow definition of organization is that it unrealistically restricts the range of phenomena that can be studied by organization theorists. One of the common themes running throughout organizational economics is comparing the efficiency characteristics of a hierarchy to those of a market in governing specific economic transactions. In this sense, hierarchies, markets, and intermediate market forms are specific alternatives among which managers can choose when deciding how to govern transactions. In organization theory, several of these alternatives are often omitted. Research is artificially restricted to considering one of several types of hierarchical responses. Markets and quasi-market alternatives are thereby excluded, perhaps prematurely.

There is, of course, a political and value laden side to including markets as transaction governance mechanisms within a broader redefined organization theory. Indeed, the neoconservative political leanings of many economists are well known (Friedman, 1970). Indeed, the organization theorist's emphasis on hierarchical governance may reflect underlying value preferences for the use of centralized control to resolve economic exchange problems or a preference for exposing the abuse of power in hierarchies. Nevertheless, as Williamson (1975) and others have shown, it is possible to separate the value and political questions from the efficiency questions of transaction governance mechanisms.

Perhaps organization theorists balk at generalizing the definition of the concept of organization to include market and quasi-market phenomena out of fear of academic incursions by economists into their protected domain. Without this broader definition, organization theory becomes just part of a general framework for analyzing economic transactions, a specialty that focuses on the more behavioral aspects of exchange. Perhaps this is appropriate. Perhaps organization theory will ultimately find itself integrated into this larger framework, its distinctiveness lost. Is this a bad thing? If, after all, the nature of the phenomena being studied requires this integration, is it not appropriate to attempt to accomplish it?

LEARNING FROM ORGANIZATION THEORY

But the learning between organizational economics and organization theory has not been one-way. Organization theory has had and continues to have important implications for organizational economics. Incorporating these points of view into organizational economics almost certainly will improve the analyses, explanations, and predictions of organizational economists.

Organizational Influences on Rational Decision Making

One of the most important contributions of organization theory to organizational economics has been recognition of the extrarational aspects of decision making. For most organizational economists, decision making is characterized by boundedly rational—but intentionally rational—utility maximizing information collectors and analyzers. While this is a description of decision making that applies in some settings, including perhaps the making of certain investment decisions, it is certainly not complete. For example, it probably does not describe how organizational economists, themselves, make a large number of decisions about their lives or careers.

Organization theorists also acknowledge bounded rationality and self-interest (Simon, 1961); but organizational research has shown that so-called rational decision making is affected by many other factors. These include the age and sex of those making decisions (Elder, 1975; Kanter, 1977), the nature of intergroup conflicts in an organization (Alderfer, 1977), the number and types of individuals making a decision (Kanter, 1977), the abilities of senior managers to encourage open discussion (Ouchi, 1981; Vroom and Yetton, 1973), and a host of other factors. Note that these factors do not create a situation in which individuals make

irrational decisions, but rather a situation in which that which is rational changes in stable and predictable ways. That is, what is rational for a woman in a large organization may not be rational for a man in that same organization. What is rational when one is twenty-five is not rational, perhaps, at age thirty or at midlife. The level of open discussion that is rational in a participatively managed firm may not be rational in an autocratically managed firm.

Including these other factors in describing decision making by organization participants will almost certainly improve the predictive capabilities of economic models. It is also likely to substantially alter the structure of those models and introduce a level of complexity and subtlety that has yet to be characteristic of organizational economics.

Empirical Research

The other major tradition in organization theory that should influence organizational economists lies in the role and use of empirical research. Organization theory is characterized by a rich tradition of both qualitative and quantitative research. Beginning with the Hawthorne studies (Roethlisberger and Dickson, 1939), this work has not only been used to test theories deductively, but also to develop concepts and ideas inductively. The number of qualitatively rich descriptions of actual organizational processes has been and continues to be a resource pool of empirical phenomena against which many theories in organization behavior and theory have been judged (Christensen and others, 1982).

In organizational economics, quantitative and qualitative empirical research has been the exception rather than the rule. . . .

On the one hand, this lack of empirical research suggests a strong theoretical focus among organizational economists, a focus which certainly can be applauded. It also reflects a level of confidence in theory that organization theorists would probably find overstated. On the other hand, this paucity of empirical research leaves much of the ultimate potential of this approach unexamined. There is, within organizational economics, a large number of interesting ideas. Whether they help explain actual organizational phenomena unfortunately remains a largely unanswered question.

. . . It is interesting to note . . . that most of the current empirical research in organizational economics, including Walker and Weber (1984), Barney (1986), and others has been conducted by organization theorists, with the important exception of Teece and his associates (Armour and Teece, 1978; Monteverde and Teece, 1982), marketing specialists, and other noneconomists. This suggests that, despite the difficulty of empirical work in this area, the paucity of such work done by economists reflects their interests and tastes as much as it does the difficulty of the research. . . .

REFERENCES

Alderfer, C. P. "Improving Organizational Communication Through Long-term Intergroup Intervention." *Journal of Applied Behavioral Science*, 1977, *13*, 193–210.

Armour, H. O., and Teece, D. J. "Organization Structure and Economic Performance: A Test of the Multidivisional Hypothesis." *Bell Journal of Economics*, 1978, *9*, 106–122.

Barney, J. B. "The Organization of Capital Acquisition." Unpublished manuscript, Graduate School of Management, University of California, Los Angeles, 1986.

Blau, P. M. *Exchange and Power in Social Life*. New York: Wiley, 1964.

Christensen, C. R., and others. *Business Policy*. Homewood, Ill.: Irwin, 1982.

Durkheim, E. *The Rules of the Sociological Method*, 8th ed. New York: Free Press, 1966.

Elder, G. H., Jr. "Age Differentiation and Life Course." In A. Inkeles, J. Coleman, and N. Smelser (eds.), *Annual Review of Sociology, 1975*, vol. 1. Palo Alto, Calif.: Annual Review, 1975.

Friedman, M. "The Social Responsibility of Business Is To Increase Its Profits." *New York Times Magazine*, Sept. 13, 1970.

Hirshleifer, J. *Price Theory and Applications*, 2nd ed. Englewood Cliffs, N.J.: Prentice-Hall, 1980.

Hoenack, S. A. *Economic Behavior Within Organizations*. New York: Cambridge University Press, 1983.

Homans, G. C. "Social Behavior as Exchange." *American Journal of Sociology*, 1958, *63*, 597–606.

Homans, G. C. *Social Behavior: Its Elementary Forms*. San Diego, Calif.: Harcourt Brace Jovanovich, 1961.

Kanter, R. *Men and Women of the Corporation*. New York: Basic, 1977.

Monteverde, K., and Teece, D. J. "Supplier Switching Costs and Vertical Integration." *Bell Journal of Economics*, 1982, *13*, 206–213.

Ouchi, W. G. *Theory Z*. Reading, Mass.: Addison-Wesley, 1981.

Ouchi, W. G. *The M-Form Society*. Reading, Mass.: Addison-Wesley, 1984.

Parsons, T. *The Social System*. New York: Free Press, 1951.

Pfeffer, J., and Salancik, G. R. *The External Control of Organizations: A Resource Dependence Perspective*. New York: Harper & Row, 1978.

Roethlisberger, F. J., and Dickson, W. J. *Management and the Worker*. Cambridge, Mass.: Harvard University Press, 1939.

Simon, H. A. *Administrative Behavior*, 2nd ed. New York: Wiley, 1961.

Vroom, V., and Yetton, P. *Leadership and Decision Making*. Pittsburgh, Penn.: University of Pittsburgh Press, 1973.

Walker, G., and Weber, D. "A Transaction Cost Approach to Make-or-Buy Decisions." *Administrative Science Quarterly*, 1984, *29*, 373–391.

Williamson, O. E. *Markets and Hierarchies: Analysis and Antitrust Implications*. New York: Free Press, 1975.

Williamson, O. E. "Franchise Bidding for Natural Monopolies—In General and with Respect to CATV." *Bell Journal of Economics*, 1976, *7*, 73–104.

Williamson, O. E. "Transaction-Cost Economics: The Governance of Contractual Relations." *Journal of Law and Economics*, 1979, *22*, 233–261.

Williamson, O. E. "The Modern Corporation: Origins, Evolution, Attributes." *Journal of Economic Literature*, 1981, *19*, 1537–1568.

28

Managing Business Transactions

Paul H. Rubin

The analysis and proposals [herein] have been based on two basic principles. First, people are self-interested and opportunistic. Second, it is impossible to write complete contracts which take account of any and all possible events and which eliminate all forms of opportunism or cheating.[1]

Since people are opportunistic, they will attempt to engross for themselves as much as possible of the benefits of any arrangement or transaction. Since contracts are not and cannot be complete, we cannot use explicit, written, legally enforceable contracts to completely eliminate shirking or other forms of opportunism. As a result, other mechanisms must be used to minimize agency costs.

These two principles imply that there will be various forms of opportunism in transactions. The varieties of opportunism are limited. The same forms occur in all the types of markets we have examined, including input markets, labor markets, capital markets, and markets for final outputs, although various forms of opportunism are called different things in different markets, and the frequency of alternative forms of opportunism varies across markets.

One form of opportunism is precontractual opportunism, sometimes called adverse selection, a situation in which people select themselves in such a way as to penalize a trading partner. In this process, one party knows more than the other (knowledge is asymmetric, one party has private knowledge), and the knowledgeable party attempts to capitalize on this additional knowledge. In the limit, such opportunism

can lead to a lemons market, and ultimately to the failure of a market to exist. There may be extreme forms of precontractual opportunism. If a party enters into a contract with the explicit intention of capitalizing on the contract and engaging in some form of holdup after the contract is begun, then this may approximate fraud.

Other forms of opportunism are postcontractual. These forms arise in situations in which parties are already transacting. General names for these forms of opportunism include shirking, agency costs, and moral hazard.

One common form of postcontractual opportunism is quasirent expropriation, in which one party to a transaction attempts to engross for herself the returns associated with a fixed, or sunk, investment. This form of opportunism is often associated with holdup problems. Attempts to avoid such exploitation should govern the make-or-buy decision, or the level of vertical integration. Shirking is the term usually applied to opportunism in labor contracts. It entails efforts to further the goals of the employee, rather than the employer. Simple forms of shirking include unwarranted leisure on the job. More extreme forms entail distorted investment patterns for the firm, including misuse of free cash flow, associated with greatly reduced profitability for a firm, and also excessively conservative or excessively risky investment patterns.

To reduce the costs of opportunism in its assorted forms, various devices have been suggested. When possible, the most powerful device available for controlling these

Source: Paul H. Rubin, *Managing Business Transactions: Controlling the Cost of Coordinating, Communication, and Decision Making* (New York: Free Press, 1990). © 1990 by Paul H. Rubin. Reprinted with the permission of The Free Press, a division of Simon & Schuster Adult Publishing Group. All rights reserved.

costs is the use of the market. Other possibilities include use of hostages and credible commitments to support exchange, so that parties who break their agreements will suffer losses. When such devices (which may take various forms, including for example joint ventures and reciprocal exchange) are available, they can reduce the costs of opportunism. Parties also engage in monitoring to control opportunism. Monitoring devices will include outside auditors and boards of directors.

Payment schemes can also be devised to reduce the costs of shirking. Most business transactions are governed by self-enforcing agreements, which, as the name suggests, are binding only because it pays for both parties to continue in the agreement. A two-part tariff (a fixed payment coupled with a variable payment) can align incentives and behavior, and so reduce shirking, although risk aversion limits the use of this method. Contests are methods of paying workers whereby relative performance is rewarded, and are useful if many workers face risks due to the same factors. Making decision makers the residual claimants is a powerful device to reduce shirking.

One of the most important tools available for controlling opportunism is creation of a reputation. A reputation for non-opportunistic behavior (for a person and, more importantly, for a firm) is an efficient method of guaranteeing that cheating will not occur, and therefore an efficient method of supporting exchange. On the other hand, it is important in vertical transactions to devise methods of eliminating incentives of one party to free ride on the reputation of other parties. Franchise contracts, for example, are aimed at reducing this sort of free riding.

In general, it is in the interests of all parties to an exchange to reduce opportunism to the lowest possible levels. Since parties to transactions are rational, they will anticipate some shirking and will adjust their payments accordingly. Therefore, the more a party can commit herself not to shirk, the higher the payment she can receive from her trading partner. Thus, you should look for ways to limit opportunism in all contracts to which you are a party, and you should explain to your trading partners ways in which suggested arrangements can work to reduce shirking.

In the special case of the behavior of management with respect to stockholders, an additional control is the law of fiduciary duties. A manager in charge of a company has particular legal obligations, in addition to those which apply to parties to arms-length contracts. These responsibilities include: duties to disclose, over and above the corresponding obligation imposed on traders under normal contracts; more open-ended duties to act in the interests of shareholders, in addition to any specific duties specified in the agreement; and greater-than-normal restrictions on rights to receive benefits associated with the position. These restrictions may be explained because of the greater-than-average power of peak managers, and the difficulty stockholders have in policing these managers. In addition, courts are more likely to use language regarding morals and other forms of normative rhetoric in finding liability for violating any of these obligations. We now turn to the role of morality in policing contracts in general.

ETHICS

To the extent that opportunism may be viewed as a form of cheating, it might appear that we could rely on ethical behavior as a way to control shirking. Nonetheless, . . . I have downplayed the role of ethics. There are several reasons for this decision. (As an economist, I may not have any particular ability to even define ethics. I will use the term as being synonymous with efficient. Any behavior which is efficient will be considered ethical. Efficient behavior is value maximizing.)

First, it does not pay for you to be more ethical than those with whom you are transacting. If all parties to transactions routinely engage in opportunism and you do not, then you will find yourself being taken advantage of and will ultimately be eliminated from the market.

Second, it will not always be possible to determine the meaning of ethical behavior. I believe that (perhaps for evolutionary reasons) humans have the ability to convince themselves that actions which are in their own interest are also moral. An outside observer (if properly trained) can sometimes determine what is truly ethical, but not always; a party to an agreement would have much more difficulty. A rule of behavior which said "Always act ethically" would not give much useful guidance. Indeed, much behavior which appears ethical to many is nonetheless inefficient (in an economic sense) and therefore leads to reduced wealth in society. (For one example, many feel that it is morally right to help farmers. The effect of policies aimed at this goal is often to increase costs of food, and the poor spend a disproportionate share of their incomes on food. Therefore, the effect of many apparently ethical policies is increased hunger.)

Third, and perhaps most important, there is little reason to rely on ethics for the types of situations . . . in which parties are already transacting with each other. In such circumstances, it is possible to devise side payments so that it will pay for parties to engage in all efficient transactions (or, in my terms, to behave ethically). Therefore, . . . it is possible to construct efficient side payments. For example, a golden parachute is a side payment to a manager to induce the manager to sell the firm when this is efficient and in the interests of stockholders. In general,

the transactions discussed here would create joint gains, and side payments can be used to ensure that the gains are indeed realized.

. . . What I have attempted to do is to indicate ways in which we can structure transactions to make it in the interests of all parties to the deal to behave ethically and efficiently. Because there is a limit to our willingness to reduce our own incomes in order to benefit others (another possible meaning of ethics), there are advantages of structuring transactions in ways which lead us to provide such benefits without harming ourselves. To an economist, this is a real benefit of efficient transactions.

NOTE

1. A third principle is that people are risk averse. This principle is less important for the analysis than the other two, and is used only to eliminate contracts which put all of the risk on one party.

REFERENCES

Clark, Robert C. "Agency Costs Versus Fiduciary Duties." In *Principals and Agents*, edited by John W. Pratt and Richard J. Zeckhauser. Boston: Harvard Business School Press, 1985.

Posner, Richard A. *The Economics of Justice*, Part 1. Boston: Harvard University Press, 1981.

Rubin, Paul H. "Evolved Ethics and Efficient Ethics." *Journal of Economic Behavior and Organization* 3 (1982):161.

CHAPTER 6

Power and Politics Organization Theory

The neatest thing about power is that we all understand it. We may have first discovered power as children when our mothers said, "Don't do that!" And we learn about power in organizations as soon as we go to school. Most of us have a good intuitive grasp of the basic concepts of organizational power by the time we reach the third grade. So the newest thing about power in organizations is not our understanding of it, but rather our intellectualizing about it.

Ordinary people as well as scholars have hesitated to talk about power. First, for many, power is not a subject for polite conversation. We have often equated power with force, brutality, unethical behavior, manipulation, connivance, and subjugation. Rosabeth Moss Kanter (1979) contends that "power is America's last dirty word. It is easier to talk about money—and much easier to talk about sex—than it is to talk about power." Besides, power doesn't fit well with our Western notion of rationality in business and government. Thus, fewer people have been exposed to analyses of organizational power. So it will be useful to start our introduction to the power and politics perspective on organization theory by contrasting some of its basic assumptions with those of the more rational "modern" structural, organizational economics, and organizations/environment schools (Chapters 4, 5, and 9 respectively).

In the "modern" structural, organizational economics, and systems/environment theories of organization, organizations are assumed to be rational institutions—institutions whose primary purpose is to accomplish established goals. People in positions of formal authority set goals. In these schools, the primary questions for organization theory involve how best to design and manage organizations so that they achieve their declared purposes effectively and efficiently. The personal preferences of organizational members are restrained by systems of formal rules, authority, and norms of rational behavior.

The power and politics school rejects these assumptions about organizations as being naive and unrealistic, and therefore of minimal practical value. Instead, organizations are viewed as complex systems of individuals and coalitions, each having its own interests, beliefs, values, preferences, perspectives, and perceptions. The coalitions continuously compete with each other for scarce organizational resources. Conflict is inevitable. Influence—as well as the power and political activities through which influence is acquired and maintained—is the primary "weapon" for use in competition and conflicts. Thus, power, politics, and influence are essential and permanent facts of organizational life.

Organization theorists from the power and politics school argue that organizational goals are only rarely established by people in positions of formal authority. Goals result from ongoing maneuvering and bargaining among individuals and coalitions. Most coalitions are transitory: they shift with issues and often cross vertical and horizontal organizational boundaries. They may, for example, include people at several levels in the organizational hierarchy and from different product, functional, and/or geographical divisions or departments. Thus, organizational goals change with shifts in the balance of power among coalitions. J. V. Baldridge (1971) noted that organizations have many conflicting goals, and different sets of goals take priority as the balance of power changes among coalitions—as different coalitions gain and use enough power to control them. *Why then are organizational goals so important in the theory of organizational power and politics?* The answer is essential for understanding this perspective on organization theory—*because they provide the official rationale and the legitimacy for resource-allocation decisions.*

Power relations are permanent features of organizations primarily because specialization and the division of labor result in the creation of many interdependent organization units with varying degrees of importance to the well-being of the organization. The units compete with each other for scarce resources as well as with the transitory coalitions. As James D. Thompson points out in *Organizations in Action* (1967), a lack of balance in the interdependence among units sets the stage for the use of power relations. Jeffrey Pfeffer, a leading organizational theorist who has written extensively on "resource dependence" in organizations, emphasizes: "Those persons and those units that have the responsibility for performing the more critical tasks in the organization have a natural advantage in developing and exercising power in the organization. . . . Power is first and foremost a structural phenomenon, and should be understood as such" (1981).

"Modern" structural theories of organization theory place high importance on "legitimate authority" (authority that flows down through the organizational hierarchy) and formal rules (promulgated and enforced by those in authority) to ensure that organizational behavior is directed toward the attainment of established organizational goals (see Chapter 4). Structuralists tend to define power as being synonymous with authority. In contrast, John Kotter (1985) argues that in today's organizational world, there is an increasing gap between the power one needs to get the job done and the power that automatically comes with the job (authority). The power and politics theories view authority as only one of the many available sources of organizational power, and power is aimed in *all* directions—not just down through the hierarchy.

Other forms of power and influence often prevail over authority-based power. Several of this chapter's selections identify different sources of power in organizations, so we list only a few here as examples: control over scarce resources (for example, office space, discretionary funds, current and accurate information, and time and skill to work on projects), access to others who are perceived as having power (for example, important customers or clients, members of the board of directors, or someone else with formal authority or who controls scarce resources), a central place in a potent coalition, ability to "work the organizational rules" (knowing how to get things done or to prevent others from getting things done), and credibility (for example, that one's word can be trusted).

Many definitions of "power" have been proposed, and Jeffrey Pfeffer explores the advantages and limitations of some of the better ones in the chapter "Understanding the Role of Power in Decision Making," from his 1981 book *Power in Organizations,* which is reprinted here. We prefer the following definition, which is a blending of definitions proposed by Gerald Salancik and Jeffrey Pfeffer (1977) and Robert Allen and Lyman Porter (1983): "Power is the ability to get things done the way one wants them done; it is the latent ability to influence people." This definition offers several advantages for understanding organizations. First, it emphasizes the relativity of power. As Pfeffer points out,

"[P]ower is context or relationship specific. A person is not 'powerful' or 'powerless' in general, but only with respect to other social actors in a specific social relationship."

Second, the phrase "the way one wants them done" is a potent reminder that conflict and the use of power often are over the choice of methods, means, approaches, and/or "turf." They are not limited to battles about outcomes. This point is important because power is primarily a structural phenomenon, a consequence of the division of labor and specialization. For example, competing organizational coalitions often form around professions: hospital nurses versus paramedics, sociologists versus mathematicians in a college of arts and sciences, business school–educated staff specialists versus generalists from the "school of hard knocks" in a production unit, or social workers versus educators in a center for incarcerated youth. Organizational conflicts among people representing different professions, educational backgrounds, genders, and ages frequently do not involve goals. They center on questions about the "right" of a profession, academic discipline, or sex or age group to exercise its perception of its "professional rights," to control the way things will be done, or to protect its turf and status. This point is crucially important because it reemphasizes that organizational behavior and decisions frequently are not "rational"—as the word is used by the "modern" structural, organizational economics, and the systems/environment schools, meaning "directed toward the accomplishment of established organizational goals." Thus, this particular definition of power highlights the primary reason why the power and politics theories reject the basic assumptions of the "modern" structural, organizational economics, and the systems/environment schools as being naive and unrealistic and downplay the importance of those theories of organization.

Pfeffer's "Understanding the Role of Power in Decision Making" provides an excellent synopsis of the power and politics perspective on organizations. We have placed it first among this chapter's selections in order to provide the reader with a macroperspective on this school. His basic theme is that power and politics are fundamental concepts for understanding behavior in organizations. He defines the concepts of power, authority, and organizational politics, and he identifies the "place of power" in the literature of organization theory.

Robert Michels, a German sociologist, is perhaps best known for his assertion that "Who says organization says oligarchy." In "Democracy and the Iron Law of Oligarchy," a chapter in *Political Parties: A Sociological Study of the Oligarchical Tendencies of Modern Democracy* (1962; originally published in 1915 in German), Michels argues from a political perspective on power in organizations. Organizations are oligarchic by their nature because majorities in organizations are not able to rule themselves.

> Organization implies the tendency to oligarchy. In every organization, . . . the aristocratic tendency manifests itself very clearly. The mechanism of the organization, while conferring a solidity of structure, induces serious changes in the organized mass, completely inverting the respective position of the leaders and the led. As a result of organization, every [political] party or professional union becomes divided into a minority of directors and a majority of the directed.

"The Bases of Social Power," by John R. P. French Jr. and Bertram Raven (1959), reprinted here, starts from the premise that power and influence involve relations between at least two agents (they limit their definition of agents to individuals), and theorizes that the reaction of the *recipient agent* is the more useful focus for explaining the phenomena of social influence and power. The core of French and Raven's chapter, however, is their identification of five bases or sources of social power: reward power, the perception of coercive power, legitimate power (organizational authority), referent power (through association with others who possess power), and expert power (power of knowledge or ability).

French and Raven examine the effects of power derived from these five different bases of *attraction* (the recipient's sentiment toward the agent who uses power) and *resistance* to the use of power. They conclude that the use of power from the different bases has different consequences. For example, coercive power typically decreases attraction and causes high resistance whereas reward power increases attraction and creates minimal levels of resistance. In what amounts to one of the earliest looks at ethical limits on the use of power, French and Raven conclude that "the more legitimate the coercion [is perceived to be] the less it will produce resistance and decreased attraction."

James March's essay "The Power of Power" is not limited to power inside of organizations. March reviews alternative definitions, concepts, and approaches for empirically studying social power in organizations and communities. His observations about "community power" are more than tangentially germane to organization theory because of the current enthusiasm for "boundaryless organizations," "virtual organizations," and networks. March discusses the advantages and limitations of three approaches to the study of power: experimental studies, community studies, and institutional studies. "The third alternative approach . . . is the analysis of the structure of institutions to determine the power structure within them." March assesses the usefulness of six types of models of social choice for arriving at empirically meaningful predictions about power. March concludes: "Although power and influence are useful concepts for many kinds of situations, they have not greatly helped us to understand many of the natural social-choice mechanisms to which they have traditionally been applied. . . . On the whole, . . . power is a disappointing concept" for social science research.

In her 1979 *Harvard Business Review* article "Power Failure in Management Circuits," which is reprinted here, Rosabeth Moss Kanter argues that executive and managerial power is a necessary ingredient for moving organizations toward their goals. "Power can mean efficacy and capacity" for organizations. The ability of managers to lead effectively cannot be predicted by studying their styles or traits; it requires knowledge of a leader's real power sources. Kanter identifies three groups of positions within organizations that are particularly susceptible to powerlessness: first-line supervisors, staff professionals, and top executives. However, she carefully distinguishes between "power" and "dominance, control, and oppression." Her primary concern is that at higher organizational levels, the power to "punish, to prevent, to sell off, to reduce, to fire, all without appropriate concern for consequences" grows, but the power needed for positive accomplishments does not. Managers who perceive themselves as being powerless and who think their subordinates are discounting them tend to use more dominating or punishing forms of influence. Thus, in larger organizations, powerlessness (or perceived powerlessness) can be a more substantive problem than possession of power. By empowering others, leaders actually can acquire more "productive power"—the power needed to accomplish organizational goals. "Power Failure in Management Circuits" also contains an embedded subarticle on the particular problems that power poses for women managers.

Henry Mintzberg describes his 1983 book *Power in and around Organizations* as a discussion of a theory of organizational power. Organizational behavior is viewed as a power game. The "players" are "influencers" with varying personal needs who attempt to control organizational decisions and actions. "Thus, to understand the behavior of the organization, it is necessary to understand which influencers are present, what needs each seeks to fulfill in the organization, and how each is able to exercise power to fulfill them." His chapter "The Power Game and the Players," which is reprinted here, focuses on the "influencers," who they are, and where their power comes from. Eleven groups of possible influencers are listed: five are in the "external coalition" and six in the "internal coalition." The external coalition consists of the owners, "associates" (suppliers, clients, trading partners, and competitors), employee associations (unions and professional associations), the organization's various publics (at large), and the corporate directors (which include representatives from the other four groups in the external coalition and also some internal influencers). The internal coalition is composed of the chief executive officer, operators (the organization's "producers"), line managers, analysts (staff specialists), the support staff, and—the final "actor" in Mintzberg's internal coalition—the ideology of the organization, that is, "the set of beliefs shared by its internal influencers that distinguishes it from other organizations." As it happens, ideology plays an important role in organizational culture, which is the topic of the next chapter.

REFERENCES

Akella, D. (2003). *Unlearning the fifth discipline: Power, politics and control in organizations*. Thousand Oaks, CA: Sage.

Allen, R. W., & L. W. Porter (1983). *Organizational influence processes*. Glenview, IL: Scott, Foresman.

Baldridge, J. V. (1971). *Power and conflict in the university*. New York: Wiley.

Cobb, A. T., & N. Margulies (1981). Organization development: A political perspective. *Academy of Management Review*, 6, 49–59.

Cohen, A. R., & D. L. Bradford (1990). *Influence without authority*. New York: Wiley.

Cohen, M. D., & J. G. March (1974). *Leadership and ambiguity: The American college president*. New York: McGraw-Hill.

Cross, R., & A. Parker. *The hidden power of social networks: Understanding how work really gets done in organizations*. Boston: Harvard Business School Press.

Cyert, R. M., & J. G. March (1963). *A behavioral theory of the firm*. Englewood Cliffs, NJ: Prentice Hall.

French, J. R. P., Jr., & B. Raven (1959). The bases of social power. In D. P. Cartwright, ed., *Studies in social power* (pp. 150–167). Ann Arbor, MI: University of Michigan, Institute for Social Research.

Hardy, C., ed. (1995). *Power and politics in organizations*. Aldershot, UK: Dartmouth.

Jay, A. (1967). *Management and Machiavelli*. New York: Holt, Rinehart & Winston.

Kanter, R. M. (1977). *Men and women of the corporation*. New York: Basic Books.

Kanter, R. M. (1979, July–August). Power failure in management circuits. *Harvard Business Review*, 57, 65–75.

Kaufman, H. (1964, March). Organization theory and political theory. *American Political Science Review*, 58, 5–14.

Korda, M. (1975). *Power! How to get it, how to use it*. New York: Random House.

Kotter, J. P. (1977, July–August). Power, dependence, and effective management. *Harvard Business Review*, 55, 125–136.

Kotter, J. P. (1985). *Power and influence: Beyond formal authority*. New York: Free Press.

March, J. G. (1966). The power of power. In David Easton, ed., *Varieties of political theory* (pp. 39–70). Englewood Cliffs, NJ: Prentice Hall, 1966.

Mechanic, D. (1962, December). Sources of power of lower participants in complex organizations. *Administrative Science Quarterly, 7*(3), 349–364.

Michels, R. (1962). Political parties: A sociological study of the oligarchical tendencies of modern democracy (Eden and Cedar Paul, trans.). New York: Free Press. Originally published in German in 1915.

Mintzberg, H. (1983). *Power in and around organizations.* Englewood Cliffs, NJ: Prentice Hall.

Ott, J. S., S. J. Parkes, & R. B. Simpson, eds. (2003). *Classic readings in organizational behavior.* 3d ed. Belmont, Calif.: Wadsworth-Thomson.

Pfeffer, J. (1981). *Power in organizations.* Boston: Pitman.

Pfeffer, J. (1992). *Managing with power: Politics and influence in organizations.* Boston: Harvard Business School Press.

Porter, L. W., R. W. Allen, & H. L. Angle (1981). The politics of upward influence in organizations. In L. L. Cummings & B. M. Staw, eds., *Research in organizational behavior,* vol. 3 (pp. 408–422). Greenwich, CT: JAI Press.

Salancik, G. R., & J. Pfeffer (1977). Who gets power—and how they hold on to it: A strategic-contingency model of power. *Organizational Dynamics, 5,* 2–21.

Siu, R. G. H. (1979). *The craft of power.* New York: Wiley.

Thompson, J. D. (1967). *Organizations in action.* New York: McGraw-Hill.

Tushman, M. L. (1977, April). A political approach to organizations: A review and rationale. *Academy of Management Review, 2,* 206–216.

Yates, D., Jr. (1985). *The politics of management.* San Francisco: Jossey-Bass.

Zaleznik, A., & M. F. R. Kets de Vries (1985). *Power and the corporate mind.* Chicago: Bonus Books.

29

Understanding the Role of Power in Decision Making

Jeffrey Pfeffer

More than 40 years ago Harold Lasswell (1936) defined politics as the study of who gets what, when, and how. Certainly, who gets what, when, and how, are issues of fundamental importance in understanding formal organizations. Nevertheless, organizational politics and organizational power are both topics which are made conspicuous by their absence in management and organization theory literature (Allen, et al., 1979). Why?

It is certainly not because the terms *power* and *politics* are concepts used infrequently in everyday conversation. Both are often used to explain events in the world around us. Richard Nixon's behavior while in the presidency has been ascribed to a need for power. Budget allocations among various federal programs are described as being the result of politics. Success in obtaining a promotion may be attributed to an individual's ability to play office politics. The fact that certain business functions (such as finance) or occupational specialties (such as law) are frequently important in organizations is taken to reflect the power of those functions or occupations. There are few events that are not ascribed to the effects of power and politics. As Dahl (1957: 201) noted, "The concept of power is as ancient and ubiquitous as any that social theory can boast." . . .

Power has been neglected for several reasons. First, the concept of power is itself problematic in much of the social science literature. In the second place, while power is something it is not everything. There are

other competing perspectives for understanding organizational decision making. These perspectives are frequently persuasive, if for no other reason than that they conform more closely to socially held values of rationality and effectiveness. And third, the concept of power is troublesome to the socialization of managers and the practice of management because of its implications and connotations. . . .

THE CONCEPT OF POWER

The very pervasiveness of the concept of power, referred to in the earlier quote from Robert Dahl, is itself a cause for concern about the utility of the concept in assisting us to understand behavior in organizations. Bierstedt (1950: 730) noted that the more things a term could be applied to the less precise was its meaning. Dahl (1957: 210) wrote, ". . . a Thing to which people attach many labels with subtly or grossly different meanings in many different cultures and times is probably not a Thing at all but many Things." March (1966) has suggested that in being used to explain almost everything, the concept of power can become almost a tautology, used to explain that which cannot be explained by other ideas, and incapable of being disproved as an explanation for actions and outcomes. . . .

It is generally agreed that power characterized relationships among social actors. A given social actor, by which we mean an individual, subunit, or organization, has more

Source: Jeffrey Pfeffer, *Power in Organizations* (Marshfield, MA: Pitman, 1981), 1–32.

power with respect to some social actors and less power with respect to others. Thus, power is context or relationship specific. A person is not "powerful" or "powerless" in general, but only with respect to other social actors in a specific social relationship. To say, for example, that the legal department in a specific firm is powerful, implies power with respect to other departments within that firm during a specific period of time. That same legal department may not be at all powerful with respect to its interactions with the firm's outside counsel, various federal and state regulatory agencies, and so forth. And, the power of the department can and probably will change over time. . . .

Most studies of power in organizations have focused on hierarchical power, the power of supervisors, or bosses over employees. The vertical, hierarchical dimension of power is important in understanding social life, but it is not the only dimension of power. As Perrow (1970: 59) wrote, "It is my impression that for all the discussion and research regarding power in organizations, the preoccupation with interpersonal power has led us to neglect one of the most obvious aspects of this subject: in complex organizations, tasks are divided up between a few major departments or subunits, and all of these subunits are not likely to be equally powerful." Implicit in this statement is the recognition that power is, first of all, a structural phenomenon, created by the division of labor and departmentation that characterize the specific organization or set of organizations being investigated. It is this more structural approach to power that constitutes the focus of this book, although at times we will consider what individual characteristics affect the exercise of structurally determined power.

It should be evident why power is somewhat tricky to measure and operationalize. In order to assess power, one must be able to estimate (a) what would have happened in the absence of the exercise of power; (b) the intentions of the actor attempting to exercise power; and (c) the effect of actions taken by that actor on the probability that

what was desired would in fact be likely to occur. . . . It should be recognized that the definition and assessment of power are both controversial and problematic.

THE CONCEPT OF AUTHORITY

It is important to distinguish between power and authority. In any social setting, there are certain beliefs and practices that come to be accepted within that setting. The acceptance of these practices and values, which can include the distribution of influence within the social setting, binds together those within the setting, through their common perspective. Activities which are accepted and expected within a context are then said to be legitimate within that context. The distribution of power within a social setting can also become legitimate over time, so that those within the setting expect and value a certain pattern of influence. When power is so legitimated, it is denoted as authority. Weber (1947) emphasized the critical role of legitimacy in the exercise of power. By transforming power into authority, the exercise of influence is transformed in a subtle but important way. In social situations, the exercise of power typically has costs. Enforcing one's way over others requires the expenditure of resources, the making of commitments, and a level of effort which can be undertaken only when the issues at hand are relatively important. On the other hand, the exercise of authority, power which has become legitimated, is expected and desired in the social context. Thus, the exercise of authority, far from diminishing through use, may actually serve to enhance the amount of authority subsequently possessed.

Dornbusch and Scott (1975), in their book on evaluation in organizations, made a similar point with respect to the evaluation process. They noted that in formal organizations, some people have the right to set criteria, to sample output, and to apply the criteria to the output that is sampled. Persons with such authority or evaluation rights are expected to engage in these authorized activities, and, instead of being punished for doing so, are punished when they fail to do so.

The transformation of power into authority is an important process, for it speaks to the issue of the institutionalization of social control. As such, we will return to this issue when political strategies are considered and when we take up the topic of institutionalized power. For the moment, it is sufficient to note that within formal organizations, norms and expectations develop that make the exercise of influence expected and accepted. Thus, social control of one's behavior by others becomes an expected part of organizational life. Rather than seeing the exercise of influence within organizations as a contest of strength or force, power, once it is transformed through legitimation into authority, is not resisted. At that point, it no longer depends on the resources or determinants that may have produced the power in the first place.

The transformation of power into authority can be seen most clearly in the relationship between supervisors and subordinates in work organizations. As Mechanic (1962) noted, lower level organizational members have, in reality, a great amount of power. If they refused to accept and accede to the instructions provided by higher level managers, those managers would have difficulty carrying out sanctions and operating the organization. Furthermore, the lower level participants have power that comes from specialized knowledge about the work process and access to information that higher level managers may not have. Thus, Mechanic (1962) argued, what is interesting is, not that subordinates accept the instructions of managers because of the greater power possessed by the managers. Rather, it is interesting that in spite of the considerable degree of power possessed by lower level employees, these employees seldom attempt to exercise their power or to resist the instructions of their managers. . . .

When social understanding and social consensus develops to accept, ratify, and even prefer the distribution of power, then the power becomes legitimated and becomes authority. Authority is maintained not only by the resources or sanctions that produced the power, but also by the social pressures and social norms that sanction the power distribution and which define it as normal and acceptable. Such social acceptance and social approval adds stability to the situation and makes the exercise of power easier and more effective. Legitimation, of course, occurs in a specific social context, and what is legitimate in one setting may be illegitimate in another. The degree and kind of supervisor-subordinate control exercised in U.S. organizations, for instance, may be perceived as illegitimate in the organizations of countries where there is more worker self-management and industrial democracy. Legitimation of power is thus ultimately problematic and far from inevitable. The examination of the conditions under which power and social control become legitimated and transformed into authority is an important undertaking in trying to understand the governance and control of organizations.

DEFINITION OF ORGANIZATIONAL POLITICS

The task of defining the term organizational politics is as difficult as that of defining power. The problem is to distinguish between political activity and organizational or administrative activity in general. As in the case of power, if politics refers to all forms of administrative or managerial action, then the term becomes meaningless because it includes every behavior.

From Lasswell's (1936) definition of politics as who gets what, when, and how, and from Wildavsky's (1979) descriptions of the politics of the budgetary process, the inference is that politics involves how differing preferences are resolved in conflicts over the allocation of scarce resources. Thus, politics involves activities which attempt to influence decisions over critical issues that are not readily resolved through the introduction of new data and in which there are differing points of view. For our purposes, organizational politics will be defined as:

> Organizational politics involves those activities taken within organizations to acquire, develop, and use power and other resources to obtain one's preferred outcomes in a situation in which there is uncertainty or dissensus about choices.

If power is a force, a store of potential influence through which events can be affected, politics involves those activities or behaviors through which power is developed and used in organizational settings. Power is a property of the system at rest; politics is the study of power in action. An individual, subunit, or department may have power within an organizational context at some period of time; politics involves the exercise of power to get something accomplished, as well as those activities which are undertaken to expand the power already possessed or the scope over which it can be exercised. This definition is similar to that provided by Allen, et al. (1979: 77): "Organizational politics involve intentional acts of influence to enhance or protect the self-interest of individuals or groups."

From the definition of power, it is clear that political activity is activity which is undertaken to overcome some resistance or opposition. Without opposition or contest within the organization, there is neither the need nor the expectation that one would observe political activity. And, because political activity is focused around the acquisition and use of power, it can be distinguished from activity involved in making decisions which uses rational or bureaucratic procedures. In both rational and bureaucratic models of choice, there is no place for and no presumed effect of political activity. Decisions are made to best achieve the organization's goals, either by relying on the best information and options that have been uncovered, or by using rules and procedures which have evolved in the organization. Political activity, by contrast, implies

the conscious effort to muster and use force to overcome opposition in a choice situation. . . .

THE PLACE OF POWER IN ORGANIZATION THEORY LITERATURE

. . . Examination of the major textbooks now current in the field will indicate that the subject of power is either not mentioned at all in the subject index or, if it is, it receives short shrift in terms of the number of pages devoted to it. When the subject of power is found in the index, it is frequently associated with a discussion of the individual bases of power (e.g., French and Raven, 1968) or the need for power. Size, technology, and environment all receive much more time and attention, even in those books with a presumably more sociological perspective. And, in specialized books dealing with topics such as organization design or organization development, power typically receives no mention at all, even though it is a particularly critical variable for some of these more specialized concerns. . . .

A likely explanation for the neglect of power in the management and organizational behavior literature is found by considering the role of management writing in the management process, and the position of a topic such as power as implied by the various functions served by management writing. The argument to be developed is relatively straightforward: management writing serves a variety of functions; in virtually all of these functions there is a strong component of ideology and values; topics such as power and politics are basically incompatible with the values and ideology being developed; therefore, it is reasonable, if not theoretically useful, to ignore topics which detract from the functions being served by the writing, and this includes tending to ignore or to downplay the topics of power and politics.

To ask what functions are served by management writing, we can begin by asking who reads management books. . . .

In the case of students, there is little doubt that one of the important functions of business education is socialization. This statement reflects both the more general importance of socialization in the educational process, and the specific prominence of socialization with respect to certain occupations and professions. It is not in just the fields of medicine and law that socialization plays an important part of the educational process. Although less frequently empirically examined, there are important considerations of socialization in the education of young, aspiring managers (e.g., Schein, 1968). Socialization involves the inculcation of norms and values that are central to the profession and that are, not incidentally, useful to the organizations in which the professionals are going to work. There is no norm so central to the existing practice and ideology of management as the norm of rationality. . . . Rationality and rational choice models focus attention on the development of technologies to more effectively achieve a goal or set of goals, such as profit or efficiency. Concern is directed toward the development of alternatives, the development of sophisticated techniques for evaluating the alternatives, their possible consequences, and the assembling of information that facilitates the evaluation of performance along these specified dimensions. . . .

To socialize students into a view of business that emphasizes power and politics would not only make the compliance to organizational authority and the acceptance of decision outcomes and procedures problematic, but also it might cause recruitment problems into the profession. It is certainly much more noble to think of oneself as developing skills toward the more efficient allocation and use of resources—implicitly for the greater good of society as a whole—than to think of oneself as engaged with other organizational participants in a political struggle over values, preferences, and definitions of technology. Technical rationality, as a component of the managerial task, provides legitimation and meaning for one's career, fulfilling a function similar to healing

the sick for doctors, or serving the nation's system of laws and justice for attorneys.

For . . . practicing managers, as well as for the student, the ideology of rationality and efficiency provides an explanation for career progress, or lack thereof, that is much more likely to lead to the acceptance of one's position rather than an attempt at making a radical change. . . .

In this way, the ideology of efficiency and rationality provides comforting explanations for practicing managers who find the progress of their careers blocked or less than what they might like, or feel a general sense of malaise about their work and their future. The invisible hands of marginal productivity and human capital have put them where they deserve to be. If power is to be considered at all, it is in terms of individually oriented political strategies (e.g., Korda, 1975), which provide the managers with the illusion that, with a few handy hints, they can improve their lot in the organization. Explanations which focus on structural variables, as most of the explanations for power and politics developed here do, are less popular, as they provide no easy palliatives and imply a need for much more fundamental change in terms of affecting decision outcomes.

For the third set of readers of the management literature, the general public, the emphasis on rationality and efficiency and the deemphasis on power and politics, assures them that the vast power and wealth controlled by organizations is, indeed, being effectively and legitimately employed. In this sense, organization theory and economic theory frequently find themselves fulfilling similar roles in explaining the status quo in terms which both justify and legitimate it. . . .

The ideology of functional rationality—decision making oriented toward the improvement of efficiency or performance—provides a legitimation of formal organizations, for the general public as well as for those working within specific organizations. Bureaucracies are, as Perrow (1972) argued, tremendous stores of resources and energy, both human and financial. Bureaucracies also represent concentrations of energy on a scale seldom seen in the history of the world. The legitimation and justification of these concentrations of power are clearly facilitated by theories arguing that efficiency, productivity, and effectiveness are the dominant dynamics underlying the operation of organizations.

To maintain that organizations are less than totally interested in efficiency, effectiveness or market performance is to suggest that it is legitimate to raise questions concerning the appropriateness of the concentration of power and energy they represent and makes it possible to introduce political concerns into the issues of corporate governance. The introduction of these concerns makes the present control arrangements less certain and permanent and would be resisted by all of those who benefit from the status quo.

The argument, then, is that the very literature of management and organizational behavior (as well, we might add, of much of economics, though that is a topic worthy of separate development) is itself political (Edelman, 1964), and causes support to be generated and opposition to be reduced as various conceptions of organizations are created and maintained in part through their very repetition. In this literature, efficiency-enhancing or profit-increasing behavior are not being taken as hypotheses about motivation and causes for action, but rather as accepted facts. Then, a theory is developed which is both consistent with these assumptions and finds excuses for why so much variation in actual decisions and behaviors is missed. . . .

Models of organizations which emphasize power and politics have their own political problems. It is important for those analyzing organizations to be able to figure out the kind of analytical framework that can be most usefully employed to diagnose the particular organization of interest. Kaplan's (1964) parable of the hammer is relevant. Because one has a hammer, one tends to use it on everything and for every task. Similarly, there is a tendency to take a noncontingent approach to the analysis of organizations, and to see them all as rational, bureaucratic, or political. Just as it is difficult to play football with baseball equipment, it is difficult to diagnose or effectively operate in an organization unless its dominant paradigm or mode of operation is understood. Furthermore, in order to evaluate the validity of a political approach to organizational analysis, there must be some alternatives with which to compare the model. For both of these reasons — to place the political model in a broader context of competing perspectives on organizational decision making and to raise issues relevant to diagnosing the form of system one is dealing with — we will describe the major contending models of organizational decision making.

RATIONAL CHOICE MODELS

The model of rational choice is prominent in the social choice literature. It is not only prescribed as being the best way to make choices in organizations, but frequently claims to be descriptive of actual choice processes as well. The rational model presumes that events are "purposive choices of consistent actors" (Allison, 1971: 11). It is important to recognize, therefore, that the rational model presumes and assumes that "behavior reflects purpose or intention" (Allison, 1971: 13). Behavior is not accidental, random, or rationalized after the fact; rather, purpose is presumed to pre-exist and behavior is guided by that purpose. With respect to understanding organizations or other social collectivities, the rational model further presumes that there is a unified purpose or set of preferences characterizing the entity taking the action. As Allison (1971: 28–29) has noted:

> What rationality adds to the concept of purpose is *consistency*: consistency among goals and objectives relative to a particular action; consistency in the application of principles in order to select the optimal alternative (emphasis in original).

The rational choice model presumes that there are goals and objectives that characterize organizations. As Friedland (1974) has noted, rationality cannot be defined apart from the existence of a set of goals. Thus, all rational choice models start with the assumption of a goal or consistent goal set. In the case of subjective expected utility maximization models (Edwards, 1954), the goals are called utilities for various outcomes, associated with the pleasure or pain producing properties of the outcomes. In the language of economics and management science, the goals are called the objectives or objective function to be maximized. Occasionally, goals are called preferences, referring to the states of the world the social actor prefers. Rational choice models require that these goals be consistent (March, 1976: 70).

Given a consistent set of goals, the next element in theories of rational choice is a set of decision-making alternatives to be chosen. Alternatives are presumed to be differentiable one from the other, so that each is uniquely identified. Such alternatives are produced by a search process. Until Simon (1957) introduced the concept of satisficing, it was generally assumed that search was costless and that large numbers of alternatives would be considered. Simon's contribution was to introduce the concept of bounded rationality, which held that persons had both limited capacities to process information and limited resources to devote to search activities. Thus a search for alternatives would be conducted only until a satisfactory alternative was uncovered. The concept of satisfaction was defined in terms of the social actor's level of aspiration (March and Simon, 1958).

Be they many or few, once a set of alternatives are uncovered, the next step in the rational decision-making process involves the assessment of the likely outcomes or consequences of the various possible courses of action. If there is risk or uncertainty involved, then estimates of the probability of the occurrence of various consequences would be used in making statements about the values of the consequences of different choices. At this stage in the decision process, it is assumed that consequences can be fully and completely anticipated, albeit with some degree of uncertainty. In other words, everything that can possibly occur as a result of the decision is presumably specified, though which of the various possibilities will actually occur may be subject to chance.

Then, a rational choice involves selecting that course of action or that alternative which maximizes the social actor's likelihood of attaining the highest value for achievement of the preferences or goals in the objective function. . . .

It is clear that in analyzing choice processes in organizations or other social collectives, the assumption of consistency and unity in the goals, information and decision processes is problematic. However, one of the advantages of the rational model is that it permits prediction of behavior with complete certainty and specificity if one knows (or assumes one knows) the goals of the other organization. Allison (1971: 13), in reviewing foreign policy analysis, has argued that this advantage is one important reason that "most contemporary analysts . . . proceed *predominantly* . . . in terms of this framework when trying to explain international events." The rational choice model facilitates the prediction of what the other social actor will do, assuming various goals; turning the model around, various goals can be inferred (though scarcely unambiguously) from the behavior of the other actor. It is inevitably the case that "an imaginative analyst can construct an account of value-maximizing choice for an action or set of actions performed" (Allison, 1971: 35). . . .

BUREAUCRATIC MODELS OF DECISION MAKING

The rational model of choice implies the need for some substantial information processing requirements in organizational decision making. These may be unrealistic or unattainable in some cases, and organizations may operate using standard operating procedures and rules rather than engaging in rational decision making on a continuous basis. The bureaucratic model of organizations substitutes procedural rationality for substantive rationality (Simon, 1979); rather than having choices made to maximize values, choices are made according to rules and processes which have been adaptive and effective in the past.

The best explication of what is meant by bureaucratically rational decision processes can be found in March and Simon (1958) and Cyert and March (1963). In this framework, goals are viewed as systems of constraints (Simon, 1964) which decisions must satisfy. Because of bounded rationality, search is limited and stops as soon as a satisfactory alternative is found. Uncertainty tends to be avoided in that, rather than making comprehensive assessments of risk and probabilities, decisions are made with relatively short time horizons. Conflict among different alternatives or points of view is never fully resolved, and priorities and objectives are attended to sequentially, first, for instance, worrying about profit, then about market share, then personnel problems, and so forth. Throughout this process, organizations learn and adapt, and their learning and knowledge takes the form of rules of action or standard operating procedures, repertoires of behavior which are activated in certain situations and which provide a program, a set of behaviors for organizational participants, that serve as a guide to action and choice.

Seen from this perspective, decisions are viewed "less as deliberate choices and more as *outputs* or large organizations functioning according to standard patterns of behavior" (Allison, 1971: 67). It is presumed that "most of the behavior is determined by previously established procedures" (Allison, 1971: 79). The model of organizations as bureaucratically rational presumes less conscious foresight and less clearly defined preferences and information. Both rely on habitual ways of doing things and the results

of past actions, and constrain how the organization proceeds to operate in the future. Decisions are not made as much as they evolve from the policies, procedures, and rules which constitute the organization and its memory. . . .

DISTINGUISHING BUREAUCRATIC ORGANIZATIONS

Distinguishing between the bureaucratic and political models of organization may be somewhat more difficult. After all, if the distribution of power is stable in the organization, which is a reasonable assumption, particularly over relatively short time periods, and if power and politics determine organizational decisions, then organizational choices will be relatively stable over time. But, this stability is also characteristic of the use of precedent in decision making, which is one of the hallmarks of bureaucratic organizations. One way of distinguishing, then, would involve looking at the correlates of the incremental changes in decisions and allocations made within the organization. While both models might be consistent with the use of precedent for the bulk of the decisions, there are some implicit differences in how incremental resources will be allocated. In bureaucratic organizations, changes in resource allocation patterns should either follow a proportional basis, be based on some standard measure of operations and performance, or reflect an attempt to shift the resources to better achieve the goals and values of the organization. By contrast, political models of organizations would suggest that power would best predict changes and shifts in decisions and allocations. . . .

DECISION PROCESS MODELS

Although they exist within much the same tradition as the bureaucratic model of organizations, decision process models differ in that they presume even less rationality and more randomness in organizational functioning. As power models depart from bureaucratic rationality by removing the assumption of consistent, overall organizational objectives and shared beliefs about technology, decision process models depart even further by removing the presumption of predefined, known preferences held by the various social actors. Decision process models posit that there are no overall organizational goals being maximized through choice, and no powerful actors with defined preferences who possess resources through which they seek to obtain those preferences. Stava (1976: 209) described decision process models as follows:

> In *decision process theories* it is presumed that policy is the outcome of a choice made by one or several decision-makers. Which choice is made is determined by the situation in which the decision-maker finds himself. This situation is, in turn, largely caused by the processes preceding the choice. It is impossible, then, to predict policies without knowing the details of the preceding processes.

March (1966: 180) argued that in such decision process models, although one might posit that the various actors have preferences and varying amounts of power, the concept of power does not add much to the prediction of behavior and choice in such systems.

More recently, March (1978) and others (e.g., Weick, 1969) have questioned whether or not the concept of preferences makes sense at any level of analysis, individual or organizational. One of the arguments raised is that instead of preferences guiding choice, choice may determine preferences. In other words, one only knows what one likes after it has been experienced; or, as Weick has argued, one only knows what one has done after he or she has done it, since the meaning of action is retrospective and follows the action rather than preceeds it. In this framework, goals are seen as the products of sense making activities which are carried on after the action has occurred to explain that action or rationalize it. The action itself is presumed to be the result of

habit, custom, or the influence of other social actors in the environment.

One example of a decision process model of social choice is the garbage can model (Cohen, March, and Olsen, 1972). The basic idea of the model is that decision points are opportunities into which various problems and solutions are dumped by organizational participants. "In a garbage can situation, a decision is an outcome of an interpretation of several relatively independent 'streams' within an organization" (Cohen, March, and Olsen, 1976: 26). The streams consist of problems, solutions (which are somebody's product), participants, and choice opportunities. The decision process models developed by March and his colleagues emphasize the problematic nature of participation by various social actors in choices. They note that systems are frequently so overloaded with problems, solutions, and decision opportunities that any given social actor will attend to only certain decisions. . . .

The garbage can model emerged largely from a study of universities and university presidents (Cohen and March, 1974). Universities were characterized as organized anarchies, and garbage can decision process models were believed to be particularly appropriate in such contexts, although the assertion is also made that elements of these models are found in most organizations. . . . "The theory holds further that problems move autonomously among choice opportunities in search for a choice process in which the problem can be resolved" (Weiner, 1976: 243). Decision making is viewed as an activity which absorbs the energy of those available, works on problems, and comes up with solutions which are determined in large measure by a random stream of events.

DISTINGUISHING ORGANIZED ANARCHIES

The key concept used in diagnosing whether or not the organization is an organized anarchy which can best be understood by using decision process organizational models is that of intention. Not only are there presumed to be no overarching organizational goals, but presumably intention is problematic even at the level of subunits and groups within the organization. Action occurs, but it is not primarily motivated by conscious choice and planning. Although not made explicit, there should be relatively little consistency or consensus over behavior in an organized anarchy. Events should unfold in ways predictable only by considering the process, and not through consideration of value maximization, precedent, power, or force. . . .

POLITICAL MODELS OF ORGANIZATIONS

One criticism that has been leveled against rational choice models is that they fail to take into account the diversity of interests and goals within organizations. March (1962) described business firms as political coalitions. The coalitional view of organizations was developed by Cyert and March (1963) in their description of organizational decision making. In bureaucratic theories of organizations, the presumption is that through control devices such as rewards based on job performance or seniority, rules that ensure fair and standardized treatment for all, and careers within the organization, the operation of self-interest can be virtually eliminated as an influence on organizational decision making. Economic or incentive theories of organizations argue that through the payment of wage, particularly when compensation is made contingent on performance, individuals hired into the organization come to accept the organization's goals. Political models of organizations assume that these control devices, as well as others such as socialization, are not wholly effective in producing a coherent and unified set of goals or definitions of technology. Rather, as Baldridge (1971: 25) has argued, political models view organizations as pluralistic and divided into various interests,

subunits, and subcultures. Conflict is viewed as normal or at least customary in political organizations. Action does not presuppose some overarching intention. Rather, action results "from games among players who perceive quite different faces of an issue and who differ markedly in the actions they prefer" (Allison, 1971: 175). Because action results from bargaining and compromise, the resulting decision seldom perfectly reflects the preferences of any group or subunit within the organization.

Political models of choice further presume that when preferences conflict, the power of the various social actors determines the outcome of the decision process. Power models hypothesize that those interests, subunits, or individuals within the organization who possess the greatest power, will receive the greatest rewards from the interplay of organizational politics. In such models, power "is an intervening variable between an initial condition, defined largely in terms of the individual components of the system, and a terminal state, defined largely in terms of the system as a whole" (March, 1966: 168–169). Power is used to overcome the resistance of others and obtain one's way in the organization.

To understand organizational choices using a political model, it is necessary to understand who participates in decision making, what determines each player's stand on the issues, what determines each actor's relative power, and how the decision process arrives at a decision; in other words, how the various preferences become combined (majority rule; unanimity; ⅔ vote; etc.) (Allison, 1971: 164). A change in any one of these aspects—relative power, the rules of decision making, or preferences—can lead to a change in the predicted organizational decision.

DISTINGUISHING POLITICAL MODELS OF ORGANIZATIONS

. . . Power models can be distinguished from rational models if it can be demonstrated that either no overarching organizational goal exists or even if such a goal does exist, decisions are made which are inconsistent with maximizing the attainment of the goal. Power can be distinguished from chance or organized anarchy models by demonstrating that actors in organizations have preferences and intentions which are consistent across decision issues and which they attempt to have implemented. Further evidence for political models would come from finding that measures of power in social systems, rather than goals, precedent, or chance, bring about decision outcomes. Indeed, the ability to measure and operationalize power is critical both for diagnosing political systems and for testing political models of organizations.

SUMMARY

One of the points of Allison's (1971) analysis of the Cuban missile crisis is that it is not necessary to choose between analytical frameworks. Each may be partly true in a particular situation, and one can obtain a better understanding of the organization by trying to use all of the models rather than by choosing among them. This point is different than saying that some organizations are characterized more by the political model and others by the rational model. Allison's argument is that insight can be gained from the application of all the frameworks in the same situation. This statement is true, but only within limits. At some point, the various perspectives will begin to make different predictions about what will occur, and will generate different recommendations concerning the strategy and tactics to be followed. At that point, the participant will need to decide where to place his or her bets. . . .

In Table 29.1, the four decision models described in this chapter are briefly summarized along eight relevant dimensions. The ability to perfectly distinguish between the models, using a single dimension in a particular situation, is likely to be limited.

However, by considering the dimensions in combination and by using comparative frames of reference, it becomes feasible to assess the extent to which the organization in question is operating according to one or the other of the models.

It is evident from the title of this book what my view is concerning the relative applicability of the four models of organizational decision making. Circumstances of bureaucratically rational decision making occur only in certain conditions on an infrequent basis. As Thompson and Tuden (1959) have argued, consensus on both goals and technology, or the connections between actions and consequences, are necessary in order for computational forms of decision making to be employed. Where there is disagreement over goals, compromise is used; when there is disagreement over technology, judgment is employed; and when there is disagreement about both, Thompson and Tuden characterize the decision situation as one requiring inspiration. In the case of judgment, compromise, and inspiration, it is the relative power of the various social actors that provides both the sufficient and necessary way of resolving the decision.

Furthermore, if intention is not always a guiding force in the taking of action and if preferences are not always clear or consistent, then there are at least some participants in organizations who know what they want and have the social power to get it. The randomness implied by the decision process model of organizations is inconsistent with the observation that in organizational decision making, some actors seem to usually get the garbage, while others manage to get the can.

Standard operating procedures, rules, and behavior repertoires clearly exist and are important in organizations. Much organizational decision making involves issues that are neither important nor contested, and in such cases, standard operating procedures are sufficient to get the decisions made in an inexpensive fashion. However, it is necessary to be aware that these various

TABLE 29.1 • OVERVIEW OF FOUR ORGANIZATIONAL
DECISION-MAKING MODELS

	Model			
Dimension	*Rational*	*Bureaucratic*	*Decision Process/ Organized Anarchy*	*Political Power*
Goals, preferences	Consistent within and across social actors	Reasonably consistent	Unclear, ambiguous, may be constructed ex post to rationalize action	Consistent within social actors; inconsistent, pluralistic within the organization
Power and control	Centralized	Less centralized with greater reliance on rules	Very decentralized, anarchic	Shifting coalitions and interest groups
Decision process	Orderly, substantively rational	Procedural rationality embodied in programs and standard operating procedures	Ad hoc	Disorderly, characterized by push and pull of interests
Rules and norms	Norm of optimization	Precedent, tradition	Segmented and episodic participation in decisions	Free play of market forces; conflict is legitimate and expected
Information and computational requirements	Extensive and systematic	Reduced by the use of rules and procedures	Haphazard collection and use of information	Information used and withheld strategically
Beliefs about action-consequence relationships	Known at least to a probability distribution	Consensually shared acceptance of routines	Unclear, ambiguous technology	Disagreements about technology
Decisions	Follow from value-maximizing choice	Follow from programs and routines	Not linked to intention; result of intersection of persons, solutions, problems	Result of bargaining and interplay among interests
Ideology	Efficiency and effectiveness	Stability, fairness, predictability	Playfulness, loose coupling, randomness	Struggle, conflict, winners and losers

rules, norms, and procedures have in themselves implications for the distribution of power and authority in organizations and for how contested decisions should be resolved. The rules and processes themselves become important focal points for the exercise of power. They are not always neutral and not always substantively rational. Sometimes they are part and parcel of the political contest that occurs within organizations.

One of the reasons why power and politics characterize so many organizations is because of what some of my students have dubbed the Law of Political Entropy: given the opportunity, an organization will tend to seek and maintain a political character. The argument is that once politics are introduced into a situation, it is very difficult to restore rationality. Once consensus is lost, once disagreements about preferences, technology, and management philosophy emerge, it is very hard to restore the kind of shared perspective and solidarity which is necessary to operate under the rational model. If rationality is indeed this fragile, and if the Law of Political Entropy is correct, then over time one would expect to see more and more organizations characterized by the political model.

REFERENCES

Allen, R. W., Madison, D. L., Porter, L. W., Renwick, P. A., & Mayes, B. T. (1979). Organizational politics: Tactics and characteristics of its actors. *California Management Review, 22,* 77–83.

Allison, G. T. (1971). *Essence of decision.* Boston: Little, Brown.

Baldridge, J. V. (1971). *Power and conflict in the university.* New York: Wiley.

Baritz, J. H. (1960). *The servants of power.* Middletown, CT: Wesleyan University Press.

Bierstedt, R. (1950). An analysis of social power. *American Sociological Review, 15,* 730–738.

Blau, P. M. (1964). *Exchange and power in social life.* New York: Wiley.

———, and Schoenherr, R. A. (1971). *The structure of organizations.* New York: Basic Books.

Burns, T., & Stalker, G. M. (1961). *The management of innovation.* London: Tavistock.

Carey, A. (1967). The Hawthorne studies: A radical criticism. *American Sociological Review, 32,* 403–416.

Cartwright, D. (1979). Contemporary social psychology in historical perspective. *Social Psychology Quarterly, 42,* 82–93.

Cohen, M. D., & March, J. G. (1974). *Leadership and ambiguity: The American college president.* New York: McGraw-Hill.

———, & Olsen, J. P. (1972). A garbage can model of organizational choice. *Administrative Science Quarterly, 17:* 1–25.

———. (1976). People, problems, solutions, and the ambiguity of relevance. In J. G. March and J. P. Olsen, (Eds.), *Ambiguity and choice in organizations* (pp. 24–37). Bergen, Norway: Universitetsforlaget.

Crecine, J. P. (1967). A computer simulation model of municipal budgeting. *Management Science, 13:* 786–815.

Crozier, M. (1964). *The bureaucratic phenomenon.* Chicago: University of Chicago Press.

Cyert, R. M., & March, J. G. (1963). *A behavioral theory of the firm.* Englewood Cliffs, NJ: Prentice-Hall.

Dahl, R. A. (1957). The concept of power. *Behavioral Science, 2,* 201–215.

Davis, O. A., Dempster, M. A. H., & Wildavsky, A. (1966). A theory of the budgeting process. *American Political Science Review, 60:* 529–547.

Dornbusch, S. M., & Scott, W. R. (1975). *Evaluation and the exercise of authority: A theory of control applied to diverse organizations.* San Francisco, CA: Jossey-Bass.

Edelman, M. (1964). *The symbolic uses of politics.* Urbana, IL: University of Illinois Press.

Edwards, W. (1954). The theory of decision making. *Psychological Bulletin, 51:* 380–417.

Emerson, R. M. (1962). Power-dependence relations. *American Sociological Review, 27,* 31–41.

French, J. R. P., Jr., & Raven, B. (1968). The bases of social power. In D. Cartwright &

A. Zander (Eds.), *Group dynamics* (3rd ed.). (pp. 259–269). New York: Harper & Row.

Friedland, E. I. (1974). *Introduction to the concept of rationality in political science*. Morristown, NJ: General Learning Press.

Galbraith, J. R. (1973). *Designing complex organizations*. Reading, MA: Addison-Wesley.

Gerwin, D. (1969). A process model of budgeting in a public school system. *Management Science, 15*: 338–361.

Kaplan, A. (1964). *The conduct of inquiry*. Scranton, PA: Chandler.

Karpik, L. (1978). Organizations, institutions and history. In Lucien Karpik (Ed.), *Organization and environment: Theory, issues and reality* (pp. 15–68). Newbury Park, CA: Sage.

Korda, M. (1975). *Power*. New York: Ballantine Books.

Lasswell, H. D. (1936). *Politics: Who gets what, when, how*. New York: McGraw-Hill.

Lawrence, P. R., & Lorsch, J. W. (1967). *Organization and environment*. Boston: Graduate School of Business Administration, Harvard University.

March, J. G. (1962). The business firm as a political coalition. *Journal of Politics, 24*, 662–678.

———. (1966). The power of power. In D. Easton (Ed.), *Varieties of political theory* (pp. 39–70). Englewood Cliffs, NJ: Prentice-Hall.

———. (1976). The technology of foolishness. In J. G. March and J. P. Olsen, (Eds.), *Ambiguity and choice in organizations* (pp. 69–81). Bergen, Norway: Universitetsforlaget.

———. (1978). Bounded rationality, ambiguity, and the engineering of choice. *Bell Journal of Economics, 9*, 587–608.

———, & Simon, H. A. (1958). *Organizations*. New York: John Wiley.

Mayes, B. T., & Allen, R. W. (1977). Toward a definition of organizational politics. *Academy of Management Review, 2*, 672–678.

Mechanic, D. (1962). Sources of power of lower participants in complex organizations. *Administrative Science Quarterly, 7*, 349–364.

Nehrbass, R. G. (1979). Ideology and the decline of management theory. *Academy of Management Review, 4*, 427–431.

Nord, W. R. (1974). The failure of current applied behavioral science: A Marxian perspective. *Journal of Applied Behavioral Science, 10*, 557–578.

Pennings, J. M. (1975). The relevance of the structural-contingency model for organizational effectiveness. *Administrative Science Quarterly, 20*, 393–410.

Perrow, C. (1961). The analysis of goals in complex organizations. *American Sociological Review, 26*, 859–866.

———. (1970). Departmental power and perspectives in industrial firms. In M. N. Zald (Ed.), *Power in organizations* (pp. 59–89). Nashville: Vanderbilt University Press.

———. (1972). *Complex organizations: A critical essay*. Glenview, IL: Scott, Foresman.

Pfeffer, J. (1978a). The micropolitics of organizations. In M. W. Meyer and Assoc., (Eds.), *Environments and organizations* (pp. 29–50). San Francisco: CA: Jossey-Bass.

Pfeffer, J., & Salancik, G. R. (1974). Organizational decision making as a political process: The case of a university budget. *Administrative Science Quarterly, 19*, 135–151.

———. (1978). *The external control of organizations: A resource dependence perspective*. New York: Harper & Row.

———, & Leblebici, H. (1976). The effect of uncertainty on the use of social influence in organizational decision making. *Administrative Science Quarterly, 21*, 227–245.

Pondy, L. R. (1969). Effects of size, complexity, and ownership on administrative intensity. *Administrative Science Quarterly, 14*, 47–60.

Pugh, D. S. (1966). Modern organization theory. *Psychological Bulletin, 66*, 235–251.

Salancik, G. R., & Pfeffer, J. (1974). The bases and use of power in organizational decision making: The case of a university. *Administrative Science Quarterly, 19*, 453–473.

———. (1977b). Who gets power—and how they hold on to it: A strategic-contingency model of power. *Organizational Dynamics, 5*, 3–21.

Schein, E. H. (1968). Organizational socialization and the profession of management. *Industrial Management Review*, 9, 1–16.

Simon, H. A. (1957). *Models of man*. New York: Wiley.

———. (1964). On the concept of organizational goal. *Administrative Science Quarterly*, 9: 1–22.

———. (1979). Rational decision making in business organizations. *American Economic Review*, 69: 493–513.

Stava, P. (1976). Constraints on the politics of public choice. In *Ambiguity and choice in organizations*, James G. March and Johan P. Olsen, pp. 206–224. Bergen, Norway: Universitetsforlaget.

Thompson, J. D. (1967). *Organizations in action*. New York: McGraw-Hill.

———, and Tuden, A. (1959). Strategies, structures, and processes of organizational decision. In J. D. Thompson, P. B. Hammond, R. W. Hawkes, B. H. Junker, and A. Tuden, (Eds.), *Comparative studies in administration* (pp. 195–216). Pittsburgh: University of Pittsburgh Press.

Weber, M. (1947). *The theory of social and economic organization*. New York: Free Press.

Weick, K. E. (1969). *The social psychology of organizing*. Reading, MA: Addison-Wesley.

Weiner, S. S. (1976). Participation, deadlines, and choice. In J. G. March and J. P. Olsen, (Eds.), *Ambiguity and choice in organizations* (pp. 225–250). Bergen, Norway: Universitetsforlaget.

Wildavsky, A. (1979). *The politics of the budgeting process*. (3rd ed.). Boston: Little, Brown.

———, and Hammond, A. (1965). Comprehensive versus incremental budgeting in the department of agriculture. *Administrative Science Quarterly*, 10: 321–346.

Williamson, O. E. (1975). *Markets and hierarchies: Analysis and antitrust implications*. New York: Free Press.

Woodward, J. (1965). *Industrial organization: Theory and practice*. London: Oxford University Press.

Zald, M. N. (1965). Who shall rule? A political analysis of succession in a large welfare organization. *Pacic Sociological Review*, 8, 52–60.

30

Democracy and the Iron Law of Oligarchy

Robert Michels

While the majority of the socialist schools believe that in a future more or less remote it will be possible to attain to a genuinely democratic order, and while the greater number of those who adhere to aristocratic political views consider that democracy, however dangerous to society, is at least realizable, we find in the scientific world a conservative tendency voiced by those who deny resolutely and once for all that there is any such possibility. . . . Those who do not believe in the god of democracy are never weary of affirming that this god is the creation of a childlike mythopœic faculty, and they contend that all phrases representing the idea of the rule of the masses, such terms as state, civic rights, popular representation, nation, are descriptive merely of a legal principle, and do not correspond to any actually existing facts. They contend that the eternal struggles between aristocracy and democracy of which we read in history have never been anything more than struggles between an old minority, defending its actual predominance, and a new and ambitious minority, intent upon the conquest of power, desiring either to fuse with the former or to dethrone and replace it. On this theory, these class struggles consist merely of struggles between successively dominant minorities. The social classes which under our eyes engage in gigantic battles upon the scene of history, battles whose ultimate causes are to be found in economic antagonism, may thus be compared to two groups of dancers executing a *chassé croisé* in a quadrille.

The democracy has an inherent preference for the authoritarian solution of important questions. It thirsts simultaneously for splendor and for power. When the English burghers had conquered their liberties, they made it their highest ambition to possess an aristocracy. Gladstone declared that the love of the English people for their liberties was equalled only by their love for the nobility. Similarly it may be said that it is a matter of pride with the socialists to show themselves capable of maintaining a discipline which, although it is to a certain extent voluntary, none the less signifies the submission of the majority to the orders issued by the minority, or at least to the rules issued by the minority in obedience to the majority's instructions. Vilfredo Pareto has even recommended socialism as a means favorable for the creation of a new working-class *élite*, and he regards the courage with which the socialist leaders face attack and persecution as a sign of their vigor, and as the first condition requisite to the formation of a new "political class."[1] . . .

This phenomenon was perhaps recognized at an earlier date, in so far as the *circulation des élites* was effected within the limits of a single great social class and took place on the political plane. In states where a purely representative government prevails, the constitutional opposition aims simply at such a circulation. In England, for instance, the opposition possesses the same simple and resistant structure as the party which holds the reins of government; its program is clearly formulated, directed to

Source: Robert Michels, "Democracy and the Iron Law of Oligarchy," in *Political Parties: A Sociological Study of the Oligarchical Tendencies of Modern Democracy,* trans. and ed. Eden and Cedar Paul (New York: Free Press, 1966), pp. 342–56. © 1962 by the Crowell-Collier Publishing Company.

purely practical and proximate ends; it is thoroughly disciplined, and is led by one lacking theoretical profundity but endowed with strategic talent; all its energies are devoted to overthrowing the government, to taking the reins of power into its own hands, while in other respects leaving matters exactly as they were; it aims, in a word, at the substitution of one clique of the dominant classes for another. Sooner or later the competition between the various cliques of the dominant classes ends in a reconciliation which is effected with the instinctive aim of retaining dominion over the masses by sharing it among themselves. The opinion is very generally held that as a result of the French Revolution, or that in any case in the Third Republic, the old order had socially speaking been completely suppressed in France. This view is utterly erroneous. In the present year of grace we find that the French nobility is represented in the cavalry regiments and in the republican diplomatic service to an extent altogether disproportionate to its numerical strength; and although in the French Chamber there does not exist, as in Germany, a declared conservative party of the nobility, we find that of 584 deputies no less than 61 belong to the old aristocracy (*noblesse d'épée and noblesse de robe*). . . .

The only scientific doctrine which can boast of ability to make an effective reply to all the theories, old or new, affirming the immanent necessity for the perennial existence of the "political class" is the Marxist doctrine. In this doctrine the state is identified with the ruling class — an identification from which Bakunin, Marx's pupil, drew the extreme consequences. The state is merely the executive committee of the ruling class, or, to quote the expression of a recent neo-Marxist, the state is merely a "trade-union formed to defend the interest of the powers-that-be."[2] It is obvious that this theory greatly resembles the conservative theory of Gaetano Mosca. Mosca, in fact, from a study of the same diagnostic signs, deduces a similar prognosis, but abstains from lamentations and recriminations

on account of a phenomenon which, in the light of his general political views, he regards not merely as inevitable, but as actually advantageous to society. Aristide Briand, in the days when he was an active member of the Socialist Party, and before he had become prime minister of the "class-state," pushed the Marxist notion of the state to its utmost limits by recommending the workers to abandon isolated and local economic struggles, to refrain from dissipating their energies in partial strikes, and to deliver a united assault upon the state in the form of the general strike, for, he said, you can reach the bourgeoisie with your weapons in no other way than by attacking the state.[3]

The Marxist theory of the state, when conjoined with a faith in the revolutionary energy of the working class and in the democratic effects of the socialization of the means of production, leads logically to the idea of a new social order which to the school of Mosca appears utopian. According to the Marxists the capitalist mode of production transforms the great majority of the population into proletarians, and thus digs its own grave. As soon as it has attained maturity, the proletariat will seize political power, and will immediately transform private property into state property. "In this way it will eliminate itself, for it will thus put an end to all social differences, and consequently to all class antagonisms. In other words, the proletariat will annul the state, *qua* state. Capitalist society, divided into classes, has need of the state as an organization of the ruling class, whose purpose it is to maintain the capitalist system of production in its own interest and in order to effect the continued exploitation of the proletariat. Thus to put an end to the state is synonymous with putting an end to the existence of the dominant class."[4] But the new collectivist society, the society without classes, which is to be established upon the ruins of the ancient state, will also need elective elements. It may be said that by the adoption of the preventive rules formulated by Rousseau in the *Contrat Sociale*, and subsequently reproduced by the French revolutionists in the *Déclaration des Droits de l'Homme*, above all by the strict application of the principle that all offices are to be held on a revocable tenure, the activity of these representatives may be confined within rigid limits.[5] It is none the less true that social wealth cannot be satisfactorily administered in any other manner than by the creation of an extensive bureaucracy. In this way we are led by an inevitable logic to the flat denial of the possibility of a state without classes. The administration of an immeasurably large capital, above all when this capital is collective property, confers upon the administrator influence at least equal to that possessed by the private owner of capital. Consequently the critics in advance of the Marxist social order ask whether the instinct which today leads the members of the possessing classes to transmit to their children the wealth which they (the parents) have amassed, will not exist also in the administrators of the public wealth of the socialist state, and whether these administrators will not utilize their immense influence in order to secure for their children the succession to the offices which they themselves hold.

The constitution of a new dominant minority would, in addition, be especially facilitated by the manner in which, according to the Marxist conception of the revolution, the social transformation is to be effected. Marx held that the period between the destruction of capitalist society and the establishment of communist society would be bridged by a period of revolutionary transition in the economic field, to which would correspond a period of political transition, "when the state could not be anything other than the revolutionary dictatorship of the proletariat."[6] To put the matter less euphemistically, there will then exist a dictatorship in the hands of those leaders who have been sufficiently astute and sufficiently powerful to grasp the scepter of dominion in the name of socialism, and to wrest it from the hand of the expiring bourgeois society. . . .

There is little difference, as far as practical results are concerned, between individ-

ual dictatorship and the dictatorship of a group of oligarchs. Now it is manifest that the concept *dictatorship* is the direct antithesis of the concept *democracy*. The attempt to make dictatorship serve the ends of democracy is tantamount to the endeavor to utilize war as the most efficient means for the defense of peace, or to employ alcohol in the struggle against alcoholism.[7] It is extremely probable that a social group which had secured control of the instruments of collective power would do all that was possible to retain that control. Theophrastus noted long ago that the strongest desire of men who have attained to leadership in a popularly governed state is not so much the acquirement of personal wealth as the gradual establishment of their own sovereignty at the expense of popular sovereignty.[8] The danger is imminent lest the social revolution should replace the visible and tangible dominant classes which now exist and act openly, by a clandestine demagogic oligarchy, pursuing its ends under the cloak of equality.

The Marxist economic doctrine and the Marxist philosophy of history cannot fail to exercise a great attraction upon thinkers. But the defects of Marxism are patent directly we enter the practical domains of administration and public law, without speaking of errors in the psychological field and even in more elementary spheres. Wherever socialist theory has endeavored to furnish guarantees for personal liberty, it has in the end either lapsed into the cloudland of individualist anarchism, or else has made proposals which (doubtless in opposition to the excellent intentions of their authors) could not fail to enslave the individual to the mass. . . .

The problem of socialism is not merely a problem in economics. In other words, socialism does not seek merely to determine to what extent it is possible to realize a distribution of wealth which shall be at once just and economically productive. Socialism is also an administrative problem, a problem of democracy, and this not in the technical and administrative sphere alone, but also in the sphere of psychology. In the individualist problem is found the most difficult of all that complex of questions which socialism seeks to answer. Rudolf Goldscheid, who aims at a renascence of the socialist movement by the strengthening of the more energetic elements in that movement, rightly draws attention to a danger which socialism incurs, however brilliantly it may handle the problems of economic organization. If socialism, he says, fails to study the problem of individual rights, individual knowledge, and individual will, it will suffer shipwreck from a defective understanding of the significance of the problem of freedom for the higher evolution of our species—will suffer shipwreck no less disastrous than that of earlier conceptions of world reform which, blinded by the general splendor of their vision, have ignored the individual light-sources which combine to produce that splendor.[9] . . .

A [political] party is neither a social unity nor an economic unity. It is based upon its program. In theory this program may be the expression of the interests of a particular class. In practice, however, anyone may join a party, whether his interests coincide or not with the principles enunciated in the party program. The Socialist Party, for example, is the ideological representative of the proletariat. This, however, does not make it a class organism. From the social point of view it is a mixture of classes, being composed of elements fulfiling diverse function in the economic process. But since the program has a class origin, an ostensible social unity is thereby conferred upon the party. All socialists as such, whatever their economic position in private life, admit in theory the absolute pre-eminence of one great class, the proletariat. Those non-proletarians affiliated to the party, and those who are but partial proletarians, "adopt the outlook of the working class, and recognize this class as predominant."[10] It is tacitly presupposed that those members of a party who do not belong to the class which that party represents will renounce their personal interests whenever these conflict with the interests of the proletarian class. On principle, the heterogeneous elements will subordinate themselves to the "idea" of a class to which they themselves do not belong. So much for theory. In practice, the acceptance of the program does not suffice to abolish the conflict of interests between capital and labor. Among the members belonging to higher social strata who have made their adhesion to the political organization of the working class, there will be some who will, when the occasion demands it, know how to sacrifice themselves, who will be able to unclass themselves. The majority of such persons, however, notwithstanding their outward community of ideas with the proletariat, will continue to pursue economic interests opposed to those of the proletariat. There is, in fact, a conflict of interests, and the decision in this conflict will be determined by the relationship which the respective interests bear towards the principal necessities of life. Consequently it is by no means impossible that an economic conflict may arise between the bourgeois members and the proletarian members of the party, and that as this conflict extends it will culminate in political dissensions. Economic antagonisms stifle the ideological superstructure. The program then becomes a dead letter, and beneath the banner of "socialism" and within the bosom of the party, a veritable class struggle goes on. We learn from actual experience that in their conduct towards persons in their employ the bourgeois socialists do not always subordinate personal interests to those of their adoptive class. When the party includes among its members the owners of factories and workshops, it may be noticed that these, notwithstanding personal goodwill and notwithstanding the pressure which is exercised on them by the party, have the same economic conflict with their employees as have those employers whose convictions harmonize with their economic status, and who think not as socialists but as bourgeois.

But there exists yet another danger. The leadership of the Socialist Party may fall into the hands of persons whose practical tendencies are in opposition with the program of the working class, so that the labor movement will be utilized for the service of interests diametrically opposed to those of the proletariat. This danger is especially great in countries where the working-class party cannot dispense with the aid and guidance of capitalists who are not economically dependent upon the party; it is least conspicuous where the party has no need of such elements, or can at any rate avoid admitting them to leadership.

When the leaders, whether derived from the bourgeoisie or from the working class, are attached to the party organism as employees, their economic interest coincides as a rule with the interest of the party. This, however, serves to eliminate only one aspect of the danger. Another aspect, graver because more general, depends upon the opposition which inevitably arises between the leaders and the rank and file as the party grows in strength.

The party, regarded as an entity, as a piece of mechanism, is not necessarily identifiable with the totality of its members, and still less so with the class to which these belong. The party is created as a means to secure an end. Having, however, become an end in itself, endowed with aims and interests of its own, it undergoes detachment, from the teleological point of view, from the class which it represents. In a party, it is far from obvious that the interests of the masses which have combined to form the party will coincide with the interests of the bureaucracy in which the party becomes personified. The interests of the body of employees are always conservative, and in a given political situation these interests may dictate a defensive and even a reactionary policy when the interests of the working class demand a bold and aggressive policy; in other cases, although these are very rare, the rôles may be reversed. By a universally applicable social law, every organ of the collectivity, brought into existence through the need for the division of labor, creates for itself, as soon as it becomes consolidated, interests peculiar to itself. The existence of these special

interests involves a necessary conflict with the interests of the collectivity. Nay, more, social strata fulfiling peculiar functions tend to become isolated, to produce organs fitted for the defense of their own peculiar interests. In the long run they tend to undergo transformation into distinct classes.

The sociological phenomena whose general characteristics have been discussed in this chapter and in preceding ones offer numerous vulnerable points to the scientific opponents of democracy. These phenomena would seem to prove beyond dispute that society cannot exist without a "dominant" or "political" class, and that the ruling class, while its elements are subject to a frequent partial renewal, nevertheless constitutes the only factor of sufficiently durable efficacy in the history of human development. According to this view, the government, or, if the phrase be preferred, the state, cannot be anything other than the organization of a minority. It is the aim of this minority to impose upon the rest of society a "legal order," which is the outcome of the exigencies of dominion and of the exploitation of the mass of helots effected by the ruling minority, and can never be truly representative of the majority. The majority is thus permanently incapable of self-government. Even when the discontent of the masses culminates in a successful attempt to deprive the bourgeoisie of power, this is after all, so Mosca contends, effected only in appearance; always and necessarily there springs from the masses a new organized minority which raises itself to the rank of a governing class.[11] Thus the majority of human beings, in a condition of eternal tutelage, are predestined by tragic necessity to submit to the dominion of a small minority, and must be content to constitute the pedestal of an oligarchy.

The principle that one dominant class inevitably succeeds to another, and the law deduced from that principle that oligarchy is, as it were, a preordained form of the common life of great social aggregates, far from conflicting with or replacing the materialist conception of history, completes that conception and reinforces it. There is no essential contradiction between the doctrine that history is the record of a continued series of class struggles and the doctrine that class struggles invariably culminate in the creation of new oligarchies which undergo fusion with the old. The existence of a political class does not conflict with the essential content of Marxism, considered not as an economic dogma but as a philosophy of history; for in each particular instance the dominance of a political class arises as the resultant of the relationships between the different social forces competing for supremacy, these forces being of course considered dynamically and not quantitatively.

The Russian socialist Alexandre Herzen, whose chief permanent claim to significance is found in the psychological interest of his writings, declared that from the day in which man became accessory to property and his life a continued struggle for money, the political groups of the bourgeois world underwent division into two camps: the owners, tenaciously keeping hold of their millions; and the dispossessed, who would gladly expropriate the owners, but lack the power to do so. Thus historical evolution merely represents an uninterrupted series of oppositions (in the parliamentary sense of this term), "attaining one after another to power, and passing from the sphere of envy to the sphere of avarice."[12]

Thus the social revolution would not effect any real modification of the internal structure of the mass. The socialists might conquer, but not socialism, which would perish in the moment of its adherents' triumph. We are tempted to speak of this process as a tragicomedy in which the masses are content to devote all their energies to effecting a change of masters. All that is left for the workers is the honor "of participating in government recruiting."[13] The result seems a poor one, especially if we take into account the psychological fact that even the purest of idealists who attains to power for a few years is unable to escape the corruption which the exercise of power carries in its train. In France, in working-class

circles, the phrase is current, *homme élu, homme foutu.* The social revolution, like the political revolution, is equivalent to an operation by which, as the Italian proverb expresses it: "Si cambia il maestro di cappella, ma la musica è sempre quella."[14] . . .

History seems to teach us that no popular movement, however energetic and vigorous, is capable of producing profound and permanent changes in the social organism of the civilized world. The preponderant elements of the movement, the men who lead and nourish it, end by undergoing a gradual detachment from the masses, and are attracted within the orbit of the "political class." They perhaps contribute to this class a certain number of "new ideas," but they also endow it with more creative energy and enhanced practical intelligence, thus providing for the ruling class an ever-renewed youth. The "political class" (continuing to employ Mosca's convenient phrase) has unquestionably an extremely fine sense of its possibilities and its means of defense. It displays a remarkable force of attraction and a vigorous capacity for absorption which rarely fail to exercise an influence even upon the most embittered and uncompromising of its adversaries. From the historical point of view, the anti-romanticists are perfectly right when they sum up their scepticism in such caustic phraseology as this: "What is a revolution? People fire guns in a street; that breaks many windows; scarcely anyone profits but the glaziers. The wind carries away the smoke. Those who stay on top push the other under. . . . It is worth the suffering to turn up so many good paving stones which otherwise could not be moved!"[15] Or we may say, as the song runs in *Madame Angot:* "It's not worth the bother to change the government!" In France, the classic land of social theories and experiments, such pessimism has struck the deepest roots.[16]

NOTES

1. V. Pareto, *Les Systèmes socialistes,* ed. cit., vol.i, pp. 62 et seq.

2. Angelo Oliviero Olivetti, *Problema del Socialismo Contemporaneo,* Canoni, Lugano, 1906, p. 41.

3. Aristide Briand, *La Grève Générale et la Révolution.* Speech published in 1907. Girard, Paris, p. 7.

4. Friedrich Engels, *Die Entwicklung des Sozialismus von der Utopie zur Wissenschaft,* Buchhandlung "Vorwärts," Berlin, 1891, 4th ed., p. 40.

5. Many believe with Hobson (*Boodle and Cant,* ed. cit., pp. 587 and 590) that the socialist state will require a larger number of leaders, including political leaders, than any other state that has hitherto existed. Bernstein declares that the administrative body of socialist society will for a long time differ very little from that of the existing state (Eduard Bernstein, *Zur Geschichte, etc.,* ed. cit., p. 212).

6. Karl Marx, *Randglossen zum Programm der deutscher Arbeiterpartei,* "Waffenkammer des Sozialismus," 10th semi-annual vol. Frankfort-on-the-Main, 1908, p. 18.

7. "There continually recurs the dream of Schiller's Marquis Posa (in *Don Carlos*), who endeavours to make absolutism the instrument of liberation; or the dream of the gentle Abbé Pierre (in Zola's *Rome*), who wishes to use the church as a lever to secure socialism" (Kropotkin, *Die historische Rolle des Staates,* Grunau, Berlin, 1898, p. 52).

8. Labruyère, *Caractères,* ed. cit., p. 28.

9. Rudolf Goldscheid, *Grundlinien zu einer Kritik de Willenskraft,* W. Braumüller, Vienna and Leipzig, 1905, p. 143.

10. Eduard Bernstein, *Wird die Sozialdemokratie Volkspartei?,* "Sozial. Monatshefte," August 1905, p. 670.

11. Gaetano Mosca, *Elemente de Scienza politica,* ed. cit., p. 62.—Among the socialists there are a few rare spirits who do not deny the truth of this axiom. One of these is the professor of philosophy, and socialist deputy of the Swedish Upper House, Gustaf F. Steffen, who declares: "Even after the victory, there will always remain in political life the leaders and the led" (Steffen, *Die Demokratie in England,* Diederichs, Jena, 1911, p. 59).

12. Alexandre Herzen, *Erinnerungen,* German translation by Otto Buek, Wiegandt u. Grieben, Berlin, 1907, vol. ii, p. 150.

13. Félicien Challaye, *Syndicalisme révolutionnaire et Syndicalisme réformiste,* Alcan, Paris, 1909, p. 16.

14. There is a new conductor, but the music is just the same.

15. Trans. from Théophile Gautier, *Les Jeunes-France,* Charpentier, Paris, 1878, p. xv.

16. The disillusionment of the French regarding democracy goes back to the Revolution. Guizot declared that this terrible experiment sufficed "to disgust the liberty-seeking world forever, and to dry up the soberest hopes of the human race at their source." (Trans. from F. Guizot, *Du Gouvernement de la France,* ed. cit., p. 165.)

31

The Bases of Social Power

John R. P. French Jr. & Bertram Raven

The processes of power are pervasive, complex, and often disguised in our society. Accordingly one finds in political science, in sociology, and in social psychology a variety of distinctions among different types of social power or among qualitatively different processes of social influence (1, 6, 14, 20, 23, 29, 30, 38, 41). Our main purpose is to identify the major types of power and to define them systematically so that we may compare them according to the changes which they produce and the other effects which accompany the use of power. The phenomena of power and influence involve a dyadic relation between two agents which may be viewed from two points of view: (a) What determines the behavior of the agent who exerts power? (b) What determines the reactions of the recipient of this behavior? We take this second point of view and formulate our theory in terms of the life space of P, the person upon whom the power is exerted. In this way we hope to define basic concepts of power which will be adequate to explain many of the phenomena of social influence, including some which have been described in other less genotypic terms. . . .

POWER, INFLUENCE, AND CHANGE

Psychological Change
Since we shall define power in terms of influence, and influence in terms of psychological change, we begin with a discussion of change. We want to define change at a level of generality which includes changes in behavior, opinions, attitudes, goals, needs, values and all other aspects of the person's psychological field. We shall use the word "system" to refer to any such part of the life space.[1] Following Lewin (26, p. 305) the state of a system at time 1 will be noted $s_1(a)$.

Psychological change is defined as any alteration of the state of some system a over time. The amount of change is measured by the size of the difference between the states of the system a at time 1 and at time 2: $ch(a) = s_2(a) - s_1(a)$.

Change in any psychological system may be conceptualized in terms of psychological forces. But it is important to note that the change must be coordinated to the resultant force of all the forces operating at the moment. Change in an opinion, for example, may be determined jointly by a driving force induced by another person, a restraining force corresponding to anchorage in a group opinion, and an own force stemming from the person's needs.

Social Influence
Our theory of social influence and power is limited to influence on the person, P, produced by a social agent, O, where O can be either another person, a role, a norm, a group or a part of a group. We do not consider social influence exerted on a group.

The influence of O on system a in the life space of P is defined as the resultant force on system a which has its source in an act of O. This resultant force induced by O consists of two components: a force to change the system in the direction induced by O and an opposing resistance set up by the same act of O.

Source: John R. P. French Jr. and Bertram Raven, "The Bases of Social Power," in *Studies in Social Power,* ed. Dorwin P. Cartwright (Ann Arbor, MI: Institute for Social Research, University of Michigan, 1959), pp. 150–167. Reprinted by permission of the publisher.

By this definition the influence of O does not include P's own forces nor the forces induced by other social agents. Accordingly the "influence" of O must be clearly distinguished from O's "control" of P. O may be able to induce strong forces on P to carry out an activity (i.e., O exerts strong influence on P); but if the opposing forces induced by another person or by P's own needs are stronger, then P will locomote in an opposite direction (i.e., O does not have control over P). Thus psychological change in P can be taken as an operational definition of the social influence of O on P only when the effects of other forces have been eliminated.

Commonly social influence takes place through an intentional act on the part of O. However, we do not want to limit our definition of "act" to such conscious behavior. Indeed, influence might result from the passive presence of O, with no evidence of speech or overt movement. A policeman's standing on a corner may be considered an act of an agent for the speeding motorist. Such acts of the inducing agent will vary in strength, for O may not always utilize all of his power. The policeman, for example, may merely stand and watch or act more strongly by blowing his whistle at the motorist.

The influence exerted by an act need not be in the direction intended by O. The direction of the resultant force on P will depend on the relative magnitude of the induced force set up by the act of O and the resisting force in the opposite direction which is generated by that same act. In cases where O intends to influence P in a given direction, a resultant force in the same direction may be termed positive influence whereas a resultant force in the opposite direction may be termed negative influence. . . .

Social Power

The strength of power of O/P in some system *a* is defined as the maximum potential ability of O to influence P in *a*.

By this definition influence is kinetic power, just as power is potential influence.

It is assumed that O is capable of various acts which, because of some more or less enduring relation to P, are able to exert influence on P.[2] O's power is measured by his maximum possible influence, though he may often choose to exert less than his full power.

An equivalent definition of power may be stated in terms of the resultant of two forces set up by the act of O: one in the direction of O's influence attempt and another resisting force in the opposite direction. Power is the maximum resultant of these two forces:

$$\text{Power of O/P(a)} = (f_{a,x} - f_{a,x})^{\max}$$

where the source of both forces is an act of O.

Thus the power of O with respect to system *a* of P is equal to the maximum resultant force of two forces set up by any possible act of O: (a) the force which O can set up on the system *a* to change in the direction x, (b) the resisting force,[3] in the opposite direction. Whenever the first component force is greater than the second, positive power exists; but if the second component force is greater than the first, then O has negative power over P.

For certain purposes it is convenient to define the range of power as the set of all systems within which O has power of strength greater than zero. A husband may have a broad range of power over his wife, but a narrow range of power over his employer. We shall use the term "magnitude of power" to denote the summation of O's power over P in all systems of his range.

The Dependence of s(a) on O

We assume that any change in the state of a system is produced by a change in some factor upon which it is functionally dependent. The state of an opinion, for example, may change because of a change either in some internal factor such as a need or in some external factor such as the arguments of O. Likewise the maintenance of the same state of a system is produced by the stability or lack of change in the internal and external factors. In general, then, psychological change and stability can be conceptualized in terms of dynamic dependence. Our interest is focused on the special case of dependence on an external agent, O (31).

In many cases the initial state of the system has the character of a quasistationary equilibrium with a central force field around $s_1(a)$ (26, p. 106). In such cases we may derive a tendency toward retrogression to the original state as soon as the force induced by O is removed.[4] . . .

Consider the example of three separated employees who have been working at the same steady level of production despite normal, small fluctuations in the work environment. The supervisor orders each to increase his production, and the level of each goes up from 100 to 115 pieces per day. After a week of producing at the new rate of 115 pieces per day, the supervisor is removed for a week. The production of employee A immediately returns to 100 but B and C return to only 110 pieces per day. Other things being equal, we can infer that A's new rate was completely dependent on his supervisor whereas the new rate of B and C was dependent on the supervisor only to the extent of 5 pieces. Let us further assume that when the supervisor returned, the production of B and of C returned to 115 without further orders from the supervisor. Now another month goes by during which B and C maintain a steady 115 pieces per day. However, there is a difference between them: B's level of production still depends on O to the extent of 5 pieces whereas C has come to rely on his own sense of obligation to obey the order of his legitimate supervisor rather than on the supervisor's external pressure for the maintenance of his 115 pieces per day. Accordingly, the next time the supervisor departs, B's production again drops to 110 but C's remains at 115 pieces per day. In cases like employee B, the degree of dependence is contingent on the perceived probability that O will observe the state of the system and note P's conformity (5, 6, 11, 12, 23). The level of observability will in turn depend on both the nature of the system (e.g., the difference between a covert opinion and overt behavior) and on the environmental barriers to observation (e.g., O is too far away from P). . . .

THE BASES OF POWER

By the basis of power we mean the relationship between O and P which is the source of that power. It is rare that we can say with certainty that a given empirical case of power is limited to one source. Normally, the relation between O and P will be characterized by several qualitatively different variables which are bases of power. . . . Although there are undoubtedly many possible bases of power which may be distinguished, we shall here define five which seem especially common and important. These five bases of O's power are: (1) reward power, based on P's perception that O has the ability to mediate rewards for him; (2) coercive power, based on P's perception that O has the ability to mediate punishments for him; (3) legitimate power, based on the perception by P that O has a legitimate right to prescribe behavior for him; (4) referent power, based on P's identification with O; (5) expert power, based on the perception that O has some special knowledge or expertness. . . .

Reward Power
Reward power is defined as power whose basis is the ability to reward. The strength of the reward power of O/P increases with the magnitude of the rewards which P perceives that O can mediate for him. Reward power depends on O's ability to administer positive valences and to remove or decrease negative valences. The strength of reward power also depends upon the probability that O can mediate the reward, as perceived by P. A common example of reward power is the addition of a piece-work rate in the factory as an incentive to increase production.

The new state of the system induced by a promise of reward (for example the factory worker's increased level of production) will be highly dependent on O. Since O mediates the reward, he controls the probability that P will receive it. Thus P's new rate of production will be dependent on his subjective probability that O will reward him for conformity minus his subjective probability that O will reward him even if he returns to his old level. Both probabilities will be greatly affected by the level of observability of P's behavior. . . .

The utilization of actual rewards (instead of promises) by O will tend over time to increase the attraction of P toward O and therefore the referent power of O over P. As we shall note later, such referent power will permit O to induce changes which are relatively independent. Neither rewards nor promises will arouse resistance in P, provided P considers it legitimate for O to offer rewards.

The range of reward power is specific to those regions within which O can reward P for conforming. The use of rewards to change systems within the range of reward power tends to increase reward power by increasing the probability attached to future promises. However, unsuccessful attempts to exert reward power outside the range of power would tend to decrease the power; for example if O offers to reward P for performing an impossible act, this will reduce for P the probability of receiving future rewards promised by O.

Coercive Power

Coercive power is similar to reward power in that it also involves O's ability to manipulate the attainment of valences. Coercive power of O/P stems from the expectation on the part of P that he will be punished by O if he fails to conform to the influence attempt. Thus negative valences will exist in given regions of P's life space, corresponding to the threatened punishment by O. The strength of coercive power depends on the magnitude of the negative valence of the threatened punishment multiplied by the perceived probability that P can avoid

the punishment by conformity, i.e., the probability of punishment for nonconformity minus the probability of punishment for conformity (11). Just as an offer of a piece-rate bonus in a factory can serve as a basis for reward power, so the ability to fire a worker if he falls below a given level of production will result in coercive power.

Coercive power leads to dependent change also; and the degree of dependence varies with the level of observability of P's conformity. An excellent illustration of coercive power leading to dependent change is provided by a clothes presser in a factory observed by Coch and French (3). As her efficiency rating climbed above average for the group the other workers began to "scapegoat" her. That the resulting plateau in her production was not independent of the group was evident once she was removed from the presence of the other workers. Her production immediately climbed to new heights.[5] . . .

The distinction between these two types of power is important because the dynamics are different. The concept of "sanctions" sometimes lumps the two together despite their opposite effects. While reward power may eventually result in an independent system, the effects of coercive power will continue to be dependent. Reward power will tend to increase the attraction of P toward O; coercive power will decrease this attraction (11, 12). The valence of the region of behavior will become more negative, acquiring some negative valence from the threatened punishment. The negative valence of punishment would also spread to other regions of the life space. Lewin (25) has pointed out this distinction between the effects of rewards and punishment. In the case of threatened punishment, there will be a resultant force on P to leave the field entirely. Thus, to achieve conformity, O must not only place a strong negative valence in certain regions through threat of punishment, but O must also introduce restraining forces, or other strong valences, so as to prevent P from withdrawing completely from O's range of coercive power.

Otherwise the probability of receiving the punishment, if P does not conform, will be too low to be effective.

Legitimate Power

. . . There has been considerable investigation and speculation about socially prescribed behavior, particularly that which is specific to a given role or position. Linton (29) distinguishes group norms according to whether they are universals for everyone in the culture, alternatives (the individual having a choice as to whether or not to accept them), or specialties (specific to given positions). Whether we speak of internalized norms, role prescriptions and expectations (34), or internalized pressures (15), the fact remains that each individual sees certain regions toward which he should locomote, some regions toward which he should not locomote, and some regions toward which he may locomote if they are generally attractive for him. This applies to specific behaviors in which he may, should, or should not engage; it applies to certain attitudes or beliefs which he may, should, or should not hold. The feeling of "oughtness" may be an internalization from his parents, from his teachers, from his religion, or may have been logically developed from some idiosyncratic system of ethics. He will speak of such behaviors with expressions like "should," "ought to," or "has a right to." In many cases, the original source of the requirement is not recalled.

Though we have oversimplified such evaluations of behavior with a positive-neutral-negative trichotomy, the evaluation of behaviors by the person is really more one of degree. This dimension of evaluation, we shall call "legitimacy." Conceptually, we may think of legitimacy as a valence in a region which is induced by some internalized norm or value. This value has the same conceptual property as power, namely an ability to induce force fields (26, p. 40–41). . . .

Legitimate power of O/P is here defined as that power which stems from internalized values in P which dictate that O has a legitimate right to influence P and that P has an obligation to accept this influence. We note that legitimate power is very similar to the notion of legitimacy of authority which has long been explored by sociologists, particularly by Weber (42), and more recently by Goldhammer and Shils (14). However, legitimate power is not always a role relation: P may accept an induction from O simply because he had previously promised to help O and he values his word too much to break the promise. In all cases, the notion of legitimacy involves some sort of code or standard, accepted by the individual, by virtue of which the external agent can assert his power. We shall attempt to describe a few of these values here.

Bases for Legitimate Power. Cultural values constitute one common basis for the legitimate power of one individual over another. O has characteristics which are specified by the culture as giving him the right to prescribe behavior for P, who may not have these characteristics. These bases, which Weber (42) has called the authority of the "eternal yesterday," include such things as age, intelligence, caste, and physical characteristics. In some cultures, the aged are granted the right to prescribe behavior for others in practically all behavior areas. In most cultures, there are certain areas of behavior in which a person of one sex is granted the right to prescribe behavior for the other sex.

Acceptance of the social structure is another basis for legitimate power. If P accepts as right the social structure of his group, organization, or society, especially the social structure involving a hierarchy of authority, P will accept the legitimate authority of O who occupies a superior office in the hierarchy. Thus legitimate power in a formal organization is largely a relationship between offices rather than between persons. And the acceptance of an office as *right* is a basis for legitimate power—a judge has a right to levy fines, a foreman should assign work, a priest is justified in prescribing religious beliefs, and it is the management's prerogative to make certain decisions (10). However, legitimate power also involves the perceived right of the person to hold the office.

Designation by a legitimizing agent is a third basis for legitimate power. An influencer O may be seen as legitimate in prescribing behavior for P because he has been granted such power by a legitimizing agent whom P accepts. Thus a department head may accept the authority of his vice-president in a certain area because that authority has been specifically delegated by the president. An election is perhaps the most common example of a group's serving to legitimize the authority of one individual or office for other individuals in the group. The success of such legitimizing depends upon the acceptance of the legitimizing agent and procedure. In this case it depends ultimately on certain democratic values concerning election procedures. The election process is one of legitimizing a person's right to an office which already has a legitimate range of power associated with it.

Range of Legitimate Power of O/P. The areas in which legitimate power may be exercised are generally specified along with the designation of that power. A job description, for example, usually species supervisory activities and also designates the person to whom the job holder is responsible for the duties described. Some bases for legitimate authority carry with them a very broad range. Culturally derived bases for legitimate power are often especially broad. It is not uncommon to find cultures in which a member of a given caste can legitimately prescribe behavior for all members of lower castes in practically all regions. More common, however, are instances of legitimate power where the range is specifically and narrowly prescribed. A sergeant in the army is given a specific set of regions within which he can legitimately prescribe behavior for his men.

The attempted use of legitimate power which is outside of the range of legitimate power will decrease the legitimate power of the authority figure. Such use of power which is not legitimate will also decrease the attractiveness of O (11, 12, 36).

Legitimate Power and Influence. The new state of the system which results from legitimate power usually has high dependence on O though it may become independent. Here, however, the degree of dependence is not related to the level of observability. Since legitimate power is based on P's values, the source of the forces induced by O include both these internal values and O. O's induction serves to activate the values and to relate them to the system which is influenced, but thereafter the new state of the system may become directly dependent on the values with no mediation by O. Accordingly this new state will be relatively stable and consistent across varying environmental situations since P's values are more stable than his psychological environment. . . .

Referent Power

The referent power of O/P has its basis in the identification of P with O. By identification, we mean a feeling of oneness of P with O, or a desire for such an identity. If O is a person toward whom P is highly attracted, P will have a feeling of membership or a desire to join. If P is already closely associated with O he will want to maintain this relationship (39, 41). P's identification with O can be established or maintained if P behaves, believes, and perceives as O does. Accordingly O has the ability to influence P, even though P may be unaware of this referent power. A verbalization of such power by P might be, "I am like O, and therefore I shall behave or believe as O does," or "I want to be like O, and I will be more like O if I behave or believe as O does." The stronger the identification of P with O the greater the referent power of O/P. . . .

We must try to distinguish between referent power and other types of power which might be operative at the same time. If a member is attracted to a group and he conforms to its norms only because he fears ridicule or expulsion from the group for nonconformity, we would call this coercive power. On the other hand if he conforms in order to obtain praise for conformity, it is a case of reward power. . . . Conformity with majority opinion is sometimes based on a respect for the collective wisdom of the group, in which case it is expert power. It is important to distinguish these phenomena, all grouped together elsewhere as "pressures toward uniformity," since the type of change which occurs will be different for different bases of power.

The concepts of "reference group" (40) and "prestige suggestion" may be treated as instances of referent power. In this case, O, the prestigeful person or group, is valued by P; because P desires to be associated or identified with O, he will assume attitudes or beliefs held by O. Similarly a negative reference group which O dislikes and evaluates negatively may exert negative influence on P as a result of negative referent power.

It has been demonstrated that the power which we designate as referent power is especially great when P is attracted to O (2, 7, 8, 9, 13, 23, 30). In our terms, this would mean that the greater the attraction, the greater the identification, and consequently the greater the referent power. In some cases, attraction or prestige may have a specific basis, and the range of referent power will be limited accordingly: a group of campers may have great referent power over a member regarding campcraft, but considerably less effect on other regions (30). However, we hypothesize that the greater the attraction of P toward O, the broader the range of referent power of O/P. . . .

Expert Power

The strength of the expert power of O/P varies with the extent of the knowledge or perception which P attributes to O within a given area. Probably P evaluates O's expertness in relation to his own knowledge as well as against an absolute standard. In any case expert power results in primary social influence on P's cognitive structure and probably not on other types of systems. Of course changes in the cognitive structure can change the direction of forces and hence of locomotion, but such a change of behavior is secondary social influence. Expert power has been demonstrated experimentally (8, 33). Accepting an attorney's advice in legal matters is a common example of expert influence; but there are many instances based on much less knowledge, such as the acceptance by a stranger of directions given by a native villager.

Expert power, where O need not be a member of P's group, is called "informational power" by Deutsch and Gerard (4). This type of expert power must be distinguished from influence based on the content of communication as described by Hovland et al. (17, 18, 24). The influence of the content of a communication upon an opinion is presumably a secondary influence produced after the *primary* influence (i.e., the acceptance of the information). Since power is here defined in terms of the primary changes, the influence of the content on a related opinion is not a case of expert power as we have defined it, but the initial acceptance of the validity of the content does seem to be based on expert power or referent power. . . .

The range of expert power, we assume, is more delimited than that of referent power. Not only is it restricted to cognitive systems but the expert is seen as having superior knowledge or ability in very specific areas, and his power will be limited to these areas, though some "halo effect" might occur. Recently, some of our renowned physical scientists have found quite painfully that their expert power in physical sciences does not extend to regions involving international politics. Indeed, there is some evidence that the attempted exertion of expert power outside of the range of expert power will reduce that expert power. An undermining of confidence seems to take place.

SUMMARY

We have distinguished five types of power: referent power, expert power, reward power, coercive power, and legitimate power. These distinctions led to the following hypotheses.

1. For all five types, the stronger the basis of power the greater the power.
2. For any type of power the size of the range may vary greatly, but in general referent power will have the broadest range.
3. Any attempt to utilize power outside the range of power will tend to reduce the power.
4. A new state of a system produced by reward power or coercive power will be highly dependent on O, and the more observable P's conformity the more dependent the state. For the other three types of power, the new state is usually dependent, at least in the beginning, but in any case the level of observability has no effect on the degree of dependence.
5. Coercion results in decreased attraction of P toward O and high resistance; reward power results in increased attraction and low resistance.
6. The more legitimate the coercion the less it will produce resistance and decreased attraction.

NOTES

1. The word "system" is here used to refer to a whole or to a part of the whole.
2. The concept of power has the conceptual property of *potentiality;* but it seems useful to restrict this potential influence to more or less enduring power relations between O and P by excluding from the definition of power those cases where the potential influence is so momentary or so changing that it cannot be predicted from the existing relationship. Power is a useful concept for describing social structure only if it has a certain stability over time; it is useless if every momentary social stimulus is viewed as actualizing social power.
3. We define resistance to an attempted induction as a force in the opposite direction which is set up by the same act of O. It must be distinguished from opposition which is defined as existing opposing forces which do not have their source in the same act of O. For example, a boy might resist his mother's order to eat spinach because of the manner of the induction attempt, and at the same time he might oppose it because he didn't like spinach.
4. Miller (32) assumes that all living systems have this character. However, it may be that some systems in the life space do not have this elasticity.
5. Though the primary influence of coercive power is dependent, it often produces secondary changes which are independent. Brainwashing, for example, utilizes coercive power to produce many primary changes in the life space of the prisoner, but these dependent changes can lead to identification with the aggressor and hence to secondary changes in ideology which are independent.

REFERENCES

1. Asch, S. E. Social psychology. New York: Prentice-Hall, 1952.
2. Back, K. W. Influence through social communication. *J. Abnorm. Soc. Psychol.,* 1951, 46, 9–23.
3. Coch, L., & French, J. R. P., Jr. Overcoming resistance to change. *Hum. Relat.,* 1948, 1, 512–532.
4. Deutsch, M., & Gerard, H. B. A study of normative and informational influences upon individual judgment. *J. Abnorm. Soc. Psychol.,* 1955, 51, 629–636.
5. Dittes, J. E., & Kelley, H. H. Effects of different conditions of acceptance upon conformity to group norms. *J. Abnorm. Soc. Psychol.,* 1956, 53, 100–107.
6. Festinger, L. An analysis of compliant behavior. In Sherif, M., & Wilson, M. O., (Eds.). *Group relations at the crossroads.* New York: Harper, 1953, 232–256.
7. Festinger, L. Informal social communication. *Psychol. Rev.,* 1950, 57, 271–282.
8. Festinger, L., Gerard, H. B., Hymovitch, B., Kelley, H. H., & Raven, B. H. The influence process in the presence of

extreme deviates. *Hum. Relat.*, 1952, 5, 327–346.

9. Festinger, L., Schachter, S., & Back, K. The operation of group standards. In Cartwright, D., & Zander, A. *Group dynamics: research and theory*. Evanston: Row, Peterson, 1953, 204–223.

10. French, J. R. P., Jr., Israel, Joachim & Ås, Dagnn. "Arbeidernes medvirkning i industribedriften. En eksperimentell undersøkelse." Institute for Social Research, Oslo, Norway, 1957.

11. French, J. R. P., Jr., Levinger, G., & Morrison, H. W. The legitimacy of coercive power. In preparation.

12. French, J. R. P., Jr., & Raven, B. H. An experiment in legitimate and coercive power. In preparation.

13. Gerard, H. B. The anchorage of opinions in face-to-face groups. *Hum. Relat.*, 1954, 7, 313–325.

14. Goldhammer, H., & Shils, E. A. Types of power and status. *Amer. J. Sociol.*, 1939, 45, 171–178.

15. Herbst, P. G. Analysis and measurement of a situation. *Hum. Relat.*, 1953, 2, 113–140.

16. Hochbaum, G. M. Self-confidence and reactions to group pressures. *Amer. Soc. Rev.*, 1954, 19, 678–687.

17. Hovland, C. I., Lumsdaine, A. A., & Shefeld, F. D. *Experiments on mass communication*. Princeton: Princeton Univer. Press, 1949.

18. Hovland, C. I., & Weiss, W. The influence of source credibility on communication effectiveness. *Publ. Opin. Quart.*, 1951, 15, 635–650.

19. Jackson, J. M., & Saltzstein, H. D. The effect of person-group relationships on conformity processes. *J. Abnorm. Soc. Psychol.*, 1958, 57, 17–24.

20. Jahoda, M. Psychological issues in civil liberties. *Amer. Psychologist*, 1956, 11, 234–240.

21. Katz, D., & Schank, R. L. *Social psychology*. New York: Wiley, 1938.

22. Kelley, H. H., & Volkart, E. H. The resistance to change of group-anchored attitudes. *Amer. Soc. Rev.*, 1952, 17, 453–465.

23. Kelman, H. Three processes of acceptance of social influence: compliance, identification and internalization. Paper read at the meetings of the American Psychological Association, August 1956.

24. Kelman, H., & Hovland, C. I. "Reinstatement" of the communicator in delayed measurement of opinion change. *J. Abnorm. Soc. Psychol.*, 1953, 48, 327–335.

25. Lewin, K. *Dynamic theory of personality*. New York: McGraw-Hill, 1935, 114–170.

26. Lewin, K. *Field theory in social science*. New York: Harper, 1951.

27. Lewin, K., Lippitt, R., & White, R. K. Patterns of aggressive behavior in experimentally created social climates. *J. Soc. Psychol.*, 1939, 10, 271–301.

28. Lasswell, H. D., & Kaplan, A. *Power and society: A framework for political inquiry*. New Haven: Yale Univer. Press, 1950.

29. Linton, R. *The cultural background of personality*. New York: Appleton-Century-Crofts, 1945.

30. Lippitt, R., Polansky, N., Redl, F., & Rosen, S. The dynamics of power. *Hum. Relat.*, 1952, 5, 37–64.

31. March, J. G. An introduction to the theory and measurement of influence. *Amer. Polit. Sci. Rev.*, 1955, 49, 431–451.

32. Miller, J. G. Toward a general theory for the behavioral sciences. *Amer. Psychologist*, 1955, 10, 513–531.

33. Moore, H. T. The comparative influence of majority and expert opinion. *Amer. J. Psychol.*, 1921, 32, 16–20.

34. Newcomb, T. M. *Social psychology*. New York: Dryden, 1950.

35. Raven, B. H. The effect of group pressures on opinion, perception, and communication. Unpublished doctoral dissertation, University of Michigan, 1953.

36. Raven, B. H., & French, J. R. P., Jr. Group support, legitimate power, and social influence. *J. Person.*, 1958, 26, 400–409.

37. Rommetveit, R. *Social norms and roles*. Minneapolis: Univer. Minnesota Press, 1953.

38. Russell, B. *Power: A new social analysis*. New York: Norton, 1938.

39. Stotland, E., Zander, A., Burnstein, E., Wolfe, D., & Natsoulas, T. Studies on the effects of identification. University of Michigan, Institute for Social Research. Forthcoming.

40. Swanson, G. E., Newcomb, T. M., & Hartley, E. L. *Readings in social psychology.* New York: Henry Holt, 1952.

41. Torrance, E. P., & Mason, R. Instructor effort to influence: an experimental evaluation of six approaches. Paper presented at USAF-NRC Symposium on Personnel, Training, and Human Engineering. Washington, D.C., 1956.

42. Weber, M. *The theory of social and economic organization.* Oxford: Oxford Univer. Press, 1947.

32
The Power of Power
James G. March

1.0 INTRODUCTION

Power is a major explanatory concept in the study of social choice. It is used in studies of relations among nations, of community decision making, of business behavior, and of small-group discussion. Partly because it conveys simultaneously overtones of the cynicism of *Realpolitik*, the glories of classical mechanics, the realism of elite sociology, and the comforts of anthropocentric theology, *power* provides a prime focus for disputation and exhortation in several social sciences.

Within this galaxy of nuances, I propose to consider a narrowly technical question: To what extent is one specific concept of power useful in the empirical analysis of mechanisms for social choice? . . .

The specific concept of power I have in mind is the concept used in theories having the following general assumptions:

1. The choice mechanism involves certain basic components (individuals, groups, roles, behaviors, labels, etc.).
2. Some amount of power is associated with each of these components.
3. The responsiveness (as measured by some direct empirical observation) of the mechanism to each individual component is monotone increasing with the power associated with the individual component. . . .

In order to explore the power of power in empirical theories of social choice, I propose to do two things: First, I wish to identify three different variations in this basic approach to power as an intervening variable to suggest the kinds of uses of *power* with

which we will be concerned. Second, I wish to examine six different classes of models of social choice that are generally consistent with what at least one substantial group of students means by *social power*. . . .

2.0 THREE APPROACHES TO THE STUDY OF POWER

2.1 The Experimental Study
. . . This brief introduction is intended simply to provide a relatively coherent characterization of a class of approaches to the study of power. . . .

Conceptual Basis. The experimental studies of power are generally Newtonian. Many of them are directly indebted to Lewin, who defined the power of *b* over *a* "as the quotient of the maximum force which *b* can induce on *a,* and the maximum resistance which *a* can offer."[1] In general, the experimental studies assume that the greater the power of the individual, the greater the changes induced (with given resistance) and the more successful the resistance to changes (with given pressure to change).

The experimental studies tend to be reductionist. Although they are ultimately (and sometimes immediately) interested in the power of one individual over another, they usually seek to reduce that relationship to more basic components. Thus, we distinguish between the power of behavior and the power of roles, and characterize specific individuals as a combination of behavior and roles.[2] Or, we distinguish factors

Source: J. G. March, "The Power of Power," in *Varieties of Political Theory,* ed. David Easton (Englewood Cliffs, NJ: Prentice-Hall, 1966), pp. 39–70. Reprinted by permission of the author.

affecting the agent of influence, the methods of influence, and the agent subjected to influence.[3] . . .

Procedures. The procedures used in this class of experimental studies are the classic ones. We determine power by some a priori measure or experimental manipulation, use a relatively simple force model to generate hypotheses concerning differences in outcomes from different treatments, and compare the observed outcomes with the predicted outcomes. . . .

Results. . . . For present purposes, two general results are particularly germane:

(1) It is possible to vary power of a specific subject systematically and (within limits) arbitrarily in an experimental setting. This can be done by manipulating some elements of his reputation[4] or by manipulating some elements of his power experience.[5] This apparently innocuous—and certainly minimal—result is in fact not so unimportant. It permits us to reject certain kinds of social-choice models for certain kinds of situations.

(2) The effectiveness of a priori power (i.e., manipulated, or a priori measured power) in producing behavior change is highly variable. Although there are indications that some kinds of leadership behavior are exhibited by some people in several different groups,[6] most studies indicate that the effectiveness of specific individuals, specific social positions, and specific behaviors in producing behavior change varies with respect to the content and relevancy of subject matter,[7] group identifications,[8] and power base.[9] . . .

2.2 The Community Study

A second major approach to the study of power can be called *the community power approach*; it is typical of, but not limited to, community studies.[10] . . .

Conceptual Basis. The conceptual definition of power implicit (and often explicit)

in the community studies is clearly Newtonian. The first two "laws" of social choice form a simple definition:

1. Social choice will be a predictable extension of past choices unless power is exerted on the choice.
2. When power is exerted, the modification of the choice will be proportional to the power.

. . . The community power studies generally assume that the decisions made by the community are a function of the power exerted on the community by various power holders. They assume some kind of "power field" in which individual powers are summed to produce the final outcome.

The community studies are analytic in the sense that they attempt to infer the power of individuals within the community by observing (either directly or indirectly) their net effects on community choice. That is, they assume that a decision is some function of individual powers and the individual preferences. Hence, they observe the decision outcome and the preferences, and estimate the powers.

The community studies are personal in the sense that power is associated with specific individuals. The estimation procedures are designed to determine the power of an individual. This power, in turn, is viewed as some function of the resources (economic, social, etc.), position (office, role, etc.), and skill (choice of behavior, choice of allies, etc.); but the study and the analysis assume that it is meaningful to aggregate resource power, position power, and skill power into a single variable associated with the individual.

Procedures. . . . The procedure most generally used involves some variation of asking individuals within the community to assess the relative power of other individuals in the community. Essentially the panel is given the following task: On the basis of past experience (both your own and that of other people with whom you have communicated), estimate the power of the following individuals.[11] . . .

A second procedure involves the direct observation of decision outcomes and prior preferences over a series of decisions.[12] Essentially, we define a model relating power to decisions, draw a sample of observations, and estimate the power of individuals on the basis of that model and those observations. . . .

Results. At a general level, the results of the community studies can be described in terms of three broad types of interests. First, we ask how power is distributed in the community. Second, we ask what relation exists between power and the possession of certain other socioeconomic attributes. Third, we ask how power is exerted.

With respect to the distribution of power, most studies indicate that most people in most communities are essentially powerless. They neither participate in the making of decisions directly nor accumulate reputations for power. Whatever latent control they may have, it is rarely exercised. . . .

With respect to the exercise of power, the studies have focused on specialization, activation, and unity of power holders. Most studies have identified significant specialization in power: Different individuals are powerful with respect to different things. But most studies also have shown "general leaders": Some individuals have significant power in several areas. Some studies have reported a significant problem associated with power activation: the more powerful members of the community are not necessarily activated to use their power, while less powerful members may be hyperactivated. . . . Some studies indicate a network of associations, consultations, and agreements among the more powerful; other studies indicate rather extensive disagreement among the more powerful.[13]

2.3 The Institutional Study

The third alternative approach to the study of power is in one sense the most common of all. It is the analysis of the structure of institutions to determine the power structure within them. Such studies are the basis of much of descriptive political science. Systematic attempts to derive quantitative indices of power from an analysis of institutional structure are limited, however. The approach will be characterized here in terms of the game-theory version. . . .

Conceptual Basis. . . . We assume the general von Neumann concept of a game: There are n players, each with a well-defined set of alternative strategies. Given the choice of strategies by the player (including the mutual choice of coalitions), there is a well-defined set of rules for determining the outcome of the game. The outcomes are evaluated by the individual players in terms of the individual orderings of preference. The Shapley value for the game to an individual player (or coalition of players) has several alternative intuitive explanations. It can be viewed as how much a rational person would be willing to pay in order to occupy a particular position in the game rather than some other position. It can be viewed as the expected marginal contribution of a particular position to a coalition if all coalitions are considered equally likely and the order in which positions are added to the coalition is random. It can be viewed as how much a rational player would expect to receive from a second rational player in return for his always selecting the strategy dictated by the second player. Or, it can be viewed simply as a computational scheme with certain desirable properties of uniqueness.

The Shapley value is impersonal. It is associated not with a specific player but rather with a specific position in the game. It is not conceived to measure the power of President Kennedy or President Eisenhower; it is conceived to measure the power of the Presidency. . . .

. . . In the standard Newtonian versions of power, power is that which induces a modification of choice by the system. Quite commonly, we measure the power by the extent to which the individual is able to induce the system to provide resources of value to him. We are aware that power, in this sense, is a function of many variables; we suspect that informal alliances and allegiances influence behavior; and we commonly allege that power is dependent on information and intelligence as well as formal position.

Suppose that we want to assess the contribution to power of formal position alone. One way to do so would be an empirical study in which we would consider simultaneously all of the various contributing factors, apply some variant of a multiple regression technique, and determine the appropriate coefficients for the position variables. A second way would be an experimental study in which nonposition factors are systematically randomized. A third way would be the one taken by Shapley and Shubik. We can imagine a game involving position variables only (e.g., the formal legislative scheme), and we can assume rationality on the part of the participants and ask for the value of each position under that assumption. Since this value is a direct measure of the resources the individual can obtain from the system by virtue of his position in the game alone, it is a reasonable measure of the power of that position. Alternatively, we can view the resources themselves as power.[14]

Procedures. There are two main ways in which we can use the Shapley-Shubik index in an empirical study: (1) We can construct some sort of empirical index of power, make some assumptions about the relation between the empirical and a priori measures, and test the consistency of the empirical results with the a priori measures. Thus, we might assume that the empirical measure consists of the a priori measure plus an error term representing various other (nonposition) factors. If we can make some assumptions about the nature of the "error," we can test the consistency. Or, (2), we can deduce some additional propositions from the model underlying the index and test those propositions. ...

Results. ... Riker has applied the basic Shapley-Shubik measure to the French Assembly to derive changes in power indices for the various parties in the French Assembly during the period 1953–54, as thirty-four migrations from one party to another produced sixty-one individual changes in affiliation.[15] ... The data did not support the hypothesis. In subsequent work, Riker has almost entirely abandoned the Shapley-Shubik approach.[16]

3.0 SIX MODELS OF SOCIAL CHOICE AND THE CONCEPT OF POWER

The three general approaches described above illustrate the range of possible uses of the concept of power, and include most of the recent efforts to use the concept in empirical research or in empirically oriented theory. I wish to use these three examples as a basis for exploring the utility of the concept of power in the analysis of systems for social choice. ...

I shall now consider six types of models of social choice, evaluate their consistency with available data, and consider the problems of the concept of power associated with them. By a *model* I mean a set of statements about the way in which individual choices (or behavior) are transformed into social choices, and a procedure for using those statements to derive some empirically meaningful predictions. The six types of models are:

1. Chance models, in which we assume that choice is a chance event, quite independent of power.
2. Basic force models, in which we assume that the components of the system exert all their power on the system with choice being a direct resultant of those powers.
3. Force activation models, in which we assume that not all the power of every component is exerted at all times.
4. Force-conditioning models, in which we assume that the power of the components is modified as a result of the outcome of past choices.

5. Force depletion models, in which we assume that the power of the components is modified as a result of the exertion of power on past choices.
6. Process models, in which we assume that choice is substantially independent of power but not a chance event. . . .

3.1 Chance Models

Let us assume that there are no attributes of human beings affecting the output of a social-choice mechanism. Further, let us assume that the only factors influencing the output are chance factors, constrained perhaps by some initial conditions. There are a rather large number of such models, but it will be enough here to describe three in skeleton form.

The Unconstrained Model. We assume a set of choice alternatives given to the system. These might be all possible bargaining agreements in bilateral bargaining, all possible appropriations in a legislative scheme, or all experimentally defined alternatives in an experimental setting. Together with this set of alternatives, we have a probability function. . . .

The Equal-Power Model. We assume a set of initial positions for the components of the system and some well-defined procedures for defining a social choice consistent with the assumption of equal power. For example, the initial positions might be arranged on some simple continuum. We might observe the initial positions with respect to wage rates in collective bargaining, with respect to legislative appropriations for space exploration, or with respect to the number of peas in a jar in an experimental group. A simple arithmetic mean of such positions is a social choice consistent with the assumption of equal power. In this chance model, we assume that the social choice is the equal-power choice plus some error term. . . .

The Encounter Model. We assume only two possible choice outcomes: We can win or lose; the bill can pass or fail; we will take the left or right branch in the maze. At each encounter (social choice) there are two opposing teams. The probability of choosing a given alternative if the teams have an equal number of members is 0.5. . . .

What are the implications of such models? Consider the encounter model. Suppose we imagine that each power encounter occurs between just two people chosen at random from the total population of the choice system. Further, assume that at each encounter we will decide who prevails by flipping a coin.[17] . . . A model of this general class has been used by Deutsch and Madow to generate a distribution of managerial performance and reputations.[18]

Similar kinds of results can be obtained from the unconstrained-chance model. If we assume that social choice is equi-probable among the alternatives and that individual initial positions are equi-probable among the alternatives, the only difference is that the number of alternatives is no longer necessarily two. In general, there will be more than two alternatives; as a result the probability of success will be less than 0.5 on every trial and the probability of a long-run record of spectacular success correspondingly less. For example, if we assume a dozen trials with ten alternatives, the probability of failing no more than once drops to about 10^{-10} (as compared with about .0032 in the two alternative cases).

Finally, generally similar results are obtained from the equal-power model. . . . Our measures of success now become not the number (or proportion) of successes but rather the mean deviation of social choices from individual positions; and we generate from the model a distribution of such distances for a given number of trials.[19] . . .

To what extent is it possible to reject the chance models in studies of social choice? . . . The answer depends on an evaluation of four properties of the chance models that are potentially inconsistent with data either from field studies or from the laboratory.

First, we ask whether power is stable over time. With most of the chance models, knowing who won in the past or who had a reputation for winning in the past would not help us to predict who would win in the future. Hence, if we can predict the outcome of future social choices by weighting current positions with weights derived from past observations or from a priori considerations, we will have some justification for rejecting the chance model. Some efforts have been made in this direction, but with mixed results.[20] . . .

Second, we ask whether power is stable over subject matter. Under the chance models, persons who win in one subject-matter area would be no more likely to win in another area than would people who lost in the first area. Thus, if we find a greater-than-chance overlap from one area to another, we would be inclined to reject the chance model. The evidence on this point is conflicting. . . .

Third, we ask whether power is correlated with other personal attributes. . . . Without any exception of which I am aware, the studies do show a greater-than-chance relation between power and such personal attributes as economic status, political office, and ethnic group. We cannot account under the simple chance model for the consistent underrepresentation of the poor, the unelected, and the Negro.

And fourth, we ask whether power is *susceptible to experimental manipulation*. If the chance model were correct, we could not systematically produce variations in who wins by manipulating power. Here the experimental evidence is fairly clear. It is possible to manipulate the results of choice mechanisms by manipulating personal attributes or personal reputations. . . .

Chance models are extremely naïve; they are the weakest test we can imagine. Yet we have had some difficulty in rejecting them, and in some situations it is not clear that we can reject them. . . . Possibly, however, our difficulty is not with the amount of order in the world, but with the concept of power. . . .

3.2 Basic Force Models

Suppose we assume that power is real and controlling, and start with a set of models that are closely linked with classical mechanics although the detailed form is somewhat different from mechanics. In purest form, the simple force models can be represented in terms of functions that make the resultant social choice a weighted average of the individual initial positions—the weights being the power attached to the various individuals. . . .

The force models . . . are reasonably well-defined and pose no great technical problems, and the estimation procedures are straightforward. The observations required are no more than the observations required by any model that assumes some sort of power. What are the implications of the models? First, unless combined with a set of constraints (such as the power-structure constraints of the French and Harary formulation), the models say nothing about the distribution of power in a choice system. Thus, there is no way to test their apparent plausibility by comparing actual power distributions with derived distributions.

Second, in all of the models, the distance between the initial position of the individual and the social choice (or expected social choice) is inversely proportional to the power when we deal with just two individuals. . . . With more than two individuals, the relation between distance and power becomes more complex, depending on the direction and magnitude of the various forces applied to the system. Since the models are directly based on the ideas of center of mass, these results are not surprising. Given these results, we can evaluate the models if we have an independent measure of power, such as the Shapley-Shubik measure. Otherwise, they become, as they frequently have, simply a definition of power.

Third, we can evaluate the reasonableness of this class of models by a few general implications. . . .

Insofar as the determinate models are concerned, both experimental and field observations make it clear that the models are not accurate portrayals of social choice. In order for the models to be accepted, the m_i (as defined in the models) must be stable. As far as I know, no one has ever reported data suggesting that the m_i are stable in a determinate model. . . .

The basis for rejecting the simple force models . . . is twofold:

(1) There seems to be general consensus that either potential power is different from actually exerted power or that actually exerted power is variable. If, while potential power is stable, there are some unknown factors that affect the actual exercise of power, the simple force models will not fit; they assume power is stable, but they also assume that power exerted is equal to power. If actually exerted power is unstable, the simple force models will fit only if we can make some plausible assertions about the nature of the instability. . . .

(2) There appears to be ample evidence that power is not strictly exogenous to the exercise of power and the results of that exercise. Most observers would agree that present reputations for power are at least in part a function of the results of past encounters. Although the evidence for the proposition is largely experimental, most observers would probably also agree that power reputation, in turn, affects the results of encounters. If these assertions are true, the simple force model will fit in the case of power systems that are in equilibrium, but it will not fit in other systems.

These objections to the simple force model are general; we now need to turn to models that attempt to deal with endogenous shifts in power and with the problem of power activation or exercise. . . . We will consider three classes of models, all of which are elaborations of the simple force models. The first class can be viewed as *activation models*. They assume that power is a potential and that the exercise of power involves some mechanism of activation. The second class can be described as *conditioning models*. They assume that power is partly endogenous—specifically that apparent power leads to actual power. The third class can be classified as *depletion models*. They assume that power is a stock, and that exercise of power leads to a depletion of the stock.

3.3 Force Activation Models

All of the models considered thus far accept the basic postulate that all power is exerted all of the time. In fact, few observers of social-choice systems believe this to be true, either for experimental groups or for natural social systems. With respect to the latter, Schulze argues that "the Cibola study appears to document the absence of any neat, constant, and direct relationship between *power as a potential for determinative action*, and *power as determinative action itself*." [21] . . .

Consider the problem of relating the activation models to observations of reality. . . .

Suppose, for example, that we have some measures of the activation of individual members of a modern community. One such measure might be the proportion of total time devoted by the individual to a specific issue of social choice. We could use such a measure, observations of initial positions and social choices, and one of the basic force models to assign power indices (potential power) to the various individuals in the community. Similarly, if we took a comparable measure in an experimental group (e.g., some function of the frequency of participation in group discussions), we could determine some power indices. Because direct observational measures of the degree of power utilization are not ordinarily the easiest of measurements to take, the partition version of the model has an important comparative advantage from the point of view of estimation problems. . . . We need only observe whether the individual involved did or did not participate in a choice, rather than the degree of his participation.

If we are unable or do not choose to observe the extent of utilization directly, we can, at least in principle, estimate it from other factors in the situation. For example, if we can determine the opportunity costs [22] to the individual of the exercise of power, we might be able to assume that the individual will exercise power only up to the point at which the marginal cost equals the marginal gain. If we can further assume something about the relation between the exercise of power and the return from that exercise, we can use the opportunity costs to estimate the power of utilization. The general idea of opportunity costs, or subjective importance,[23] as a dimension of power has considerable intuitive appeal. . . .

The second major alternative, given the assumption of constant potential power, is also to assume a constant utilization of power over all choices. . . . If both utilization and potential power are constant, we are back to the simple force model and can estimate the product . . . in the same way we previously established the m_i. Under such circumstances, the introduction of the concepts of power utilization and power potential is unnecessary and we can deal directly with power exercised as the core variable.[24]

The force activation model has been compared with empirical data to a limited extent. Hanson and Miller undertook to determine independently the potential power and power utilization of community members and to predict from those measures the outcome of social choices.[25] Potential power was determined by a priori theory; utilization was determined by interviews and observation. The results, as previously noted, were consistent not only with the force activation model but also with a number of other models. The French and Harary graph theory models are essentially activation force models (with activation associated with a communication structure) and they have been compared generally with experimental data for the equal potential power case. The comparison suggests a general consistency of the data with several alternate models. . . .

It is clear from a consideration both of the formal properties of activation models and of the problems observers have had with such models that they suffer from their excessive a posteriori explanatory power. If we observe that power exists and is stable and if we observe that sometimes weak people seem to triumph over strong people, we are tempted to rely on an activation hypothesis to explain the discrepancy. But if we then try to use the activation hypothesis

to predict the results of social-choice procedures, we discover that the data requirements of "plausible" activation models are quite substantial. As a result, we retreat to what are essentially degenerate forms of the activation model — retaining some of the form but little of the substance. This puts us back where we started, looking for some device to explain our failures in prediction. Unfortunately, the next two types of models simply complicate life further rather than relieve it.

3.4 Force-Conditioning Models

The conditioning models take as given either the basic force model or the force activation model. The only modification is to replace a constant power resource with a variable power resource. The basic mechanisms are simple: (1) People have power because they are believed to have power. (2) People are believed to have power because they have been observed to have power. . . .

Furthermore, it is clear that if power is accurately specified by observations and if social choices are precisely and uniquely specified by the power distribution, then the conditioning models are relatively uninteresting. They become interesting because of non-uniqueness in the results of the exercise of power or because of non-uniqueness in the attributions of power. . . .

Models of this general class have not been explored in the power literature. Experimental studies have demonstrated the realism of each of the two mechanisms — success improves reputation, reputation improves success. As a result, conditioning models cannot be rejected out of hand. Moreover, they lead directly to some interesting and relevant predictions.

In most of the literature on the measurement of power, there are two nagging problems — the problem of the chameleon who frequently jumps in and agrees with an already decided issue and the satellite who, though he himself has little power, is highly correlated with a high-power person. Since these problems must be at least as compelling for the individual citizen as they are for the professional observer, they have served as a basis for a number of strong attacks on the reputational approach to the attribution of power. But the problem changes somewhat if we assume that reputations affect outcomes. Now the chameleon and the satellite are not measurement problems but important phenomena. The models will predict that an association with power will lead to power. Whether the association is by chance or by deliberate imitation, the results are substantially the same.

To the best of my knowledge, no formal efforts have been made to test either the satellite prediction in a real-world situation, or to test some of its corollaries, which include:

1. Informal power is unstable. Let the kingmaker beware of the king.
2. Unexercised power disappears. Peace is the enemy of victory.
3. Undifferentiated power diffuses. Beware of your allies lest they become your equals. . . .

3.5 Force Depletion Models

Within the conditioning models, success breeds success. But there is another class of plausible models in which success breeds failure. As in the conditioning models, we assume that power varies over time. As in the force activation models, we assume that not all power is exercised at every point in time.

The basic idea of the model is plausible. We consider power to be a resource. The exercise of power depletes that resource. Subject to additions to the power supply, the more power a particular component in the system exercises, the less power there is available for that component to use. . . .

Under this scheme, it is quite possible for power to shift as a result of variations in the rates of power utilization. So long as additions to the power supply are independent of the exercise of power, the use of power today means that we will have less to use tomorrow. We can show various conditions for convergence and divergence of power resources or exercised power. We can also

generate a set of aphorisms parallel to—but somewhat at variance with—the conditioning model aphorisms:

1. Formal power is unstable. Let the king beware of the kingmaker.
2. Exercised power is lost. Wars are won by neutrals.
3. Differentiation wastes power. Maintain the alliance as long as possible. . . .

Some of the studies of interpersonal relations in organizations indicate that the exercise of power is often dysfunctional with regard to the effective exercise of power in the future. In those cases, the mechanism ordinarily postulated involves the impact of power on sentiments[26] rather than our simple resource notion. Nonetheless the grosser attributes of observed behavior in such studies are consistent with the gross predictions of models that view power as a stock. . . .

. . . From a simple concept of power in a simple force model, we have moved to a concept of power that is further and further removed from the basic intuitive notions captured by the simple model, and to models in which simple observations of power are less and less useful. It is only a short step from this point to a set of models that are conceptually remote from the original conception of a social-choice system.

3.6 Process Models

Suppose that the choice system we are studying is not random. Suppose further that power really is a significant phenomenon in the sense that it can be manipulated systematically in the laboratory and can be used to explain choice in certain social-choice systems. I think that both those suppositions are reasonable. But let us further suppose that there is a class of social-choice systems in which power is insignificant. Unless we treat *power* as true by definition, I think that suppression is reasonable. If we treat *power* as a definition, I think it is reasonable to suppose there is a class of social-choice systems in which power measurement will be unstable and useless.

Consider the following process models of social choice as representative of this class:

An Exchange Model. We assume that the individual components in the system prefer certain of the alternative social choices, and that the system has a formal criterion for making the final choices (e.g., majority vote, unanimity, clearing the market). We also assume that there is some medium of exchange by which individual components seek to arrange agreements (e.g., exchanges of money or votes) that are of advantage to themselves. These agreements, plus the formal criterion for choice, determine the social decision. This general type of market system is familiar enough for economic systems and political systems.[27] It is also one way of viewing some modern theories of interpersonal influence[28] in which sentiments on one dimension ("I like you") are exchanged for sentiments on another ("You like my pots") in order to reach a social choice ("We like us and we like my pots").

A Problem-Solving Model. We assume that each of the individual components in the system has certain information and skills relevant to a problem of social choice, and that the system has a criterion for solution. We postulate some kind of process by which the system calls forth and organizes the information and skills so as systematically to reduce the difference between its present position and a solution. This general type of system is familiar to students of individual and group problem solving.[29]

A Communication-Diffusion Model. We assume that the components in the system are connected by some formal or informal communication system by which information is diffused through the system. We postulate some process by which the information is sent and behavior modified, one component at a time, until a social position is reached. This general type of system is familiar to many students of individual behavior in a social context.[30]

A Decision-Making Model. We assume that the components in the system have preferences with respect to social choices, and that the system has a procedure for rendering choices. The system and the components operate under two limitations:

1. Overload: They have more demands on their attention than they can meet in the time available.

2. Undercomprehension: The world they face is much more complicated than they can handle.

Thus, although we assume that each of the components modifies its behavior and its preferences over time in order to achieve a subjectively satisfactory combination of social choices, it is clear that different parts of the system contribute to different decisions in different ways at different times. This general type of system is a familiar model of complex organizations.[31]

In each of these process models, it is possible to attribute power to the individual components. We might want to say that a man owning a section of land in Iowa has more power in the economic system than a man owning a section of land in Alaska. We might want to say that, in a pot-selling competition, a man with great concern over his personal status has less power than a man with less concern. We might want to say that a man who knows Russian has more power than a man who does not in a group deciding the relative frequency of adjectival phrases in Tolstoi and Dostoievski. Or, we might want to say that, within an organization, a subunit that has problems has more power than a subunit that does not have problems. But I think we would probably not want to say any of these things. The concept of power does not contribute much to our understanding of systems that can be represented in any of these ways.

I am impressed by the extent to which models of this class seem to be generally consistent with the reports of . . .[32] students of political systems and other relatively large (in terms of number of people involved) systems of social choice. "Observation of certain local communities makes it appear that inclusive over-all organization for many general purposes is weak or nonexistent," Long writes. "Much of what occurs seems to just happen with accidental trends becoming cumulative over time and producing results intended by nobody. A great deal of the communities' activities consist of undirected cooperation of particular social structures, each seeking particular goals and, in doing so, meshing with the others."[33]

Such descriptions of social choice have two general implications. On the one hand, if a system has the properties suggested by such students as Coleman, Long, Riesman, Lindblom, and Dahl, power will be a substantially useless concept. In such systems, the measurement of power is feasible, but it is not valuable in calculating predictions. . . .

On the other hand, the process models — and particularly the decision-making process models — look technically more difficult with regard to estimation and testing than the more complex modifications of the force model. We want to include many more discrete and nominal variables, many more discontinuous functions, and many more rare combinations of events. . . .

4.0 THE POWER OF POWER

. . . Although *power* and *influence* are useful concepts for many kinds of situations, they have not greatly helped us to understand many of the natural social-choice mechanisms to which they have traditionally been applied.

The extent to which we have used the concept of power fruitlessly is symptomatic of three unfortunate temptations associated with power:

Temptation No. 1: The Obviousness of Power. To almost anyone living in contemporary society, power is patently real. We can scarcely talk about our daily life or major political and social phenomena without talking about power. Our discussions of political machinations consist largely of stories of negotiations among the influentials. Our analyses of social events are punctuated with calculations of power. Our interpretations of organizational life are built on evaluations of who does and who does not have power. Our debates of the grand issues of social, political, and economic systems are funneled into a consideration of whether *i* has too little power and *j* has too much.

Because of this ubiquity of power, we are inclined to assume that it is real and meaningful.

There must be some fire behind the smoke. "I take it for granted that in every human organization some individuals have more influence over key decisions than do others."[34] Most of my biases in this regard are conservative, and I am inclined to give some credence to the utility of social conceptual validation. I think, however, that we run the risk of treating the social validation of power as more compelling than it is simply because the social conditioning to a simple force model is so pervasive.

Temptation No. 2: The Importance of Measurement. The first corollary of the obviousness of power is the importance of the measurement problem. Given the obviousness of power, we rarely reexamine the basic model by which social choice is viewed as some combination of individual choices, the combination being dependent on the power of the various individuals. Since we have a persistent problem discovering a measurement procedure that consistently yields results which are consistent with the model, we assert a measurement problem and a problem of the concept of power. We clarify and reclarify the concept, and we define and redefine the measures. . . .

Although I have some sympathy with these efforts, I think our perseveration may be extreme. At the least, we should consider whether subsuming all our problems under the rubric of conceptual and measurement problems may be too tempting. I think we too often ask *how* to measure power when we should ask *whether* to measure power. The measurement problem and the model problem have to be solved simultaneously.

Temptation No. 3: The Residual Variance. The second corollary of the obviousness of power is the use of *power* as a residual category for explanation. We always have some unexplained variance in our data — results that simply cannot be explained within the theory. It is always tempting to give that residual variance some name. Some of us are inclined to talk about God's will; others talk about errors of observation; still others talk about some named variable (e.g., power, personality, extrasensory perception). Such naming can be harmless; we might just as well have some label for our failures. But where the unexplained variance is rather large, as it often is when we consider social-choice systems, we can easily fool ourselves into believing that we know something simply because we have a name for our errors. In general, I think we can roughly determine the index of the temptation to label errors by computing the ratio of uses of the variable for prediction to the uses for a posteriori explanation. On that calculation, I think power exhibits a rather low ratio, even lower than such other problem areas as personality and culture. . . .

I have tried to suggest that the power of power depends on the extent to which a predictive model requires and can make effective use of such a concept. Thus, it depends on the kind of system we are confronting, the amount and kinds of data we are willing or able to collect, and the kinds of estimation and validation procedures we have available to us. Given our present empirical and test technology, power is probably a useful concept for many short-run situations involving the direct confrontations of committed and activated participants. Such situations can be found in natural settings, but they are more frequent in the laboratory. Power is probably not a useful concept for many long-run situations involving problems of component-overload and undercomprehension. Such situations can be found in the laboratory but are more common in natural settings. Power may become more useful as a concept if we can develop analytic and empirical procedures for coping with the more complicated forms of force models, involving activation, conditioning, and depletion of power.

Thus, the answer to the original question is tentative and mixed. Provided some rather restrictive assumptions are met, the concept of power and a simple force model represent a reasonable approach to the study of social choice. Provided some rather substantial estimation and analysis problems can be solved, the concept of power and more elaborate force models represent a reasonable approach. On the whole, however, power is a disappointing concept. It gives us surprisingly little purchase in reasonable models of complex systems of social choice.

NOTES

1. Kurt Lewin, *Field Theory in Social Science* (New York: Harper & Row, Publishers, 1951), p. 336.

2. See J. G. March, "Measurement Concepts in the Theory of Influence," *Journal of Politics*, 14 (1957), 202–26.

3. Dorwin Cartwright, "Influence, Leadership, Control," in *Handbook of Organizations*, ed. J. G. March (Chicago: Rand McNally & Co., 1965).

4. See C. I. Hovland, I. L. Janis, and H. H. Kelley, *Communication and Persuasion* (New Haven: Yale University Press, 1953).

5. See B. Mausner, "The Effect of Prior Reinforcement on the Interaction of Observer Pairs," *Journal of Abnormal and Social Psychology*, 49 (1954), 65–68, and "The Effects of One Partner's Success or Failure in a Relevant Task on the Interaction of Observer Pairs," *Journal of Abnormal and Social Psychology*, 49 (1954), 577–60.

6. See E. F. Borgatta, A. S. Couch, and R. F. Bales, "Some Findings Relevant to the Great Man Theory of Leadership," *American Sociological Review*, 19 (1954), 755–59.

7. J. G. March, "Influence Measurement in Experimental and Semi-Experimental Groups," *Sociometry*, 19 (1956), 260–71.

8. Cartwright, *Studies in Social Power*.

9. Cartwright, *Studies in Social Power*.

10. For reviews of the literature, see P. H. Rossi, "Community Decision Making," *Administrative Science Quarterly*, 1 (1957), 415–43; and L. J. R. Henson, "In the Footsteps of Community Power," *American Political Science Review*, 55 (1961), 817–30.

11. See F. Hunter, *Community Power Structures* (Chapel Hill: University of North Carolina Press, 1953).

12. See R. A. Dahl, *Who Governs?* (New Haven: Yale University Press, 1961).

13. See W. H. Form and W. V. D'Antonio, "Integration and Cleavage among Community Influentials in Two Border Cities," *American Sociological Review*, 24 (1959), 804–14; and H. Scoble, "Leadership Hierarchies and Political Issues in a New England Town," in *Community Political Systems*, ed. Morris Janowitz (New York: Free Press of Glencoe, Inc., 1961).

14. See R. D. Luce, "Further Comments on Power Distributions for a Stable Two-Party Congress," Paper read at American Political Science Association meetings (1956); and W. H. Riker, "A Test of the Adequacy of the Power Index," *Behavioral Science*, 9 (1959), 276–90.

15. Riker, "A Test of the Adequacy of the Power Index."

16. W. H. Riker, *The Theory of Political Coalitions* (New Haven: Yale University Press, 1962).

17. See H. White, "Uses of Mathematics in Sociology," in *Mathematics and the Social Sciences*, ed. J. C. Charlesworth (Philadelphia: American Academy of Political and Social Science, 1963).

18. K. W. Deutsch and W. G. Madow, "A Note on the Appearance of Wisdom in Large Organizations," *Behavioral Science*, 6 (1961), 72–78.

19. See D. MacRae, Jr., and H. D. Price, "Scale Positions and 'Power' in the Senate," *Behavioral Science*, 4 (1959), 212–18.

20. See, for example, Hanson, "Predicting a Community Decision: A Test of the Miller-Form Theory," *American Sociological Review*, 24 (1959), 662–71.

21. R. O. Schulze, "The Role of Economic Dominants in Community Power Structure," *American Sociological Review*, 23 (1958), 9.

22. See J. C. Harsanyi, "Measurement of Social Power, Opportunity Costs, and the Theory of Two-Person Bargaining Games," *Behavioral Science*, 7 (1962), 67–80.

23. See R. Dubin, "Power and Union-Management Relations," *Administrative Science Quarterly*, II (1957), 60–81; and A. S. Tannenbaum, "An Event Structure Approach to Social Power and to the Problem of Power Comparability," *Behavioral Science*, 7 (1962), 315–31.

24. See Dahl, *Who Governs?* and R. E. Wolfinger, "Reputation and Reality in the Study of 'Community Power,'" *American Sociological Review*, 25 (1960), 636–44.

25. Hanson, "Predicting a Community Decision"; D. C. Miller, "The Prediction of Issue Outcome in Community Decision-Making," *Research Studies of the State College of Washington*, 25 (1957), 137–47.

26. See W. G. Bennis, "Effecting Organizational Change: A New Role for the Behavioral Sciences," *Administrative Science Quarterly*, 8 (1963).

27. See, for example, Anthony Downs, *An Economic Theory of Democracy* (New York: Harper & Row, Publishers, 1957); J. M. Buchanan and Gordon Tullock, *The Calculus of Consent* (Ann Arbor: University of Michigan Press, 1962); and Riker, *The Theory of Political Coalitions*.

28. Dale Carnegie, *How to Win Friends and Influence People* (New York: Simon and Schuster, Inc., 1936); Leon Festinger, *A Theory of Cognitive Dissonance* (New York: Harper & Row, Publishers, 1957).

29. See, for example, A. Newell, J. C. Shaw, and H. A. Simon, "Elements of a Theory of Human Problem Solving," *Psychological Review*, 65 (1958), 151–66; and D. W. Taylor, "Decision Making and Problem Solving," in *Handbook of Organizations*, ed. March.

30. See, for example, Elihu Katz and P. F. Lazarsfeld, *Personal Influence* (New York: Free Press of Glencoe, Inc., 1955); and Angus Campbell, Philip Converse, W. E. Miller, and Donald Stokes, *The American Voter* (New York: John Wiley & Sons, Inc., 1960).

31. See C. E. Lindblom, "The Science of Muddling Through," *Public Administration Review*, 19 (1959), 79–88; and R. M. Cyert and J. G. March, *A Behavioral Theory of the Firm* (Englewood Cliffs, N.J.: Prentice-Hall, Inc., 1963).

32. For example, David Riesman, *The Lonely Crowd* (New Haven: Yale University Press, 1951).

33. N. E. Long, "The Local Community as an Ecology of Games," *American Journal of Sociology*, 44 (1958), 252.

34. R. A. Dahl, "A Critique of the Ruling Elite Model," *American Political Science Review*, 52 (1958).

33
The Power Game and the Players
Henry Mintzberg

The core of this book is devoted to the discussion of a theory of organizational power. It is built on the premise that organizational behavior is a power game in which various players, called *influencers*, seek to control the organization's decisions and actions. The organization first comes into being when an initial group of influencers join together to pursue a common mission. Other influencers are subsequently attracted to the organization as a vehicle for satisfying some of their needs. Since the needs of influencers vary, each tries to use his or her own levers of power—*means or systems of influence*—to control decisions and actions. How they succeed determines what configuration of organizational power emerges. Thus, to understand the behavior of the organization, it is necessary to understand which influencers are present, what needs each seeks to fulfill in the organization, and how each is able to exercise power to fulfill them.

Of course, much more than power determines what an organization does. But our perspective in this book is that power is what matters, and that, if you like, everyone exhibits a lust for power (an assumption, by the way, that I do not personally favor, but that proves useful for the purposes of this book). When our conclusions here are coupled with those of the first book in this series, *The Structuring of Organizations* (Mintzberg 1979a, which will subsequently be referred to as the *Structuring book*), a more complete picture of the behavior of organizations emerges.

THE EXERCISE OF POWER

Hirschman (1970) notes in a small but provocative book entitled *Exit, Voice, and Loyalty*, that the participant in any system has three basic options:

> To stay and contribute as expected, which Hirschman calls *loyalty* (in the vernacular, "Shut up and deal")
>
> To leave, which Hirschman calls *exit* ("Take my marbles and go")
>
> To stay and try to change the system, which Hirschman refers to as *voice* ("I'd rather fight than switch")

Should he or she choose voice, the participant becomes what we call an influencer.[1] Those who exit—such as the client who stops buying or the employee who seeks work elsewhere—cease to be influencers, while those who choose loyalty over voice—the client who buys without question at the going rate, the employees who do whatever they are told quietly—choose not to participate as active influencers (other than to support implicitly the existing power structure).

> To resort to voice, rather than exit, is for the customer or member to make an attempt at changing the practices, policies, and outputs of the firm from which one buys or of the organization to which one belongs. Voice is here defined as any attempt at all to change, rather than to escape from, an objectionable state of affairs. . . . (Hirschman 1970, p. 30)[2]

For those who stay and fight, what gives power to their voice? Essentially the influencer requires (1) some source or basis of

Source: Henry Mintzberg, *Power in and Around Organizations* (Englewood Cliffs, NJ: Prentice Hall, 1983), pp. 22–30. © 1983 Prentice-Hall. Reprinted by permission of Pearson Education, Inc., Upper Saddle River, NJ.

power, coupled with (2) the expenditure of energy in a (3) politically skillful way when necessary. These are the three basic conditions for the exercise of power. In Allison's concise words, "Power . . . is an elusive blend of . . . bargaining advantages, skill and will in using bargaining advantages. . . ." (1971, p. 168).

The General Bases of Power

In the most basic sense, the power of the individual in or over the organization reflects some *dependency* that it has—some gap in its own power as a system, in Crozier's view, an "uncertainty" that the organization faces (Crozier 1964; also Crozier and Friedberg 1977). This is especially true of three of the five bases of power we describe here.[3] Three prime bases of power are control of (1) a resource, (2) a technical skill, or (3) a body of knowledge, any one critical to the organization. For example, a monopolist may control the raw material supply to an organization, while an expert may control the repair of important and highly complex machinery. To serve as a basis of power, a resource, skill or body of knowledge must first of all be *essential* to the functioning of the organization. Second, it must be *concentrated*, in short supply or else in the hands of one person or a small number of people who cooperate to some extent. And third it must be *nonsubstitutable*, in other words irreplaceable. These three characteristics create the dependency—the organization needs something, and it can get it only from the few people who have it.

A fourth general basis of power stems from legal prerogatives—exclusive rights or privileges to impose choices. Society, through its governments and judicial system, creates a whole set of legal prerogatives which grant power—*formal power*—to various influencers. In the first place governments reserve for themselves the power to authorize the creation of the organization and thereafter impose regulations of various sorts on it. They also vest owners and/or the directors of the organization with certain powers, usually including the right to hire and fire the top executives. And these executives, in turn, usually have the power to hire and perhaps fire the rest of the employees, and to issue orders to them, tempered by other legal prerogatives which grant power to employees and their associations.

The fifth general basis of power derives from access to those who can rely on the other four. That access may be personal. For example, the spouses and friends of government regulators and of chief executives have power by virtue of having the ear of those who exercise legal prerogatives. The control of an important constituency which itself has influence—the customers who buy or the accountants who control the costs—can also be an important basis for power. Likewise power flows to those who can sway other influencers through the mass media—newspaper editors, TV commentators, and the like.

Sometimes access stems from favors traded: Friends and partners grant each other influence over their respective activities. In this case, power stems not from dependency but from *reciprocity*, the gaining of power in one sphere by the giving up of power in another. As we shall see in many examples in this book, the organizational power game is characterized as much by reciprocal as by dependency—onesided, or "asymmetrical"—relationships.[4]

Will and Skill

But having a basis for power is not enough. The individual must act in order to become an influencer, he or she must expend energy, use the basis for power. When the basis is formal, little effort would seem to be required to use it. But many a government has passed legislation that has never been respected, in many cases because it did not bother to establish an agency strong enough to enforce it. Likewise managers often find that their power to give orders means little when not backed up by the effort to ensure that these are in fact carried out. On the other hand, when the basis of power is informal, much effort would seem to be required to use it. If orders cannot be given, battles will have to be won. Yet here too, sometimes the reverse is true. In universities, for example, power often flows to those who take the trouble to serve on the committees. As two researchers noted in one study: "Since few people were involved and those who were involved wandered in and out, someone who was willing to spend time being present could often become influential" (March and Romelaer 1976, p. 272). In the game of power, it is often the squeaky wheel that gets the grease.

In effect, the requirement that energy be expected to achieve outcomes, and the fact that those with the important bases of power have only so much personal energy to expend, means that power gets distributed more widely than our discussions of the bases of power would suggest. Thus, one article shows how the attendants in a mental hospital, at the bottom of the formal hierarchy, could block policy initiatives from the top because collectively they were willing and able to exert far more effort than could the administrators and doctors (Scheff 1961). What this means is that influencers pick and choose their issues, concentrating their efforts on the ones most important to them, and, of course, those they think they can win. Thus Patchen (1974) finds that each influencer stakes out those areas that affect him or her most, deferring elsewhere to other influencers.

Finally, the influencer must not only have some basis for power and expend some energy, but often he or she must also do it in a clever manner, with political skill. Much informal and even formal power backed by great effort has come to naught because of political ineptness. Managers, by exploiting those over whom they have formal power, have often provoked resistance and even mutiny; experts regularly lose reasonable issues in meetings because they fail to marshall adequate support. Political skill means the ability to use the bases of power

effectively—to convince those to whom one has access, to use one's resources, information, and technical skills to their fullest in bargaining, to exercise formal power with a sensitivity to the feelings of others, to know where to concentrate one's energies, to sense what is possible, to organize the necessary alliances.

Related to political skill is a set of intrinsic leadership characteristics —charm, physical strength, attractiveness, what Kipnis calls "personal resources" (1974, p. 88). *Charisma* is the label for that mystical quality that attracts followers to an individual. Some people become powerful simply because others support them; the followers pledge loyalty to a single voice.

Thus power derives from some basis for it is coupled with the efforts and the abilities to use the basis. We shall assume this in the rest of the book, and look more concretely at the channels through which power is exercised, what we call the *means* and *the systems of influence*—the specific instruments influencers are able to use to effect outcomes.

THE CAST OF PLAYERS IN ORDER OF APPEARANCE

Who are these influencers to whom we have referred? We can first distinguish *internal* from *external* influencers. The internal influencers are the full-time employees who use voice, those people charged with making the decision and taking the actions on a permanent, regular basis; it is they who determine the outcomes, which express the goals pursued by the organization. The external influencers are nonemployees who use their bases of influence to try to affect the behavior of the employees.[5] The first two sections of our theory, on the elements of power, describe respectively the *External Coalition*, formed by the external influencers, and the *Internal Coalition*, formed by the internal influencers.

As the word *coalition* was retained in this book only after a good deal of consideration, it is worth explaining here why it was chosen. In general, an attempt was made to avoid jargon whenever it was felt to be possible—for example, employing "chief executive officer" instead of "peak coordinator." "Coalition" proved to be a necessary exception. Because there are no common labels—popular or otherwise—to distinguish the power in from that around the organization, one had to be selected. But why *coalition?* Because it seems to fit best, even though it may be misleading to the reader at first. The word *coalition* is normally used for a group of people who band together to win some issue. As the Hickson research team at the University of Bradford notes, it has the connotation of "engineered agreements and alliances" (Astley et al. 1980, p. 21). Ostensibly, we are not using the word in this sense, at least not at first. We use it more in the sense that Cyert and March (1963) introduced it, as a set of people who bargain among themselves to determine a certain distribution of organizational power. But as we proceed in our discussion, the reader will find the two meanings growing increasingly similar. For one thing, in the External or Internal Coalition, the various influencers band together around or within the same organization to satisfy their needs. They do form some sort of "coalition." As Hickson et al. note in an earlier publication, "it is their coalition of interests that sustains (or destroys) [the] organization" (1976, p. 9).[6] More importantly, we shall see that the external and internal influencers each typically form rather stable systems of power, usually focussed in nature. These become semipermanent means to distribute benefits, and so resemble coalitions in the usual meaning of the term.

Our power play includes ten groups of possible influencers, listed below in order of appearance. The first four are found in the External Coalition:

- First are the owners, who hold the legal title to the organization. Some of them perhaps conceived the idea of founding the organization in the first place and served as

brokers to bring the initial influencers together.
- Second are the *associates*, the suppliers of the organization's input resources, the clients for its output products and services, as well as its trading partners and competitors. It should be noted that only those associates who resort to voice—for example, who engage in contacts of other than a purely economic nature—are counted as influencers in the External Coalition.
- Third are the *employee associations*, that is, unions and professional associations. Again these are included as influencers to the extent that they seek to influence the organization in other than purely economic ways, that is, to use voice to affect decisions and actions directly. Such employee associations see themselves as representatives of more than simple suppliers of labor resources. Note that employee associations are themselves considered *external* influencers, even though they represent people who can be internal influencers. Acting collectively, through their representatives, the employees choose to exert their influence on the organization from outside of its regular decision-making and action-taking channels, much as do owners and clients. (Singly, or even collectively but in different ways, the employees can of course bring their influence to bear directly on these processes, as internal influencers. Later we shall in fact see that it is typically their impotence in the Internal Coalition that causes them to act collectively in the External Coalition.)
- A fourth category comprises the organization's various *publics*, groups representing special or general interests of the public at large. We can divide these into three: (1) such general groups as families, opinion leaders, and the like; (2) special interest groups such as conservation movements or local community institutions; and (3) government in all of its forms—national, regional, local, departments and ministries, regulatory agencies, and so on.
- Another group of influencers, which is really made up of representatives from among the other four, as well as from the internal influencers, are the *directors* of the organization. These constitute a kind of "formal coalition." This group stands at the interface of the External and Internal

Coalitions, but because it meets only intermittently, . . . it is treated as part of the External Coalition.

The Internal Coalition comprises six groups of influencers:

- First is the top or general management of the organization, Papandreou's peak coordinator. We shall refer to this by the single individual at the top of the hierarchy of authority, in standard American terminology, the *chief executive officer*, or CEO.[7]
- Second are the *operators*, those workers who actually produce the products and services, or who provide the direct support to them, such as the machine operators in the manufacturing plant or the doctors and nurses in the hospital.
- Third are the managers who stand in the hierarchy of line authority from the CEO down to the first-line supervisors to whom the operators formally report. We shall refer to these simply as the *line managers*.
- Fourth are the *analysts of the technostructure*, those staff specialists who concern themselves with the design and operation of the systems for planning and for formal control, people such as work study analysts, cost accountants, and long-range planners.
- Fifth is the *support staff*, comprising those staff specialists who provide indirect support to the operators and the rest of the organization, in a business firm, for example, the mailroom staff, the chef in the cafeteria, the researchers, the public relation officers, and the legal counsel.[8]
- Finally, there is an eleventh actor in the organizational power system, one that is technically inanimate but in fact shows every indication of having a life of its own, namely the *ideology* of the organization—the set of beliefs shared by its internal influencers that distinguishes it from other organizations.

Figure 33.1 shows the position of each of these eleven groups schematically. The Internal Coalition is shown in the center, with the Chief Executive Officer at the top, followed, according to the formal hierarchy of authority, by the line managers and then the operators. (In some parts of the discussion, we shall accept these notions of formal

authority, in others, we shall not. For now, we retain them.) Shown at either side to represent their roles as staff members are the analysts and the support staff. Above the CEO is shown the board of directors to which the CEO formally reports. And emanating from the organization is a kind of aura to represent its ideology. Surrounding all this are the various groups of the External Coalition. The owners are shown closest to the top of the hierarchy, and to the board of directors, where they are often inclined to exert their influence. The associates are shown surrounding the operating core where the operators work, the suppliers on the left (input) side and the clients on the right (output) side, with the partners and competitors in between. The employee associations are shown closest to the operators, whom they represent, while the various publics are shown to form a ring around the entire power system, in effect influencing every part of it. Thus the organization of Figure 33.1 can be seen to exist in a complex field of influencer forces.

Each of these eleven groups of players in the organizational power game will be discussed in turn, together with the means of influence they have at their disposal. We assume in this discussion that each is driven by the needs inherent in the roles they play. For example, owners will be described as owners, not as fathers, or Episcopalians, or powerhungry devils. People are of course driven by a variety of needs—by intrinsic values such as the need for control or autonomy, or in Maslow's (1954) needs hierarchy theory, by physiological, safety, love, esteem, and self-actualization needs; by the values instilled in them as children or developed later through socialization and various identifications; by the need to exploit fully whatever skills and abilities they happen to have; by their desire to avoid repetition of painful experiences or to repeat successful ones; by opportunism, the drive to exploit whatever opportunities happen to present themselves. All of these needs contribute to the makeup of each influencer and lead to an infinite variety of behaviors.

FIGURE 33.1 • THE CAST OF PLAYERS

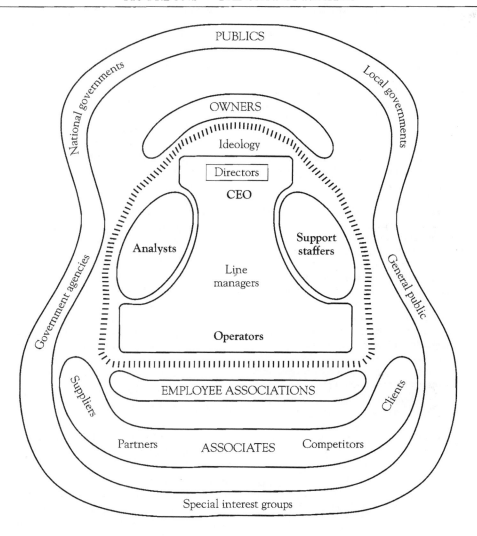

All are, therefore, important to understand. But they are beyond the scope of this book. Here we focus on those behaviors that are dictated strictly by role. We assume throughout that each group discussed above is driven to gain power in or over the organization — in other words, is an influencer; our discussion then focuses on what ends each seeks to attain, what means or systems of influence each has at its disposal, and how much power each tends to end up with by virtue of the role it plays in the power coalition to

which it happens to belong. This is the point of departure for the discussion of our theory.

NOTES

1. Some writers call the influencer a "stakeholder" since he or she maintains a stake in the organization the way a shareholder maintains shares. Others use the term "claimant," in that he or she has a claim on the organization's benefits. Both these

terms, however, would include those who express loyalty as well as voice.

2. There are some interesting linkages among these three options, as Hirschman points out. Exit is sometimes a last resort for frustrated voice, or in the case of a strike (temporary exit), a means to supplement voice. The effect of exit can be "galvanizing" when voice is the norm, or vice versa, as in the case of Ralph Nader who showed consumers how to use voice instead of exit against the automobile companies (p. 125). Of course, an inability to exit forces the disgruntled individual to turn to voice. Hirschman also makes the intriguing point that exit belongs to the study of economics, voice to that of political science. In economic theory, the customer or employee dissatisfied with one firm is supposed to shift to another: ". . . one either exits or one does not; it is impersonal" (p. 15). In contrast, voice is "a far more 'messy' concept because it can be graduated, all the way from hint grumbling to violent protest . . . voice is political action par excellence" (p. 16). But students of political science also have a "blind spot": " . . . exit has often been branded as *criminal*, for it has been labelled desertion, defection, and treason" (p. 17).

3. Related discussions of bases of power can be found in Allison (1971), Crozier and Friedberg (1977), Jacobs (1974), Kipnis (1974), Mechanic (1962), and Pfeffer and Salancik (1978).

4. French and Raven's (1959) five categories of power, as perhaps the most widely quoted typology of power, should be related to these five bases of power. Their "reward" and "coercive" power are used formally by those with legal prerogatives and may be used informally by those who control critical resources, skills, or knowledge (for example, to coerce by holding these back). Their "legitimate" power corresponds most closely to our legal prerogatives and their "expert" power to our critical skills and knowledge. Their fifth category, "referent" power, is not discussed here.

5. As we shall soon see, there are some circumstances in which external influencers can impose decisions directly on the organization, and others in which full-time employees acting in concert through their associations behave as external influencers by trying to affect the behavior of the senior managers. As Pfeffer and Salancik (1978, p. 30) point out, actors can be part of the organization as well as its environment. Nevertheless, the distinction between full-time employees — those individuals with an intensive and regular commitment to the organization — and others will prove to be a useful and important one in all that follows.

6. It might be noted that the Hickson group in the 1980 publication cited earlier (as Astley et al.) decided to replace the word *coalition* by *constellation*. That was tried in this book, but dropped as not having quite the right ring to it.

7. An alternate term which appears frequently in the more recent literature is *dominant coalition*. But we have no wish to prejudice the discussion of the power of one of our groups of influencers by the choice of its title.

8. For a more elaborate description of each of these five groups as well as clarification of the differences between technocratic and support staff and of line and staff in general, see Chapter 2 of the *Structuring* book [Mintzberg, 1979a].

REFERENCES

Allison, G. T. (1971). *Essence of decision: Explaining the Cuban missile crisis*. Boston: Little, Brown.

Astley, W. G., Axelsson, R., Butler, R. J., Hickson, D. J., & Wilson, D. C. (1980). Decision making: Theory III. Working Paper, University of Bradford Management Centre.

Crozier, M. (1964). *The bureaucratic phenomenon*. Chicago: University of Chicago Press.

———. (1974). Why is France blocked? In H. J. Leavitt, L. Pinfield, & E. J. Webb (Eds.). *Organizations of the future: Interaction with the external environment*. New York: Praeger.

———, & Friedberg, E. (1977). *L'acteur et le système*. Paris: Editions du Seuil.

Cyert, R. M., & March, J. G. (1963). *A behavioral theory of the firm*. Englewood Cliffs, NJ: Prentice-Hall.

French, J. R. P., Jr., & Raven, B. (1959). The bases of social power. In D. Cartwright (Ed.). *Studies in social power* (pp. 150–167). Ann Arbor: Institute for Social Research, University of Michigan.

Hickson, D. J., Butler, R. J., Axelsson, R., & Wilson, D. (1976). Decisive coalitions. Paper presented to International Conference on Coordination and Control of Group and Organizational Performance, Munich, West Germany.

Hirschman, A. O. (1970). *Exit, voice, and loyalty: Responses to decline in firms, organizations, and states*. Cambridge, MA: Harvard University Press.

Jacobs, D. (1974). Dependency and vulnerability: An exchange approach to the control of organizations. *Administrative Science Quarterly*, 45–59.

Kipnis, D. (1974). The powerholder. In J. T. Tedeschi (Ed.), *Perspectives on social power* (pp. 82–122). Chicago: Aldine.

March, J. G., & Romelaer, P. J. (1976). Position and presence in the drift of decisions. In J. G. March & J. P. Olsen (Eds.), *Ambiguity and choice in organizations*. Bergen, Norway: Universitetsforlaget.

Maslow, A. H. (1954). *Motivation and personality*. New York: Harper & Row.

Mechanic, D. (1962). Sources of power of lower participants in complex organizations. *Administrative Science Quarterly*, 349–364.

Mintzberg, H. (1979a). *The structuring of organizations: A synthesis of the research*. Englewood Cliffs, NJ: Prentice-Hall.

Patchen, M. (1974). The locus and basis of influence on organizational decisions. *Organizational Behavior and Human Performance*, 195–221.

Pfeffer, N., and Salancik, G. R. (1978). *The external control of organizations: A resource dependence perspective*. New York: Harper & Row.

Scheff, T. J. (1961). Control over policy by attendants in a mental hospital. *Journal of Health and Human Behavior*, 93–105.

34

Power Failure in Management Circuits

Rosabeth Moss Kanter

Power is America's last dirty word. It is easier to talk about money—and much easier to talk about sex—than it is to talk about power. People who have it deny it; people who want it do not want to appear to hunger for it; and people who engage in its machinations do so secretly.

Yet, because it turns out to be a critical element in effective managerial behavior, power should come out from undercover. Having searched for years for those styles or skills that would identify capable organization leaders, many analysts, like myself, are rejecting individual traits or situational appropriateness as key and finding the sources of a leader's real power.

Access to resources and information and the ability to act quickly make it possible to accomplish more and to pass on more resources and information to subordinates. For this reason, people tend to prefer bosses with "clout." When employees perceive their manager as influential upward and outward, their status is enhanced by association and they generally have high morale and feel less critical or resistant to their boss.[1] More powerful leaders are also more likely to delegate (they are too busy to do it all themselves), to reward talent, and to build a team that places subordinates in significant positions.

Powerlessness, in contrast, tends to breed bossiness rather than true leadership. In large organizations, at least, it is powerlessness that often creates ineffective, desultory management and petty, dictatorial, rules-minded managerial styles. Accountability without power—responsibility for results without the resources to get them—creates frustration and failure. People who see themselves as weak and powerless and find their subordinates resisting or discounting them tend to use more punishing forms of influence. If organizational power can "ennoble," then, recent research shows, organizational powerlessness can (with apologies to Lord Acton) "corrupt."[2]

So perhaps power, in the organization at least, does not deserve such a bad reputation. Rather than connoting only dominance, control, and oppression, *power* can mean efficacy and capacity—something managers and executives need to move the organization toward its goals. Power in organizations is analogous in simple terms to physical power: it is the ability to mobilize resources (human and material) to get things done. The true sign of power, then, is accomplishment—not fear, terror, or tyranny. Where power is "on," the system can be productive; where the power is "off," the system bogs down. . . .

WHERE DOES POWER COME FROM?

The effectiveness that power brings evolves from two kinds of capacities: first, access to resources, information, and support necessary to carry out a task; and, second, ability to get cooperation in doing what is necessary. (Table 34.1 identifies some symbols of an individual manager's power.) . . .

TABLE 34.1 • SOME COMMON SYMBOLS OF A MANAGER'S ORGANIZATIONAL
POWER (INFLUENCE UPWARD AND OUTWARD)

To What Extent a Manager Can—

Intercede favorably on behalf of someone in trouble with the organization.

Get a desirable placement for a talented subordinate.

Get approval for expenditures beyond the budget.

Get above-average salary increases for subordinates.

Get items on the agenda at policy meetings.

Get fast access to top decision makers.

Get regular, frequent access to top decision makers.

Get early information about decisions and policy shifts.

We can regard the uniquely organizational sources of power as consisting of three "lines":

1. *Lines of Supply.* Influence outward, over the environment, means that managers have the capacity to bring in the things that their own organizational domain needs—materials, money, resources to distribute as rewards, and perhaps even prestige.
2. *Lines of Information.* To be effective, managers need to be "in the know" in both the formal and the informal sense.
3. *Lines of Support.* In a formal framework, a manager's job parameters need to allow for nonordinary action, for a show of discretion or exercise of judgment. Thus managers need to know that they can assume innovative, risk-taking activities without having to go through the stifling multilayered approval process. And, informally, managers need the backing of other important figures in the organization whose tacit approval becomes another resource they bring to their own work unit as well as a sign of the manager's being "in."

Note that productive power has to do with *connections* with other parts of a system. Such systemic aspects of power derive from two sources—job activities and political alliances:

1. Power is most easily accumulated when one has a job that is designed and located to allow discretion (nonroutinized action permitting flexible, adaptive, and creative contributions), recognition (visibility and notice), and relevance (being central to pressing organizational problems).
2. Power also comes when one has relatively close contact with sponsors (higher-level people who confer approval, prestige, or backing), peer networks (circles of acquaintanceship that provide reputation and information, the grapevine often being faster than formal communication channels), and subordinates (who can be developed to relieve managers of some of their burdens and to represent the manager's point of view).

When managers are in powerful situations, it is easier for them to accomplish more. Because the tools are there, they are likely to be highly motivated and, in turn, to be able to motivate subordinates. Their activities are more likely to be on target and to net them successes. They can flexibly interpret or shape policy to meet the needs of particular areas, emergent situations, or sudden environmental shifts. They gain the respect and cooperation that attributed power brings. Subordinates' talents are resources rather than threats. And, because powerful managers have so many lines of connection and thus are oriented outward, they tend to let go of control downward, developing more independently functioning lieutenants.

The powerless live in a different world. Lacking the supplies, information, or support to make things happen easily, they may turn instead to the ultimate weapon of those who lack productive power—oppressive

TABLE 34.2 • WAYS ORGANIZATIONAL FACTORS CONTRIBUTE TO POWER OR POWERLESSNESS

Factors	Generates Power When Factor Is	Generates Powerlessness When Factor Is
Rules inherent in the job	few	many
Predecessors in the job	few	many
Established routines	few	many
Task variety	high	low
Rewards for reliability/predictability	few	many
Rewards for unusual performance/innovation	many	few
Flexibility around use of people	high	low
Approvals needed for nonroutine decisions	few	many
Physical location	central	distant
Publicity about job activities	high	low
Relation of tasks to current problem areas	central	peripheral
Focus of tasks	outside work unit	inside work unit
Interpersonal contact in the job	high	low
Contact with senior officials	high	low
Participation in programs, conferences, meetings	high	low
Participation in problem-solving task forces	high	low
Advancement prospects of subordinates	high	low

power: holding others back and punishing with whatever threats they can muster.

Table 34.2 summarizes some of the major ways in which variables in the organization and in job design contribute to either power or powerlessness.

POSITIONS OF POWERLESSNESS

Understanding what it takes to have power and recognizing the classic behavior of the powerless can immediately help managers make sense out of a number of familiar organizational problems that are usually attributed to inadequate people:

The ineffectiveness of first-line supervisors.
The petty interest protection and conservatism of staff professionals.
The crises of leadership at the top.

Instead of blaming the individuals involved in organizational problems, let us look at the positions people occupy. . . .

First-line Supervisors

Because an employee's most important work relationship is with his or her supervisor, when many of them talk about "the company," they mean their immediate boss. Thus a supervisor's behavior is an important determinant of the average employee's relationship to work and is in itself a critical link in the production chain.

Yet I know of no U.S. corporate management entirely satisfied with the performance of its supervisors. Most see them as supervising too closely and not training their people. In one manufacturing company where direct laborers were asked on a survey how they learned their job, on a list of seven possibilities "from my supervisor" ranked next to last. (Only company training programs ranked worse.) Also, it is said that supervisors do not translate company policies into practice—for instance, that they do not carry out the right of every employee to frequent performance reviews or to career counseling.

In court cases charging race or sex discrimination, first-line supervisors are frequently cited as the "discriminating official."[3] And, in studies of innovative work redesign and quality of work life projects, they often appear as the implied villains; they are the ones who are said to undermine the program or interfere with its effectiveness. In short, they are often seen as "not sufficiently managerial." . . .

A large part of the problem lies in the position itself—one that almost universally creates powerlessness.

First-line supervisors are "people in the middle," and that has been seen as the source of many of their problems.[4] But by recognizing that first-line supervisors are caught between higher management and workers, we only begin to skim the surface of the problem. There is practically no other organizational category as subject to powerlessness.

First, these supervisors may be at a virtual dead end in their careers. Even in companies where the job used to be a stepping stone to higher-level management jobs, it is now common practice to bring in MBAs from the outside for those positions. Thus moving from the ranks of direct labor into supervision may mean, essentially, getting "stuck" rather than moving upward. Because employees do not perceive supervisors as eventually joining the leadership circles of the organization, they may see them as lacking the high-level contacts needed to have clout. Indeed, sometimes turnover among supervisors is so high that workers feel they can outwait—and outwit—any boss.

Second, although they lack clout, with little in the way of support from above, supervisors are forced to administer programs or explain policies that they have no hand in shaping. In one company, as part of a new personnel program supervisors were required to conduct counseling interviews with employees. But supervisors were not trained to do this and were given no incentives to get involved. Counseling was just

another obligation. Then managers suddenly encouraged the workers to bypass their supervisors or to put pressure on them. The personnel staff brought them together and told them to demand such interviews as a basic right. If supervisors had not felt powerless before, they did after that squeeze from below, engineered from above.

The people they supervise can also make life hard for them in numerous ways. This often happens when a supervisor has himself or herself risen up from the ranks. Peers that have not made it are resentful or derisive of their former colleague, whom they now see as trying to lord it over them. Often it is easy for workers to break the rules and let a lot of things slip.

Yet first-line supervisors are frequently judged according to rules and regulations while being limited by other regulations in what disciplinary actions they can take. They often lack the resources to influence or reward people; after all, workers are guaranteed their pay and benefits by someone other than their supervisors. Supervisors cannot easily control events; rather, they must react to them. . . .

It is not surprising, then, that supervisors frequently manifest symptoms of powerlessness: overly close supervision, rules-mindedness, and a tendency to do the job themselves rather than to train their people (since job skills may be one of the few remaining things they feel good about). Perhaps this is why they sometimes stand as roadblocks between their subordinates and the higher reaches of the company.

Staff Professionals

Also working under conditions that can lead to organizational powerlessness are the staff specialists. As advisers behind the scenes, staff people must sell their programs and bargain for resources, but unless they get themselves entrenched in organizational power networks, they have little in the way of favors to exchange. They are seen as useful adjuncts to the primary tasks of the organization but inessential in a day-

Women Managers Experience Special Power Failures

The traditional problems of women in management are illustrative of how formal and informal practices can combine to engender powerlessness. Historically, women in management have found their opportunities in more routine, low-profile jobs. In staff positions, where they serve in support capacities to line managers but have no line responsibilities of their own, or in supervisory jobs managing "stuck" subordinates, they are not in a position either to take the kinds of risks that build credibility or to develop their own team by pushing bright subordinates.

Such jobs, which have few favors to trade, tend to keep women out of the mainstream of the organization. This lack of clout, coupled with the greater difficulty anyone who is "different" has in getting into the information and support networks, has meant that merely by organizational situation women in management have been more likely than men to be rendered structurally powerless. This is one reason those women who have achieved power have often had family connections that put them in the mainstream of the organization's social circles.

A disproportionate number of women managers are found among first-line supervisors or staff professionals; and they, like men in those circumstances, are likely to be organizationally powerless. But the behavior of other managers can contribute to the powerlessness of women in management in a number of less obvious ways.

One way other managers can make a woman powerless is by patronizingly overprotecting her: putting her in "a safe job," not giving her enough to do to prove herself, and not suggesting her for high-risk, visible assignments. This protectiveness is sometimes born of "good" intentions to give her every chance to succeed (why stack the deck against her?). Out of managerial concerns, out of awareness that a woman may be up against situations that men simply do not have to face, some very well-meaning managers protect their female managers ("It's a jungle, so why send her into it?").

Overprotectiveness can also mask a manager's fear of association with a woman should she fail. One senior bank official at a level below vice president told me about his concerns with respect to a high-performing, financially experienced woman reporting to him. Despite *his* overwhelmingly positive work experiences with her, he was still afraid to recommend her for other assignments because he felt it was a personal risk. "What if other managers are not as accepting of women as I am?" he asked. "I know I'd be sticking my neck out; they would take her more because of my endorsement than her qualifications. And what if she doesn't make it? My judgment will be on the line."

Overprotection is relatively benign compared with rendering a person powerless by providing obvious signs of lack of managerial support. For example, allowing someone supposedly in authority to be bypassed easily means that no one else has to take him or her seriously. If a woman's immediate supervisor or other managers listen willingly to criticism of her and show they are concerned every time a negative comment comes up and that they assume she must be at fault, then they are helping to undercut her. If managers let other people know that they have concerns about this person or that they are testing her to see how she does, then they are inviting other people to look for signs of inadequacy or failure.

Furthermore, people assume they can afford to bypass women because they "must be uninformed" or "don't know the ropes." Even though women may be respected for their competence or expertise, they are not necessarily seen as being informed beyond the technical requirements of the job. There may be a grain of historical truth in this. Many women come to senior management positions as "outsiders" rather than up through the usual channels.

Also, because until very recently men have not felt comfortable seeing women as businesspeople (business clubs have traditionally excluded women), they have tended to seek each other out for informal socializing. Anyone, male or female, seen as organizationally naive and lacking sources of "inside dope" will find his or her own lines of information limited.

Finally, even when women are able to achieve some power on their own, they have not necessarily been able to translate such personal credibility into an organizational power base. To create a network of supporters out of individual clout requires that a person pass on and share power, that subordinates and peers be empowered by virtue of their connection with that person. Traditionally, neither men nor women have seen women as capable of sponsoring others, even though they may be capable of achieving and succeeding on their own. Women have been viewed as the *recipients of sponsorship rather than as the sponsors themselves.* . . .

Viewing managers in terms of power and powerlessness helps explain two familiar stereotypes about women and leadership in organizations: that no one wants a woman boss (although studies show that anyone who has ever had a woman boss is likely to have had a positive experience), and that the reason no one wants a woman boss is that women are "too controlling, rules-minded, and petty."

The first stereotype simply makes clear that power is important to leadership. Underneath the preference for men is the assumption that, given the current distribution of people in organizational leadership positions, men are more likely than women to be in positions to achieve power and, therefore, to share their power with others. Similarly, the "bossy woman boss" stereotype is a perfect picture of powerlessness. All of those traits are just as characteristic of men who are powerless, but women are slightly more likely, because of circumstances I have mentioned, to find themselves powerless than are men. Women with power in the organization are just as effective — and preferred — as men.

Recent interviews conducted with about 600 bank managers show that, when a woman exhibits the petty traits of powerlessness, people assume that she does so "because she is a woman." A striking difference is that, when a man engages in the same behavior, people assume the behavior is a matter of his own individual style and characteristics and do not conclude that it reflects on the suitability of men for management.

---

to-day operating sense. This disenfranchisement occurs particularly when staff jobs consist of easily routinized administrative functions which are out of the mainstream of the currently relevant areas and involve little innovative decision making.

Furthermore, in some organizations, unless they have had previous line experience, staff people tend to be limited in the number of jobs into which they can move. Specialists' ladders are often very short, and professionals are just as likely to get "stuck" in such jobs as people are in less prestigious clerical or factory positions.

Staff people, unlike those who are being groomed for important line positions, may be hired because of a special expertise or particular background. But management rarely pays any attention to developing them into more general organizational resources. Lacking growth prospects themselves and working alone or in very small teams, they are not in a position to develop others or pass on power to them. They miss out on an important way that power can be accumulated. . . .

Staff people tend to act out their powerlessness by becoming turf-minded. They create islands within the organization. They set themselves up as the only ones who can control professional standards and judge their own work. They create sometimes false distinctions between themselves as experts (no one else could possibly do what they do) and lay people, and this continues to keep them out of the mainstream.

One form such distinctions take is a combination of disdain when line managers attempt to act in areas the professionals think are their preserve and of subtle refusal to support the managers' efforts. Or staff groups battle with each other for control of new "problem areas," with the result that no one really handles the issue at all. To cope with their essential powerlessness, staff groups may try to evaluate their own status and draw boundaries between themselves and others.

When staff jobs are treated as final resting places for people who have reached their level of competence in the organization — a good shelf on which to dump managers who are too old to go anywhere but too young to retire — then staff groups can also become pockets of conservatism, resistant to change. Their own exclusion from the risk-taking action may make them resist *anyone's* innovative proposals. In the past, personnel departments, for example, have sometimes been the last in their organization to know about innovations in human resource development or to be interested in applying them.

Top Executives

Despite the great resources and responsibilities concentrated at the top of an organization, leaders can be powerless for reasons that are not very different from those that affect staff and supervisors: lack of supplies, information, and support.

We have faith in leaders because of their ability to make things happen in the larger world, to create possibilities for everyone else, and to attract resources to the organization. These are their supplies. But influence outward—the source of much credibility downward—can diminish as environments change, setting terms and conditions out of the control of the leaders. Regardless of top management's grand plans for the organization, the environment presses. At the very least, things going on outside the organization can deflect a leader's attention and drain energy. And more detrimental, decisions made elsewhere can have severe consequences for the organization and affect top management's sense of power and thus its operating style inside. . . .

As powerlessness in lower levels of organizations can manifest itself in overly routinized jobs where performance measures are oriented to rules and absence of change, so it can at upper levels as well. Routine work often drives out nonroutine work. Accomplishment becomes a question of nailing down details. Short-term results provide immediate gratifications and satisfy stockholders or other constituencies with limited interests.

It takes a powerful leader to be willing to risk short-term deprivations in order to bring about desired long-term outcomes. Much as first-line supervisors are tempted to focus on daily adherence to rules, leaders are tempted to focus on short-term fluctuations and lose sight of long-term objectives. The dynamics of such a situation are self-reinforcing. The more the long-term goals go unattended, the more a leader feels powerless and the greater the scramble to prove that he or she is in control of daily events at least. The more he is involved in the organization as a short-term Mr. Fix-it, the more out of control of long-term objectives he is, and the more ultimately powerless he is likely to be.

Credibility for the top executives often comes from doing the extraordinary: exercising discretion, creating, inventing, planning, and acting in nonroutine ways. But since routine problems look easier and more manageable, require less change and consent on the part of anyone else, and lend themselves to instant solutions that can make any leader look good temporarily, leaders may avoid the risk by taking over what their subordinates should be doing. Ultimately, a leader may succeed in getting all the trivial problems dumped on his or her desk. This can establish expectations even for leaders attempting more challenging tasks. When Warren Bennis was president of the University of Cincinnati, a professor called him when the heat was down in a classroom. In writing about this incident, Bennis commented, "I suppose he expected me to grab a wrench and fix it."[5]

People at the top need to insulate themselves from the routine operations of the organization in order to develop and exercise power. But this very insulation can lead to another source of powerlessness—lack of information. In one multinational corporation, top executives who are sealed off in a large, distant office, flattered and virtually babied by aides, are frustrated by their distance from the real action.[6]

At the top, the concern for secrecy and privacy is mixed with real loneliness. In one bank, organization members were so accustomed to never seeing the top leaders that when a new senior vice president went to the branch offices to look around, they had suspicion, even fear, about his intentions.

Thus leaders who are cut out of an organization's information networks understand neither what is really going on at lower levels nor that their isolation may be having negative effects. All too often top executives design "beneficial" new employee programs or declare a new humanitarian policy (e.g., "Participatory management is now our style") only to find the policy ignored or mistrusted because it is perceived as coming from uncaring bosses.

The information gap has more serious consequences when executives are so insulated from the rest of the organization or from other decision makers that, as Nixon so dramatically did, they fail to see their own impending downfall. Such insulation is partly a matter of organizational position and, in some cases, of executive style.

For example, leaders may create closed inner circles consisting of "doppelgängers," people just like themselves, who are their principal sources of organizational information and tell them only what they want to know. The reasons for the distortions are varied: key aides want to relieve the leader of burdens, they think just like the leader, they want to protect their own positions of power, or the familiar "kill the messenger" syndrome makes people close to top executives reluctant to be the bearers of bad news.

Finally, just as supervisors and lower-level managers need their supporters in order to be and feel powerful, so do top executives. But for them sponsorship may not be so much a matter of individual endorsement as an issue of support by larger sources of legitimacy in the society. For top executives the problem is not to fit in among peers; rather, the question is whether the public at large and other organization members perceive a common interest which they see the executives as promoting. . . .

When common purpose is lost, the system's own politics may reduce the capacity of those at the top to act. Just as managing decline seems to create a much more passive and reactive stance than managing growth, so does mediating among conflicting inter-ests. When what is happening outside and inside their organizations is out of control, many people at the top turn into decline managers and dispute mediators. Neither is a particularly empowering role.

Thus when top executives lose their own lines of supply, lines of information, and lines of support, they too suffer from a kind of powerlessness. The temptation for them then is to pull in every shred of power they can and to decrease the power available to other people to act. Innovation loses out in favor of control. Limits rather than targets are set. Financial goals are met by reducing "overhead" (people) rather than by giving people the tools and discretion to increase their own productive capacity. Dictatorial statements come down from the top, spreading the mentality of powerlessness farther until the whole organization becomes sluggish and people concentrate on protecting what they can. . . .

TO EXPAND POWER, SHARE IT

In no case am I saying that people in the three hierarchical levels described are always powerless, but they are susceptible to common conditions that can contribute to powerlessness. Table 34.3 summarizes the most common symptoms of powerlessness for each level and some typical sources of that behavior. . . .

The absence of ways to prevent individual and social harm causes the polity to feel it must surround people in power with constraints, regulations, and laws that limit the arbitrary use of their authority. But if oppressive power corrupts, then so does the absence of productive power. In large organizations, powerlessness can be a bigger problem than power. . . .

Organizational power can grow, in part, by being shared. We do not yet know enough about new organizational forms to say whether productive power is infinitely expandable or where we reach the point of diminishing returns. But we do know that sharing power is different from giving or

TABLE 34.3 • COMMON SYMPTOMS AND SOURCES OF POWERLESSNESS
FOR THREE KEY ORGANIZATIONAL POSITIONS

Position	Symptoms	Sources
First-line supervisors	Close, rules-minded supervision	Routine, rules-minded jobs with little control over lines of supply
	Tendency to do things oneself, blocking of subordinates' development and information	Limited lines of information
	Resistant, underproducing subordinates	Limited advancement or involvement prospects for oneself/subordinates
Staff professionals	Turf protection, information control	Routine tasks seen as peripheral to "real tasks" of line organization
		Retreat into professionalism
		Block careers
	Conservative resistance to change	Easy replacement by outside experts
Top executives	Focus on internal cutting, short-term results, "punishing"	Uncontrollable lines of supply because of environmental changes
	Dictatorial top-down communications	Limited or blocked lines of information about lower levels of organization
	Retreat to comfort of like-minded lieutenants	Diminished lines of support because of challenges to legitimacy (e.g., from the public or special interest groups)

throwing it away. Delegation does not mean abdication.

Some basic lessons could be translated from the field of economics to the realm of organizations and management. Capital investment in plants and equipment is not the only key to productivity. The productive capacity of nations, like organizations, grows if the skill base is upgraded. People with the tools, information, and support to make more informed decisions and act more quickly can often accomplish more. By empowering others, a leader does not decrease his power; instead he may increase it—especially if the whole organization performs better. . . .

Also, if the powerless bosses could be encouraged to share some of the power they do have, their power would grow. Yet, of course, only those leaders who feel secure about their own power outward—their lines of supply, information, and support—can see empowering subordinates as a gain rather than as a loss. The two sides of power (getting it and giving it) are closely connected.

There are important lessons here for both subordinates and those who want to change organizations, whether executives or change agents. Instead of resisting or criticizing a powerless boss, which only increases the boss's feeling of powerlessness and need to control, subordinates instead might concentrate on helping the boss become more powerful. Managers might make pockets of ineffectiveness in the organization more productive not by training or replacing individuals but by structural solutions such as opening supply and support lines.

Similarly, organizational change agents who make a new program or policy to succeed should make sure that the change itself does not render any other level of the organization powerless. In making changes, it is wise to make sure that the key people in the level or two directly above and in neighboring functions are sufficiently involved, informed, and taken into account, so that the program can be used to build their own sense of power also. If such involvement is impossible, then it is better to move these people out of the territory altogether than to leave behind a group from whom some power has been removed and who might resist and undercut the program.

In part, of course, spreading power means educating people to this new definition of it. But words alone will not make the difference; managers will need the real experience of a new way of managing. . . .

Naturally, people need to have power before they can learn to share it. Exhorting managers to change their leadership styles is rarely useful by itself. In one large plant of a major electronics company, first-line production supervisors were the source of numerous complaints from managers who saw them as major roadblocks to overall plant productivity and as insufficiently skilled supervisors. So the plant personnel staff undertook two pilot programs to increase the supervisor's effectiveness. The first program was based on a traditional competency and training model aimed at teaching the specific skills of successful supervisors. The second program, in contrast, was designed to empower the supervisors by directly affecting their flexibility, access to resources, connections with higher-level officials, and control over working conditions. . . .

One might wonder why more organizations do not adopt such empowering strategies. There are standard answers: that giving up control is threatening to people who

have fought for every shred of it; that people do not want to share power with those they look down on; that managers fear losing their own place and special privileges in the system; that "predictability" often rates higher than "flexibility" as an organizational value; and so forth.

But I would also put skepticism about employee abilities high on the list. Many modern bureaucratic systems are designed to minimize dependence on individual intelligence by making routine as many decisions as possible. So it often comes as a genuine surprise to top executives that people doing the more routine jobs could, indeed, make sophisticated decisions or use resources entrusted to them in intelligent ways. . . .

NOTES

1. Donald C. Pelz, "Influence: A Key to Effective Leadership in the First-Line Supervisor," *Personnel*, November 1952, p. 209.
2. See my book, *Men and Women of the Corporation* (New York: Basic Books, 1977), pp. 164–205; and David Kipnis, *The Powerholders* (Chicago: University of Chicago Press, 1976).
3. William E. Fulmer, "Supervisory Selection: The Acid Test of Affirmative Action," *Personnel*, November-December 1976, p. 40.
4. See my chapter (coauthor, Barry A. Stein), "Life in the Middle: Getting In, Getting Up, and Getting Along," in *Life in Organizations*, eds. Rosabeth M. Kanter and Barry A. Stein (New York: Basic Books, 1979).
5. Warren Bennis, *The Unconscious Conspiracy: Why Leaders Can't Lead* (New York: AMACOM, 1976).
6. See my chapter, "How the Top Is Different," in *Life in Organizations*.

CHAPTER 7

Organizational Culture Theory

Organizational culture is the culture that exists in an organization, something akin to a societal culture. It is composed of many intangible phenomena, such as values, beliefs, assumptions, perceptions, behavioral norms, artifacts, and patterns of behavior. It is the unseen and unobservable force that is always behind the organizational activities that can be seen and observed. According to Kilmann and others (1985), organizational culture is a social energy that moves people to act. "Culture is to the organization what personality is to the individual—a hidden, yet unifying theme that provides meaning, direction, and mobilization."

The organizational culture perspective is a set of organization theories with its own assumptions about organizational realities and relationships. It is yet another way of viewing, thinking about, studying, and trying to understand organizations. Like power and politics organization theory (Chapter 6), the organizational culture perspective represents a counterculture within organization theory. Its assumptions, units of analysis, research methods, and approaches are very different from those of the dominant, rational, "modern" structural, organizational economics, and systems/environment theories. The organizational culture perspective challenges the basic views of these more rational perspectives about, for example, how organizations make decisions and how and why organizations— and people in organizations—act as they do.

In the "modern" structural, organizational economics, and systems/environment theories of organization, organizations are assumed to be rational-utilitarian institutions whose primary purpose is to accomplish established goals. People in positions of formal authority set goals. The primary questions for organization theory thus involve how best to design and manage organizations so that they achieve their declared purposes effectively and efficiently. The personal preferences of organizational members are restrained by systems of formal rules, authority, and norms of rational behavior. In a 1982 *Phi Delta Kappan* article, however, Karl Weick argues that four organizational conditions must exist in order for the basic assumptions of the rational theories to be valid:

1. a self-correcting system of interdependent people;
2. consensus on objectives and methods;
3. coordination achieved through sharing information; and
4. predictable organizational problems and solutions.

But, Weick concludes, these conditions seldom if ever exist in large modern organizations.

Thus, the organizational culture perspective rejects the assumptions of the "modern" structural, organizational economics, and systems/environment theories—as does the power and politics perspective. Instead, it assumes that many organizational behaviors and decisions are in effect predetermined by the patterns of basic assumptions held by members of an organization. These patterns of assumptions continue to exist and to influence behaviors in an organization because they repeatedly have led people to make decisions that "worked in the past." With repeated use, the assumptions slowly drop out of people's consciousness but continue to influence organizational decisions and behaviors even when the environment changes and different decisions are needed. They become the underlying, unquestioned, but largely forgotten, reasons for "the way we do things here"—even when the ways may no longer be appropriate. They are so basic, so ingrained, and so completely accepted that no one thinks about or remembers them.

A strong organizational culture can control organizational behavior; for example, an organizational culture can block an organization from making changes that are needed to adapt to new market dynamics or new information technologies. From the organizational culture perspective, systems of formal rules, authority, and norms of rational behavior do not restrain the personal preferences of organizational members. Instead, they are controlled by cultural norms, values, beliefs, and assumptions. In order to understand or predict how an organization will behave under varying circumstances, one must know and understand the organization's patterns of basic assumptions—its organizational culture.

Organizational cultures differ for several reasons. First, what has worked repeatedly for one organization may not for another, so basic assumptions may differ. Second, an organization's culture is shaped by many factors, including, for example, the societal culture in which it resides; its technologies, markets, and competition; and the personality of its founder(s) or dominant early leaders. Some organizational cultures are more distinctive than others; some organizations have strong, unified, pervasive cultures, whereas others have weaker or less pervasive ones; some organizational cultures are quite pervasive, whereas others may have many *subcultures* existing in different functional or geographical areas (Ott, 1989, Chapter 4).

Knowledge of an organization's structure, information systems, strategic planning processes, markets, technology, goals, and so forth can provide clues about an organization's culture, but not accurately or reliably. As a consequence, an organization's behavior cannot be understood or predicted by studying its structural or systems elements; its organizational culture must be studied. And the positivist, quantitative, quasi-experimental research methods favored by the "modern" structural, organizational economics, and systems/environment schools cannot identify or measure unconscious, virtually forgotten basic assumptions. Yet, quantitative research using quasi-experimental designs, control groups, computers, multivariate analyses, heuristic models, and the like are the essential tools of the rational schools. The organizational culture theories (along with theories from the power and politics school) have relied principally on qualitative research methods such as ethnography and participant observation.

Earlier, we said that organizational culture represents a counterculture within the field of organization theory. The reasons should be becoming evident. The organizational culture perspective believes that the "modern" structural, organizational economics, and systems/environment schools of organization theory are using the wrong tools (or the wrong "lenses") to look at the wrong organizational elements in their attempts to understand and predict organizational behavior.

It takes courage to challenge the basic views of the more mainstream rational schools. Yet this is what the organizational culture and the power and politics perspectives are doing when they advocate different ways or means of looking at and working with organizations.

For example, from the organizational culture perspective, AT&T's basic problems follow-ing deregulation and court-ordered splintering of the Bell system were not in its structure, information systems, or people. Rather, it was an organizational culture that no longer was appropriate for AT&T's deregulated world. The longstanding AT&T culture had been centered on assumptions about (1) the value of technical superiority, (2) AT&T's posses-sion of technical superiority, and thus (3) AT&T's rightful dominance in the telephone and telecommunications market. Therefore, working to improve such things as AT&T's goals, structure, differentiation and integration processes, strategic plans, and information systems could not solve AT&T's monumental problems. The solution required changing an ingrained organizational culture — changing basic unconscious assumptions about what was required to be successful in a competitive telecommunications market.

Almost all of the literature about the organizational culture perspective has been pub-lished in the last twenty-five years. Thus, the organizational culture perspective suffers from the problems and limitations of youthfulness. Although phrases such as *organizational culture* and *culture of a factory* can be found in a few books on management written as early as the 1950s (for example, Elliott Jaques's 1951 book *The Changing Culture of a Factory* and William H. Whyte Jr.'s 1956 book about conformity in business, *The Organization Man*), few students of management or organizations paid attention to the nature and content of organizational culture until about 1981.

During the 1960s and early 1970s, several books on organizational and professional socialization processes received wide attention. As useful as these earlier works were, they *assumed* the presence of organizational or professional cultures and proceeded to examine issues involving the match between individuals and cultures. Some of the more widely read of these included the 1961 book by Becker, Geer, Hughes, and Strauss, *Boys in White*, which chronicled the processes used to socialize students into the medical profession; Herbert Kaufman's 1960 study, *The Forest Ranger*, of how the United States Forest Service developed the "will and capacity to conform" among its remotely stationed rangers; Ritti and Funkhouser's 1977 humorous-but-serious look at organizations, *The Ropes to Skip and the Ropes to Know*; and John Van Maanen's "Police Socialization" (1975) and "Breaking In: Socialization to Work" (1976).

During this same period, Edgar H. Schein contributed significantly to the knowledge about organizational and professional socialization processes in numerous writings, includ-ing, for example, "How to Break In the College Graduate" (1964), "Organizational Social-ization and the Profession of Management" (1968), and *Career Dynamics: Matching Individ-ual and Organizational Needs* (1978). Once again, however, these earlier writings did not address important questions such as how cultures are formed or changed, how cultures affect leadership, or the relationship between culture and strategic planning (establishing organi-zational directions); rather, they focused on the process of socializing employees into exist-ing organizational cultures and the impacts of existing cultures on organizational members.

A different orientation to cultures in organizations started to appear in the organization theory literature during the late 1970s, and it developed into a "wave" in the mid-1980s. This orientation is known as the symbolic frame, symbolic management, or organizational symbolism. Bolman and Deal (1997) identify the basic tenets of symbolic management as follows:

1. The meaning or the interpretation of what is happening in organizations is more important than what actually is happening.

2. Ambiguity and uncertainty, which are prevalent in most organizations, preclude rational problem-solving and decision-making processes.
3. People use symbols to reduce ambiguity and to gain a sense of direction when they are faced with uncertainty.

Peter Berger and Thomas Luckmann paved the way for this perspective in their 1967 book, *The Social Construction of Reality* (1967), in which they define meanings as "socially constructed realities." Things are not real in and of themselves; the perceptions of them are, in fact, reality. As W. I. Thomas wrote (1923), "If people believe things are real, they are real in their consequences." According to the organizational culture perspective, meaning (reality) is established by and among the people in organizations—by the organizational culture. Experimenters have shown that there is a strong relationship between culturally determined values and the perception of symbols. People will distort the perceptions of symbols according to the need for what is symbolized (Davis, 1963). Thus, organizational symbolism is an integral part of the organizational culture perspective.

The turning point for the organizational culture/symbolic management perspective arrived almost overnight in the 1980s. Organizational culture became a hot topic in books, journals, and periodicals aimed at management practitioners and academicians, including the 1982 best-seller by Thomas Peters and Robert Waterman Jr. *In Search of Excellence* and its sequels; Terrence Deal and Allan Kennedy's 1982 book *Corporate Cultures*; *Fortune* magazine's 1983 story "The Corporate Culture Vultures"; and *Business Week's* May 14, 1984, cover story "Changing a Corporate Culture." The first comprehensive, theoretically based, integrative writings on organizational culture were published in 1984–1986, including Thomas Sergiovanni and John Corbally's heady reader *Leadership and Organizational Culture* (1984); Edgar Schein's pioneering *Organizational Culture and Leadership* (1985); Vijay Sathe's *Culture and Related Corporate Realities* (1985); the first of Ralph Kilmann's series of books built from interactive conference papers, *Gaining Control of the Corporate Culture* (1985); and the first edition of Gareth Morgan's highly influential book on organizational metaphors, *Images of Organization* (1986).

"Total Quality Management" (TQM) and "Reinventing Government" thrust organizational culture further onto the front pages of the management and organizational literature in the 1980s and 1990s (see Chapter 8). Several professional management and behavioral sciences journals began to carry articles regularly on a variety of issues that reflected the organizational culture and symbolic management perspective. Books with useful insights rolled off publishers' presses, for example, *Developing Corporate Character*, by Alan Wilkins (1989); *Cultures in Organizations*, by Joanne Martin; *Organisational Cultures in Theory and Practice*, by Pedersen and Sorensen (1989); *Organizational Climate and Culture*, edited by Schneider (1990); *Corporate Culture and Organizational Effectiveness*, by Denison (1990); *Cultural Knowledge in Organizations*, by Sackman (1991); *The Four Cultures of the Academy*, by William Bergquist (1992); and *The Cultures of Work Organizations* (1993), by Trice and Beyer—to cite only a few.

The first selection reprinted here is a chapter from the second edition of Edgar H. Schein's book *Organizational Culture and Leadership*, titled "Defining Organizational Culture" (1993). Schein proposes a "formal definition" of organizational culture that has gained wide—but not universal—acceptance. His definition consists of a model with three levels of culture that is particularly useful for sorting through myriad methodological and substantive problems associated with identifying an organizational culture. Schein also takes a unique stand on behalf of using a "clinical" rather than an "ethnographic" perspective for gaining knowledge about an organization's culture. He argues that an ethnographer seeks to understand an organizational culture for "intellectual and scientific" reasons, and organization members "have no particular stake in the intellectual issues that may have motivated the study." Thus, the ethnographer must work to obtain cooperation. In contrast, when clients call in an "outsider" (a consultant) to help solve problems, "the nature of the psychological contract between client and helper is completely different from that between researcher and subject, leading to a different kind of relationship between them, the revelation of different kinds of data, and the use of different criteria for when enough has been 'understood' to terminate the inquiry."

Scott Cook and Dvora Yanow use the case of three small workshops that make "the finest flutes in the world" to explore the relationship between organizational culture and organizational learning. "Our intention here is to outline a 'cultural perspective' on organizational learning." Traditionally, theories of organizational learning have taken one of two approaches. One approach focuses on learning by individuals in organizational contexts. The second focuses on individual learning as a model for organizational action. The authors explain, however, that organizations learn in ways that are neither like individuals learning in organizations nor like organizations employing processes similar to learning by individuals. "Organizational learning, as we use the term, refers to the capacity of an organization to learn how to do what it does, where what it learns is possessed not by individual members of the organization but by the aggregate itself." Thus, Cook and Yanow derive their own definition of organizational learning as "the acquiring, sustaining, or changing of intersubjective meanings through the artifactual vehicles of their expression and transmission and the collective actions of the group."

Eight "prescriptive aphorisms" or "specific considerations in changing [organizational] cultures" form the core of Harrison Trice and Janice Beyer's 1993 chapter, "Changing Organizational Cultures":

- capitalize on propitious moments;
- combine caution with optimism;
- understand resistance to culture change;
- change many elements, but maintain some continuity;
- recognize the importance of implementation;
- select, modify, and create appropriate cultural forms;
- modify socialization tactics; and
- find and cultivate innovative leadership.

Trice and Beyer's selection also provides a preview of issues addressed in Chapter 8, "Organizational Reform through Culture Change." Whereas this chapter concentrates specifically on organizational culture, Chapter 8 explores theories that assume organizational cultures need to be reformed before organizations can be changed. Altered organizational culture is merely the first—but essential—step in reshaping organizations to become more flexible, responsive, and customer driven. Trice and Beyer remind us that changing an organizational culture is not a task to be undertaken lightly.

In this chapter's concluding reading, "Organizational Culture: Pieces of the Puzzle," Joanne Martin attempts to answer the questions "what is culture, and what is not culture?"

using the intellectual traditions of functionalism, critical theory, and postmodernism. Martin takes a metaphorical approach to organizational culture rather than approaching culture as a variable to be studied. "What distinguishes a cultural study from an inventory . . . is a willingness to look beneath the surface, to gain an in-depth understanding of how people interpret the meanings of . . . manifestations and how . . . interpretations form patterns of clarity, inconsistency, and ambiguity that can be used to characterize understandings of working lives." She concludes that the current state of organizational culture research is problematic: "Because culture researchers do not agree what we should study when we claim to be studying culture, and because our definitions of culture do not always agree with how we operationalize the concept, it is no wonder that we also disagree about what we have learned, so far, about culture."

REFERENCES

Aaltio-Marjosola, I., & A. Mills, eds. (2003). *Gender, identity and the culture of organizations*. London: Routledge.

Acker, J. (1992). Gendering organizational theory. In A. J. Mills & P. Tancred, eds., *Gendering organizational analysis* (pp. 248–260). Thousand Oaks, CA: Sage.

Alvesson, M. (2002). *Understanding organizational culture*. Thousand Oaks, CA: Sage.

Becker, H. S., B. Geer, E. C. Hughes, & A. L. Strauss (1961). *The boys in white: Student culture in medical school*. Chicago: University of Chicago Press.

Bennis, W. G. (1984). Transformative power and leadership. In T. J. Sergiovanni & J. E. Corbally, eds., *Leadership and organizational culture* (pp. 64–71). Urbana, IL: University of Illinois Press.

Berger, P. L., & T. Luckman (1967). *The social construction of reality*. Garden City, NY: Doubleday Anchor.

Bergquist, W. H. (1992). *The four cultures of the academy*. San Francisco: Jossey-Bass.

Bolman, L. G., & T. D. Deal (1997). *Reframing organizations: Artistry, choice, and leadership*. 2d ed. San Francisco: Jossey-Bass.

Business Week (May 14, 1984). Changing a corporate culture: Can J&J move from Band-aids to high tech? 130–138.

Clark, B. R. (1970). *The distinctive college: Antioch, Reed, and Swarthmore*. Chicago: Aldine.

Cook, S. D. N., & D. Yanow (1993, December). Culture and organizational learning. *Journal of Management Inquiry, 2*(4), 373–390.

Cooper, C. L., S. Cartwright, & P. C. Earley, eds. (2001). *The international handbook of organizational culture and climate*. New York: Wiley.

Crossan, M. M., H. W. Lane, & R. E. White (1999, July). An organizational learning framework: From intuition to institution. *Academy of Management Review, 24*(3), 522–537.

Czarniawska-Joerges, B. (1992). *Exploring complex organizations: A cultural perspective*. Newbury Park, CA: Sage.

Davis, J. C. (1963). *Human nature in politics: The dynamics of political behavior*. New York; Wiley.

Deal, T. E., & A. A. Kennedy (1982). *Corporate cultures*. Reading, MA: Addison-Wesley.

Denison, D. R. (1990). *Corporate culture and organizational effectiveness*. New York: Wiley.

Elsmore, P. J. A. (2001). *Organisational culture: Organisational change?* Aldershot, UK: Ashgate.

Fortune (October 17, 1983). The corporate culture vultures, 66–71.

Gannon, M. J. (1994). *Understanding global cultures: Metaphorical journeys through seventeen countries*. Thousand Oaks, CA: Sage.

Gore, A. (1993). *The Gore report on reinventing government*. New York: Times Books.

Graves, D. (1986). *Corporate culture: Diagnosis and change*. New York: St. Martin's.

Handy, C. (1978). *The Gods of management: Who they are, how they work, and why they fail*. London: Souvenir Press.

Handy, C. (1989). *The age of unreason*. Boston: Harvard Business School Press.

Hatch, M. J. (1997). *Organization theory: Modern symbolic and postmodern perspectives*. Oxford, UK: Oxford University Press.

Hummel, R. P. (1991, January/February). Stories managers tell: Why they are as valid as science. *Public Administration Review, 51*, 31–41.

Hunt, J. G., D. M. Hosking, C. A. Schriesheim, & R. Stewart, eds. (1984). *Leaders and managers*. New York: Pergamon.

Ingersoll, V. H., & G. B. Adams (1992). *The tacit organization*. Greenwich, CT: JAI Press.

Jaques, E. (1951). *The changing culture of a factory*. London: Tavistock Institute.

Kaufman, H. (1960). *The forest ranger*. Baltimore, MD: Johns Hopkins University Press.

Khademian, A. M. (2002). *Working with culture: The way the job gets done in public programs*. Washington, DC: CQ Press.

Kilmann, R. H., M. J. Saxton, & R. Serpa, eds. (1985). *Gaining control of the corporate culture*. San Francisco: Jossey-Bass.

Kotkin, J. (1992). *Tribes: How race, religion, and identity determine success in the new global economy*. New York: Random House.

Louis, M. R. (June 1980). Surprise and sense making: What newcomers experience in entering unfamiliar organizational settings. *Administrative Science Quarterly, 25*, 226–251.

Louis, M. R. (1983). Organizations as culture-bearing milieux. In L. R. Pondy, P. J. Frost, G. Morgan, & T. C. Dandridge, eds., *Organizational symbolism* (pp. 39–54). Greenwich, CT: JAI Press.

Martin, J. (1992). *Cultures in organizations: Three perspectives*. New York: Oxford University Press.

Martin, J. (2002). *Organizational culture: Mapping the terrain*. Thousand Oaks, CA: Sage.

Morgan, G. (1986). *Images of organization*. Thousand Oaks, CA: Sage.

Neuhauser, P. C. (1993). *Corporate legends and lore: The power of storytelling as a management tool*. New York: McGraw-Hill.

Ott, J. S. (1989). *The organizational culture perspective*. Fort Worth, TX: Harcourt Brace.

Ott, J. S., S. J. Parkes, & R. B. Simpson, eds. (2003). *Classic readings in organizational behavior*. 3d ed. Belmont, CA: Wadsworth-Thomson.

Pearson, C. (2003). *Introduction to archetypes in organizational settings: A guide to interpreting the organizational and team culture instrument*. Gainsville, FL: Center for Applications of Psychological Type.

Pedersen, J. S., & J. S. Sorensen (1989). *Organisational cultures in theory and practice*. Aldershot, UK: Gower.

Peters, T. J. (1978, Autumn). Symbols, patterns, and settings: An optimistic case for getting things done. *Organizational Dynamics*, 3–23.

Peters, T. J., & R. H. Waterman Jr. (1982). *In search of excellence*. New York: Harper & Row.

Pheysey, D. C. (1993). *Organizational cultures: Types and transformations*. London: Routledge.

Pondy, L. R., P. J. Frost, G. Morgan, & T. C. Dandridge, eds. (1983). *Organizational symbolism*. Greenwich, CT: JAI Press.

Quinn, R. E., & K. S. Cameron, eds. (1988). *Paradox and transformation: Toward a theory of change in organization and management*. Cambridge, MA: Ballinger.

Ritti, R. R., & G. R. Funkhouser (1977). *The ropes to skip and the ropes to know*. New York: Wiley.

Sackman, S. A. (1991). *Cultural knowledge in organizations: Exploring the collective mind*. Thousand Oaks, CA: Sage.

Sackman, S. A., ed. (1997). *Cultural complexity in organizations*. Thousand Oaks, CA: Sage.

Sathe, V. (1985). *Culture and related corporate realities*. Homewood, IL: Richard D. Irwin.

Schein, E. H. (1964). How to break in the college graduate. *Harvard Business Review, 42*, 68–76.

Schein, E. H. (1968). Organizational socialization and the profession of management. *Industrial Management Review, 9,* 1–15.

Schein, E. H. (1978). *Career dynamics: Matching individual and organizational needs.* Reading, MA: Addison-Wesley.

Schein, E. H. (1985; 1993). *Organizational culture and leadership.* San Francisco: Jossey-Bass.

Schein, E. H. (1999). *The corporate culture survival guide: Sense & nonsense about culture change.* San Francisco: Jossey-Bass.

Schneider, B., ed. (1990). *Organizational climate and culture.* San Francisco: Jossey-Bass.

Schultz, M. (1995). *On studying organizational cultures: Diagnosis and understanding.* Berlin: de Gruyter.

Sergiovanni, T. J., & J. E. Corbally, eds. (1984). *Leadership and organizational culture.* Urbana, IL: University of Illinois Press.

Siehl, C., & J. Martin (1984). The role of symbolic management: How can managers effectively transmit organizational culture? In J. G. Hunt, D. M. Hosking, C. A. Schriesheim, & R. Stewart, eds., *Leaders and managers* (pp. 227–239). New York: Pergamon.

Smircich, L. (1983). Organizations as shared meanings. In L. R. Pondy, P. J. Frost, G. Morgan, & T. C. Dandridge, eds., *Organizational symbolism* (pp. 55–65). Greenwich, CT: JAI Press.

Stivers, C. (1993). *Gender images in public administration.* Thousand Oaks, CA: Sage.

Thomas, W. I. (1923). *The unadjusted girl.* New York: Harper Torchbooks, 1967.

Tichy, N. M., & D. O. Ulrich (1984, Fall). The leadership challenge: A call for the transformational leader. *Sloan Management Review, 26*(1), 59–68.

Trice, H. M. (1993). *Occupational subcultures in the workplace.* Ithaca, NY: ILR Press.

Trice, H. M., & J. M. Beyer (1993). *The cultures of work organizations.* Englewood Cliffs, NJ: Prentice Hall.

Van Maanen, J. (1975). Police socialization. *Administrative Science Quarterly, 20,* 207–228.

Van Maanen, J. (1976). Breaking in: Socialization to work. In R. Dubin, ed., *Handbook of work, organization, and society* (pp. 67–130). Chicago: Rand McNally.

Van Maanen, J., ed. (1979; 1983). *Qualitative methodology.* Thousand Oaks, CA: Sage.

Van Maanen, J., J. M. Dabbs Jr., & R. R. Faulkner, eds. (1982). *Varieties of qualitative research.* Thousand Oaks, CA: Sage.

Weick, K. E. (1982, June). Administering education in loosely coupled schools. *Phi Delta Kappan,* 673–676.

Weick, K. E. (1995). *Sensemaking in organizations.* Thousand Oaks, CA: Sage.

Whyte, W. H., Jr. (1956). *The organization man.* New York: Simon & Schuster.

Wilkins, A. L. (1989). *Developing corporate character: How to successfully change an organization without destroying it.* San Francisco: Jossey-Bass.

35
Defining Organizational Culture
Edgar H. Schein

Culture as a concept has had a long and checkered history. It has been used by the lay person as a word to indicate sophistication, as when we say that someone is very "cultured." It has been used by anthropologists to refer to the customs and rituals that societies develop over the course of their history. In the last decade or so it has been used by some organizational researchers and managers to indicate the climate and practices that organizations develop around their handling of people or to refer to the espoused values and credo of an organization.

In this context managers speak of developing the "right kind of culture" or a "culture of quality," suggesting that culture is concerned with certain values that managers are trying to inculcate in their organizations. Also implied in this usage is the assumption that there are better or worse cultures, stronger or weaker cultures, and that the "right" kind of culture will influence how effective organizations are.

If a new and abstract concept is to be useful to our thinking, it should refer to a set of events that are otherwise mysterious or not well understood. From this point of view, I will argue that we must avoid the superficial models of culture and build on the deeper, more complex anthropological models. Culture will be most useful as a concept if it helps us better understand the hidden and complex aspects of organizational life. This understanding cannot be obtained if we use superficial definitions.

Most of us in our roles as students, employees, managers, researchers, or consultants work in and deal with organizations of all kinds. Yet we continue to find it amazingly difficult to understand and justify much of what we observe and experience in our organizational life. Too much seems to be bureaucratic, or political, or just plain irrational. People in positions of authority, especially our immediate bosses, often frustrate us or act incomprehensibly, and those we consider the leaders of our organizations often disappoint us.

If we are managers who are trying to change the behavior of subordinates, we often encounter resistance to change at a level that seems beyond reason. We observe departments in our organization that seem to be more interested in fighting with each other than getting the job done. We see communication problems and misunderstandings between group members that should not be occurring between "reasonable" people.

If we are leaders who are trying to get our organizations to become more effective in the face of severe environmental pressures, we are sometimes amazed at the degree to which individuals and groups in the organization will continue to behave in obviously ineffective ways, often threatening the very survival of the organization. As we try to get things done that involve other groups, we often discover that they do not communicate with each other and that the level of conflict between groups in organizations and in the community is often astonishingly high.

If we are teachers, we encounter the sometimes mysterious phenomenon that different classes behave completely differently from each other even though our material and teaching style remain the same. If

Source: E. H. Schein, *Organizational Culture and Leadership,* 2d ed. (San Francisco: Jossey-Bass, 1993), pp. 3–15. Reprinted by permission of John Wiley & Sons, Inc.

we are employees considering a new job, we realize that companies differ greatly in their approach, even in the same industry and geographical area. We feel these differences even as we walk in the door of different organizations such as restaurants, banks, and stores.

The concept of culture helps explain all of these phenomena and to "normalize" them. If we understand the dynamics of culture, we will be less likely to be puzzled, irritated, and anxious when we encounter the unfamiliar and seemingly irrational behavior of people in organizations, and we will have a deeper understanding not only of why various groups of people or organizations can be so different but also why it is so hard to change them.

A deeper understanding of cultural issues in groups and organizations is necessary to decipher what goes on in them but, even more important, to identify what may be the priority issues for leaders and leadership. Organizational cultures are created in part by leaders, and one of the most decisive functions of leadership is the creation, the management, and sometimes even the destruction of culture.

Neither culture nor leadership, when one examines each closely, can really be understood by itself. In fact, one could argue that the only thing of real importance that leaders do is to create and manage culture and that the unique talent of leaders is their ability to understand and work with culture. If one wishes to distinguish leadership from management or administration, one can argue that leaders create and change cultures, while managers and administrators live within them.

By defining leadership in this manner, I am not implying that culture is easy to create or change or that leaders are the only determiners of culture. On the contrary, as we will see, culture refers to those elements of a group or organization that are most stable and least malleable. Culture is the result of a complex group learning process that is only partially influenced by leader behavior. But if the group's survival is threatened because elements of its culture have become maladapted, it is ultimately the function of leadership to recognize and do something about the situation. It is in this sense that leadership and culture are conceptually intertwined.

TWO BRIEF EXAMPLES

To illustrate how "culture" helps illuminate organizational situations, I will describe two situations I encountered in my experience as a consultant. In the first case (the Action Company), I was called in to help a management group improve its communication, interpersonal relationships, and decision making. After sitting in on a number of meetings, I observed among other things (1) high levels of interrupting, confrontation, and debate; (2) excessive emotionalism about proposed courses of action; (3) great frustration over the difficulty of getting a point of view across; and (4) a sense that every member of the group wanted to win all the time.

Over a period of several months, I made many suggestions about better listening, less interrupting, more orderly processing of the agenda, the potential negative effects of high emotionalism and conflict, and the need to reduce the frustration level. The group members said that the suggestions were helpful, and they modified certain aspects of their procedure, such as lengthening some of their meetings. However, the basic pattern did not change. No matter what kind of intervention I attempted, the group's basic style remained the same.

In the second case (the Multi Company), I was asked, as part of a broader consultation project, to help create a climate for innovation in an organization that felt a need to become more flexible in order to respond to its increasingly dynamic business environment. The organization consisted of many different business units, geographical units, and functional groups. As I got to know more about these units and their problems, I observed that some very innovative things were occurring in many places in the company. I wrote several memos describing these innovations, added other ideas from my own experience, and gave the memos to my contact person in the company with the request that he distribute them to the various business unit and geographical managers who needed to be made aware of these ideas.

After some months, I discovered that the managers to whom I had personally given a memo thought it was helpful and on target, but rarely if ever did they pass it on. Moreover, none of the memos were ever distributed by my contact person. I also suggested meetings of managers from different units to stimulate lateral communication but found no support at all for such meetings. No matter what I did, I could not seem to get information flowing, especially laterally across divisional, functional, or geographical boundaries. Yet everyone agreed in principle that innovation would be stimulated by more lateral communication and encouraged me to keep on "helping."

I did not really understand what happened in either of these cases until I began to examine *my own assumptions* about how things should work in these organizations and began to test whether my assumptions fitted those operating in my client systems. This step of examining the shared assumptions in the organization or group one is dealing with takes one into "cultural" analysis and will be the focus from here on.

It turned out that in the Action Company senior managers and most of the other members of the organization shared the assumption that one cannot determine whether or not something is true unless one subjects that idea or proposal to intensive debate. Only ideas that survive such debate are worth acting on, and only ideas that survive such scrutiny will be implemented. The group assumed that what they were doing was discovering truth, and in this context being polite to each other was relatively less important.

In the case of the Multi Company I eventually discovered that there was a strong shared assumption that each manager's job was his or her private turf, not to be infringed on. Articulated was the strong image that one's job is like one's home, and if someone gives one unsolicited information, it is like walking into one's home uninvited. Sending memos to people implies that they do not already know what is in the memo and that is potentially insulting. In this organization managers prided themselves on knowing whatever they needed to know to do their job.

In both of these cases I did not understand what was going on because my basic assumptions about truth and turf differed from the shared assumptions of the group members. Cultural analysis, then, is the encountering and deciphering of such shared basic assumptions.

TOWARD A FORMAL DEFINITION OF CULTURE

The word *culture* has many meanings and connotations. When we apply it to groups and organizations, we are almost certain to have conceptual and semantic confusion because groups and organizations are also difficult to define unambiguously. Most people have a connotative sense of what culture is but have difficulty defining it abstractly. In talking about organizational culture with colleagues and members of organizations, I often find that we agree "it" exists and that "it" is important in its effects but that we have completely different ideas of what "it" is. I have also had colleagues tell me pointedly that they do not use the concept of culture in their work, but when I ask them what it is they do not use, they cannot define "it" clearly.

To make matters worse, the concept of culture has been the subject of considerable academic debate in the last five years, and there are various approaches to defining and studying culture (for example, Barley, Meyer, and Gash, 1988; Martin, 1991; Ott, 1989; Smircich and Calas, 1987). This debate is a healthy sign in that it testifies to the importance of culture as a concept. At the same time, however, it creates difficulties for both the scholar and the practitioner if definitions are fuzzy and uses are inconsistent. . . .

Commonly used words relating to culture emphasize one of its critical aspects—the idea that certain things in groups are *shared or held in common*. The major categories of such overt phenomena that are associated with culture in this sense are the following:

1. *Observed behavioral regularities* when *people interact*: the *language* they use, the *customs and traditions* that evolve, and the *rituals* they employ in a wide variety of situations. . . .
2. *Group norms*: the implicit standards and values that evolve in working groups, such as the particular norm of "a fair day's work for a fair day's pay" that evolved among workers in the Bank Wiring Room in the Hawthorne studies. . . .
3. *Espoused values*: the articulated, publicly announced principles and values that the group claims to be trying to achieve, such as "product quality" or "price leadership." . . .
4. *Formal philosophy*: the broad policies and ideological principles that guide a group's actions toward stockholders, employees, customers, and other stakeholders, such as the highly publicized "HP Way" of Hewlett-Packard. . . .
5. *Rules of the game*: the implicit rules for getting along in the organization, "the ropes" that a newcomer must learn to become an accepted member, "the way we do things around here." . . .
6. *Climate*: the feeling that is conveyed in a group by the physical layout and the way in which members of the organization interact with each other, with customers, or with other outsiders. . . .
7. *Embedded skills*: the special competencies group members display in accomplishing certain tasks, the ability to make certain things that gets passed on from generation to generation without necessarily being articulated in writing. . . .
8. *Habits of thinking, mental models, and/ or linguistic paradigms*: the shared cognitive frames that guide the perceptions, thought, and language used by the

members of a group and are taught to new members in the early socialization process. . . .
9. *Shared meanings*: the emergent understandings that are created by group members as they interact with each other. . . .
10. *"Root metaphors" or integrating symbols*: the ideas, feelings, and images groups develop to characterize themselves, that may or may not be appreciated consciously but that become embodied in buildings, office layout, and other material artifacts of the group. This level of the culture reflects group members' emotional and aesthetic responses as contrasted with their cognitive or evaluative response. . . .

All of these concepts relate to culture and/or reflect culture in that they deal with things that group members share or hold in common, but none of them are "the culture" of an organization or group. If one asks oneself why one needs the word *culture* at all when we have so many other words such as *norms, values, behavior patterns, rituals, traditions*, and so on, one recognizes that the word *culture* adds two other critical elements to the concept of sharing.

One of these elements is that culture implies some level of *structural stability* in the group. When we say that something is "cultural," we imply that it is not only shared but deep and stable. By deep I mean less conscious and therefore less tangible and less visible. The other element that lends stability is *patterning or integration* of the elements into a larger paradigm or gestalt that ties together the various elements and that lies at a deeper level. Culture somehow implies that rituals, climate, values, and behaviors bind together into a coherent whole. This patterning or integration is the *essence* of what we mean by "culture." How then do we think about this essence and formally define it?

The most useful way to think about culture is to view it as the accumulated shared learning of a given group, covering behavioral, emotional, and cognitive elements of the group members' total psychological functioning. For shared learning to occur, there must be a history of shared experience, which in turn implies some stability of membership in the group. Given such stability and a shared history, the human need for parsimony, consistency, and meaning will cause the various shared elements to form into patterns that eventually can be called a culture.

I am not arguing, however, that all groups develop integrated cultures in this sense. We all know of groups, organizations, and societies where cultural elements work at cross purposes with other elements, leading to situations full of conflict and ambiguity (Martin, 1991; Martin and Meyerson, 1988). This may result from insufficient stability of membership, insufficient shared history of experience, or the presence of many subgroups with different kinds of shared experiences. Ambiguity and conflict also result from the fact that each of us belongs to many groups so that what we bring to any given group is influenced by the assumptions that are appropriate to our other groups.

If the concept of culture is to have any utility, however, it should draw our attention to those things that are the product of our human need for stability, consistency, and meaning. Culture formation, therefore, is always, by definition, a *striving toward patterning and integration*, even though the actual history of experiences of many groups prevents them from ever achieving a clear-cut paradigm.

If a group's culture is that group's accumulated learning, how do we describe and catalogue the content of that learning? All group and organizational theories distinguish two major sets of problems that all groups, no matter what their size, must deal with: (1) survival, growth, and adaptation in their environment and (2) internal integration that permits daily functioning and the ability to adapt.

In conceptualizing group learning, we have to note that because of the human capacity to abstract and to be self-conscious, learning occurs not only at the behavioral level but also at an abstract level internally. Once people have a common system of communication and a language, learning can take place at a conceptual level and shared

concepts become possible. Therefore, the deeper levels of learning that get us to the essence of culture must be thought of as concepts or, as I will define them, shared basic assumptions.

The process by which shared basic assumptions evolve is illustrated in detail in later chapters. For the present, I need only summarize that the learning process for the group starts with one or more members taking a leadership role in proposing courses of action and as these continue to be successful in solving the group's internal and external problems, they come to be taken for granted and the assumptions underlying them cease to be questioned or debated. A group has a culture when it has had enough of a shared history to have formed such a set of *shared assumptions*.

Shared assumptions derive their power from the fact that they begin to operate outside of awareness. Furthermore, once formed and taken for granted, they become a defining property of the group that permits the group to differentiate itself from other groups, and in that process, value is attached to such assumptions. They are not only "our" assumptions, but by virtue of our history of success, they must be right and good. In fact, as we will see, one of the main problems in resolving intercultural issues is that we take culture so much for granted and put so much value on our own assumptions that we find it awkward and inappropriate even to discuss our assumptions or to ask others about their assumptions. We tend not to examine assumptions once we have made them but to take them for granted, and we tend not to discuss them, which makes them seemingly unconscious. If we are forced to discuss them, we tend not to examine them but to defend them because we have emotionally invested in them (Bohm, 1990).

CULTURE FORMALLY DEFINED

The **culture** of a group can now be defined as

A pattern of shared basic assumptions that the group learned as it solved its problems of external adaptation and internal integration, that has worked well enough to be considered valid and, therefore, to be taught to new members as the correct way to perceive, think, and feel in relation to those problems.

Note that this definition introduces three elements not previously discussed.

1. *The problem of socialization.* It is my view that what we think of as culture is primarily what is passed on to new generations of group members (Louis, 1980, 1990; Schein, 1968; Van Maanen, 1976; Van Maanen and Schein, 1979). Studying what new members of groups are taught is, in fact, a good way to discover some of the elements of a culture, but one only learns about surface aspects of the culture by this means. This is especially so because much of what is at the heart of a culture will not be revealed in the rules of behavior taught to newcomers. It will only be revealed to members as they gain permanent status and are allowed to enter the inner circles of the group, where group secrets are shared.

On the other hand, *how* one learns and the socialization *processes* to which one is subjected may indeed reveal deeper assumptions. To get at those deeper levels one must try to understand the perceptions and feelings that arise in critical situations, and one must observe and interview regular members or old-timers to get an accurate sense of which deeper-level assumptions are shared.

Can culture be learned through anticipatory socialization or self-socialization? Can new members discover for themselves what the basic assumptions are? Yes and no. We certainly know that one of the major activities of any new member when she enters a new group is to decipher the norms and assumptions that are operating. But this deciphering can only be successful through the rewards and punishments that long-time members mete out to new members as they experiment with different kinds of behavior. In this sense, a teaching process is always going on, even though it may be quite implicit and unsystematic.

If the group does not have shared assumptions, as is sometimes the case, the new members' interaction with old members

will be a more creative process of building a culture. Once shared assumptions exist, however, the culture survives through teaching them to newcomers. In this regard culture is a mechanism of social control and can be the basis of explicitly manipulating members into perceiving, thinking, and feeling in certain ways (Van Maanen and Kunda, 1989; Kunda, 1992). Whether or not we approve of this as a mechanism of social control is a separate question that will be addressed later.

2. *The problem of "behavior."* Note that the definition of culture that I have given does *not* include overt behavior patterns, though some such behavior, especially formal rituals, would reflect cultural assumptions. Instead, the definition emphasizes that the critical assumptions deal with how we perceive, think about, and feel about things. Overt behavior is always determined both by the cultural predisposition (the perceptions, thoughts, and feelings that are patterned) and by the situational contingencies that arise from the immediate external environment.

Behavioral regularities could thus be as much a reflection of separate but similar individual experiences and/or common situational stimuli arising from the environment. For example, suppose we observe that all members of a group cower in the presence of a large and loud leader. Such cowering could be based on biological reflex reactions to sound and size, or individual learning, or shared learning. Such a behavioral regularity should not, therefore, be the basis for defining culture, though we might later discover that in a given group's experience, cowering is indeed a result of shared learning and therefore a manifestation of deeper shared assumptions. To put it another way, when we observe behavior regularities, we do not know whether we are dealing with a cultural manifestation. Only after we have discovered the deeper layers that I am defining as the essence of culture can we specify what is and what is not an "artifact" that reflects the culture.

3. *Can a large organization have one culture?* The definition provided does not spec-

ify the size of social unit to which it can legitimately be applied. Our experience with large organizations tells us that at a certain size, the variations among the subgroups are substantial, suggesting that it is not appropriate to talk of "the culture" of an IBM or a General Motors or a Shell Oil. My view is that this question should be handled empirically. If we find that certain assumptions are shared across all the units of an organization, then we can legitimately speak of an organizational culture, even though at the same time we may find a number of discrete subcultures that have their own integrity. In fact, as we will see, with time any social unit will produce subunits that will produce subcultures as a normal process of evolution. Some of these subcultures will typically be in conflict with each other, as is often the case with higher management and unionized labor groups. Yet in spite of such conflict one will find that organizations have common assumptions that come into play when a crisis occurs or when a common enemy is found.

SUMMARY AND CONCLUSIONS

The concept of culture is most useful if it helps to explain some of the more seemingly incomprehensible and irrational aspects of groups and organizations. Analysts of culture have a wide variety of ways of looking at the concept. My formal definition brings many of these various concepts together, putting the emphasis on shared, taken-for-granted basic assumptions held by the members of the group or organization. In this sense, any group with a stable membership and a history of shared learning will have developed some level of culture, but a group having either a great deal of turnover of members and leaders or a history without any kind of challenging events may well lack any shared assumptions. Not every collection of people develops a culture; in fact, we tend to use the term *group* rather than *crowd* or *collection of people* only when there has been enough of a shared

history so that some degree of culture formation has taken place.

Culture and leadership are two sides of the same coin in that leaders first create cultures when they create groups and organizations. Once cultures exist, they determine the criteria for leadership and thus determine who will or will not be a leader. But if cultures become dysfunctional, it is the unique function of leadership to perceive the functional and dysfunctional elements of the existing culture and to manage cultural evolution and change in such a way that the group can survive in a changing environment.

The bottom line for leaders is that if they do not become conscious of the cultures in which they are embedded, those cultures will manage them. Cultural understanding is desirable for all of us, but it is essential to leaders if they are to lead.

REFERENCES

Barley, S. R., Meyer, G. W., and Gash, D. "Cultures of Culture: Academics, Practitioners, and the Pragmatics of Normative Control." *Administrative Science Quarterly,* 1988, *33,* 24–60.

Bohm, D. *On Dialogue.* Ojai, Calif.: David Bohm Seminars, 1990.

Kunda, G. *Engineering Culture.* Philadelphia: Temple University Press, 1992.

Louis, M. R. "Surprise and Sense Making." *Administrative Science Quarterly,* 1980, *25,* 226–251.

Louis, M. R. "A Cultural Perspective on Organizations." *Human Systems Management,* 1981, *2,* 246–258.

Louis, M. R. "Organizations as Culture Bearing Milieux." In L. R. Pondy and others (eds.), *Organizational Symbolism.* Greenwich, Conn.: JAI Press, 1983.

Louis, M. R. "Newcomers as Lay Ethnographers: Acculturation During Organizational Socialization." In B. Schneider (ed.), *Organizational Climate and Culture.* San Francisco: Jossey-Bass, 1990.

Martin, J. "A Personal Journey: From Integration to Differentiation to Fragmentation to Feminism." In P. Frost and others (eds.), *Reframing Organizational Culture*. Newbury Park, Calif.: Sage, 1991.

Martin, J., and Meyerson, D. "Organizational Cultures and the Denial, Channeling and Acknowledgment of Ambiguity." In L. R. Pondy, R. J. Boland, Jr., and H. Thomas (eds.), *Managing Ambiguity and Change*. New York: Wiley, 1988.

Ott, J. S. *The Organizational Culture Perspective*. Belmont, Calif.: Dorsey Press, 1989.

Schein, E. H. "Organizational Socialization and the Profession of Management." *Industrial Management Review*, 1968, 9, 1–15.

Schein, E. H. "The Role of the Founder in Creating Organizational Culture." *Organizational Dynamics*, Summer 1983, pp. 13–28.

Schein, E. H. "Innovative Cultures and Adaptive Organizations." *Sri Lanka Journal of Development Administration*, 1990, 7 (2), 9–39.

Schein, E. H. "Legitimating Clinical Research in the Study of Organizational Culture." Massachusetts Institute of Technology Sloan School of Management Working Paper, no. 3288–91, 1991.

Schein, E. H. "The Role of the CEO in the Management of Change." In T. A. Kochan and M. Useem (eds.), *Transforming Organizations*. New York: Oxford University Press, 1992.

Smircich, L. "Concepts of Culture and Organizational Analysis." *Administrative Science Quarterly*, 1983, 28, 339–358.

Smircich, L., and Calas, M. B. "Organizational Culture: A Critical Assessment." In F. M. Jablin, L. L. Putnam, K. H. Roberts, and L. W. Porter (eds.), *Handbook of Organizational Communication*. Newbury Park, Calif.: Sage, 1987.

Van Maanen, J. "Breaking In: Socialization to Work." In R. Dubin (ed.), *Handbook of Work, Organization and Society*. Skokie, Ill.: Rand McNally, 1976.

Van Maanen, J., and Barley, S. R. "Occupational Communities: Culture and Control in Organizations." In B. M. Staw and L. L. Cummings (eds.), *Research in Organizational Behavior*. Vol. 6. Greenwich, Conn.: JAI Press, 1984.

Van Maanen, J., and Kunda, G. "'Real Feelings': Emotional Expression and Organizational Culture." in B. Staw (ed.), *Research in Organizational Behavior*. Vol. 11. Greenwich, Conn.: JAI Press, 1989.

Van Maanen, J., and Schein, E. H. "Toward a Theory of Organizational Socialization." In B. M. Staw and L. L. Cummings (eds.), *Research in Organizational Behavior*. Vol. 1. Greenwich, Conn.: JAI Press, 1979.

36

Culture and Organizational Learning

Scott D. N. Cook & Dvora Yanow

Two questions underlie the phrase "organizational learning": Can organizations learn? What is the nature of learning when it is done by organizations? . . .

In writing on organizational learning, most authors . . . have examined how individuals learn in organizational contexts or have explored ways that theories of individual learning can be applied to organizations or both. In the first instance, the typical argument is that organizational learning is a particular sort of learning done in organizations by key individuals whose learning is tied to subsequent organizational change. The second approach holds that organizations can learn because they possess capacities that are identical or equivalent to the capacities that individuals possess that enable them to learn — that is, with respect to learning, this approach treats organizations *as if* they were individuals. Despite their differences, both approaches tend to address the questions just mentioned from a common perspective: They typically base their account of the nature of *organizational* learning, explicitly or implicitly, on an understanding of what it means for an *individual* to learn. This grounding in learning by individuals suggests a link between discussions of organizational learning and theories of cognition: For this reason, we call this orientation the "cognitive perspective" on organizational learning.

Although the cognitive perspective has been and continues to be a wellspring of insight and utility, we have found it less useful in efforts to understand a phenomenon that we believe is central to the subject of organizational learning: specifically, where learning is understood to be done by the organization as a whole, not by individuals in it, and where the organization is not understood as if it were an individual (that is, as if it were in some way ontologically a cognitive entity). We hold that learning can indeed be done by organizations; that this phenomenon is neither conceptually nor empirically the same as either learning by individuals or individuals learning within organizations; and that to understand organizational learning as learning by organizations, theorists and practitioners need to see organizations not primarily as cognitive entities but as cultural ones.

Our intention here is to outline a "cultural perspective" on organizational learning (in keeping with recent attention to organizational culture; e.g., Frost, Moore, Louis, Lundberg, & Martin, 1985, 1991; Schein, 1985). We see this perspective as a complement to, not a substitute for, the cognitive perspective. From the cultural perspective, we argue, the question, "Can organizations learn?" is not an epistemological one about cognitive capacities, but an empirical one about organizational actions — to which the answer is, yes. Further, we hope to show that the second question, "What is the nature of learning as done by organizations?" can be addressed from the cultural perspective in a way that avoids some specific conceptual difficulties found in the cognitive perspective, while also suggesting some new avenues for exploration.

The theoretical argument presented here has grown out of our analysis of three small

Source: S. D. N. Cook & D. Yanow, "Culture and Organizational Learning," *Journal of Management Inquiry* 2 (December 1993), 373–390. Reprinted by permission of Sage Publications, Inc.

companies manufacturing flutes. In the sections that follow, we describe what we see as some of the conceptual difficulties inherent in the cognitive view, discuss the meanings of the concept of organizational learning, and outline a cultural perspective on organizational learning, which we illustrate through the case example of the flute companies.

THE COGNITIVE PERSPECTIVE

. . . There are problems inherent in transferring to organizations concepts whose origin is cognition by individuals. . . .

A fundamental problem derives from the fact that it is impossible to *see* cognition taking place in the actions of organizations. This has led to the common assertion in the literature that organizational learning has taken place when actions by organizationally key individuals that are understood to entail learning are followed by observable changes in the organization's pattern of activities. In this vein, Miles and Randolph (1981), drawing on Simon's work, define organizational learning as individuals' insights reflected "in the structural elements and outcomes of the organization itself" (p. 50).

Having accepted generally the inference that organizational learning entails observable organizational change linked to individual cognition, the cognitive perspective splits into two major approaches. One approach has focused on individual learning in an organizational context. The other has used individual learning as a model for understanding certain types of collective organizational activity. Most authors have followed one approach or the other; a few have explored both.

The first approach treats organizational learning explicitly as learning by individuals within an organizational context. . . .

Some authors state that they take organizational learning to be different in some sense from individual learning. . . . Organizational learning as approached in such cases, although conceived of as different

from individual learning, is nevertheless described as a form of learning by individuals; it is not treated as learning by organizations.[1]

The second approach develops theories of organizational action largely by applying to organizations concepts that are commonly found in models of individual learning. Hedberg (1981) and Gahmberg (1980), for example, extend stimulus-response models of individual learning to explain organizational selection of stimuli and choice of responses. . . .

It is clear that individuals do indeed learn within the context of organizations, that this context influences the character of that learning and, in turn, that such learning can have operational consequences for the activities of the organization. . . . In drawing on individual cognition as a way of understanding organizational phenomena, we must take care not to lose sense of the "as if" quality of the metaphor, forgetting that organizations and individuals are not the same sorts of entities. The nature of the difference, as we will argue later, bears on how each can be understood to learn.

In both approaches, the application to organizations of a model of learning based on cognition by individuals entails, in our view, at least three substantive problems. First, it raises a set of complex arguments concerning the ontological status of organizations as cognitive entities—specifically, arguments about how organizations exist and how the nature of their existence entails an ability to learn that is identical or akin to the human cognitive abilities associated with learning. In other words, because the cognitive perspective adopts its understanding of learning from theories about individuals, it follows that to discuss cognitive organizational learning, one must first show how, in their capacity to learn, organizations are like individuals.

Further, because theories of cognition already carry with them an understanding of learning, many who have adopted the cognitive perspective on organizational learning have seen *organizations*, although not always *learning*, as the term called for explanation. In this vein, Argyris and Schön (1978) begin their discussion of organizational learning with the section, "What is an organization that it may learn?" Others (e.g., Duncan & Weiss, 1979; Gahmberg, 1980) similarly begin with definitions and discussions of the concept of organization that, in part, constitute arguments concerning the ontological status of organizations with respect to learning. Morgan (1986) looks at how organizations can be understood to be brains (metaphorically at least) and how this might help us design organizations "so that they can learn and self-organize in the manner of a fully functioning brain" (p. 105). . . .

Second, the study of individual learning is itself complex, in flux, and bounded by its own theoretical constraints. . . . Linking our understanding of organizational learning to cognitive theory, at the very least, obligates us to account in organizational terms for developments in that theory or to explain why this is not necessary.

Apart from the problems posed by debates concerning organizational ontology and the nature of theories of individual learning, the cognitive perspective presents a third difficulty: its proposition (often implicit) that learning for organizations is the same as learning for individuals. This is a difficulty for several reasons. In a fundamental sense, it does not follow from anything essential about organizations or about learning that learning must be the same for individuals and organizations. Nor is it clear how two things that are in so many ways so obviously different as individuals and organizations could nonetheless carry out identical or even equivalent activities. Further, even if it were shown that organizations and individuals are ontologically equivalent in the possession of cognitive capacities required for learning, it would not necessarily follow that they would both learn in the same fashion or, as Weick (1991) notes, that the results of their learning would be the same. Indeed, even among individuals, we can observe significantly different "learning styles."[2] This issue has

been left largely unaddressed by theorists of organizational learning.

There is a further problematic point that is found in many parts of the literature that derives, we believe, in large measure from its systems origins. Although the idea is not inherent in the concept of cognition itself, organizational learning has typically been linked to organizational change and, particularly, to increased effectiveness. . . .

Although change is often associated with individual learning, it seems clear that some forms of learning entail little or no change that is meaningfully discernible, particularly in observable behavior. . . . Change does not always accompany learning by organizations, and moreover, equating learning with change may leave out much of interest.[3] Here, we turn to an exploration of learning by organizations.

KNOWING AND LEARNING BY ORGANIZATIONS

Organizations act. The Boston Celtics play basketball. The Concertgebouw Orchestra performs Mahler symphonies. These are activities done by groups; they are not and cannot be done by single individuals. A single basketball player cannot play a game of basketball by herself; only the several players, together as a team, are able to carry out the team's strategies, moves, and style of play. A violinist alone cannot perform Mahler's Third Symphony; the execution of the phrasing, dynamics, and tempi of the piece requires the collective actions of the orchestra as a group.

Further, the ability to play basketball games or perform symphonies, we argue, is only meaningfully attributed to a group, not to individual players. It is not meaningful to say that the ability to play Mahler symphonies is possessed by an individual musician, because no individual person can perform symphonies. An individual musician possesses the ability to carry out merely a portion of what only an orchestra can do. Moreover, musicians can act on that ability only in the context of the orchestra: They may each play their parts alone (to practice, say), but to perform the symphony they must participate in an activity of the orchestra.

Although it has become more common to attribute abilities to groups, there has been an equally common reluctance to attribute to them any form of knowledge or knowing associated with those abilities: Traditionally, it has been accepted, usually unquestioningly, that matters of knowing are exclusively matters about what or how individuals know. This reluctance is consistent with the cognitive perspective's origins in theories of individual cognition. From this perspective, therefore, it would typically be argued that it is the knowledge of all the individuals in an orchestra taken together that constitutes the know-how behind the ability to perform symphonies — and thus it is not know-how possessed by a group. This argument has two shortcomings. First, it implies that the performance of a symphony is meaningfully reducible to the playing of 100 different parts by individuals. This is an implication that belies the experiential reports of musicians and their audiences, and it can never be meaningfully tested because the performance of symphonies is always a group activity. Second, it is conceptually unsound to attribute to individuals know-how that no individual can demonstrate. Just as the ability to perform symphonies is meaningfully attributed only to a group, so is possession of the know-how necessary to do so. Removed from the traditional assumptions of the cognitive perspective, the same reasoning that supports the concept of group abilities would also suggest the concept of group know-how.

In this sense, the statement, "The Celtics know how to play basketball" is meaningful as a statement about organizational knowing. Other "ensembles" that are more commonly thought of as organizations, such as IBM or Saab or the U.S. Environmental Protection Agency, similarly know how to do what they do. The know-how entailed in producing a computer, a Saab 9000, or a set of standards for air quality resides in the organization as a whole, not in individual members of the organization.[4] These are propositions about organizational knowing.

Learning is related to knowing; in one sense, it is the act of acquiring knowledge. Thus the knowledge demonstrated by the Concertgebouw when it plays a symphony or by Saab when it produces a car can be understood as having been learned. The individuals in the organization were not born with the ability to perform their parts of these activities, nor has the organization always possessed these abilities. What can be said of the abilities can be said of the know-how associated with them: It has to be acquired; it has to be learned. The statement, "The Celtics know how to play basketball" suggests something about organizational learning as well as organizational knowing. Organizational learning, then, describes a category of activity that can only be done by a group. It cannot be done by an individual.

In this respect, organizational learning, as we use the term, refers to the capacity of an organization to learn how to do what it does, where what it learns is possessed not by individual members of the organization but by the aggregate itself. That is, when a group acquires the know-how associated with its ability to carry out its collective activities, that constitutes organizational learning.[5]

From the perspective of this understanding, the foregoing examples of organizational activities are descriptions of things that organizations as collectives actually do that can be meaningfully understood as learning. The answer to our initial question is, yes, organizations do indeed learn. . . . Specifically, we believe that organizational learning is not essentially a cognitive activity, because, at the very least, organizations lack the typical wherewithal for undertaking cognition: They do not possess what people possess and use in knowing and learning — that is, actual bodies, perceptive organs, brains, and so forth. . . .

At this juncture, three additional points can be raised. First, in our view, organizational learning, like individual learning, does not necessarily imply change, particularly observable change. An organization can, for example, learn something in order *not* to change. Second, organizational learning need not, as the systems notion of feedback would suggest, be a response to an environmental stimulus (such as error detection). The impetus for learning can also come from within the organization itself. Third, in a significant measure, organizational knowledge or know-how is unique to each organization. That is, two organizations performing the same task do not necessarily perform it identically. Even two very similar organizations know how to do somewhat different things. The Celtics do not play basketball in the same way as do the 76ers. The Concertgebouw and the New York Philharmonic perform the same Mahler Symphony differently. IBM and Apple have different management styles, although both manufacture computers. Organizational knowing and learning are always in some part intimately bound to a particular organization.

In the case analysis that follows, we examine in greater detail how understanding organizational learning in terms of organizational culture helps address the issues we have identified so far. Organizational culture has been defined and treated in many ways (see, for example, Frost et al., 1985, 1991; Ouchi & Wilkins, 1985; Schein, 1985; Smircich, 1983). For our purposes at hand, we define culture in application to organizations as a set of values, beliefs, and feelings, together with the artifacts of their expression and transmission (such as myths, symbols, metaphors, rituals), that are created, inherited, shared, and transmitted within one group of people and that, in part, distinguish that group from others. This definition is in keeping with an interpretive approach to human action and social reality (see, for example, Berger & Luckmann, 1966; Mead, 1934; Taylor, 1979).[6]

Such an approach to organizational learning builds on the following. Human action includes the ability to act in groups. Over time and in the course of joint action or practice, a group of people creates a set of intersubjective meanings that are expressed in and through their artifacts (objects, language, and acts). Such artifacts include the symbols, metaphors, ceremonies, myths, and so forth with which organizations and groups transmit their values, beliefs, and feelings to new and existing members, as well as in part to strangers. As new members join the group, each acquires a sense of these meanings through the everyday practices in which the organization's artifacts are engaged. Through such "artifactual interactions," shared meanings are continually maintained or modified; these are acts that create, sustain, or modify the organization's culture.[7] . . .

. . . The focus of the cultural theorist concerned with organizational learning shifts to the second question, "What is the nature of learning when it is done by organizations?" and the task is to develop concepts with which to describe how a group of individuals acting collectively, as an organization, does those things that might meaningfully and usefully be understood as learning.

THE FINEST FLUTES IN THE WORLD: ORGANIZING CRAFTSMANSHIP

Most of the finest flutes produced in this century have been made in a style reminiscent of old world craftsmanship by three small workshops in and around Boston, Massachusetts: the Wm. S. Haynes Company; Verne Q. Powell Flutes, Inc.; and Brannen Brothers—Flutemakers, Inc. Haynes, the oldest of the three, was founded in 1900. In 1927, Verne Q. Powell, who was shop foreman for Haynes, left the company to make flutes on his own. Two of Powell's mastercraftsmen, Bickford and Robert Brannen, founded Brannen Brothers in 1977.[8]

Instruments made by these three companies have been regarded by flutists internationally as the "best flutes in the world." The idea of excellence has been central to the identities of all three companies. Until the early 1980s, when changing economics and a growing challenge by large-scale, highly tooled Japanese flute manufacturers affected demand, it was common for the Boston companies to have a 5-year backlog of orders. . . .

The flutemakers themselves are in many ways a varied lot. The range of ages has been wide, yet most of the flutemakers have been in their 20s or 30s. Until recently, they were almost exclusively men; now, at Brannen Brothers, for example, about 40% are women. Some flutemakers are musicians; very few have ever been flutists. A growing number have been to college. . . .

In all three shops, flutes have been made following similar procedures and organization of production. The tube that becomes the body of the flute is made outside the shop to each company's precise specifications. Screws and steel rods for the key mechanism and strips of silver for various parts are also brought in. The parts are collected, carefully inspected, and given an initial polishing. Next, the body is formed. Tone holes are put into the tube, and the structure that holds the key mechanism is soldered on. The key mechanism is assembled and precisely fit to the body. Then, pads are put into the keys and the mechanism adjusted by hand to remarkably fine tolerances. Meanwhile, the head joint and embouchure hole are put together and delicately hand finished. Finally, the flute is polished, packed up, and shipped to its new owner.

At Powell (which we will use here as the primary example), it would take about 2 weeks to make an instrument from start to finish. At all times there would be several flutes at each step of manufacture. Typically, each flute would be worked on by several flutemakers in succession. Each individual craftsman, typically skilled in only a few aspects of the process, would work on his part of a flute (or a small batch) until that work was finished, whereupon the flute (or batch) would be handed on to the next craftsman. The second flutemaker would base her work on the former's. And so on down the line. If at any point a flutemaker felt that ear-

lier work was not right, that person would return the piece to the appropriate prior flutemaker to be reworked to their mutual satisfaction.

In describing why a piece might need to be reworked, a flutemaker would typically make only cryptic remarks, such as, "It doesn't feel right" or "This bit doesn't look quite right." The first flutemaker would then rework the piece until both were in agreement that it had "the right feel" or "the right look." In working on a portion of the key mechanism, say, one flutemaker might tell the previous one that a key "doesn't feel right; it's cranky." This would lead the other to check the key over until he got a sense of how the feel was off. Ultimately he would trace the problem down, for example, to a need for adjusting the way the key fit into the mechanism or, perhaps, to a need to reset the tension on the spring that operates the key. The language in such interchanges is inexact in no small part because many of the actual physical dimensions and tolerances of the flutes have never been made explicit; and many that have been are not commonly referred to in explicit terms by the flutemakers in daily practice. Yet the extremely precise standards of the instruments, on which the flute's ultimate style and quality depend, have been maintained through just these sorts of individual and mutual judgments of hand and eye.

This process has resulted in two very important things. First, it has made sure that at any one step of manufacture not only had work been done properly with respect to the work each flutemaker needed to accomplish, but it was also done properly from the perspective of the next flutemaker who needed to base her work on that of the former. The second result has been that when a flute reached the final inspection at the end of manufacture, almost without exception, it required no further work. The hand-to-hand checking of the flutes has amounted to a very successful, informal quality control system.

Apprentices have typically been trained by sitting at a workbench to do one of the steps of manufacture as would any other flutemaker. As an apprentice finished each piece of work, he would show it to a master craftsman who would judge it, just as she would judge the work of any other flutemaker: If it did not feel right or look right, it would be handed back to the apprentice to be reworked until it did. Eventually, the apprentice would become a judge of his own work (this would be a mark of the end of his apprenticeship). Similarly, he would become able to judge work by other flutemakers on flutes coming to him for work and be able to recognize when they needed to be taken back because the look or feel was "not right." In this way, at one and the same time, an apprentice would both acquire a set of skills in flutemaking and become a member of the informal quality control system that has unfalteringly maintained the style and quality of these instruments.

No two Powell flutes are exactly alike. Each has its own strengths and quirks, its own personality. Yet a knowledgeable fluteplayer would never fail to recognize a Powell by the way it feels and plays, nor would she confuse a Powell with a Haynes or a Brannen Brothers. Each Powell flute, although unique, shares an unambiguous family resemblance with all other Powells. This family resemblance is the essence of Powell style and quality. And although each Powell has its own personality and aspects of the flute's physical design have been changed from time to time, the Powell style has been maintained. In this sense, a Powell flute made 50 years ago plays and feels the same as one made recently.

This principle is equally true of Haynes and Brannen Brothers flutes. Each company has developed a distinctly recognizable product, transcending individual variations among flutes and design changes over time. Further, this constancy of style and quality has been maintained through the years, even though each instrument has typically been the product of several flutemakers and the workshops have passed through several generations of flutemakers.

ORGANIZATIONAL LEARNING IN THE FLUTE WORKSHOP

Like playing basketball or a symphony, the knowledge needed to make these flutes of the finest quality resides not in any one individual, but in the organization as a whole. The organization was not "born" with that knowledge; it had to learn it.

We may say that each of the Boston companies, as an organization, knows how to make flutes. Indeed, the know-how required to make one of their instruments from start to finish rarely has been known by a single flutemaker; typically, producing a flute has been a group effort.

Each organization has learned how to produce a flute. The knowledge has been learned collectively, not individually. It is true that each flutemaker knows how to perform his or her individual tasks; but the know-how required to make the flute as a whole resides with the organization, not with the individual flutemaker because only the workshop as a whole can make the flute. This is demonstrated in the fact that when flutemakers have left one of the workshops, the know-how needed to make the flute has not been lost to the organization, as evidenced in the sameness of play and feel of instruments produced by that workshop over the years. The workshop has continued to make flutes of the same quality and style as before because it—the organization, not the individual—possesses the know-how and the ability to make its own particular style of instrument. Typically, neither the flutes nor the way they are made have changed when flutemakers have left one of the workshops.

Moreover, the organizational know-how entailed in flutemaking at each workshop is, in a significant measure, different from that at the others. Although all three know how to make flutes and all follow similar production operations, each makes its own particular flute, one with a unique, unambiguously recognizable style. Thus part of what each workshop knows is unique to it.

Further, such organizational know-how is not meaningfully transferable from one shop to the next; it is deeply embedded in the practices of each workshop. A Haynes flutemaker, for example, could not walk into the Powell workshop, sit down at a bench, and begin making Powell flutes. Over the years, several flutemakers have, in fact, moved from one company to another, and in every instance they have had to be partially retrained, even to do the same jobs they were doing at the other company. They have had to learn a new "feel," a different way of "handling the pieces." Overall, this know-how has been learned not by being given explicit measurements and tolerances, but tacitly, in the hand-to-hand judgments of feel and eye, by working on flutes and having that work judged by the other flutemakers. These judgments are typically expressed in terms of the right look or right feel that are unique to that workshop.

What such a flutemaker knows can be learned only within the context of a specific workshop and only by joining in the collective activity of the workshop as a whole, making its particular instrument. The knowledge of how a finished mechanism, say, should feel can be used only in that workshop. Although each individual possesses the know-how needed to do her portion of the work on the flute, she cannot use that knowledge to produce an entire flute on her own, nor could she produce quality work in the style of a particular workshop except in that particular organizational context.

In this lies an example of organizational learning that does not require overt change on the part of the organization. As a new member, for example, is socialized or acculturated into the organization, learning by the organization takes place: The organization learns how to maintain the style and quality of its flutes through the particular skills, character, and quirks of a new individual. The organization engages in a dynamic process of maintaining the norms and practices that assure the constancy of its product. This is learning in a sense quite

different from change-oriented learning: It is the active reaffirmation or maintenance of the know-how that the organization already possesses. We argue that such organizational learning is better explained from a cultural perspective that assumes the group and group attributes as its unit of analysis than from an individually oriented cognitive perspective. . . .

REFLECTIONS ON CULTURAL LEARNING

Several aspects of the cultural perspective on organizational learning can be noted at this point. First, intuitively it is a much shorter conceptual leap to see organizations as cultural entities than it is to see them as cognitive ones. Organizations, being human groups, are more readily understood as being like tribes than they are as being like individuals or brains. Second, because organizational learning here is understood to involve shared meanings associated with and carried out through cultural artifacts, it is understood as an activity *of* the organization, that is, an activity at the level of the group, not at the level of the individual. Accordingly, it is seen as conceptually and empirically distinct from learning by individuals in the organization. Third, it is also, then, unnecessary to argue that organizations learn in a way that is fundamentally the same as or similar to individual learning. The cultural perspective makes it possible to explore the meaning of organizational learning by beginning with empirical observations of group action rather than relying on conceptual arguments about likenesses between theories of individual cognition and theories of organizations. Fourth, it allows us to view organizational learning as both an innovative and a preservative activity, thus incorporating into the discussion of organizational learning the rather considerable amount of effort that organizations, like all human groups, put into maintaining the patterns of activity that are unique to each organization.

The cultural perspective and the cognitive perspective both include the study of the activities of individuals. The difference is one of focus: The cognitive perspective takes individual action as its primary point of reference; the cultural perspective focuses on a group of individuals moving within a "net of expectations" ranging from the organization's "explicit constitution to the most subtle mutual understandings between its members" (Vickers, 1976, p. 6). Within the cultural perspective, organizational knowledge is not held by an individual, nor do we see it as the aggregated knowledge of many individuals. What is known is known and made operational only by several individuals acting "in congregate."

The case analysis presented here exemplifies organizational learning as a collective activity rather than an individual one and, quite importantly, as an activity of preservation as well as one of innovation. From this analysis we derive a definition of organizational learning as *the acquiring, sustaining, or changing of intersubjective meanings through the artifactual vehicles of their expression and transmission and the collective actions of the group*.

These meanings, whether they are acquired by new members or created by existing ones, come about and are maintained through interactions among members of the organization. They need not be face-to-face verbal interactions: meaning-making and meaning-sustaining interactions take place just as importantly through the medium of the artifacts of the organization's culture — its symbolic objects, symbolic language, and symbolic acts. Such "artifactual interaction" happens not only in exceptional circumstances of disruption or change but also routinely as part of "normal" day-to-day work (whether that be production, management, marketing, etc.). Such was the case at Powell.

This means that much of organizational learning, in our view, is tacit, occasioned through experiences of the artifacts of the organization's culture that are part of its daily work. No one says during the course of a typical working day, for example, "Powell values its identity as producer of the flutes with a particular feel to the mechanism." Rather, that part of Powell's culture is incorporated into the artifacts of daily life in the organization. It is reflected, for example, in the company's stories and myths, in the daily judgments of feel and eye, and in the ceremony of making a prototype Powell with a Cooper scale. Through such largely tacit practice and interpretation of artifactual interaction, the members of each workshop sustain their shared "web of meanings" and the group's expectations concerning the quality of workmanship and the style of its product. This sense of artifactual interaction follows Polanyi's formulation (Polanyi & Prosch, 1975) for tacit knowledge: something learned while focusing on something else.[9] Similarly, we argue, organizations learn tacitly, while focusing on "normal" work.

This incorporation of tacit expression and communication is a further point of distinction from the cognitive perspective, which typically requires that those things essential to organizational learning be made explicit, so that they can be communicated. What is to be learned must be "capable *of being stated* [italics added] in terms that are in principle understandable to other members of the organization" (Duncan & Weiss, 1979, p. 86). By contrast, the cultural perspective we propose here argues that what the organization learns may be, and often is, tacitly known, communicated, and understood. In the flute case, not only do the daily hand-to-hand judgments constitute tacit expressions of organizational know-how, but learning and knowing how to recognize the right feel are also transmitted tacitly — for example, in the mastercraftsman's judgments of an apprentice's work. Indeed, in large measure, it was such tacit knowledge that guided the decision making around the adoption of the Cooper scale.

A central concern of organizational learning from this cultural perspective is how an organization constitutes and reconstitutes itself. We have described organizational learning as the acquiring, sustaining, and changing, through collective actions, of the meanings embedded in the organization's cultural artifacts. Following this, organizational activities, from ordinary daily tasks to major innovations, can be seen to entail the ongoing reconstitution of what is essential to the organization's identity and its ability to do what it does.

One way in which organizations reconstitute themselves is through the acquisition of new members. As new members are successfully integrated into an organization, their actions increasingly exhibit aspects of the group's or organization's culture. Accordingly, the meanings embedded in a new member's actions become compatible with—indeed, become part of—the "web of meaning" embedded in the actions of the group. This is what happens, for example, when an apprentice at one of the workshops begins to use that workshop's metaphors successfully in interactions with other flute-makers or when he becomes able to work within the informal quality control system by judging his own work and that of others as having the right feel, without checking with a mastercraftsman. When a new member's actions "fit in" to group activity, the organization's concerns are thereby confirmed and sustained; that is to say, the organization has reconstituted itself. Organizations also reconstitute themselves through the ordinary day-to-day activities of veteran members. Such activities and their underlying web of meaning mutually confirm and sustain each other.

The flute workshops have engaged in a form of organizational learning that amounts to organizational reconstitution over time as they have passed through successive generations of flutemakers. The personnel have undergone a complete turnover (in some cases more than once), whereas the form of workmanship and the style and quality of the products have remained constant. A provocative parallel can be found in Weick's (1979) example of the Duke Ellington Orchestra continuing long after the Duke had been replaced by his son. Weick

reasons that this has been possible because the concept of that orchestra has been continually recreated by the perceptions of its audiences. We suggest that another likely factor is that the orchestra has sustained its identity through long-term organizational learning. Specifically, the ongoing maintenance of the patterns of collective action among the players, intimately bound up with performance itself, has enabled the organization to survive over the years and through a change in personnel (indeed, its leadership!) because the orchestra continued to learn what it needed to do—how it needed to play—to be the Duke Ellington Orchestra.[10]

The focus here is less on what goes on inside the heads of individuals and more on what goes on in the practices of the group (including how those practices are manifested, in part, in individual action). To paraphrase Douglas (1986), rather than seeing the organization as the individual writ large, we would do well to see the individual as the group writ small, each individual carrying those parts of the collective knowledge that make possible individual action with respect to organizational concerns.[11]

Further, organizational reconstitution can be seen as an important feature of organizational change. . . . A significant part of the effort put into mastering what is new is often concerned with keeping stable what is old.

CULTURE AND ORGANIZATIONAL LEARNING: CONCLUSION

We began this article by focusing on two questions: Can organizations learn? What is the nature of learning when it is done by organization? It is our view that in addressing these questions, most authors have adopted a cognitive perspective. . . .

By comparison, from a cultural perspective, we have argued (a) that one aspect of the human capacity to act is the ability to act in groups; (b) that a group of people with a history of joint action or practice is meaningfully understood as a culture; (c) that a culture is constituted, at least in part, from the intersubjective meanings that its members express in their common practice through objects, language, and acts; (d) that such meaning-bearing objects, language, and acts are cultural artifacts through which an organization's collective knowledge or know-how is transmitted, expressed, and put to use; and (e) that organizations are constantly involved in activities of modifying or maintaining those meanings and their embodiments — that is, of changing or preserving their cultural identity. Finally, it has been our position that such activities constitute organizational learning. That is, when organizations are seen as cultures, they are seen to learn through activities involving cultural artifacts, and that learning, in turn, is understood to entail organizations' acquiring, changing, or preserving their abilities to do what they know how to do.

This is not to suggest that an organization has only one culture — there is always the possibility that an organization will have multiple cultures, no one of which is dominant, or that there will be a dominant culture and one or more subcultures — nor does it indicate that organizational cultures are created only by managers or founders (see Davis, 1985; Louis, 1985; Yanow, 1992, for discussions and examples of multiple cultures, including those not managerially created). Indeed, the flute case illustrates the role of members in sustaining an organization's culture, even when the original ones are long gone. . . .

. . . Because we see culture as the values, beliefs, and feelings of the organization's members along with their artifacts, we do find culture in the case. . . .

We find a cultural understanding of organizational learning to be a fruitful approach that suggests further areas of exploration. We would like to speculate on some of these.

Organizations commonly acquire new members. As we noted above, such occasions present an opportunity for an organization to learn, where that learning can be understood to constitute the maintenance

or preservation of the know-how associated with an organization's activities and abilities. There is a need for a fuller understanding of how the group and the individual come to hold the shared intersubjective meanings that constitute organizational cultures, as well as of processes by which both "agree to disagree." This cultural perspective suggests that organizational socialization is not simply a question of "How do you socialize Smith into IBM?" (because that constitutes learning by Smith, the individual, not IBM, the organization) but rather the fuller question, "How does IBM renourish itself with new members, yet ensure its continuity?" Socialization typically suggests movement in a single direction: IBM socializes Smith, where Smith is relatively passive, a receptive vessel. From the cultural perspective, for Smith to become a member of IBM (or of a unit within IBM), she must form an understanding of the meaning of those elements of IBM's culture that enable her to carry out her role effectively within it (a point where individual cognition may properly and profitably enter the discussion). IBM, meanwhile, must learn how to make Smith's actions compatible with the actions (and underlying meanings) of other members of its culture and to do so in a way that fosters its own continuity, flourishing, and survival. Cultural organizational learning would focus on the *mutual* creation of compatible and shared meanings.

Would one find the same tacit, artifactual interaction in a larger, more highly differentiated organization? We agree with Ed Schein (personal communication, June 1988) that the theoretical premises remain the same, regardless of differences in size and structure. We suggest, however, that cultural learning as we have described it may be more easily seen when size is small and structure is simple. Such would be the case with subunits of large organizations. . . .

. . . We do not mean to suggest that organizations have only single cultures. It does seem to us, however, that cultural learning across subcultures within a single organization, even in the presence of differences, disagreements, perhaps hostility, will take place—if at all—through the tacit processes of artifactual interaction we have discussed. The question indeed is whether learning will take place under such circumstances, whether it will be preservative or not, and if so, of what. How and whether it happens is likely to be context specific; that it might be preservative learning is a possibility to entertain in any context. As the field of organizational culture itself develops theories of power, our understanding of cultural learning will benefit.

Finally, from the emphasis on error detection and correction inherited from the systems view, it has been a logical step for the cognitive perspective to develop the normative position that organizations *ought* to have the ability to detect and correct errors. This, in turn, has supported the claim that when organizations detect and correct errors, they have "learned." In this fashion, the cognitive perspective has evolved a substantially problem-oriented and problem-solving understanding of organizational learning: If learning is about correcting errors, then learning is about things that have gone wrong.

But, as Vickers (personal communication, January 1981) has pointed out, an orientation toward what goes wrong does not necessarily yield the sum total of what is interesting or vital about organizational life. What goes right can also be of interest, and is so, we would argue, for the very reason that it accounts for much of what organizations do. We hold that a cultural theory of organizational learning enables one to focus as much on the right as on the wrong and as much on continuity and preservation as on change. We believe this to be a fruitful area for further exploration.

Vickers (1976) intended his focus on the cultural nature of institutional change "to challenge some widely held beliefs about the role and dominance of cognition" (p. 7). We do not assume for ourselves the whole of this challenge, but we would be pleased if our observations were to further

the current explorations of the role that culture plays in our lives, particularly that growing portion that is spent in maintaining and changing our institutions.

NOTES

1. Duncan and Weiss (1979) develop a similar critique in their finding that individual learning within an organizational setting, as presented by March and Olsen (1976) and Argyris and Schön (1978), has limitations for producing understanding of "systematic organization action."

2. For that matter, even within research on individual cognition there is a great deal of attention given to variations in how learning occurs across individuals and within one individual over time (see, for example, Gardner, 1983).

3. It seems to us that the concept of organizational learning began to attract attention in the mid-1970s, in part in response to theories of organizational change from the previous decade that called for radical changes in the social, political, and corporate worlds. The concept of organizational *learning* provided a noncontroversial, conservative, yet dynamic, alternative for addressing the issue of change because, traditionally, learning is not seen as a controversial or radical activity. It also provided a tool for intervention. Its psychological origins made it a manageable tool, in that it targeted problems in single individuals, who could be helped to learn, in contrast with radical change theories rooted in analyses of the sociopolitical structure that demanded change in "the system."

4. Although inventions and innovations are often the products of single individuals, part of the process of building an organization is a matter of embedding the know-how required for the ongoing production and adaptation of these products into the organization itself. Karl Weick has called to our attention a series of social psychological experiments that modeled cultural transmission within a group, similar to our discussion here, as subjects are replaced over successive generations of the experi-

ment. The research found that the small group's simple strategy survived changes in membership. This research is reported in Weick and Gilfillan (1971).

5. Bateson (1958) was perhaps the first to analyze the problem of learning by a group, in his 1936 study of how the Iatmul culture learned to accommodate change. In his epilogue to the later edition of the book, he elaborated on the concept of "schismo-genesis" to describe this process. Much influenced by his interim studies in psychology, Bateson introduced the concept of "deutero-learning"—"learning to learn"—as the way in which groups and individuals manage a changing environment.

6. There is no single definition or theory of culture in either the interdisciplinary field of organizational culture studies or in its disciplinary "homes" of anthropology or sociology. Ouchi and Wilkins (1985) noted this quite thoroughly in their review of the several literatures whose theories and debates underlie and inform work in organizationally oriented culture studies. We place ourselves in the school that considers both meanings and their artifactual expressions to be necessary components of culture. When we refer to a cultural perspective in this essay, we have in mind one informed by such an interpretative theoretical position. We cannot in this article explore the ways in which cultural learning might look different according to one's theoretical position regarding the nature of culture, but we wish to acknowledge that this might be the case and might be a useful area for further research.

7. Properly speaking, symbols, rituals, myths, and so forth are *not* the artifacts of an organization's culture; annual reports, statements of corporate philosophy, award celebrations, daily talk about the specifics of work, and so forth are the artifacts. The former terms are analytic vocabulary that characterize and categorize the actual artifacts. As tools of research, these terms draw attention to certain features of organizational life; in fact, they incorporate the rules and conventions by which such categories are formed. This point is germane to a central methodological issue in the study of organizational cultures: Because the analytic categories are essentially constructs of

the observer, care must be taken not to confuse them with organizational experience itself.

8. This case is based on extensive observation and interviewing over a period of several years, including numerous visits to all three workshops, detailed interviews with all key personnel, and "shop floor" interviews with flutemakers and apprentices at all levels. The case as presented here draws, as well, on Cook (1982). Our theoretical interest in culture as an approach to organizational learning initially grew out of our considerations of the flute case. Since then, we have moved back and forth between theory building and exploration of the case in developing the view presented here. In this sense, both our experience and the form of this essay reflect a recursive interpretive, or hermeneutic, circle.

9. One of Polanyi's examples is of bicycle riding, where balance is learned tacitly while focusing on pedaling or steering or some other target of attention. On a related subject, Brown and Duguid (1991) have explored ways that practitioners communicate and learn skills tacitly in daily practice.

10. We have had this point further confirmed in a personal conversation with a member of the Juilliard String Quartet. Over more than two decades the quartet has replaced all but one of its original members. One of the newest members reports that his experience of learning to play in the style of the Juilliard and his contributions to the evolution of that style were never a subject of explicit conversation but were carried out through the playing of the music itself in rehearsal and performance.

11. For Douglas (1986), such concerns in a societal context include classification systems, institutional memory and forgetfulness, and group identity. She addresses the issue of attributing emotions, behaviors, or thought to institutions, and argues that thinking itself forms the social bond among individuals and binds them in a corporate entity. In a similar sense, Bougon, Weick, and Binkhorst (1977) held that "what ties an organization together is what ties thought together" (p. 626). What we are suggesting is an approach that adds to thinking what Vickers (1973) called

"appreciating," that would include values and feelings along with artifacts and practices as the organizational glue.

REFERENCES

Argyris, C., & Schön, D. A. (1978). *Organizational learning*. Reading, MA: Addison-Wesley.

Bateson, G. (1958). *Naven* (2nd ed.). Stanford, CA: Stanford University Press.

Berger, P. L., & Luckmann, T. (1966). *The social construction of reality*. New York: Doubleday.

Bougon, M., Weick, K., & Binkhorst, D. (1977). Cognition in organizations: An analysis of the Utrecht Jazz Orchestra. *Administrative Science Quarterly, 22*, 606–639.

Brown, J. S., & Duguid, P. (1991). Organizational learning and communities-of-practice: Toward a unified view of working, learning, and innovation. *Organizational Science, 2*, 40–57.

Cook, S. D. N. (1982). *Part of what judgment is*. Doctoral dissertation, Massachusetts Institute of Technology.

Davis, T. R. V. (1985). Managing culture at the bottom. In R. H. Kilmann, M. J. Saxton, R. Serpa, & Associates (Eds.), *Gaining control of the corporate culture*. San Francisco: Jossey-Bass.

Douglas, M. (1986). *How institutions think*. Syracuse, NY: Syracuse University Press.

Duncan, R., & Weiss, A. (1979). Organizational learning. *Research in Organizational Behavior, 1*, 75–123.

Frost, P. J., Moore, L. F., Louis, M. R., Lundberg, C. C., & Martin, J. (1985). *Organizational culture*. Beverly Hills, CA: Sage.

Frost, P. J., Moore, L. F., Louis, M. R., Lundberg, C. C., & Martin, J. (1991). *Reframing organizational cultures*. Newbury Park, CA: Sage.

Gahmberg, H. (1980). *Contact patterns and learning in organizations: With a network analysis in two industrial organizations*. Helsinki, Finland: Helsinki School of Economics.

Gardner, H. (1983). *Frames of mind*. New York: Basic Books.

Hamilton, E., & Cairns, H. (Eds.). (1961). *The collected dialogues of Plato*. Princeton, NJ: Princeton University Press.

Hedberg, B. (1981). How organizations learn and unlearn. In P. C. Nystrom & W. H. Starbuck (Eds.), *Handbook of organizational design*. London: Oxford University Press.

Louis, M. R. (1985). Sourcing workplace cultures. In R. H. Kilmann, M. J. Saxton, R. Serpa, & Associates (Eds.), *Gaining control of the corporate culture*. San Francisco: Jossey-Bass.

March, J. G., & Olsen, J. P. (1976). Organizational learning and the ambiguity of the past. In *Ambiguity and choice in organizations*. Oslo, Norway: Universitetsforlaget.

Mead, G. H. (1934). *Mind, self and society*. Chicago: University of Chicago.

Miles, R. H., & Randolph, W. A. (1981). Influence of organizational learning styles on early development. In J. R. Kimberly & R. H. Miles (Eds.), *The organizational life cycle*. San Francisco: Jossey-Bass.

Morgan, G. (1986). *Images of organization*. Beverly Hills, CA: Sage.

Ouchi, W. G., & Wilkins, A. L. (1985). Organizational culture. *Annual Review of Sociology, 11*, 457–483.

Polanyi, M., & Prosch, H. (1975). *Meaning*. Chicago: University of Chicago Press.

Schein, E. H. (1985). Organizational culture and leadership. San Francisco: Jossey-Bass.

Smircich, L. (1983). Concepts of culture and organizational analysis. *Administrative Science Quarterly, 28*(3), 339–358.

Taylor, C. (1979). Interpretation and the sciences of man. In P. Rabinow & W. M. Sullivan (Eds.), *Interpretive social science: A reader*. Berkeley: University of California Press.

Vickers, G. (1973). *Making institutions work*. London: Associated Business Programmes.

Vickers, G. (1976, November). *Institutional learning as controlled cultural change*. Paper presented at the Division for Study in Research and Education, Massachusetts Institute of Technology.

Weick, K. E. (1979). Cognitive processes in organizations. *Research in Organizational Behavior, 1*, 41–74.

Weick, K. E. (1991). The nontraditional quality of organizational learning. *Organizational Science, 2*(1), 41–73.

Weick, K. E., & Gilfillan, D. P. (1971). Fact of arbitrary traditions in a lab microculture. *Journal of Personality and Social Psychology, 17,* 179–191.

Yanow, D. (1992). Supermarkets and culture clash: The epistemological role of metaphors in administrative practice. *American Review of Public Administration, 22*(2), 89–109.

37
Changing Organizational Cultures
Harrison M. Trice & Janice M. Beyer

Because it entails introducing something new and substantially different from what prevails in existing cultures, cultural innovation is bound to be more difficult than cultural maintenance. Managers who want to change existing cultures need to find ways to incorporate new elements into prevalent ideologies and cultural forms. Managers who want to create cultures need to figure out how to develop and inculcate distinctive sets of ideologies and cultural forms that will fit their circumstances and membership. Whether changing or creating cultures, managers inevitably need to replace some of the existing ideologies, symbols, and customs with new ones. Even in new organizations, members do not arrive without cultural baggage from their pasts.

The underlying duality of creation and destruction that is required by innovation is often downplayed by those who preach it. But when innovation occurs, some things replace or displace others. . . . People often resist such changes. They have good reasons to. It is realistic for people to expect that any change will bring some losses as well as possible gains. Often the losses are more certain than the gains. The successful management of the processes of culture change or creation thus often entails convincing people that likely gains outweigh the losses. . . .

WAYS OF THINKING ABOUT CULTURE CHANGE

A Definition of Culture Change
Discussing culture change can be very confusing unless we define what we mean by change. . . . Cultures are dynamic entities; they naturally give rise to all kinds of incremental changes. Furthermore, . . . attempts to maintain a culture inevitably involve some adjustments in ideologies and cultural forms that could be considered changes. Neither of these forms of change, however, are what most experts and managers mean when they refer to culture change. Most mean something more deliberate, drastic, and profound than incremental changes or cultural adjustments. We will reserve the term *culture change* to refer to planned, more encompassing, and more substantial kinds of changes than those which arise spontaneously within cultures or as a part of conscious efforts to keep an existing culture vital. Culture change involves a break with the past; cultural continuity is noticeably disrupted. It is an inherently disequilibriating process.

Considering what culture change is not is one way to begin the search for a definition. One observer concluded that ". . . a few examples of new practices here and there throughout an organization do not represent 'culture change'; they need to be woven into the entire fabric of the system" (Kanter 1984, p. 196). Thus, culture change amounts to more than a reduction in litter and vandalism, the promotion of executive health, or the turnaround of an unprofitable two-year history. On the positive side, other analysts suggest culture change is marked by

> . . . real changes in the behavior of people throughout the organization. In a technical sense we mean people in the organization identifying with new role-model heroes . . . telling different stories to one another . . .

Source: Harrison M. Trice & Janice M. Beyer, *The Cultures of Work Organizations* (Upper Saddle River, NJ: Prentice-Hall, 1993), pp. 393–428. ©1993 Prentice-Hall, Inc. Reprinted by permission of Pearson Education, Inc., Upper Saddle River, NJ.

spending their time differently on a day-to-day basis . . . asking different questions and carrying out different work rituals. (Deal and Kennedy 1982, p. 158).

Like the description of culture change that opened this chapter, these analyses make it clear that culture change in organizations is not an easy process; rather it is a difficult, complicated, and demanding effort that may not succeed. It involves not one change, but many changes in many cultural elements so that ". . . *together* [they] reflect a new pattern of values, norms, and expectations" (Kanter 1984, p. 196). Such concerted, widespread changes don't happen spontaneously. Rather they are planned and consciously carried out—usually at the instigation of top management.

Because it involves such wholesale change, culture change is a relatively drawn out and slow process. The popular press during the 1980s seemed to suggest the possibility that new "designer cultures" could be produced quickly. More cautious thinking has challenged such facile promises, but they have not entirely disappeared. Most experts now agree that culture change usually takes several years to accomplish.

Types of Culture Change

Accounts describe at least three different types of culture change efforts in organizations. Some of these efforts seek to bring about massive changes in whole organizations with as much speed as possible. Others are just as radical, but are confined to only parts of an organization. Still others involve many smaller changes that are spread out over years and decades. The descriptions seem to fall into three basic types: (1) revolutionary and comprehensive efforts to change the cultures of entire organizations; (2) efforts confined largely to changing specific subcultures or subunits within organizations; and (3) efforts that are gradual and incremental, but nevertheless cumulate in a comprehensive reshaping of an entire organization's culture. The changes made at the post office in the 1970s . . . exemplify the

first type—revolutionary, comprehensive culture change. Efforts that transformed the L-1011 plant at Lockheed, . . . which will be described later in this chapter exemplify the second type—culture change limited to subcultures or subunits. The last type is exemplified by Cadbury, Limited, the British chocolate confectionery company that continuously and self-consciously modified its culture over a period of almost thirty years to fit its changing environment (Child and Smith 1987). . . .

Assessing Amounts of Change

If culture change is viewed as an ongoing process, and not a discrete event or outcome, it becomes easier to disaggregate different aspects of the process. Change processes can be described along four dimensions that help to clarify the amount of change involved in a planned culture change. These dimensions . . . are the pervasiveness, magnitude, innovativeness, and duration of a change process (Beyer and Trice 1978, pp. 18–20). By analyzing an envisioned change in terms of these dimensions, managers will have a better understanding of the amounts of change they are taking on.

The *pervasiveness* of an envisioned culture change is the proportion of the activities in an organization that will be affected by it. This proportion is determined by at least two factors: how many members are expected to change their cultural understandings and behaviors, and how frequently these changes will call upon them to behave differently in doing their work. . . .

The *magnitude* of a change involves the distance between old understandings and behaviors and the new ones members are expected to adopt. Will organizational members see the new desired ideologies and values as close to ones they already hold or as very different and distant from them? Are some existing ideologies and values now so incompatible with the desired culture that members must stop subscribing to them and put others in their place? In effect, must parts of the existing cultures be destroyed or just displaced somewhat? Looking at the behavioral side, how much replacement or displacement of programs and activities that act as cultural forms is involved? How much will the status quo be disturbed in regard to time allocations, status, power, and other resources?

Innovativeness refers to the degree to which the ideas and behaviors required by a desired culture are unprecedented or have some similarity to what already happened somewhere. If a desired culture is similar to that used by other groups or organizations, managers and members can adapt what others have learned about how such a culture works. In particular, they can perhaps imitate some of the cultural forms that help to communicate and affirm such a culture.[1] If it is not similar, originality will be required to devise cultural forms with novel content. Also relevant is whether some groups inside the organization already have a subculture similar to the desired culture. If any internal examples exist, managers and other members can learn something from them. But if a totally new and radical culture is envisioned, managers and members must invent new networks of ideologies and values to give it substance. They may also have to invent variations of cultural forms no one has ever tried before. . . .

Duration refers to how long a change effort is likely to take and how permanent the change will be. While all radical organizationwide culture changes take years, some are more protracted than others. We would expect that culture change in organizations with poor performance or rapidly changing environments would proceed more rapidly than that in other organizations. While management usually intends cultural changes to persist over the foreseeable future, some cultures are temporary—either because they deal with temporary circumstances that are clearly recognized as such, or because they grow up in temporary organizations. . . .

Because the four dimensions of change are conceptually distinct, we should not expect any given change to be either high or low on all dimensions. In assessing amounts of culture change, managers will want to especially consider the magnitude and innovativeness of a change; together these dimensions indicate how much the envisioned changes represent a break with the past. If magnitude is high and innovativeness is low or medium, managers are facing a culture change effort. If innovativeness is high, managers may need to create a new culture, especially if the change will also be pervasive. This is what General Motors chose to do in founding the Saturn Corporation. Saturn represents GM's attempt to build cars in what is a radically new way for that company and its employees. If both magnitude and innovativeness are low, managers are dealing with cultural maintenance rather than innovation. The pervasiveness of an envisioned change indicates how comprehensive it will be. High pervasiveness indicates that the whole organization must be persuaded to change; low pervasiveness indicates that the change effort can be targeted to certain subunits or groups. Table 37.1 combines the three types of

TABLE 37.1 • TYPES AND DIMENSIONS OF CULTURE CHANGE

Types of Culture Change	Placement on Dimensions
1. Revolutionary, comprehensive	Pervasiveness: high Magnitude: high Innovativeness: variable Duration: variable
2. Subunit or subculture	Pervasiveness: low Magnitude: moderate to high Innovativeness: variable Duration: variable
3. Cumulative comprehensive reshaping	Pervasiveness: high Magnitude: moderate Innovativeness: moderate Duration: high

change discussed in the last section with the four dimensions just discussed. The table shows that different dimensions of change are key indicators of the types of culture change described in the literature. While other combinations of dimensions are possible, these appear to be the most common.

The third type of culture change is the least discontinuous of the three. The culture breaks that occur are numerous, but each is moderate in magnitude. Also, this type of change tends to seek pervasive changes — ones intended to affect virtually all employees to some degree. Because the cultural reshaping occurs gradually, through many changes that accumulate and are internalized over time, this type of change may be easiest to implement and most enduring.

SPECIFIC CONSIDERATIONS IN CHANGING CULTURES

Capitalize on Propitious Moments

Culture change is best initiated at propitious moments, when some obvious problem, opportunity, or change in circumstances makes change seem desirable. . . . By the time that John Egan and his new management team took over at Jaguar, performance was so poor that another cultural change could be readily justified. Many analyses of all kinds of social changes point to the presence of accumulated excesses or deficiencies of the past social order as triggers to cultural revolutions (Lundberg 1985; Miller and Friesen 1980; Meyer 1982; Kuhn 1970).

Managers should be cautious not only about whether culture change is appropriate and really needed . . . but also about whether they can persuade members and outside constituents that a culture change is justified. They should not assume that because the need for change seems obvious to them it is obvious to others. Proponents of culture change often need to dramatize the circumstances that call for change to various stakeholders in order to win their support and cooperation. This may require sharing some bad news about the organization that

management is reluctant to disclose lest it reflect badly on their performance. Fortunately, any problems that have accumulated can often be blamed on environmental change of some sort (Salancik and Meindl 1984). . . .

Combine Caution with Optimism

Once they have decided to embark on a cultural change effort, managers need to create an optimistic outlook on what the change effort will bring. While cultures are undoubtedly difficult to change (Uttal 1983; Barley and Louis 1983; Beyer 1981; Martin and Siehl 1983), managers must have confidence that they can succeed or they will likely communicate their doubts to others. A thorough understanding of the various leverage points they have available to them should help to create such confidence. It will also help if they realize that cultures inevitably change anyway, and that it is natural for them as managers to attempt to channel and initiate such change (Jones 1984). Consistency and persistence in their efforts is absolutely essential in conveying optimism and confidence.

One way to resolve doubts about whether an organization's culture can be changed is to realize that the truth lies roughly halfway between extreme views on the subject. Recall that some analysts claim it is practically impossible to change cultures deliberately. According to this argument, cultures are too elusive and hidden to be accurately described, managed, or changed (Uttal 1983). Other analyses, however, imply that cultures can be readily manipulated, suggesting that managers can use direct, intentional actions to change their cultures (Peters and Waterman 1982: Deal and Kennedy 1982; Kilmann 1982). A consensus seems to be emerging that the middle ground between these two viewpoints is realistic. Thus, both caution and optimism are warranted. . . .

Understand Resistance to Culture Change

. . . Research on organizational change of all kinds has documented many reasons that

TABLE 37.2 • COMMON SOURCES OF RESISTANCE TO CHANGE

At the individual level:
  Fear of the unknown
  Self-interest
  Selective attention and retention
  Habit
  Dependence
  Need for security
At the organization or group level:
  Threats to power and influence
  Lack of trust
  Different perceptions and goals
  Social disruption
  Resource limitations
  Fixed investments
  Interorganizational agreements

Source: Adapted from Hellriegel, Slocum, and Woodman, 1986; and Daft and Steers, 1986.

people resist change. Table 37.2 gives a fairly comprehensive listing of common sources of such resistance. All of them may come into play in culture change efforts. . . .

Change Many Elements, But Maintain Some Continuity

One way to honor the past and maintain continuity is to identify the principles that will remain constant "in the midst of turbulence, both internal and external" (Wilkins 1989, p. 56). Hewlett-Packard, for example, has been forced by its growth to develop large corporate structures that require increased coordination between far-flung operations. Despite these changed conditions, HP management has made substantial efforts to continue the "HP way"—an emphasis on decentralized operations, autonomous management, and the promotion of employee welfare. By increasing the number of meetings and coordinating efforts among division general managers, HP has been able to maintain division autonomy. "By focusing upon what will remain un-

changed, and showing that these commitments will be kept inviolate, the company has apparently been able to significantly improve coordination between divisions" (Wilkins 1989, p. 57). . . .

Of course, changing organizational cultures requires not one change, but many changes in many different cultural elements. In particular, change efforts must encompass both ideologies and the accumulated cultural forms that express them. It is not easy to keep cultural practices and associated meanings consistent with each other and with new ideologies as changes occur. Since ideologies lie at the core of culture, change efforts must be aimed directly at changing "the experiences people have and what they learn from them so that assumptions and core values are altered" (Wilkins and Patterson 1985, p. 289). Detailed studies of cultural change at Jaguar and at a British merchant bank showed that attempts to alter cultures by attending only to cultural beliefs have little success. "Those efforts which are directed towards the essence of . . . values, *as well as* the logics, languages, metaphors or status patterns in which they are embodied promise greater return" (Whipp, Rosenfeld, and Pettigrew 1989, p. 581 [emphasis added]). . . .

Recognize the Importance of Implementation

An informal survey of management consultants found that over 90 percent of American companies have been unable to carry out changes in corporate strategies (Kiechel 1979). This astonishing figure dramatizes the fact that many adopted changes are never successfully implemented. Initial acceptance and enthusiasm are insufficient to carry change forward. Many carefully adopted changes are subsequently abandoned.

Every stage of any change process carries the hazard of omission, abandonment, or return to an earlier stage. A simplified three-stage model of a change process begins with adoption—the decision to make some change. The next stage is implementation—the actions required to put the change in place. The last stage is institutionalization—the persistent incorporation of the change into the daily routines and cultures of the organization (Beyer and Trice 1978). While these stages may overlap, especially in culture change efforts, the model is useful in showing that how thoroughly and well a logically prior stage is executed is likely to affect the next stage. In particular, it suggests that the institutionalization of a culture change effort depends heavily on how well it is implemented. . . .

The kinds of strategies that can be employed to diffuse a cultural innovation are well illustrated by what happened when Blount set out to change the U.S. Post Office (Biggart, 1977). His implementation strategies employed extensive communications and training. Because unhappy mailers frequently complained to members of Congress, the new United States Postal Service (USPS) created a consumer advocate position in an effort to funnel complaints away from Congress. It also established an Office of Advertising to propagate its new image of autonomy from outsiders and from Congress. At the same time, it dispatched top level executives on media tours to hold briefings in all regions of the country. Finally, training of supervisors focused upon learning new businesslike attitudes and unlearning old practices of relating to employees, customers, and work itself. A large training institute was established in Bethesda, Maryland with a 75-member faculty of specialists in training, development, and technical areas. They trained approximately 20,000 supervisors a year. Also, members of this faculty often went to major post offices and conducted on-site training in decision making directed explicitly at reducing the accumulated emphasis on authoritarianism in the organization.

Despite the many avenues Blount used to implement culture change, critics of the post office see considerable cultural persistence. Many feel the post office has not entirely shed its old ways and that its com-

petitors are still more efficient and businesslike. But it is hard to deny that the post office has changed. What critics see are residues of the old culture. It is unrealistic to expect a complete disappearance of an existing culture without total destruction of the group or organization involved or dispersal of its members. Even then, members will carry much of what they learned in that culture with them as they enter new organizations or join new groups. All culture change is partial; it cannot reasonably be expected to achieve total eradication of a prior culture. Even when envisioned changes are pervasive and of great magnitude, culture change usually amounts to some degree of modification of a culture. Changes that entail innovative responses—unprecedented and genuinely unfamiliar understandings and behaviors—are likely to result in the most radical cultural change.

Select, Modify, and Create Appropriate Cultural Forms

Numerous scholars have suggested that cultural change comes about by managers' employing symbols, rituals, languages, and stories to modify cultural meanings. Some argue that the manipulation of symbols is the "very stuff" of managerial behavior (Peters 1978, p. 10; Schein 1985). The actions of managers can also symbolically legitimate changes in the culture (Pfeffer 1981; Jones 1984). Their calendar and phone behavior, the apportionment of their time, and their control of settings are powerful symbolic tools managers can use to change organizational cultures. The presence or absence of top managers, the location of meetings, who attends, what types of questions managers ask—all of these act as "mundane tools" that can be consciously "packaged and managed" (Peters 1978, p. 10). Other scholars advise that managers should "be seen as spending a lot of time on matters visibly related to the values they preach" (Deal and Kennedy 1982, p. 169).

Metaphors can also be effective vehicles for change (Krefting and Frost 1985, p. 155).

By changing or eliminating long-standing metaphors that depict an old organizational ideology, a culture can be moved toward change. For example, the elimination of the family metaphor "Ma Bell" signaled that AT&T was modifying its protective ideology relative to employees and customers. A new symbol was chosen for the new culture—a globe girdled by electronic communications. Long-standing metaphors can be hard to eradicate, however. As pointed out earlier, the press still regularly refers to the regional companies spun off from AT&T more than ten years ago as Baby Bells.

Devising and promulgating new myths has also been advocated as a particularly effective way to change cultures (Boje, Fedor, and Rowland 1982). Through myths, managers can invent new explanations for the way things are. They can also change existing myths in various ways (Hedberg 1981, p. 12). Ruling myths can be undermined when the actions they support fail to materialize. New leaders and new political coalitions can then discredit old myths as the doubts about them spread. Also, competing myths from outside the organization can be introduced to challenge the old myths.

Although rites and ceremonials can also act as levers for change (Moore and Myerhoff 1977), change is clearly not their usual purpose. They usually maintain and celebrate current, traditional ideologies (Trice and Beyer 1985). For this reason it seems unrealistic to expect that rites composed entirely of forms that express new ideologies will seem appropriate and appealing to members of a culture. Instead, new messages can be combined with accepted, ongoing cultural elements. Either existing rites can be modified to incorporate new values, or entirely new rites that consciously combine elements of the old and the new can be established. . . .

While rites of passage are usually used to maintain the continuity of cultures, there is no inherent reason why they cannot be used to instill new ideologies and values. . . .

Other possibilities for resocializing members include rites of passage to mark any

changes of status of existing members and rites of enhancement that reward those behaviors most in accord with desired ideologies. The latter are likely to be most effective when they reinforce behaviors already instilled in some employees through rites of passage. Of course, all of the other culture forms can also be used to support and facilitate cultural change. Uniforms can be changed, new jargon created, new stories circulated, new songs written, and so on. Readers have probably seen some of these uses and can readily think of ideas for others.

In general, it seems that establishing rites of creation and transition, and new rites of passage and enhancement for individuals may be the best way to begin cultural change efforts. Both newcomers and current employees can learn about and be indoctrinated into new understandings with demanding training that readies members for the changes that will be required.

Rites of degradation logically complete this cluster of rites, but probably should ordinarily not follow until members have had a chance to learn the new expectations. Even when a jolt would be desirable to signal that quick change is imperative, and rites of degradation look like a logical starting point, early use may make members of the organization feel that those degraded are being treated unfairly. If firings must take place, it may be better to delay and then gloss over them as quickly as possible (Gooding 1972) while getting on to positive celebrations of new culture. . . .

Modify Socialization Tactics
Because the primary way that people learn their cultures is through the socialization processes they experience (Van Maanen 1973), if these processes are changed, an organization's cultures will begin to change. We have already discussed the crucial role that cultural forms, especially rites, play in socializing new members and resocializing old ones during a planned culture change. Rites of passage are, of course, the cultural form most directly aimed at socializing peo-

ple into new roles. One reason that they tend to function to ensure cultural continuity rather than change is that they are often structured as institutionalized tactics, which tend to produce custodial role orientations. In work organizations, rites of passage often consist of collective, formal training of a fixed duration that prepares a group of recruits for one of a sequence of established statuses. They may also employ experienced members of the culture to communicate expectations and provide role models, and often endeavor to divest recruits of past identities. It is easy to see how socialization structured in this way is likely to produce cultural continuity.

However, it is far from clear that changing all of these tactics is advisable to further planned culture change. More individualized tactics may produce more innovative role orientations by individual members but are too random and dissimilar in their effects across individuals to be very helpful in instilling desired cultural beliefs and values uniformly throughout an organization. Rather, persons who experience individualized tactics are freer to develop their own ideas about how to carry out their roles. If management already has a set of new cultural ideologies, values, and norms it wishes to instill throughout an organization, some of the institutionalized tactics are still appropriate because a relatively uniform response to socialization is desirable. Collective and formal tactics of a fixed duration can be used to impart new cultural substance in addition to those elements of the old culture that are desirable to retain. . . .

Although we have focused on the socialization of newcomers, most of the considerations discussed also apply to socialization of present members for new roles and responsibilities or their general resocialization into a desired new culture. Members cannot be expected to change their convictions without some organized presentation and discussion of the new ideas they are expected to internalize. General resocialization efforts usually begin at the top levels of large organizations and work downwards, for it

seems unrealistic to expect lower level managers and employees to subscribe to values different from those evidenced by their superiors' behaviors and decisions.

Find and Cultivate Innovative Leadership

Probably the most important quality of an innovative cultural leader is that he or she be able to convince members of the organization to follow new visions. "Members are unlikely to give up whatever security they derive from existing cultures and follow a leader in new directions unless that leader exudes self-confidence, has strong convictions, a dominant personality, and can preach the new vision with drama and eloquence" (Trice and Beyer 1991, p. 163). . . .

Managers who seek to change an existing culture often have to find ways to discredit and destroy parts of the old culture. One way to do so is to remove prominent persons representing those aspects of the old culture. Their removal has both symbolic and practical consequences. It communicates to other members that certain values and beliefs are no longer acceptable. It also typically eliminates powerful persons who might generate resistance to the new culture. As already mentioned, there are some dangers, however, that firing prominent members of the old culture may cause widespread resentment. Some new CEOs, like Blount in the U.S. Postal Service, used incentives to persuade old-guard members to retire. Others force out those who oppose their managerial ideologies with rites of degradation. They assemble evidence to discredit those they want to dismiss, make it public, and then fire them. . . .

SUMMARY

Cultural innovation involves the duality of creation and destruction. Whether old cultures are being changed or new cultures are being created in new organizations, members will need to replace or displace ideologies and customary behaviors they bring from past roles and experiences in different cultures. There is, however, a range of degrees of creation and destruction — of displacements and innovations — involved in what people caught up in them experience as "changes." Because cultures inevitably change incrementally and people within them adjust their behaviors and beliefs in various ways, discussing cultural innovation and change can be confusing if we do not draw a line somewhere to separate substantial changes from minor fluctuations and adjustments. Also, managers need to be clear about which they are attempting because substantial change and minor adjustments in cultures involve different issues and require different behaviors.

Culture change involves a noticeable break with the past; it also inevitably involves changes in both ideologies and cultural forms. Three types of cultural change have been identified: (1) relatively fast, revolutionary, comprehensive change; (2) subunit or subcultural change; and (3) a more gradual cumulative but comprehensive reshaping of a culture. Each of these types has a characteristic pattern along four dimensions of change processes: pervasiveness, magnitude, innovativeness, and duration. . . .

NOTE

1. The imitation of Japanese quality circles provides a well-known example of such cultural borrowing. U.S. users did not invent this cultural form; therefore it was not a totally new cultural innovation. However, the first U.S. users of quality circles did confront a more innovative change than later users because the first users had to figure out how to adapt this cultural form to the U.S. culture. The hazards of borrowing cultural forms are also evident from this example. Most observers agree that quality circles have had only modest success in the United States and have not been successfully grafted onto U.S. organizational cultures (Lawler and Mohrman 1987, Shea 1986).

REFERENCES

Barley Stephen R., and Meryl Louis (1983). Many in one: Organizations as multicultural entities. Paper presented at the annual meeting of the Academy of Management, August 14–17, Dallas, Tex.

Beyer, Janice M. (1981). Ideologies, values and decison-making in organizations. Pp. 166–97 in Nystrom, Paul, and William H. Starbuck (eds.) *Handbook of Organizational Design*, vol. 2. London: Oxford University Press.

Beyer, Janice M., and Harrison M. Trice (1978). *Implementing Change: Alcoholism Programs in Work Organizations*. New York: Free Press.

Biggart, Nicole W. (1977). The creative-destructive process of organizational change: The case of the post office. *Administrative Science Quarterly*, 22: 410–26.

Boje, David M., Donald B. Fedor, and Kendrith M. Rowland (1982). Mythmaking: A qualitative step in OD interventions. *Journal of Applied Behavioral Science*, 18: 17–28.

Child, John, and Chris Smith (1987). The context and process of organizational transformation — Cadbury Limited in its sector. *Journal of Management Studies*, 24(November): 565–93.

Daft, Richard L., and Richard M. Steers (1986). *Organizations: A Micro/Macro Approach*. Glenview, Ill.: Scott, Foresman.

Deal, Terrence E., and Allan A. Kennedy (1982). *Corporate Cultures: The Rites and Rituals of Corporate Life*. Reading, Mass.: Addison-Wesley.

Gooding, Judson (1972). The art of firing an executive. *Fortune*, October, Pp. 22–30.

Hedberg, Bo (1981). How organizations learn and unlearn. Pp. 3–27 in Nystrom, Paul C., and William H. Starbuck (eds.) *Handbook of Organizational Design*. London: Oxford University Press.

Hellriegel, Don, John W. Slocum, Jr., and Richard W. Woodman (1986). *Organizational Behavior*, 4th ed. New York: West Publishing Co.

Jones, Michael O. (1984). Corporate natives confer on culture. *The American Folklore Society Newsletter*, 13(October): 6, 8.

Kanter, Rosabeth M. (1984). Managing transitions in organizational culture: The case of participative management at Honeywell. Pp. 195–217 in Kimberly, John R., and Robert Quinn (eds.) *New Futures: The Challenges of Managing Corporate Transitions*. Homewood, Ill.: Dow Jones-Irwin.

Kiechel, Walter (1979). Playing the rules of the corporate strategy game. *Fortune*, September, 24, Pp. 110–15.

Kilmann, Ralph H. (1982). Getting control of the corporate culture. *Managing*, 3: 11–17.

Krefting, Linda A., and Peter J. Frost (1985). Untangling webs, surfing waves, and wildcatting: A multiple-metaphor perspective on managing organizational cultures. Pp. 155–68 in Frost, Pester, et al. (eds.) *Organizational Culture*. Beverly Hills, Calif.: Sage Publications, Inc.

Kuhn, Thomas (1970). *The Structure of Scientific Revolutions*. Chicago: University of Chicago Press.

Lawler, Edward E., and Susan A. Mohrman (1987). Quality circles: After the honeymoon. *Organizational Dynamics*, 15(Spring): 42–54.

Lundberg, Craig C. (1985). How should organizational culture be studied? Pp. 197–200 in Frost, Peter J., et al. (eds.) *Organizational Culture*. Beverly Hills, Calif.: Sage Publications, Inc.

Martin, Joanne, and Caren Siehl (1983). Organizational culture and counterculture: An uneasy symbiosis. *Organizational Dynamics*, 12(2): 52–65.

Meyer, Alan D. (1982). How ideologies supplant formal structures and shape responses to environments. *Journal of Management Studies*, 19(1): 45–61.

Miller, Danny, and Peter H. Friesen (1980). Momentum and revolution in organizational adaptation. *Academy of Management Journal*, 23(4): 591–614.

Moore, Sally F., and Barbara G. Myerhoff (1977). Secular ritual: Forms and Meaning. Pp. 3–25 in Moore, Sally F., and Barbara G. Myerhoff (eds.) *Secular Ritual*. Assen, Amsterdam, The Netherlands: Van Gorcum.

Peters, Thomas J. (1978). Symbols, patterns, and settings. *Organizational Dynamics*, 7: 3–23.

Peters, Thomas J., and Robert H. Waterman (1982). *In Search of Excellence: Lessons from America's Best Run Companies*. New York: Harper & Row, Pub.

Pfeffer, Jeffrey (1977). The ambiguity of leadership. *Academy of Management Review*, 2(1): 104–12.

——— (1981). Management as symbolic action: The creation and maintenance of organizational paradigms. *Research in Organizational Behavior*, 3: 1–52.

Salancik, Gerald R., and J. R. Meindl (1984). Corporate attributions as strategic illusions of management control. *Administrative Science Quarterly*, 29: 238–54.

Schein, Edgar H. (1985). *Organizational Culture and Leadership*. San Francisco: Jossey-Bass.

Shea, Gregory P. (1986). Quality circles: The danger of bottled change. *Sloan Management Review*, Spring: 33–46.

Trice, Harrison M., and Janice M. Beyer (1985). Using six organizational rites to change cultures. Pp. 370–99 in Kilmann, Ralph H., Mary J. Saxton, and Roy Serpa (eds.) *Gaining Control of the Corporate Culture*. San Francisco: Jossey-Bass Publishers.

——— (1991). Cultural leadership in organizations. *Organization Science*, 2(2): 149–69.

Uttal, Bro (1983). The corporate culture vultures. *Fortune*, October, 17, Pp. 66–72.

Van Maanen, John (1973). Observations on the making of policemen. *Human Organization*, 32(Winter): 407–17.

Whipp, Richard, Robert Rosenfeld, and Andrew Pettigrew (1989). Culture and Competitiveness: Evidence from two mature U.K. Industries. *Journal of Management Studies*, 26(November): 561–85.

Wilkins, Alan L. (1989). *Developing Corporate Character: How to Successfully Change an Organization without Destroying It*. San Francisco: Jossey-Bass.

Wilkins, Alan L., and Kerry J. Patterson (1985). You can't get there from here: What will make culture-change projects fail. Pp. 262–91 in Kilmann, Ralph H., and Associates (eds.) *Gaining Control of the Corporate Culture*. San Francisco: Jossey-Bass.

38

Organizational Culture: Pieces of the Puzzle

Joanne Martin

When organizations are examined from a cultural viewpoint, attention is drawn to aspects of organizational life that historically have often been ignored or understudied, such as the stories people tell to newcomers to explain "how things are done around here," the ways in which offices are arranged and personal items are or are not displayed, jokes people tell, the working atmosphere (hushed and luxurious or dirty and noisy), the relations among people (affectionate in some areas of an office and obviously angry and perhaps competitive in another place), and so on. Cultural observers also often attend to aspects of working life that other researchers study, such as the organization's official policies, the amounts of money different employees earn, reporting relationships, and so on. A cultural observer is interested in the surfaces of these cultural manifestations because details can be informative, but he or she also seeks an in-depth understanding of the patterns of meanings that link these manifestations together, sometimes in harmony, sometimes in bitter conflicts between groups, and sometimes in webs of ambiguity, paradox, and contradiction.

CULTURE AS A METAPHOR AND CULTURE AS A VARIABLE

The long-winded definition of culture in the prior paragraph takes positions on some of the issues that divide cultural researchers. One of the most important is Smircich's (1983a) distinction between studies of culture as a metaphor for organizational life

and studies of culture as a variable. Studies that assume culture can be treated as a variable are usually assuming a functionalist viewpoint. Functionalist studies of culture offer the promise, to the delight of many managers, that a "strong" culture (one that generates much consensus among employees of an organization) will lead to outcomes most top executives desire to maximize, such as greater productivity and profitability. Functionalist studies bring a kind of cultural research into the mainstream of organizational behavior, where research streams that fail to establish a causal link to performance-related outcomes have seldom managed to achieve long-term prominence. Critics of functional cultural research react with dismay at the intrusion of mainstream preoccupations into "their" cultural domain. For example, Calás and Smircich (1987) declared that cultural research had, by the end of the 1980s, become "dominant, but dead." Although this death knell was premature, many cultural researchers continue to oppose a functionalist approach to the study of culture. Cultural studies that eschew functionalism generally prefer a symbolic approach (Alvesson & Berg, 1992; Pondy, Frost, Morgan, & Dandridge, 1983; Schultz & Hatch, 1996), focusing on the symbolic meanings associated with cultural forms such as rituals and physical arrangements (Schultz, 1995). Although functional approaches often treat culture as a variable, used to predict outcomes, symbolic approaches tend to view culture as a lens for studying organizational life (Smircich, 1983b).

Source: Joanne Martin, *Organizational Culture: Mapping the Terrain* (Thousand Oaks, CA: Sage, 2002), pp. 3–7; 55–92, ©2002 by Sage Publications, Inc. Reprinted by permission of Sage Publications, Inc.

The definition I previously offered assumes that culture is a metaphor, a lens for examining organizational life. That does not mean that culture encompasses and eclipses all other ways of studying organizations. . . . What distinguishes a cultural study from an inventory, however, is a willingness to look beneath the surface, to gain an in-depth understanding of how people interpret the meanings of these manifestations and how these interpretations form patterns of clarity, inconsistency, and ambiguity that can be used to characterize understandings of working lives. . . .

CULTURES IN ORGANIZATIONS AS A VORTEX

When culture is defined as a way of studying everyday life in organizations, the question of scope quickly arises. What is not culture? Is culture just another word for organization? Does cultural theory and research encompass all organizational theory and research? The scope of cultural studies of organizations is much narrower than these questions imply. Cultural theory and research is just one of many organizational domains, and it certainly does not encompass all the others. People cannot learn all they need to know about organizations by studying culture. Simultaneously, however, cultural theory and research is a broad area of organizational inquiry. The field has become a vortex, drawing in people who are studying culture for very different reasons and working from very different scholarly assumptions.

Some people have been drawn to the study of culture in organizations because they find noncultural studies of organizations—for example, those that focus on variables such as size, structure, technology, and demography—dry and narrowly focused. These researchers revel in the kinds of topics—rituals, symbolic meanings, and humor—that some cultural studies examine. Some researchers have been drawn to cultural studies because this domain has been open to qualitative methods,

such as long-term participant observation, discourse analysis, and textual deconstruction, that have not readily been accepted in many mainstream organizational topic domains. These qualitative methods seemed to offer particularly useful ways to deepen understanding of cultural phenomena. For some, cultural research fills a void—offering the promise of clarity and unity in a confusing and ambiguous world. For others, culture offers a way to capture and express complexities central to everyday life in organizations. Many applied researchers have been excited by the potential of culture research to provide some solutions for managers searching for new ways to motivate and control employees, using values to generate commitment and increase productivity and perhaps even profitability. These are not the only reasons for studying culture, but they are representative.

Because of the range of reasons why organizational researchers have been drawn to cultural studies, the major controversies that have polarized and sometimes revolutionized disciplines in the humanities and other social sciences are represented within the field of organizational culture studies as well. Neopositivist cultural research (like much of mainstream organizational research) uses the scientific method to develop and test theory, working from deductively derived hypotheses that can be empirically tested and potentially proven false. Therefore, a neopositivist cultural study's empirically based conclusions are usually described as objectively true ("Our study demonstrated that . . . "), with the goal of developing generalizable theory. In contrast, interpretive studies of culture describe a context in great detail, usually seeking to develop context-specific understandings rather than generalizable theory. Interpretive studies focus on socially constructed knowledge—how people interpret what happens to them. Some interpretive studies frame their conclusions in terms that implicitly claim to be the best available or even an objectively true representation of the culture studied. Other interpretive studies of culture, including those written from a postmodern position, implicitly or explicitly challenge any objective truth claim, explaining that other subjective interpretations are always possible. Postmodern cultural studies, for example, use deconstruction to show how a study's textual rhetoric hides its own inevitable weaknesses if it attempts to claim an inviolable place from which objective truth can be presented. Such postmodern analysis attempts to show that literally any argument contains the seeds of its own destruction. Intellectual traditions, such as neopositivism, interpretive approaches, and postmodernism, all have contributed to cultural studies of organizations and to other domains of organizational research.

Because of the range of scholarly assumptions these researchers hold, the body of literature that focuses on organizational culture is large and diverse, crossing disciplinary and methodological barriers. Also, given that the field of organizational culture research has become a vortex, drawing in scholars who take differing positions on the controversies that have polarized the humanities and social sciences during the past few decades, it can sometimes be difficult to discern which disputes pertain only to the study of culture and which pertain, more broadly, to the study of organizations. . . .

WHAT IS CULTURE? WHAT IS NOT CULTURE?

. . . What is culture? . . . What is not culture? In the course of defining and giving examples of . . . cultural manifestations, three intellectual traditions of relevance to cultural theory will be introduced: functionalism, critical theory, and postmodernism. Manifestations of culture include rituals, stories, humor, jargon, physical arrangements, and formal structures and policies, as well as informal norms and practices. Content themes (such as values or basic assumptions) are used to capture and show the relation-

ships among interpretations of the meanings of these manifestations. These are the building blocks needed for you to understand the theoretical assumptions underlying a culture study, summarize the content of any cultural portrait, and, if you wish, develop your own answers to the questions: What is culture? What is not culture?

Defining Culture

Table 38.1 lists a variety of definitions of culture. I use this table to make it easier to read this section of the chapter, referring to each definition by the number of the definition in the table. These definitions were selected because they reflect the range of definitions of culture currently in use among organizational culture researchers. Definition 1 (Sathe, 1985) and Definition 2 (Louis, 1985) in Table 38.1 illustrate two theoretical features common to most such definitions: the use of the word "shared" and a reference to culture as that which is distinctive or unique to a particular context. Not all researchers agree that culture is shared and unique, however, as will become evident in the following discussion.

Ideational and Materialistic Approaches. The first two definitions have another characteristic in common: Culture is conceptualized in terms of meanings or understandings. These are cognitive aspects of culture, and therefore such definitions are referred to as ideational. Ideational definitions of culture emphasize subjective interpretations, whereas material aspects of culture can be described in objectivist terms, or their meanings can be interpreted subjectively. Definition 3 (Sergiovanni & Corbally, 1984) is similar to Definitions 1 and 2 in that culture is defined as shared, but Definition 3 adds to this ideational emphasis a consideration of the material conditions in which these ideas develop. Materialist manifestations include the material conditions of work (e.g., the plush carpet of an executive suite and the noise and dirt on an assembly line) and the size of employees'

TABLE 38.1 • DEFINITIONS OF ORGANIZATIONAL CULTURE

1. "Culture is the set of important understandings (often unstated) that members of a community share in common" (Sathe, 1985, p. 6).

2. "[Culture is] a set of understandings or meanings shared by a group of people. The meanings are largely tacit among the members, are clearly relevant to a particular group, and are distinctive to the group" (Louis, 1985, p. 74).

3. "A standard definition of culture would include the system of values, symbols, and shared meanings of a group including the embodiment of these values, symbols, and meanings into material objects and ritualized practices. . . . The 'stuff' of culture includes customs and traditions, historical accounts be they mythical or actual, tacit understandings, habits, norms and expectations, common meanings associated with fixed objects and established rites, shared assumptions, and intersubjective meanings" (Sergiovanni & Corbally, 1984, p. viii).

4. "Cultural arrangements, of which organizations are an essential segment, are seen as manifestations of a process of ideational development located within a context of definite material conditions. It is a context of dominance (males over females/owners over workers) but also of conflict and contradiction in which class and gender, autonomous but overdetermined, are vital dynamics. Ideas and cultural arrangements confront actors as a series of rules of behavior; rules that, in their contradictions, may variously be enacted, followed, or resisted" (Mills, 1988, p. 366).

5. "An organization might then be studied by discovering and synthesizing its rules of social interaction and interpretation, as revealed in the behavior they shape. Social interaction and interpretation are communication activities, so it follows that the culture could be described by articulating communication rules" (Schall, 1983, p. 3).

6. "[Culture is] the pattern of shared beliefs and values that give members of an institution meaning, and provide them with the rules for behavior in their organization" (Davis, 1984, p. 1).

7. "To analyze *why* members behave the way they do, we often look for the *values* that govern behavior, which is the second level. . . . But as the values are hard to observe directly, it is often necessary to infer them by interviewing key members of the organization or to content analyze artifacts such as documents and charters. However, in identifying such values, we usually note that they represent accurately only the manifest or *espoused* values of a culture. That is, they focus on what people *say* is the reason for their behavior, what they ideally would like those reasons to be, and what are often their rationalizations for their behavior. Yet, the underlying reasons for their behavior remain concealed or unconscious. To really *understand* a culture and to ascertain more completely the group's values and overt behavior, it is imperative to delve into the *underlying assumptions*, which are typically unconscious but which actually determine how group members perceive, think, and feel" (Schein, 1985, p. 3).

8. "In a particular situation the set of meanings that evolves gives a group its own ethos, or distinctive character, which is expressed in patterns of belief (ideology), activity (norms and rituals), language and other symbolic forms through which organization members both create and sustain their view of the world and image of themselves in the world. The development of a worldview with its shared understanding of group identity, purpose, and direction are products of the unique history, personal interactions, and environmental circumstances of the group" (Smircich, 1983a, p. 56).

9. "Culture does not necessarily imply a uniformity of values. Indeed quite different values may be displayed by people of the same culture. In such an instance, what is it that holds together the members of the organization? I suggest that we look to the existence of a common frame of reference or a shared recognition of relevant issues. There may not be agreement about whether these issues should be relevant or about whether they are positively or negatively valued. . . . They may array themselves differently with respect to that issue, but whether positively or negatively, they are all oriented to it" (Feldman, 1991, p. 154).

10. "Culture is a loosely structured and incompletely shared system that emerges dynamically as cultural members experience each other, events, and the organization's contextual features" (Anonymous reviewer, 1987).

TABLE 38.1 (*continued*)

11. "Members do not agree upon clear boundaries, cannot identify shared solutions, and do not reconcile contradictory beliefs and multiple identities. Yet, these members contend they belong to a culture. They share a common orientation and overarching purpose, face similar problems, and have comparable experiences. However, these shared orientations and purposes accommodate different beliefs and incommensurable technologies, these problems imply different solutions, and these experiences have multiple meanings. . . . Thus, for at least some cultures, to dismiss the ambiguities in favor of strictly what is clear and shared is to exclude some of the most central aspects of the members' cultural experience and to ignore the essence of their cultural community" (Meyerson, 1991a, pp. 131–132).

12. "When organizations are examined from a cultural viewpoint, attention is drawn to aspects of organizational life that historically have often been ignored or understudied, such as the stories people tell to newcomers to explain 'how things are done around here,' the ways in which offices are arranged and personal items are or are not displayed, jokes people tell, the working atmosphere (hushed and luxurious or dirty and noisy), the relations among people (affectionate in some areas of an office and obviously angry and perhaps competitive in another place), and so on. Cultural observers also often attend to aspects of working life that other researchers study, such as the organization's official policies, the amounts of money different employees earn, reporting relationships, and so on. A cultural observer is interested in the surfaces of these cultural manifestations because details can be informative, but he or she also seeks an in-depth understanding of the patterns of meanings that link these manifestations together, sometimes in harmony, sometimes in bitter conflicts between groups, and sometimes in webs of ambiguity, paradox, and contradiction" (Martin, Chapter 1, this volume, p. 3).

Source: Adapted and expanded from materials presented in Martin (1992a).

paychecks and other indicators of their material well-being. Advocates of including material manifestations of culture argue that an exclusive emphasis on ideational elements of culture would foster misunderstanding by permitting a de-emphasis on the vastly different material conditions that characterize work at different levels of an organization's hierarchy. Czarniawaska-Joerges (1992) explains why it is important to include material manifestations:

> Organizational theorists have located new aspects of organizational life and its function to study during the second half of the decade. Among these we can find jokes, coffee breaks, how people are dressed, how they behave at the corporation's Christmas party, how they sit at meetings, how they get fired (the "rite" of getting fired), what stories about present and former figures of authority are told, and so on. . . . It could be argued that these are of marginal importance compared to, for example, the organization's hierarchy and the way in which work is organized, controlled, and carried out. (p. 108)

For example, materialist culture researchers would argue the low pay, dirt, and noise that assembly line workers often endure, or the relative quiet and luxury of the executive suite, must be considered if a cultural study is to offer a rich understanding of these disparate working experiences. In this way, material definitions of culture facilitate discussion of intergroup conflicts. Therefore, Definition 4 (Mills, 1988) is important because it stresses conflict in addition to what is shared, at least within subcultures; Definition 4 also includes both ideational and material aspects of culture.

Two kinds of materialist approaches to the study of culture can be distinguished. Some materialist definitions include material manifestations as part of culture, as can be seen in Definition 3's inclusion of "material objects" and Definition 4's incorporation of "definite material conditions." Other materialist approaches assume that ideational considerations constitute culture (the cultural "superstructure"), whereas material aspects of working life are essential to consider but are not defined as part of culture (the structural "base"). According to this latter point of view, the materialist base consists of attributes such as job descriptions, reporting relationships, pay practices, and formally mandated policies and procedures, which are not part of the cultural superstructure. Culture, then, consists of the ideational elements, such as beliefs and values, that emerge to explain and reinforce a materialist base. Whether one defines material conditions as important to study but not part of culture or includes material conditions as manifestations of a culture, materialist approaches agree that it is essential to examine the material conditions that characterize a cultural context. In contrast, ideational definitions of culture exclude such material conditions.

Focus and Breadth. When many types of cultural manifestations are studied, including informal norms, rituals, stories, physical arrangements, and formal and informal practices, this produces a holistic view of a cultural context, referred to sometimes as a "generalist" study of culture. Materialist studies of culture, for example, are likely to include many types of cultural manifestations, as can be seen in Definitions 3 and 4. In contrast, other more narrow studies define culture in terms of just one or two manifestations, as can be seen in Definition 5 (Schall, 1983) and Definition 6 (Davis, 1984). Definition 5 defines culture as communication rules, whereas Definition 6 has an emphasis on beliefs and values. Studies that rely on narrow definitions of culture are referred to as "specialist" studies. Specialist studies assume that one or a few manifestations can stand in for, or represent, an entire culture because interpretations of more types of manifestations would be consistent. Consistency is a crucial and highly debatable theoretical assumption....

Level of Depth of Interpretation. Depth is also an important component of some

definitions of culture, as can be seen in Definition 7.... Schein's (1985) approach to depth in Definition 7 (see also Schein, 1999) distinguishes three levels of depth: artifacts, values, and basic assumptions.... I argue that this approach to the question of depth confounds the content of a manifestation, such as a story, with the depth of the interpretation of that manifestation. I and others argue that any cultural manifestation can be interpreted superficially, or its interpretation can reflect deeply held, unconscious assumptions....

Areas of Theoretical Disagreement Implicit in Definitions of Culture

Is Culture Shared? We can examine these definitions of culture and see how they imply fundamental theoretical disagreements. Most definitions of organizational culture include an explicit focus on what is shared (e.g., Definitions 1–3, 6, and 8). In contrast, some definitions stress conflict between opposing points of view rather than that which is shared (e.g., Definition 4). Even conflict definitions, however, tacitly presume that some views are shared by subcultures (e.g., owners and workers). Culture is less often defined as an incompletely shared system, allowing for a wide variation across interpretations. An example of this last "incompletely shared" view is given in Definitions 9 (Feldman, 1991), 10 (Anonymous reviewer, 1987), and 11 (Meyerson, 1991a). Although these three definitions allow for a "common frame of reference" concerning which issues are relevant, no clear unity and no clear conflicts characterize this view of culture as ambiguity; cultural members may agree that certain issues are an important part of their frames of reference but disagree regarding the particulars of each of those issues, creating ambiguity. Thus, even the word "shared" fails to elicit agreement among cultural researchers. My definition of culture ... is listed as Definition 12 in Table 38.1. Mine is a generalist rather than a specialist definition, including a broad range of ideational and material manifestations of culture, emphasizing depth of interpretation but allowing for shared meanings, conflict, and an ambiguity similar to that described in Definitions 9, 10, and 11. Thus, I believe that culture includes conflict and ambiguity as well as that which is shared. . . .

Is a Culture Unique? Many definitions and discussions of culture include a second common characteristic: the assertion that a culture is "unique" or "distinctive," claiming (usually without evidence) that its characteristics are seldom, if ever, to be found in other organizations (i.e., Definitions 2 and 8) (see also Clark, 1972; Gregory, 1983; Schein, 1985; Selznick, 1957; Van Maanen & Barley, 1984). This emphasis on uniqueness is important because if a culture is unique, then its study is likely to yield few theoretical generalizations. One reason why definitions of culture often include the assertion of uniqueness is that cultural members often believe, and take pride in, the idea that their organization's culture is unique (Martin, 1992a, pp. 109–110; Martin, Feldman, Hatch, & Sitkin, 1983). For example, Young (1991) found that women working on an assembly line in Britain had formed a close-knit culture that, they were sure, was unique:

> **Production director:** Oh, I'll tell you, it's a unique little world of its own down there. They all have their own little events which they organize, and they've got their own lot of interests. (p. 93)
> **Machinist:** All that stuff over on the [bulletin] board, that's all old biddies really. They all do that. It's their way of sayin' 'ow special they think they are; 'ow they've been 'ere longest an' all that. Just sort of tryin' to put all the others down. (p. 102)

There are many reasons why cultural members like to think of their culture as unique. An organization often defines the goods or services it produces as distinctive to carve out a well-defined niche in a market. In a similar fashion, members often view their

cultures as distinctive (e.g., Clark, 1972; Gregory, 1983; Selznick, 1957). Particularly in individualistic societies, people generally want to be viewed as separate and special— a "unique" individual (e.g., Snyder & Fromkin, 1980).[1] All these factors combine to make cultural uniqueness desirable. Of course, because cultural members work within the boundaries of their culture, and probably have intimate knowledge of only a few other cultures, it is difficult for them to know whether their cultural uniqueness claims are justified.

Cultural researchers are presumably in a better position to assess the validity of uniqueness claims because they read case studies of many cultures and can determine that a cultural manifestation, claimed to be unique in one context, is observed in a variety of other contexts. Cultural researchers, however, often seem to take uniqueness claims at face value, including uniqueness or distinctiveness as one aspect of their definitions of culture and claiming that the perception of uniqueness increases organizational identification and commitment (e.g., Clark, 1972; Schein, 1985; Selznick, 1957, p. 8). So many cultural researchers include uniqueness claims as part of their definition of culture that Ott (1989, p. 52; see also Pedersen & Dobbin, 1997) concluded that one of the "very few areas of general consensus about organizational culture [is that] each organizational culture is relatively unique."

Contrary to Ott's (1989) claim, however, here too there is dissensus. For example, in Table 38.1, Definitions 1, 3 through 7, 9, and 10 do not include explicit claims of uniqueness. Many researchers challenge the assumption of uniqueness (e.g., Bockus, 1983; Martin et al., 1983; Riley, 1983; Trice & Beyer, 1984; Van Maanen & Barley, 1985, p. 32). Cultural members may believe their organization's culture is unique, but often what is believed to be unique to a particular context is found elsewhere as well (Martin, 1992a, p. 111), a contradiction labeled the "uniqueness paradox" (Martin et al., 1983). For example, when people tell stories that illustrate "what makes this place special," these anecdotes share the characteristics of the seven common story types found in most organizations. Similarly, when people describe rituals that they think of as unique, the basic dramatic structure, roles, and scripts of the ritual usually fit within one of several common ritual types (Trice & Beyer, 1984). Studies of the cultures of large corporations reveal that certain value themes (such as concern for quality of goods and services or customer satisfaction) are commonplace. In accord with the uniqueness paradox, members cite these common themes as evidence of the "uniqueness" of their culture (e.g., Bockus, 1983; Siehl & Martin, 1990). (These common types of stories, rituals, and content themes will be described later.) These examples suggest that claims of cultural uniqueness should be met with some skepticism, as some scholars have done: Turner (1986, p. 111) stated, "We note, then, that organizational entities may not be possessed of a distinctive and uniquely unified culture," and Van Maanen and Barley (1985, p. 32) noted, "The phrase 'organizational culture' suggests that organizations bear unitary and unique cultures. Such a stance, however, is difficult to justify empirically." The work of these authors suggests, for example, that claims of uniqueness might not be found as frequently in nations in which collectivist, rather than individualist, values predominate. . . .

WHAT CULTURE RESEARCHERS STUDY WHEN THEY CLAIM TO BE STUDYING CULTURE

The fundamental nature of theoretical issues raised by these varying definitions of culture is underscored by a final source of conceptual confusion. Conceptual definitions should correspond to the way those concepts are operationalized in a particular study. Unfortunately, cultural studies often define culture one way and operationalize the concept differently, further contributing to the theoretical and empirical confusion

that characterizes this domain of research. Therefore, I will ignore definitions for the moment and examine what researchers actually study when they claim to be studying culture.

. . . Four types of cultural manifestations will be described: cultural forms (such as rituals, organizational stories, jargon, humor, and physical arrangements), formal practices (such as pay schemes and hierarchical reporting structures), informal practices (such as norms), and content themes.

Cultural Forms: The Esoterica of Cultural Analysis
Cultural forms include rituals, organizational stories, jargon, humor, and physical arrangements including architecture, interior decor, and dress codes. Forms are the esoterica of cultural analysis. Until the 1980s, most organizational researchers and practitioners studied formal practices (such as written policies and formal organizational structures) and informal practices (behavioral norms—the unwritten rules). The espoused values of leaders, managers, and other employees have also been studied, often through attitude surveys. Until the 1980s, however, most organizational researchers did not study cultural forms, such as rituals and stories (as exceptions, see Clark, 1972; Pettigrew, 1979; Selznick, 1957). Since then, it has become clear that such an omission is a mistake. These cultural forms can provide important clues to what employees are thinking, believing, and doing.

Rituals: The Celebration and Sanctification of the Mundane. . . . MFC, Inc., (a pseudonym) is a very small company that makes relatively large amounts of money by manufacturing metal foam. Even after years of refining the manufacturing process, MFC employees sometimes have trouble in the crucial last step, and if this happens the foam can fail to form properly—an expensive mistake. The "pour time" ritual at MFC transforms this last step of the manufacturing process into an elaborate rite. Every workday, as this crucial step in the process approaches, the beginning of a ritual is

> signaled by a call, "pour time." Workers in the machine shop promptly stop their work and head for the pouring area. The half-dozen participants include all of the production personnel: two shop machinists, two foam technicians, the shop supervisor, and Bryan Anderson [a pseudonym], vice-president for production. The men don white smocks, safety glasses, and asbestos mitts. A roughly cylindrical vessel is removed from an oven and placed on a special altar. A crucible filled with molten metal is lifted from a furnace in a carefully orchestrated motion requiring two men, one at each end of a special, 6-foot long caliper. The two men carefully pour the molten metal into the waiting vessel and then move quickly away. Seconds after the pouring is complete, flames shoot out from the bottom of the vessel. Two of the watching men use fire extinguishers to douse the flames, while two others rush in to encircle the bottom of the vessel with putty. A cap is then placed on top and insulation is wrapped around it. Various machines are turned on, in sequence, to assist formation of the foam, and the vessel is left to cool. (adapted from Rifkin, 1985, p. 6)

A ritual is like a drama (Rosen, 1985; Trice & Beyer, 1984). It consists of a carefully planned and executed set of activities, carried out in a social context (an audience), with well-demarcated beginnings and endings (like a play) and well-defined roles for organizational members (like a script). Sometimes, costumes and props are even used. Rifkin's (1985) description of the foam-making ritual exhibits all these dramatic characteristics. From the opening line, "pour time," the spectacle is carefully choreographed. Props and costumes have a religious aura. Attention is riveted on a sacred vessel, which the costumed high priests place on an "altar." The dangers of fire and molten metal (not to mention financial loss) raise the level of dramatic tension until the possibility of failure has been eliminated—temporarily—and the sealed vessel is put aside to cool.

Rituals have another distinguishing characteristic: They are repeated. For example, the foam-making ritual is enacted daily. Such repeated rituals have been referred to as rites to distinguish them from ceremonies, which are ritualized events that occur only once (Trice & Beyer, 1984). . . . Rituals . . . often include other cultural forms, such as stories or jargon. For example, participants in a wake often give speeches that include jargon only cultural insiders could decipher. Organizational stories, featuring key events in the company's history, may be told. Humor is used to relieve the tension and sadness, often with jokes only insiders would understand. Sometimes, employees' personal office spaces are dismantled and, more rarely, company property may be defaced or destroyed. Photographs of friends may be taken to keep memories alive.

Rituals such as wakes usually mark transition points in employees' careers, the life cycle of products, or the history of the organization as a whole. For example, the "pour time" ritual marks a daily transition point in a manufacturing process, whereas a wake marks a transition in the life cycle of an organization. Other common types of transition rituals are defined in Table 38.2.

The annual sales convention held by the Mary Kay cosmetics company combines many of the common types of rituals described in Table 38.2. New and newly promoted employees are introduced (initiation). Mary Kay rewards high performers (enhancement) with prizes, such as diamonds and pink Cadillacs. This convention can also be seen as a renewal ritual, drawing attention to and renewing the enthusiasm of the sales force while drawing attention away from other more problematic issues (product development delays, missed shipping deadlines, or competition from other cosmetics companies). It is also an integration ritual because even those employees who are not singled out for recognition join in the fun and build relationships with each other and with the company as a whole.

TABLE 38.2 • COMMON TYPES OF RITUALS

Initiation rituals focus on the indoctrination of new or newly promoted employees, such as police recruits or a Japanese bank's newest crop of recent college graduates (e.g., Rohlene, 1974; Van Maanen, 1976).

Enhancement rituals bring recognition to good performance, such as when valued employees are flown to the Caribbean or young professors are given tenure (e.g., Trice & Beyer, 1984; Van Maanen & Kunda, 1989).

Degradation rituals celebrate the opposite — the defamation and removal of poor performers, particularly those in leadership positions (e.g., Gephart, 1978).

Renewal rituals, such as the "pour time" ritual, seek to strengthen group functioning by resolving one set of problems while drawing attention away from others.

Integration rituals provide an opportunity for employees to solidify their interpersonal relationships in a context in which family members are (usually) welcome and the formality of hierarchical relationships can safely and temporarily be suspended. For example, at a Christmas party, top executives chat informally with subordinates and their spouses, often talking of hobbies or children. At a party with music, male and female employees often dance and even flirt with each other, partially and temporarily suspending some of the sexual taboos associated with relationships at work. At a company softball game, the star of the day or the captain of a team may be a low-ranking employee, while the president of the company may be exposed as a poor batter. It is important that top executives participate in integration rituals, in part because hierarchical relations cannot be temporarily suspended or reversed in their absence. Too much insubordination, flirtation, or loss of control is usually not condoned. Not surprisingly, alcohol is often involved in these events.

Conflict reduction rituals are a special kind of integration ritual designed to repair relationships strained by a conflict or by work-induced stress, such as a deadline, a controversial decision, or a bad outcome. They provide a context in which it is safe to relax, rebuild good feelings among participants, and let off steam. As in other integration rituals, if conflict is to be successfully reduced, hierarchical relationships need to be minimized or temporarily suspended; food and alcohol are often involved. For example, a work team may decide to go out for drinks or dinner after a difficult meeting.

Ending rituals mark a transition from insider to outsider, for example, when a transferred employee is given a good-bye party by coworkers, a newly retired employee is given a ceremony and a gift, or an organization about to dissolve gives its employees a wake.

Compound rituals include two or more of the ritual types mentioned previously. Many of the most involving rituals are compound. For example, the Mary Kay company holds a noisy, fun-filled annual convention for the sales force employees who sell the firm's cosmetics door to door in their neighborhoods. Most of these sales-people are women, usually with no more than a high school degree. They work hard, often combining their work for Mary Kay with the usual responsibilities of a stay-at-home spouse. For these employees, the convention is a rare opportunity to leave family responsibilities behind and be recognized for their other accomplishments. The convention is designed to heighten the sense that this is a special event, in part by incorporating other cultural forms. For example, physical arrangements are used to give the event glitz and glamor, like that associated with the Academy Awards in Hollywood. Mary Kay wears a floor-length sequined gown. As the music reaches a crescendo, she appears, slowly rising from below the stage, on a dais. The audience also dresses up. In this setting, pink feather boas and bunny ears are normal.

Source: Adapted from Trice and Beyer (1984).

Rituals offer an opportunity to show how the functionalist intellectual tradition has influenced cultural theory and research. The typology of rituals offered in Table 38.2 is an example of a functional cultural analysis. . . . The typology is based on the outcomes anticipated from each type of ritual—enhancement, integration, and so on. A ritual fitting the descriptions in Table 38.2 would not, of course, be a unique cultural manifestation, although specific details of its implementation might be distinctive. Trice and Beyer (1984) expand this functional analysis, adding depth of interpretation, by arguing that rituals can have both technical and emotional, manifest and latent functions. The usefulness and the limitations of this kind of functional analysis can be demonstrated by analyzing the "pour time" ritual in these terms. The purpose of the "pour time" ritual may seem purely technical—to complete the last step of the foam manufacturing process. Also, undoubtedly, this manifest technical objective explains much about what is going on. . . .

So far, this functional analysis of manifest and latent, technical and emotional outcomes has tacitly assumed a managerial point of view. For example, it is in management's interest to reinforce current systems of power and authority. The functions of this ritual can also be analyzed from a critical theory viewpoint, however. Critical theory offers a critique of efforts by managers to control the minds and behaviors of employees, particularly those who labor at the bottom of organizational hierarchies. Critical theory has its roots in Marxism, the Frankfurt school (Adorno, Horkheimer, Marcuse, and Habermas), and the theories of Foucault. (Alvesson and Willmott [1992] and Alvesson and Deetz [1996] offer good introductions to critical theory.) When critical perspectives are applied to cultural studies, the focus is on interpretations of meaning that differ according to one's status within an organization, with particular attention paid to the interests and opinions of lower-status employees (e.g., Rosen, 1985; Young, 1989).

The focus and power of critical analysis can be illustrated with the "pour time" ritual. A critical analyst might note that the boss, Bryan Anderson, is present in order to observe any mistakes made by the workers at a time when such errors would be particularly costly to the company. The description of the ritual reinforces the inequality between labor and management by referring to the boss, but not the workers, by a proper name. The boss's presence is a visible, although silent, threat that mistakes will be noticed and perhaps punished. In addition, a critical theorist might note that there is an egalitarian twist to the legitimation of power and authority in this ritual. Higher-ranking employees such as Bryan Anderson are temporarily standing aside, whereas lower-level employees take center stage. For the purpose of this ritual, they all wear the same uniform—white smocks and safety equipment. This can be interpreted as a temporary reduction of management-labor inequality and as a tacit acknowledgment of the importance and difficulty of lower-ranking jobs. In this way, the ritual may serve to increase workers' commitment to the firm without any adjustment in the magnitude of inequality between labor and management pay rates. . . .

. . . Before proceeding to the next cultural form, organizational stories, it is important to note that not all analyses of rituals are functional and that most rituals can be interpreted from managerial, critical, and ambiguous points of view.

Organizational Stories and Scripts. Organizational stories consist of two elements: a narrative, describing a sequence of events, and a set of meanings or interpretations—the morals to the story. The details of a narrative and the interpretations of its meanings may vary, depending on who is telling the story, the audience, and the context. Some variations on a story theme will help illustrate these ideas. Some IBM employees tell the "green badge" story about a security supervisor who dared to challenge Thomas Watson, Jr., the intimidating chairman of the board of the company.[2] According to one version of this story (Rodgers, 1969), the supervisor was

> a 22-year-old bride weighing 90 pounds, whose husband had been sent overseas and who, in consequence, had been given a job until his return. . . . The young woman, Lucille Burger, was obliged to make certain that

people entering security areas wore the correct clearance identification.

Surrounded by his usual entourage of white-shirted men, Watson approached the doorway to an area where she was on guard, wearing an orange badge acceptable elsewhere in the plant, but not a green badge, which alone permitted entrance at her door.

"I was trembling in my uniform, which was far too big," she recalled. "It hid my shakes but not my voice. 'I'm sorry,' I said to him. I knew who he was all right. 'You cannot enter. Your admittance is not recognized.' That's what we were supposed to say."

The men accompanying Watson were stricken; the moment held unpredictable possibilities. "Don't you know who he is?" someone hissed. Watson raised his hand for silence, while one of the party strode off and returned with the appropriate badge. (pp. 153–154)

This story can be interpreted many different ways. IBM employees might conclude, "Even Watson obeys the rules, so you certainly should" or "Uphold the rules, no matter who is breaking them."

Organizational stories, such as the green badge narrative, are often confused with organizational sagas, myths, and personal anecdotes, which may not be known to large numbers of employees and/or which do not claim to represent what actually happened to organizational members or both.[3] To avoid this conceptual confusion and clarify what is being discussed here, it is important to define an organizational story as follows:

1. The central elements of an organizational story are known by a large number of people. For this reason, organizational stories are more informative about a cultural context than are personal anecdotes about a storyteller's experiences, which are not known to many other employees.
2. An organizational story focuses on a single event sequence. In contrast, an organizational saga (or the biography of a company founder or leader) summarizes years of events and is far more lengthy than a single organizational story.
3. An organizational story's central characters are members of the organization. An organizational story does not concern people or events outside the organization, restricting attention to narratives that are more likely to be informative about a particular cultural context.
4. An organizational story is ostensibly true. Organizational stories implicitly claim to be an accurate representation of "the facts." Of course, others may disagree.

The green badge story is of particular interest because versions of this story are told in a wide variety of large and small, public and private organizations. . . .

Wherever I have found this story, there are two central roles in it: the high-status rule breaker and the lower-level employee who challenges the infraction. The attributes of the two protagonists amplify the status differences between them, although exact details may be unique to a particular culture. In all versions of the story I can find, the high-status figure is an older male. In the beginning of the story, he does something that makes his status clear. For example, Watson enters accompanied by an entourage. . . . Furthermore, the lower-status employee is usually a young female. Story details pinpoint her lower status. Lucille Burger is young, she weighs only 90 pounds, her marital status (new bride) is mentioned, and her uniform is too large. . . . (As more women enter high-status executive positions, it will be interesting to see if this kind of story persists and if status remains associated with gender in the same ways.)

. . . The inequality between the two protagonists sets up a tension: Will the high-status person pull rank and be angry at the attempt to enforce the rules? In the versions of the rule-breaking story presented previously, rather than pulling rank, the authority figure complied with the rule. This outcome could be different, however, as shown in [another] version of the rule-breaking story. Charles Revson, the head of the Revlon Corporation, was worried that employees were not coming to work on time, although he seldom arrived much before noon (Tobias, 1976):

Everyone was required to sign in in the morning. Everyone. Even Charles signed in. One day, when Revlon was in the process of moving from 666 Fifth Avenue up to the General Motors Building, in 1969, Charles sauntered in and began to look over the sign-in sheet. The receptionist, who was new, says "I'm sorry, sir, you can't do that." Charles says, "Yes, I can." "No, sir," she says, "I have strict orders that no one is to remove the list; you'll have to put it back." This goes back and forth for a while with the receptionist being very courteous, as all Revlon receptionists are, and finally Charles says, "Do you know who I am?" and she says, "No, sir, I don't." "Well, when you pick up your final paycheck this afternoon, ask 'em to tell ya." (pp. 98–99)

The green badge [version] of the rule-breaking story [seems] to portray the high-status employee, and by implication the focal organization, in a relatively favorable light. In contrast, the "sign-in sheet" version places Mr. Revson, and by implication the Revlon organization, in a more negative light. These similarities and differences among the various versions of the rule-breaking story can be captured using the concept of a script. A *script* is a cognitive framework that underlies an organizational story, the skeleton of a story that remains after the nonessential details have been stripped away (Schank & Abelson, 1977). A script has four defining characteristics:

1. A script specifies a well-defined set of characters or roles.
2. It contains a single, fixed sequence of events.
3. In addition, some events in a sequence may be optional.
4. When one of several alternatives may occur, these options are referred to as script branches.

These four elements can be seen in all the versions of the rule-breaking story presented previously. Two roles are well-defined: a high-status executive and a lower-status subordinate who has responsibility for ensuring rule compliance. Four events always occur in a fixed sequence. First, the high-status person did something that drew attention to his or her authority. Second, the high-status person broke a company rule. Third, the subordinate challenged the

rule infraction. Fourth, the high-status person either did or did not comply. This either/or action alternative provides an example of a script branch, like a branch in a decision tree analysis. In an optional fifth step, evident in the . . . sign-in sheet [version] of the story, the high-status person reacted to the confrontation either by complimenting or by condemning the subordinate.

Script analysis has been used to develop a typology of stories frequently told in a wide range of organizations (Martin et al., 1983). These common story types include the rule-breaking story discussed previously and stories concerning the following: Is the big boss human? Can the little person rise to the top? Will the employee be fired? Will the organization help an employee to move? How will the boss react to mistakes? How will the organization react to obstacles? In accord with the uniqueness paradox, these common stories are often presented as evidence of a culture's uniqueness. . . .

Although script theory and classifications of common types of stories can help capture similarities, and some kinds of differences among stories, other kinds of differences, particularly in interpretation, are more effectively captured with other sets of conceptual and methodological tools. For example, a story might be told differently depending on who the storyteller is. Furthermore, a storyteller may vary the content of a story, and therefore its meanings, depending on the context in which the story is told. What you might say to the boss might be different than what you might say to a coworker. Imagine how a story's details might vary depending on whether it is told on a stage, in the men's room, or at the water cooler. Such differences in interpretation apply to other cultural manifestations as well.

Other meanings of stories emerge if an analysis considers what the story does not say. Such a focus on silences and on reading between the lines of a story text is characteristic of postmodern analysis. . . . *Postmodernism* is an intellectual movement that has spread from Europe to North America and beyond, offering a serious challenge to any theory that makes a truth claim, forcing scholars from the humanities and many social sciences to rethink the basic assumptions of their disciplines. Postmodern scholars (such as Baudrillard, Lyotard, and, his protestations to the contrary, Derrida) have used textual deconstruction (a precise form of logical analysis of language use) to show how theoretical rhetoric hides its own weaknesses as it attempts to claim an inviolable place from which objective truth can be espoused. . . .

Postmodern work has great relevance for cultural studies. Postmodernists could deconstruct any cultural theory using analysis of metaphors, dichotomies, silences, marginal asides, and footnotes in a scholarly text to show what complications and difficulties are being elided (merged together, without drawing attention to this melding) and masked by these abstractions. . . . Deconstruction is a powerful tool, as yet underused by cultural scholars. In addition, postmodernism has deep implications for how we write about the cultures we study. . . .

Jargon: The Special Language of Initiates. When outsiders enter a culture, one of the first manifestations of culture they will notice is jargon, the special language that only cultural insiders seem to comprehend (Clark, 1998). Despite this salience, relatively little cultural research has focused on jargon. Two types of jargon can be distinguished: technical and emotional. *Technical jargon* is task oriented and appears to be emotionally neutral. For example, lawyers and secretaries at the Neighborhood Legal Assistance Foundation spoke of "intake dispositions" and "litigation cost requests." At the Center for Community Self-Help, members became familiar with the "alphabet soup" of organizations involved in the worker-ownership movement: PACE, ICA, NCEO, AWOK, and WOSCO.[4]

In contrast, *emotionally laden jargon* is more overtly concerned with feelings (e.g., Ignatow & Jost, 2000). For example, "idea hamsters" on the "bleeding edge" are meta-

phors of life and death in Silicon Valley, the U.S. mecca for high-technology entrepreneurship. Nicknames are another type of emotional jargon. Many organizations use family names to refer to top management, a choice that can reflect familial closeness, conventional sex roles, the hierarchical distance and emotional ambivalence usually associated with patriarchal corporate relationships, or all these. For example, at B. F. Goodrich, business expenses charged to the company were "compliments of Uncle Benny," a reference to Benjamin Franklin Goodrich, the founder of the firm. Phillips Petroleum employees referred to "Uncle Frank" Phillips, whereas Honda had both an "uncle" and a "dad." Other emotional nicknames draw a line between cultural outsiders and insiders. For example, U.S. Navy personnel derogatively referred to members of the Marines, a rival service, as "jar heads." Land-loving civilian workers in a Navy yard were dismissed as "sand crabs." . . .

Jargon also refers to place or position names. For example, at IBM, the "penalty box" was a temporary, unexciting position in which an employee paid for inadequate performance, whereas "Siberia" was a dead-end position — so useless that the offender usually resigned. At Revlon Corporation, the negative atmosphere, evident in the rule-breaking story discussed previously, also permeated the jargon. For example, the headquarters building at 666 Fifth Avenue was called "sick, sick, sick."

Jargon may seem trivial, or at best a necessary precursor to understanding a culture, but it can be used to develop unexpected insights. For example, at a large high-tech corporation named GEM Company (a pseudonym), some jargon appeared to be purely technical and emotionally neutral (e.g., "Master Order Form"). Other terms were more obviously emotional and value laden (e.g., "working the issue," which referred to the value placed on confronting disagreement and continuing discussion until consensus was reached). At GEM Company, Siehl and Martin (1988) tested new employees' familiarity with various cultural manifestations after 2 and 8 weeks on the job. The new hires were given multiple-choice vocabulary tests asking for the meanings of both technical and emotional jargon terms (with different versions of the test appropriately counterbalanced so respondents were not tested twice on the same words). Results indicated that new employees became familiar with cultural manifestations in a predictable order. Technical jargon was learned first, perhaps because it was essential for getting tasks done. Next, emotional jargon was learned. Other cultural manifestations were learned much later. For example, knowledge of the "correct" (most common) interpretation of organizational stories increased rapidly during the 6-week period of the study. A more difficult test attempted to assess general knowledge of the culture. Selected words in memos and letters from top management were blacked out. New employees had to fill in the blanks. After 2 weeks of employment, error rates were very high, and 4 weeks later they had improved significantly, although many errors were still being made. These results suggest that jargon may provide a linguistic foundation for other, more complex forms of cultural knowledge. This study, however, was conducted in an established, large, and stable corporation. It is important to learn if such results would be found (I doubt it) in a turbulent industry, such as high technology, or in a rapidly growing start-up company in which employees are constantly being hired and lines between old guard and newcomers are blurred.

There has been some research on jargon use in companies that are distinctive due to the intensity of the ideological commitment of their employees. In these companies, technical jargon and emotional jargon sometimes merge. . . .

Some jargon relies on metaphors. For example, violent language permeates the jargon used to describe mergers and acquisitions (Hirsch & Andrews, 1983). "Sharks" are extremely predatory takeover experts, the worst of whom is called "Jaws." "Shark

repellent" is a protective strategy used to keep sharks away. Other metaphors of violence use the language of cowboy movies. "Hired guns" are the lawyers and investment bankers that specialize in this business. An "ambush" is a clever, premeditated, and swift takeover attempt. A "shootout" determines the final outcome of the battle for control. Other metaphors for mergers and acquisitions are sexual. "Studs" are aggressive potential acquirers, and "sleeping beauties" are vulnerable target companies. "Cupid" is a role played by merger brokers. "Sex without marriage" is an extended negotiation for a friendly takeover that is never finalized. "Rape" is a hostile takeover, sometimes accompanied by looting of a firm's financial resources. Finally, "afterglow" is the postmerger euphoria of acquiring or acquired companies or both, which usually soon dissipates. These metaphors stress sex and violence, with strong overtones of competitiveness and aggression. In this way, metaphors tap the emotional aspects of life in particular kinds of organizations and industries, alluding to emotions that may not be socially acceptable to express more directly. . . .

Humor: Drawing the Line With Laughter. Intriguingly, sex and violence surface in another cultural manifestation: humor. In contrast to studies of humor in organizations, examples of organizational stories, rituals, and even jargon are often intrinsically interesting. The same cannot be said for organizational humor, which is usually unfunny to an outsider. It is probably therefore fortunate that few organizational studies have focused on humor (as an exception, see Hatch and Ehrlich [1993]). You have been warned.

Much humor research has focused on blue-collar workers. For example, a 6-year ethnographic study in a machine shop found that most humorous incidents involved either physical slapstick or "dirty tricks" (Boland & Hoffman, 1983). One favorite joke involved the "goosing" of coworkers with broomsticks or steel tubes. Another popular trick was "bluing." The perpetrators would surreptitiously cover a machine handle with indelible blue steel marking ink and then laugh gleefully when the unsuspecting operator grabbed the "blued" handle and then touched his face or clothes. Recent research has begun to analyze the sexual associations of this kind of humor, focusing on the ways men enact their masculinity at work. Collinson (1992), for example, studied humor in a truck assembly plant, exploring the ways men used humor to express conformity, resistance, and control, particularly in situations in which their masculinity was undermined by low status and low pay. . . .

This kind of humor is not limited to blue-collar workers. Newly hired sales executives at GEM Company also favored ethnic and sexual jokes (Siehl & Martin, 1988). During a 2-week training program for these executives, all instances of laughter were recorded. At first, most newcomers who attempted to be funny offered familiar ethnic jokes and sexual innuendoes with little explicitly organizational content. After just a few days, however, the trainees' humor changed. The jokes were still familiar, but now the ethnic and sexual targets were members of competitive organizations or people from other divisions of GEM Company. Both at the start of the training program and after a few days, jokes were being used to distinguish insiders from outsiders, and at both time periods women and minorities were the focus of these jokes. Racial, ethnic, and sexist jokes are a widespread characteristic of humor inside and outside organizations, at least in settings in which members of some demographic groups are numerically rare. What distinguishes organizational versions of these jokes is that outsider status is also being defined by membership in competing organizations or other parts of the employing organization; telling and laughing at these kinds of jokes may be a subtle measure of the extent to which employees are feeling identification with the organization for which they work.

Humor bridges uncomfortable moments, offers a way of releasing tension, and permits people to express that which they otherwise might be forbidden to say. Meyerson (1991a), for example, explored the ways social workers used humor to release the inevitable tensions of working in a profession in which success with clients was ill defined and in many cases unlikely. Meyerson, unlike the humor researchers cited previously, focused on groups of social workers, examining the helpful, tension-breaking role a single cynical joker played in group meetings. The social workers' jokes were full of irony and multiple meanings; the space created by these ambiguities permitted laughter. . . .

Physical Arrangements: Architecture, Decor, and Dress. Architecture, interior decor, and dress norms are particularly powerful cultural clues, in part because they are so easy to see. Some consultants, for example, pride themselves on being able to "size up" an organization's culture during the brief time it takes to drive up to a building, greet the receptionist, and walk to the office of the person they are meeting. Even a brief, "bare bones" description of an organization's physical arrangements can be quite informative. For example, descriptions of General Motor's (GM) architecture, interior decor, and dress codes suggest much about this firm's culture (Wright, 1979):

> The General Motors Building, where about 7,000 people work, is the most impressive structure in midtown Detroit whether viewed from air, the windows of skyscrapers in downtown Detroit 4 miles to the south, or the cement channels of the nearby Edsel Ford and John Lodge Freeways. The giant letters "GENERAL MOTORS" atop the building can be seen 20 miles away on a clear night. (p. 16)

In this headquarters building, as described by Martin and Siehl (1983), the offices of GM's top management team were

> located in an I-shaped end of the fourteenth floor of this building. . . . Even on this floor, office decor was standardized. The carpeting

was a nondescript blue-green and the oak paneling was faded beige. When (one executive requested something different) the man in charge of office decoration was apologetic, but firm, "We decorate the offices only every few years. And they are all done the same. It's the same way with the furniture. Maybe I can get you an extra table or lamp." (pp. 57–58).

Dress norms at GM were also strongly enforced (Martin & Siehl, 1983):

GM's dress norms in the 1960s required a dark suit, a light shirt, and a muted tie. This was a slightly more liberal version of the famous IBM dress code that required a dark suit, a sparkling white shirt, and a narrow blue or black tie. (p. 57)

Even within GM, some diversity in decor and dress was allowed. One GM executive, John DeLorean, used physical arrangements to facilitate the development of a counterculture, different from the rest of the company (Martin & Siehl, 1983). For example, when he was promoted to head the Chevrolet division, DeLorean used decor changes to symbolize his declaration of independence. The division's lobby and executive offices were refurbished with bright carpets, the paneling was sanded and restained, and modern furniture was brought in. Executives were allowed "within reasonable limits" to decorate their offices to fit their individual tastes. Because physical arrangements are so visible, subtle variations can have a major impact. In his own dress, DeLorean role modeled an apparently carefully calibrated willingness to deviate from GM's dress norms (Martin & Siehl, 1983):

DeLorean's dark suits had a continental cut. His shirts were off-white with wide collars. His ties were suitably muted, but wider than the GM norm. His deviations were fashionable, for the late 1960s, but they represented only a slight variation on the executive dress norms. (p. 61)

The previous examples illustrate the ways in which physical arrangements, such as dress norms and interior decor, can be a rich source of information about a culture. The DeLorean study also suggests that phys-

ical arrangements can be used by skilled managers to signal what kind of cultural changes they would like to see evolve in their own organizational domains. Despite evidence of the power of physical arrangements, research in this area is rare. . . .

. . . Cultural forms are not really esoterica. They can provide important clues to what employees are thinking, believing, and doing. Because these aspects of culture are just beginning to be studied, however, they offer many opportunities for research. On a map of the cultural terrain, cultural forms would be labeled "terra incognita." I would add to the map "Dig here" for intellectual treasure hunters.

Formal and Informal Practices

Although cultural forms have traditionally been dismissed as esoteric and therefore not important, practices have long been the primary focus of attention in organizational research. In contrast to informal practices, formal practices are written and are therefore more easily controlled by management. Four types of formal practices have been of particular interest to culture researchers: structure, task and technology, rules and procedures, and financial controls. . . .

In contrast to formal practices, informal practices evolve through interaction and are not written down. Informal practices often take the form of social rules (e.g., Lundberg, in press). These rules are seldom written down because this would reveal an inconsistency between what is formally required and what actually happens. For example, when DeLorean was promoted at GM he tried to change the formal performance appraisal system to include only objective criteria, such as sales figures, rather than the subjective criteria, such as "gets along well with coworkers," that had been so important to the rest of GM. Although DeLorean's subordinates appeared to go along with this change in formal practice, informally they continued to let subjective factors influence their judgments. Obviously, they did not leave a written trace of this unapproved deviation from formal requirements (Martin & Siehl, 1983). Sometimes, informal practices create a limited or temporary space in which formal requirements can be relaxed. For example, British police are formally prohibited from drinking alcohol while on duty. They do so, however, both on and off the job and, while drinking, certain forms of behavior become temporarily acceptable. If a policeman is drunk or is drinking, he can make jokes about authority figures and express anger, fear, and affection in ways that would otherwise be unacceptable. These informal practices cannot be found in any handbook of police procedures, but they provide an important outlet for the pressures associated with this kind of work (Van Maanen, 1986). Similar drinking practices are found in Japan. As both these examples indicate, formal and informal practices are often inconsistent.

Some cultural studies are open to finding that interpretations are inconsistent across various manifestations, and, not surprisingly, these studies are more likely to include both formal and informal practices. Cultural studies that assume that interpretations of various cultural manifestations are consistent seldom examine both formal and informal practices; when they do, they tend to focus only on those formal and informal practices that are mutually consistent. This is indicative of a common problem in cultural studies: Researchers operationalize culture by focusing on types of manifestations that are more likely to produce results that confirm, rather than contradict, their theoretical presuppositions.

Content Themes: Espoused and Inferred

A content theme is a common thread of concern that underlies interpretations of several cultural manifestations. Content themes can be cognitive (beliefs or tacit assumptions), or they can be attitudinal (values). Sometimes, themes are espoused—for example, when top managers offer a list of their company's "core values." Other themes are inferred deductively by a researcher or

an employee, such as when assumptions are inferred from behavior. Usually, espoused themes are relatively superficial because they are espoused to make an impression on an audience, whereas themes that are inferred deductively, by researchers or employees, reflect a deeper level of interpretation.

When content themes are espoused deliberately to external audiences, such as the general public or members of the immediately surrounding community, these themes may be sincerely espoused as an accurate reflection of an organization's activities, or they may be "corporate propaganda" that bears little relationship to what actually happens within the organization. In either case, espoused values represent an attempt to influence an individual or an organization's "aura" or "reputation" (Christensen & Kreiner, 1984). As Schein explains (1985) in one of his definitions of culture cited previously, espoused values

> focus on what people *say* is the reason for their behavior, what they ideally would like those reasons to be, and what are often their rationalizations for their behavior. Yet, the underlying reasons for their behavior remain concealed or unconscious. (p. 14)

Because espoused values are an attempt to create an impression on an audience, usually portraying the organization in an attractive light, they tend to be highly abstract and somewhat platitudinous—the organizational equivalent of motherhood and apple pie. . . .

Content themes can be expressed at a variety of levels of abstraction. . . . For example, in a study of 21 U.S. corporations of varying sizes (Goodhead, 1985), larger firms tended to discuss employee well-being in language that stressed hierarchy (valuing elite status), paternalistic values (such as a familial type of loyalty to the firm), or "Protestant ethic" (calling for hard work and sacrifice). Smaller firms and organizations composed primarily of professionals discussed employee well-being in terms that were meritocratic (rewards for contribution and professionalism) or cooperative (teamwork). A few smaller firms preferred an egalitarian form of employee well-being (ideas from anyone and freedom).

It is interesting to consider trade-offs among content themes. Some data suggest that executives may place greater stress on humanitarian values, such as warmth and friendliness, in contexts in which pay inequality between labor and management is particularly large (Martin & Harder, 1994). In other words, to reverse the slogan adopted by a union of secretaries, employees may be given roses (gestures of friendliness) as a substitute for more bread (pay). This cynical interpretation of externally espoused values has caused many cultural researchers to worry about the ways in which externally espoused values can be manipulated. These researchers prefer to infer themes deductively from what is observed. For example, employees may take a short-term time perspective whenever decisions are made, or they may assume the best, or the worst, about their fellow employees. Espoused content themes and inferred content themes may be quite different. For example, in an organization in which top management is articulating "corporate value statements" that do not reflect employees' values and experiences, espoused and inferred values will be inconsistent.

In summary, content themes can be externally, self-consciously espoused, or they can be inferred deductively from what people do and how they interpret their surroundings. . . .

Summary: The Question of Depth of Interpretation

I believe that cultural forms, such as stories, rituals, and physical arrangements (which are sometimes referred to as artifacts), are not necessarily more superficial or less important than deeply held assumptions. Thus, the various cultural manifestations described previously do not represent separable, varying levels of depth. A cultural researcher should seek deep interpretations associated with each type of cultural manifestation. A cultural study can be superficial, focusing on interpretations that reflect, for example, formulaic expressions of espoused values in a "corporate values" statement. Alternatively, a cultural study can focus on deep interpretations that take the form of basic assumptions, sometimes so taken for granted that they are difficult to articulate. Such basic assumptions may include "walking the talk"—when a person's expressed values and assumptions are consistent with how he or she behaves. Other kinds of interpretations of events and artifacts are less value laden and more like cognitive conclusions about "how things are." In each of these examples, what is important is not the cultural manifestation itself but how people interpret it. The depth of a researcher's analysis of interpretations of manifestations can (and I argue should) approach the depth of understanding that Schein terms "basic assumptions."

From Definitions and Operationalizations to Theories of Culture

This chapter has covered a lot of ground. We have seen that many culture researchers define culture in approximately the same way—in terms of cultural manifestations that are shared by most cultural members. Often, they will also define culture as that which is unique about a context. We have seen that if we analyze how culture researchers operationalize culture—that is, examining what they actually study when they claim to be studying culture—we find a great variety of approaches. Some researchers study the meanings employees give to stories about leaders and colleagues or rituals they engage in at work; other researchers also examine more familiar attributes of organizations, such as hierarchical structures, the physical layout of the workplace, and pay systems, claiming that they too are studying manifestations of an organization's culture. To make matters more confusing, we have seen that cultural studies sometimes break a taboo, defining culture in ways that do not coincide with the ways they operationalize the concept and/or the results they find. For example, some interpretations of a cultural manifestation may not, in fact, be shared by most cultural members; some cultural manifestations studied may not be unique.

For these reasons, it is a good idea to disregard how culture researchers define culture and examine instead how they operationalize it. When this analysis of operationalizations is done systematically, often glimpses of a cultural theory emerge. Cultural manifestations are consistent or not, cultural members appear to agree or not, and interpretations are singular and clear or ultiple and ambiguous. Because culture researchers do not agree what we should study when we claim to be studying culture, and because our definitions of culture do not always agree with how we operationalize the concept, it is no wonder that we also disagree about what we have learned, so far, about culture. . . .

NOTES

1. Individuation has been conceptualized as an essential stage in the maturation process, whereby a child separates from parents (Maslach, 1974), and "deindividuation" has been studied as a potentially harmful loss of individual identity that can facilitate the expression of antisocial aggression (Zimbardo, 1969).

2. This material on stories and scripts is adapted from Martin (1982) and Martin et al. (1983).

3. An organizational story is a type of narrative—that is, a way of encapsulating knowledge organized around the intentionality of human action, expressed in a plot, which is the basic means by which specific events are put into one meaningful whole (Czarniawska, 1999). Narratives that are not organizational stories can be defined as follows: Organizational sagas are lengthy corporate histories containing many organizational stories (Clark, 1972). Myths are narratives presumed to be false; although myths are literally untrue, at their best they capture an underlying logic that

expresses a kind of truth. Personal anecdotes are stories about the storyteller, not widely known by others.

4. Unless otherwise mentioned, examples of jargon are taken from material collected by students in my organizational culture class at Stanford University's Graduate School of Business.

REFERENCES

Alvesson, M., & Berg, P. (1992). *Corporate culture and organizational symbolism*. Berlin: de Gruyter.

Alvesson, M., & Deetz, S. (1996). Critical theory and postmodern approaches to organization studies. In S. Clegg, C. Hardy, & W. Nord (Eds.), *Handbook of organization studies* (pp. 191–217). London: Sage.

Alvesson, M., & Willmott, H. (Eds.). (1992). *Critical management studies*. London: Sage.

Bockus, S. (1983). *Corporate values: A refutation of uniqueness theory*. Unpublished manuscript, Stanford University, Stanford, CA.

Boland, R., & Hoffman, R. (1983). Humor in a machine shop: An interpretation of symbolic action. In L. Pondy, P. Frost, G. Morgan, & T. Dandridge (Eds.), *Organizational symbolism*. Greenwich, CT: JAI.

Calás, M., & Smircich, L. (1987). *Post-culture: Is the organizational culture literature dominant but dead?* Paper presented at the International Conference on Organizational Symbolism and Corporate Culture, Milan.

Christensen, S., & Kreiner, K. (1984). *On the origin of organizational cultures*. Paper presented at the International Conference on Organizational Symbolism and Corporate Culture, Lund, Sweden.

Clark, B. (1972). The organizational saga in higher education. *Administrative Science Quarterly, 17*, 178–184.

Clark, H. (1998). Communal lexicons. In K. Malmkjaer & J. Williams (Eds.), *Context in language learning and language understanding* (pp. 63–87). Cambridge, UK: Cambridge University Press.

Collinson, D. (1992). *Managing the shop floor: Subjectivity, masculinity and workplace culture*. New York: de Gruyter.

Czarniawska-Joerges, B. (1992). *Exploring complex organizations: A cultural perspective.* Newbury Park, CA: Sage.

Davis, S. (1984). *Managing corporate culture.* Cambridge, MA: Ballinger.

Feldman, M. (1991). The meanings of ambiguity: Learning from stories and metaphors. In P. Frost, L. Moore, M. Louis, C. Lundberg, & J. Martin (Eds.), *Reframing organizational culture* (pp. 145–156). Newbury Park, CA: Sage.

Gephart, R. (1978). Status degradation and organizational succession: An ethnomethodological approach. *Administrative Science Quarterly, 23,* 553–581.

Goodhead, G. (1985). *What do corporations believe?* Unpublished manuscript, Stanford University, Stanford, CA.

Gregory, K. (1983). Native-view paradigms: Multiple cultures and culture conflicts in organizations. *Administrative Science Quarterly, 28,* 359–376.

Hatch, M., & Ehrlich, S. (1993). Spontaneous humour as an indicator of paradox and ambiguity. *Organization Studies, 14,* 505–526.

Hirsch, P., & Andrews, A. (1983). Ambushes, shootouts, and knights of the roundtable: The language of corporate takeovers. In L. Pondy, M. Luis, P. Frost, & T. Dandridge (Eds.), *Organizational symbolism.* Greenwich, CT: JAI.

Ignatow, G., & Jost, J. (2000). *"Idea hamsters" on the "bleeding edge": Metaphors of life and death in Silicon Valley* (Research Paper No. 1628). Stanford, CA: Stanford University, Graduate School of Business.

Louis, M. (1985). An investigator's guide to workplace culture. In P. Frost, L. Moore, M. Louis, C. Lundberg, & J. Martin (Eds.), *Organizational culture* (pp. 73–94). Beverly Hills, CA: Sage.

Martin, J. (1992a). *Cultures in organizations.* New York: Oxford University Press.

Martin, J., Feldman, M., Hatch, M., & Sitkin, S. (1983). The uniqueness paradox in organizational stories. *Administrative Science Quarterly, 28,* 438–453.

Martin, J., & Harder, J. (1994). Bread and roses: Justice and the distribution of financial and socio-emotional rewards in organizations. *Social Justice Research, 7,* 241–264.

Martin, J., & Siehl, C. (1983). Organizational culture and counterculture: An uneasy symbiosis. *Organizational Dynamics, 12,* 52–64.

Meyerson, D. (1991a). "Normal" ambiguity? A glimpse of an occupational culture. In P. Frost, L. Moore, M. Louis, C. Lundberg, & J. Martin (Eds.), *Reframing organizational culture* (pp. 131–144). Newbury Park, CA: Sage.

Mills, A. (1988). Organization, gender, and culture. *Organization Studies, 9,* 351–370.

Ott, J. (1989). *The organizational culture perspective.* Pacific Grove, CA: Brooks/Cole.

Pedersen, J., & Dobbin, F. (1997). *Constructing organizations: Neo-institutionalism and organizational culture* (Papers in Organization No. 21). Copenhagen: Copenhagen Business School, Institute of Organization and Industrial Sociology.

Pettigrew, A. (1979). On studying organizational culture. *Administrative Science Quarterly, 24,* 570–581.

Pondy, L., Frost, P., Morgan, G., & Dandridge, T. (Eds.). (1983). *Organizational symbolism.* Greenwich, CT: JAI.

Rifkin, C. (1985). *Rituals in organizations.* Unpublished manuscript, Stanford University, Stanford, CA.

Riley, P. (1983). A structurationist account of political cultures. *Administrative Science Quarterly, 28,* 414–437.

Rodgers, W. (1969). *Think.* New York: Stein & Day.

Rofel, L. (1989). *Eating out of one big pot: Hegemony and resistance in a Chinese factory.* Unpublished doctoral dissertation, Stanford University, Stanford, CA.

Rohlene, T. (1974). *For harmony and strength: Japanese white-collar organizations in anthropological perspective.* Berkeley: University of California Press.

Rosen, M. (1985). Breakfast at Spiro's: Dramaturgy and dominance. *Journal of Management, 11,* 31–48.

Sathe, V. (1985). *Culture and related corporate realities: Text, cases, and readings on organizational entry, establishment, and change.* Homewood, IL: Irwin.

Schall, M. (1983). A communication rules approach to organizational culture. *Administrative Science Quarterly, 8,* 557–581.

Schank, R., & Abelson, R. (1977). *Scripts, plans, and knowledge.* Hillsdale, NJ: Lawrence Erlbaum.

Schein, E. (1985). *Organizational culture and leadership.* San Francisco: Jossey-Bass.

Schein, E. (1999). *The corporate culture survival guide: Sense & nonsense about culture change.* San Francisco: Jossey-Bass.

Schultz, M. (1995). *On studying organizational cultures: Diagnosis and understanding.* Berlin: de Gruyter.

Schultz, M., & Hatch, M. (1996). Living with multiple paradigms: The case of paradigm interplay in organizational culture studies. *Academy of Management Review, 21,* 529–557.

Selznick, P. (1957). *Leadership and administration.* Evanston, IL: Row & Peterson.

Sergiovanni, T., & Corbally, J. (Eds.). (1984). *Leadership and organizational culture.* Urbana: University of Illinois Press.

Siehl, C., & Martin, J. (1988). Measuring organizational culture: Mixing qualitative and quantitative methods. In M. Jones, M. Moore, & R. Snyder (Eds.), *Inside organizations: Understanding the human dimension* (pp. 79–104). Newbury Park, CA: Sage.

Siehl, C., & Martin, J. (1990). Organizational culture: A key to financial performance? In B. Schneider (Ed.), *Organizational climate and culture* (pp. 241–281). San Francisco: Jossey-Bass.

Smircich, L. (1983a). Concepts of culture and organizational analysis. *Administrative Science Quarterly, 28,* 339–358.

Smircich, L. (1983b). Organizations as shared meanings. In L. Pondy, P. Frost, G. Morgan, & T. Dandridge (Eds.), *Organizational symbolism* (pp. 55–65). Greenwich, CT: JAI.

Smircich, L., & Calás, M. (1987). Organizational culture: A critical assessment. In F. Jablin, L. Putnam, K. Roberts, & L. Porter (Eds.), *Handbook of organizational communication* (pp. 228–263). Newbury Park, CA: Sage.

Snyder, C., & Fromkin, H. (1980). *Uniqueness: The human pursuit of difference.* New York: Plenum.

Tobias, A. (1976). *Fire and ice.* New York: William Morrow.

Trice, H., & Beyer, J. (1984). Studying organizational cultures through rites and ceremonials. *Academy of Management Review, 9,* 653–669.

Turner, B. (1986). Sociological aspects of organizational symbolism. *Organizational Studies, 7,* 101–115.

Van Maanen, J. (1976). Breaking-in: Socialization to work. In R. Dubin (Ed.), *Handbook of work, organization, and society* (pp. 67–130). Chicago: Rand McNally.

Van Maanen, J. (1986). Power in the bottle. In S. Srivasta (Ed.), *Executive power.* San Francisco: Jossey-Bass.

Van Maanen, J., & Barley, S. (1984). Occupational communities: Culture and control in organizations. In B. Staw & L. Cummings (Eds.), *Research in organizational behavior* (Vol. 6, pp. 287–366). Greenwich, CT: JAI.

Van Maanen, J., & Barley, S. (1985). Cultural organization: Fragments of a theory. In P. Frost, L. Moore, M. Louis, C. Lundberg, & J. Martin (Eds.), *Organizational culture* (pp. 31–54). Beverly Hills, CA: Sage.

Van Maanen, J., & Kunda, G. (1989). "Real feelings": Emotional expression and organizational culture. In L. Cummings & B. Staw (Eds.), *Research in organizational behavior* (Vol. 11, pp. 43–103). Greenwich, CT: JAI.

Wright, J. (1979). *On a clear day you can see General Motors.* Grosse Point, MI: Wright.

Young, E. (1989). On the naming of the rose: Interests and multiple meanings as elements of organizational culture. *Organization Studies, 10,* 187–206.

Young, E. (1991). On the naming of the rose: Interests and multiple meanings as elements of organizational culture. In P. Frost, L. Moore, M. Louis, C. Lundberg, & J. Martin (Eds.), *Reframing organizational culture* (pp. 90–103). Newbury Park, CA: Sage.

CHAPTER 8

Reform Through Changes in Organizational Culture

The diverse "reform movements" presented in this chapter all share a common theme — *lasting organizational reform requires changes in organizational culture*. Organizational cultures that reflect unwanted values, such as hierarchy, rigidity, homogeneity, power based on authority and associations in closed networks, and reliance on rules, must be replaced with cultures where horizontal relations, open and accessible networks, flexibility, responsiveness, individual and group empowerment, diversity, and customer service are valued. Thus they share a commitment to increasing organizational effectiveness, competitiveness, flexibility, and responsiveness by changing organizational cultures. "Command-and-control" cultures must be replaced with cultures that encourage and support widespread use of an increasingly diverse workforce, and employee participation and empowerment approaches for individuals in work teams. First we look at the post-TQM-type organizational reform movements, and then we turn to the feminist and multicultural perspectives on organizational reform.

THE CONTEXT OF THE 1980s AND 1990s

The approaches to reforming organizations that dominated in the 1980s and through most of the 1990s shared their origins in the realization that U.S. companies and government agencies had lost their competitiveness and agility during the last three decades of the twentieth century, as well as the understanding that organizational change required more than structural or functional "tweaking"—that organizational cultures had to be reformed.

The recognition that American industry was losing — or had already lost—its competitiveness (and the fear that accompanied the realization) began in the late 1970s as globalism became a reality. Where once U.S. firms had competed mostly with each other, they now were forced to compete in global markets against worthy competitors. The competitive marketplace had become a worldwide economic playing field on which all competitors were not bound by the same rules. Of equal concern, however, was the mounting evidence that U.S. productivity was not increasing and in some industries was actually decreasing. Declining productivity in the United States coincided with noticeable productivity gains in many industrialized nations, particularly in Asia but also in several European countries. Overwhelming evidence pointed to the loss of U.S. position in the global marketplace. In the late 1980s, 53 of the top 100 corporations in the world were Japanese.

The problem for U.S. industries was twofold. The decline in the U.S. competitive position resulted from an absolute failure to increase productivity as well as an even larger relative decline in comparison with other industrialized nations (Ingle, 1987). The United

States faced a competitiveness crisis, and the general public was becoming aware that unless the current trend was reversed, it could result in a lower standard of living for all Americans (American Productivity & Quality Center, 1988). The real or perceived ineffectiveness of government, although seemingly around forever, emerged during the decade of the 1980s as a public policy issue that could not be ignored (Ott, Boonyarak & Dicke, 2001; Peters, 1996; Savas, 1982).

ORIGINS OF THE POST-TQM-TYPE ORGANIZATIONAL CULTURE REFORM MOVEMENTS

Although the various organizational reform movements that require changes in organizational culture have taken different shapes, used different jargon, and emphasized different techniques, their origins can all be traced back to Dr. W. Edwards Deming's 1950 trip to Japan. Deming succeeded in convincing a number of Japanese executives to adopt his approach to statistical quality control. Joseph Juran, who emphasized the "management" part of "quality," followed Deming to Japan in 1954. In turn, Val Feigenbaum followed Juran with "total quality control" (TQC), a management approach that allowed employees across organizations to participate in quality improvement activities—from the chair of the board to hourly workers, from suppliers to customers, and the community.

By 1975, Japan had developed into the world leader in quality and productivity. "Deming's popularity in Japan was in contrast to an almost total ignorance about him in the United States. . . . Deming remained in the quality wilderness of America for a whole generation" (Bhote, 1994, p. 156). The turning point for the "total quality movement" in the United States was a June 24, 1980, NBC television documentary, "If Japan Can . . . Why Can't We?" The program documented Deming's experience and successes in Japan. The response was overwhelming. Within months, hundreds of major U.S. corporations and government agencies had scrambled aboard the quality bandwagon (Al-Khalaf, 1994). Quality circles—voluntary work groups that cut across organizational layers and boundaries to analyze and recommend solutions to organizational problems—appeared everywhere as if by magic, in industry and government alike.

A FEW OF THE POST-TQM-TYPE REFORM MOVEMENTS THAT REQUIRE CHANGES IN ORGANIZATIONAL CULTURE

Several of the best-known reform movements that require changes in organizational culture and that followed the early work with Japanese industries by Deming, Juran, and Feigenbaum, and the NBC documentary, include:

- Total Quality Management (TQM): (Crosby, 1979, 1984; Deming, 1986, 1993; Joiner, 1994; Juran, 1992; Walton, 1986);
- Japanese Management: (Ouchi, 1981; Pascale & Athos, 1981);
- The Search for Excellence: (Peters & Waterman, 1982; Peters, 1987);
- Sociotechnical Systems or Quality of Work Life (QWI): (Weisbord, 1991);
- Learning Organizations: (Cohen & Sproull, 1996; Senge, 1990);
- Productivity Measurement/Balanced Scorecard: (Berman, 1998; Cohen & Eimicke, 1998; Eccles, 1991; Kaplan & Norton, 1992, 1993, 1996);

- Reinventing Government: (Barzelay, 1992; Gore, 1993; Osborne & Gaebler, 1992); and
- Reengineering, Process Reengineering, or Business Reengineering: (Hammer & Champy, 1993).

Virtually all of these reform movements seek to increase productivity, flexibility, responsiveness, and customer service by reshaping organizational cultures (see Chapter 7). Most—but not all—advocate the empowerment of individual employees and work groups or contracted individuals and firms. Empowered employees and work teams are granted autonomy and discretion to make decisions. Work teams coordinate tasks and discipline their own members. Policies, procedures, and layers of hierarchy are eliminated. Accountability to bosses is replaced by accountability to customers or clients. Data-based information systems provide the information needed to coordinate and correct actions in real time (see Burton & Obel, 1998, reprinted in Chapter 4). Levels of middle managers and supervisors are eliminated because they are not needed, do not add value, cost too much, and get in the way of empowered workers.

Several of the most popular examples of the literature on reform through changes in organizational culture are included in this chapter: William Ouchi's *The Z Organization*, Peters and Waterman's *In Search of Excellence*, Peter Senge's *The Fifth Discipline*, and Al Gore's *Reinventing Government*, or as it was titled formally, *Report of the National Performance Review*.

We begin our exploration of the organizational culture reform movements, though, with the original "driving force"—W. Edwards Deming's *Total Quality Management*.

Total Quality Management (TQM)

In 1991, the United States Government Accounting Office defined "quality management" as:

> A leadership philosophy that demands a relentless pursuit of quality and the stamina for continuous improvement in all aspects of operations: product, service, processes, and communications. The major components of quality management are leadership, a customer focus, continuous improvement, employee empowerment, and management by fact (pp. 41, 42).

For most people who are familiar with TQM, Deming's now-famous fourteen points of management represent its essence. Thus, instead of reproducing an article here by Deming, we introduce Deming's "theory of TQM" by listing and elaborating briefly on his fourteen points (Al-Khalaf, 1994; adapted from Deming, 1986, pp. 24–92).

1. *Create constancy of purpose for improvement of product and service*. If organizations are to survive, they must allocate resources for long-term planning research and education, and for the constant improvement of the design of their products and services.
2. *Adopt the new philosophy*. Government regulations that represent obstacles to competitiveness must be revised. Transformation of companies is needed.
3. *Cease dependence on mass inspections*. Quality needs to be designed and built into the processes, preventing defects rather than attempting to detect them after they have occurred.
4. *End the practice of awarding business on the basis of price tag alone*. Lowest bids lead to low quality. Organizations should establish long-term relationships with single suppliers.
5. *Improve constantly and forever the system of production and service*. Management and employees must search continuously for ways to improve quality and productivity.

6. *Institute training.* Training at all organizational levels is a necessity, not an option.
7. *Adopt and institute leadership.* Management's job is to lead, not to supervise. Leaders should eliminate barriers that prevent people from doing the job well and from learning new methods.
8. *Drive out fear.* Unless employees feel secure enough to express ideas and ask questions, they will do things the wrong way or not do them at all.
9. *Break down barriers between staff areas.* Working in teams will solve problems and thus improve quality and productivity.
10. *Eliminate slogans, exhortations, and targets for the workforce.* Problems with quality and productivity are caused by the system, not by individuals. Posters and slogans generate frustration and resentment.
11. *Eliminate numerical quotas for the work force and numerical goals for people in management.* In order to meet quotas, people produce defective products. Instead, management must take decisive steps to replace work standards, rates, and piecework with intelligent leadership.
12. *Remove barriers that rob people of pride of workmanship.* Deming views individual performance appraisals as one of the greatest of the barriers to pride of achievement.
13. *Encourage education and self-improvement for everyone.* Education should never end, for people at all levels of the organization.
14. *Take action to accomplish the transformation.* Commitment on the part of both top management and employees is required.

Japanese Management

The titles of the "Japanese management" movement's two best-selling books reflected the 1980s fears of declining competitiveness and the economic challenge from the Pacific Rim: *Theory Z: How American Business Can Meet the Japanese Challenge* (Ouchi, 1981), and *The Art of Japanese Management: Applications for American Executives* (Pascale and Athos, 1981).

In 1980, William Ouchi turned his attention to a key practical question: Could Japanese management methods (as introduced by Deming and Juran) be utilized in the United States? At the time, most scholars and businessmen were convinced that they could not. The differences between the cultures of Japan and the United States were too great. Ouchi's "objective became to separate the culturally specific principles from those universally applicable to economic organizations" (1981, viii). Ouchi began from the premise that organizations are social beings. "The Z Organization," which is reprinted in this chapter, describes the style and substance of companies that achieved a high state of consistency in their organizational cultures. "In the sense that Z organizations are more like clans than markets or bureaucracies, they foster close interchange between work and social life." While acknowledging the differences between the United States and Japan, Ouchi contends that "social organizations are incompatible with formality, distance, and contractualism. They proceed smoothly only with intimacy, subtlety, and trust."

The Search for Excellence

Like Ouchi, Tom Peters and Bob Waterman were driven by the twin swords of declining American corporate productivity and the rising overall excellence of Japanese companies, products, services, and quality. These quotations from *In Search of Excellence: Lessons from*

America's Best-Run Companies reflect their concern with competition from Japan but also their optimism that the United States could compete with Japanese corporations:

> There is good news from America. Good management practice today is not resident only in Japan (p. xxiii).
>
> Finally, it dawned on us that we did not have to look all the way to Japan for models with which to attack the corporate malaise that has us in its viselike grip (p. xx).
>
> What really fascinated us as we began to pursue our survey of corporate excellence was that . . . these [excellent U.S.] companies had cultures as strong as any Japanese organization (pp. xix, xx).

While Deming built his quality movement on fourteen points of management, the foundations of the Peters and Waterman movement are "eight attributes of management excellence":

- *a bias for action;*
- *close to the customer;*
- *autonomy and entrepreneurship;*
- *productivity through people;*
- *hands-on, value-driven;*
- *stick to the knitting;*
- *simple form, lean staff; and*
- *simultaneous loose-tight properties.*

Peters and Waterman describe "Simultaneous Loose-Tight Properties" (the title of a chapter from *In Search of Excellence* that is reprinted here) as a summary point of the other seven. "It is in essence the coexistence of firm central direction and maximum individual autonomy. . . . Organizations that live by the loose-tight principle are on the one hand rigidly controlled, yet at the same time allow (indeed, insist on) autonomy, entrepreneurship, and innovation from the rank and file." The "auras" of Deming, TQM, and Ouchi are readily evident in this reading, but the approach and style of Peters and Waterman are uniquely their own. Their message to managers (Tom Peters's, in particular) remained a powerful force through the 1990s.

Learning Organizations

Peter Senge's 1990 book, *The Fifth Discipline*, rivaled *In Search of Excellence* in its influence with management practitioners and academicians. For Senge, change occurs through teaming, and learning is change—for people and organizations. Thus, it is possible for organizations to learn to change because "deep down, we are all learners." Senge's purpose in *The Fifth Discipline* is "to destroy the illusion that the world is created of separate, unrelated forces. When we give up this illusion—we can then build 'learning organizations,' organizations where people continually expand their capacity to create the results they truly desire, where new and expansive patterns of thinking are nurtured, where collective aspiration is set free, and where people are continually learning how to learn together" (Senge, 1990, p. 3). To do so, managers must learn to detect seven organizational "learning disabilities" and how to use five "disciplines" as antidotes to them.

In a chapter from *The Fifth Discipline*, "A Shift of Mind," (reprinted here), Senge argues that five new "component technologies" are gradually converging that will collectively permit the emergence of learning organizations. He labels these component technologies the "five disciplines":

- *systems thinking;*
- *personal mastery:* people approaching life and work "as an artist would approach a work of art" (p. 7);
- *mental models:* deeply ingrained assumptions or mental images "that influence how we understand the world and how we take action" (p. 8);
- *building shared vision:* "when there is a genuine vision . . . people excel and learn, not because they are told to, but because they want to" (p. 9); and
- *team learning:* team members engaging in true dialogue with their assumptions suspended.

A true learning organization employs all five of the disciplines in a never-ending quest to expand its capacity to create its future. "Systems thinking" is the fifth discipline—the integrative discipline that fuses the others into a coherent body of theory and practice. Learning organizations are organizations that are able to move past mere survival learning to engage in generative learning—"learning that enhances our capacity to create" (p. 14).

Reinventing Government

Whereas Ouchi, Peters and Waterman, and Senge focused on private industry, David Osborne and Ted Gaebler elected to take on government. Their concept was straightforward. Governments that are tall, sluggish, over-centralized, and preoccupied with rules and regulations don't work well. We designed public agencies to protect against abuses of power such as misusing public funds. "In making it difficult to steal the public's money, we made it virtually impossible to manage the public's money. . . . In attempting to control virtually everything, we became so obsessed with dictating how things should be done—regulating the process, controlling the inputs—that we ignored the outcomes, the results." Osborne and Gaebler argued persuasively for the emergence of "entrepreneurial government," government that can—and must—compete with for-profit businesses, nonprofit agencies, and other units of government. "We must turn bureaucratic institutions into entrepreneurial institutions, ready to kill off obsolete initiatives, willing to do more with less, eager to absorb new ideas."

All of the reform movements that require changes in organizational culture have their lists of essential points, including Osborne and Gaebler. Their ten "principles" of reinvention are:

1. *Catalytic government:* steering rather than rowing
2. *Community-owned government:* empowering rather than serving
3. *Competitive government:* injecting competition into service delivery
4. *Mission-driven government:* transforming rule-driven organizations
5. *Results-oriented government:* funding outcomes, not inputs
6. *Customer-driven government:* meeting the needs of the customer, not the bureaucracy
7. *Enterprising government:* earning rather than spending
8. *Anticipatory government:* prevention rather than cure
9. *Decentralized government:* from hierarchy to participation and teamwork
10. *Market-oriented government:* leveraging change through the market

Osborne and Gaebler's message fell on receptive ears in Washington, D.C. Although Democrats won the White House in 1992, Republicans swept into power in both houses of the Congress, and "bloated, unresponsive government" was a popular theme with the electorate. President Bill Clinton assigned the task of "reinventing government" to Vice President Al Gore, who promptly invited Osborne and Gaebler to help organize the implementation of massive changes in the U.S. government. On September 7, 1993, Vice President Gore and the National Performance Review (NPR) released a report that had taken six months of study: *From Red Tape to Results: Creating a Government That Works Better and Costs Less*, or, *The Gore Report on Reinventing Government*. The wave of government management reform that followed "reinventing government" was uncreatively labeled "new public management" (Farazmand, 2001; Kearney & Hays, 1998; Light, 1998; Savas, 2000).

In its early years, the National Performance Review (NPR) was indeed a "cultural change movement." Its goal was improved productivity, quality of services, and "customer" satisfaction. It was easy to be cynical about NPR's potential for creating change. No "blue-ribbon task forces" of business executives were brought in to lead the effort, and the usual armies of consultants were noticeably absent. Instead, the NPR initiative relied on existing employees to identify problems, propose solutions, and implement changes. *The Gore Report* (1993), parts of which are reprinted here, was an early effort to explain NPR's purposes and strategies. Subsequent reports documented surprising improvements across many branches of the executive branch. As the 1994 election approached, however, the Clinton-Gore administration was being criticized vigorously by the Republicans for failing to reduce the size of government. House Speaker Newt Gingrich was especially articulate in challenging the White House incumbents. The task was not to "improve" government, but to shrink it. Clinton-Gore responded politically. In 1994, one of NPR's announced goals became the reduction of the government workforce by 250,000 employees. The same employees who were "solving problems" for NPR thus learned that their jobs might well be eliminated. Although vestiges of NPR remain in 2005, it is not the same movement that it started out to be in 1992–1993.

THE FEMINIST AND MULTICULTURAL PERSPECTIVES ON ORGANIZATIONAL REFORM

Two readings are included here that are written from the feminist and multicultural perspectives of organization theory. They examine the need for cultural reforms that will enable women and minority employees to participate fully and thereby strengthen organizations: Joan Acker's *Gendering Organization Theory* and Taylor Cox Jr.'s, *Creating the Multicultural Organization: The Challenge of Managing Diversity*.

Joan Acker's "Gendering Organizational Theory" (1992) reflects a theme popularized by Gareth Morgan (1986): "The way we 'read' organizations influences how we produce them." Feminist organization theorists argue that longstanding male control of organizations has been accompanied and maintained by male perspectives of organization theory. Thus it is through male lenses that we *see* and analyze organizations. At least four sets of gendered processes perpetuate this male reality of organizations: (1) gender divisions that produce gender patterning of jobs, (2) creation of symbols and images, (3) interactions characterized by dominance and subordination, and (4) "the internal mental work of individuals as they consciously construct their understandings of the organization's

gendered structure of work and opportunity and the demands for gender-appropriate behaviors and attitudes." Ordinary activities in organizations are not gender neutral. They
perpetuate the "gendered substructure within the organization itself and within the wider
society," as well as in organization theory.

Taylor Cox Jr. argues that the ability to manage diversity is a requirement—a crucial
competency—for managers in today's organizations, but it has been far more difficult to
master this competency than many had expected following the clarion calls that were
spawned by the "Workforce 2000" report of the Hudson Institute (Johnston & Packer,
1987). Many organizations have found the goal of a multicultural work culture highly
elusive. Cox advocates that "making fairness and respect for all people a reality is a part of
business strategy in its own right, independent of the linkage of these ideals to financial performance." Yet, strategically managed diversity also is desirable as a strategy for improving
the performance of organizations on many dimensions, including problem solving, creativity and innovation, flexibility, overall quality of personnel, and marketing strategies. On
the other hand, ". . . the presence of diversity in an organization or work group can create
obstacles to high performance." In "Creating the Multicultural Organization: The Challenge of Managing Diversity," Cox asserts that although "bigoted and insensitive people do
exist, and they are a significant barrier to the presence of diversity and to realization of its
benefits, but this is a very superficial diagnosis of the problem. The more significant problem is that *most employers have an organizational culture that is somewhere between toxic and
deadly when it comes to handling diversity.* The result is that the presence of real diversity is
unsustainable. . . ." (emphasis in original).

REFERENCES

Acker, J. (1992). Gendering organizational theory. In A. J. Mills & P. Tancred, eds., *Gendering orga-
nizational analysis* (pp. 248–260). Thousand Oaks, CA: Sage.
Al-Khalaf, A. (1994). Factors that affect the success and failure of TQM implementation in small
U.S. cities. Unpublished doctoral dissertation, Graduate School of Public and International
Affairs, University of Pittsburgh.
American Productivity & Quality Center. (1988). Results of a national survey: American people
aware of competitiveness problem. *The Letter, APQC,* 8 (September), 1–9.
Barzelay, M. (1992). *Breaking through bureaucracy.* Berkeley, CA: University of California Press.
Berman, E. M. (1998). *Productivity in public and nonprofit organizations: Strategies and techniques.*
Thousand Oaks, CA: Sage.
Bhote, K. R. (Spring 1994). Dr. W. Edwards Deming: A prophet with belated honor in his own coun-
try. *National Productivity Review,* 13, 153–159.
Cohen, M. D., & L. S. Sproull, eds. (1996). *Organizational learning.* Thousand Oaks, CA: Sage.
Cohen, S., and W. Eimicke (1998). *Tools for innovators.* San Francisco: Jossey-Bass.
Cox, T., Jr. (2001). *Creating the multicultural organization: A strategy for capturing the power of diversity.*
San Francisco: Jossey-Bass.
Crosby, P. B. (1979). *Quality is free.* New York: McGraw-Hill.
Crosby, P. B. (1984). *Quality without tears.* New York: McGraw-Hill.
Deming, W. E. (1986). *Out of the crisis.* Cambridge, MA: MIT Press.
Deming, W. E. (1993). *The new economics.* Cambridge, MA: MIT Press.
Eccles, R. G. (1991, January–February). The performance measurement manifesto. *Harvard Business
Review,* 131–137.
Eismore, P. J. A. (2001). *Organisational culture: Organisational change?* Aldershot, UK: Ashgate.

Farazmand, A., ed. (2001). *Privatization or public enterprise reform?* Westport, CT: Greenwood Press.

Gore, A. (1993). *The Gore report on reinventing government.* New York: Times Books.

Hammer, M., & Champy, J. (1993). *Reengineering the corporation.* New York: Harper-Business.

Head, Simon (1999, August–September). Big Brother in a black box. *Civilization,* 52–55.

Ingle, S. (1987, December). Training. *The Journal for Quality and Participation,* 10, 4–6.

Johnston, W. B., & A. H. Packer (1987). *Workforce 2000: Work and workers for the twenty-first century.* Indianapolis, IN: Hudson Institute; Washington, DC: U. S. Department of Labor.

Joiner, B. L. (1994). *Fourth generation management.* New York: McGraw-Hill.

Juran, J. M. (1992). *Juran on quality by design.* New York: Free Press.

Kaplan, R. S., & D. P. Norton (1992, January–February). The balanced scorecard: Measures that drive performance. *Harvard Business Review,* 71–79.

Kaplan, R. S., & D. P. Norton (1993, September–October). Putting the balanced scorecard to work. *Harvard Business Review,* 134–147.

Kaplan, R. S., & D. P. Norton (1996, January–February). Using the balanced scorecard as a strategic management system. *Harvard Business Review,* 75–85.

Kearney, R. C., & S. W. Hays (1998, Fall). Reinventing government, the new public management and civil service systems in international perspective. *Review of Public Personnel Administration,* 18(4), 39–54.

Light, P. C. (1998). *The tides of reform: Making government work 1945–1995.* New Haven, CT: Yale University Press.

Lindsay, W. M., R. K. Curtis, & G. E. Manning (1989, June). A participative management primer. *Journal for Quality and Participation,* 12, 78–84.

Mroczkowski, T. (1984–1985, Winter). Productivity and quality improvement at GE's Video Products Division: The cultural change component. *National Productivity Review,* 4, 15–23.

Nadler, D. A., M. S. Gerstein, & R. B. Shaw, eds. (1992). *Organizational architecture: Designs for changing organizations.* San Francisco: Jossey-Bass.

Osborne, D., & T. Gaebler (1992). *Reinventing government.* Reading, MA: Addison-Wesley.

Ott, J. S., P. Boonyarak, & L. A. Dicke (2001, Summer). Public sector reform, and moral and ethical accountability. *Public Integrity,* 3(3), 277–289.

Ott, J. S., S. J. Parkes, and R. B. Simpson, eds. (2003). *Classic readings in organizational behavior.* 3d ed. Belmont, CA: Wadsworth/Thomson.

Ouchi, W. G. (1981). *Theory Z: How American business can meet the Japanese challenge.* Reading, MA: Addison-Wesley.

Pascale, R. T., & A. G. Athos (1981). *The art of Japanese management: Applications for American executives.* New York: Simon & Schuster.

Peters, B. G. (1996). *The future of governing: Four emerging models.* Lawrence, KS: University Press of Kansas.

Peters, T. J. (1987). *Thriving on chaos.* New York: Knopf.

Peters, T. J., & R. H. Waterman Jr. (1982). *In search of excellence: Lessons from America's best-run companies.* New York: Harper & Row.

Savas, E. S. (1982). *Privatizing the public sector: How to shrink government.* Chatham, NJ: Chatham House.

Savas, E. S. (2000). *Privatization and public-private partnerships.* New York: Chatham House.

Senge, P. M. (1990). *The fifth discipline: The art and practice of the learning organization.* New York: Doubleday Currency.

U. S. General Accounting Office (GAO) (1991). *Management practices: U.S. companies improve performance through quality efforts.* Washington, DC, GAO/OCG941.

Walton, M. (1986). *The Deming management method.* New York: Putnam.

Weisbord, M. R. (1991). *Productive workplaces: Organizing and managing for dignity, meaning, and community.* San Francisco: Jossey-Bass.

39

The Z Organization

William G. Ouchi

Each Type Z company has its own distinctiveness—the United States military has a flavor quite different from IBM or Eastman Kodak. Yet all display features that strongly resemble Japanese firms. Like their Japanese counterparts, Type Z companies tend to have long-term employment, often for a lifetime, although the lifetime relationship is not formally stated. The long-term relationship often stems from the intricate nature of the business; commonly, it requires lots of learning-by-doing. Companies, therefore, want to retain employees, having invested in their training to perform well in that one unique setting. Employees tend to stay with the company, since many of their skills are specific to that one firm with the result that they could not readily find equally remunerative nor challenging work elsewhere. These task characteristics that produce the life-long employment relationship also produce a relatively slow process of evaluation and promotion. Here we observe one important adaptation of the Japanese form. Type Z companies do not wait ten years to evaluate and promote: any Western firm that did so would not retain many of its talented employees. Thus such firms frequently provide the sorts of explicit performance interviews that are commonplace. However, promotions are slower in coming. . . .

Career paths in Type Z companies display much of the "wandering around" across functions and offices that typifies the Japanese firm. This effectively produces more company-specific skills that work toward intimate coordination between steps in the design, manufacturing, and distribution process. An employee who engages in such "non-professional" development takes the risk that the end skills will be largely non-marketable to other companies. Therefore, long-term employment ties into career development in a critical way.

Typically Type Z companies are replete with the paraphernalia of modern information and accounting systems, formal planning, management by objectives, and all of the other formal, explicit mechanisms of control. . . . Yet in Z companies these mechanisms are tended to carefully for their information, but rarely dominate in major decisions. By contrast, managers in big companies, hospitals, and government agencies often complain about feeling powerless to exercise their judgement in the face of quantitative analysis, computer models, and numbers, numbers, numbers. Western management seems to be characterized for the most part by an ethos which roughly runs as follows: rational is better than non-rational, objective is more nearly rational than subjective, quantitative is more objective than nonquantitative, and thus quantitative analysis is preferred over judgements based on wisdom, experience, and subtlety. Some observers, such as Professor Harold Leavitt of Stanford University, have written that the penchant for the explicit and the measurable has gone well beyond reasonable limits, and that a return to the subtle and the subjective is in order.[1]

In a Type Z company, the explicit and the implicit seem to exist in a state of balance. While decisions weigh the complete analysis of facts, they are also shaped

Source: William G. Ouchi, *Theory Z: How American Business Can Meet the Japanese Challenge* (Reading, MA: Addison-Wesley, 1981), pp. 71–94. © 1981 by Addison-Wesley Publishing Company, Inc. Reprinted by permission.

by serious attention to questions of whether or not this decision is "suitable," whether it "fits" the company. A company that isolates sub-specialities is hardly capable of achieving such fine-grained forms of understanding. Perhaps the underlying cause is the loss of the ability for disparate departments within a single organization to communicate effectively with one another. They communicate in the sparse, inadequate language of numbers, because numbers are the only language all can understand in a reasonably symmetrical fashion. Let us consider one example.

A MATTER OF COMPANY STYLE

One of the more dramatic new businesses to develop during the decade of the 1970s was the digital watch industry. At the outset, the digital or electronic watch presented a mystery to everyone in the business. The old, main-line watch firms such as Timex and Bulova were suspicious of the new semiconductor technology which replaced the mainspring and the tuning fork. The semiconductor firms that knew this technology supplied parts to other companies and did not know the business of selling goods to the individual consumer. I watched the reaction of two of these semiconductor firms to a new business opportunity. . . .

The digital watch seemed from the first to hold out the promise of a huge new industry. This new watch, which was more accurate, more reliable, and cheaper than the conventional timepiece, held the promise of replacing almost all timepieces in the Western world. Company A performed a careful analysis of the potential market, estimating the number of digital watches that could be sold at various prices, the cost of manufacturing and distributing these watches to retail outlets, and thus the potential profits to be earned by the firm. Company A, already a supplier of the central electronic component, possessed the necessary technical skill. The executives of the company knew that the business of selling consumer goods

was unfamiliar to them, but they felt that they could develop the necessary knowledge. Following their analysis of the situation, they proceeded to go out and buy a company that manufactured watch cases, another that manufactured wrist bands for watches, and within weeks after their go-ahead decision, were in the watch business. Starting from zero, Company A rapidly gained a major share of the watch business and, eighteen months after the decision, was a major factor in the new industry and earned large profits on digital watches.

The executives of Company Z also recognized the opportunities in digital watches; they too manufactured the key electronic component that is the heart of the digital watch. Their analyses of the market promised very great rewards should they enter the business. But at Company Z, the numbers never dominate. The top executives at the firm asked whether this business really fit their "style." They saw the anticipated profits but wondered whether this would be a one-shot success or whether the company could continue to be an innovator and a leader in the watch business in the years to come. Most importantly, entering the watch business seemed to conflict with the company's philosophy. In Company Z, talking about the company philosophy is not considered soft-headed, wishful, or unrealistic. Rather, the company consists of a set of managers who see clearly that their capacity to achieve close cooperation depends in part on their agreeing on a central set of objectives and ways of doing business. These agreements comprise their philosophy of business, a broad statement that contemplates the proper relationship of the business to its employees, its owners, its customers, and to the public-at-large. This general statement must be interpreted to have meaning for any specific situation, and it is therefore important that managers be sufficiently familiar with the underlying corporate culture so that they can interpret the philosophy in ways which produce cooperation rather than conflict. One element of the philosophy concerns the kinds of products the company should manufacture, and that statement seemed clearly to exclude a product like the digital watch. On that basis, it seemed, the philosophy outweighed the financial analysis, and the watch project should have ended there.

But it didn't. A second major element of this corporation's philosophy had to do with preserving the freedom of employees to pursue projects they felt would be fruitful. In particular, the freedom of a unit manager to set goals and pursue them to their conclusion is cherished. In this case, a young general manager with a proven record of success wanted to take the company into the watch business. The top executives of the company disagreed with his judgement but were unwilling to sacrifice the manager's freedom. Two very central values conflicted in their implications for action. What was striking about this case was that values, not market share or profitability, lay at the heart of the conflict in Company Z.

Let me not seem to imply that Company Z is unconcerned with profitability. The record is clear. Company Z is among the fastest-growing, most profitable of major American firms. Every manager knows that projects survive only as long as they produce profits well above what other companies demand. But at Company Z, profits are regarded not as an end in itself nor as the method of "keeping score" in the competitive process. Rather, profits are the reward to the firm if it continues to provide true value to its customers, to help its employees to grow, and to behave responsibly as a corporate citizen. Many of us have heard these words and are by now cynical about that kind of a public face which frequently shields a far less attractive internal reality. One of the distinctive features of Company Z is that these values are not a sham, not cosmetic, but they are practiced as the standard by which decisions are made. Again, the process is not faultless. Some managers within the firm are skeptical about the wisdom of these values and about the firm's true commitment to them, but by and large, the culture is intact and operating effectively.

Why a philosophy of management when firms in a free enterprise economy are supposed to seek profits only? In a large organization, it is impossible to determine over the period of a few months or a year whether a business segment is profitable or not. Suppose that you become the manager in charge of a new division created to enter the digital watch market. You buy the electronics from another division, you share salespersons with other divisions, you draw on a central engineering staff to design and maintain both your product and your manufacturing process, you rely heavily on the good name of the company to promote your product, and you staff your new operation with skilled managers and technicians who are products of the company's training programs. How much should you be charged for each of these inputs to your business? No one can know. Someone, inevitably, will come up with some numbers, sometimes referred to as "transfer prices" and other times referred to as "magic numbers," and these numbers will be used to calculate your costs in order to subtract those from your sales revenues so that a profit can be measured. Everyone, however, knows that the stated profits are a very inexact measure of your true profits, and that your true profits are unknowable.

Suppose that your company is in fact run by a strict profitability standard. If you are being undercharged for the central engineering services, then you will use as much engineering as you can, thereby taking that service away from some other use in the company. If another division manager asks to borrow three of your experienced staff, you may deny this request or send three not very skilled persons instead, since another's success is not reflected in your profits. In many ways, large and small, the inexact measurement of value will result in an explicit, formal mechanism that yields low coordination, low productivity, and high frustration.

Organizational life is a life of interdependence, of relying upon others. It is also a life of ambiguity. Armen Alchian and Harold Demsetz, two distinguished economists at UCLA, have argued that where teamwork is involved the measurement of individual performance will inevitably be ambiguous. Knowing this, and understanding the extreme complexity of interdependence in their business, the top management of Company Z has determined that explicit measures not be the final arbiter of decision making. They feel that if most of the top managers agree on what the company ought to be trying to do and how, in general, it ought to go about that set of tasks, then they will be able to rely on their mutual trust and goodwill to reach decisions far superior to anything that a formal system of control could provide.

They furthermore understand that the informal, implicit mechanisms of control cannot succeed alone. They can develop only under the conditions of stable employment, slow evaluation and promotion, and low career specialization. Even with those aids, however, the subtle and the implicit must be supported with the crutch of formal control and analysis in a large, multiproduct, multi-national, multi-technology organization in which a complete agreement on values and beliefs can never be fully realized.

In the end, Company Z authorized the general manager to enter a relatively small and specialized segment of the digital watch market. He had the opportunity to "grow" his new venture if it succeeded, but the initial venture was small enough that its failure would not jeopardize the health of the company overall. Three years after the initial decisions by both companies, the picture was quite different. Following a dramatic surge in sales and profits, Company A had encountered stiff competition from other firms who were more experienced than they in this industry. Eighteen months after their initial success, they had taken severe losses and had sold their watch business to a competitor. They were, once again, back to zero in watches. Company Z also experienced an early success with its more limited digital watch venture, and after the initial success

they, too, experienced stiff competition and a decline in profits. Rather than sell off the business, however, they slowly de-emphasized it, continuing to service the watches that they already had sold and, perhaps, maintaining the skeletal business as a valuable lesson from which future managers could learn.

A MATTER OF COMPANY SUBSTANCE

In Type Z organizations, as we have seen, the decision-making process is typically a consensual, participative one. Social scientists have described this as a democratic (as opposed to autocratic or apathetic) process in which many people are drawn into the shaping of important decisions. This participative process is one of the mechanisms that provides for the broad dissemination of information and of values within the organization, and it also serves the symbolic role of signaling in an unmistakable way the cooperative intent of the firm. Many of the values central to a corporate culture are difficult to test or to display. Some do not come into play more than once every few years, when a crisis appears (for example, the commitment to long-term employment, which is tested only during a recession), while others, such as the commitment to behave unselfishly, are difficult to observe. These values and beliefs must be expressed in concrete ways if they are to be understood and believed by new employees, particularly since new employees arrive with the expectation that all companies are basically the same: they are not to be trusted, not to be believed. Consensual decision making both provides the direct values of information and value sharing and at the same time openly signals the commitment of the organization to those values. When people get together in one room to discuss a problem or to make a decision, that meeting is often noticed and even talked about: it is a highly visible form of commitment to working together. Typically, Type Z organizations devote a great deal of energy to developing the interpersonal skills necessary to effective group decision making, perhaps in part for this symbolic reason.

In Type Z companies, the decision making may be collective, but the ultimate responsibility for decision still resides in one individual. It is doubtful that Westerners could ever tolerate the collective form of responsibility that characterizes Japanese organizations. This maintenance of the sense of individual responsibility remains critical to Western society but it also creates much tension in the Type Z organization. When a group engages in consensual decision making, members are effectively being asked to place their fate to some extent in the hands of others. Not a common fate but a set of individual fates is being dealt with. Each person will come from the meeting with the responsibility for some individual targets set collectively by the group. The consensual process, as defined by Professor Edgar Schein of M.I.T., is one in which members of the group may be asked to accept responsibility for a decision that they do not prefer, but that the group, in an open and complete discussion, has settled upon.[2] This combination of collective decision making with individual responsibility demands an atmosphere of trust. Only under a strong assumption that all hold basically compatible goals and that no one is engaged in self-serving behavior will individuals accept personal responsibility for a group decision and make enthusiastic attempts to get the job done.

The wholistic orientation of Type Z companies is in many ways similar to that found in the Japanese form but with some important differences. The similarity has to do with orientation of superior to subordinates and of employees at all levels to their co-workers. Type Z companies generally show broad concern for the welfare of subordinates and of co-workers as a natural part of a working relationship. Relationships between people tend to be informal and to emphasize that whole people deal with one another at work, rather than just managers with workers and clerks with machinists.

This wholistic orientation, a central feature of the organization, inevitably maintains a strong egalitarian atmosphere that is a feature of all Type Z organizations.

If people deal with one another in segmented ways, as one role to another rather than as one human being to another, then these dehumanized relationships easily become authoritarian. Feelings of superiority and inferiority prevail in relationships narrowly defined and constrained to "my" duties as department head and "your" duties as worker. That attitude, out of step in a democratic society, implies class distinctions. The subordinate will inevitably be alienated both from the superior who takes such an attitude and from the company that he or she represents. The superior is often relieved of some of the anxiety and stress that come with having to respond to the needs of others, whether those are superiors, subordinates, or peers. Most of us cannot block off the requests or complaints of superiors and peers, but if we become impersonal and formal and thus distant from the needs of subordinates, that gives one less thing to worry about. Of course we recognize that feeling as being improper, unfair, and unproductive, but short-term pressures will often beckon in that direction.

An organization that maintains a wholistic orientation and forces employees at all levels to deal with one another as complete human beings creates a condition in which de-personalization is impossible, autocracy is unlikely, and open communication, trust, and commitment are common. In one Type Z company with which I am familiar, each plant in the company holds a monthly "beer bust" at the end of a working day. Beer and snacks are consumed, neither in large quantities, and informal games and skits are frequently offered. Any manager who regularly fails to take part in the beer bust will fail to achieve success and continued promotion. Is this an example of "politics at work," of "it's who you know, not what you know," or is it simply a holdover from earlier days?

The beer bust, as I interpret it, is similar to the cocktails after work shared by bosses and subordinates in Japan. Both have the same group of people who work together each day now cast in different roles. The hierarchy of work, somewhat relaxed in this setting, gives people the opportunity to interact more as equals, or at least without the familiar hierarchical roles. Technicians can express their willingness to regard foremen as regular people rather than as superiors to be suspected. Managers show subordinates their acceptance of them as equals, as whole human beings. In this particular company with the beer bust, managers must be willing to engage in frivolous games and skits in which their obvious lack of skill and their embarrassment bring them down to earth both in their own eyes and in the eyes of their subordinates.

Very few of us are superior to our fellow workers in every way. As long as we cling to our organizational roles, we can maintain the fiction that we are indeed superior in every way. But if we engage these people in social intercourse, the fiction is dispelled. The natural force of organizational hierarchy promotes a segmented relationship and a hierarchical attitude. A wholistic relationship provides a counterbalance that encourages a more egalitarian attitude.

Egalitarianism is a central feature of Type Z organizations. Egalitarianism implies that each person can apply discretion and can work autonomously without close supervision, because they are to be trusted. Again, trust underscores the belief that goals correspond, that neither person is out to harm the other. This feature, perhaps more than any other, accounts for the high levels of commitment, of loyalty, and of productivity in Japanese firms and in Type Z organizations. . . .

The central importance of trust is revealed in a study of utopian societies by Rosabeth Moss Kanter.[3] Kanter described the Amana (refrigerators), the Oneida (tableware), and other utopian communities that succeeded as commercial enterprises. In these communities one of the key values was egalitarianism—equality of influence and of power. Consistent with this value, all

explicit forms of supervision and of direction were forgone. Now the problem was how to ensure a high level of discipline and hard work without hierarchical supervision and monitoring of production. The chief danger was of self-interest in the form of laziness, shirking, and selfishness at work. Such behavior could not readily be corrected without hierarchy, and other means had to be found to limit such tendencies. The answer was to develop a complete unity of goals between individuals and the community such that an autonomous individual would naturally seek to work hard, cooperate, and benefit the community. In order to accomplish this complete socialization, utopian communities engaged in a variety of practices that had the objective of developing common goals. Open sex or complete celibacy, the most dramatic of these, both have characterized all successful utopian communes in the United States. From Kanter's point of view, open sex and complete celibacy are functionally equivalent: each prevents the formation of loyalties to another individual and so preserves the loyalty of all to the community. Open sex allows no free choice of partners but rather a strict assignment of older men to younger women and older women to younger men. As soon as partners begin to show preference for one another in this system, they are reassigned. The example illustrates both the great difficulty of achieving complete goal integration in a Western society and the central importance of selfless goals in nonhierarchical organizations.

Type Z organizations, unlike utopian communities, do employ hierarchical modes of control, and thus do not rely entirely upon goal congruence among employees for order. Nevertheless, they do rely extensively upon symbolic means to promote an attitude of egalitarianism and of mutual trust, and they do so in part by encouraging a wholistic relation between employees. Self-direction replaces hierarchical direction to a great extent, which enhances commitment, loyalty, and motivation.

Argyris challenged managers to integrate individuals into organizations, not to create alienating, hostile, and impersonally bureaucratic places of work. In a real sense, the Type Z organization comes close to realizing that ideal. It is a consent culture, a community of equals who cooperate with one another to reach common goals. Rather than relying exclusively upon hierarchy and monitoring to direct behavior, it relies also upon commitment and trust.

THE THEORY BEHIND THE THEORY Z ORGANIZATION

The difference between a hierarchy—or bureaucracy—and Type Z is that Z organizations have achieved a high state of consistency in their internal culture. They are most aptly described as clans in that they are intimate associations of people engaged in economic activity but tied together through a variety of bonds.[4] *Clans* are distinct from *hierarchies*, and from *markets*, which are the other two fundamental social mechanisms through which transactions between individuals can be governed. In a market, there will be competitive bidding for, say, an engineer's services as well as for a weaver's baskets. Each will know the true value of their products according to the terms the market sets. In a bureaucracy, however, workers lack any clear sense of the value of their services. No competitive bidding sets the yearly wage for an engineering vice-president, for example. Since each job is unique, companies instead rely upon the hierarchy to evaluate performance and to estimate the amount that an employee is worth. The hierarchy succeeds only to the extent that we trust it to yield equitable outcomes, just as the marketplace succeeds only because we grant legitimacy to it. As long as the vice-president regards the president as a fair and well-informed person who will arrive at a fair appraisal of his performance, the contented employee will let the hierarchy operate unobstructed. However, mistrust will bring about prespecified

contractual protections such as those written when selling some service to an outside firm. The writing and enforcement of that contract will vastly increase the costs of managing the vice-president.

More common is the example of the hourly employee who learns, over time, that the corporate hierarchy cannot be trusted to provide equitable treatment and insists upon union representation and contractual specification of rights. The employee pays additional costs in the form of union dues, the company pays additional costs in the form of more industrial relations staff, and everyone pays more costs in the form of less cooperation, less productivity, and less wealth to be shared. Thus the success of a hierarchy, or bureaucracy, can be costly. But whatever the financial cost, these protective mechanisms take over when individual contribution can be equitably assessed only through the somewhat more subtle form of bureaucratic surveillance.

By comparison clans succeed when teamwork and change render individual performance almost totally ambiguous. At these times long-term commitment, supported by agreement on goals and operating methods, is necessary to achieve an equitable balance. Individual performance and reward can be judged equitably only over a period of several years, thus relationships must be long-term and trust must be great.

In a market each individual is in effect asked to pursue selfish interests. Because the market mechanism will exactly measure the contribution of each person to the common good, each person can be compensated exactly for personal contributions. If one chooses not to contribute anything, then one is not compensated and equity is achieved.

In a clan, each individual is also effectively told to do just what that person wants. In this case, however, the socialization of all to a common goal is so complete and the capacity of the system to measure the subtleties of contributions over the long run is so exact that individuals will naturally seek to do that which is in the common good.

Thus the monk, the marine, or the Japanese auto worker who appears to have arrived at a self-less state is, in fact, achieving selfish ends quite thoroughly. Both of these governance mechanisms realize human potential and maximize human freedom because they do not constrain behavior.

Only the bureaucratic mechanism explicitly says to individuals, "Do not do what you want, do what we tell you to do because we pay you for it." The bureaucratic mechanism alone produces alienation, anomie, and a lowered sense of autonomy. This is the reason that the employees of Z companies report a higher sense of personal autonomy and freedom than do the employees of Type A companies. Feelings of autonomy and freedom make the employees in Japanese firms work with so much more enthusiasm than their counterparts in many Western firms.

In the sense that Z organizations are more like clans than markets or bureaucracies, they foster close interchange between work and social life. Consider this example: Chinese-American entrepreneurs appear in greater numbers than would be expected, based on their fraction of the population as a whole. For many years, the explanation offered by social scientists was that by contrast black Americans were systematically denied access to banks and other sources of capital necessary to start a small business, whereas Asian-Americans had better access to these capital markets. As a number of studies have shown, however, both blacks and Asians find the same difficulties in raising capital for businesses.[5] Yet Asian-Americans brought with them from their homelands the tradition of informal revolving-credit societies, the *Tanomoshi* for the Japanese-Americans and the *Hui* for the Chinese-Americans. A *Tanomoshi* or *Hui* typically consists of about one dozen individuals, each one wanting to own his own service station, a one-truck hauling service, or other such small businesses. Once each month, the group gathers at one member's home for dinner, and each person brings with him a prespecified sum of money, per-

haps $1,000. The host of the evening keeps the whole sum — say, $12,000 — which he then uses to buy a second truck or open his service station. The group meets in this fashion for twelve successive months until each person has put in $12,000 and has taken out $12,000. In this manner, people who would have great difficulty saving the whole sum of $12,000 are able to raise capital.

The process on closer scrutiny has some unusual properties. First, the earlier recipients of the pot effectively pay a lower interest rate than do the later recipients. The first host has the use of $11,000 of other people's money for one month without interest, then $10,000 (as he adds his $1,000 to the second dinner), and so on. By comparison the last host has to put $11,000 dollars into the pot, money that he could have left in the bank to draw interest, before he receives his pot. Surely this is an inequitable process, yet it persists. The second interesting property is that no contracts are signed, no collateral is offered, even though the late borrowers willingly turn over large sums of money to others with no assurance that they will be paid. They have no evidence of even having made a loan that would stand up in a court of law, should there be a default.

Japanese-Americans' membership in a *Tanomoshi* is limited strictly by the geographical regions of birth in Japan, and by the region in Japan from which one's ancestors came. Among the Chinese-Americans, membership in a *Hui* is limited to those within the kinship network. Thus one can only be born into a *Tanomoshi* or a *Hui*, and one can never escape from the network of familiar, communal, social, religious, and economic ties that bind those groups together. If a member should fail to make good on his obligations, members of his family would certainly take up his obligation or else pay the very high price of having all branches of the family shut out of the economic and social network of the community. This ethnically bound community thus obviates the need for contracts or collateral to protect a loan. But what about the unfair difference in the implicit interest rates paid by the early versus late borrowers? We can understand this phenomenon in two ways. First, we note that these short-run inequities are made up in the long run. Because each adult in these ethnic communities typically participates in a large number of *Huis* or *Tanomoshis* over his lifetime, at times simultaneously participating in two or more, many opportunities arise to repay past debts by taking a later position in the chain. In addition, a debt incurred to one person may be repaid to that person's son or brother, who in turn has the capacity to repay the initial creditor through one of a thousand favors. What is critical is that there be a communal memory—much like that of the corporate memory in Theory Z—and that the community have a stable membership. The effects of this memory mechanism are far-reaching. Depending on his behavior as a borrower and lender, an individual may or may not be invited to participate in various other groups and may be included in or left out of religious and social activities that could affect the marital prospects of his children, the economic prospects of his business, and so on. In fact the more valuable his *Tanomoshi* membership, the higher the price he can command in the form of sought-after affiliations. Although the individuals in a *Hui* or *Tanomoshi* do not share complete goal congruence, they are at once largely committed to a congruent set of goals which have to do with maintaining the social structure of the community, and they are also subject to the long-run evaluation of an ethnically bound marketplace.

These clans also work largely on the basis of trust. Marcel Mauss, a French anthropologist, has noted that the willingness to be in someone's debt is an important signal of trust.[6] For instance, in most societies it is considered rude to rush over to repay a neighbor for a favor just received. To do so implies lack of trust in that neighbor and a fear that the neighbor may abuse your obligation by asking in return something you find particularly difficult or distasteful.

Thus, the leaving of many debts between people amounts to evidence of their trust of one another, and the evidence of trust in turn serves as the oil that lubricates future social transactions.

The point is that organizations are social organisms and, like any other social creations, are profoundly shaped by the social environment in which they exist. As we will see, the Type Z organization succeeds only under social conditions that support lifetime employment. The *Hui* and the *Tanomoshi* succeed in the United States only because the Chinese and Japanese immigrants found themselves living together in ethnic ghettoes.

DIFFICULTIES IN TRANSLATION

Despite its remarkable properties, the clan form in industry possesses a few potentially disabling weaknesses. A clan always tends to develop xenophobia, a fear of outsiders. In the words of the president of one major Type Z company: "We simply can't bring in an outsider at top levels. We've tried it, but the others won't accept him. I consider that to be one of our biggest problems." In other ways, too, the Type Z resists deviance in all forms. Because the glue that holds it together is consistency of belief rather than application of hierarchy, it tends indiscriminately to reject all inconsistency. The trouble is that it is difficult, perhaps impossible, to discriminate in advance between a deviant idea that is useful and adaptive and one that is simply stupid and immoral. Companies such as IBM, General Motors, and Xerox, in which innovation is critical, typically segregate their researchers and those who come up with new product ideas, sometimes locating them on the opposite end of the continent from headquarters in order to shield them from the sometimes oppressive corporate culture. What happens, of course, is that those scientists indeed become deviant from the mainline culture, develop lots of different ideas, and then discover that the headquarters decision-makers reject their ideas as being too deviant.

In a Type Z organization, changing people's behavior by changing a measure of performance or by changing the profit calculation is an impossibility: The only way to influence behavior is to change the culture. A culture changes slowly because its values reach deeply and integrate into a consistent network of beliefs that tends to maintain the status quo. Therefore, a Type Z organization runs the risk of becoming an industrial dinosaur, unable to react quickly enough to a major shift in the environment. Where operating changes are involved, Type Z organizations tend to be unusually adaptive. A better way to accomplish some task can be adopted without having to rewrite a book of rules specifying job descriptions and without worrying about whether this change will hurt the current way of measuring our performance. This is one of the greatest strengths of the Japanese firm. Japanese companies in the United States are fast becoming legendary for their capacity to quickly adopt changes in procedure, unencumbered by bureaucratic paraphernalia. However, the coordination in this system is provided by adherence to an underlying set of values that are deeply held and closely followed. If adaptation required a change in those values, then Type Z organizations would be at a severe disadvantage. . . .

Every Type Z organization that I know experiences some loss of professionalism.[7] Whether it is a financial analyst, a salesperson, a personnel specialist, or an engineer, a Type Z company manifests a lower level of professionalism. I systematically interviewed everyone at the level of vicepresident and above at two high-technology companies, one a pure Type A and one a pure Type Z (or as nearly pure as possible). I also interviewed a random selection of employees in each company. At Company A, each person was introduced to me with pride as being, ". . . the top public relations man in the industry," or ". . . the most innovative electrical engineer, the holder of twenty patents on circuit design," or ". . . the

personnel manager who set the pattern for industry in performance appraisal." At Company Z, by comparison, the emphasis was on how the individuals comprised a working team, with little mention of specialized skills, although great emphasis was placed on the company's practice of hiring only the most skilled and able young people and then developing them. The offices of Company A managers were typically filled with shelves of books and journals, and people would often offer me an article that they had written on their speciality. At Company Z people read fewer journals, wrote fewer articles, and attended fewer professional meetings. At the extreme, Type Z companies will express the "notinvented-here" mentality: "We have most of the top people in the field right here, so why should I go talk to anyone else?" The trouble, of course, comes if the company starts to slip. They will not know it, since they have no external point of comparison.

With respect to sex and race, Type Z companies have a tendency to be sexist and racist. This is another paradox, because while Type Z companies typically work much harder and care much more about offering equality of opportunity to minorities, in some ways they have much greater obstacles to overcome than do Type A companies. As I visited the managers in the high technology Type A, I was struck by the ethnic diversity among the upper levels of management: Spanish-Americans, Asian-Americans, Hungarian-Americans, and Anglo-Saxon-Americans. At Company A, new promotion opportunity is simply awarded to that candidate who has had the best "bottom line" for the past few periods. Whether that manager is obnoxious or strange, succeeds by abusing his employees or by encouraging them, doesn't matter. The only thing that counts is the bottom line, and thus a diverse group of people make it to the top. How well they are able to work with one another once at the top is another question.

At Company Z the cast of top managers is so homogeneous that one member of my research team characterized the dominant culture as "Boy Scout Macho." That is, the top management is wholesome, disciplined, hard-working, and honest, but unremittingly white, male, and middle class. Company Z has affirmative action goals at the top of its list and devotes great time and expense to recruiting, training, and developing women and ethnic minorities. Why is it nonetheless typical of "Boy Scout Macho"? Imagine that you are a general manager at Company Z. In your division you have an opening for a new manager in charge of marketing. Both a white male engineer and a female Mexican-American are completely qualified for the promotion. The difference between them is past experience. You have evaluated forty or fifty white male engineers in the past, you have worked with them day in and day out for twenty years, and you know how to calibrate them, how to read their subtle instincts, values, and beliefs. You are quite certain that you have correctly evaluated this white male engineer as being fully qualified for the job of marketing manager. But how about the female Mexican-American? How many of them have you evaluated or worked with at this level? She is probably the first. You cannot be sure that what you regard as initiative is truly that; you cannot be sure that the signs you see of ambition, of maturity, or of integrity are what they seem to be. It takes time and experience to learn to read subtleties in one who is culturally different, and because subtleties are everything in the Type Z organization, you cannot be confident that you have correctly appraised this candidate, and she is therefore at a considerable disadvantage, since no one in his right mind will choose an uncertainty over a certainty.

Probably no form of organization is more sexist or racist than the Japanese corporation. They do not intentionally shut out those who are different nor do they consider male Japanese to be superior. Their organizations simply operate as culturally homogeneous social systems that have very weak explicit or hierarchical monitoring properties and thus can withstand no internal cultural

diversity. To the extent that women or ethnic minorities (caucasians or Koreans, for example) are culturally different, they cannot succeed in Japan. The Japanese firm in the United States has a considerably greater tolerance for heterogeneity and thus can operate successfully with white people and women in high positions, but the tendency toward sameness is still present. The Type Z organization is still more open to heterogeneity, but it too requires a high level of homogeneity. Perhaps the other extreme, the cultural opposite of the Japanese firm in Japan, is the United States federal bureaucracy.

In a sense the federal bureaucracy is a microcosm of our society. Here our values of equality of opportunity for all people are crystallized, if not always realized. Much the same is true of state and local government agencies, but let us consider the federal agencies for a moment. Equality of opportunity and of treatment is taken far more seriously in the federal agencies than in almost any private sector organizations. What this means is that the government must promulgate a series of bureaucratic rules that should ordinarily prevent, insofar as humanly possible, the application of capricious or unfair standards that will harm women and ethnic minorities. Unfortunately, this set of bureaucratic rules must be geared to catch the lowest common denominator. That is, they cannot leave any rule ambiguous, to be decided on the discretion of an individual manager, since that leaves open the possibility of the manager arriving at a discriminatory interpretation. Thus the bureaucratic rules are not only explicit and inflexible but also constraining and impersonal. This thoroughgoing bureaucratization rests on the assumption that bureaucrats cannot be trusted to share the society's egalitarian goals nor to enact an egalitarian form of organization. Thus they are directed not to use their discretion and judgement. If we place a priceless value on equality in our public institutions, then we will pay any price to keep them democratic.

The price that we pay, of course, is in inefficiency, inflexibility, indolence, and impersonality. All too often a federal bureau will fail to do that which makes sense because common sense does not fit the rules. All too often bureaucrats, trained not to allow personal values to intrude on decisions, will treat us, their customers, in an unfeeling manner. All too often the machinery of government will respond slowly and inefficiently with poor coordination between agencies, because they have learned not to trust one another, not to rely on subtlety, not to develop intimacy.

Social organizations are incompatible with formality, distance, and contractualism. They proceed smoothly only with intimacy, subtlety, and trust. But these conditions can develop only over a long period of cultural homogenization during which the people of a nation become accustomed to one another and come to espouse a common body of values and beliefs. In a nation as young and as heterogeneous as ours, that level of cultural agreement is yet some distance away. The United States is not Japan. We are not a homogeneous body of people. Our institutions cannot operate in a wholly synchronized manner. On the other hand, we cannot allow our institutions to become so thoroughly unfeeling and unthinking that they make work and social intercourse unbearable for all of us most of the time. We must find those organizational innovations which can permit a balance between freedom and integration, which go beyond our current interpretation of individualism.

NOTES

1. See Harold J. Leavitt, *Managerial Psychology*, 4th ed. (Chicago: University of Chicago, 1978).

2. See Edgar Schein, *Process Consultation* (Reading, Mass.: Addison-Wesley, 1969).

3. See Rosabeth Moss Kanter, *Commitment and Community* (Cambridge: Harvard University Press, 1972).

4. Here and elsewhere . . . I refer to industrial clans. The meaning of *clan* I derive from the use by the sociologist Emile Durkheim. In this usage, a disorganized aggregation of individuals is a *horde*, the smallest organized unit is a *band*, and a clan is a group of bands. A clan is an intimate association of individuals who are connected to each other through a variety of ties. The members of a clan may or may not share blood relations. Here I refer to an intimate group of industrial workers who know one another well but who typically do not share blood relations.

5. See Ivan H. Light, *Ethnic Enterprise in America* (Berkeley: University of California Press, 1972).

6. See Marcel Mauss, *The Gift* (New York: W. W. Norton, 1967).

7. I have developed this work in collaboration with Jerry B. Johnson. For a complete description of the initial study, see W. G. Ouchi and Jerry B. Johnson, "Types of Organizational Control and Their Relationship to Emotional Well-Being," *Administrative Science Quarterly*, Vol. 23 (June 1978). We were assisted in this work by Alan Wilkins, David Gibson, Alice Kaplan, and Raymond Price, to whom I am grateful.

40

In Search of Excellence: Simultaneous Loose-Tight Properties

Thomas J. Peters & Robert H. Waterman Jr.

Simultaneous loose-tight properties, . . . is in essence the co-existence of firm central direction and maximum individual autonomy—what we have called "having one's cake and eating it too." Organizations that live by the loose-tight principle are on the one hand rigidly controlled, yet at the same time allow (indeed, insist on) autonomy, entrepreneurship, and innovation from the rank and file. They do this literally through "faith"—through value systems, which . . . most managers avoid like the plague. They do it also through painstaking attention to detail, to getting the "itty-bitty, teeny-tiny things" right, as Alabama's inimitable football coach, Bear Bryant, stresses.

Loose-tight? Most businessmen's eyes glaze over when the talk turns to value systems, culture, and the like. Yet ours light up: we recall ex-chairman Bill Blackie of Caterpillar talking about Cat's commitment to "Forty-eight-hour parts service anywhere in the world." We are drawn back to a minus 60° chill factor day in Minneapolis–St. Paul, where 3M's Tait Elder talked to us about the "irrational champions" running around 3M. And we see Rene McPherson speaking to a class at Stanford. He is animated. The class asks him for the magic prescriptions with which he mastered productivity problems at Dana. He sticks his hands out in front of him, palms upright, and says, "You just keep pushing. You just keep pushing. I made every mistake that could be made. But I just kept pushing." You suspect he is serious: that really *is* all there was to it.

You think of Tom Watson, Sr., coming in after a hard day of selling pianos to farmers, and reporting to his headquarters in Painted Post, New York. And you think of what he became and why. You picture J. Willard Marriott, Sr., at that first food stand in Washington, D.C. And you see him now, at eighty-two, still worrying about a single lobby's cleanliness, although his food stand is a $2 billion enterprise. You picture Eddie Carlson working as a page boy at a Western International Hotel, the Benjamin Franklin in 1929, and marvel at the legend he has become.

Carlson doesn't blush when he talks about values. Neither did Watson—he said that values are really all there is. They lived by their values, these men—Marriott, Ray Kroc, Bill Hewlett and Dave Packard, Levi Strauss, James Cash Penney, Robert Wood Johnson. And they meticulously applied them within their organizations. They *believed* in the customer. They *believed* in granting autonomy; room to perform. They *believed* in open doors, in quality. But they were stern disciplinarians, every one. They gave plenty of rope, but they accepted the chance that some of their minions would hang themselves. Loose-tight is about rope. Yet in the last analysis, it's really about culture. Now, culture is the "softest" stuff around. Who trusts its leading analysts—anthropologists and sociologists—after all? Businessmen surely don't. Yet culture is the hardest stuff around, as well. Violate the lofty phrase, "IBM Means Service," and you

Source: Thomas J. Peters and Robert H. Waterman Jr., "Simultaneous Loose-Tight Properties," from *In Search of Excellence: Lessons from America's Best-Run Companies* (New York: Harper & Row, 1982), pp. 318–25. © 1982 by Thomas J. Peters and Robert H. Waterman Jr. Reprinted by permission of HarperCollins Publishers, Inc.

are out of a job, the company's job security program to the contrary notwithstanding. Digital is crazy (soft). Digital is anarchic (soft). "People at Digital don't know who they work for," says a colleague. But they do know quality: the products they turn out work (hard). So "Soft is hard."

Patrick Haggerty says the only reason that OST (hard) works at Texas Instruments is because of TI's "innovative culture" (soft). Lew Lehr, 3M's chairman, goes around telling tales of people who have failed monumentally—but gone on, after decades of trying, to become vice presidents of the company. He's describing the loose-tight, soft-hard properties of the 3M culture.

We have talked about lots of soft traits, lots of loose traits. We have mentioned clubby, campus-like environments, flexible organizational structures (hiving off new divisions, temporary habit-breaking devices, regular reorganizations), volunteers, zealous champions, maximized autonomy for individuals, teams and divisions, regular and extensive experimentation, feedback emphasizing the positive, and strong social networks. All of these traits focus on the positive, the excitement of trying things out in a slightly disorderly (loose) fashion.

But at the same time, a remarkably tight—culturally driven/controlled set of properties marks the excellent companies. Most have rigidly shared values. The action focus, including experimentation itself, emphasizes extremely regular communication and very quick feedback; nothing gets very far out of line. Concise paperwork and the focus on realism are yet other, nonaversive ways of exerting extremely tight control. If you have only three numbers to live by, you may be sure they are all well checked out. A predominant discipline or two is in itself another crucial measure of tightness. The fact that the vast majority of the management group at 3M consists of chemical engineers, at Fluor of mechanical engineers, is another vital assurance of realism, a form of tight control.

Intriguingly, the focus on the outside, the external perspective, the attention to the customer, is one of the tightest properties of all. In the excellent companies, it is perhaps the most stringent means of self-discipline. If one is really paying attention to what the customer is saying, being blown in the wind by the customer's demands, one may be sure he is sailing a tight ship. And then there is the peer pressure: weekly Rallies at Tupperware, Dana's twice-annual Hell Weeks. Although this is not control via massive forms and incalculable numbers of variables, it is the toughest control of all. As McPherson said, it's easy to fool the boss, but you can't fool your peers. These are the apparent contradictions that turn out in practice not to be contradictions at all.

Take the quality versus cost trade-off, for example, or small versus big (i.e., effectiveness versus efficiency). They turn out in the excellent companies not to be trade-offs at all. There is a story about a GM foundry manager who led a remarkable economic turnaround; he painted the grimy interior of his foundry white, insisting that he would pay attention to quality (and housekeeping, safety), and that cost would follow. As he pointed out: "To begin with, if you are making it with good quality, you don't have to make everything twice." There is nothing like quality. It is the most important word used in these companies. Quality leads to a focus on innovativeness—to doing the best one can for every customer on every product; hence it is a goad to productivity, automatic excitement, an external focus. The drive to make "the best" affects virtually every function of the organization.

In the same way, the efficiency/effectiveness contradiction dissolves into thin air. Things of quality are produced by craftsmen, generally requiring small-scale enterprise, we are told. Activities that achieve cost efficiencies, on the other hand, are reputedly best done in large facilities, to achieve economies of scale. Except that that is not the way it works in the excellent companies. In the excellent companies, small *in almost every case* is beautiful. The small facility turns out to be the most efficient; its turned-on, motivated, highly productive worker, in communication (and competition) with his peers, outproduces the worker in the big facilities time and again. It holds for plants, for project teams, for divisions—for the entire company. So we find that in this most vital area, there really is no conflict. Small, quality, excitement, autonomy—and efficiency—are all words that belong on the same side of the coin. Cost and efficiency, over the long run, *follow* from the emphasis on quality, service, innovativeness, result sharing, participation, excitement, and an external problem-solving focus that is tailored to the customer. The revenue line does come first. But once the ball gets rolling, cost control and innovation effectiveness become fully achievable, parallel goals.

Surprisingly, the execution versus autonomy contradiction becomes a paradox, too. Indeed, one can appreciate this paradox almost anywhere. Studies in the classroom, for example, suggest that effective classes are the ones in which discipline is sure: students are expected to come to class on time; homework is regularly turned in and graded. On the other hand, those same classrooms as a general rule emphasize positive feedback, posting good reports, praise, and coaching by the teacher. Similarly, when we look at McDonald's or virtually any of the excellent companies, we find that *autonomy is a product of discipline. The discipline (a few shared values) provides the framework. It gives people confidence (to experiment, for instance) stemming from stable expectations about what really counts.*

Thus a set of shared values and rules about discipline, details, and execution can provide the framework in which practical autonomy takes place routinely. Regular experimentation takes place at 3M in a large measure because of all the tight things that surround it—extraordinarily regular communication (nothing gets far out of line), the shared values that result from the common denominator of the engineering degree, the consensus on customer problem solving that comes from a top management

virtually all of whom started as down-the-line salesmen.

3M is, indeed, the tightest organization we have seen, tighter by far, in our opinion, than ITT under Geneen. At ITT, there were countless rules and variables to be measured and filed. But the dominant theme there was gamesmanship—beating the system, pulling end runs, joining together with other line officers to avoid the infamous staff "flying squads." Too much overbearing discipline of the wrong kind will kill autonomy. But the more rigid discipline, the discipline based on a small number of shared values that marks a 3M, an HP, a J&J, or a McDonald's, in fact, induces practical autonomy and experimentation throughout the organization and beyond.

The nature of the rules is crucial here. The "rules" in the excellent companies have a positive cast. They deal with quality, service, innovation, and experimentation. Their focus is on building, expanding, the opposite of restraining; whereas most companies concentrate on controlling, limiting, constraint. We don't seem to understand that rules can reinforce positive traits as well as discourage negative ones, and that the former kind are far more effective.

Even the external versus internal contradiction is resolved in the excellent companies. Quite simply, these companies are simultaneously externally focused and internally focused—externally in that they are truly driven by their desire to provide service, quality, and innovative problem solving in support of their customers; internally in that quality control, for example, is put on the back of the individual line worker, not primarily in the lap of the quality control department. Service standards likewise are substantially self-monitored. The organization thrives on internal competition. And it thrives on intense communication, on the family feeling, on open door policies, on informality, on fluidity and flexibility, on nonpolitical shifts of resources. This constitutes the crucial internal focus: the focus on people.

The skill with which the excellent companies develop their people recalls that grim conflict . . . our basic need for security versus the need to stick out, the "essential tension" that the psychoanalyst Ernest Becker described. Once again the paradox, as it is dealt with in the excellent companies, holds. By offering meaning as well as money, they give their employees a mission as well as a sense of feeling great. Every man becomes a pioneer, an experimenter, a leader. The institution provides guiding belief and creates a sense of excitement, a sense of being a part of the best, a sense of producing something of quality that is generally valued. And in this way it draws out the best— from Ken Ohmae's "worker at the frontier" as from Kyoto Ceramic chairman Kazuo Inamori's "fifty percent man." The *average* worker in these companies is expected to contribute, to add ideas, to innovate in service to the customer and in producing quality products. In short, each individual— like the 9,000 leaders of PIP teams at Texas Instruments—is expected to stand out and contribute, to be distinctive. At the same time he is part of something great: Caterpillar, IBM, 3M, Disney Productions.

Finally, the last of our paradoxes involves the short-term versus long-term "trade-off." Again, we found there was no conflict at all. We found that the excellent companies are not really "long-term thinkers." They don't have better five-year plans. Indeed, the formal plans at the excellent companies are often marked by little detail, or don't exist at all (recall the complete absence of corporate level planners in many of them).

But there is a value set—and it is a value set for all seasons. (Remember the content areas: quality, innovativeness, informality, customer service, people.) However, it is executed by attention to mundane, nitty-gritty details. Every minute, every hour, every day is an opportunity to act in support of overarching themes.

We will conclude with one strange contradiction that may really hold. We call it the smart-dumb rule. Many of today's managers—MBA-trained and the like—may be a little bit too smart for their own good. The smart ones are the ones who shift direction all the time, based upon the latest output from the expected value equation. The ones who juggle hundred-variable models with facility; the ones who design complicated incentive systems; the ones who wire up matrix structures. The ones who have 200-page strategic plans and 500-page market requirement documents that are but step one in product development exercises.

Our "dumber" friends are different. They just don't understand why every product can't be of the highest quality. They just don't understand why every customer can't get personalized service, even in the potato chip business. They are personally affronted . . . when a bottle of beer goes sour. They can't understand why a regular flow of new products isn't possible, or why a worker can't contribute a suggestion every couple of weeks. Simple-minded fellows, really; simplistic even. Yes, simplistic has a negative connotation. But the people who lead the excellent companies *are* a bit simplistic. They are seemingly unjustified in what they believe the worker is capable of doing. They are seemingly unjustified in believing that every product can be of the highest quality. They are seemingly unjustified in believing that service can be maintained at a high standard for virtually every customer, whether in Missoula, Montana, or Manhattan. They are seemingly unjustified in believing that virtually every worker can contribute suggestions regularly. It is simplistic. But it may be the true key to inducing astonishing contributions from tens of thousands of people.

Of course, what one is simplistic about is vitally important. It's a focus on the external, on service, on quality, on people, on informality, those value content words we noted. And those may very well be things— the only things—worth being simplistic about. Remember the executive James Brian Quinn interviewed: he said that it was important for his people to want to be "the best" at something. He doesn't really care very much what.

But so many can't see it. There are always practical, justifiable, inevitable, sensible, and sane reasons to compromise on any of these variables. Only those simplistic people—like Watson, Hewlett, Packard, Kroc, Mars, Olsen, McPherson, Marriott, Procter, Gamble, Johnson—stayed simplistic. And their companies have remained remarkably successful.

41

The Fifth Discipline: A Shift of Mind

Peter M. Senge

SEEING THE WORLD ANEW

There is something in all of us that loves to put together a puzzle, that loves to see the image of the whole emerge. The beauty of a person, or a flower, or a poem lies in seeing all of it. It is interesting that the words "whole" and "health" come from the same root (the Old English *hal*, as in "hale and hearty"). So it should come as no surprise that the unhealthiness of our world today is in direct proportion to our inability to see it as a whole.

Systems thinking is a discipline for seeing wholes. It is a framework for seeing interrelationships rather than things, for seeing patterns of change rather than static "snapshots." It is a set of general principles— distilled over the course of the twentieth century, spanning fields as diverse as the physical and social sciences, engineering, and management. It is also a set of specific tools and techniques, originating in two threads: in "feedback" concepts of cybernetics and in "servo-mechanism" engineering theory dating back to the nineteenth century. During the last thirty years, these tools have been applied to understand a wide range of corporate, urban, regional, economic, political, ecological, and even physiological systems.[1] And systems thinking is a sensibility—for the subtle interconnectedness that gives living systems their unique character.

Today, systems thinking is needed more than ever because we are becoming overwhelmed by complexity. Perhaps for the first time in history, humankind has the capacity to create far more information than anyone can absorb, to foster far greater interdependency than anyone can manage, and to accelerate change far faster than anyone's ability to keep pace. Certainly the scale of complexity is without precedent. All around us are examples of "systemic breakdowns"—problems such as global warming, ozone depletion, the international drug trade, and the U.S. trade and budget deficits—problems that have no simple local cause. Similarly, organizations break down, despite individual brilliance and innovative products, because they are unable to pull their diverse functions and talents into a productive whole.

Complexity can easily undermine confidence and responsibility—as in the frequent refrain, "It's all too complex for me," or "There's nothing I can do. It's the system." Systems thinking is the antidote to this sense of helplessness that many feel as we enter the "age of interdependence." Systems thinking is a discipline for seeing the "structures" that underlie complex situations, and for discerning high from low leverage change. That is, by seeing wholes we learn how to foster health. To do so, systems thinking offers a language that begins by restructuring how we think.

I call systems thinking the fifth discipline because it is the conceptual cornerstone that underlies all of the five learning disciplines. . . . All are concerned with a shift of mind from seeing parts to seeing wholes, from seeing people as helpless reactors to seeing them as active participants in shaping their reality, from reacting to the present to creating the future. Without systems thinking, there is neither the incentive nor the means to integrate the learning disciplines once they have come into practice. As the fifth discipline, systems thinking is the cornerstone of how learning organizations think about their world. . . .

Sophisticated tools of forecasting and business analysis, as well as elegant strategic plans, usually fail to produce dramatic breakthroughs in managing a business. They are all designed to handle the sort of complexity in which there are many variables: *detail complexity. But there are two types of complexity.* The second type is *dynamic complexity,* situations where cause and effect are subtle, and where the effects over time of interventions are not obvious. Conventional forecasting, planning, and analysis methods are not equipped to deal with dynamic complexity. Mixing many ingredients in a stew involves detail complexity, as does following a complex set of instructions to assemble a machine, or taking inventory in a discount retail store. But none of these situations is especially complex dynamically.

When the same action has dramatically different effects in the short run and the long, there is dynamic complexity. When an action has one set of consequences locally and a very different set of consequences in another part of the system, there is dynamic complexity. When obvious interventions produce nonobvious consequences, there is dynamic complexity. A gyroscope is a dynamically complex machine: If you push downward on one edge, it moves to the left; if you push another edge to the left, it moves upward. Yet, how trivially simple is a gyroscope when compared with the complex dynamics of an enterprise, where it takes days to produce something, weeks to develop a new marketing promotion, months to hire and train new people, and years to develop new products, nurture management talent, and build a reputation for quality—and all of these processes interact continually.

The real leverage in most management situations lies in understanding dynamic complexity, not detail complexity. Balancing market growth and capacity expansion is a dynamic

problem. Developing a profitable mix of price, product (or service) quality, design, and availability that makes a strong market position is a dynamic problem. Improving quality, lowering total costs, and satisfying customers in a sustainable manner is a dynamic problem.

Unfortunately, most "systems analyses" focus on detail complexity not dynamic complexity. Simulations with thousands of variables and complex arrays of details can actually distract us from seeing patterns and major interrelationships. In fact, sadly, for most people "systems thinking" means "fighting complexity with complexity," devising increasingly "complex" (we should really say "detailed") solutions to increasingly "complex" problems. In fact, this is the antithesis of real systems thinking. . . .

The essence of the discipline of systems thinking lies in a shift of mind:

- seeing interrelationships rather than linear cause-effect chains, and
- seeing processes of change rather than snapshots

The practice of systems thinking starts with understanding a simple concept called "feedback" that shows how actions can reinforce or counteract (balance) each other. *It builds to learning to recognize types of "structures" that recur again and again:* the arms race is a generic or archetypal pattern of escalation, at its heart no different from turf warfare between two street gangs, the demise of a marriage, or the advertising battles of two consumer goods companies fighting for market share. Eventually, systems thinking forms a rich language for describing a vast array of interrelationships and patterns of change. Ultimately, *it simplifies life* by helping us see the deeper patterns lying behind the events and the details. . . .

SEEING CIRCLES OF CAUSALITY[2]

Reality is made up of circles but we see straight lines. Herein lie the beginnings of our limitation as systems thinkers.

One of the reasons for this fragmentation in our thinking stems from our language. Language shapes perception. What we *see* depends on what we are prepared to see. Western languages, with their subject-verb-object structure, are biased toward a linear view.[3] If we want to see systemwide interrelationships, we need a language of interrelationships, a language made up of circles. Without such a language, our habitual ways of seeing the world produce fragmented views and counterproductive actions—as it has done for decision makers in the arms race. Such a language is important in facing dynamically complex issues and strategic choices, especially when individuals, teams, and organizations need to see beyond events and into the forces that shape change.

To illustrate the rudiments of the new language, consider a very simple system—filling a glass of water. You might think, "That's not a system—it's too simple." But think again.

From the linear viewpoint, we say, "I am filling a glass of water." . . .

But, in fact, as we fill the glass, we are watching the water level rise. We monitor the "gap" between the level and our goal, the "desired water level." As the water approaches the desired level, we adjust the faucet position to slow the flow of water, until it is turned off when the glass is full. In fact, when we fill a glass of water we operate in a "water-regulation" system involving five variables: our desired water level, the glass's current water level, the gap between the two, the faucet position, and the water flow. These variables are organized in a circle or loop of cause-effect relationships which is called a "feedback process." The process operates continuously to bring the water level to its desired level.

People get confused about "feedback" because we often use the word in a somewhat different way—to gather opinions about an act we have undertaken. "Give me some feedback on the brewery decision," you might say. "What did you think of the way I handled it?" In that context, "positive feedback" means encouraging remarks and "negative feedback" means bad news. But in systems thinking, feedback is a broader concept. It means any reciprocal flow of influence. In systems thinking it is an axiom that every influence is both *cause* and *effect*. Nothing is ever influenced in just one direction. . . .

Though simple in concept, the feedback loop overturns deeply ingrained ideas—such as causality. In everyday English we say, "I am filling the glass of water" without thinking very deeply about the real meaning of the statement. It implies a one-way causality—"I am causing the water level to rise." More precisely, "My hand on the faucet is controlling the rate of flow of water into the glass." Clearly, this statement describes only half of the feedback process: the linkages from "faucet position" to "flow of water" to "water level."

But it would be just as true to describe only the other "half" of the process: "The level of water in the glass is controlling my hand."

Both statements are equally incomplete. The more complete statement of causality is that my intent to fill a glass of water creates a system that causes water to flow in when the level is low, then shuts the flow off when the glass is full. In other words, the structure causes the behavior. This distinction is important because seeing only individual actions and missing the structure underlying the actions . . . lies at the root of our powerlessness in complex situations.

In fact, all causal attributions made in everyday English are highly suspect! Most are embedded in linear ways of seeing. They are at best partially accurate, inherently biased toward describing portions of reciprocal processes, not the entire processes.

Another idea overturned by the feedback perspective is anthropocentrism—or seeing ourselves as the center of activities. The simple description, "I am filling the glass of water," suggests a world of human actors standing at the center of activity, operating on an inanimate reality. *From the systems perspective, the human actor is part of the feedback process, not standing apart from it. This represents a profound shift in awareness.* It allows us to see how we are continually both influenced by and influencing our reality. It is the shift in awareness so ardently advocated by ecologists in their cries that we see ourselves as part of nature, not separate from nature. It is the shift in awareness recognized by many (but not all) of the world's great philosophical systems—for example, the *Bhagavad Gita's* chastisement:

> All actions are wrought by the qualities of nature only. The self, deluded by egoism, thinketh: "I am the doer."[4]

In addition, the feedback concept complicates the ethical issue of responsibility. In the arms race, who is responsible? From each side's linear view, responsibility clearly lies with the other side: "It is their aggressive actions, and their nationalistic intent, that are causing us to respond by building our arms." A linear view always suggests a simple locus of responsibility. When things go wrong, this is seen as blame—"he, she, it did it"—or guilt—"I did it." At a deep level, there is no difference between blame and guilt, for both spring from linear perceptions. From the linear view, we are always looking for someone or something that must be responsible—they can even be directed toward hidden agents within ourselves. When my son was four years old, he used to say, "My stomach won't let me eat it," when turning down his vegetables. We may chuckle, but is his assignment of responsibility really different from the adult who says, "My neuroses keep me from trusting people."

In mastering systems thinking, we give up the assumption that there must be an individual, or individual agent, responsible. The feedback perspective suggests that *everyone shares responsibility for problems generated by a system.* That doesn't necessarily imply that everyone involved can exert equal leverage in changing the system. But it does imply that the search for scapegoats—a particularly alluring pastime in individualistic cultures such as ours in the United States—is a blind alley.

Finally, the feedback concept illuminates the limitations of our language. When we try to describe in words even a very simple system, such as filling the water glass, it gets very awkward: "When I fill a glass of water, there is a feedback process that causes me to adjust the faucet position, which adjusts the water flow and feeds back to alter the water position. The goal of the process is to make the water level rise to my desired level." This is precisely why a new language for describing systems is needed. If it is this awkward to describe a system as simple as filling a water glass, *imagine our difficulties using everyday English to describe the multiple feedback processes in an organization.*

All this takes some getting used to. We are steeped in a linear language for describing our experience. We find simple statements about causality and responsibility familiar and comfortable. It is not that they must be given up, anymore than you give up English to learn French. There are many situations where simple linear descriptions suffice and looking for feedback processes would be a waste of time. But not when dealing with problems of dynamic complexity.

REINFORCING AND BALANCING FEEDBACK AND DELAYS: THE BUILDING BLOCKS OF SYSTEMS THINKING

There are two distinct types of feedback processes: reinforcing and balancing. *Reinforcing* (or amplifying) feedback processes are the engines of growth. Whenever you are in a situation where things are growing, you can be sure that reinforcing feedback is at work. Reinforcing feedback can also generate accelerating decline—a pattern of decline where small drops amplify themselves into larger and larger drops, such as the decline in bank assets when there is a financial panic.

Balancing (or stabilizing) feedback operates whenever there is a goal-oriented behavior. If the goal is to be not moving, then balancing feedback will act the way the brakes in a car do. If the goal is to be moving at sixty miles per hour, then balancing feedback will cause you to accelerate to sixty but no faster. The "goal" can be an explicit target, as when a firm seeks a desired market share, or it can be implicit, such as a bad habit, which despite disavowing, we stick to nevertheless.

In addition, many feedback processes contain "*delays,*" interruptions in the flow of influence which make the consequences of actions occur gradually.

All ideas in the language of systems thinking are built up from these elements, just as English sentences are built up from nouns and verbs. Once we have learned the building blocks, we can begin constructing stories: the systems archetypes . . .

REINFORCING FEEDBACK: DISCOVERING HOW SMALL CHANGES CAN GROW

If you are in a reinforcing feedback system, you may be blind to how small actions can grow into large consequences—for better or for worse. Seeing the system often allows you to influence how it works.

For example, managers frequently fail to appreciate the extent to which their own expectations influence subordinates' performance. If I see a person as having high potential, I give him special attention to develop that potential. When he flowers, I feel that my original assessment was correct and I help him still further. Conversely, those I regard as having lower potential languish in disregard and inattention, perform in a disinterested manner, and further justify, in my mind, the lack of attention I give them.

Psychologist Robert Merton first identified this phenomenon as the "self-fulfilling prophecy."[5] It is also known as the "Pygmalion effect," after the famous George Bernard Shaw play (later to become *My Fair Lady*). Shaw in turn had taken his title from Pygmalion, a character in Greek and Roman mythology, who believed so strongly in the beauty of the statue he had carved that it came to life. . . .

In *reinforcing processes* such as the Pygmalion effect, a small change builds on itself. Whatever movement occurs is amplified, producing more movement in the same direction. A small action snowballs, with more and more and still more of the same, resembling compounding interest. Some reinforcing (amplifying) processes are "vicious cycles," in which things start off badly and grow worse. The "gas crisis" was a classic example. Word that gasoline was becoming scarce set off a spate of trips to the local service station, to fill up. Once people started seeing lines of cars, they were convinced that the crisis was here. Panic and hoarding then set in. Before long, everyone was "topping off" their tanks when they were only one-quarter empty, lest they be caught when the pumps went dry. A run on a bank is another example, as are escalation structures such as the arms race or price wars.

But there's nothing inherently bad about reinforcing loops. There are also "virtuous cycles"—processes that reinforce in desired directions. For instance, physical exercise can lead to a reinforcing spiral; you feel better, thus you exercise more, thus you're rewarded by feeling better and exercise still more. The arms race run in reverse, if it can be sustained, makes another virtuous circle. The growth of any new product involves reinforcing spirals. For example, many products grow from "word of mouth." Word of mouth about a product can reinforce a snowballing sense of good feeling (as occurred with the Volkswagen Beetle and more recent Japanese imports) as satisfied customers tell others who then become satisfied customers, who tell still others. . . .

The behavior that results from a reinforcing loop is either accelerating growth or accelerating decline. . . .

Positive word of mouth produced rapidly rising sales of Volkswagens during the 1950s, and videocassette recorders during the 1980s. A bank run produces an accelerating decline in a bank's deposits.

Folk wisdom speaks of reinforcing loops in terms such as "snowball effect," "bandwagon effect," or "vicious circle," and in phrases describing particular systems: "the rich get richer and the poor get poorer." In business, we know that "momentum is everything," in building confidence in a new product or within a fledgling organization. We also know about reinforcing spirals running the wrong way. "The rats are jumping ship" suggests a situation where, as soon as a few people lose confidence, their defection will cause others to defect in a vicious spiral of eroding confidence. Word of mouth can easily work in reverse, and (as occurred with contaminated over-the-counter drugs) produce marketplace disaster.

Both good news and bad news reinforcing loops accelerate so quickly that they often take people by surprise. A French schoolchildren's jingle illustrates the process. First there is just one lily pad in a corner of a pond. But every day the number of lily pads doubles. It takes thirty days to fill the pond, but for the first twenty-eight days, no one even notices. Suddenly, on the twenty-ninth day, the pond is half full of lily pads and the villagers become concerned. But by this time there is little that can be done. The next day their worst fears come true. That's why environmental dangers are so worrisome, especially those that follow reinforcing patterns (as many environmentalists fear occurs with such pollutants as CFCs). By the time the problem is noticed, it may be too late. Extinctions of species often follow patterns of slow, gradually accelerating decline over long time periods, then rapid demise. So do extinctions of corporations.

But pure accelerating growth or decline rarely continues unchecked in nature, because reinforcing processes rarely occur in isolation. Eventually, limits are encountered—which can slow growth, stop it, divert it, or even reverse it. Even the lily pads stop growing when the limit of the pond's perimeter is encountered. These limits are one form of *balancing feedback,* which, after reinforcing processes, is the second basic element of systems thinking.

BALANCING PROCESSES: DISCOVERING THE SOURCES OF STABILITY AND RESISTANCE

If you are in a balancing system, you are in a system that is seeking stability. If the system's goal is one you like, you will be happy. If it is not, you will find all your efforts to change matters frustrated—until you can either change the goal or weaken its influence.

Nature loves a balance—but many times, human decision makers act contrary to these balances, and pay the price. For example, managers under budget pressure often cut back staff to lower costs, but eventually discover that their remaining staff is now overworked, and their costs have not gone down at all—because the remaining work has been farmed out to consultants, or because overtime has made up the difference. The reason that costs don't stay down is that *the system has its own agenda.* There is an implicit goal, unspoken but very real—the amount of work that is expected to get done.

In a balancing (stabilizing) system, there is a self-correction that attempts to maintain some goal or target. Filling the glass of water is a balancing process with the goal of a full glass. Hiring new employees is a balancing process with the goal of having a target work force size or rate of growth. Steering a car and staying upright on a bicycle are also examples of balancing processes, where the goal is heading in a desired direction.

Balancing feedback processes are everywhere. They underlie all goal-oriented behavior. Complex organisms such as the human body contain thousands of balancing feedback processes that maintain temperature and balance, heal our wounds, adjust our eyesight to the amount of light, and alert us to threat. A biologist would say that all of these processes are the mechanisms by which our body achieves *homeostasis*—its ability to maintain conditions for survival in a changing environment. Balancing feedback prompts us to eat when we need food, and to sleep when we need rest, or . . . to put on a sweater when we are cold.

As in all balancing processes, the crucial element—our body temperature—gradually adjusts itself toward its desired level.

Organizations and societies resemble complex organisms because they too have myriad balancing feedback processes. In corporations, the production and materials ordering process is constantly adjusting in response to changes in incoming orders; short-term (discounts) and long-term (list) prices adjust in response to changes in demand or competitors' prices; and borrowing adjusts with changes in cash balances or financing needs.

Planning creates longer-term balancing processes. A human resource plan might establish long-term growth targets in head count and in skill profile of the work force to match anticipated needs. Market research and R&D plans shape new product development and investments in people, technologies, and capital plant to build competitive advantage.

What makes balancing processes so difficult in management is that the goals are often implicit, and no one recognizes that the balancing process exists at all. I recall a good friend who tried, fruitlessly, to reduce burnout among professionals in his rapidly growing training business. He wrote memos, shortened working hours, even closed and locked offices earlier—all attempts to get people to stop overworking. But all these actions were offset—people ignored the memos, disobeyed the shortened hours, and took their work home with them when the offices were locked. Why? Because an unwritten norm in the organization stated that the *real* heros, the people who really cared and who got ahead in the organization, worked seventy hours a week—a norm that my friend had established himself by his own prodigious energy and long hours.

To understand how an organism works we must understand its balancing processes—those that are explicit *and* implicit. We could master long lists of body parts, organs, bones, veins, and blood vessels and yet we would not understand how the body functions—until we understand how the neuromuscular system maintains balance, or how the cardiovascular system maintains blood pressure and oxygen levels. This is why many attempts to redesign social systems fail. The state-controlled economy fails because it severs the multiple self-correcting processes that operate in a free market system.[6] This is why corporate mergers often fail. . . .

Though simple in concept, balancing processes can generate surprising and problematic behavior if they go undetected.

In general, balancing loops are more difficult to see than reinforcing loops because it often *looks* like nothing is happening. There's no dramatic growth of sales and marketing expenditures, or nuclear arms, or lily pads. Instead, the balancing process maintains the status quo, even when all participants want change. The feeling, as Lewis Carroll's Queen of Hearts put it, of needing "all the running you can do to keep in the same place," is a clue that a balancing loop may exist nearby.

Leaders who attempt organizational change often find themselves unwittingly caught in balancing processes. To the leaders, it looks as though their efforts are clashing with sudden resistance that seems to come from nowhere. In fact, as my friend found when he tried to reduce burnout, the resistance is a response by the system, trying to maintain an implicit system goal. Until this goal is recognized, the change effort is doomed to failure. So long as the leader continues to be the "model," his work habits will set the norm. Either he must change his habits, or establish new and different models.

Whenever there is "resistance to change," you can count on there being one or more "hidden" balancing processes. Resistance to change is neither capricious nor mysterious. It almost always arises from threats to traditional norms and ways of doing things. Often these norms are woven into the fabric of established power relationships. The norm is entrenched because the distribution of authority and control is entrenched. Rather than pushing harder to overcome resistance to change, artful leaders discern the source of the resistance. They focus directly on the implicit norms and power relationships within which the norms are embedded.

DELAYS: WHEN THINGS HAPPEN . . . EVENTUALLY

As we've seen, systems seem to have minds of their own. Nowhere is this more evident than in delays—interruptions between your actions and their consequences. Delays can make you badly overshoot your mark, or they can have a positive effect if you recognize them and work with them. . . .

Delays, when the effect of one variable on another takes time, constitute the third basic building block for a systems language. Virtually all feedback processes have some form of delay. But often the delays are either unrecognized or not well understood. This can result in "overshoot," going further than needed to achieve a desired result. The delay between eating and feeling full has been the nemesis of many a happy diner; we don't yet feel full when we should stop eating, so we keep going until we are overstuffed. The delay between starting a new construction project and its completion results in overbuilding real estate markets and an eventual shakeout. . . .

Unrecognized delays can also lead to instability and breakdown, especially when they are long. Adjusting the shower temperature, for instance, is far more difficult when there is a ten-second delay before the water temperature adjusts, then when the delay takes only a second or two.

During that ten seconds after you turn up the heat, the water remains cold. You receive no response to your action; so you *perceive* that your act has had no effect. You respond by continuing to turn up the heat. When the hot water finally arrives, a 190-degree water gusher erupts from the faucet. You jump out and turn it back; and, after another delay, it's frigid again. On and on you go, through the balancing loop process.

Each cycle of adjustments compensates somewhat for the cycle before. . . .

The more aggressive you are in your behavior—the more drastically you turn the knobs—the longer it will take to reach the right temperature. That's one of the lessons of balancing loops with delays: that aggressive action often produces exactly the opposite of what is intended. It produces instability and oscillation, instead of moving you more quickly toward your goal.

Delays are no less problematic in reinforcing loops. In the arms race example, each side perceives itself as gaining advantage from expanding its arsenal because of the delay in the other side's response. This delay can be as long as five years because of the time required to gather intelligence on the other side's weaponry, and to design and deploy new weapons. It is this temporary perceived advantage that keeps the escalation process going. If each side were able to respond instantly to buildups of its adversary, incentives to keep building would be nil.

The systems viewpoint is generally oriented toward the long-term view. That's why delays and feedback loops are so important. In the short term, you can often ignore them; they're inconsequential. They only come back to haunt you in the long term.

Reinforcing feedback, balancing feedback, and delays are all fairly simple. They come into their own as building blocks for the "systems archetypes"—more elaborate structures that recur in our personal and work lives again and again.

NOTES

1. A comprehensive summary of the "cybernetic" and "servo-mechanism" schools of thought in the social sciences can be found in George Richardson, *Feedback Thought in Social Science and Systems Theory* (Philadelphia: University of Pennsylvania Press), 1990.

2. The principles and tools of systems thinking have emerged from diverse roots

in physics, engineering, biology, and mathematics. The particular tools presented in this chapter come from the "system dynamics" approach pioneered by Jay Forrester at MIT. See, for example, *Industrial Dynamics* (Cambridge, Mass.: MIT Press), 1961; *Urban Dynamics* (Cambridge, Mass.: MIT Press), 1969; and "The Counterintuitive Behavior of Social Systems," *Technology Review* (January 1971), 52–68. This particular section owes a special debt to Donella Meadows, whose earlier article "Whole Earth Models and Systems," *Co-Evolution Quarterly* (Summer 1982), 98–108 provided the model and the inspiration for its development.

3. By contrast, many "Eastern" languages such as Chinese and Japanese do not build up from subject-verb-object linear sequences.

David Crystal, *The Cambridge Encyclopedia of Language* (New York: Cambridge University Press), 1987.

4. The *Bhagavad-Gita*, or "The Lord's Song," translated by Annie Besant, reprinted in Robert O. Ballou, *The Bible of the World* (New York: Viking), 1939.

5. Robert K. Merton, "The Self-Fulfilling Prophecy," in Robert K. Merton, editor, *Social Theory and Social Structure* (New York: Free Press), 1968.

6. This does not suggest that free-market forces are sufficient for all forms of balance and control needed in modern societies — delays, inadequate information, unrealistic expectations, and distortions such as monopoly power also reduce efficiency of "free markets."

42

Gendering Organizational Theory

Joan Acker

Although early critical analyses of organizational theory (e.g., Acker and Van Houten 1974; Kanter 1977a) led to few immediate further efforts, feminist examination of organizational theory has developed rapidly in the last few years (Ferguson 1984; Calás and Smircich 1989a, 1989b; Hearn and Parkin 1983, 1987; Burrell 1984, 1987; Mills 1988b; Hearn et al. 1989; Acker 1990; Martin 1990a, 1990b). The authors of these critiques are responding to and helping to create the conditions for a fundamental reworking of organizational theories to account for the persistence of male advantage in male organizations and to lay a base for new critical and gendered theories of organizations that can better answer questions about how we humans come to organize our activities as we do in contemporary societies.

The conditions for a new critique began with the rapid proliferation of studies about women and work, conceptualized in theoretical terms of prefeminist social science. For example, studies of women's economic and occupational inequality, sex segregation, and the wage gap document the extent of the problems but give us no convincing explanations for their persistence or for the apparently endless reorganization of gender and permutations of male power. Similarly, the extensive literature on women and management documents difficulties and differences but provides no adequate theory of gendered power imbalance. The need for new theory was implicit in the inadequacies of old theory.

Developments within feminist theory also provide foundations for a new criticism of organizational theory. . . .

THINKING ABOUT GENDER

Gender refers to patterned, socially produced, distinctions between female and male, feminine and masculine. Gender is not something that people are, in some inherent sense, although we may consciously think of ourselves in this way. Rather, for the individual and the collective, it is a daily accomplishment (West and Zimmerman 1987) that occurs in the course of participation in work organizations as well as in many other locations and relations.

. . . Gender, as patterned differences, usually involves the subordination of women, either concretely or symbolically, and, as Joan Scott (1986) points out, gender is a pervasive symbol of power.

The term *gendered processes* "means that advantage and disadvantage, exploitation and control, action and emotion, meaning and identity, are patterned through and in terms of a distinction between male and female, masculine and feminine" (Acker 1990: 146; see also Scott 1986; Harding 1986; Connell 1987; Flax 1990). Gendered processes are concrete activities, what people do and say, and how they think about these activities, for thinking is also an activity. The daily construction, and sometimes deconstruction, of gender occurs within material and ideological constraints that set the limits of possibility. For example, the boundaries of sex segregation, themselves continually constructed and reconstructed, limit the actions of particular women and men at particular times. Gendered processes do not occur outside other social processes but are integral parts of these processes —for example, class and race relations—which cannot be fully understood without a comprehension of gender (Connell 1987). At the same time, class and race processes are integral to gender relations. The links between class and race domination and gender are ubiquitous. For example, at the top of the typical Southern California high-tech firm stands the rational, aggressive, controlling white man (occasionally a woman but one who has learned how to operate in the class/gender structure), while at the very bottom there are often women of color working on a production line where they have little control over any aspect of their working lives (Fernandez Kelly and Garcia 1988). Examining how the organization was started and is controlled by these particular men and how these particular women came to be the production workers leads us back into the class/gender/race relations of that time and place. Similarly, if we look at the work processes and organizational controls that keep the firm going, we will see the intertwining of gender, race, and class.

Gendered processes and practices may be open and overt, as when managers choose only men or only women for certain positions or when sexual jokes denigrating women are part of the work culture. On the other hand, gender may be deeply hidden in organizational processes and decisions that appear to have nothing to do with gender. For example, deregulation and internationalization of banking has altered the gender structure of banks in both Sweden (Acker 1991) and Britain (Morgan and Knights 1991). In Sweden, these changes contributed to a growing wage gap between women and men, as women remained in low-wage branch banking and men, chosen more often for the growing international banking departments, were rewarded with disproportionate salary increases. In Britain, deregulation, and the resulting increase in competitiveness in the industry, was an important cause of reorganization in one bank that gave women new tasks at the expense of some men but still protected the privileges of men in traditional managerial

positions. To understand the persistence of gender patterns, even as external changes cause internal organizational restructuring, I think we should consider the gender substructure of organizations and the ways that gender is used as an organizational resource, topics discussed below.

ELEMENTS IN A THEORY OF GENDERED ORGANIZATIONS

Gendered Processes

Gendered organizations can be described in terms of four sets of processes that are components of the same reality, although, for purposes of description, they can be seen as analytically distinct. As outlined above, gendering may occur in gender-explicit or gender-neutral practices; it occurs through concrete organizational activities; and its processes usually have class and racial implications as well. Sexuality, in its diverse forms and meanings, is implicated in each of these processes of gendering organizations.

The first set of processes is the production of gender divisions. Ordinary organizational practices produce the gender patterning of jobs, wages, and hierarchies, power, and subordination (e.g., Kanter 1977a). Managers make conscious decisions that re-create and sometimes alter these patterns (Cohn 1985); unions, where they exist, often collude, whether intentionally or not. For example, while employers can no longer, by law, advertise for female workers for some jobs and male workers for others, many still perceive women as suited for certain work and men as suited for other work. These perceptions help to shape decisions. The introduction of new technology may offer the possibility for the reduction of gender divisions but most often results in a reorganization, not an elimination, of male predominance (e.g., Cockburn 1983, 1985). The depth and character of gender divisions vary dramatically from one society to another and from one time to another. In Britain, for example, when women first began to enter clerical work, separate offices were often set up so that women and men would not have to meet on the job, thus avoiding the possibility of sexual encounters and resulting in extreme gender segregation (Cohn 1985). Whatever the variation, there is overwhelming evidence that hierarchies are gendered and that gender and sexuality have a central role in the reproduction of hierarchy.

Gendering also involves the creation of symbols, images, and forms of consciousness that explicate, justify, and, more rarely, oppose gender divisions. Complex organizations are one of the main locations of the production of such images and forms of consciousness in our societies. Television, films, and advertising are obvious examples, but all organizations are sites of symbolic production. Gender images, always containing implications of sexuality, infuse organizational structure. The top manager or business leader is always strong, decisive, rational, and forceful—and often seductive (Calás and Smircich 1989b). The organization itself is often defined through metaphors of masculinity of a certain sort. Today, organizations are lean, mean, aggressive, goal oriented, efficient, and competitive but rarely empathetic, supportive, kind, and caring. Organizational participants actively create these images in their efforts to construct organizational cultures that contribute to competitive success.

The third set of processes that reproduce gendered organizations are interactions between individuals, women and men, women and women, men and men, in the multiplicity of forms that enact dominance and subordination and create alliances and exclusions. In these interactions, at various levels of hierarchy, policies that create divisions are developed and images of gender are created and affirmed. Sexuality is involved here, too, in overt or hidden ways; links between dominance and sexuality shape interaction and help to maintain hierarchies favoring men (Pringle 1989). Interactions may be between supervisors and subordinates, between coworkers, or between workers and customers, clients, or other outsiders. Interactions are part of the

concrete work of organization, and the production of gender is often "inside" the activities that constitute the organization itself.

The fourth dimension of gendering of organizations is the internal mental work of individuals as they consciously construct their understandings of the organization's gendered structure of work and opportunity and the demands for gender-appropriate behaviors and attitudes (e.g., Pringle 1989; Cockburn 1991). This includes creating the correct gendered persona and hiding unacceptable aspects of one's life, such as homosexuality. As Pringle (1989: 176) says, "Sexual games are integral to the play of power at work, and success for women depends on how they negotiate their sexuality." Such internal work helps to reproduce divisions and images even as it ensures individual survival.

Gender and Sexuality as Organizational Resources

Gender, sexuality, and bodies can be thought of as organizational resources, primarily available to management but also used by individuals and groups of workers. Simultaneously, however, gender, sexuality, and bodies are problems for management. Solutions to these problems become resources for control. Both female and male bodies have physical needs on the job. Management often controls lunch and toilet breaks as well as physical movement around the workplace as integral elements in furthering productivity. Numbers of researchers, from Crozier on (Acker and Van Houten 1974), have observed that women workers are more tightly controlled in these ways than men workers. Higher-level employees are often rewarded with fewer bodily constraints and special privileges in regard to physical needs—for example, the executive washroom and dining room.

Reproduction and sexuality are often objects of and resources for control. As Burrell (1984: 98) argues, "Individual organizations inaugurate mechanisms for the control of sexuality at a very early stage in their development." Reproduction and sexuality may disrupt ongoing work and seriously undermine the orderly and rational pursuit of organizational goals. Women's bodies, sexuality, and procreative abilities are used as grounds for exclusion or objectification. On the other hand, men's sexuality dominates most workplaces and reinforces their organizational power (Collinson and Collinson 1989). In addition, talk about sex and male sexual superiority helps construct solidarity and cooperation from the bottom to the top of many organizations, thus promoting organizational stability and control.

Gender is also a resource in organizational change. Hacker (1979) showed how technological transformation at AT&T in the 1970s was facilitated by moving women into formerly male jobs slated to be eliminated. Today, in the drive for organizational "flexibility," managements often consciously create part-time jobs, low paid and dead end, to be filled by women (see, e.g., Cockburn 1991). It is gender, and often race, that makes women ideal employees. These are only examples from a multiplicity of processes that suggest the possibilities for research about gender and sexuality in organizational control and change.

The Gendered Substructure of Organization

The more or less obvious manifestations of gender in organizational processes outlined above are built upon, and in turn help to reproduce, a gendered substructure of organization. The gendered substructure lies in the spatial and temporal arrangements of work, in the rules prescribing workplace behavior, and in the relations linking workplaces to living places. These practices and relations, encoded in arrangements and rules, are supported by assumptions that work is separate from the rest of life and that it has first claim on the worker. Many people, particularly women, have difficulty making their daily lives fit these expectations

and assumptions. As a consequence, today, there are two types of workers, those, mostly men, who, it is assumed, can adhere to organizational rules, arrangements, and assumptions, and those, mostly women, who, it is assumed, cannot, because of other obligations to family and reproduction.

Organizations depend upon this division, for, in a free market economy, in contrast to a slave economy, they could not exist without some outside organization of reproduction to take care of supplying workers. In this sense, the gender substructure of organization is linked to the family and reproduction. This relationship is not simply a functional link. It is embedded in and re-created daily in ordinary organizational activities, most of which do not appear on the surface to be gendered. In the exploration of some of these processes, it is possible to see how integral to modern organization this gendered substructure is, and how relatively inaccessible to change it remains.

I began this discussion by considering some of the problems posed by the gendered nature of existing, ostensibly gender-neutral, organizational theory and processes. Feminist critics of traditional theory now widely recognize that this body of theory is gendered, that it implicitly assumes that managers and workers are male, with male-stereotypic powers, attitudes, and obligations (e.g., Acker 1990; Calás and Smircich 1992; Mills 1989).

What is problematic is the discontinuity, even contradiction, between organizational realities obviously structured around gender and ways of thinking and talking about these same realities as though they were gender neutral. What activities or practices produce the facade of gender neutrality and maintain this disjuncture between organizational life and theory? These questions can provide a point of entry into the underlying processes that maintain gender divisions, images, interactions, and identities.

This analytic strategy is based on Dorothy Smith's *The Conceptual Practices of Power* (1990) in which she argues that concepts that feminists may see as misrepresenting reality—here the concept of gender-neutral structure—indicate something about the social relations they represent. That is, such concepts are not "wrong." On the contrary, they are constructed out of the working knowledge of those who manage and control, thus they say something about processes of power, including the suppression of knowledge about gender. While it is important to "deconstruct"these concepts, revealing hidden meanings, we can, in addition, investigate the concrete activities that produce them.

The break between a gendered reality and gender-neutral thought is maintained, I believe, through the impersonal, objectifying practices of organizing, managing, and controlling large organizations. As Smith (1987) argues, these processes are increasingly textually mediated. Bureaucratic rules and written guides for organizational processes have been around for a long time, but their proliferation continues as rationalization of production and management expands on a global scale. The fact that much of this is now built into computer programs may mystify the process but only increases objectification and the appearance of gender neutrality. The continuing replication of the assumption of gender neutrality is part of the production of texts that can apply to workers, work processes, production, and management as general phenomena. Thus gender neutrality, the suppression of knowledge about gender, is embedded in organizational control processes.

This work of re-creating gender neutrality as part of the construction of general phenomena that can be organized and controlled through the application of documentary processes is evident in job evaluation,[1] a textual tool used by management to rationalize wage setting and the construction of organizational hierarchies. Other managerial processes produce assumptions of gender neutrality, but job evaluation provides a particularly good example because it is widely used in every industrial country (International Labour Office 1986).

Job evaluators use documents, or instruments, that describe general aspects of jobs, such as knowledge, skill, complexity, and responsibility, to assess the "value" of particular, concrete jobs in comparison with other particular, concrete jobs. The content of the documents and the way evaluators discuss and interpret them in the course of the job evaluation process provide an illustration of how concrete organizational activities reproduce the assumption of gender neutrality (Acker 1989, 1990).

Job evaluation, as most experts will tell you, evaluates jobs, not the people who do the jobs. Job evaluation consultants and trainers admonish evaluators to consider only the requirements of the job, not the gender or other characteristics of the incumbent. The tasks, skill requirements, and responsibilities of a job can be reliably described and assessed, while people who fill the jobs vary in their knowledge and commitment. Jobs can be rationalized and standardized; people cannot. A job exists separate from those who fill it, as a position in the hierarchy of an organizational chart. It is a reified, objectified category. But the abstract job must contain the assumption of an abstract worker if it is to be more than a set of tasks written on a piece of paper. Such a worker has no obligations outside the demands of the job, which is a bounded, abstract entity. To fit such demands, the abstract worker does not eat, urinate, or procreate, for these activities are not part of the job. Indeed, the abstract worker has no body and thus no gender. Jobs and hierarchies are represented as gender neutral, and every time such a job evaluation system is used, the notion of gender-neutral structure and the behavior based on that notion are re-created within the organization. Gender-neutral organizational theories reflect this gender-neutral rendering of organizational reality.

Real jobs and real workers are, of course, deeply gendered and embodied. The abstract worker transformed into a concrete worker turns out to be a man whose work is his life and whose wife takes care of everything else. Thus the concept of a job is gendered, in spite of its presentation as gender neutral, because only a male worker can begin to meet its implicit demands. Hidden within the concept of a job are assumptions about separations between the public and private spheres and the gendered organization of reproduction and production. Reproduction itself, procreation, sexuality, and caring for children, the ill, and the aged, unless transferred to the public sphere, are outside job and organizational boundaries. Too much involvement in such activities makes a person unsuitable for the organization. Women do not fit the assumptions about the abstract worker. Thus they are less than ideal organization participants, best placed in particular jobs that separate them from "real" workers.

The exclusion of reproduction is, as I argue above, linked to the ideology of the gender-neutral, abstract worker who has no body and no feelings, along with no gender. This abstraction facilitates the idea that the organization and its goals come first before the reproductive needs of individuals and society, such as, for example, the need to preserve and restore the natural environment. The concept of the abstract worker, completely devoted to the job, also supports the idea that strong commitment to the organization over and above commitment to family and community are necessary and normal. . . . As a consequence, management can more easily make the tough decisions, such as those to close factories while opposing all efforts to protect actual, concrete bodies and minds through plant closure legislation.

The theory and practice of gender neutrality covers up, obscures, the underlying gender structure, allowing practices that perpetuate it to continue even as efforts to reduce gender inequality are also under way (e.g., Cockburn 1991). The textual tools of management, as they are employed in everyday organizational life, not only help to create and then obscure gender structures that disadvantage women but are also part of complex processes that

daily re-create the subordination of reproduction to production and justify the privileging of production over all other human necessities.

The gender-neutral character of the job and the worker, central to organizational processes and theories discussed above, depends upon the assumption that the worker has no body. This disembodied worker is a manifestation of the universal "citizen" or "individual" fundamental to ideas of democracy and contract. As Carole Pateman (1986: 8) points out, the most fundamental abstraction in the concept of liberal individualism is "the abstraction of the 'individual' from the body. In order for the individual to appear in liberal theory as a universal figure, who represents anyone and everyone, the individual must be disembodied." If the individual had bodily form, it would be clear that he represents one gender and one sex rather than a universal being. The universal individual is "constructed from a male body so that his identity is always masculine" (Pateman 1988: 223). Even with the full rights of citizens, women stand in an ambiguous relation to this universal individual. In a similar way, the concept of the universal worker, so common in talk about work organizations, "excludes and marginalizes women who cannot, almost by definition, achieve the qualities of a real worker because to do so is to become like a man" (Acker 1990: 150).

SUMMARY AND CONCLUSIONS

A gendered organization theory should produce better answers to questions about both the organization of production and the reproduction of organization (Burrell and Hearn 1989). I have suggested one strategy for developing such a theory, starting with an inventory of gendered processes that necessarily include manifestations of sexuality. In any concrete organization, these processes occur in complex interrelations. Gendered processes are often resources in organizational control and transformation.

Underlying these processes, and intimately connected to them, is a gendered substructure of organization that links the more surface gender arrangements with the gender relations in other parts of the society. Ostensibly gender neutral, everyday activities of organizing and managing large organizations reproduce the gendered substructure within the organization itself and within the wider society. I think that this is the most important part of the process to comprehend, because it is hidden within abstract, objectifying, textually mediated relations and is difficult to make visible. The fiction of the universal worker obscures the gendered effects of these ostensibly gender-neutral processes and helps to banish gender from theorizing about the fundamental character of complex organizations. Gender, sexuality, reproduction, and emotionality of women are outside organizational boundaries, continually and actively consigned to that social space by ongoing organizational practices. Complex organizations play an important role, therefore, in defining gender and women's disadvantage for the whole society.

What are the practical implications of analyses, such as mine, in which ordinary organizational practices and thinking about those practices are grounded in the prior exclusion of women? The implications are not a return to an imaginary, utopian past where production is small scale and reproduction and production are fully integrated in daily life. Nor are the implications an Orwellian future where sexuality, procreation, and child raising would be integrated in superorganizations where all of life is paternalistically regulated.

Instead, we might think about alternative possibilities, some short term and others long term. Short-term, new strategies to transform parts of large organizations from the inside are possible.[2] One way to do this is to take control of, or at least to influence and use, the textual tools of management. This is what comparable worth activists aim to do, as they attempt to affect

the construction and use of job evaluation instruments to increase the value placed on women's jobs. Comparable worth experience shows that this is difficult and time consuming but not impossible (Acker 1989; Blum 1991). Many other practices could be similarly altered, but union organization controlled by women is the essential condition for doing such things. In the meantime, individual women can become experts in using and manipulating organizational texts; superior knowledge of rules and procedures can often facilitate change. . . .

Long-term strategies will have to challenge the privileging of the "economy" over life and raise questions about the rationality of such things as organizational and work commitment . . . as well as the legitimacy of organizations' claims for the priority of their goals over other broader goals. The gendered structure of organizations will only be completely changed with a fundamental reorganization of both production and reproduction. The long term is very long term and impossible to specify, but this should not lead us to abandon the search for other ways of organizing complex collective human activities.

NOTES

1. The following discussion of job evaluation is based on Acker (1989).
2. This has been suggested by Beatrice Halsaa, Hildur Ve, and Cynthia Cockburn, who are proposing an international feminist activist/researcher conference on the topic.

REFERENCES

Acker, J. 1980. "Women and Stratification: A Review of Recent Literature." *Contemporary Sociology* 9:25–34.

———. 1988. "Class, Gender, and the Relations of Distribution." *Signs: Journal of Women in Culture and Society* 13:473–97.

————. 1989. *Doing Comparable Worth: Gender, Class and Pay Equity.* Philadelphia: Temple University Press.

————. 1990. "Hierarchies, Jobs, Bodies: A Theory of Gendered Organizations." *Gender & Society* 4:139–58.

————. 1991. "Thinking About Wages: The Gendered Wage Gap in Swedish Banks." *Gender & Society* 5:390–407.

Acker, J., and D. R. Van Houten. 1974. "Differential Recruitment and Control: The Sex Structuring of Organizations." *Administrative Science Quarterly* 19(2): 152–63.

Blum, L. M. 1991. *Between Feminism and Labor: The Significance of the Comparable Worth Movement.* Berkeley: University of California Press.

Burrell, G. 1980. "Radical Organization Theory." In *The International Yearbook of Organization Studies 1979,* edited by D. Dunkerley and G. Salaman. London: Routledge & Kegan Paul.

————. 1984. "Sex and Organizational Analysis." *Organization Studies* 5(2):97–118.

————. 1987. "No Accounting for Sexuality." *Accounting, Organizations, and Society* 12:89–101.

Burrell, G., and J. Hearn. 1989. "The Sexuality of Organization." In *The Sexuality of Organization,* edited by J. Hearn, D. L. Sheppard, P. Tancred-Sheriff, and G. Burrell. London: Sage.

Butler, J. 1990. *Gender Trouble: Feminism and the Subversion of Identity.* New York: Routledge.

Calás, M. B., and L. Smircich. 1989a. "Voicing Seduction to Silence Leadership." Paper presented at the Fourth International Conference on Organizational Symbolism and Corporate Culture, Fountainbleau, France.

————. 1989b. "Using the 'F' Word: Feminist Theories and the Social Consequences of Organizational Research." Pp. 355–59. In *Academy of Management Best Papers Proceedings.* Washington, DC: Academy of Management.

————. 1992. "Re-writing Gender into Organization Theorizing: Directions from Feminist Perspectives." In *Re-thinking Organization: New Directions in Organizational*

Research and Analysis, edited by M. I. Reed and M. D. Hughes. London: Sage.

Cockburn, C. 1981. "The Material of Male Power." *Feminist Review* 9:51.

————. 1983. *Brothers: Male Dominance and Technological Change.* London: Pluto.

————. 1985. *Machinery of Dominance.* London: Pluto.

————. 1991. *In the Way of Women: Men's Resistance to Sex Equality in Organizations.* Ithaca: ILR Press.

Cohn, S. 1985. *The Process of Occupational Sex-Typing.* Philadelphia: Temple University Press.

Collinson, D. L., and M. Collinson. 1989. "Sexuality in the Workplace: The Domination of Men's Sexuality." In *The Sexuality of Organization,* edited by J. Hearn, D. L. Sheppard, P. Tancred-Sheriff, and G. Burrell. London: Sage.

Connell, R. W. 1987. *Gender and Power.* Stanford, CA: Stanford University Press.

Czarniawska-Joerges, B. 1991. "Gender, Power, Organizations: An Interruptive Interpretation." Paper presented at the New Theory in Organizations Conference at Keele, England.

Ferguson, K. E. 1984. *The Feminist Case Against Bureaucracy.* Philadelphia: Temple University Press.

————. 1988. "Knowledge, Politics and Personhood." Presented at the conference, The Feminine in Public Administration and Policy, Washington, DC, May 7.

Fernandez Kelly, M. P., and A. M. Garcia. 1988. "Invisible Amidst the Glitter: Hispanic Women in the Southern California Electronics Industry." In *The Worth of Women's work,* edited by A. Statham, E. M. Miller, and H. O. Mauksch. Albany: SUNY Press.

Flax, J. 1987. "Postmodernism and Gender Relations in Feminist Theory." *Signs: Journal of Women in Culture and Society* 12:621–43.

————. 1990. *Thinking Fragments: Psychoanalysis, Feminism, and Postmodernism in the Contemporary West.* Berkeley: University of California Press.

Foucault, M. 1972. *The Archeology of Knowledge.* New York: Pantheon.

————. 1979. *The History of Sexuality*. Vol. 1. London: Allen Lane.

Hacker, S. L. 1979. "Sex Stratification, Technology and Organizational Change: A Longitudinal Case Study of AT&T." *Social Problems* 26:539–57.

Harding, S. 1986. *The Science Question in Feminism*. Ithaca, NY: Cornell University Press.

Hearn, J., and P. W. Parkin. 1983. "Gender and Organizations: A Selective Review and a Critique of a Neglected Area." *Organization Studies* 4(3):219–42.

————. 1987. *"Sex" at "Work": The Power and Paradox of Organizational Sexuality*. Brighton: Wheatsheaf.

————. 1991. "Women, Men and Leadership: A Critical Review of Assumptions, Practices and Changes in the Industrialized Nations." In *Women in Management Worldwide*. 2nd ed., edited by N. J. Adler and D. Izraeli. New York: M. E. Sharpe.

Hearn, J., D. Sheppard, P. Tancred-Sheriff, and G. Burrell, eds. 1989. *The Sexuality of Organization*. London: Sage.

Hill-Collins, P. 1989. "The Social Construction of Black Feminist Thought." *Signs: Journal of Women in Culture and Society* 14:745–73.

————. 1990. *Black Feminist Thought: Knowledge, Consciousness, the Politics of Empowerment*. Boston: Unwin Hyman.

International Labour Office. 1986. *Job Evaluation*. Geneva: Author.

Kanter, R. M. 1977a. *Men and Women of the Corporation*. New York: Basic Books.

————. 1977b. "Some Effects of Proportions of Group Life: Skewed Sex-Ratios and Responses to Token Women." *American Journal of Sociology* 82:965–90.

MacKinnon, C. 1979. *Sexual Harassment of Working Women*. New Haven, CT: Yale University Press.

————. 1982. "Feminism, Marxism, Method and the State: An Agenda for Theory." *Signs: Journal of Women in Culture and Society* 7:515–44.

Martin, J. 1988. "The Suppression of Gender Conflict in Organizations: Deconstructing the Fissure Between Public and Private."
Paper presented at the Academy of Management Meeting, Anaheim, CA, August.

————. 1990a. "Deconstructing Organizational Taboos: The Suppression of Gender Conflict in Organizations." *Organizational Science* 1:1–21.

————. 1990b. "Re-reading Weber: Searching for Feminist Alternatives to Bureaucracy." Paper presented at the annual meeting of the Academy of Management, San Francisco.

————. 1990c. "Organizational Taboos: The Suppression of Gender Conflict in Organizations." *Organization Science* 1:334–59.

Mills, A. J. 1988a. "Organizational Acculturation and Gender Discrimination." Pp. 1–22 in *Canadian Issues, Vol. 11, Women and the Workplace*, edited by P. K. Kresl. Montreal: Association of Canadian Studies/International Council for Canadian Studies.

————. 1988b. "Organization, Gender and Culture." *Organization Studies* 9(3): 351–69.

————. 1989. "Gender, Sexuality and Organization Theory." In *The Sexuality of Organization*, edited by J. Hearn, D. L. Sheppard, P. Tancred-Sheriff, and G. Burrell. London: Sage.

Morgan, G. and D. Knights. 1991. "Gendering Jobs: Corporate Strategy, Managerial Control and the Dynamics of Job Segregation." *Work, Employment & Society* 5: 181–200.

Pateman, C. 1981. "The Concept of Equality." In *A Just Society? Essays on Equity in Australia*, edited by P. N. Troy. Sydney: George Allen and Unwin.

————. 1986. "Introduction: The Theoretical Subversiveness of Feminism." In *Feminist Challenges*, edited by C. Pateman and E. Gross. Winchester, MA: Allen & Unwin.

————. 1988. *The Sexual Contract*. Cambridge, MA: Polity.

Pringle, R. 1989. "Bureaucracy, Rationality and Sexuality: The Case of Secretaries." In *The Sexuality of Organization*, edited by J. Hearn, D. L. Sheppard, P. Tancred-Sheriff, and G. Burrell. London: Sage.

Scott, J. 1986. "Gender: A Useful Category of Historical Analysis." *American Historical Review* 91:1053–75.

Smith, D. 1975. "Analysis of Ideological Structures and How Women Are Excluded: Considerations for Academic Women." *Canadian Review of Sociology and Anthropology* 12:353–69.

———. 1977. "Women, the Family and Corporate Capitalism." In *Women in Canada.* Rev. ed., edited by M. Stephenson. Don Mills, Ontario: General Publishing.

———. 1987. *The Everyday World as Problematic: A Feminist Sociology.* Toronto: University of Toronto Press.

———. 1990. *The Conceptual Practices of Power: A Feminist Sociology of Knowledge.* Toronto: University of Toronto Press.

West, C., and D. H. Zimmerman. 1987. "Doing Gender." *Gender & Society* 1:125–51.

43

Creating a Government That Works Better & Costs Less: Report of the National Performance Review

Vice President Al Gore

Our goal is to make the entire federal government both less expensive and more efficient, and to change the culture of our national bureaucracy away from complacency and entitlement toward initiative and empowerment. We intend to re-design, to reinvent, to reinvigorate the entire national government.

President Bill Clinton
Remarks announcing the
National Performance Review
March 3, 1993

Public confidence in the federal government has never been lower. The average American believes we waste 48 cents of every tax dollar. Five of every six want "fundamental change" in Washington. Only 20 percent of Americans trust the federal government to do the right thing most of the time—down from 76 percent 30 years ago.[1]

We all know why. Washington's failures are large and obvious. For a decade, the deficit has run out of control. The national debt now exceeds $4 trillion—$16,600 for every man, woman, and child in America.

But the deficit is only the tip of the iceberg. Below the surface, Americans believe, lies enormous unseen waste. The Defense Department owns more than $40 billion in unnecessary supplies.[2] The Internal Revenue Service struggles to collect billions in unpaid bills. A century after industry replaced farming as America's principal business, the Agriculture Department still operates more than 12,000 field service offices, an average of nearly 4 for every county in the nation—rural, urban, or suburban. The federal government seems unable to abandon the obsolete. It knows how to add, but not to subtract.

And yet, waste is not the only problem. The federal government is not simply broke; it is broken. Ineffective regulation of the financial industry brought us the savings and loan debacle. Ineffective education and training programs jeopardize our competitive edge. Ineffective welfare and housing programs undermine our families and cities.

We spend $25 billion a year on welfare, $27 billion on food stamps, and $13 billion on public housing—yet more Americans fall into poverty every year.[3] We spend $12 billion a year waging war on drugs—yet see few signs of victory. We fund 150 different employment and training programs—yet the average American has no idea where to get job training, and the skills of our workforce fall further behind those of our competitors.[4]

It is almost as if federal programs were *designed* not to work. In truth, few are "designed" at all; the legislative process simply churns them out, one after another, year after year. It's little wonder that when asked if "government always manages to mess things up," two-thirds of Americans say "yes."[5]

To borrow the words of a recent Brookings Institution book, we suffer not only a budget deficit but a performance deficit.[6] Indeed, public opinion experts argue that

Source: Vice President Al Gore, *Creating a Government That Works Better & Costs Less: Report of the National Performance Review* (September 7, 1993). Washington, DC: U.S. Government Printing Office.

we are suffering the deepest crisis of faith in government in our lifetimes. In past crises—Watergate or the Vietnam War, for example—Americans doubted their leaders on moral or ideological grounds. They felt their government was deceiving them or failing to represent their values. Today's crisis is different: people simply feel that government doesn't work.[7]

In Washington, debate rarely focuses on the performance deficit. Our leaders spend most of their time debating policy issues. But if the vehicle designed to carry out policy is broken, new policies won't take us anywhere. If the car won't run, it hardly matters where we point it; we won't get there. Today, the central issue we face is not *what* government does, but *how* it works.

We have spent too much money for programs that don't work. It's time to make our government work for the people, learn to do more with less, and treat taxpayers like customers.

President Clinton created the National Performance Review to do just that. In this report we make hundreds of recommendations for actions that, if implemented, will revolutionize the way the federal government does business. They will reduce waste, eliminate unneeded bureaucracy, improve service to taxpayers, and create a leaner but more productive government. As noted in the preface, they can save $108 billion over 5 years if those which will be enacted by the President and his cabinet are added to those we propose for enactment by Congress. Some of these proposals can be enacted by the President and his cabinet, others will require legislative action. We are going to fight for these changes. We are determined to create a government that works better and costs less.

A CURE WORSE THAN THE DISEASE

Government is not alone in its troubles. As the Industrial Era has given way to the Information Age, institutions—both public and private—have come face to face with obsolescence. The past decade has witnessed profound restructuring: In the 1980s, major American corporations reinvented themselves; in the 1990s, governments are struggling to do the same.

In recent years, our national leaders responded to the growing crisis with traditional medicine. They blamed the bureaucrats. They railed against "fraud, waste, and abuse." And they slapped ever more controls on the bureaucracy to prevent it.

But the cure has become indistinguishable from the disease. The problem is not lazy or incompetent people; it is red tape and regulation so suffocating that they stifle every ounce of creativity. No one would offer a drowning man a drink of water. And yet, for more than a decade, we have added red tape to a system already strangling in it.

The federal government is filled with good people trapped in bad systems: budget systems, personnel systems, procurement systems, financial management systems, information systems. When we blame the people and impose more controls, we make the systems worse. Over the past 15 years, for example, Congress has created within each agency an independent office of the inspector general. The idea was to root out fraud, waste, and abuse. The inspectors general have certainly uncovered important problems. But as we learned in conversation after conversation, they have so intimidated federal employees that many are now afraid to deviate even slightly from standard operating procedure.

Yet innovation, by its nature, requires deviation. Unfortunately, faced with so many controls, many employees have simply given up. They do everything by the book—whether it makes sense or not. They fill out forms that should never have been created, follow rules that should never have been imposed, and prepare reports that serve no purpose—and are often never even read. In the name of controlling waste, we have created paralyzing inefficiency. It's time we found a way to get rid of waste and encourage efficiency.

THE ROOT PROBLEM: INDUSTRIAL-ERA BUREAUCRACIES IN AN INFORMATION AGE

Is government inherently incompetent? Absolutely not. Are federal agencies filled with incompetent people? No. The problem is much deeper: Washington is filled with organizations designed for an environment that no longer exists—bureaucracies so big and wasteful they can no longer serve the American people.

From the 1930s through the 1960s, we built large, top-down, centralized bureaucracies to do the public's business. They were patterned after the corporate structures of the age: hierarchical bureaucracies in which tasks were broken into simple parts, each the responsibility of a different layer of employees, each defined by specific rules and regulations. With their rigid preoccupation with standard operating procedure, their vertical chains of command, and their standardized services, these bureaucracies were steady—but slow and cumbersome. And in today's world of rapid change, lightning-quick information technologies, tough global competition, and demanding customers, large, top-down bureaucracies—public or private—don't work very well. Saturn isn't run the way General Motors was. Intel isn't run the way IBM was.

Many federal organizations are also monopolies, with few incentives to innovate or improve. Employees have virtual lifetime tenure, regardless of their performance. Success offers few rewards; failure, few penalties. And customers are captive; they can't walk away from the air traffic control system or the Internal Revenue Service and sign up with a competitor. Worse, most federal monopolies receive their money without any direct input from their customers. Consequently, they try a lot harder to please Congressional appropriations subcommittees than the people they are meant to serve. Taxpayers pay more than they should and get poorer service.

Politics intensifies the problem. In Washington's highly politicized world, the greatest risk is not that a program will perform poorly, but that a scandal will erupt. Scandals are front-page news, while routine failure is ignored. Hence control system after control system is piled up to minimize the risk of scandal. The budget system, the personnel rules, the procurement process, the inspectors general—all are designed to prevent the tiniest misstep. We assume that we can't trust employees to make decisions, so we spell out in precise detail how they must do virtually everything, then audit them to ensure that they have obeyed every rule. The slightest deviation prompts new regulations and even more audits.

During Vice President Gore's town hall meeting with employees of the Department of Housing and Urban Development (HUD), the following exchange took place:

Participant: *We had an article in our newsletter several months ago that said—the lead story was "I'd rather have a lobotomy than have another idea." And that was reflecting the problem of our Ideas Program here in HUD.*

Many of the employees have wonderful ideas about how to save money and so on, but the way it works is that it has to be approved by the supervisor and the supervisor's supervisor and the supervisor's supervisor's supervisor before it ever gets to the Ideas Program . . .

Many of the supervisors feel threatened because they didn't think of this idea, and this money is wasted in their office, and they didn't believe or didn't know it was happening and didn't catch it. So they are threatened and feel that it will make them look bad if they recognize the idea.

Vice President Gore: *So they strangle that idea in the crib, don't they?*

Participant: *And then they strangle the person that had the idea. . . .*

Before long, simple procedures are too complex for employees to navigate, so we hire more budget analysts, more personnel experts, and more procurement officers to make things work. By then, the process involves so much red tape that the smallest action takes far longer and costs far more than it should. Simple travel arrangements require endless forms and numerous signatures. Straightforward purchases take months; larger ones take years. Routine printing jobs can take dozens of approvals.

This emphasis on process steals resources from the real job: serving the customer. Indeed, the federal government spends billions paying people who control, check up on, or investigate others — supervisors, headquarters staffs, budget officers, personnel officers, procurement officers, and staffs of the General Accounting Office (GAO) and the inspectors general.[8] Not all this money is wasted, of course. But the real waste is no doubt larger, because the endless regulations and layers of control consume every employee's time. Who pays? The taxpayer.

Consider but one example, shared with Vice President Gore at a meeting of federal employees in Atlanta. After federal marshals seize drug dealers' homes, they are allowed to sell them and use the money to help finance the war on drugs. To sell the houses, they must keep them presentable, which includes keeping the lawns mowed.

In Atlanta, the employee explained, most organizations would hire neighborhood teenagers to mow a lawn for $10. But procurement regulations require the U.S. Marshals Service to bid out all work competitively, and neighborhood teenagers don't compete for contracts. So the federal government pays $40 a lawn to professional landscape firms. Regulations designed to save money waste it, because they take decisions out of the hands of those responsible for doing the work. And taxpayers lose $30 for every lawn mowed.

What would happen if the marshals used their common sense and hired neighborhood teenagers? Someone would notice — perhaps the Washington office, perhaps the inspector general's office, perhaps even the GAO. An investigation might well follow — hindering a career or damaging a reputation.

In this way, federal employees quickly learn that common sense is risky — and creativity is downright dangerous. They learn that the goal is not to produce results, please customers, or save taxpayers' money,

but to avoid mistakes. Those who dare to innovate do so quietly.

This is perhaps the saddest lesson learned by those who worked on the National Performance Review: Yes, innovators exist within the federal government, but many work hard to keep their innovations quiet. By its nature, innovation requires a departure from standard operating procedure. In the federal government, such departures invite repercussions.

The result is a culture of fear and resignation. To survive, employees keep a low profile. They decide that the safest answer in any given situation is a firm "maybe." They follow the rules, pass the buck, and keep their heads down. They develop what one employee, speaking with Vice President Gore at a Department of Veterans Affairs meeting, called "a government attitude."

THE SOLUTION: CREATING ENTREPRENEURIAL ORGANIZATIONS

How do we solve these problems? It won't be easy. We know all about government's problems, but little about solutions. The National Performance Review began by compiling a comprehensive list of problems. We had the GAO's 28-volume report on federal management problems, published last fall. We had GAO's *High-Risk Series,* a 17-volume series of pamphlets on troubled programs and agencies. We had the House Government Operations Committee's report on federal mismanagement, called *Managing the Federal Government: A Decade of Decline.* And we had 83 notebooks summarizing just the tables of contents of reports published by the inspectors general, the Congressional Budget Office, the agencies, and think tanks.

Unfortunately, few of these studies helped us design solutions. Few of the investigating bodies had studied success stories — organizations that had solved their problems. And without studying success, it is hard to devise real solutions. For years, the federal government has studied failure, and for years, failure has endured. Six of every ten major agencies have programs on the Office of Management and Budget's "high-risk" list, meaning they carry a significant risk of runaway spending or fraud.

The National Performance Review approached its task differently. Not only did we look for potential savings and efficiencies, we searched for success. We looked for organizations that produced results, satisfied customers, and increased productivity. We looked for organizations that constantly learned, innovated, and improved. We looked for effective, entrepreneurial public organizations. And we found them: in local government, in state government, in other countries—and right here in our federal government.

At the Air Combat Command, for example, we found units that had doubled their productivity in 5 years. Why? Because the command measured performance everywhere; squadrons and bases competed proudly for the best maintenance, flight, and safety records; and top management had empowered employees to strip away red tape and redesign work processes. A supply system that had once required 243 entries by 22 people on 13 forms to get one spare part into an F-15 had been radically simplified and decentralized. Teams of employees were saving millions of dollars by moving supply operations to the front line, developing their own flight schedules, and repairing parts that were once discarded.[9]

At the Internal Revenue Service, we found tax return centers competing for the best productivity records. Performance on key customer service criteria—such as the accuracy of answers provided to taxpayers—had improved dramatically. Utah's Ogden Service Center, to cite but one example, had more than 50 "productivity improvement teams" simplifying forms and reengineering work processes. Not only had employees saved more than $11 million, they had won the 1992 Presidential Award for Quality.[10]

At the Forest Service, we found a pilot project in the 22-state Eastern Region that had increased productivity by 15 percent in just 2 years. The region had simplified its budget systems, eliminated layers of middle management, pared central headquarters staff by a fifth, and empowered front-line employees to make their own decisions. At the Mark Twain National Forest, for instance, the time needed to grant a grazing permit had shrunk from 30 days to a few hours—because employees could grant permits themselves rather than process them through headquarters.[11]

We discovered that several other governments were also reinventing themselves, from Australia to Great Britain, Singapore to Sweden, the Netherlands to New Zealand. Throughout the developed world, the needs of information-age societies were colliding with the limits of industrial-era government. Regardless of party, regardless of ideology, these governments were responding. In Great Britain, conservatives led the way. In New Zealand, the Labor Party revolutionized government. In Australia and Sweden, both conservative and liberal parties embraced fundamental change.

In the United States, we found the same phenomenon at the state and local levels. The movement to reinvent government is as bipartisan as it is widespread. It is driven not by political ideology, but by absolute necessity. Governors, mayors, and legislators of both parties have reached the same conclusion: Government is broken, and it is time to fix it.

Where we found success, we found many common characteristics. Early on, we articulated these in a one-page statement of our commitment. In organizing this report, we have boiled these characteristics down to four key principles.

1. Cutting Red Tape

Effective, entrepreneurial governments cast aside red tape, shifting from systems in which people are accountable for following rules to systems in which they are accountable for achieving results. They streamline their budget, personnel, and procurement systems—liberating organizations to pursue their missions. They reorient their control systems to prevent problems rather than simply punish those who make mistakes. They strip away unnecessary layers of regulation that stifle innovation. And they deregulate organizations that depend upon them for funding, such as lower levels of government.

2. Putting Customers First

Effective, entrepreneurial governments insist on customer satisfaction. They listen carefully to their customers—using surveys, focus groups, and the like. They restructure their basic operations to meet customers' needs. And they use market dynamics such as competition and customer choice to create incentives that drive their employees to put customers first.

By "customer," we do not mean "citizen." A citizen can participate in democratic decisionmaking; a customer receives benefits from a specific service. All Americans are citizens. Most are also customers: of the U.S. Postal Service, the Social Security Administration, the Department of Veterans Affairs, the National Park Service, and scores of other federal organizations.

In a democracy, citizens and customers both matter. But when they vote, citizens seldom have much chance to influence the behavior of public institutions that directly affect their lives: schools, hospitals, farm service agencies, social security offices. It is a sad irony: citizens own their government, but private businesses they do not own work much harder to cater to their needs.

3. Empowering Employees to Get Results

Effective, entrepreneurial governments transform their cultures by decentralizing authority. They empower those who work on the front lines to make more of their own decisions and solve more of their own problems. They embrace labor-management cooperation, provide training and other tools employees need to be effective, and humanize the workplace. While stripping away layers and empowering front-line employees, they hold organizations accountable for producing results.

4. Cutting Back to Basics: Producing Better Government for Less

Effective, entrepreneurial governments constantly find ways to make government work better and cost less—reengineering how they do their work and reexamining programs and processes. They abandon the obsolete, eliminate duplication, and end special interest privileges. They invest in greater productivity, through loan funds and long-term capital investments. And they embrace advanced technologies to cut costs.

These are the bedrock principles on which the reinvention of the federal bureaucracy must build—and the principles around which we have organized our actions. They fit together much like the pieces of a puzzle: if one is missing, the others lose their power. To create organizations that deliver value to American taxpayers, we must embrace all four.

Our approach goes far beyond fixing specific problems in specific agencies. Piecemeal efforts have been underway for years, but they have not delivered what Americans demand. The failure in Washington is embedded in the very systems by which we organize the federal bureaucracy. In recent years, Congress has taken the lead in reinventing these systems. In 1990, it passed the Chief Financial Officers Act, designed to overhaul financial management systems; in July 1993, it passed the Government Performance and Results Act, which will introduce performance measurement throughout the federal government. With Congress's leadership, we hope to reinvent government's other basic systems, such as budget, personnel, information, and procurement.

Principles of the National Performance Review

We will invent a government that puts people first, by:

- Cutting unnecessary spending
- Serving its customers
- Empowering its employees
- Helping communities solve their own problems
- Fostering excellence

Here's how. We will:

- Create a clear sense of mission
- Steer more, row less
- Delegate authority and responsibility
- Replace regulations with incentives
- Develop budgets based on outcomes
- Expose federal operations to competition
- Search for market, not administrative, solutions
- Measure our success by customer satisfaction

Our approach has much in common with other management philosophies, such as quality management and business process reengineering. But these management disciplines were developed for the private sector, where conditions are quite different. In business, red tape may be bad, but it is not the suffocating presence it is in government. In business, market incentives already exist; no one need invent them. Powerful incentives are always at work, forcing organizations to do more with less. Indeed, businesses that fail to increase their productivity—or that tie themselves up in red tape—shrink or die. Hence, private sector management doctrines tend to overlook some central problems of government: its monopolies, its lack of a bottom line, its obsession with process rather than results. Consequently, our approach goes beyond private sector methods. It is aimed at the heart and soul of government.

The National Performance Review also shares certain goals with past efforts to cut costs in government. But our mission goes beyond cost-cutting. Our goal is not simply to weed the federal garden; it is to create a regimen that will *keep* the garden free of weeds. It is not simply to trim *pieces* of government, but to reinvent the way government does everything. It is not simply to produce a more efficient government, but to create a more *effective* one. After all, Americans don't want a government that fails more efficiently. They want a government that *works*.

To deliver what the people want, we need not jettison the traditional values that underlie democratic governance—values such as equal opportunity, justice, diversity, and democracy. We hold these values dear. We seek to transform bureaucracies precisely *because* they have failed to nurture these values. We believe that those who resist change for fear of jeopardizing our democratic values doom us to a government that continues—through its failures—to subvert those very values.

OUR COMMITMENT: A LONG-TERM INVESTMENT IN CHANGE

This is not the first time Americans have felt compelled to reinvent their government. In 1776, our founding fathers rejected the old model of a central power issuing edicts for all to obey. In its place, they created a government that broadly distributed power. Their vision of democracy, which gave citizens a voice in managing the United States, was untried and untested in 1776. It required a tremendous leap of faith. But it worked.

Later generations extended this experiment in democracy to those not yet enfranchised. As the 20th century dawned, a generation of "Progressives" such as Teddy Roosevelt and Woodrow Wilson invented the modern bureaucratic state, designed to meet the needs of a new industrial society. Franklin Roosevelt brought it to full flower. Indeed, Roosevelt's 1937 announcement of his Committee on Administrative

Management sounds as if it were written today:

> The time has come to set our house in order. The administrative management of the government needs overhauling. The executive structure of the government is sadly out of date. . . . If we have faith in our republican form of government . . . we must devote ourselves energetically and courageously to the task of making that government efficient.

Through the ages, public management has tended to follow the prevailing paradigm of private management. The 1930s were no exception. Roosevelt's committee—and the two Hoover commissions that followed—recommended a structure patterned largely after those of corporate America in the 1930s. In a sense, they brought to government the GM model of organization.

By the 1980s, even GM recognized that this model no longer worked. When it created Saturn, its first new division in 67 years, GM embraced a very different model. It picked its best and brightest and asked them to create a more entrepreneurial organization, with fewer layers, fewer rules, and employees empowered to do whatever was necessary to satisfy the customer. Faced with the very real threat of bankruptcy, major American corporations have revolutionized the way they do business.

Confronted with our twin budget and performance deficits—which so undermine public trust in government—President Clinton intends to do the same thing. He did not staff the Performance Review primarily with outside consultants or corporate experts, as past presidents have. Instead, he chose federal employees to take the lead. They consulted with experts from state government, local government, and the private sector. But as Vice President Gore said over and over at his meetings with federal employees: "The people who work closest to the problem know the most about how to solve the problem."

Nor did the effort stop with the men and women who staffed the Performance Review. President Clinton asked every cabinet member to create a Reinvention Team to redesign his or her department, and Reinvention Laboratories to begin experimenting immediately. Since April, people all across our government have been working full time to reinvent the federal bureaucracy.

The process is not easy, nor will it be quick. There are changes we can make immediately, but even if all of our actions are enacted, we will only have begun to reinvent the federal government. Our efforts are but a down payment—the first installment of a long-term investment in change. Every expert with whom we talked reminded us that change takes time. In a large corporation, transformation takes 6 to 8 years at best. In the federal government, which has more than 7 times as many employees as America's largest corporation, it will undoubtedly take longer to bring about the historic changes we propose.[12]

Along the way, we will make mistakes. Some reforms will succeed beyond our wildest dreams; others will not. As in any experimental process, we will need to monitor results and correct as we go. But we must not confuse mistakes with failure. As Tom Peters and Robert Waterman wrote in *In Search of Excellence*, any organization that is not making mistakes is not trying hard enough. Babe Ruth, the Sultan of Swat, struck out 1,330 times.

With this report, then, we begin a decade-long process of reinvention. We hope this process will involve not only the thousands of federal employees now at work on Reinvention Teams and in Reinvention Labs, but millions more who are not yet engaged. We hope it will transform the habits, culture, and performance of all federal organizations.

Some may say that the task is too large; that we should not attempt it because we are bound to make mistakes; that it cannot be done. But we have no choice. Our government is in trouble. It has lost its sense of mission; it has lost its ethic of public service; and, most importantly, it has lost the faith of the American people.

In times such as these, the most dangerous course is to do nothing. We must have
the courage to risk change.

NOTES

1. Data taken from the following sources:
"The average American . . .," Senator
William Roth, vol. 138 no. 51, Cong. Rec.
(April 7, 1992), p. S1; "Five out of every
six Americans . . .," CBS News Poll, unpublished, May 27–30, 1992, released June
1, 1992; "Only 20 percent . . .," an ABC
News-Washington Post poll, taken April
23–26, 1993, asked: "How much of the
time do you trust the government in
Washington to do what is right: Just about
always, most of the time, or only some of
the time?" Four percent said "just about
always," 16 percent said "most of the time,"
74 percent said "only some of the time,"
and 6 percent volunteered "none of the
time;" 1963 figure, University of Michigan
poll, cited in "From Camelot to Clinton:
A Statistical Portrait of the United
States," *Washington Post* (August 23, 1993),
p. A15.

2. U.S. General Accounting Office (GAO),
*High-Risk Series: Defense Inventory Manage-
ment*, GAO/HR-93-12 (December 1992).

3. U.S. Office of Management and Budget
(OMB), *Budget of the U.S. Government FY
93* (Washington, D.C., 1992) and *Budget of
the U.S. Government FY 94* (Washington,
D.C., 1993); and interview with Department of Housing and Urban Development
Budget Officer Herbert Purcell, August
26, 1993.

4. U.S. Congress, Senate, Committee on Ap-
propriations, Subcommittee on Education,
Labor and Health and Human Services,
testimony of Clarence C. Crawford, U.S.
GAO, "Multiple Employment Programs:
National Employment Training Strategy
Needed," June 18, 1993.

5. Democratic Leadership Council, *The Road
to Realignment: The Democrats and the Perot
Voters* (Washington, D.C.: Democratic
Leadership Council, July 1993), p. III-12.

Pollster Stanley Greenberg asked people if
they agreed that "government always manages to mess things up." Seventy-two percent of Perot voters agreed, 64 percent of
Clinton voters agreed, and 66 percent of
Bush voters agreed.

6. Dilulio, John J., Jr., Gerald Garvey, and
Donald F. Kettl, *Improving Government
Performance: An Owner's Manual* (Washington, D.C.: Brookings Institution,
1993), p. 79.

7. Yankelovich, Daniel, *American Values and
Public Policy* (Washington, D.C.: Democratic Leadership Council, 1992), p. 7.

8. National Performance Review Accompanying Report, *Transforming Organizational
Structures* (Washington, D.C.: U.S. Government Printing Office [GPO], September
1993).

9. Finegan, Jay, "Four-Star Management," *Inc.*
(January 1987), pp. 42–51; Osborne, David, and Ted Gaebler, *Reinventing Government: How the Entrepreneurial Spirit is
Transforming the Public Sector* (Reading,
MA: Addison-Wesley Publishing Company, Inc., 1992), pp. 255–259; and
Creech, General W. L., "Leadership and
Management—The Present and the Future," address presented at the Armed Services Leadership and Management Symposium (October 11–14, 1983) (available
from the Office of the Assistant Secretary
of Defense for Installations, Pentagon,
Washington, D.C.).

10. National Performance Review Accompanying Report, *Improving Customer Service*
(Washington, D.C. U.S. GPO, September
1993).

11. U.S. Department of Agriculture, Forest
Service, Regional Office, *Profile of a Reinvented Government Organization* (Milwau-
kee, WI, May 24, 1993); "The U.S. Forest
Service: Decentralizing Authority," *Government Executive* (March 1993), pp. 23–4;
and interviews with Forest Service officials.

12. The President's Fiscal 1994 budget (page
40) estimates 2.1 million Federal non-
postal workers and 1.8 million military for
1994. Manpower, Inc. employs 560,000.
General Motors employs 362,000.

44

Creating the Multicultural Organization: The Challenge of Managing Diversity

Taylor Cox Jr.

As we enter the twenty-first century, human capital has taken center stage in the business strategies of enlightened organizations. Attracting, retaining, and effectively using people are increasingly the top priorities of leaders in all kinds of organizations, from high-tech firms to universities, from government agencies to heavy manufacturing firms. In the United States a very tight labor market has intensified the focus on leveraging human capital in recent years. Compounding the challenges posed by more jobs chasing fewer people are additional challenges posed by the increasing diversity of people with the skills to do the work those jobs require.

Consider, for example, the case of gender diversity. In the 1950s three of every four college degrees in the United States went to men; in recent years the majority (around 54 percent) of college graduates have been women. Similarly, in 1971 U.S. women earned fewer than 4 percent of all graduate-level business management degrees; by the early 1990s this figure had multiplied more than sevenfold to around 30 percent. In hot technical fields like engineering, the rates of increase in the participation of women have been even greater.

The shift of worker identity is not limited to gender. Fueled by a variety of factors, including differential birth rates, work groups are increasingly diverse in terms of race and national origin.[1] In addition, more and more organizations are reorganizing work so that it is performed by teams composed of people from different organizational levels and work specializations.

These trends and others, such as increases in the number of working mothers and dual-career couples, make managing diversity a critical competency for today's organizations. Although forward-thinking executives have acknowledged the importance of an effective response to these trends for years, many are finding that the challenges of diversity are not easily met. After more than a decade of work following the clarion calls spawned by the Workforce 2000 report of the Hudson Institute in 1987,[2] many organizations are finding that the goal of creating a multicultural work culture that both welcomes and leverages diversity remains elusive. . . .

DEFINING DIVERSITY

The term *diversity* has many interpretations. I believe it is neither so broad as to mean *any* difference between people nor so narrow as to be limited to differences of gender and race. Diversity is not another name for affirmative action, nor a name for nontraditional or "minority group" members of organizations, nor a synonym for EEO (equal employment opportunity). Rather, I define diversity as follows:

> Diversity is the variation of social and cultural identities among people existing together in a defined employment or market setting.

Source: Taylor Cox Jr., *Creating the Multicultural Organization* (John Wiley & Sons, 2001), pp. 1–15. © 2001. This material is used by permission of John Wiley & Sons, Inc.

In this definition the phrase *social and cultural identity* refers to the personal affiliations with groups that research has shown to have significant influence on people's major life experiences. These affiliations include gender, race, national origin, religion, age cohort, and work specialization, among others. *Employment and market systems* include churches, schools, factory work teams, industrial customers, end-use consumers, baseball teams, military units, and so on. The geographic scope of the employment-market settings includes local, regional, national, and global settings.

As a characteristic of work groups, diversity creates challenges and opportunities that are not present in homogeneous work groups. By *managing diversity* I mean understanding its effects and implementing behaviors, work practices, and policies that respond to them in an effective way.

PROBLEMS AND OPPORTUNITIES OF DIVERSITY

Although the existence of diversity in the workforce is now widely recognized in organizations throughout the world, it is too often viewed only in terms of legal compliance and human rights protection. In reality the implications of diversity are much more demanding and much more interesting. Increasing diversity presents a double-edged sword; hence the challenge of managing diversity is to create conditions that *minimize* its potential to be a performance barrier while *maximizing* its potential to enhance organizational performance.

Diversity as a Potential Performance Barrier
Theory and research indicate that the presence of diversity in an organization or work group can create obstacles to high performance for several reasons. To begin, diversity can reduce the effectiveness of communication and increase conflict among workers. Compared to more homogeneous work

groups, workers in diverse work groups may also experience lower levels of social attraction and display lower levels of commitment to the group. In addition, diversity-related effects such as identity harassment and discrimination behaviors can increase organizations' costs.[3] . . .

Diversity as Value-Added Activity
The other side of the double-edged sword is that managing diversity well can improve the performance of organizations on a variety of criteria.

First and foremost in the minds of many executives I work with is the criterion of implementing the values of fairness and respect for all people. These values are ubiquitous in formal statements of policy in organizations throughout the world. Too often, however, they are just words on laminated cards that draw snickers from the workforce because they have no real substance. These values will never be anything but meaningless platitudes unless the organization has an effective and ongoing strategy for managing diversity.

Because the achievement of all core values is a key part of the mission of organizations, making fairness and respect for all people a reality is a part of business strategy in its own right, independent of the linkage of these ideals to financial performance. This is an important principle. . . .

In addition to fulfilling organizational values, well-managed diversity can add value to an organization by (1) improving problem solving, (2) increasing creativity and innovation, (3) increasing organizational flexibility, (4) improving the quality of personnel through better recruitment and retention, and (5) improving marketing strategies, especially for organizations that sell products or services to end users. . . .

Problem Solving. First, diversity in work groups can increase revenues through improved problem solving and decision making. Diverse groups have a broader and richer base of experience from which to approach a problem. In addition, diversity enhances critical analysis in decision-making groups. In a series of research studies, Charlene Nemeth found that groups subjected to minority views were better at critically analyzing decision issues and alternatives than those that were not. The presence of minority views improved the quality of the decision-making process, regardless of whether or not the minority view ultimately prevailed. Although Nemeth was studying the effects of minority opinions and not differences of social or cultural group identity per se, the fact that members of minority identity groups often hold different worldviews from majority group members makes this research relevant to diversity in work groups.[4]

The prospective benefits of diversity in problem solving do not necessarily happen by simply mixing people together who are culturally different. Research also suggests that the effect of diversity on the quality of problem solving depends greatly on the extent to which the diversity is proactively managed. In one of the classic studies of this type, Harry Triandis and his colleagues compared the problem-solving scores of homogeneous groups with those of two types of more diverse groups: (1) diverse with training and (2) diverse without training. They found that the diverse groups that were not trained on the existence and implications of their differences actually produced lower problem-solving scores than the homogeneous groups. In contrast, the diverse groups that were trained produced scores that averaged six times higher than those of the homogeneous groups. A similar result was found in some recent research on diversity of ethnicity and national origin.[5] This research suggests that beyond simply diversifying the workforce, organizations need to manage diversity proactively in order to reap its potential benefits for better problem solving.

Creativity and Innovation. Creativity and innovation can enhance virtually all organizational activities. . . . If there is evidence suggesting that diversity in work teams promotes creativity and innovation, then diversity is a potential resource to improve these important organizational activities. I will cite a few examples of such evidence.

In her 1983 book *The Change Masters* (Simon & Schuster), Rosabeth Moss Kanter notes that high levels of innovation occur in companies that

- Have done a better job of eradicating racism, sexism, and classism
- Tend to have workforces that are more diverse with respect to race and gender
- Are more deliberate than less innovative companies in taking steps to create heterogeneous work teams

In a similar vein, research on educational institutions in the late 1970s shows that the most innovative schools are also the most tolerant of diversity.[6] My own research comparing ethnically diverse teams to all-Anglo teams doing a marketing task shows that the diverse teams outperformed the homogeneous ones by about 10 percent.[7]

Organizational Flexibility. The existence of diversity and the adaptations organizations make to accommodate it should lead to greater flexibility. One way that diversity can make organizations more flexible is through changes in the patterns of employees' cognitive structures, that is, their typical ways of organizing and responding to information. For example, there is some evidence that women tend to have more tolerance for ambiguity than men—a quality that has been linked to both higher levels of cognitive complexity and the ability to perform ambiguous tasks.[8] Similarly, studies on bilingual and monolingual cultural groups in various nations have shown that bilingual individuals tend to have higher levels of cognitive flexibility and of divergent thinking than monolinguals. Because diversifying the workforce increases the presence of people who speak two or more languages, it indirectly increases flexibility of thought.[9]

The responses an organization makes to diversity can also lead to greater flexibility as a kind of by-product. For example, broadening policies and reducing standardization tend to make the organization more fluid and adaptable. This increased fluidity should allow the organization to respond to environmental changes faster and at lower cost. Although this line of reasoning is somewhat speculative and not based on research, the logic seems compelling.

Human Talent. Given today's increasingly diverse labor market, organizations that are best at attracting, retaining, and using the skills of diverse workers will enjoy a competitive advantage. . . .

. . . Organizations that are effective at attracting, retaining, and using people from only one or two social-cultural groups will be at a disadvantage compared to those that are equally effective with people from a variety of backgrounds. This is a quality issue because the capabilities of employed people are a major raw material in all organizations. . . .

Marketing Strategy. An important consequence of the rising globalization of business is that consumer markets, like the workplace, are becoming increasingly diverse. An automobile manufacturer in Japan cannot afford to ignore the fact that nearly half of all new-car buyers in the United States are women, regardless of the gender composition of car buyers in Japan. Likewise, no reasonable person in the consumer goods industry can afford to ignore the fact that roughly a quarter of the world's population is Chinese or that immigration to the United States from mostly Asian and Latin American countries is occurring at the rate of more than one million people per year. In the United States, Asians, blacks, and Hispanics now collectively represent nearly $500 billion annually in consumer spending. Because research on consumer behavior has consistently shown that sociocultural identities affect buying behavior, marketing success will depend, to some de-

gree, on the ability of companies to understand and respond effectively to the cultural nuances of the diverse marketplace.[10] . . .

This brief review of some of the pertinent research makes the point that managing diversity well can lead to better results on a variety of performance dimensions. Achieving these results, however, requires that organizations manage the complex challenges of diversity far more effectively than most firms have been able to. Why past efforts have often fallen short is the subject of the next section.

WHY PAST EFFORTS HAVE FAILED

Although recognition of the potential problems and benefits of diversity has increased in recent years, many organizations have been disappointed with the results they have achieved in their efforts to meet the diversity challenge. A case in point is Alcoa Inc. When I was asked in December of 1996 to begin working with Alcoa's corporate diversity committee, the message to me went something like this:

> We have been working on improving our company to include and utilize the full skills of people who are different from our traditional workforce for many years, but despite what seems to us like a lot of effort, we still have a workforce that is dominated by white, U.S.-born men, and our progress in moving people of other backgrounds into top positions in the company has been very slow. In addition, we continue to get feedback from the workforce, including some of our highest-ranking women and nonwhite men, that the company is not very hospitable to people who come from different social and cultural backgrounds than our traditional workforce. What are we doing wrong? How can we move this to another level of accomplishment?

. . . My contacts with hundreds of managers from dozens of companies in recent years tell me that Alcoa is far from alone in its frustration about less-than-hoped-for results on diversity goals.

I have learned that there are three main reasons why many past efforts have been disappointing: (1) misdiagnosis of the problem, (2) wrong solution (that is, failure to use a systemic approach), and (3) failure to understand the shape of the learning curve for leveraging diversity work. . . .

Misdiagnosis of the Problem

The root cause of many failures to manage and leverage diversity is a misdiagnosis of the problem. The problem posed by diversity is not simply that there are not enough people of certain social-cultural identity groups in the organization. Nor is it primarily one of making insensitive people more aware that identity matters, although this is certainly a part of what needs to happen. Bigoted and insensitive people do exist, and they are a significant barrier to the presence of diversity and to realization of its benefits, but this is a very superficial diagnosis of the problem. The more significant problem is that *most employers have an organizational culture that is somewhere between toxic and deadly when it comes to handling diversity*. The result is that the presence of real diversity is unsustainable as a characteristic of the organization.

Let me say more about what I mean by *real* diversity. Research has shown that differences of social-cultural identity such as gender, national origin, race, and work specialization represent real differences in *culture*. These group identities should therefore be regarded as micro-culture groups.[11] Organizations, however, tend to hire people who are perceived as fitting the existing culture of their firm. Moreover, because many organizations deal with cultural differences by exerting strong pressure on new employees to assimilate to existing organizational norms (acculturation by assimilation), real differences tend to diminish over time.[12] Due to the pressure to conform, members who have high cultural distance from prevailing norms of the work culture tend to either leave the organization or modify their thinking—and their behavior—to achieve acceptance. The result is that apparent differences of cultural groups, such as

an increasing presence of women, may represent only small differences in worldviews.

The presence of a diversity-toxic culture is the ultimate cause of the failure of organizations to successfully embrace diversity in its members. . . .

Wrong Approach

The second major reason for past failure to manage diversity effectively is the selection of the wrong approach to meeting the challenge of diversity. This mistake follows directly from the failure to accurately diagnose the problem. In the typical case, the problem diagnosis is limited to "insufficient diversity," and the solution consequently focuses on changing inputs to the system. This involves such actions as creating multifunctional and cross-level work teams, placing foreign nationals on the board and in key developmental assignments in the host country, and recruiting more women and racial-minority men. There is no question that this change in the composition of human inputs is an important step toward changing the culture, especially if the changes include positions of high decision-making authority. However, this is only one element of the system. Systems theory tells us that the elements of a system are highly interdependent so that change in one element requires adjustments in all the others if the system is to function effectively (and, I would add, if the new elements are to survive and prosper).[13] Unfortunately, the approach of new inputs has usually not been accompanied by corresponding changes in the other elements of the system. The result is a predictable suboptimization or even outright failure of the change effort.

Here is a simple example to illustrate what I mean. Recruiting is an element of the organizational system that has received great emphasis in past efforts to manage diversity. A typical scenario in the United States is that the organization makes an effort to hire more racial minorities and women for management and professional jobs. However, as the hiring criteria remain otherwise unchanged, the organization continues to hire and promote people who have a low tolerance for working with women and racial-minority men. The result is that the cultural minority hires encounter unnecessary barriers to contribution that at best are overcome with extra effort and at worst lead to turnover or subpar job performance. Extend this logic to other system elements, such as employee development, performance appraisal, compensation, mentoring, and so on, and you can begin to see the startling implications.

What organizations need, therefore, is an approach to change that aggressively pursues the deliberate and knowledgeable alignment of all other elements in the system with the changes in human inputs. . . .

Misunderstanding of the Learning Curve

The third major reason for past failures is misunderstanding the shape of the learning curve for leveraging diversity. Here I use the term *learning curve* in a broad sense to capture the development of the organization and its members toward competence to welcome and use diversity as a resource. Leaders often act as though the learning curve is steep, with the achievement of a high level of competence occurring after only a few months or a year of concerted effort. On the contrary, I have found that the learning curve on diversity work is much flatter, requiring years of conscientious effort to achieve a high level of proficiency. For example, at the time of this writing, my work with Alcoa is entering its fifth year, and yet there is general agreement that many areas of the company are still in the early stages of the curve.

When leaders make the mistake of acting as though a flat learning curve is steep, their behavior becomes dysfunctional. They become impatient about seeing results, tend to shift their focus to other things, and prematurely withdraw attention to the process being used to create change. All of these responses are deadly to the prospect of creating real, sustainable change.

This point highlights once again how important it is to diagnose the problem accurately. Misdiagnosis leads to the wrong approach for action and the wrong timetable for seeing results. In addition, I challenge you to be sincere about what you are doing when you tackle the challenges of diversity. Leaders often say they understand that creating a welcoming climate for diversity is a culture change and requires years of intense effort, but their actions contradict their words. For instance, if after just one year of work, progress on diversity is no longer a topic of significant discussion when business plans are reviewed, this sends the wrong message about priorities and suggests a naïve notion of what it takes to institutionalize diversity competency.

Of course, meeting the challenges of diversity involves more than correctly diagnosing the problem and having the will and determination for long-term commitment to the effort. Those who lead this change work must know how to go about the process of changing the organizational culture. The next chapter presents a model to meet this need that is already producing measurable results.

NOTES

1. William B. Johnston, "Global Work Force 2000: The New World Labor Market," *Harvard Business Review* (March-April 1991): 115–127.

2. William B. Johnston and Arnold H. Packer, *Workforce 2000: Work and Workers for the Twenty-First Century* (Indianapolis, Ind.: Hudson Institute; Washington, D.C.: U.S. Department of Labor, 1987).

3. For reviews and references see Taylor Cox Jr. and Ruby L. Beale, *Developing Competency to Manage Diversity: Readings, Cases & Activities* (San Francisco: Berrett-Koehler, 1997) and Kathleen Williams and Charles O'Reilly, "1998 Demography and Diversity in Organizations: A Review of 40 Years of Research," in *Research in Organizational Behavior* 20 (1997): 77–140.

4. For Nemeth's research see Charlene J. Nemeth, "Dissent, Group Process, and Creativity," *Advances in Group Processes* 2 (1985): 57–75; "Differential Contributions of Majority and Minority Influence," *Psychological Review* 93 (1986): 23–32; Charlene J. Nemeth and J. Wachter, "Creative Problem Solving as a Result of Majority Versus Minority Influence," *European Journal of Social Psychology* 13 (1983): 45–55.

5. See Harry C. Triandis, E. R. Hall, and R. B. Ewen, "Member Heterogeneity and Dyadic Creativity," *Human Relations* 18 (1965): 33–55; Nancy Adler, *International Dimensions of Organization Behavior* (Boston: Kent Publishing, 1986).

6. Saul Siegel and William Kammerer, "Measuring the Perceived Support for Innovation in Organizations," *Journal of Applied Psychology* 63 (1978): 553–562.

7. Poppy L. McLeod, Sharon A. Lobel, and Taylor Cox Jr., "Ethnic Diversity and Creativity in Small Groups," *Small Group Research* 27 (1996): 248–264.

8. See, for example, N. G. Rotter and A. N. O'Connell, "The Relationships Among Sex-Role Orientation, Cognitive Complexity and Tolerance for Ambiguity," *Sex Roles* 8 (1982): 1209–1220; David Shaffer, Clyde Hendrick, Robert Regula, and Joseph Freconna, "Interactive Effects of Ambiguity Tolerance and Task Effort on Dissonance Reduction," *Journal of Personality* 41 (1973): 224–233.

9. See the review of this research by Wallace Lambert, "The Effects of Bilingualism on the Individual: Cognitive and Sociocultural Consequences," in P. A. Hurnbey (ed.), *Bilingualism: Psychological, Social and Educational Implications* (San Diego: Academic Press, 1977), pp. 15–27.

10. See Richard A. Levy, "Ethnic & Racial Differences in Response to Medicines: Preserving Individualized Therapy in Managed Pharmaceutical Programs" (Reston, Virginia: National Pharmaceutical Council, 1993); John A. McCarty, "Current Theory and Research on Cross-Cultural Factors in Consumer Behavior," in *Advances in Consumer Research* 16 (1989), pp. 127–129; David K. Tse, Kam-hon Lee, Illan Vertinsky, and Donald A. Wehrung, "Does Culture Matter? A Cross-Cultural Study of Executives' Choice, Decisiveness, and Risk Adjustment in International Marketing," *Journal of Marketing* 52 (October 1988): 81–85.

11. For examples of this research see the following: Taylor Cox Jr. and Joycelyn Finley, "An Analysis of Work Specialization and Organization Level as Dimensions of Workforce Diversity," in Martin Chemers, Stuart Oskamp, and Mark Costanzo (eds.), *Diversity in Organizations* (Newbury Park, Calif.: Sage, 1995): pp. 62–90; J. Barnett, "Understanding Group Effects Within Organizations: A Study of Group Attitudes and Behaviors of Engineers and Scientists," (Ph.D. diss., The Fielding Institute, Santa Barbara, Calif., 1994); Sally Helgesen, *The Female Advantage: Women's Ways of Leadership* (New York: Doubleday, 1990); Deborah Tannen, *Talking from 9 to 5* (New York: Avon, 1995); Rosalie L. Tung, "People's Republic of China," in R. Nath (ed.), *Comparative Management: A Regional View* (Cambridge, Mass.: Ballinger, 1988a): pp. 139–168; Stephen B. Knouse, Paul Rosenfeld, and Amy L. Culbertson (eds.), *Hispanics in the Workplace* (Sage, 1992).

12. See the following for a detailed discussion of organizational acculturation processes: Taylor Cox Jr. and J. Finley-Nickelson, "Models of Acculturation for Intra-Organizational Cultural Diversity," *Canadian Journal of Administrative Sciences* 8 (1991): 90–100.

13. For example, see Daniel Katz and Robert Kahn, *The Social Psychology of Organizations*, 2nd ed. (New York: Wiley, 1978).

CHAPTER 9

Theories of Organizations and Environments

Theoretical models of organizations underwent a major change starting during the decade of the 1960s when the "open systems perspective" gained support and essentially displaced the "closed system models" (Scott, 2003). The primary focus of research and theory building shifted from the internal characteristics of organizations to the external dynamics of organizational competition, interaction, and interdependency. The *organizations as open systems* perspective views organizations as systems of interdependent activities embedded in and dependent on wider environments. Organizations not only acquire material, financial, and human resources from their environment, they also gain social support and legitimacy. Thus, the focus of theory and research from the open systems perspective inevitably moved to the interactions and interdependencies among organizations and their environments.

Most observers concur that the open systems perspective began to dominate organization theory in 1966–1967 when two of the most influential modern works in organization theory were published: Daniel Katz and Robert Kahn's *The Social Psychology of Organizations* (1966), which articulated the concept of organizations as open systems; and James D. Thompson's coherent statement of the rational systems/contingency perspective of organizations, in *Organizations in Action* (1967). Systems theories of organization have two major conceptual themes or components: (1) applications of Ludwig von Bertalanffy's (1951, 1968) general systems theory to organizations and (2) the use of quantitative tools and techniques to understand complex relationships among organizational and environmental variables and thereby to optimize decisions.

A *system* is any organized collection of parts united by prescribed interactions and designed for the accomplishment of specific goals or general purposes (Boulding, 1956). Thus, it is easy to see why general systems theory provides an important perspective for understanding modern organizations. Systems theory views an organization as a complex set of dynamically intertwined and interconnected elements, including its inputs, processes, outputs, and feedback loops, and the environment in which it operates and with which it continuously interacts. A change in any element of the system causes changes in other elements. The interconnections tend to be complex, dynamic, and often unknown; thus, when management makes decisions involving one organizational element, unanticipated impacts usually occur throughout the organizational system. Systems theorists study these interconnections, frequently using organizational decision processes and information and control systems as their focal points of analysis.

Whereas classical organization theory tends to be single-dimensional and somewhat simplistic, open systems theories tend to be multidimensional and complex in their assumptions about organizational cause-and-effect relationships. The classicalists viewed organizations as static structures; systems theorists see organizations as always-changing processes of interactions among organizational and environmental elements. Organizations are not static, but rather are in constantly shifting states of dynamic equilibrium. They are adaptive systems that are integral parts of their environments. Organizations must adjust to changes in their environment if they are to survive; in turn, virtually all of their decisions and actions affect their environment.

Norbert Wiener's classic model of an organization as an adaptive system, from his 1948 book *Cybernetics*, epitomizes these basic theoretical perspectives of the systems perspective. *Cybernetics*, from a Greek word meaning "steersman," was used by Wiener to mean the multidisciplinary study of the structures and functions of control and information-processing systems in animals and machines. The basic concept behind cybernetics is self-regulation—through biological, social, or technological systems that can identify problems, do something about them, and receive feedback to adjust themselves automatically. Wiener, a mathematician, developed the concept of cybernetics while working on antiaircraft systems during World War II. Variations on this simple model of a system have been used extensively by systems theorists for many years, particularly around the development and use of management information systems, but we have not been able to locate anyone who used it before Wiener did in 1948.

The search for order among complex variables has led to an extensive reliance on quantitative analytical methods and models. The systems approach is strongly cause-and-effect oriented ("positivist") in its philosophy and methods (Ott, 1989, Chapter 5). In these respects, systems theories have close ties to the scientific management approach of Frederick Winslow Taylor. Whereas Taylor used quantitative scientific methods to find "the one best way," the systems theorist uses quantitative scientific methods to identify cause-and-effect relationships and to find *optimal solutions*. In this sense, the conceptual approaches and purposes between the two perspectives are strikingly similar. Systems theories are often called *management sciences* or *administrative sciences*.

Computers, models, and interdisciplinary teams of analysts are the *tools* of the systems perspective. Studies of organizations done by its proponents typically use the scientific method and quasi-experimental research techniques, or computer models. This quantitative orientation reflects the systems school's origins in the years immediately following World War II, when the first serious attempts were made to apply mathematical and statistical probability models to organizational processes and decision making. Many of the early efforts started under the label of operations analysis, or operations research, in defense industry–related "think tanks" such as the RAND Corporation of Santa Monica, California. *Operations research* or *operations analysis* refers to the use of mathematical and scientific techniques to develop a quantitative basis for organizational decision making (Raiffa, 1968). During the subsequent decades, defense and aerospace programs provided the development and testing settings for many of the tools and techniques of operations research, including PERT (Program Evaluation and Review Technique), CPM (Critical Path Method), statistical inference, linear programming, gaming, Monte Carlo methods, and simulation.

Katz and Kahn provided the intellectual basis for merging classical, neoclassical, human relations/behavioral, "modern" structural, and systems perspectives of organizations. They balanced these perspectives through their concept of organizations as open systems—systems that include organizations and their environments. Because organizations are open systems, they must continuously adapt to changing environmental factors, and managers must recognize that all organizational decisions and actions in turn influence their environments. Reprinted here is "Organizations and the System Concept," a chapter from *The Social Psychology of Organizations*, wherein Katz and Kahn conclude that the traditional closed-system view of organizations has led to a failure to fully appreciate the interdependencies and interactions between organizations and their environments. Katz and Kahn's concept of open systems has influenced the thinking of many organization theorists.

Classical organization theorists saw organizations as rational but closed systems that pursued the goal of economic efficiency. Because the systems were viewed as "closed" and thus not subject to influence from the external environment, major attention could be focused on such functions as planning and/or controlling. James D. Thompson, in his influential 1967 book *Organizations in Action*, classifies most organizations as open systems. Reprinted here are the book's first two chapters, in which he suggests that the closed-system approach may be realistic only at the technical level of organizational operations. Thompson seeks to bridge the gap between open and closed systems by postulating that organizations "abhor uncertainty" and deal with it in the environment by creating specific elements designed to cope with the outside world, while other elements are able to focus on the rational nature of technical operations. The dominant technology used by an organization strongly influences its structure, activities, and evaluation/control processes.

Meyer and Rowan (1977) emphasize cultural and institutional environmental influences while arguing that the modern world contains socially constructed practices and norms that provide the framework for the creation and elaboration of formal organizations. As open systems, organizations gain legitimacy and support to the extent that they accept these norms as appropriate ways to organize. This line of argument, called *institutional theory*, asserts that the world is a product of our ideas and conceptions; our socially created and validated meanings *define* reality. The rise of the modern world as we know it was not caused solely by new production technologies and administrative structures for coordinating complex activities. The growth of certain beliefs and cognitions about the nature of the world and the way things happen—and *should* happen—also shaped the modern world. Beliefs about organizations and institutions are created and reinforced by a wide range of actors and forces, including universities, professional groups, public opinion, the mass media, the state, and laws (Scott, 2003). According to institutional theory, an organization's life chances are significantly improved by an organization's demonstrated conformity to the norms and social expectations of the institutional environments. Thus, environments are sources of legitimacy and support. Many of the environmental forces that affect organizations are not based on the values of efficiency or effectiveness but instead on social and cultural pressures to conform to a prescribed structural form.

Another open system theory, *resource dependency theory*, stresses that all organizations exchange resources with their environment as a condition for survival. Pfeffer and Salancik (1978) explain that one cannot understand the structure and behavior of an organization without understanding the context within which it operates. No organizations are self-sufficient, and thus they must engage in exchanges with their environment in order to survive. Organizations need to acquire resources from their environment, and the importance and scarcity of these resources determine the extent of organizational dependency in and on their environment. For example, "information" is a resource organizations need to reduce uncertainty and dependency. Therefore, organizations seek information to survive.

In the final reading on organizations and environment, Carroll and Hannan (2000) draw on the theories of *organizational ecology* to explore theories, models, methods, and data used in demographic approaches to organizational studies. Organizational ecologists assess the applicability of bioecological models to the study of organization-environment relations. From this perspective, organizational environments are the loci of competition, selection, and survival of the fittest. Organizational ecological models resemble Darwinian theories of evolution in which natural selection processes operate in and among organizations. Organizations do not adapt to their changing environments by making decisions; instead, the environment selects the fittest among different organizational forms.

Carroll and Hannan explain how "populations of organizations" change over time through the processes of founding, growth, decline, transformation, and mortality. The organizational ecology approach differs from other open systems theory approaches in that it focuses on populations of organizations rather than individual organizational units. Organizational ecology attempts to explain why certain types or species of organizations survive and multiply whereas others languish and die. Environmental selection is the prime process by which change occurs in organizations; for example, variation in structural forms is more likely to be caused by environmental selection than by adaptation. Environments differentially select organizations for survival on the basis of the fit between organization forms and environmental characteristics. The stronger the pressures are from within or outside an organization, the less flexibly adaptive it can be and the higher the likelihood that environmental selection will prevail (Hannan & Freeman, 1977). The general factors leading to higher mortality rates among organizations are: the liability of newness, the liability of smallness, and the density dependence.

REFERENCES

Bertalanffy, L. von (1951, December). General systems theory: A new approach to unity of science. *Human Biology, 23*, 303–361.

Bertalanffy, L. von (1968). *General systems theory: Foundations, development, applications.* New York: George Braziller.

Boulding, K. E. (1956, April). General systems theory: The skeleton of science. *Management Science, 2*(3), 197–208.

Carroll, G. R., & M. T. Hannan (2000). *Demography of corporations and industries.* Princeton, NJ: Princeton University Press.

Hannan, M. T., & J. Freeman (1989). *Organizational ecology.* Cambridge, MA: Harvard University Press.

Katz, D., & R. L. Kahn (1966). *The social psychology of organizations.* New York: Wiley.

Meyer, J. W., & B. Rowan (1977). Institutionalized organizations: Formal structures as myth and ceremony. *American Journal of Sociology, 83*, 340–363.

Ott, J. S. (1989). *The organizational culture perspective.* Ft. Worth, TX: Harcourt Brace.

Pfeffer, J., & G. R. Salancik (1978). *The external control of organizations: A resource dependence perspective.* New York: Harper & Row.

Raiffa, H. (1968). *Decision analysis.* Reading, MA: Addison-Wesley.

Scott, W. R. (2003). *Organizations: Rational, natural, and open systems* (5th ed.). Upper Saddle River, NJ: Prentice Hall.

Thompson, J. D. (1967). *Organizations in action.* New York: McGraw-Hill.

Wiener, N. (1948). *Cybernetics.* Cambridge, MA: MIT Press.

45

Organizations and the System Concept

Daniel Katz & Robert L. Kahn

The aims of social science with respect to human organizations are like those of any other science with respect to the events and phenomena of its domain. The social scientist wishes to understand human organizations, to describe what is essential in their form, aspects, and functions. He wishes to explain their cycles of growth and decline, to predict their effects and effectiveness. Perhaps he wishes as well to test and apply such knowledge by introducing purposeful changes into organizations—by making them, for example, more benign, more responsive to human needs.

Such efforts are not solely the prerogative of social science, however; common sense approaches to understanding and altering organizations are ancient and perpetual. They tend, on the whole, to rely heavily on two assumptions: that the location and nature of an organization are given by its name; and that an organization is possessed of built-in goals—because such goals were implanted by founders, decreed by its present leaders, or because they emerged mysteriously as the purposes of the organizational system itself. These assumptions scarcely provide an adequate basis for the study of organizations and at times can be misleading and even fallacious. We propose, however, to make use of the information to which they point.

The first problem in understanding an organization or a social system is its location and identification. How do we know that we are dealing with an organization? What are its boundaries? What behavior belongs to the organization and what behavior lies outside it? Who are the individuals whose

actions are to be studied and what segments of their behavior are to be included?

The fact that popular names exist to label social organizations is both a help and a hindrance. These popular labels represent the socially accepted stereotypes about organizations and do not specify their role structure, their psychological nature, or their boundaries. On the other hand, these names help in locating the area of behavior in which we are interested. Moreover, the fact that people both within and without an organization accept stereotypes about its nature and functioning is one determinant of its character.

The second key characteristic of the common sense approach to understanding an organization is to regard it simply as the epitome of the purposes of its designer, its leaders, or its key members. The teleology of this approach is again both a help and a hindrance. Since human purpose is deliberately built into organizations and is specifically recorded in the social compact, the bylaws, or other formal protocol of the undertaking, it would be inefficient not to utilize these sources of information. In the early development of a group, many processes are generated which have little to do with its rational purpose, but over time there is a cumulative recognition of the devices for ordering group life and a deliberate use of these devices.

Apart from formal protocol, the primary mission of an organization as perceived by its leaders furnishes a highly informative set of clues for the researcher seeking to study organizational functioning. Nevertheless, the stated purposes of an organization as

Source: Daniel Katz and Robert L. Kahn, *The Social Psychology of Organizations* (New York: John Wiley & Sons, 1966), pp. 14–29 (footnotes renumbered). © 1966 John Wiley & Sons, Inc. Reprinted by permission of John Wiley & Sons, Inc.

given by its by-laws or in the reports of its leaders can be misleading. Such statements of objectives may idealize, rationalize, distort, omit, or even conceal some essential aspects of the functioning of the organization. Nor is there always agreement about the mission of the organization among its leaders and members. The university president may describe the purpose of his institution as one of turning out national leaders; the academic dean sees it as imparting the cultural heritage of the past, the academic vice-president as enabling students to move toward self-actualization and development, the graduate dean as creating new knowledge, the dean of men as training youngsters in technical and professional skills which will enable them to earn their living, and the editor of the student newspaper as inculcating the conservative values which will preserve the status quo of an outmoded capitalistic society.

The fallacy here is one of equating the purposes or goals of organizations with the purposes and goals of individual members. The organization as a system has an output, a product or an outcome, but this is not necessarily identical with the individual purposes of group members. Though the founders of the organization and its key members do think in teleological terms about organization objectives, we should not accept such practical thinking, useful as it may be, in place of a theoretical set of constructs for purposes of scientific analysis. Social science, too frequently in the past, has been misled by such short-cuts and has equated popular phenomenology with scientific explanation.

In fact, the classic body of theory and thinking about organizations has assumed a teleology of this sort as the easiest way of identifying organizational structures and their functions. From this point of view an organization is a social device for efficiently accomplishing through group means some stated purpose; it is the equivalent of the blueprint for the design of the machine which is to be created for some practical objective. The essential difficulty with this purposive or design approach is that an or-

ganization characteristically includes more and less than is indicated by the design of its founder or the purpose of its leader. Some of the factors assumed in the design may be lacking or so distorted in operational practice as to be meaningless, while unforeseen embellishments dominate the organizational structure. Moreover, it is not always possible to ferret out the designer of the organization or to discover the intricacies of the design which he carried in his head. The attempt by Merton to deal with the latent function of the organization in contrast with its manifest function is one way of dealing with this problem.[1] The study of unanticipated consequences as well as anticipated consequences of organizational functioning is a similar way of handling the matter. Again, however, we are back to the purposes of the creator or leader, dealing with unanticipated consequences on the assumption that we can discover the consequences anticipated by him and can lump all other outcomes together as a kind of error variance.

It would be much better theoretically, however, to start with concepts which do not call for identifying the purposes of the designers and then correcting for them when they do not seem to be fulfilled. The theoretical concepts should begin with the input, output, and functioning of the organization as a system and not with the rational purposes of its leaders. We may want to utilize such purposive notions to lead us to sources of data or as subjects of special study, but not as our basic theoretical constructs for understanding organizations.

Our theoretical model for the understanding of organizations is that of an energic input-output system in which the energic return from the output reactivates the system. Social organizations are flagrantly open systems in that the input of energies and the conversion of output into further energic input consist of transactions between the organization and its environment.

All social systems, including organizations, consist of the patterned activities of a number of individuals. Moreover, these patterned activities are complementary or interdependent with respect to some common output or outcome; they are repeated, relatively enduring, and bounded in space and time. If the activity pattern occurs only once or at unpredictable intervals, we could not speak of an organization. The stability or recurrence of activities can be examined in relation to the *energic input* into the system, the *transformation of energies within the system*, and the *resulting product or energic output*. In a factory the raw materials and the human labor are the energic input, the patterned activities of production the transformation of energy, and the finished product the output. To maintain this patterned activity requires a continued renewal of the inflow of energy. This is guaranteed in social systems by the energic return from the product or outcome. Thus the outcome of the cycle of activities furnishes new energy for the initiation of a renewed cycle. The company which produces automobiles sells them and by doing so obtains the means of securing new raw materials, compensating its labor force, and continuing the activity pattern.

In many organizations outcomes are converted into money and new energy is furnished through this mechanism. Money is a convenient way of handling energy units both on the output and input sides, and buying and selling represent one set of social rules for regulating the exchange of money. Indeed, these rules are so effective and so widespread that there is some danger of mistaking the business of buying and selling for the defining cycles of organization. It is a commonplace executive observation that businesses exist to make money, and the observation is usually allowed to go unchallenged. It is, however, a very limited statement about the purposes of business.

Some human organizations do not depend on the cycle of selling and buying to maintain themselves. Universities and public agencies depend rather on bequests and legislative appropriations, and in so-called voluntary organizations the output reenergizes the activity of organization members in a more direct fashion. Member activities

and accomplishments are rewarding in themselves and tend therefore to be continued, without the mediation of the outside environment. A society of bird watchers can wander into the hills and engage in the rewarding activities of identifying birds for their mutual edification and enjoyment. Organizations thus differ on this important dimension of the source of energy renewal, with the great majority utilizing both intrinsic and extrinsic sources in varying degree. Most large-scale organizations are not as self-contained as small voluntary groups and are very dependent upon the social effects of their output for energy renewal.

Our two basic criteria for identifying social systems and determining their functions are (1) tracing the pattern of energy exchange or activity of people as it results in some output and (2) ascertaining how the output is translated into energy which reactivates the pattern. We shall refer to organizational functions or objectives not as the conscious purposes of group leaders or group members but as the outcomes which are the energic source for a maintenance of the same type of output.

This model of an energic input-output system is taken from the open system theory as promulgated by von Bertalanffy.[2] Theorists have pointed out the applicability of the system concepts of the natural sciences to the problems of social science. It is important, therefore, to examine in more detail the constructs of system theory and the characteristics of open systems.

System theory is basically concerned with problems of relationships, of structure, and of interdependence rather than with the constant attributes of objects. In general approach it resembles field theory except that its dynamics deal with temporal as well as spatial patterns. Older formulations of system constructs dealt with the closed systems of the physical sciences, in which relatively self-contained structures could be treated successfully as if they were independent of external forces. But living systems, whether biological organisms or social organizations, are acutely dependent upon their external environment and so must be conceived of as open systems.

Before the advent of open-system thinking, social scientists tended to take one of two approaches in dealing with social structures; they tended either (1) to regard them as closed systems to which the laws of physics applied or (2) to endow them with some vitalistic concept like entelechy. In the former case they ignored the environmental forces affecting the organization and in the latter case they fell back upon some magical purposiveness to account for organizational functioning. Biological theorists, however, have rescued us from this trap by pointing out that the concept of the open system means that we neither have to follow the laws of traditional physics, nor in deserting them do we have to abandon science. The laws of Newtonian physics are correct generalizations but they are limited to closed systems. They do not apply in the same fashion to open systems which maintain themselves through constant commerce with their environment, i.e., a continuous inflow and outflow of energy through permeable boundaries.

One example of the operation of closed versus open systems can be seen in the concept of entropy and the second law of thermodynamics. According to the second law of thermodynamics a system moves toward equilibrium; it tends to run down, that is, its differentiated structures tend to move toward dissolution as the elements composing them become arranged in random disorder. For example, suppose that a bar of iron has been heated by the application of a blowtorch on one side. The arrangement of all the fast (heated) molecules on one side and all the slow molecules on the other is an unstable state, and over time the distribution of molecules becomes in effect random, with the resultant cooling of one side and heating of the other, so that all surfaces of the iron approach the same temperature. A similar process of heat exchange will also be going on between the iron bar and its environment, so that the bar will gradually approach the temperature of the room in which it is located, and in so doing will elevate somewhat the previous temperature of the room. More technically, entropy increases toward a maximum and equilibrium occurs as the physical system attains the state of the most probable distribution of its elements. In social systems, however, structures tend to become more elaborated rather than less differentiated. The rich may grow richer and the poor may grow poorer. The open system does not run down, because it can import energy from the world around it. Thus the operation of entropy is counteracted by the importation of energy and the living system is characterized by negative rather than positive entropy.

COMMON CHARACTERISTICS OF OPEN SYSTEMS

Though the various types of open systems have common characteristics by virtue of being open systems, they differ in other characteristics. If this were not the case, we would be able to obtain all our basic knowledge about social organizations through the study of a single cell.

The following nine characteristics seem to define all open systems.

1. Importation of Energy

Open systems import some form of energy from the external environment. The cell receives oxygen from the blood stream; the body similarly takes in oxygen from the air and food from the external world. The personality is dependent upon the external world for stimulation. Studies of sensory deprivation show that when a person is placed in a darkened soundproof room, where he has a minimal amount of visual and auditory stimulation, he develops hallucinations and other signs of mental stress.[3] Deprivation of social stimulation also can lead to mental disorganization.[4] Kohler's studies of the figural after-effects of continued stimulation show the dependence of perception upon its energic support from the external world.[5] Animals deprived of visual experience from birth for a prolonged period never fully recover their visual capacities.[6] In other words, the functioning personality is heavily dependent upon the continuous inflow of stimulation from the external environment. Similarly, social organizations must also draw renewed supplies of energy from other institutions, or people, or the material environment. No social structure is self-sufficient or self-contained.

2. The Through-Put

Open systems transform the energy available to them. The body converts starch and sugar into heat and action. The personality converts chemical and electrical forms of stimulation into sensory qualities, and information into thought patterns. The organization creates a new product, or processes materials, or trains people, or provides a service. These activities entail some reorganization of input. Some work gets done in the system.

3. The Output

Open systems export some products into the environment, whether it be the invention of an inquiring mind or a bridge constructed by an engineering firm. Even the biological organism exports physiological products such as carbon dioxide from the lungs, which helps to maintain plants in the immediate environment.

4. Systems as Cycles of Events

The pattern of activities of the energy exchange has a cyclic character. The product exported into the environment furnishes the sources of energy for the repetition of the cycle of activities. The energy reinforcing the cycle of activities can derive from some exchange of the product in the external world or from the activity itself. In the former instance, the industrial concern utilizes raw materials and human labor to turn out a product which is marketed, and the monetary return is used to obtain more raw

materials and labor to perpetuate the cycle of activities. In the latter instance, the voluntary organization can provide expressive satisfactions to its members so that the energy renewal comes directly from the organizational activity itself.

The problem of structure, or the relatedness of parts, can be observed directly in some physical arrangement of things where the larger unit is physically bounded and its subparts are also bounded within the larger structure. But how do we deal with social structures, where physical boundaries in this sense do not exist? It was the genius of F. H. Allport which contributed the answer, namely that the structure is to be found in an interrelated set of events which return upon themselves to complete and renew a cycle of activities.[7] It is events rather than things which are structured, so that social structure is a dynamic rather than a static concept. Activities are structured so that they comprise a unity in their completion or closure. A simple linear stimulus-response exchange between two people would not constitute social structure. To create structure, the responses of A would have to elicit B's reactions in such a manner that the responses of the latter would stimulate A to further responses. Of course the chain of events may involve many people, but their behavior can be characterized as showing structure only when there is some closure to the chain by a return to its point of origin with the probability that the chain of events will then be repeated. The repetition of the cycle does not have to involve the same set of phenotypical happenings. It may expand to include more subevents of exactly the same kind or it may involve similar activities directed toward the same outcomes. In the individual organism the eye may move in such a way as to have the point of light fall upon the center of the retina. As the point of light moves, the movements of the eye may also change but to complete the same cycle of activity, i.e., to focus upon the point of light.

A single cycle of events of a self-closing character gives us a simple form of structure. But such single cycles can also combine to give a larger structure of events or an event system. An event system may consist of a circle of smaller cycles or hoops, each one of which makes contact with several others. Cycles may also be tangential to one another from other types of subsystems. The basic method for the identification of social structures is to follow the energic chain of events from the input of energy through its transformation to the point of closure of the cycle.

5. Negative Entropy

To survive, open systems must move to arrest the entropic process; they must acquire negative entropy. The entropic process is a universal law of nature in which all forms of organization move toward disorganization or death. Complex physical systems move toward simple random distribution of their elements and biological organisms also run down and perish. The open system, however, by importing more energy from its environment than it expends, can store energy and can acquire negative entropy. There is then a general trend in an open system to maximize its ratio of imported to expended energy, to survive and even during periods of crisis to live on borrowed time. Prisoners in concentration camps on a starvation diet will carefully conserve any form of energy expenditure to make the limited food intake go as far as possible.[8] Social organizations will seek to improve their survival position and to acquire in their reserves a comfortable margin of operation.

The entropic process asserts itself in all biological systems as well as in closed physical systems. The energy replenishment of the biological organism is not of a qualitative character which can maintain indefinitely the complex organizational structure of living tissue. Social systems, however, are not anchored in the same physical constancies as biological organisms and so are capable of almost indefinite arresting of the entropic process. Nevertheless the number of organizations which go out of existence every year is large.

6. Information Input, Negative Feedback, and the Coding Process

The inputs into living systems consist not only of energic materials which become transformed or altered in the work that gets done. Inputs are also informative in character and furnish signals to the structure about the environment and about its own functioning in relation to the environment. Just as we recognize the distinction between cues and drives in individual psychology, so must we take account of information and energic inputs for all living systems.

The simplest type of information input found in all systems is negative feedback. Information feedback of a negative kind enables the system to correct its deviations from course. The working parts of the machine feed back information about the effects of their operation to some central mechanism or subsystem which acts on such information to keep the system on target. The thermostat which controls the temperature of the room is a simple example of a regulatory device which operates on the basis of negative feedback. The automated power plant would furnish more complex examples. Miller emphasizes the critical nature of negative feedback in his proposition: "When a system's negative feedback discontinues, its steady state vanishes, and at the same time its boundary disappears and the system terminates."[9] If there is no corrective device to get the system back on its course, it will expend too much energy or it will ingest too much energic input and no longer continue as a system.

The reception of inputs into a system is selective. Not all energic inputs are capable of being absorbed into every system. The digestive system of living creatures assimilates only those inputs to which it is adapted. Similarly, systems can react only to those information signals to which they are attuned. The general term for the selective mechanisms of a system by which incoming materials are rejected or accepted and translated for the structure is coding. Through the coding process, the "blooming, buzzing confusion" of the world is simplified into a few meaningful and simplified categories for a given system. The nature of the functions performed by the system determines its coding mechanisms, which in turn perpetuate this type of functioning.

7. The Steady State and Dynamic Homeostasis

The importation of energy to arrest entropy operates to maintain some constancy in energy exchange, so that open systems which survive are characterized by a steady state. A steady state is not motionless or a true equilibrium. There is a continuous inflow of energy from the external environment and a continuous export of the products of the system, but the character of the system, the ratio of the energy exchanges and the relations between parts, remains the same. The catabolic and anabolic processes of tissue breakdown and restoration within the body preserve a steady state so that the organism from time to time is not the identical organism it was but a highly similar organism. The steady state is seen in clear form in the homeostatic processes for the regulation of body temperature; external conditions of humidity and temperature may vary, but the temperature of the body remains the same. The endocrine glands are a regulatory mechanism for preserving an evenness of physiological functioning. The general principle here is that of Le Châtelier who maintains that any internal or external factor making for disruption of the system is countered by forces which restore the system as closely as possible to its previous state.[10] Krech and Crutchfield similarly hold, with respect to psychological organization, that cognitive structures will react to influences in such a way as to absorb them with minimal change to existing cognitive integration.[11]

The homeostatic principle does not apply literally to the functioning of all complex living systems, in that in counteracting entropy they move toward growth and expansion. This apparent contradiction can be resolved, however, if we recognize the complexity of the subsystems and their interaction in anticipating changes necessary for the maintenance of an overall steady state. Stagner has pointed out that the initial disturbance of a given tissue constancy within the biological organism will result in mobilization of energy to restore the balance, but that recurrent upsets will lead to actions to anticipate the disturbance:

> We eat before we experience intense hunger pangs. . . . energy mobilization for forestalling tactics must be explained in terms of a *cortical tension* which reflects the visceral-proprioceptive pattern of the original biological disequilibration. . . . *Dynamic homeostasis* involves the maintenance of tissue constancies by establishing a constant physical environment—by reducing the variability and disturbing effects of external stimulation. Thus the organism does not simply restore the prior equilibrium. A new, more complex and more comprehensive equilibrium is established.[12]

Though the tendency toward a steady state in its simplest form is homeostatic, as in the preservation of a constant body temperature, the basic principle is *the preservation of the character of the system*. The equilibrium which complex systems approach is often that of a quasi-stationary equilibrium, to use Lewin's concept.[13] An adjustment in one direction is countered by a movement in the opposite direction and both movements are approximate rather than precise in their compensatory nature. Thus a temporal chart of activity will show a series of ups and downs rather than a smooth curve.

In preserving the character of the system, moreover, the structure will tend to import more energy than is required for its output, as we have already noted in discussing negative entropy. To insure survival, systems will operate to acquire some margin of safety beyond the immediate level of existence. The body will store fat, the social organization will build up reserves, the society will increase its technological and cultural base. Miller has formulated the proposition that the rate of growth of a system—within certain ranges—is exponential if it exists in a medium which makes available unrestricted amounts of energy for input.[14]

In adapting to their environment, systems will attempt to cope with external forces by ingesting them or acquiring control over them. The physical boundedness of the single organism means that such attempts at control over the environment affect the behavioral system rather than the biological system of the individual. Social systems will move, however, towards incorporating within their boundaries the external resources essential to survival. Again the result is an expansion of the original system.

Thus, the steady state which at the simple level is one of homeostasis over time, at more complex levels becomes one of preserving the character of the system through growth and expansion. The basic type of system does not change directly as a consequence of expansion. The most common type of growth is a multiplication of the same type of cycles or subsystems—a change in quantity rather than in quality. Animal and plant species grow by multiplication. A social system adds more units of the same essential type as it already has. Haire has studied the ratio between the sizes of different subsystems in growing business organizations.[15] He found that though the number of people increased in both the production subsystem and the subsystem concerned with the external world, the ratio of the two groups remained constant. Qualitative change does occur, however, in two ways. In the first place, quantitative growth calls for supportive subsystems of a specialized character not necessary when the system was smaller. In the second place, there is a point where quantitative changes produce a qualitative difference in the functioning of a system. A small college which triples its size is no longer the same institution in terms of the relation between its administration and faculty, relations among the various academic departments, or the nature of its instruction.

In time, living systems exhibit a growth or expansion dynamic in which they maximize their basic character. They react to change or they anticipate change through growth which assimilates the new energic inputs to the nature of their structure. In terms of Lewin's quasi-stationary equilibrium the ups and downs of the adjustive process do not always result in a return to the old level. Under certain circumstances a solidification or freezing occurs during one of the adjustive cycles. A new base line level is thus established and successive movements fluctuate around this plateau which may be either above or below the previous plateau of operation.

8. Differentiation

Open systems move in the direction of differentiation and elaboration. Diffuse global patterns are replaced by more specialized functions. The sense organs and the nervous system evolved as highly differentiated structures from the primitive nervous tissues. The growth of the personality proceeds from primitive, crude organizations of mental functions to hierarchically structured and well-differentiated systems of beliefs and feelings. Social organizations move toward the multiplication and elaboration of roles with greater specialization of function. In the United States today medical specialists now outnumber the general practitioners.

One type of differentiated growth in systems is what von Bertalanffy terms progressive mechanization. It finds expression in the way in which a system achieves a steady state. The early method is a process which involves an interaction of various dynamic forces, whereas the later development entails the use of a regulatory feedback mechanism. He writes:

> It can be shown that the primary regulations in organic systems, that is, those which are most fundamental and primitive in embryonic development as well as in evolution, are of such nature of dynamic interaction. . . . Superimposed are those regulations which we may call secondary, and which are controlled by fixed arrangements, especially of the feedback type. This state of affairs is a consequence of a general principle of organization which may be called progressive mechanization. At

first, systems—biological, neurological, psychological or social—are governed by dynamic interaction of their components; later
on, fixed arrangements and conditions of
constraint are established which render the
system and its parts more efficient, but also
gradually diminish and eventually abolish its
equipotentiality.[16]

9. Equifinality

Open systems are further characterized by
the principle of equifinality, a principle suggested by von Bertalanffy in 1940.[17] According to this principle, a system can reach
the same final state from differing initial
conditions and by a variety of paths. The
well-known biological experiments on the
sea urchin show that a normal creature of
that species can develop from a complete
ovum, from each half of a divided ovum, or
from the fusion product of two whole ova.
As open systems move toward regulatory
mechanisms to control their operations,
the amount of equifinality may be reduced.

SOME CONSEQUENCES OF
VIEWING ORGANIZATIONS
AS OPEN SYSTEMS

[In a later chapter] we shall inquire into
the specific implications of considering organizations as open systems and into the
ways in which social organizations differ
from other types of living systems. At this
point, however, we should call attention to
some of the misconceptions which arise
both in theory and practice when social organizations are regarded as closed rather
than open systems.

The major misconception is the failure
to recognize fully that the organization is
continually dependent upon inputs from
the environment and that the inflow of materials and human energy is not a constant.
The fact that organizations have built-in
protective devices to maintain stability and
that they are notoriously difficult to change
in the direction of some reformer's desires

should not obscure the realities of the dynamic interrelationships of any social structure with its social and natural environment. The very efforts of the organization
to maintain a constant external environment produce changes in organizational
structure. The reaction to changed inputs
to mute their possible revolutionary implications also results in changes.

The typical models in organizational theorizing concentrate upon principles of internal functioning as if these problems were
independent of changes in the environment and as if they did not affect the maintenance inputs of motivation and morale.
Moves toward tighter integration and coordination are made to insure stability,
when flexibility may be the more important
requirement. Moreover, coordination and
control become ends in themselves rather
than means to an end. They are not seen in
full perspective as adjusting the system to
its environment but as desirable goals
within a closed system. In fact, however,
every attempt at coordination which is not
functionally required may produce a host of
new organizational problems.

One error which stems from this kind of
misconception is the failure to recognize
the equifinality of the open system, namely
that there are more ways than one of producing a given outcome. In a closed physical system the same initial conditions must
lead to the same final result. In open systems this is not true even at the biological
level. It is much less true at the social level.
Yet in practice we insist that there is one
best way of assembling a gun for all recruits,
one best way for the baseball player to hurl
the ball in from the outfield and that we
standardize and teach these best methods.
Now it is true under certain conditions that
there is one best way, but these conditions
must first be established. The general principle, which characterizes all open systems,
is that there does not have to be a single
method for achieving an objective.

A second error lies in the notion that irregularities in the functioning of a system
due to environmental influences are error

variances and should be treated accordingly. According to this conception, they should be controlled out of studies of organizations. From the organization's own operations they should be excluded as irrelevant and should be guarded against. The decisions of officers to omit a consideration of external factors or to guard against such influences in a defensive fashion, as if they would go away if ignored, is an instance of this type of thinking. So is the now outmoded "public be damned" attitude of businessmen toward the clientele upon whose support they depend. Open system theory, on the other hand, would maintain that environmental influences are not sources of error variance but are integrally related to the functioning of a social system, and that we cannot understand a system without a constant study of the forces that impinge upon it.

Thinking of the organization as a closed system, moreover, results in a failure to develop the intelligence or feedback function of obtaining adequate information about the changes in environmental forces. It is remarkable how weak many industrial companies are in their market research departments when they are so dependent upon the market. The prediction can be hazarded that organizations in our society will increasingly move toward the improvements of the facilities for research in assessing environmental forces. The reason is that we are in the process of correcting our misconception of the organization as a closed system.

Emery and Trist have pointed out how current theorizing on organizations still reflects the older closed system conceptions. They write:

> In the realm of social theory, however, there has been something of a tendency to continue thinking in terms of a "closed" system, that is, to regard the enterprise as sufficiently independent to allow most of its problems to be analyzed with reference to its internal structure and without reference to its external environment. . . . In practice the system theorists in social science . . . did "tend to focus on the statics of social structure and to neglect the study of structural change." In an attempt

to overcome this bias, Merton suggested that "the concept of strain, stress and tension on the structural level, provides an analytical approach to the study of dynamics and change." This concept has been widely accepted by system theorists but while it draws attention to sources of imbalance within an organization it does not conceptually reflect the mutual permeation of an organization and its environment that is the cause of such imbalance. It still retains the limiting perspectives of "closed system" theorizing. In the administrative field the same limitations may be seen in the otherwise invaluable contributions of Barnard and related writers.[18]

SUMMARY

The open-system approach to organizations is contrasted with common-sense approaches, which tend to accept popular names and stereotypes as basic organizational properties and to identify the purpose of an organization in terms of the goals of its founders and leaders.

The open-system approach, on the other hand, begins by identifying and mapping the repeated cycles of input, transformation, output, and renewed input which comprise the organizational pattern. This approach to organizations represents the adaptation of work in biology and in the physical sciences by von Bertalanffy and others.

Organizations as a special class of open systems have properties of their own, but they share other properties in common with all open systems. These include the importation of energy from the environment, the through-put or transformation of the imported energy into some product form which is characteristic of the system, the exporting of that product into the environment, and the reenergizing of the system from sources in the environment.

Open systems also share the characteristics of negative entropy, feedback, homeostasis, differentiation, and equifinality. The law of negative entropy states that systems survive and maintain their characteristic internal order only so long as they import from the environment more energy than they expend in the process of transformation and exportation. The feedback principle has to do with information input, which is a special kind of energic importation, a kind of signal to the system about environmental conditions and about the functioning of the system in relation to its environment. The feedback of such information enables the system to correct for its own malfunctioning or for changes in the environment, and thus to maintain a steady state or homeostasis. This is a dynamic rather than a static balance, however. Open systems are not at rest but tend toward differentiation and elaboration, both because of subsystem dynamics and because of the relationship between growth and survival. Finally, open systems are characterized by the principle of equifinality, which asserts that systems can reach the same final state from different initial conditions and by different paths of development.

Traditional organizational theories have tended to view the human organization as a closed system. This tendency has led to a disregard of differing organizational environments and the nature of organizational dependency on environment. It has led also to an overconcentration on principles of internal organizational functioning, with consequent failure to develop and understand the processes of feedback which are essential to survival.

NOTES

1. Merton, R. K. 1957. *Social theory and social structure*, rev. ed. New York: Free Press.

2. von Bertalanffy, L. 1956. General system theory. *General Systems*. Yearbook of the Society for the Advancement of General System Theory, *1*, 1–10.

3. Solomon, P., *et al.* (Eds.) 1961. *Sensory deprivation*. Cambridge, Mass: Harvard University Press.

4. Spitz, R. A. 1945. Hospitalism: an inquiry into the genesis of psychiatric conditions in early childhood. *Psychoanalytic Study of the Child*, *1*, 53–74.

5. Kohler, W., & H. Wallach. 1944. Figural after-effects: an investigation of visual processes. *Proceedings of the American Philosophical Society*, 88, 269–357. Also, Kohler, W., & D. Emery. 1947. Figural after-effects in the third dimension of visual space. *American Journal of Psychology*, 60, 159–201.

6. Melzack, R., & W. Thompson. 1956. Effects of early experience on social behavior. *Canadian Journal of Psychology*, 10, 82–90.

7. Allport, F. H. 1962. A structuronomic conception of behavior: individual and collective. I. Structural theory and the master problem of social psychology. *Journal of Abnormal and Social Psychology*, 64, 3–30.

8. Cohen, E. 1954. *Human behavior in the concentration camp*. London: Jonathan Cape.

9. Miller, J. G. 1955. Toward a general theory for the behavioral sciences. *American Psychologist*, 10, 513–531; quote from p. 529.

10. See Bradley, D. F., & M. Calvin. 1956. Behavior: imbalance in a network of chemical transformations. *General Systems*. Yearbook of the Society for the Advancement of General System Theory, *1*, 56–65.

11. Krech, D., & R. Crutchfield. 1948. *Theory and problems of social psychology*. New York: McGraw-Hill.

12. Stagner, R. 1951. Homeostasis as a unifying concept in personality theory. *Psychological Review*, 58, 5–17; quote from p. 5.

13. Lewin, K. 1947. Frontiers in group dynamics. *Human Relations*, *1*, 5–41.

14. Miller, *op. cit.*

15. Haire, M. 1959. Biological models and empirical histories of the growth of organizations. In M. Haire (Ed.), *Modern organization theory*, New York: Wiley, 272–306.

16. von Bertalanffy. 1956, *op. cit*, p. 6.

17. von Bertalanffy, L. 1940. Der organismus als physikalisches system betrachtet. *Naturwissenschaften*, 28, 521 ff.

18. Emery, F. E., & E. L. Trist. 1960. Sociotechnical systems. In *Management sciences models and techniques*. Vol. 2, London: Pergamon Press; quote from p. 84.

46

Organizations in Action

James D. Thompson

STRATEGIES FOR STUDYING ORGANIZATIONS

Complex organizations—manufacturing firms, hospitals, schools, armies, community agencies—are ubiquitous in modern societies, but our understanding of them is limited and segmented.

The fact that impressive and sometimes frightening consequences flow from organizations suggests that some individuals have had considerable insight into these social instruments. But insight and private experiences may generate private understandings without producing a public body of knowledge adequate for the preparation of a next generation of administrators, for designing new styles of organizations for new purposes, for controlling organizations, or for appreciation of distinctive aspects of modern societies.

What we know or think we know about complex organizations is housed in a variety of fields or disciplines, and communication among them more nearly resembles a trickle than a torrent.[1] Although each of the several schools has its unique terminology and special heroes, Gouldner was able to discern two fundamental models underlying most of the literature.[2] He labeled these the "rational" and "natural-system" models of organizations, and these labels are indeed descriptive of the results.

To Gouldner's important distinction we wish to add the notion that the rational model results from a *closed-system strategy* for studying organizations, and that the natural-system model flows from an *open-system strategy*.

Closed-System Strategy

The Search for Certainty. If we wish to predict accurately the state a system will be in presently, it helps immensely to be dealing with a *determinate system*. As Ashby observes, fixing the present circumstances of a determinate system will determine the state it moves to next, and since such a system cannot go to two states at once, the transformation will be unique.[3]

Fixing the present circumstances requires, of course, that the variables and relationships involved be few enough for us to comprehend and that we have control over or can reliably predict all of the variables and relations. In other words, it requires that the system be closed or, if closure is not complete, that the outside forces acting on it be predictable.

Now if we have responsibility for the future states or performances of some system, we are likely to opt for a closed system. Bartlett's research on mental processes, comparing "adventurous thinking" with "thinking in closed systems," suggests that there are strong human tendencies to reduce various forms of knowledge to the closed-system variety, to rid them of all ultimate uncertainty.[4] If such tendencies appear in puzzle-solving as well as in everyday situations, we would especially expect them to be emphasized when responsibility and high stakes are added. Since much of the literature about organizations has been generated as a by-product of the search for improved efficiency or performance, it is not surprising that it employs closed-system assumptions—employs a rational model—about orga-

Source: James D. Thompson, *Organizations in Action* (Piscataway, NJ: Transaction Publishers, 2003), pp. 3–24. Used by permission of Transaction Publishers.

nizations. Whether we consider *scientific management*,[5] *administrative management*,[6] or *bureaucracy*,[7] the ingredients of the organization are deliberately chosen for their necessary contribution to a goal, and the structures established are those deliberately intended to attain highest efficiency.

Three Schools in Caricature. Scientific management, focused primarily on manufacturing or similar production activities, clearly employs economic efficiency as its ultimate criterion, and seeks to maximize efficiency by planning procedures according to a technical logic, setting standards, and exercising controls to ensure conformity with standards and thereby with the technical logic. Scientific management achieves conceptual closure of the organization by assuming that goals are known, tasks are repetitive, output of the production process somehow disappears, and resources in uniform qualities are available.

Administrative-management literature focuses on structural relationships among production, personnel, supply, and other service units of the organization; and again employs as the ultimate criterion economic efficiency. Here efficiency is maximized by specializing tasks and grouping them into departments, fixing responsibility according to such principles as span of control or delegation, and controlling action to plans. Administrative management achieves closure by assuming that ultimately a master plan is known, against which specialization, departmentalization, and controls are determined. (That this master plan is elusive is shown by Simon.[8]) Administrative management also assumes that production tasks are known, that output disappears, and that resources are automatically available to the organization.

Bureaucracy also follows the pattern noted above, focusing on staffing and structure as means of handling clients and disposing of cases. Again the ultimate criterion is efficiency, and this time it is maximized by defining offices according to jurisdiction and place in a hierarchy, appointing experts to offices, establishing rules for categories of activity, categorizing cases or clients, and then motivating proper performance of expert officials by providing salaries and patterns for career advancement. [The extended implications of the assumptions made by bureaucratic theory are brought out by Merton's discussion of "bureaucratic personality."[9]] Bureaucratic theory also employs the closed system of logic. Weber saw three holes through which empirical reality might penetrate the logic, but in outlining his "pure type" he quickly plugged these holes. Policymakers, somewhere above the bureaucracy, could alter the goals, but the implications of this are set aside. Human components—the expert office-holders—might be more complicated than the model describes, but bureaucratic theory handles this by divorcing the individual's private life from his life as an officeholder through the use of rules, salary, and career. Finally, bureaucratic theory takes note of outsiders—clientele—but nullifies their effects by depersonalizing and categorizing clients.

It seems clear that the rational-model approach uses a closed-system strategy. It also seems clear that the developers of the several schools using the rational model have been primarily students of performance or efficiency, and only incidentally students of organizations. Having focused on control of the organization as a target, each employs a closed system of logic and conceptually closes the organization to coincide with that type of logic, for this elimination of uncertainty is the way to achieve determinateness. The rational model of an organization results in everything being functional—making a positive, indeed an optimum, contribution to the overall result. All resources are appropriate resources, and their allocation fits a master plan. All action is appropriate action, and its outcomes are predictable.

It is no accident that much of the literature on the management or administration of complex organization centers on the concepts of *planning* or *controlling*. Nor is it any accident that such views are dismissed by those using the open-system strategy.

Open-System Strategy

The Expectation of Uncertainty. If, instead of assuming closure, we assume that a system contains more variables than we can comprehend at one time, or that some of the variables are subject to influences we cannot control or predict, we must resort to a different sort of logic. We can, if we wish, assume that the system is determinate by nature, but that it is our incomplete understanding which forces us to expect surprise or the intrusion of certainty. In this case we can employ a natural-system model.

Approached as a natural system, the complex organization is a set of interdependent parts which together make up a whole because each contributes something and receives something from the whole, which in turn is interdependent with some larger environment. Survival of the system is taken to be the goal, and the parts and their relationships presumably are determined through evolutionary processes. Dysfunctions are conceivable, but it is assumed that an offending part will adjust to produce a net positive contribution or be disengaged, or else the system will degenerate.

Central to the natural-system approach is the concept of homeostasis, or self-stabilization, which spontaneously, or naturally, governs the necessary relationships among parts and activities and thereby keeps the system viable in the face of disturbances stemming from the environment.

Two Examples in Caricature. Study of the *informal organization* constitutes one example of research in complex organizations using the natural-system approach. Here attention is focused on variables which are not included in any of the rational models — sentiments, cliques, social controls via informal norms, status and status striving, and so on. It is clear that students of informal organization regard these variables not as random deviations or error, but as pat-

terned, adaptive responses of human beings in problematic situations.[10] In this view the formal organization is a spontaneous and functional development, indeed a necessity, in complex organizations, permitting the system to adapt and survive.

A second version of the natural-system approach is more global but less crystallized under a label. This school views the organization as a unit in interaction with its environment, and its view was perhaps most forcefully expressed by Chester Barnard[11] and by the empirical studies of Selznick[12] and Clark.[13] This stream of work leads to the conclusion that organizations are not autonomous entities; instead, the best laid plans of managers have unintended consequences and are conditioned or upset by other social units — other complex organizations or publics — on whom the organization is dependent.

Again it is clear that in contrast to the rational-model approach, this research area focuses on variables not subject to complete control by the organization and hence not contained within a closed system of logic. It is also clear that students regard interdependence of organization and environment as inevitable or natural, and as adaptive or functional.

Choice or Compromise?

The literature about organizations, or at least much of it, seems to fall into one of the two categories, each of which at best tends to ignore the other and at worse denies the relevance of the other. The logics associated with each appear to be incompatible, for one avoids uncertainty to achieve determinateness, while the other assumes uncertainty and indeterminateness. Yet the phenomena treated by each approach, as distinct from the explanations of each, cannot be denied.

Viewed in the large, complex organizations are often effective instruments for achievement, and that achievement flows from planned, controlled action. In every sphere — educational, medical, industrial, commercial, or governmental — the quality or costs of goods or services may be challenged and questions may be raised about the equity of distribution within the society of the fruits of complex organizations. Still millions live each day on the assumption that a reasonable degree of purposeful, effective action will be forthcoming from the many complex organizations on which they depend. Planned action, not random behavior, supports our daily lives. Specialized, controlled, patterned action surrounds us.

There can be no question but that the rational model of organizations directs our attention to important phenomena—to important "truth" in the sense that complex organizations viewed in the large exhibit some of the patterns and results to which the rational model attends, but which the natural-system model tends to ignore. But it is equally evident that phenomena associated with the natural-system approach also exist in complex organizations. There is little room to doubt the universal emergence of the informal organization. The daily news about labor-management negotiations, interagency jurisdictional squabbles, collusive agreements, favoritism, breeches of contract, and so on, are impressive evidence that complex organizations are influenced in significant ways by elements of their environments, a phenomenon addressed by the natural-system approach but avoided by the rational. Yet most versions of the natural-system approach treat organizational purposes and achievements as peripheral matters.

It appears that each approach leads to some truth, but neither alone affords an adequate understanding of complex organizations. Gouldner calls for a synthesis of the two models, but does not provide the synthetic model.

Meanwhile, a serious and sustained elaboration of Barnard's work [14] has produced a newer tradition which evades the closed-versus open-system dilemma.

A Newer Tradition

What emerges from the Simon-March-Cyert stream of study is the organization as a problem-facing and problem-solving phenomenon. The focus is on organizational processes related to choice of courses of action in an environment which does not fully disclose the alternatives available or the consequences of those alternatives. In this view, the organization has limited capacity to gather and process information or to predict consequences of alternatives. To deal with situations of such great complexity, the organization must develop processes for *searching* and *learning,* as well as for *deciding.* The complexity, if fully faced, would overwhelm the organization, hence it must set limits to its definitions of situations; it must make decisions in *bounded rationality.*[15] This requirement involved replacing the maximum-efficiency criterion with one of satisfactory accomplishment, decision-making now involving *satisficing* rather than *maximizing.*[16]

These are highly significant notions, and it will become apparent that this book seeks to extend this "newer tradition." The assumptions it makes are consistent with the open-system strategy, for it holds that the processes going on within the organization are significantly affected by the complexity of the organization's environment. But this tradition also touches on matters important in the closed-system strategy; performance and deliberate decisions.

But despite what seem to be obvious advantages, the Simon-March-Cyert stream of work has not entirely replaced the more extreme strategies, and we need to ask why so many intelligent men and women in a position to make the same observations we have been making should continue to espouse patently incomplete views of complex organizations.

The Cutting Edge of Uncertainty. Part of the answer to that question undoubtedly lies in the fact that supporters of each strategy have had different purposes in mind, with open-system strategists attempting to understand organizations per se, and closed-system strategists interested in organizations mainly as vehicles for rational achievements. Yet this answer does not seem completely satisfactory, for these students could not have been entirely unaware of the challenges to their assumptions and beliefs.

We can suggest now that rather than reflecting weakness in those who use them, the two strategies reflect something fundamental about the cultures surrounding complex organizations—the fact that our culture does not contain concepts for simultaneously thinking about rationality and indeterminateness. These appear to be incompatible concepts, and we have no ready way of thinking about something as half-closed, half-rational. One alternative, then, is the closed-system approach of ignoring uncertainty to see rationality; another is to ignore rational action in order to see spontaneous processes. The newer tradition with its focus on organizational coping with uncertainty is indeed a major advance. It is notable that a recent treatment by Crozier starts from the bureaucratic position but focuses on coping with uncertainty as its major topic.[17]

Yet in directing our attention to processes for meeting uncertainty, Simon, March, and Cyert may lead us to overlook the useful knowledge amassed by the older approaches. If the phenomena of rational models are indeed observable, we may want to incorporate some elements of those models; and if natural-system phenomena occur, we should also benefit from the relevant theories. For purposes of this volume, then, *we will conceive of complex organizations as open systems, hence indeterminate and faced with uncertainty, but at the same time as subject to criteria of rationality and hence needing determinateness and certainty.*

The Location of Problems

As a starting point, we will suggest that the phenomena associated with open- and closed-system strategies are not randomly distributed through complex organizations, but instead tend to be specialized by location. To introduce this notion we will start with Parsons' suggestion that organizations exhibit three distinct levels of responsibil-ity and control—*technical, managerial,* and *institutional.*[18]

In this view, every formal organization contains a suborganization whose "problems" are focused around effective performance of the technical function—the conduct of classes by teachers, the processing of income tax returns and the handling of recalcitrants by the bureau, the processing of material and supervision of these operations in the case of physical production. The primary exigencies to which the technical suborganization is oriented are those imposed by the nature of the technical task, such as the materials, which must be processed and the kinds of cooperation of different people required to get the job done effectively.

The second level, the managerial, *services* the technical suborganization by (1) mediating between the technical suborganization and those who use its products—the customers, pupils, and so on—and (2) procuring the resources necessary for carrying out the technical functions. The managerial level *controls,* or administers, the technical suborganization (although Parsons notes that its control is not unilateral) by deciding such matters as the broad technical task which is to be performed, the scale of operations, employment and purchasing policy, and so on.

Finally, in the Parsons formulation, the organization which consists of both technical and managerial suborganizations is also part of a wider social system which is the source of the "meaning," or higher-level support which makes the implementation of the organization's goals possible. In terms of "formal" controls, an organization may be relatively independent; but in terms of the meaning of the functions performed by the organization and hence of its "rights" to command resources and to subject its customers to discipline, it is never wholly independent. This overall articulation of the organization and the institutional structure and agencies of the community is the function of the third, or institutional, level of the organization.

Parsons' distinction of the three levels becomes more significant when he points out that at each of the two points of articulation between them there is a *qualitative* break in the simple continuity of "line" authority because the functions at each level are qualitatively different. Those at the second level are not simply lower-order spellings-out of the top level functions. Moreover, the articulation of levels and functions rests on a two-way interaction, with each side, by withholding its important contribution, in a position to interfere with the functioning of the other and of the larger organization.

If we now reintroduce the conception of the complex organization as an open system subject to criteria of rationality, we are in a position to speculate about some dynamic properties of organizations. As we suggested, the logical model for achieving complete technical rationality uses a closed system of logic—closed by the elimination of uncertainty. In practice, it would seem, the more variables involved, the greater the likelihood of uncertainty, and it would therefore be advantageous for an organization subject to criteria of rationality to remove as much uncertainty as possible from its *technical core* by reducing the number of variables operating on it. Hence if both resource-acquisition and output-disposal problems—which are in part controlled by environmental elements and hence to a degree uncertain or problematic—can be removed from the technical core, the logic can be brought closer to closure, and the rationality, increased.

Uncertainty would appear to be greatest, at least potentially, at the other extreme, the institutional level. Here the organization deals largely with elements of the environment over which it has no formal authority or control. Instead, it is subjected to generalized norms, ranging from formally codified law to informal standards of good practice, to public authority, or to elements expressing the public interest.

At this extreme the closed system of logic is clearly inappropriate. The organization is open to influence by the environment (and vice versa) which can change independently

of the actions of the organization. Here an open system of logic, permitting the intrusion of variables penetrating the organization from outside, and facing up to uncertainty, seems indispensable.

If the closed-system aspects of organizations are seen most clearly at the technical level, and the open-system qualities appear most vividly at the institutional level, it would suggest that a significant function of the managerial level is to mediate between the two extremes and the emphases they exhibit. If the organization must approach certainty at the technical level to satisfy its rationality criteria, but must remain flexible and adaptive to satisfy environmental requirements, we might expect the managerial level to mediate between them, ironing out some irregularities stemming from external sources, but also pressing the technical core for modifications as conditions alter. One exploration of this notion was offered in Thompson.[19]

Possible Sources of Variation. Following Parsons' reasoning leads to the expectation that differences in technical functions, or *technologies*, cause significant differences among organization, and since the three levels are interdependent, differences in technical functions should also make for differences at managerial and institutional levels of the organization. Similarly, differences of the institutional structures in which organizations are imbedded should make for significant variations among organizations at all three levels.

Relating this back to the Simon-March-Cyert focus on organizational processes of searching, learning, and deciding, we can also suggest that while these adaptive processes may be generic, the ways in which they proceed may well vary with differences in technologies or in environments.

Recapitulation
Most of our beliefs about complex organizations follow from one or the other of two distinct strategies. The closed-system strategy seeks certainty by incorporating only

those variables positively associated with goal achievement and subjecting them to a monolithic control network. The open-system strategy shifts attention from goal achievement to survival, and incorporates uncertainty by recognizing organizational interdependence with environment. A newer tradition enables us to conceive of the organization as an open system, indeterminate and faced with uncertainty, but subject to criteria of rationality and hence needing certainty.

With this conception the central problem for complex organizations is one of coping with uncertainty. As a point of departure, we suggest that organizations cope with uncertainty by creating certain parts specifically to deal with it, specializing other parts in operating under conditions of certainty or near certainty. In this case, articulation of these specialized parts becomes significant.

We also suggest that technologies and environments are major sources of uncertainty for organizations, and that differences in those dimensions will result in differences in organizations. To proceed, we now turn to a closer examination of the meaning of "rationality," in the context of complex organizations.

RATIONALITY IN ORGANIZATIONS

Instrumental action is rooted on the one hand in *desired outcomes* and on the other hand in *beliefs about cause/effect relationships*. Given a desire, the state of man's knowledge at any point in time dictates the kinds of variables required and the manner of their manipulation to bring that desire to fruition. To the extent that the activities thus dictated by man's beliefs are judged to produce the desired outcomes, we can speak of technology, or *technical rationality*.

Technical rationality can be evaluated by two criteria: instrumental and economic. The essence of the instrumental question is whether the specified actions do in fact produce the desired outcome, and the instrumentally perfect technology is one which inevitably achieves such results. The economic question in essence is whether the results are obtained with the least necessary expenditure of resources, and for this there is no absolute standard. Two different routes to the same desired outcome may be compared in terms of cost, or both may be compared with some abstract ideal, but in practical terms the evaluation of economy is relative to the state of man's knowledge at the time of evaluation.

We will give further consideration to the assessment of organizational action in a later chapter, but it is necessary to distinguish at this point between the instrumental and economic questions because present literature and organization gives considerable attention to the economic dimension of technology but hides the importance of the instrumental question, which in fact takes priority. The cost of doing something can be considered only after we know that the something can be done.

Complex organizations are built to operate technologies which are found to be impossible or impractical for individuals to operate. This does not mean, however, that technologies operated by complex organizations are instrumentally perfect. The instrumentally perfect technology would produce the desired outcome inevitably, and this perfection is approached in the case of continuous processing of chemicals or in mass manufacturing—for example, of automobiles. A less perfect technology will produce the desired outcome only part of the time; nevertheless, it may be incorporated into complex organizations, such as the mental hospital, because the desire for the possible outcome is intense enough to settle for possible rather than highly probable success. Sometimes the intensity of desire for certain kinds of outcomes, such as world peace, leads to the creation of complex organizations, such as the United Nations to operate patently imperfect technologies.

Variations in Technologies
Clearly, technology is an important variable in understanding the actions of complex

organizations. In modern societies the variety of desired outcomes for which specific technologies are available seems infinite. A complete but simple typology of technologies which has found order in this variety would be quite helpful. Typologies are available for industrial production[20] and for mental therapy[21] but are not general enough to deal with the range of technologies found in complex organizations. Lacking such a typology, we will simply identify three varieties which are (1) widespread in modern society and (2) sufficiently different to illustrate the propositions we wish to develop.

The Long-linked Technology.[22] A long-linked technology involves serial interdependence in the sense that act Z can be performed only after successful completion of act Y, which in turn rests on act X, and so on. The original symbol of technical rationality, the mass production assembly line, is of this long-linked nature. It approaches instrumental perfection when it produces a single kind of standard product, repetitively and at a constant rate. Production of only one kind of product means that a single technology is required, and this in turn permits the use of clear-cut criteria for the selection of machines and tools, construction of work-flow arrangements, acquisition of raw materials, and selection of human operators. Repetition of the productive process provides experience as a means of eliminating imperfections in the technology; experience can lead to the modification of machines and provide the basis for scheduled preventive maintenance. Repetition means that human motions can also be examined, and through training and practice, energy losses and errors minimized. It is in this setting that the scientific-management movement has perhaps made its greatest contribution.

The constant rate of production means that, once adjusted, the proportion of resources involved can be standardized to the point where each contributes to its capacity; none need be underemployed. This

of course makes important contributions to the economic aspect of the technology.

The Mediating Technology. Various organizations have, as a primary function, the linking of clients or customers who are or wish to be interdependent. The commercial bank links depositors and borrowers. The insurance firm links those who would pool common risks. The telephone utility links those who would call and those who would be called. The post office provides a possible linkage of virtually every member of the modern society. The employment agency mediates the supply of labor and the demand for it.

Complexity in the mediating technology comes not from the necessity of having each activity geared to the requirements of the next but rather from the fact that the mediating technology requires operating in *standardized ways*, and *extensively*; e.g., with multiple clients or customers distributed in time and space.

The commercial bank must find and aggregate deposits from diverse depositors; but however diverse the depositors, the transaction must conform to standard terms and to uniform bookkeeping and accounting procedures. It must also find borrowers; but no matter how varied their needs or desires, loans must be made according to standardized criteria and on terms uniformly applied to the category appropriate to the particular borrower. Poor risks who receive favored treatment jeopardize bank solvency. Standardization permits the insurance organization to define categories of risk and hence to sort its customers or potential customers into appropriate aggregate categories; the insured who is not a qualified risk but is so defined upsets the probabilities on which insurance rests. The telephone company became viable only when the telephone became regarded as a necessity, and this did not occur until equipment was standardized to the point where it could be incorporated into one network. Standardization enables the employment agency to aggregate job applicants into categories which can be matched against standardized requests for employees.

Standardization makes possible the operation of the mediating technology over time and through space by assuring each segment of the organization that other segments are operating in compatible ways. It is in such situations that the bureaucratic techniques of categorization and impersonal application of rules have been most beneficial.[23]

The Intensive Technology. This third variety we label *intensive* to signify that a variety of techniques is drawn upon in order to achieve a change in some specific object; but the selection, combination, and order of application are determined by feedback from the object itself. When the object is human, this intensive technology is regarded as "therapeutic," but the same technical logic is found also in the construction industry[24] and in research where the objects of concern are nonhuman. . . .

The intensive technology is a custom technology. Its successful employment rests in part on the availability of all the capacities potentially needed, but equally on the appropriate custom combination of selected capacities as required by the individual case or project.

Boundaries of Technical Rationality. Technical rationality, as a system of cause/effect relationships which lead to a desired result, is an abstraction. It is instrumentally perfect when it becomes a closed system of logic. The closed system of logic contains all relevant variables, and only relevant variables. All other influences, or *exogenous variables*, are excluded; and the variables contained in the system vary only to the extent that the experimenter, the manager, or the computer determines they should.

When a technology is put to use, however, there must be not only desired outcomes and knowledge of relevant cause/effect relationships, but also power to control

the empirical resources which correspond to the variables in the logical system. A closed system of action corresponding to a closed system of logic would result in instrumental perfection in reality.

The mass production assembly operation and the continuous processing of chemicals are more nearly perfect, in application, than the other two varieties discussed above because they achieve a high degree of control over relevant variables and are relatively free from disturbing influences. Once started, most of the action involved in the long-linked technology is dictated by the internal logic of the technology itself. With the mediating technology, customers or clients intrude to make difficult the standardized activities required by the technology. And with the intensive technology, the specific case defines the component activities and their combination from the larger array of components contained in the abstract technology.

Since technical perfection seems more nearly approachable when the organization has control over all the elements involved,

> Proposition 2.1: Under norms of rationality, organizations seek to seal off their core technologies from environmental influences.

Organizational Rationality

When organizations seek to translate the abstractions called technologies into action, they immediately face problems for which the core technologies do not provide solutions.

Mass production manufacturing technologies are quite specific, *assuming* that certain inputs are provided and finished products are somehow removed from the premises before the productive process is clogged; but mass production technologies do not include variables which provide solutions to either the input- or output-disposal problems. The present technology of medicine may be rather specific if certain tests indicate an appendectomy is in order, if the condition of the patient meets certain criteria, and if certain medical staff, equipment, and medications are present. But medical technology contains no cause/effect statements about bringing sufferers to the attention of medical practitioners, or about the provision of the specified equipment, skills, and medications. The technology of education rests on abstract systems of belief about relationships among teachers, teaching materials, and pupils; but learning theories assume the presence of these variables and proceed from that point.

One or more technologies constitute the core of all purposive organizations. But this technical core is always an incomplete representation of what the organization must do to accomplish desired results. Technical rationality is a necessary component but never alone sufficient to provide *organizational rationality*, which involves acquiring the inputs which are taken for granted by the technology, and dispensing outputs which again are outside the scope of the core technology.

At a minimum, then, organizational rationality involves three major component activities, (1) input activities, (2) technological activities, and (3) output activities. Since these are interdependent, organizational rationality requires that they be appropriately geared to one another. The inputs acquired must be within the scope of the technology, and it must be within the capacity of the organization to dispose of the technological production.

Not only are these component activities interdependent, but both input and output activities are interdependent with environmental elements. Organizational rationality, therefore, never conforms to closed-system logic but demands the logic of an open system. Moreover, since the technological activities are embedded in and interdependent with activities which are open to the environment, the closed system can never be completely attained for the technological component. Yet we have offered the proposition that organizations subject to rationality norms seek to seal off their core technologies from environmental

influences. How do we reconcile these two contentions?

> Proposition 2.2: Under norms of rationality, organizations seek to buffer environmental influences by surrounding their technical cores with input and output components.

To maximize productivity of a manufacturing technology, the technical core must be able to operate as if the market will absorb the single kind of product at a continuous rate, and as if inputs flowed continuously, at a steady rate and with specified quality. Conceivably both sets of conditions could occur; realistically they do not. But organizations reveal a variety of devices for approximating these "as if" assumptions, with input and output components meeting fluctuating environments and converting them into steady conditions for the technological core.

Buffering on the input side is illustrated by the stockpiling of materials and supplies acquired in an irregular market, and their steady insertion into the production process. Preventive maintenance, whereby machines or equipment are repaired on a scheduled basis, thus minimizing surprise, is another example of buffering by the input component. The recruitment of dissimilar personnel and their conversion into reliable performers through training or indoctrination is another; it is most dramatically illustrated by basic training or boot camp in military organizations.[25]

Buffering on the output side of long-linked technologies usually takes the form of maintaining warehouse inventories and items in transit or in distributor inventories, which permits the technical core to produce at a constant rate, but distribution to fluctuate with market conditions.

Buffering on the input side is an appropriate and important device available to all types of organizations. Buffering on the output side is especially important for mass-manufacturing organizations, but is less feasible when the product is perishable or when the object is inextricably involved in the technological process, as in the therapeutic case.

Buffering of an unsteady environment obviously brings considerable advantages to the technical core, but it does so with costs to the organization. A classic problem in connection with buffering is how to maintain inventories, input or output, sufficient to meet all needs without recurring obsolescence as needs change. Operations research recently has made important contributions toward this problem of "run out versus obsolescence," both of which are costly.

Thus while a fully buffered technological core would enjoy the conditions for maximum technical rationality, organizational rationality may call for compromises between conditions for maximum technical efficiency and the energy required for buffering operations. In an unsteady environment, then, the organization under rationality norms must seek other devices for protecting its technical core.

> Proposition 2.3: Under norms of rationality, organizations seek to smooth out input and output transactions.

Whereas buffering absorbs environmental fluctuations, smoothing or leveling involves attempts to reduce fluctuations in the environment. Utility firms—electric, gas, water, or telephone—may offer inducements to those who use their services during "trough" periods, or charge premiums to those who contribute to "peaking." Retailing organizations faced with seasonal or other fluctuations in demand, may offer inducements in the form of special promotions or sales during slow periods. Transportation organizations such as airlines may offer special reduced fare rates on light days or during slow seasons.

Organizations pointed toward emergencies, such as fire departments, attempt to level the need for their services by activities designed to prevent emergencies, and by emphasis on the early detection so that demand is not allowed to grow to the point that would overtax the capacity of the organization. Hospitals accomplish some smoothing through the scheduling of nonemergency admissions.

Although action by the organization may thus reduce fluctuations in demand, complete smoothing of demand is seldom possible. But a core technology interrupted by constant fluctuation and change must settle for a low degree of technical rationality. What other services do organizations employ to protect core technologies?

> Proposition 2.4: Under norms of rationality, organizations seek to anticipate and adapt to environmental changes which cannot be buffered or leveled.

If environmental fluctuations penetrate the organization and require the technical core to alter its activities, then environmental fluctuations are exogenous variables within the logic of technical rationality. To the extent that environmental fluctuations can be anticipated, however, they can be treated as *constraints* on the technical core within which a closed system of logic can be employed.

The manufacturing firm which can correctly forecast demand for a particular time period can thereby plan or schedule operations of its technical core at a steady rate during that period. Any changes in technical operations due to changes in the environment can be made at the end of the period on the basis of forecasts for the next period.

Organizations often learn that some environmental fluctuations are patterned, and in these cases forecasting and adjustment appear almost automatic. The post office knows, for example, that in large commercial centers large volumes of business mail are posted at the end of the business day, when secretaries leave offices. Recently the post office has attempted to buffer that load by promising rapid treatment of mail posted in special locations during morning hours. Its success in buffering is not known at this writing, but meanwhile the post office schedules its technical activities to meet known daily fluctuations. It can also anticipate heavy demand during November and December, thus allowing its input components lead time in acquiring additional resources.

Banks likewise learn that local conditions and customs result in peak loads at predictable times during the day and week, and can schedule their operations to meet these shifts.[26]

In cases such as these, organizations have amassed sufficient experience to know that fluctuations are patterned with a high degree of regularity or probability; but when environmental fluctuations are the result of combinations of more dynamic factors, anticipation may require something more than the simple projection of previous experience. It is in these situations that forecasting emerges as a specialized and elaborate activity, for which some of the emerging management-science or statistical-decision theories seem especially appropriate.

To the extent that environmental fluctuations are unanticipated they interfere with the orderly operation of the core technology and thereby reduce its performance. When such influences are anticipated and considered as constraints for a particular period of time, the technical core can operate as if it enjoyed a closed system.

Buffering, leveling, and adaptation to anticipated fluctuations are widely used devices for reducing the influence of the environment on the technological cores of organizations. Often they are effective, but there are occasions when these devices are not sufficient to ward off environmental penetration.

> Proposition 2.5: When buffering, leveling, and forecasting do not protect their technical cores from environmental fluctuations, organizations under norms of rationality resort to rationing.

Rationing is most easily seen in organizations pointed toward emergencies, such as hospitals. Even in nonemergency situations hospitals may ration beds to physicians by establishing priority systems for nonemergency admissions. In emergencies, such as community disasters, hospitals may ration pharmaceutical dosages or nursing services by dilution—by assigning a fixed number of nurses to a larger patient population. Mental hospitals, especially state mental hospitals, may ration technical services by employing primarily organic-treatment procedures—electroshock, drugs, insulin—which can be employed more economically than psychoanalytic or *milieu* therapies.[27] Teachers and caseworkers in social welfare organizations may ration effort by accepting only a portion of those seeking service, or if not empowered to exercise such discretion, may concentrate their energies on the more challenging cases or on those which appear most likely to yield satisfactory outcomes.[28]

But rationing is not a device reserved for therapeutic organizations. The post office may assign priority to first-class mail, attending to lesser classes only when the priority task is completed. Manufacturers of suddenly popular items may ration allotments to wholesalers or dealers, and if inputs are scarce, may assign priorities to alternative uses of those resources. Libraries may ration book loans, acquisitions, and search efforts.[29]

Rationing is an unhappy solution, for its use signifies that the technology is not operating at its maximum. Yet some system of priorities for the allocation of capacity under adverse conditions is essential if a technology is to be instrumentally effective—if action is to be other than random.

The Logic of Organizational Rationality. Core technologies rest on closed systems of logic, but are invariably embedded in a larger organizational rationality which pins the technology to a time and place, and links it with the larger environment through input and output activities. Organizational rationality thus calls for an open-system logic, for when the organization is opened to environmental influences, some of the factors involved in organizational action become *constraints*; for some meaningful period of time they are not variables but fixed conditions to which the organization must adapt. Some of the factors become *contingencies*, which may or may not vary, but are not subject to arbitrary control by the organization.

Organizational rationality therefore is some result of (1) constraints which the organization must face, (2) contingencies which the organization must meet, and (3) variables which the organization can control.

Recapitulation

Perfection in technical rationality requires complete knowledge of cause/effect relations plus control over all of the relevant variables, or closure. Therefore, under norms of rationality (Prop. 2.1), organizations seek to seal off their core technologies from environmental influences. Since complete closure is impossible (Prop. 2.2), they seek to buffer environmental influences by surrounding their technical cores with input and output components.

Because buffering does not handle all variations in an unsteady environment, organizations seek to smooth input and output transactions (Prop. 2.3), and to anticipate and adapt to environmental changes which cannot be buffered or smoothed (Prop. 2.4), and finally, when buffering, leveling, and forecasting do not protect their technical cores from environmental fluctuations (Prop. 2.5), organizations resort to rationing.

These are maneuvering devices which provide the organization with some self-control despite interdependence with the environment. But if we are to gain understanding of such maneuvering, we must consider both the direction toward which maneuvering is designed and the nature of the environment in which maneuvering takes place.

NOTES

1. William R. Dill, "Desegregation or Integration? Comments about Contemporary Research in Organizations," in *New Perspectives in Organization Research*, eds. W. W. Cooper, Harold J. Leavitt, & Maynard W. Shelly II (New York: John Wiley & Sons, Inc., 1964). James G. March, "Introduction," in *Handbook of Organizations*, ed. James G. March (Chicago: Rand McNally, 1965).

2. Alvin W. Gouldner, "Organizational Analysis," in *Sociology Today*, eds. Robert K. Merton, Leonard Broom, and Leonard S. Cottrell, Jr. (New York: Basic Books, 1959).

3. W. Ross Ashby, *An Introduction to Cybernetics* (London: Chapman and Hall, Ltd., 1956).

4. Sir Frederic Bartlett, *Thinking: An Experimental and Social Study* (New York: Basic Books, 1958).

5. Frederick W. Taylor, *Scientific Management* (New York: Harper & Row, 1911).

6. Luther Gulick, & L. Urwick, eds., *Papers on the Science of Administration* (New York: Institute of Public Administration, 1937).

7. Max Weber, *The Theory of Social and Economic Organization*, ed. Talcott Parsons, trans. A. M. Henderson and Talcott Parsons (New York: Free Press, 1947).

8. Herbert A. Simon, *Administrative Behavior*, 2nd ed. (New York: Macmillan, 1957).

9. Robert K. Merton, "Bureaucratic Structure and Personality," in *Social Theory and Social Structure*, rev. ed., ed. Robert K. Merton (New York: Free Press, 1957).

10. Fritz J. Roethlisberger, & W. J. Dickson, *Management and the Worker* (Cambridge, Mass.: Harvard University Press, 1939).

11. Chester I. Barnard, *The Functions of the Executive* (Cambridge, Mass.: Harvard University Press, 1938).

12. Philip Selznick, *TVA and the Grass Roots* (Berkeley, Calif.: University of California Press, 1949).

13. Burton R. Clark, *Adult Education in Transition* (Berkeley, Calif.: University of California Press, 1956).

14. Herbert A. Simon, *Administrative Behavior*. James G. March, & Herbert A. Simon, *Organizations* (New York: Wiley, 1958). Richard M. Cyert, & James G. March, *A Behavioral Theory of the Firm* (Englewood Cliffs, N.J.: Prentice-Hall, 1963).

15. Herbert A. Simon, *Models of Man, Social and Rational* (New York: Wiley, 1957).

16. *Ibid.*

17. Michel Crozier, *The Bureaucratic Phenomenon* (Chicago: The University of Chicago Press, 1964).

18. Talcott Parsons, *Structure and Process in Modern Societies* (New York: Free Press, 1960).

19. James D. Thompson, "Decision-making, the Firm, and the Market," in *New Perspectives in Organization Research*, eds., W. W. Cooper et al. (New York: Wiley, 1964).

20. Joan Woodward, *Industrial Organization: Theory and Practice* (London: Oxford University Press, 1965).

21. Robert W. Hawkes, "Physical Psychiatric Rehabilitation Models Compared" (Paper presented at the Ohio Valley Sociological Society, 1962).

22. The notions in this section rest especially on conversations some years ago with Frederick L. Bates. For a different but somewhat parallel analysis of work flows, see

Robert Dubin, "Stability of Human Organizations," in *Modern Organization Theory*, ed. Mason Haire (New York: Wiley, 1959).

23. Weber, *Theory of Organization*. Merton, *Social Theory and Structure*.

24. Arthur L. Stinchcombe, "Bureaucratic and Craft Administration of Production: A Comparative Study," *Administrative Science Quarterly* 4 (September 1959): 168–187.

25. Sanford M. Dornbusch, "The Military Academy as an Assimilating Institution," *Social Forces* 33 (May 1955): 316–321.

26. Chris Argyris, *Organization of a Bank* (New Haven, Conn.: Labor and Management Center, Yale University, 1954).

27. Ivan Belknap, *The Human Problems of a State Mental Hospital* (New York: McGraw-Hill, 1956).

28. Peter M. Blau, *The Dynamics of Bureaucracy* (Chicago: The University of Chicago Press, 1955).

29. Richard L. Meier, "Communications Overload," *Administrative Science Quarterly* 7 (March 1963): 521–544.

47

Institutionalized Organizations: Formal Structure as Myth and Ceremony

John W. Meyer and Brian Rowan

. . . Formal organizations are generally understood to be systems of coordinated and controlled activities that arise when work is embedded in complex networks of technical relations and boundary-spanning exchanges. But in modern societies formal organizational structures arise in highly institutionalized contexts. Professions, policies, and programs are created along with the products and services that they are understood to produce rationally. This permits many new organizations to spring up and forces existing ones to incorporate new practices and procedures. That is, organizations are driven to incorporate the practices and procedures defined by prevailing rationalized concepts of organizational work and institutionalized in society. Organizations that do so increase their legitimacy and their survival prospects, independent of the immediate efficacy of the acquired practices and procedures.

Institutionalized products, services, techniques, policies, and programs function as powerful myths, and many organizations adopt them ceremonially. But conformity to institutionalized rules often conflicts sharply with efficiency criteria and, conversely, to coordinate and control activity in order to promote efficiency undermines an organization's ceremonial conformity and sacrifices its support and legitimacy. To maintain ceremonial conformity, organizations that reflect institutional rules tend to buffer their formal structures from the uncertainties of technical activities by becoming loosely coupled, building gaps between their formal structures and actual work activities.

This paper argues that the formal structures of many organizations in postindustrial society (Bell 1973) dramatically reflect the myths of their institutional environments instead of the demands of their work activities. The first part describes prevailing theories of the origins of formal structures and the main problem the theories confront. The second part discusses an alternative source of formal structures: myths embedded in the institutional environment. The third part develops the argument that organizations reflecting institutionalized environments maintain gaps between their formal structures and their ongoing work activities. The final part summarizes by discussing some research implications.

Throughout the paper, institutionalized rules are distinguished sharply from prevailing social behaviors. Institutionalized rules are classifications built into society as reciprocated typifications or interpretations (Berger and Luckmann 1967, p. 54). Such rules may be simply taken for granted or may be supported by public opinion or the force of law (Starbuck 1976). Institutions inevitably involve normative obligations but often enter into social life primarily as facts which must be taken into account by actors. Institutionalization involves the processes by which social processes, obligations, or actualities come to take on a rule-like status in social thought and action. So, for example, the social status of doctor is a

Source: John W. Meyer and Brian Rowan, "Institutionalized Organizations: Formal Structure as Myth and Ceremony," *American Journal of Sociology* 83, no. 2 (1977): 340–363. © 1977 by The University of Chicago. Reprinted by permission of University of Chicago Press.

highly institutionalized rule (both norma-tive and cognitive) for managing illness as well as a social role made up of particular behaviors, relations, and expectations. . . . In a smaller way, a No Smoking sign is an institution with legal status and impli-cations, as well as an attempt to regulate smoking behavior. It is fundamental to the argument of this paper that institutional rules may have effects on organizational structures and their implementation in ac-tual technical work which are very different from the effects generated by the networks of social behavior and relationships which compose and surround a given organization.

PREVAILING THEORIES
OF FORMAL STRUCTURE

A sharp distinction should be made between the formal structure of an organization and its actual day-to-day work activities. Formal structure is a blueprint for activities which includes, first of all, the table of organiza-tion: a listing of offices, departments, posi-tions, and programs. These elements are linked by explicit goals and policies that make up a rational theory of how, and to what end, activities are to be fitted together. The essence of a modern bureaucratic or-ganization lies in the rationalized and im-personal character of these structural ele-ments and of the goals that link them.

One of the central problems in organiza-tion theory is to describe the conditions that give rise to rationalized formal structure. In conventional theories, rational formal structure is assumed to be the most effective way to coordinate and control the complex relational networks involved in modern technical or work activities (see Scott 1975 for a review). This assumption derives from Weber's (1930, 1946, 1947) discussions of the historical emergence of bureaucracies as consequences of economic markets and centralized states. Economic markets place a premium on rationality and coordination. As markets expand, the relational networks in a given domain become more complex

and differentiated, and organizations in that domain must manage more internal and boundary-spanning interdependencies. Such factors as size (Blau 1970) and tech-nology (Woodward 1965) increase the com-plexity of internal relations, and the divi-sion of labor among organizations increases boundary-spanning problems (Aiken and Hage 1968; Freeman 1973; Thompson 1967). Because the need for coordination increases under these conditions, and be-cause formally coordinated work has com-petitive advantages, organizations with ra-tionalized formal structures tend to develop.

The formation of centralized states and the penetration of societies by political centers also contribute to the rise and spread of formal organization. When the relational networks involved in economic exchange and political management become ex-tremely complex, bureaucratic structures are thought to be the most effective and rational means to standardize and control subunits. Bureaucratic control is especially useful for expanding political centers, and standardi-zation is often demanded by both centers and peripheral units (Bendix 1964, 1968). Political centers organize layers of offices that manage to extend conformity and to displace traditional activities throughout societies.

The problem. *Prevailing theories assume that the coordination and control of activity are the critical dimensions on which formal orga-nizations have succeeded in the modern world.* This assumption is based on the view that organizations function according to their formal blueprints: coordination is routine, rules and procedures are followed, and ac-tual activities conform to the prescriptions of formal structure. But much of the empir-ical research on organizations casts doubt on this assumption. An earlier generation of researchers concluded that there was a great gap between the formal and the infor-mal organization (e.g., Dalton 1959; Downs 1967; Homans 1950). A related observa-tion is that formal organizations are often loosely coupled (March and Olsen 1976; Weick 1976): structural elements are only loosely linked to each other and to activities, rules are often violated, decisions are often unimplemented, or if implemented have uncertain consequences, technologies are of problematic efficiency, and evaluation and inspection systems are subverted or rendered so vague as to provide little coordination.

Formal organizations are endemic in modern societies. There is need for an explanation of their rise that is partially free from the assumption that, in practice, formal structures actually coordinate and control work. Such an explanation should account for the elaboration of purposes, positions, policies, and procedural rules that characterizes formal organizations, but must do so without supposing that these structural features are implemented in routine work activity.

INSTITUTIONAL SOURCES OF FORMAL STRUCTURE

By focusing on the management of complex relational networks and the exercise of coordination and control, prevailing theories have neglected an alternative Weberian source of formal structure: the legitimacy of rationalized formal structures. In prevailing theories, legitimacy is a given: assertions about bureaucratization rest on the assumption of norms of rationality (Thompson 1967). When norms do play causal roles in theories of bureaucratization, it is because they are thought to be built into modern societies and personalities as very general values, which are thought to facilitate formal organization. But norms of rationality are not simply general values. They exist in much more specific and powerful ways in the rules, understandings, and meanings attached to institutionalized social structures. The causal importance of such institutions in the process of bureaucratization has been neglected.

Formal structures are not only creatures of their relational networks in the social organization. In modern societies, the elements of rationalized formal structure are deeply ingrained in, and reflect, widespread understandings of social reality. Many of the positions, policies, programs, and procedures of modern organizations are enforced by public opinion, by the views of important constituents, by knowledge legitimated through the educational system, by social prestige, by the laws, and by the definitions of negligence and prudence used by the courts. Such elements of formal structure are manifestations of powerful institutional rules which function as highly rationalized myths that are binding on particular organizations.

In modern societies, the myths generating formal organizational structure have two key properties. First, they are rationalized and impersonal prescriptions that identify various social purposes as technical ones and specify in a rulelike way the appropriate means to pursue these technical purposes rationally (Ellul 1964). Second, they are highly institutionalized and thus in some measure beyond the discretion of any individual participant or organization. They must, therefore, be taken for granted as legitimate, apart from evaluations of their impact on work outcomes.

Many elements of formal structure are highly institutionalized and function as myths. Examples include professions, programs, and technologies:

Large numbers of rationalized professions emerge (Wilensky 1965; Bell 1973). These are occupations controlled, not only by direct inspection of work outcomes but also by social rules of licensing, certifying, and schooling. The occupations are rationalized, being understood to control impersonal techniques rather than moral mysteries. Further, they are highly institutionalized: the delegation of activities to the appropriate occupations is socially expected and often legally obligatory over and above any calculations of its efficiency.

Many formalized organizational programs are also institutionalized in society. Ideologies define the functions appropriate to a business—such as sales, production, advertising, or accounting; to a university—such as instruction and research in history, engineering, and literature; and to a hospital—such as surgery, internal medicine, and obstetrics. Such classifications of organizational functions, and the specifications for conducting each function, are prefabricated formulae available for use by any given organization.

Similarly, technologies are institutionalized and become myths binding on organizations. Technical procedures of production, accounting, personnel selection, or data processing become taken-for-granted means to accomplish organizational ends. Quite apart from their possible efficiency, such institutionalized techniques establish an organization as appropriate, rational, and modern. Their use displays responsibility and avoids claims of negligence.

The impact of such rationalized institutional elements on organizations and organizing situations is enormous. These rules define new organizing situations, redefine existing ones, and specify the means for coping rationally with each. They enable, and often require, participants to organize along prescribed lines. And they spread very rapidly in modern society as part of the rise of postindustrial society (Bell 1973). New and extant domains of activity are codified in institutionalized programs, professions, or techniques, and organizations incorporate the packaged codes. For example:

The discipline of psychology creates a rationalized theory of personnel selection and certifies personnel professionals. Personnel departments and functionaries appear in all sorts of extant organizations, and new specialized personnel agencies also appear.

As programs of research and development are created and professionals with expertise in these fields are trained and defined, organizations come under increasing pressure to incorporate R & D units.

As the prerational profession of prostitution is rationalized along medical lines, bureaucratized organizations—sex-therapy clinics, massage parlors, and the like—spring up more easily.

As the issues of safety and environmental pollution arise, and as relevant professions and programs become institutionalized in laws, union ideologies, and public opinion, organizations incorporate these programs and professions.

The growth of rationalized institutional structures in society makes formal organizations more common and more elaborate. Such institutions are myths which make formal organizations both easier to create and more necessary. After all, the building blocks for organizations come to be littered around the societal landscape; it takes only a little entrepreneurial energy to assemble them into a structure. And because these building blocks are considered proper, adequate, rational, and necessary, organizations must incorporate them to avoid illegitimacy. Thus, the myths built into rationalized institutional elements create the necessity, the opportunity, and the impulse to organize rationally, over and above pressures in this direction created by the need to manage proximate relational networks:

Proposition 1. As *rationalized institutional rules arise in given domains of work activity, formal organizations form and expand by incorporating these rules as structural elements.*

Two distinct ideas are implied here: (1A) As institutionalized myths define new domains of rationalized activity, formal organizations emerge in these domains. (1B) As rationalizing institutional myths arise in existing domains of activity, extant organizations expand their formal structures so as to become isomorphic with these new myths.

To understand the larger historical process it is useful to note that:

Proposition 2. *The more modernized the society, the more extended the rationalized institutional structure in given domains and the greater the number of domains containing rationalized institutions.*

Modern institutions, then, are thoroughly rationalized, and these rationalized elements act as myths giving rise to more formal organization. When propositions 1 and 2 are combined, two more specific ideas follow: (2A) Formal organizations are more likely to emerge in more modernized societies, even with the complexity of immedi-

FIGURE 47.1 • THE ORIGINS AND ELABORATION OF FORMAL ORGANIZATIONAL STRUCTURES

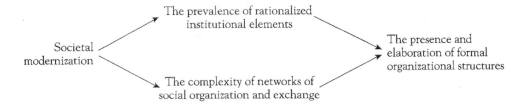

ate relational networks held constant. (2B) Formal organizations in a given domain of activity are likely to have more elaborated structures in more modernized societies, even with the complexity of immediate relational networks held constant.

Combining the ideas above with prevailing organization theory, it becomes clear that modern societies are filled with rationalized bureaucracies for two reasons. First, as the prevailing theories have asserted, relational networks become increasingly complex as societies modernize. Second, modern societies are filled with institutional rules which function as myths depicting various formal structures as rational means to the attainment of desirable ends. Figure 47.1 summarizes these two lines of theory. Both lines suggest that the postindustrial society — the society dominated by rational organization even more than by the forces of production — arises both out of the complexity of the modern social organizational network and, more directly, as an ideological matter. Once institutionalized, rationality becomes a myth with explosive organizing potential, as both Ellul (1964) and Bell (1973) — though with rather different reactions — observe.

The Relation of Organizations to Their Institutional Environments

The observation is not new that organizations are structured by phenomena in their environments and tend to become isomorphic with them. One explanation of such isomorphism is that formal organizations become matched with their environments by technical and exchange interdependencies. This line of reasoning can be seen in the works of Aiken and Hage (1968), Hawley (1968), and Thompson (1967). This explanation asserts that structural elements diffuse because environments create boundary-spanning exigencies for organizations, and that organizations which incorporate structural elements isomorphic with the environment are able to manage such interdependencies.

A second explanation for the parallelism between organizations and their environments — and the one emphasized here — is that organizations structurally reflect socially constructed reality (Berger and Luckmann 1967). This view is suggested in the work of Parsons (1956) and Udy (1970), who see organizations as greatly conditioned by their general institutional environments and therefore as institutions themselves in part. Emery and Trist (1965) also see organizations as responding directly to environmental structures and distinguish such effects sharply from those that occur through boundary-spanning exchanges. According to the institutional conception as developed here, organizations tend to disappear as distinct and bounded units. Quite beyond the environmental interrelations suggested in open-systems theories, institutional theories in their extreme forms define organizations as dramatic enactments of the rationalized myths pervading modern societies, rather than as units involved in exchange — no matter how complex — with their environments.

The two explanations of environmental isomorphism are not entirely inconsistent. Organizations both deal with their environments at their boundaries and imitate environmental elements in their structures. However, the two lines of explanation have very different implications for internal organizational process, as will be argued below.

The Origins of Rational Institutional Myths

Bureaucratization is caused in part by the proliferation of rationalized myths in society, and this in turn involves the evolution of the whole modern institutional system. Although the latter topic is beyond the scope of this paper, three specific processes that generate rationalized myths of organizational structure can be noted.

The elaboration of complex relational networks.—As the relational networks in societies become dense and interconnected, increasing numbers of rationalized myths arise. Some of them are highly generalized: for example, the principles of universalism (Parsons 1971), contracts (Spencer 1897), restitution (Durkheim 1933), and expertise (Weber 1947) are generalized to diverse occupations, organizational programs, and organizational practices. Other myths describe specific structural elements. These myths may originate from narrow contexts and be applied in different ones. For example, in modern societies the relational contexts of business organizations in a single industry are roughly similar from place to place. Under these conditions a particularly effective practice, occupational specialty, or principle of coordination can be codified into mythlike form. The laws, the educational and credentialing systems, and public opinion then make it necessary or advantageous for organizations to incorporate the new structures.

The degree of collective organization of the environment.—The myths generated by particular organizational practices and diffused through relational networks have legitimacy based on the supposition that they are rationally effective. But many myths also have official legitimacy based on legal mandates. . . . Legislative and judicial authorities create and interpret legal mandates; administrative agencies—such as state and federal governments, port authorities, and school districts—establish rules of practice; and licenses and credentials become necessary in order to practice occupations. The stronger the rational-legal order, the greater the extent to which rationalized rules and procedures and personnel become institutional requirements. New formal organizations emerge and extant organizations acquire new structural elements.

Leadership efforts of local organizations.—The rise of the state and the expansion of collective jurisdiction are often thought to result in domesticated organizations (Carlson 1962) subject to high levels of goal displacement (Clark 1956; Selznick 1949; and Zald and Denton 1963). This view is misleading: organizations do often adapt to their institutional contexts, but they often play active roles in shaping those contexts (Dowling and Pfeffer 1975; Parsons 1956; Perrow 1970; Thompson 1967). Many organizations actively seek charters from collective authorities and manage to institutionalize their goals and structures in the rules of such authorities.

Efforts to mold institutional environments proceed along two dimensions. First, powerful organizations force their immediate relational networks to adapt to their structures and relations. For instance, automobile producers help create demands for particular kinds of roads, transportation systems, and fuels that make automobiles virtual necessities; competitive forms of transportation have to adapt to the existing relational context. But second, powerful organizations attempt to build their goals and procedures directly into society as institutional rules. Automobile producers, for instance, attempt to create the standards in public opinion defining desirable cars, to influence legal standards defining satisfactory cars, to affect judicial rules defining cars adequate enough to avoid manufacturer liability, and to force agents of the collectivity to purchase only their cars. Rivals must then compete both in social networks or markets and in contexts of institutional rules which are defined by extant organizations. In this fashion, given organizational forms perpetuate themselves by becoming institutionalized rules. . . .

The Impact of Institutional Environments on Organizations

Isomorphism with environmental institutions has some crucial consequences for organizations: (*a*) they incorporate elements which are legitimated externally, rather than in terms of efficiency; (*b*) they employ external or ceremonial assessment criteria to define the value of structural elements; and (*c*) dependence on externally fixed institutions reduces turbulence and maintains stability. As a result, it is argued here, institutional isomorphism promotes the success and survival of organizations. Incorporating externally legitimated formal structures increases the commitment of internal participants and external constituents. And the use of external assessment criteria — that is, moving toward the status in society of a subunit rather than an independent system — can enable an organization to remain successful by social definition, buffering it from failure.

Changing formal structures. — By designing a formal structure that adheres to the prescriptions of myths in the institutional environment, an organization demonstrates that it is acting on collectively valued purposes in a proper and adequate manner (Dowling and Pfeffer 1975; Meyer and Rowan 1975). The incorporation of institutionalized elements provides an account (Scott and Lyman 1968) of its activities that protects the organization from having its conduct questioned. The organization becomes, in a word, legitimate, and it uses its legitimacy to strengthen its support and secure its survival.

From an institutional perspective, then, a most important aspect of isomorphism with environmental institutions is the evolution of organizational language. The labels of the organization chart as well as the vocabulary used to delineate organizational goals, procedures, and policies are analogous to the vocabularies of motive used to account for the activities of individuals (Blum and McHugh 1971; Mills 1940). Just as jealousy, anger, altruism, and love are myths that interpret and explain the actions of individuals, the myths of doctors, of accountants, or of the assembly line explain organizational activities. Thus, some can say that the engineers will solve a specific problem or that the secretaries will perform certain tasks, without knowing who these engineers or secretaries will be or exactly what they will do. Both the speaker and the listeners understand such statements to describe how certain responsibilities will be carried out.

Vocabularies of structure which are isomorphic with institutional rules provide prudent, rational, and legitimate accounts. Organizations described in legitimated vocabularies are assumed to be oriented to collectively defined, and often collectively mandated, ends. The myths of personnel services, for example, not only account for the rationality of employment practices but also indicate that personnel services are valuable to an organization. Employees, applicants, managers, trustees, and governmental agencies are predisposed to trust the hiring practices of organizations that follow legitimated procedures — such as equal opportunity programs, or personality testing — and they are more willing to participate in or to fund such organizations. On the other hand, organizations that omit environmentally legitimated elements of structure or create unique structures lack acceptable legitimated accounts of their activities. Such organizations are more vulnerable to claims that they are negligent, irrational, or unnecessary. Claims of this kind, whether made by internal participants, external constituents, or the government, can cause organizations to incur real costs. For example:

> With the rise of modern medical institutions, large organizations that do not arrange

medical-care facilities for their workers come to be seen as negligent—by the workers, by management factions, by insurers, by courts which legally define negligence, and often by laws. The costs of illegitimacy in insurance premiums and legal liabilities are very real.

Similarly, environmental safety institutions make it important for organizations to create formal safety rules, safety departments, and safety programs. No Smoking rules and signs, regardless of their enforcement, are necessary to avoid charges of negligence and to avoid the extreme of illegitimation: the closing of buildings by the state.

The rise of professionalized economics makes it useful for organizations to incorporate groups of economists and econometric analyses. Though no one may read, understand, or believe them, econometric analyses help legitimate the organization's plans in the eyes of investors, customers (as with Defense Department contractors), and internal participants. Such analyses can also provide rational accountings after failures occur: managers whose plans have failed can demonstrate to investors, stockholders, and superiors that procedures were prudent and that decisions were made by rational means.

Thus, rationalized institutions create myths of formal structure which shape organizations. Failure to incorporate the proper elements of structure is negligent and irrational; the continued flow of support is threatened and internal dissidents are strengthened. At the same time, these myths present organizations with great opportunities for expansion. Affixing the right labels to activities can change them into valuable services and mobilize the commitments of internal participants and external constituents.

Adopting external assessment criteria.—In institutionally elaborated environments organizations also become sensitive to, and employ, external criteria of worth. Such criteria include, for instance, such ceremonial awards as the Nobel Prize, endorsements by important people, the standard prices of professionals and consultants, or the prestige of programs or personnel in external social circles. For example, the conventions of modern accounting attempt to assign value

to particular components of organizations on the basis of their contribution—through the organization's production function—to the goods and services the organization produces. But for many units—service departments, administrative sectors, and others—it is utterly unclear what is being produced that has clear or definable value in terms of its contribution to the organizational product. In these situations, accountants employ shadow prices: they assume that given organizational units are necessary and calculate their value from their prices in the world outside the organization. Thus modern accounting creates ceremonial production functions and maps them onto economic production functions: organizations assign externally defined worth to advertising departments, safety departments, managers, econometricians, and occasionally even sociologists, whether or not these units contribute measurably to the production of outputs. Monetary prices, in postindustrial society, reflect hosts of ceremonial influences, as do economic measures of efficiency, profitability, or net worth (Hirsch 1975).

Ceremonial criteria of worth and ceremonially derived production functions are useful to organizations: they legitimate organizations with internal participants, stockholders, the public, and the state, as with the IRS or the SEC. They demonstrate socially the fitness of an organization. The incorporation of structures with high ceremonial value, such as those reflecting the latest expert thinking or those with the most prestige, makes the credit position of an organization more favorable. Loans, donations, or investments are more easily obtained. Finally, units within the organization use ceremonial assessments as accounts of their productive service to the organization. Their internal power rises with their performance on ceremonial measures (Salancik and Pfeffer 1974).

Stabilization.—The rise of an elaborate institutional environment stabilizes both external and internal organizational relationships. Centralized states, trade associations, unions, professional associations, and coalitions among organizations standardize and stabilize (see the review by Starbuck 1976).

Market conditions, the characteristics of inputs and outputs, and technological procedures are brought under the jurisdiction of institutional meanings and controls. Stabilization also results as a given organization becomes part of the wider collective system. Support is guaranteed by agreements instead of depending entirely on performance. For example, apart from whether schools educate students, or hospitals cure patients, people and governmental agencies remain committed to these organizations, funding and using them almost automatically year after year.

Institutionally controlled environments buffer organizations from turbulence (Emery and Trist 1965; Terreberry 1968). Adaptations occur less rapidly as increased numbers of agreements are enacted. Collectively granted monopolies guarantee clienteles for organizations like schools, hospitals, or professional associations. The taken-for-granted (and legally regulated) quality of institutional rules makes dramatic instabilities in products, techniques, or policies unlikely. And legitimacy as accepted subunits of society protects organizations from immediate sanctions for variations in technical performance:

> Thus, American school districts (like other governmental units) have near monopolies and are very stable. They must conform to wider rules about proper classifications and credentials of teachers and students, and of topics of study. But they are protected by rules which make education as defined by these classifications compulsory. Alternative or private schools are possible, but must conform so closely to the required structures and classifications as to be able to generate little advantage.
>
> Some business organizations obtain very high levels of institutional stabilization. A large defense contractor may be paid for following agreed-on procedures, even if the product is ineffective. In the extreme, such organizations may be so successful as to survive bankruptcy intact—as Lockheed and

Penn Central have done—by becoming partially components of the state. More commonly, such firms are guaranteed survival by state-regulated rates which secure profits regardless of costs, as with American public utility firms.

> Large automobile firms are a little less stabilized. They exist in an environment that contains enough structures to make automobiles, as conventionally defined, virtual necessities. But still, customers and governments can inspect each automobile and can evaluate and even legally discredit it. Legal action cannot as easily discredit a high school graduate.

Organizational success and survival.— Thus, organizational success depends on factors other than efficient coordination and control of productive activities. Independent of their productive efficiency, organizations which exist in highly elaborated institutional environments and succeed in becoming isomorphic with these environments gain the legitimacy and resources needed to survive. In part, this depends on environmental processes and on the capacity of given organizational leadership to mold these processes (Hirsch 1975). In part, it depends on the ability of given organizations to conform to, and become legitimated by, environmental institutions. In institutionally elaborated environments, sagacious conformity is required: leadership (in a university, a hospital, or a business) requires an understanding of changing fashions and governmental programs. But this kind of conformity—and the almost guaranteed survival which may accompany it— is possible only in an environment with a highly institutionalized structure. In such a context an organization can be locked into isomorphism, ceremonially reflecting the institutional environment in its structure, functionaries, and procedures. Thus, in addition to the conventionally defined sources of organizational success and survival, the following general assertion can be proposed:

Proposition 3. *Organizations that incorporate societally legitimated rationalized elements in their formal structures maximize their legitimacy and increase their resources and survival capabilities.*

FIGURE 47.2 • ORGANIZATIONAL SURVIVAL

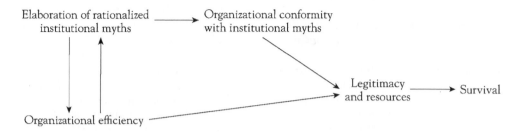

This proposition asserts that the long-run survival prospects of organizations increase as state structures elaborate and as organizations respond to institutionalized rules. In the United States, for instance, schools, hospitals, and welfare organizations show considerable ability to survive, precisely because they are matched with — and almost absorbed by — their institutional environments. In the same way, organizations fail when they deviate from the prescriptions of institutionalizing myths: quite apart from technical efficiency, organizations which innovate in important structural ways bear considerable costs in legitimacy.

Figure 47.2 summarizes the general argument of this section, alongside the established view that organizations succeed through efficiency.

INSTITUTIONALIZED STRUCTURES AND ORGANIZATIONAL ACTIVITIES

Rationalized formal structures arise in two contexts. First, the demands of local relational networks encourage the development of structures that coordinate and control activities. Such structures contribute to the efficiency of organizations and give them competitive advantages over less efficient competitors. Second, the interconnectedness of societal relations, the collective organization of society, and the leadership of organizational elites create a highly institutionalized context. In this context rationalized structures present an acceptable account of organizational activities, and organizations gain legitimacy, stability, and resources.

All organizations, to one degree or another, are embedded in both relational and institutionalized contexts and are therefore concerned both with coordinating and controlling their activities and with prudently accounting for them. Organizations in highly institutionalized environments face internal and boundary-spanning contingencies. Schools, for example, must transport students to and from school under some circumstances and must assign teachers, students, and topics to classrooms. On the other hand, organizations producing in markets that place great emphasis on efficiency build in units whose relation to production is obscure and whose efficiency is determined, not by a true production function, but by ceremonial definition.

Nevertheless, the survival of some organizations depends more on managing the demands of internal and boundary-spanning relations, while the survival of others depends more on the ceremonial demands of highly institutionalized environments. The discussion to follow shows that whether an organization's survival depends primarily on relational or on institutional demands determines the tightness of alignments between structures and activities.

Types of Organizations
Institutionalized myths differ in the completeness with which they describe cause and effect relationships, and in the clarity

with which they describe standards that should be used to evaluate outputs (Thompson 1967). Some organizations use routine, clearly defined technologies to produce outputs. When output can be easily evaluated a market often develops, and consumers gain considerable rights of inspection and control. In this context, efficiency often determines success. Organizations must face exigencies of close coordination with their relational networks, and they cope with these exigencies by organizing around immediate technical problems.

But the rise of collectively organized society and the increasing interconnectedness of social relations have eroded many market contexts. Increasingly, such organizations as schools, R & D units, and governmental bureaucracies use variable, ambiguous technologies to produce outputs that are difficult to appraise, and other organizations with clearly defined technologies find themselves unable to adapt to environmental turbulence. The uncertainties of unpredictable technical contingencies or of adapting to environmental change cannot be resolved on the basis of efficiency. Internal participants and external constituents alike call for institutionalized rules that promote trust and confidence in outputs and buffer organizations from failure (Emery and Trist 1965).

Thus, one can conceive of a continuum along which organizations can be ordered. At one end are production organizations under strong output controls (Ouchi and McGuire 1975) whose success depends on the management of relational networks. At the other end are institutionalized organizations whose success depends on the confidence and stability achieved by isomorphism with institutional rules. For two reasons it is important not to assume that an organization's location on this continuum is based on the inherent technical properties of its output and therefore permanent. First, the technical properties of outputs are socially defined and do not exist in some concrete sense that allows them to be empirically discovered. Second,

environments and organizations often redefine the nature of products, services, and technologies. Redefinition sometimes clarifies techniques or evaluative standards. But often organizations and environments redefine the nature of techniques and output so that ambiguity is introduced and rights of inspection and control are lowered. For example, American schools have evolved from producing rather specific training that was evaluated according to strict criteria of efficiency to producing ambiguously defined services that are evaluated according to criteria of certification (Callahan 1962; Tyack 1974; Meyer and Rowan 1975).

Structural Inconsistencies in Institutionalized Organizations

Two very general problems face an organization if its success depends primarily on isomorphism with institutionalized rules. First, technical activities and demands for efficiency create conflicts and inconsistencies in an institutionalized organization's efforts to conform to the ceremonial rules of production. Second, because these ceremonial rules are transmitted by myths that may arise from different parts of the environment, the rules may conflict with one another. These inconsistencies make a concern for efficiency and tight coordination and control problematic.

Formal structures that celebrate institutionalized myths differ from structures that act efficiently. Ceremonial activity is significant in relation to categorical rules, not in its concrete effects (Merton 1940; March and Simon 1958). A sick worker must be treated by a doctor using accepted medical procedures; whether the worker is treated effectively is less important. A bus company must service required routes whether or not there are many passengers. A university must maintain appropriate departments independently of the departments' enrollments. Activity, that is, has ritual significance: it maintains appearances and validates an organization.

Categorical rules conflict with the logic of efficiency. Organizations often face the dilemma that activities celebrating institutionalized rules, although they count as virtuous ceremonial expenditures, are pure costs from the point of view of efficiency. For example, hiring a Nobel Prize winner brings great ceremonial benefits to a university. The celebrated name can lead to research grants, brighter students, or reputational gains. But from the point of view of immediate outcomes, the expenditure lowers the instructional return per dollar expended and lowers the university's ability to solve immediate logistical problems. . . .

Yet another source of conflict between categorical rules and efficiency is the inconsistency among institutionalized elements. Institutional environments are often pluralistic (Udy 1970), and societies promulgate sharply inconsistent myths. As a result, organizations in search of external support and stability incorporate all sorts of incompatible structural elements. Professions are incorporated although they make overlapping jurisdictional claims. Programs are adopted which contend with each other for authority over a given domain. For instance, if one inquires who decides what curricula will be taught in schools, any number of parties from the various governments down to individual teachers may say that they decide.

In institutionalized organizations, then, concern with the efficiency of day-to-day activities creates enormous uncertainties. Specific contexts highlight the inadequacies of the prescriptions of generalized myths, and inconsistent structural elements conflict over jurisdictional rights. Thus the organization must struggle to link the requirements of ceremonial elements to technical activities and to link inconsistent ceremonial elements to each other.

Resolving Inconsistencies

. . . An organization can resolve conflicts between ceremonial rules and efficiency by employing two interrelated devices: decoupling and the logic of confidence.

Decoupling.—Ideally, organizations built around efficiency attempt to maintain close alignments between structures and activities. Conformity is enforced through inspection, output quality is continually monitored, the efficiency of various units is evaluated, and the various goals are unified and coordinated. But a policy of close alignment in institutionalized organizations merely makes public a record of inefficiency and inconsistency.

Institutionalized organizations protect their formal structures from evaluation on the basis of technical performance: inspection, evaluation, and control of activities are minimized, and coordination, interdependence, and mutual adjustments among structural units are handled informally.

Proposition 4. *Because attempts to control and coordinate activities in institutionalized organizations lead to conflicts and loss of legitimacy, elements of structure are decoupled from activities and from each other.*

Some well-known properties of organizations illustrate the decoupling process:

Activities are performed beyond the purview of managers. In particular, organizations actively encourage professionalism, and activities are delegated to professionals.

Goals are made ambiguous or vacuous, and categorical ends are substituted for technical ends. Hospitals treat, not cure, patients. Schools produce students, not learning. In fact, data on technical performance are eliminated or rendered invisible. Hospitals try to ignore information on cure rates, public services avoid data about effectiveness, and schools deemphasize measures of achievement.

Integration is avoided, program implementation is neglected, and inspection and evaluation are ceremonialized.

Human relations are made very important. The organization cannot formally coordinate activities because its formal rules, if applied, would generate inconsistencies. Therefore individuals are left to work out technical interdependencies informally. The ability to coordinate things in violation of the rules—that is, to get along with other people—is highly valued.

The advantages of decoupling are clear. The assumption that formal structures are really working is buffered from the inconsistencies and anomalies involved in technical activities. Also, because integration is avoided disputes and conflicts are minimized, and an organization can mobilize support from a broader range of external constituents.

Thus, decoupling enables organizations to maintain standardized, legitimating, formal structures while their activities vary in response to practical considerations. The organizations in an industry tend to be similar in formal structure — reflecting their common institutional origins — but may show much diversity in actual practice.

The logic of confidence and good faith. — Despite the lack of coordination and control, decoupled organizations are not anarchies. Day-to-day activities proceed in an orderly fashion. What legitimates institutionalized organizations, enabling them to appear useful in spite of the lack of technical validation, is the confidence and good faith of their internal participants and their external constituents.

Considerations of face characterize ceremonial management (Goffman 1967). Confidence in structural elements is maintained through three practices — avoidance, discretion, and overlooking (Goffman 1967, pp. 12–18). Avoidance and discretion are encouraged by decoupling autonomous subunits; overlooking anomalies is also quite common. Both internal participants and external constituents cooperate in these practices. Assuring that individual participants maintain face sustains confidence in the organization, and ultimately reinforces confidence in the myths that rationalize the organization's existence.

Delegation, professionalization, goal ambiguity, the elimination of output data, and maintenance of face are all mechanisms for absorbing uncertainty while preserving the formal structure of the organization (March and Simon 1958). They contribute to a general aura of confidence within and outside the organization. . . .

Decoupling and maintenance of face, in other words, are mechanisms that maintain the assumption that people are acting in good faith. Professionalization is not merely a way of avoiding inspection — it binds both supervisors and subordinates to act in good faith. So in a smaller way does strategic leniency (Blau 1956). And so do the public displays of morale and satisfaction which are characteristic of many organizations. Organizations employ a host of mechanisms to dramatize the ritual commitments which their participants make to basic structural elements. These mechanisms are especially common in organizations which strongly reflect their institutionalized environments.

Proposition 5. *The more an organization's structure is derived from institutionalized myths, the more it maintains elaborate displays of confidence, satisfaction, and good faith, internally and externally.*

The commitments built up by displays of morale and satisfaction are not simply vacuous affirmations of institutionalized myths. Participants not only commit themselves to supporting an organization's ceremonial facade but also commit themselves to making things work out backstage. The committed participants engage in informal coordination that, although often formally inappropriate, keeps technical activities running smoothly and avoids public embarrassments. In this sense the confidence and good faith generated by ceremonial action is in no way fraudulent. It may even be the most reasonable way to get participants to make their best efforts in situations that are made problematic by institutionalized myths that are at odds with immediate technical demands.

Ceremonial inspection and evaluation. — All organizations, even those maintaining high levels of confidence and good faith, are in environments that have institutionalized the rationalized rituals of inspection and evaluation. And inspection and evaluation can uncover events and deviations that undermine legitimacy. So institutionalized organizations minimize and ceremonialize inspection and evaluation.

FIGURE 47.3 • THE EFFECTS OF INSTITUTIONAL
ISOMORPHISM ON ORGANIZATIONS

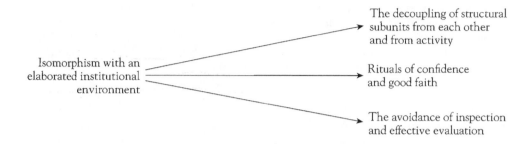

In institutionalized organizations, in fact, evaluation accompanies and produces illegitimacy. The interest in evaluation research by the American federal government, for instance, is partly intended to undercut the state, local, and private authorities which have managed social services in the United States. The federal authorities, of course, have usually not evaluated those programs which are completely under federal jurisdiction; they have only evaluated those over which federal controls are incomplete. Similarly, state governments have often insisted on evaluating the special fundings they create in welfare and education but ordinarily do not evaluate the programs which they fund in a routine way.

Evaluation and inspection are public assertions of societal control which violate the assumption that everyone is acting with competence and in good faith. Violating this assumption lowers morale and confidence. Thus, evaluation and inspection undermine the ceremonial aspects of organizations.

Proposition 6. *Institutionalized organizations seek to minimize inspection and evaluation by both internal managers and external constituents.*

Decoupling and the avoidance of inspection and evaluation are not merely devices used by the organization. External constituents, too, avoid inspecting and controlling institutionalized organizations (Meyer and Rowan 1975). Accrediting agencies, boards of trustees, government agencies, and individuals accept ceremonially at face value the credentials, ambiguous goals, and categorical evaluations that are characteristic of ceremonial organizations. In elaborate institutional environments these external constituents are themselves likely to be corporately organized agents of society. Maintaining categorical relationships with their organizational subunits is more stable and more certain than is relying on inspection and control.

Figure 47.3 summarizes the main arguments of this section of our discussion.

SUMMARY AND RESEARCH IMPLICATIONS

Organizational structures are created and made more elaborate with the rise of institutionalized myths, and, in highly institutionalized contexts, organizational action must support these myths. But an organization must also attend to practical activity. The two requirements are at odds. A stable solution is to maintain the organization in a loosely coupled state.

No position is taken here on the overall social effectiveness of isomorphic and loosely coupled organizations. To some extent such structures buffer activity from efficiency criteria and produce ineffectiveness. On the other hand, by binding participants to act in good faith, and to adhere to the larger rationalities of the wider structure, they may maximize long-run effectiveness. It should not be assumed that the creation of microscopic rationalities in the daily activity of workers effects social ends more efficiently than commitment to larger institutional claims and purposes. . . .

NOTE

Work on this paper was conducted at the Stanford Center for Research and Development in Teaching (SCRDT) and was supported by the National Institute of Education (contract no. NE-C-00-3-0062). The views expressed here do not, of course, reflect NIE positions. Many colleagues in the SCRDT, the Stanford Organizations Training Program, the American Sociological Association's work group on Organizations and Environments, and the NIE gave help and encouragement. In particular, H. Acland, A. Bergesen, J. Boli-Bennett, T. Deal, J. Freeman, P. Hirsch, J. G. March, W. R. Scott, and W. Starbuck made helpful suggestions.

REFERENCES

Aiken, Michael, and Jerald Hage. 1968. "Organizational Interdependence and Intraorganizational Structure." *American Sociological Review* 33 (December): 912–30.

Bell, Daniel. 1973. *The Coming of Post-industrial Society*. New York: Basic.

Bendix, Reinhard. 1964. *Nation-Building and Citizenship*. New York: Wiley.

———. 1968. "Bureaucracy." Pp. 206–19 in *International Encyclopedia of the Social Sciences*, edited by David L. Sills. New York: Macmillan.

Berger, Peter L., and Thomas Luckmann. 1967. *The Social Construction of Reality*. New York: Doubleday.

Blau, Peter M. 1956. *Bureaucracy in Modern Society*. New York: Random House.

———. 1970. "A Formal Theory of Differentiation in Organizations." *American Sociological Review* 35 (April): 201–18.

Blum, Alan F., and Peter McHugh. 1971. "The Social Ascription of Motives." *American Sociological Review* 36 (December): 98–109.

Callahan, Raymond E. 1962. *Education and the Cult of Efficiency*. Chicago: University of Chicago Press.

Carlson, Richard O. 1962. *Executive Succession and Organizational Change*. Chicago: Midwest Administration Center, University of Chicago.

Clark, Burton R. 1956. *Adult Education in Transition*. Berkeley: University of California Press.

Dalton, Melville. 1959. *Men Who Manage*. New York: Wiley.

Dowling, John, and Jeffrey Pfeffer. 1975. "Organizational Legitimacy." *Pacific Sociological Review* 18 (January): 122–36.

Downs, Anthony. 1967. *Inside Bureaucracy*. Boston: Little, Brown.

Durkheim, Émile. 1933. *The Division of Labor in Society*. New York: Macmillan.

Ellul, Jacques. 1964. *The Technological Society*. New York: Knopf.

Emery, Fred L., and Eric L. Trist. 1965. "The Causal Texture of Organizational Environments." *Human Relations* 18 (February): 21–32.

Freeman, John Henry. 1973. "Environment, Technology and Administrative Intensity of Manufacturing Organizations." *American Sociological Review* 38 (December): 750–63.

Goffman, Erving. 1967. *Interaction Ritual*. Garden City, N.Y.: Anchor.

Hawley, Amos H. 1968. "Human Ecology." Pp. 328–37 in *International Encyclopedia of the Social Sciences*, edited by David L. Sills. New York: Macmillan.

Hirsch, Paul M. 1975. "Organizational Effectiveness and the Institutional Environment." *Administrative Science Quarterly* 20 (September): 327–44.

Homans, George C. 1950. *The Human Group*. New York: Harcourt, Brace.

March, James G., and Johan P. Olsen. 1976. *Ambiguity and Choice in Organizations*. Bergen: Universitetsforlaget.

March, James G., and Herbert A. Simon. 1958. *Organizations*. New York: Wiley.

Merton, Robert K. 1940. "Bureaucratic Structure and Personality." *Social Forces* 18 (May): 560–68.

Meyer, John W., and Brian Rowan. 1975. "Notes on the Structure of Educational Organizations." Paper presented at annual meeting of the American Sociological Association, San Francisco.

Mills, C. Wright. 1940. "Situated Actions and Vocabularies of Motive." *American Sociological Review* 5 (February): 904–13.

Ouchi, William, and Mary Ann Maguire. 1975. "Organizational Control: Two Functions." *Administrative Science Quarterly* 20 (December): 559–69.

Parsons, Talcott. 1956. "Suggestions for a Sociological Approach to the Theory of Organizations I." *Administrative Science Quarterly* 1 (June): 63–85.

———. 1971. *The System of Modern Societies.* Englewood Cliffs, N.J.: Prentice-Hall.

Perrow, Charles. 1970. *Organizational Analysis: A Sociological View.* Belmont, Calif.: Wadsworth.

Salancik, Gerald R., and Jeffrey Pfeffer. 1974. "The Bases and Use of Power in Organizational Decision Making." *Administrative Science Quarterly* 19 (December): 453–73.

Scott, Marvin B., and Stanford M. Lyman. 1968. "Accounts." *American Sociological Review* 33 (February): 46–62.

Scott, W. Richard. 1975. "Organizational Structure." Pp. 1–20 in *Annual Review of Sociology.* Vol. 1, edited by Alex Inkeles. Palo Alto, Calif.: Annual Reviews.

Selznick, Philip. 1949. *TVA and the Grass Roots.* Berkeley: University of California Press.

Spencer, Herbert. 1897. *Principles of Sociology.* New York: Appleton.

Starbuck, William H. 1976. "Organizations and their Environments." Pp. 1069–1123 in *Handbook of Industrial and Organizational Psychology,* edited by Marvin D. Dunnette. New York: Rand McNally.

Swanson, Guy E. 1971. "An Organizational Analysis of Collectivities." *American Sociological Review* 36 (August): 607–24.

Terreberry, Shirley. 1968. "The Evolution of Organizational Environments." *Administrative Science Quarterly* 12 (March): 590–613.

Thompson, James D. 1967. *Organizations in Action.* New York: McGraw-Hill.

Tyack, David B. 1974. *The One Best System.* Cambridge, Mass.: Harvard University Press.

Udy, Stanley H., Jr. 1970. *Work in Traditional and Modern Society.* Englewood Cliffs, N.J.: Prentice-Hall.

Weber, Max. 1930. *The Protestant's Ethic and the Spirit of Capitalism.* New York: Scribner's.

———. 1946. *Essays in Sociology.* New York: Oxford University Press.

———. 1947. *The Theory of Social and Economic Organization.* New York: Oxford University Press.

Weick, Karl E. 1976. "Educational Organizations as Loosely Coupled Systems." *Administrative Science Quarterly* 21 (March): 1–19.

Wilensky, Harold L. 1965. "The Professionalization of Everyone?" *American Journal of Sociology* 70 (September): 137–58.

Woodward, Joan. 1965. *Industrial Organization, Theory and Practice.* London: Oxford University Press.

Zald, Mayer N., and Patricia Denton. 1963. "From Evangelism to General Service: The Transformation of the YMCA." *Administrative Science Quarterly* 8 (September): 214–34.

48
External Control of Organizations: A Resource Dependence Perspective

Jeffrey Pfeffer and Gerald R. Salancik

. . . To understand the behavior of an organization you must understand the context of that behavior—that is, the ecology of the organization. This point of view is important for those who seek to understand organizations as well as for those who seek to manage and control them. Organizations are inescapably bound up with the conditions of their environment. Indeed, it has been said that all organizations engage in activities which have as their logical conclusion adjustment to the environment (Hawley, 1950:3).

At first glance, this position seems obvious. An open-systems perspective on organizations is not new (Katz and Kahn, 1966), and it is generally accepted that contexts, organizational environments, are important for understanding actions and structures. One of the purposes of [this chapter] is to note that, in spite of the apparent obviousness of this position, much of the literature on organizations still does not recognize the importance of context; indeed, there are some reasons why such a neglect of contextual factors is likely to be maintained.

OVERVIEW

Most books about organizations describe how they operate, and the existence of the organizations is taken for granted. This book discusses how organizations manage to survive. Their existence is constantly in question, and their survival is viewed as problematic. How managers go about ensuring their organization's survival is what this book is about.

Our position is that organizations survive to the extent that they are effective. Their effectiveness derives from the management of demands, particularly the demands of interest groups upon which the organizations depend for resources and support. As we shall consider, there are a variety of ways of managing demands, including the obvious one of giving in to them.

The key to organizational survival is the ability to acquire and maintain resources. This problem would be simplified if organizations were in complete control of all the components necessary for their operation. However, no organization is completely self-contained. Organizations are embedded in an environment comprised of other organizations. They depend on those other organizations for the many resources they themselves require. Organizations are linked to environments by federations, associations, customer-supplier relationships, competitive relationships, and a social-legal apparatus defining and controlling the nature and limits of these relationships. Organizations must transact with other elements in their environment to acquire needed resources, and this is true whether we are talking about public organizations, private organizations, small or large organizations, or organizations which are bureaucratic or organic (Burns and Stalker, 1961). . . .

The fact that organizations are dependent for survival and success on their environments does not, in itself, make their

Source: Jeffrey Pfeffer and Gerald R. Salancik, *The External Control of Organizations* (New York: Harper & Row, 1978), pp. 1–22. © 1978 Harper and Row. © 2003 by the Board of Trustees of the Leland Stanford Jr. University. Used with the permission of Stanford University Press.

existence problematic. If stable supplies were assured from the sources of needed resources, there would be no problem. If the resources needed by the organization were continually available, even if outside their control, there would be no problem. Problems arise not merely because organizations are dependent on their environment, but because this environment is not dependable. Environments can change, new organizations enter and exit, and the supply of resources becomes more or less scarce. When environments change, organizations face the prospect either of not surviving or of changing their activities in response to these environmental factors. . . .

Both problems of using resources and problems of acquiring them face organizations, but the use of resources always presupposes their existence. A good deal of organizational behavior, the actions taken by organizations, can be understood only by knowing something about the organization's environment and the problems it creates for obtaining resources. What happens in an organization is not only a function of the organization, its structure, its leadership, its procedures, or its goals. What happens is also a consequence of the environment and the particular contingencies and constraints deriving from that environment.

Consider the following case, described by a student at the University of Illinois. The student had worked in a fast-food restaurant near the campus and was concerned about how the workers (himself) were treated. Involved in what he was studying the student read a great deal about self-actualizing, theories of motivation, and the management of human resources. He observed at the restaurant that workers would steal food, make obscene statements about the boss behind his back, and complain about the low pay. The student's analysis of the situation was a concise report summarizing the typical human relations palliatives: make the boring, greasy work more challenging and the indifferent management more democratic. The student was asked why he thought

management was unresponsive to such suggestions. He considered the possibility that management was cruel and interested only in making a profit (and the operation was quite profitable). He was then asked why the employees permitted management to treat them in such a fashion—after all, they could always quit. The student responded that the workers needed the money and that jobs were hard to obtain.

This fact, that the workers were drawn from an almost limitless labor pool of students looking for any kind of part-time employment was nowhere to be found in the student's discussion of the operation of the restaurant. Yet, it was precisely this characteristic of the labor market which permitted the operation to disregard the feelings of the workers. Since there were many who wanted to work, the power of an individual worker was severely limited. More critical to the organization's success was its location and its ability both to keep competition to a minimum and to maintain a steady flow of supplies to serve a virtually captive market. If the workers were unsatisfied, it was not only because they did not like the organization's policies; in the absence of any base of power and with few alternative jobs, the workers had neither the option of voice nor exit (Hirschman, 1970).

More important to this organization's success than the motivation of its workers was its location on a block between the campus and dormitories, the path of thousands of students. Changes in policies and facilities for housing and transportation of students would have a far greater effect than some disgruntled employees. Our example illustrates, first, the importance of attending to contextual variables in understanding organizations, but also that organizational survival and success are not always achieved by making internal adjustments. Dealing with and managing the environment is just as important a component of organizational effectiveness.

A comparison of the phonograph record and the pharmaceutical industries (Hirsch,

1975) illustrates this point more directly. These two industries, Hirsch noted, are strikingly different in profitability. This difference in profits is more striking because the industries in many ways are otherwise similar: both sell their products through intermediaries, doctors in the case of pharmaceuticals, disc jockeys in the case of records; both introduce many new products; both protect their market positions through patent or copyright laws. What could account for the difference in profit? Hirsch argued that the pharmaceutical industry's greater profits came from its greater control of its environment; a more concentrated industry, firms could more effectively restrict entry and manage distribution channels. Profits resulted from a favorable institutional environment. Aware of the importance of the institutional environment for success, firms spent a lot of strategic effort maintaining that environment. They would engage in activities designed to modify patent laws to their advantage and in other efforts to protect their market positions.

The Environment as Treated in the Social Sciences

The social sciences, even if not frequently examining the context of behavior, have long recognized its importance. The demography of a city has been found to affect the particular form of city government used, and particularly the use of a city manager (Kessel, 1962; Schnore and Alford, 1963). Some political economists have argued that party positions are developed with reference to the distribution of preferences for policies in the population (e.g., Davis and Hinich, 1966), which means that political platforms are affected by context. The importance of external influences on individual voting behaviors has been recognized, while participation in political activities, as well as other forms of voluntary associations, is also partially determined by the context, particularly the demographic and socioeconomic dimensions of the community.

As in the case of political science, some theorists writing about organizational behavior have recognized that the organization's context shapes the activities and structures of formal organizations. Katz and Kahn (1966) argued for the necessity of viewing organizations as open systems, and Perrow (1970) forcefully illustrated the analytical benefits to be gained by considering the environment of the organization in addition to its internal operating characteristics. Bendix (1956) showed how ideologies shaped the use of authority in organizations, and Weber (1930) proposed a theory of economic development that held the religion of a country to be critical. He suggested that the development of mercantile capitalism depended on a legitimating ideology which stressed hard work and delayed gratification, such as that provided by Protestantism, as contrasted with Catholicism.

Economists were even more explicit in giving critical importance to the context of organizations, but they tended to take the environment as a given. Competition is a critical variable distinguishing between the applicability of models of monopoly, oligopoly, imperfect competition, or perfectly competitive behavior. The study of oligopoly is explicitly the study of interorganizational behavior (e.g., Phillips, 1960; Williamson, 1965; Fellner, 1949). And, the study of antitrust policy implicitly recognizes the fact that organizations do make efforts to limit or otherwise manage the competitiveness of their environments.

In recent years, it has become fashionable for those writing about management and organizations to acknowledge the importance of the open-systems view and the importance of the environment, particularly in the first chapter or in a special section of the book. Except for some special terminology, however, the implications of the organization's context for analyzing and managing organizations remains undeveloped. . . . Prescriptions for, and discussions of, the operation of organizations remain predominantly concerned with the internal activities, organizational adjustments, and the behavior of individuals.

INTERNAL VERSUS EXTERNAL PERSPECTIVES ON ORGANIZATIONS

The interest in intraorganizational phenomena is not difficult to understand. First, internal processes are the most visible. Walking into any organization, one finds people who are involved in a variety of activities important to the performance of the organization. As Perrow (1970) aptly noted, at first glance, the statement that organizations are, after all, composed of people is patently obvious. . . . People inside the organization are visible, accessible, and willing to express their opinions. They are a convenient, if not always adequate, research focus.

In addition to convenience, attention to intraorganizational phenomena is fostered by a cognitive bias to attribute causality to the actions of individuals. Research on the behavior of individuals asked to select causative factors suggests that while actors and participants in an event tend to attribute the outcome to situational factors, observers tend to interpret outcomes as the result of the personal motivation and capabilities of the actors (Jones and Nisbett, 1971). The observers of organizations and organizational behavior share this bias. In one recent illustration of this phenomenon (Wolfson and Salancik, 1977), individuals were given the task of controlling an electric car as it traveled over a model track. Unknown to the individuals, their performance was controlled by alterations in the amount of electrical power reaching various sections of the track. All the actual subjects were motivated to do well, but observers tended to see a performer's success as reflecting the amount of effort expended. In fact, it was the result of the experimenter's manipulation of electricity. . . .

Kelley (1971) perceptively noted that attributions are guided not only by the desire to be correct, but also to provide a feeling of control over situations. Clearly, by attributing outcomes to individual action, the observer has a theory of behavior that implies how to control outcomes. When one does not like what is going on, the simple solution is to replace the individual or change the activities. When, on the other hand, a model is used which attributes causality to contextual factors, one faces a much more difficult task in altering activities or outcomes. Therefore, the feelings of control that derive from attributing organizational actions to individuals reinforce the perceptual and cognitive biases, tending to produce a consistent, self-reinforcing system of perception and attribution that emphasizes the importance of individual action. . . .

The Importance of Individuals in Organizations

The basic, important question of how much of the variance in organizational activities or outcomes is associated with context and how much with individuals has been infrequently addressed. Pfeffer (1977) noted various theoretical reasons for expecting that individuals would have less effect on organizational outcomes than would an organization's context. First, he argued that both personal and organizational selection processes would lead to similarity among organizational leaders. This means that there is a restriction on the range of skills, characteristics, and behaviors of those likely to achieve positions of importance in organizations. Second, even when a relatively prominent position in the organization has been achieved, the discretion permitted to a given individual is limited. Decisions may require the approval of others in the organization; information used in formulating the decisions comes from others; and persons may be the targets of influence attempts by others in their role set — these social influences further constrain the individual's discretion. Finally, it is simply the case that many of the things that affected organizational results are not controlled by organizational participants. In the case of business firms, the economic cycle, tariff and other regulations, and tax policies are either not subject to control by the organization or are controlled only indirectly through persuasion. In school districts, budgets and educational demands, which are largely a function of state legislative action, local economic growth, and demographic factors are largely outside the control of the district administration. Considering all these factors, it is not likely administrators would have a large effect on the outcomes of most organizations.

In a study of 167 companies, Lieberson and O'Connor (1972) attempted to partition variance in sales, profit, and profit margin to the effects of year (economic cycle), industry, company, and finally, administrators. While the estimate of administrative impact varied by industry and was largest in the case of profit margin, the magnitude of the administrative effect was dwarfed by the impact of the organization's industry and the stable characteristics of a given organization. Extending this perspective, Salancik and Pfeffer (1977) examined the effects of mayors on city budget categories for a sample of 30 United States cities. These authors found that the mayoral impact was greatest for budget items such as parks and libraries not directly the subject of powerful interest-group demands, but that, in general, the mayor accounted for less than 10 percent of the variation in most city budget expenditures.

The conditions under which there would be more or less administrative effect is an important issue, and the theoretical perspective developed in this book will suggest some answers. But, it is fair to state that, based on the presently available research evidence, there is much less evidence for profound administrative effects than is reflected in the predominance of an internal orientation in the literature on organizations.

BASIC CONCEPTS FOR A CONTEXTUAL PERSPECTIVE

. . . In the remainder of this chapter, we will briefly describe a number of key concepts that develop this perspective. These concepts will assist in bringing coherence to the large body of work on organization and environment and will provide us with the tools for systematically understanding the effect of environments on organizations and the effect of organizations on environments.

Organizational Effectiveness

The first concept is organizational effectiveness. . . . The effectiveness of an organization is its ability to create acceptable outcomes and actions. It is important to avoid confusing organizational effectiveness with organizational efficiency, a confusion that is both widespread and more a real than a semantic problem. The difference between the two concepts is at the heart of the external versus internal perspective on organizations. Organizational effectiveness is an *external* standard of how well an organization is meeting the demands of the various groups and organizations that are concerned with its activities. When the automobile as a mode of transportation is questioned by consumers and governments, this is an issue of the organizational effectiveness of automobile manufacturers. The most important aspect of this concept of organizational effectiveness is that the acceptability of the organization and its activities is ultimately judged by those outside the organization. As we shall see, this does not imply that the organization is at the mercy of outsiders. The organization can and does manipulate, influence, and create acceptability for itself and its activities.

The effectiveness of an organization is a sociopolitical question. It may have a basis in economic considerations, as when an individual declines purchase of a product because it is priced too high. The concept is not restricted, however, to decisions that are economically motivated. Rather, it reflects both an assessment of the usefulness of what is being done and of the resources that are being consumed by the organization.

Organizational efficiency is an *internal* standard of performance. The question whether what is being done should be done is not posed, but only how well is it being done. Efficiency is measured by the ratio of resources utilized to output produced. Efficiency is relatively value free and independent of the particular criteria used to evaluate input and output. Because efficiency involves doing better what the organization is currently doing, external pressures on the organization are often defined internally as ·requests for greater efficiency. . . .

The difference between efficiency and effectiveness can be illustrated easily. In the late 1960s, Governor Ronald Reagan of California curtailed the amount of money going to the state university system. He was concerned that state university campuses, particularly Berkeley, were indoctrinating students in radical, left-wing ideas. In response to these political pressures and to forestall further budget cuts, the administrators attempted to demonstrate that they were educating students at an ever lower cost per student. Not surprisingly, this argument had little impact on the governor; indeed, it missed the point of his criticism. Producing revolutionaries at lower cost was not what the governor wanted; rather, he questioned whether the universities produced anything that justified giving them state funds.

Organizational Environment

The external basis for judging organizational effectiveness makes the concept of environment important. The concept of environment, however, is elusive. In one sense, the environment includes every event in the world which has any effect on the activities or outcomes of the organization. Primary schools are a part of other organizations' environment. Thus, when primary schools fail to teach reading and grammar properly, some organizations may be affected more than others. An organization which does not require people to read as part of their task may be minimally affected. Other organizations may feel profound effects, as in the case of universities which found themselves spending more and more resources teaching basic reading, grammar, and mathematics skills. Even

more affected were publishers, who found it necessary to rewrite many of their textbooks at a seventh- or eighth-grade reading level. The Association of American Publishers had to revise the pamphlet "How to Get the Most Out of Your Textbook" because the college students for whom it was written could not understand it.

Although one can conceive of an organization's environment as encompassing every event that affects it, doing so would not be useful for understanding how the organization responds. Every event confronting an organization does not necessarily affect it. A baking company which has a large inventory of sugar will be less affected by changes in the price of sugar than one which must purchase supplies on the open market continually. Thus, one reason why elements of an environment may have little impact is that the organization is isolated or buffered from them. A second reason why organizations do not respond to every event in the environment is that they do not notice every event, nor are all occurrences important enough to require a response. The term "loosely coupled" has been used to denote the relationship between elements in a social system, such as those between organizations. The effects of organizations on one another are frequently filtered and imperfect (March and Olsen, 1975; Weick, 1976). Loose-coupling is an important safety device for organizational survival. If organizational actions were completely determined by every changing event, organizations would constantly confront potential disaster and need to monitor every change while continually modifying themselves. The fact that environmental impacts are felt only imperfectly provides the organization with some discretion, as well as the capability to act across time horizons longer than the time it takes for an environment to change.

Perhaps one of the most important influences on an organization's response to its environment is the organization itself. Organizational environments are not given realities; they are created through a process of attention and interpretation. Organizations have information systems for gathering, screening, selecting, and retaining information. By the existence of a department or a position, the organization will attend to some aspects of its environment rather than others. Organizations establish subunits to screen out information and protect the internal operations from external influences. Organizational perception and knowledge of the environment is also affected because individuals who attend to the information occupy certain positions in the organization and tend to define the information as a function of their position. If the complaint department is located in the sales division, the flow of information may be interpreted as problems with the marketing and promotion of the product. If it is located in the public relations department, the complaints may be seen as a problem in corporate image. If the function were located in the production department, the complaints might be interpreted as problems of quality control or product design. Since there is no way of knowing about the environment except by interpreting ambiguous events, it is important to understand how organizations come to construct perceptions of reality.

Organizational information systems offer insight to those seeking to analyze and diagnose organizations. Information which is not collected or available is not likely to be used in decision making, and information which is heavily represented in the organization's record keeping is likely to emphatically shape decisions. Some organizations, such as Sears, collect information on a regular basis about worker opinions and morale, while others do not. It is inevitable that those organizations not collecting such information will make decisions that do not take those factors into account. Information systems both determine what will be considered in organizational choice and also provide information about what the organization considers important. . . . Information, regardless of its actual validity, comes to take on an importance and meaning just because of its collection and availability.

The kind of information an organization has about its environment will also vary with its connections to the environment. Organizational members serve on boards of directors, commissions, and are members of clubs and various other organizations. By sending representatives to governmental hearings or investigatory panels, organizations learn about policies that may affect their operations. Research personnel in industry maintain regular contacts with university research projects that may result in knowledge vital to their interests. In one instance, the director of research for the Petroleum Chemicals Research Division of the Ethyl Corporation, a major producer of lead additives for gasoline, made a personal visit to a university research group one month after it had received a large grant to study the impact of lead in the environment (Salancik and Lamont, 1974). Ethyl had learned of the project from contacts in the government. As the project's major objective was to determine the impact of lead on the environment so that policies regarding the manufacture, sale, and distribution of lead might be assessed, the project was of obvious concern to Ethyl.

How an organization learns about its environment, how it attends to the environment, and how it selects and processes information to give meaning to its environment are all important aspects of how the context of an organization affects its actions.

Constraints

A third concept important for understanding organization-environment relationships is constraint. Actions can be said to be constrained whenever one response to a given situation is more probable than any other response to the situation, regardless of the actor responding. That is, constraint is present whenever responses to a situation are not random. A person driving down a city street will tend to drive between 25 and 35 miles per hour. The same person on a state or federal highway will tend to drive between 50 and 65 miles per hour. Whatever the reason, the fact that behavior — of drivers, for example — is not random or, in other words, is somewhat predictable suggests that something is constraining behavior in these situations.

Constraints on behavior are often considered to be undesirable, restricting creativity and adaptation. However, in most cases action is not possible without constraints, which can facilitate the choice and decision process. Consider an undergraduate student attempting to decide on a course of study for a given semester. At a large university, there may be hundreds of courses, and if there were no constraint, literally millions of possible program combinations could be constructed. Deciding among these millions of programs would, of course, be difficult and time consuming, if not impossible. Fortunately, program choices are constrained. First, there may be a limit on the number of courses a student is allowed to take, and then, there is the constraint of not being able to be in two places at the same time. A third constraint is that some courses are defined as being appropriate for certain categories of student, such as graduate courses or freshman courses, while others have necessary prerequisites that limit their being chosen. Further constraints are added by general university requirements, and then, requirements particular to the student's own department and chosen degree program. Thus, out of millions of possible programs of study, only a few options will be feasible, permitted by all the various constraints. Instead of facing a difficult information-processing task, the student need choose only among a very limited set of alternatives.

Behavior is almost inevitably constrained — by physical realities, by social influence, by information and cognitive capacity, as well as by personal preferences. And, in many cases, constraints can be manipulated to promote certain behaviors. In the study of human behavior, when an experimenter designs an experimental situation, he presupposes that he has imposed enough constraints on the situation so that most individuals will behave as he predicts. In a similar fashion, the behavior of larger social units, such as groups and formal organizations, is generally constrained by the interests of others — governments, consumers, unions, competitors, etc.

The concept of constraint explains why individuals account for relatively little variance in the performance and activities of organizational systems. Every individual operates under constraint. Even leaders are not free from it. In a recent study of leadership behavior in an insurance company, it was found that the extent to which supervisors were able to do as their workers wanted was inversely related to the extent to which the supervisors were constrained by other departments (Salancik et al., 1975). Supervisors forced to coordinate and meet the demands of other departments had to behave in ways necessary to meet those demands; they did not have the opportunity to satisfy the desires of their subordinates. The point is that behaviors are frequently constrained by situational contingencies and the individual's effect is relatively small.

THE ROLE OF MANAGEMENT

We have emphasized the importance of contexts, or situational contingencies, as determinants of organizational behavior. We have attempted to question the internal perspective of organizational functioning and the concomitant belief in the omnipotence of individual administrative action. We have not, however, defined the role of the manager out of existence. It is important to conclude this introductory chapter by making explicit our view of the role of the manager within the theoretical perspective we are developing.

The Symbolic Role of Management
As has been noted by others (e.g., Kelley, 1971; Lieberson and O'Connor, 1972), individuals apparently desire a feeling of control over their social environments. The

tendency to attribute great effect to individual action, particularly action taken by persons in designated leadership positions, may be partially accounted for by this desire for a feeling of personal effectiveness and control. Thus, one function of the leader or manager is to serve as a symbol, as a focal point for the organization's successes and failures—in other words, to personify the organization, its activities, and its outcomes. Such personification of social causation enhances the feeling of predictability and control, giving observers an identifiable, concrete target for emotion and action. . . .

The symbolic role of administrators is, occasionally, constructed with elaborate ritual and ceremony. The inauguration of the president is an uncommon event invested with pomp and expectation. This even though three months earlier both voters and commentators were saying that there was no difference between the candidates. The ritual, however, is necessary.

Why organizations vary in the ritual they associate with their offices of power is little understood. One possibility is that more care and trouble is taken in selecting and installing organizational leaders when they do have influence. Another possibility is just the reverse. The very impotence of leadership positions requires that a ritual indicating great power be performed. People desire to believe in the effectiveness of leadership and personal action. When, in fact, administrators have only minor effects, it might be plausibly argued that ritual, mythology, and symbolism will be most necessary to keep the image of personal control alive. When the administrator really does make a difference and really does affect organizational performance, his effect will be obvious to all and there will be little need to make a show of power and control. It is only when the administrator makes little or no difference that some symbol of control and effectiveness is needed.

It is interesting to note that the ritual of the inauguration of American presidents has grown over time as the executive bureaucracy has grown. The president personally probably has come to have less and less effect on the basic operations of government, while the rituals associated with the office have increased in scope and grandeur.

That managers serve as symbols is not to deny their importance. Important social functions are served by the manipulation of symbols. The catharsis achieved by firing the unsuccessful football coach or the company executive, or by not reelecting some political figure, is too real to dismiss as unimportant. Those who remain in the organization are left with the hope that things will be improved. And, belief in the importance of individual action itself is reinforced—a belief which, even if not completely true, is necessary to motivate individuals to act at all.

The manager who serves as a symbol exposes himself to personal risks. He is accountable for things over which he has no control, and his personal career and fortunes may suffer as a consequence. The sportscasters' cliche that managers are hired to be fired reflects a great amount of truth about all managers. One of the reasons for having a manager is to have someone who is responsible, accountable for the organization's activities and outcomes. If the manager has little influence over these activities or outcomes, it is still useful to hold him responsible. His firing itself may permit loosening some of the constraints facing the organization.

Since most organizational researchers have assumed that managers were the critical element in actual organizational outcomes, the symbolic role of management has been virtually neglected, except for the brief mention by Mintzberg (1973). We would argue that this is one of the more important functions of management, deserving of more explicit empirical attention.

The Possibilities of Managerial Action

Saying that managers are symbols to be held accountable does not suggest many purposeful actions for them; yet, there are many possibilities for managerial action, even given the external constraints on most organizations. Constraints are not predestined and irreversible. Most constraints on organizational actions are the result of prior decision making or the resolution of various conflicts among competing interest groups. For instance, the requirement for companies doing business with the government to develop (and, possibly, implement) affirmative action hiring plans for recruiting minorities and women did not suddenly materialize. This constraint has a lengthy history and resulted from the interaction of a variety of groups and individuals. The fact that a constraint exists indicates that sufficient social support has been mustered to bring it into existence. In the social context of organizations, behind every constraint there is an interest group that has managed to have that constraint imposed. Since this is the case, the constraint is potentially removable if it is possible to organize the social support and resources sufficient to remove it.

The social context of an organization is, itself, the outcome of the actions of social actors. Since many constraints derive from the actions of others, one important function of management is influencing these others as a means of determining one's own environment. Organizations frequently operate on their environments to make them more stable or more munificent. One function of management, then, is to guide and control this process of manipulating the environment. Much of this book will describe just how organizations attempt to influence and control their social context.

Another component of managerial action involves both the recognition of the social context and constraints within which the organization must operate and the choice of organizational adjustments to these social realities. Even when there is no possibility for managerial alteration of the social environment, management can still be difficult, for recognizing the realities of the social context is not easy or assured. Many organizations have gotten into difficulty by failing to understand those groups

or organizations on which they depended for support or by failing to adjust their activities to ensure continued support.

One image of the manager we have developed is that of an advocator, an active manipulator of constraints and of the social setting in which the organization is embedded. Another image is that of a processor of the various demands on the organization. In the first, the manager seeks to enact or create an environment more favorable to the organization. In the second, organizational actions are adjusted to conform to the constraints imposed by the social context. In reality, both sets of managerial activities are performed. We would like to emphasize that both are problematic and difficult. It requires skill to perceive and register accurately one's social context and to adjust organizational activities accordingly. And, it requires skill to alter the social context that the organization confronts. Both images of the role of management imply a sensitivity to the social context in which the organization is embedded and an understanding of the relationship between the organization and its environment. Both, in other words, require the adoption of an external orientation to guide the understanding of organizational functioning.

SUMMARY

. . . We have noted that we are dealing with the problems of the acquisition of resources by social organizations, of the organization's survival, as well as of the use of such resources within organizations to accomplish something. To acquire resources, organizations must inevitably interact with their social environments. No organization is completely self-contained or in complete control of the conditions of its own existence. Because organizations import resources from their environments, they depend on their environments. Survival comes when the organization adjusts to, and copes with, its environment, not only when it makes efficient internal adjustments.

The context of an organization is critical for understanding its activities. Despite considerable pro forma acknowledgement of the environment, managers and researchers continue to attribute organizational actions and outcomes to internal factors. Such attributional processes flow from cognitive and perceptual biases that accompany the observation of organizations, as well as from the desire to view social behavior with a feeling of control. These attributions have led to the neglect and serious underestimation of the importance of social context for understanding organizational behavior. Studies estimating the effects of administrators (e.g., Lieberson and O'Connor, 1972; Salancik and Pfeffer, 1977) have found them to account for about 10 percent of the variance in organizational performance, a striking contrast to the 90 percent of the intellectual effort that has been devoted to developing theories of individual action.

While organizational actions are constrained, and contextual factors do predict organizational outcomes and activities, there are several perspectives on the role of management in organizations consistent with such a theoretical position. In the first place, management serves as a symbol of the organization and its actions. Managers are people to fire when things go poorly, an act that reinforces the feeling of control over organizational actions and results. The symbolic role of management, though as yet unexplored, can be systematically empirically examined. In addition to its symbolic role, management can adjust and alter the social context surrounding the organization or can facilitate the organization's adjustment to its context. Both activities require understanding the social context and the interrelationship between context and the organization. Even as a processor of external demands, management has a problematic task. Many organizational troubles stem from inaccurate perceptions of external demands or from patterns of dependence on the environment. Indeed, we would argue that the image of management as a processor of demands is one that

implies a high degree of skill and intelligence. After all, anyone can make decisions or take actions—it requires much more skill to be correct.

REFERENCES

Bendix, R. 1956. *Work and Authority in Industry*. New York: Wiley.

Burns, T., and G. M. Stalker. 1961. *The Management of Innovation*. London: Tavistock.

Davis, O. A., and M. Hinich. 1966. "A mathematical model of policy formulation in a democratic society." In J. L. Bernd (ed.), *Mathematical Applications in Political Science II*, 175–208. Dallas, Tex.: Southern Methodist University Press.

Fellner, W. 1949. *Competition Among the Few*. New York: Knopf.

Hawley, A. H. 1950. *Human Ecology*. New York: Ronald Press.

Hirsch, P. M. 1975. "Organizational effectiveness and the institutional environment." *Administrative Science Quarterly*, 20: 327–344.

Hirschman, A. O. 1970. *Exit, Voice, and Loyalty*. Cambridge: Harvard University Press.

Jones, E. E., and R. E. Nisbett. 1971. *The Actor and the Observer: Divergent Perceptions of the Causes of Behavior*. Morristown, N.J.: General Learning Press.

Katz, D., and R. L. Kahn. 1966. *The Social Psychology of Organizations*. New York: Wiley.

Kelley, H. H. 1971. *Attribution in Social Interaction*. Morristown, N.J.: General Learning Press.

Kessel, J. H. 1962. "Government structure and political environment: a statistical note about American cities." *American Political Science Review*, 56: 615–620.

Lieberson, S., and J. F. O'Connor. 1972. "Leadership and organizational performance: a study of large corporations." *American Sociological Review*, 37: 117–130.

March J. G., and J. P. Olsen. 1975. "Choice situations in loosely coupled worlds." Unpublished manuscript, Stanford University.

Mintzberg, H. 1973. *The Nature of Managerial Work*. New York: Harper & Row.

Perrow, C. 1970. *Organizational Analysis: A Sociological View.* Belmont, Calif.: Wadsworth.

Pfeffer, J. 1977. "The ambiguity of leadership." *Academy of Management Review*, 2: 104–112.

Phillips, A. 1960. "A theory of interfirm organization." *Quarterly Journal of Economics*, 74: 602–613.

Salancik, G. R., B. J. Calder, K. M. Rowland, H. Leblebici, and M. Conway. 1975. "Leadership as an outcome of social structure and process: a multidimensional approach." In J. G. Hunt and L. Larson (eds.), *Leadership Frontiers*, 81–102. Ohio: Kent State University Press.

Salancik, G. R., and V. Lamont. 1975. "Conflicts in societal research: a study of one RANN project suggests that benefitting society may cost universities." *Journal of Higher Education*, 46: 161–176.

Salancik, G. R., and J. Pfeffer. 1977. "Constraints on administrator discretion: the limited influence of mayors on city budgets." *Urban Affairs Quarterly*, June.

Schnore, L. F., and R. R. Alford. 1963. "Forms of government and socio-economic characteristics of suburbs." *Administrative Science Quarterly*, 8: 1–17.

Weber, M. 1930. *The Protestant Ethic and the Spirit of Capitalism.* New York: Scribner.

Weick, K. E. 1976. "Educational organizations as loosely coupled systems." *Administrative Science Quarterly*, 21: 1–19.

Williamson, O. E. 1965. "A dynamic theory of interfirm behavior." *Quarterly Journal of Economics*, 79: 579–607.

Wolfson, M. R., and G. R. Salancik. 1977. "Actor-observer and observer-observer attributional differences about an achievement task." *Journal of Experimental Social Psychology*, June.

49

Demography of Corporations and Industries

Glenn R. Carroll and Michael T. Hannan

. . . At its most general level, the notion of environment summarizes the relevant parts of the social and physical world that lie outside the organization. In social science applications, the environment includes other organizations, natural actors, political structures, technologies, and physical environments. Analyses of organizations often define environments with reference to identifiable social units such as nation-states, economies, industries, and markets. Environmental variations are typically assessed by measuring and assessing the relationships of measures of these dimensions with vital rates.

We distinguish two broad classes of environmental processes. The first class, discussed in this chapter, we call exogenous processes. These environmental processes shape and change organizations and organizational populations, but they are not directly affected by organizations themselves (at least in known, systematic ways). The second class, reviewed [elsewhere], we call endogenous processes. In these types of environmental processes, the organizational population comprises the primary environment for organizational activity and demography. In endogenous processes, as organizations and populations change, so too do their environments. . . .

This chapter takes a very basic, but essential, approach to considering the ways environments affect corporate activity. It starts with an illustration, one that shows some of the unexpected ways that environments shape organizational populations.

It then discusses how demographic researchers typically analyze and model the effects of environmental factors. It touches on the dimensions associated with large variations in demographic activity among organizations across the social units commonly used to define environments. These are resource availability, ethnic identity, technology, and political forces. General theoretical understanding of the effects of these factors is somewhat limited. However, we believe that, as corporate demography develops and stronger empirical patterns emerge, deeper theoretical insights will be forthcoming. The final parts of the chapter deal with a specific type of environmental effect that plays a large role in determining organizational life chances: environmental imprinting, especially at the time of organizational founding.

ENVIRONMENTS AND TELEPHONE COMPANIES

The early American telephone industry provides an interesting point of departure for discussion of environmental effects in corporate demography. The early industry saw dramatic differences in the number of telephone companies operating in various states. Some states—for example, Alaska, Delaware, Nevada, and Rhode Island—had fewer than 10 telephone companies in 1908. Others—including Illinois, Indiana, Iowa, New York, Wisconsin, and Ohio—were each home to more than 500 companies.

Source: Glenn R. Carroll and Michael T. Hannon, *The Demography of Corporations and Industries* (Princeton, NJ: Princeton University Press, 2000), pp. 193–212. © by Princeton University Press. Reprinted by permission of Princeton University Press.

Did environmental factors produce these variations in organizational populations across states? If so, how? . . .

. . . Urban population has a positive effect on large independents and commercial companies. The effects of the average value of farmland and buildings are more robust across type, showing positive effects on both large and small independents (but these are not significant for commercial and mutual forms). So, resource variables show some effects of munificence, but these are not consistent across all measures.

. . . The number of rural incorporated places has a strong positive effect in every equation. Moreover, this effect is larger for the small companies than for the large ones. The number of counties also usually has a positive effect, although it is not significant. The effect of the number of urban incorporated places is negative and significant in three of the four equations. Overall, the pattern of findings suggests that large and small telephone companies operated in different "niches," with the large companies being organized around city boundaries and the small companies around towns and villages. To the extent that there were many cities in a state, the niche of the large organizational form apparently encroached on that of the small form.[1]

Social scientists (Stinchcombe 1965; Hannan and Freeman 1977) typically expect resource factors to increase the market's capacity to support a given form of organization. So, the positive relationship between telephone-market variables and numbers of organizations seems natural. Why do the numbers of political units (incorporated places and counties) within a state also show a positive relationship to the number of telephone companies? Barnett and Carroll (1993) argue that the political boundaries of towns, cities, and counties constrained the expansion of individual telephone companies—and so greater political differentiation led to great numbers of companies— for at least two institutional reasons.

First, local political units must have affected and reflected, at least in part, the taken-for-granted normative conceptions of the market; entrepreneurs would have readily adopted these boundaries when thinking of organizing telephone companies (Meyer and Rowan 1977). This was especially likely for the mutual telephone companies, which often sprang up in populist fashion in places where Bell and the commercial independents refused to locate (Fischer 1994).

A second reason has to do with the fact that local governments were the first regulators of the telephone industry (Brooks 1976). This came about because the initial proliferation of companies resulted in direct price competition in some places (Gabel 1969). In fact, nearly one-half of the nation's 1051 incorporated places with telephone service had more than one company by 1902 (Phillips 1985). To attract customers in these places, companies reduced prices— sometimes offering service at no charge— which often resulted in poor-quality service (Gabel 1969). In other cases, opportunistic entrepreneurs would enter local markets intending simply to prompt existing competitors to buy them out. Consequently, local governments began requiring telephone companies to obtain charters— often for a fee—that controlled rates, acquisitions and mergers, and rights-of-way for cable (Stehman 1925).

The combined effect of many such local constraints creates at the state level what Meyer and Scott (1992) call *institutional fragmentation*. Empirical research in a variety of contexts has demonstrated that such a fragmentation makes it difficult to design, monitor, and enforce a unified and coherent public policy (Meyer, Scott, and Strang 1987; Carroll, Delacroix, and Goodstein 1988). Therefore, states with greater numbers of political units would have been less capable of rationalizing the telephone industry.

Political boundaries also prevented market factors from operating freely. For example, the Pittsburgh and Allegheny Telephone Company served most of the market in Pittsburgh by 1910. Unconstrained, one would expect that this company would also have served the entire metropolitan area surrounding Pittsburgh in Allegheny County. However, the area was very fragmented politically; it included 120 distinct political units in 1910. As a result, this area was not completely dominated by the Pittsburgh and Allegheny Telephone Company, but instead was served by 11 different telephone companies at that time.

MODELING ENVIRONMENTAL CONDITIONS

The usual corporate demography study examines organizational life histories and the rates at which vital events occur, not the type of cross-sectional distribution investigated above for telephone companies. . . .

Most corporate demographers also attempt to incorporate environmental variations into the analysis. Environmental conditions often change substantially over the periods for which corporations and organizational populations are at risk of experiencing the relevant events. When environmental characteristics can be measured directly, these changes can be modeled as time-varying covariates.[2] To the extent that relevant theory gets developed, it might provide guidance about the functional form relating environmental covariates to vital rates. We illustrate such arguments with brief discussions of each of the four major classes of exogenous environmental factors: (1) resources, (2) political forces, (3) technology, and (4) ethnic identity.

Resources
Building and sustaining organizations depends on the availability of resources, both human and material (Weber 1968; Stinchcombe 1965). Resource availability for new organization means that levels of potentially mobilizable resources are ample and claims on these resources by other social units can be contested. Under norms of rationality, the founding rate of new organizations in-

creases when the levels of resources rise and other groups and organizations do not control them. Population growth and economic development are classic examples of environmental conditions in which resources rise: however, these conditions obviously do not always result in new organization because existing firms often hold entrenched and advantaged competitive positions that allow them to absorb the resources before new firms can.

Consider, for example, the resources available to the early American automobile industry. Technological knowledge, labor, and consumer wealth all increased rapidly and steadily throughout much of the twentieth century—and so too did the number of cars built and sold. Nonetheless, the number of automobile producers did not grow with resources; instead it declined through much of this period. . . . A major research question for corporate demography thus involves identifying the conditions under which growth in resources generates growth among existing firms or population expansion in the form of new organizations.

Durkheim's theory about the causes of the division of labor in society provides one version of an argument relating the size of the resource base to organizational diversity. According to Durkheim (1947, 266), "if work becomes divided more as societies become more voluminous and denser, it is not because external circumstances are more varied, but because the struggle for existence is more acute." Durkheim developed the imagery of a set of isolated communities whose economic enterprises have expanded to the limits of the local markets and local competitive interactions. When these isolated communities are brought into close contact by declines in the costs of communication and transportation, a competitive struggle ensues. . . .

To the extent that new specializations come about by the creation of new enterprises, increased "moral density" increases rates of both organizational founding and failure (Hawley 1950).

Political Forces

Another broad type of environmental change that potentially creates pervasive organizational change reflects political processes, especially those associated with political discontinuities in national government. The major political forces that affect organizational diversity are tied to social revolutions, that is, processes by which some class structures and political structures are destroyed and others built. Social revolutions and political crisis almost invariably change the mix of organizations in society. . . .

In contrast to revolution, political change by ordinary institutional means (in response to political and social crises) usually involves the addition of new organizations and new organizational forms without the destruction of much existing organization. That is, solving political crises usually means constructing new organizations either to repress dissent or to incorporate contending groups into the polity. For example, the incorporation of organized labor into the polity in the United States during the 1930s involved the creation of numerous state and local agencies designed to enforce the newly won rights of unions. Subsequent attempts by conservative governments to roll back New Deal concessions to labor unions often involved attempts to eliminate agencies. Similar reactions followed the War on Poverty program development.

Less profound organizational change often occurs with routine regime change. Once in power, new governments frequently provide the authority and funds to proliferate their preferred organizational forms. For instance, the dramatic increase in offshore commercial banks in Singapore after 1971 . . . is directly attributable to the government's establishment of the Monetary Authority of Singapore. . . .

Technology

A third broad class of important environmental changes involves technological developments occurring through innovations and other discontinuities. Often arising from the periphery of an industry, these major breakthroughs in technology typically substitute for and eventually supplant an existing technology. The initial discovery is often called paradigmatic because it renders obsolete previous ways of doing things (Dosi 1982). Further technological progress proceeds incrementally down a few uncertain but directed trajectories to an accepted regime. The organizational structures associated with the new technology differ from those associated with the old technology (Tushman and Anderson 1986; Utterback and Suarez 1993; Klepper and Simons 1997).

A well-known example of technological change severely affecting organizational change involves the modern evolution of the world watch industry. From the industry's earliest days until about 1950, mechanical watches using pin-lever and jewel-lever technologies dominated the market. Swiss firms overwhelmingly produced these watches; they tended to be fairly small operations consisting of highly trained craftsmen who were not involved in the distribution of their products. Between 1950 and 1970, alternative types of watches appeared, using new electric and tuning-fork technologies. These watches were produced primarily by large American firms, which usually had their own distribution and retail networks. The biggest technological change occurred in the 1970s, however, with the successful development of quartz-watch technology, resulting in numerous electronic watches, many inexpensive. The popularity of this new technology virtually eliminated the old Swiss watchmaking companies whose products suddenly seemed less reliable and much more expensive. The quartz-technology regime in the world watch industry was initially dominated by large, vertically integrated Japanese firms such as Hattori-Seiko. Hong Kong companies also participated in this reorganized industry.

Technical innovation plays a key role in the creation of new organizations and especially new forms of organization (Sutton 1999). Each wave of technical innovation produces new sets of opportunities. Sometimes these new opportunities get exploited by members of existing organizational forms. Quite often, however, only new organizational strategies and structures can meet the demands of efficiently producing, servicing and marketing the new products and services that arise from application of the new techniques. Recent examples of technology-driven organization building come from biotechnology, which depends on new knowledge of recombinant DNA biochemistry, and from the overnight delivery business, which depends critically on extensive computer networks and scheduling algorithms.

Ethnic Identity

Changes in the distributions of socially constructed identities in human populations also often constitute important environmental changes for organizations. Consider, for instance, the effects of the changing demography of ethnic groups for the demography of corporations. Often these changes occur as a result of large-scale immigration of minority groups into advanced economies, but they can also involve the increased salience of identities or the activation of new or latent identities (e.g., the black power movement). In any case, blocked-upward mobility channels (because of discrimination directed against the minority group), labor market competition, and ethnic solidarity by ethnic consumers (reinforced by concentrated geographic settlement patterns, caused in part by discrimination) create new ethnic-based forms of organization often situated in ethnic enclaves and providing numerous sources of opportunity (Olzak 1989).

An example of organizational change following from ethnic change can be found in the history of the U.S. newspaper industry. Waves of ethnic (often foreign-language) papers were generated by waves of immigration. . . .

Measurement Issues

Organizational populations—and even individual organizations—sometimes span centuries of time. In these cases, environments commonly develop and change in many dramatic ways. However, it is often difficult to find systematic data that record environmental variables in reliable and consistent fashion across the entire period. . . .

Corporate demographers often use a combination of . . . two strategies, relying on those covariates that can be measured consistently for the entire observation window but also introducing period effects to pick up other unmeasured environmental changes. For example, our studies of the automobile industries (Carroll et al. 1996; Hannan et al. 1998a) relied on measured variables such as gross national product and human population size as well as period dummies representing the industry regimes identified by Altshuler, Anderson, Jones, Roos, and Womack (1984). Both types of variables show strong and significant effects, as is typically the case.

Estimation Issues

Some theoretical analyses of organizational environments postulate that the competitive structure of an industry has much to do with the types of resources, technologies, institutions, and regulatory structures that develop and evolve within that industry. Those very same factors might influence and change later competition. For instance, institutional theorists seek to explain how specific organizations and organizational forms get institutionalized and become sociopolitically legitimated. In its usual form, this type of analysis relies on historical understanding of the authority structures prevailing over an organizational population, be they governmental, professional, or normative. Analysts seek to identify those specific endorsement actions by the authority leading to institutionalization of the organization or organizational form (for example, certification of a hospital by Medicare or recognition of acupuncture as an acceptable treatment mode by insurance companies). Theory presumes that institutionalization accords favorable treatment by social actors or other important advantages, often generating more resources. Hypotheses typically link organizational fates to the specific endorsement actions, predicting that particular organizations will show lower mortality rates as a result. . . .

As one imagines solving these technical problems, it becomes apparent that accommodating full endogeneity requires specifying the processes that generate acts of sociopolitical legitimation. Current research practice entails identifying specific relevant acts by assessing their likely beneficial consequences on an organizational population (for example, lower death rates because of greater legal protection or more resources). Theory constructed in this way does not usually contemplate the general causes of the endorsement acts or factors affecting their timing. Indeed, such theory does not often even describe the general characteristics of endorsement acts leading to sociopolitical legitimation, making it difficult for other analysts to develop theory or to connect the research program to other areas of potential application, such as positive political theory. So, even if one could estimate the simultaneous system of equations required to make sociopolitical legitimation endogenous, it would be difficult (based on the current state of development of the field) to specify models of endorsement acts. Accordingly, the research problem is underdeveloped theoretically and needs to pay more attention to modeling sociopolitical legitimation appropriately.

ENVIRONMENTAL IMPRINTING

Imprinting refers to a process in which events occurring at certain key developmental stages have persisting, possibly lifelong, consequences. Environmental imprinting is a form of imprinting whereby specific environmental characteristics get mapped onto

an organization's structure and affect its development and life chances. Research on corporate demography has identified several types of environmental imprinting including imprinting at founding, an exogenous process which we discuss at length here.

Imprinting at Founding

The idea that firms and other kinds of organizations tend to be imprinted by their environmental conditions at founding comes from Stinchcombe (1965). This seminal essay argued that social and economic structures have their maximal impact on new organizations. . . .

Stinchcombe (1965; 1979) examined this process for employment relations at the industry level. He noted that industries formed in different centuries still reflect today some of the character of their formative periods. For instance, those formed after the "organizational revolution" of the closing years of the nineteenth century and the early years of the twentieth century typically employ a higher fraction of administrative workers than those with earlier origins.[3]

If Stinchcombe is right, then certain features of the employment relation get imprinted. Moreover, the character of the employment relation gets set, at least implicitly, very early in the organization's existence, when the first employees join, and later when jobs are formalized. Arrangements made at that time might have long-lasting consequences.

Baron and colleagues' investigation of employment systems in agencies of the California state government found such an imprinting effect. Baron and Newman (1990) found that jobs with mainly female incumbents tended to have lower prescribed pay rates and that this effect increased significantly with the age of the job. Baron and Newman (1990, 172) interpret this effect as indicating that

. . . notions of imprinting and inertia thus might fruitfully be extended to the study of work roles: cohorts of jobs founded during the same period might be expected to evince common features, such as shared selection and promotion criteria and similar degrees of ascription.

Organizational age also affected the rate at which gender composition of jobs changed in response to changing composition of the relevant work force. Baron, Mittman, and Newman (1991) reported that the youngest and oldest state agencies integrated their work forces more quickly than agencies of intermediate age. They interpreted the effect for younger jobs as agreeing with the idea that inertial pressures on youthful structures are weaker than on older ones.[4] This study makes clear that organizational age matters for the employment relationship and that the observed patterns are consistent with the hypothesis of inertia in organizational structures and practices.

Modeling Environmental Imprinting

Environmental imprinting requires two conditions: (1) a mapping of an environmental condition onto the organization, and (2) inertia (or at least a fair degree of hysteresis) in the imprinted characteristics. If the second condition does not hold, then later modifications of the structure will erode the association of founding conditions and those features.

Environmental imprinting can be detected by estimating the effects of covariates measuring environmental characteristics on life changes over temporally defined observation windows. The simplest case is imprinting at *founding*. Here the observation window is defined as the moment of founding. Covariates are measured at founding and then treated as fixed for the life of the organization. A simple case of importance to corporate demography involves density at time of founding. . . .

A related idea says that *experience* at some later time has enduring effects (Barnett 1997; Barnett and Hansen 1996). When the organization's entire life experience matters, then the window must be wide enough to include all previous experience. The covariates vary over time and get updated in every new period of the organization's existence. That is, the relevant information is summarized across the organization's lifetime. The more common case specifies a historical period of specific length over which observations are made (say, the last five years) and updates values as warranted.

IMPRINTING IN HIGH-TECHNOLOGY FIRMS

The Stanford Project on Emerging Companies (SPEC) provides an opportunity to examine how organizational design features get imprinted. This panel study of more than 170 young, high-technology firms in California's Silicon Valley (Baron, Burton, and Hannan 1999) seeks to understand how founding conditions and early decisions affect organizational evolution, which necessitates information about the earliest days of the organization. The sample was restricted to firms no more than 10 years old and with at least 10 employees when sampled. The focus on firms in a single region and sector of economic activity controls for many labor market and environmental conditions that might be relevant to organizational design. In 1994/5, semistructured interviews were conducted with a founder, the current chief executive officer (CEO), and a key informant whom the CEO nominated to provide information about human-resource practices.

Models of Organizing in Young Technology Firms

Founders were asked about how they had thought about the organization-building process and about employment relations, including whether or not they had "an organizational model or blueprint in mind when . . . founding the company." A large fraction reported that they had a specific organizational model in mind, often patterned to reflect — or diverge from — a par-

ticular firm with which they had prior experience. Analyses of transcripts from these
interviews suggested that their organizational models reflect a set of premises about
three dimensions of the employment relationship:

- *Attachment.* Is the primary intended basis
  of employee attachment and retention: (a)
  monetary rewards (money); (b) opportunities for challenging work and professional
  development (work); or (c) a strong emotional bond to the organization and its
  members (love)?
- *Selection.* Was the primary consideration in
  selecting employees to be: (a) their command of specific skills necessary to perform
  well defined and immediately needed tasks
  effectively; (b) the potential to perform
  effectively on a series of projects (often
  not yet even envisioned) through which
  the employee would move over time; or
  (c) values and organizational fit?
- *Basis of control.* Is control and coordination
  of work to be achieved principally through:
  (a) direct oversight; (b) formal rules, systems, and procedures; (c) informal mechanisms (peers or organizational culture); or
  (d) professionalism?

Premises about the employment relation
can thus be classified into three types of attachment, three types of selection, and four
types of control, yielding $3 \times 3 \times 4 = 36$
possible combinations. The observations
turn out to be highly clustered. Roughly
half of the responses fall in five of the 36
cells. These five cells, which Baron et al.
(1999) call basic model types, correspond
with well-known images:

- *Engineering model:* attachment through
  challenging work, peer group control, and
  selection based on specific task abilities.
  This is generally thought to represent the
  default blueprint for a high-tech Silicon
  Valley start-up, and it is the most prevalent
  model among the SPEC founders (espoused
  by roughly a third of them).
- *Star model:* attachment based on challenging work, reliance on autonomy and professional control, and selection of elite personnel based on their longterm potential.
- *Commitment model:* emotional or familial attachments to the organization, selec-

tion based on values or fit, and peer group
control.
- *Bureaucracy model:* attachment based on
  challenging work and/or opportunities for
  development, selection based on qualifications for a particular role, and formalized
  control.
- *Autocracy model:* monetary motivations,
  control and coordination through direct
  oversight, and employees who are selected
  to perform a set of prespecified tasks.

Most of the responses that do not correspond to one of these basic model types differ from a single type on only one of the
three dimensions. . . .

Founders' Models and Subsequent Events

Founders' models of employment relations
significantly affected the early careers of
their firms. Hannan, Burton, and Baron
(1996) reported analysis for the 100 firms
sampled in 1994 (analysis for the full sample is ongoing). They concentrated on the
rate of transition from a founder as CEO to
a nonfounder CEO and the rate of initial
public offering (IPO) of stock. They examined the effects of the employment models
of founders. They also analyzed the employment models of the then-current CEOs
(who had been asked similar questions about
their organizational blueprint for their
companies). For each outcome, they found
that the founders' models matter but the
CEOs' models do not. In other words, the
initial premises matter more than the premises employed by those who are best posi-
tioned to control later events.

In the case of the transition to a nonfounder CEO, the commitment, engineering, and star models of employment have
higher transition rates than the bureaucratic and autocratic models. If the bureaucratic and autocratic models stand at one
extreme, the star model stands at the other.
Estimates imply that the transition rate
for firms with star-model founders is approximately 8.5 times higher than for firms
with bureaucratic and autocratic founders.
This difference in rates is highly significant.

The difference between the commitment model and the bureaucratic and autocratic models is also large (the ratio of the rates is roughly 3). . . .

The founder's model of employment also has a surprisingly strong impact on the rate at which firms manage to conduct an initial public offering. The rate of IPO for the firms founded with commitment, engineering, or star models is much higher than that for the bureaucratic and autocratic models. The difference is large and statistically significant for the star and commitment models. Holding constant age, size, and industry, firms whose founders had star or commitment models go public at roughly ten times the rate of firms whose founders had either a bureaucratic or autocratic model.

Effects of Founders' Models on Managerial/Administrative Intensity

The founders' models (or blueprints) vary in how strongly they presume that control and coordination will be effected through the standard devices of bureaucratic administration—rules, procedures, reporting relations, specialization of tasks, performance evaluation, and the like—rather than through informal, tacit means of generating commitment or through personal oversight by the founders themselves or their agents. Empirically, these blueprints profoundly shape the extent (and speed) of some aspects of formalization and bureaucratization in firms over their early years, even controlling for other features of organizations and their environments likely to influence organizational design. Indeed, the current level of managerial and administrative intensity in these enterprises is more strongly related to the founders' espoused organizational blueprints than it is to the contemporaneous organizational models of the current CEOs. Founders' early premises about employment relations exert enduring effects on the managerial and administrative intensity of the organizations they build, even when/after the initial founder(s) departs.

Managerial or administrative intensity provides a handy summary measure of the tendency toward bureaucratization. Baron, Hannan, and Burton (1999) examined the relationship of founders' and CEOs' models on bureaucratization by estimating multivariate regressions relating the (ln) number of managerial and administrative full-time equivalent positions (FTEs) in 1994/5 to the founder's organizational model, controlling for the (ln) number of nonmanagerial, nonadministrative FTEs in 1994/5. . . .

As hypothesized, the bureaucracy and commitment models were at opposite extremes in terms of managerial intensity. Firms whose founders championed a bureaucratic model had significantly more managerial and administrative specialists by 1994/5 than otherwise-comparable firms. At the other end of the spectrum, commitment firms were significantly less administratively intense than otherwise-comparable firms (with the exception of star firms, where the contrast was not statistically significant).

Baron et al. (1999) also examined the impact of the employment models of the then-current CEOs. . . . How the founder conceptualized the organization at its inception, not how the then-CEO conceived of it, predicts bureaucratization in 1994/5. Baron et al. (1999) construe this result as providing quite compelling evidence of imprinting at founding.

It turns out that patterns of bureaucratization and formalization are also influenced by the social composition of the work force (specifically, in this sample, the gender mix) early in a firm's history. Women's proportional representation in the labor force at the end of the firm's first year of operations has a significant negative effect on managerial and administrative intensity, even controlling for founder's model, industry, strategy, organizational age, and whether the firm had gone public. The results imply fairly dramatic differences in administrative intensity for firms of a given size by 1994/5, based on women's proportionate representation in the first year.

As was the case in contrasting the effects of founders' versus CEOs' organizational models, early work-force demography was more decisive than the current state of affairs. That is, the present-day gender mix was less relevant to current managerial intensity than was the gender mix at the firm's inception.

Effects of Founders' Models on the Formalization of Human-Resources Policies

The SPEC researchers also examined how founders' organizational models and the firm's early gender mix affected the rate of formalization of the employment relationship.[5] The researchers constructed scales (ranging from 0 to 11) indicating how many of the relevant employment practices each firm had adopted: (a) by the end of its first year of operations; and (b) by the time it was first interviewed by the SPEC research team in 1994/5. Analysis of the number of formalized HR practices adopted by each firm by 1994/5 reveals that commitment-model firms display less employment formalization than all other types. However, the differences across organizational models are small and far from statistically significant.

In a parallel analysis, the SPEC research team analyzed the hazard of adding practices using a monthly split-spell file built using information on the month and year of adoption (if ever) of each of the 11 human-resource practices comprising the index of employment formalization. This kind of analysis focuses on rates of adoption (rather than on the total count of practices adopted over some period), and it controls for the number of practices adopted at the start of each monthly spell and uses information on changes within the study period for some covariates. . . . [This analysis] finds that firms founded along commitment-model lines add employment practices at a somewhat lower rate than firms whose founders espoused other models. The estimated model implies that the rate of formalization in commitment firms is 0.47 that of

otherwise-identical firms founded along bureaucratic lines.

In sum, early differences in the overall extent of employment formalization, reflecting founders' organizational blueprints, are essentially absent after a period that averages around six years. This suggests a pattern of convergence, rather than path-dependent development, as was found for managerial intensity. Event-history analyses suggest that it is not primarily a matter of how much, but rather how fast, technology companies adopt various standard HR practices designed to formalize and routinize employment relations. In particular, commitment-model firms resemble firms founded along bureaucratic lines in doing somewhat more extensive organization-building early on. However, commitment-model firms are somewhat slower to formalize, presumably reflecting the capacity for self-organizing and self-managing that such firms seek to cultivate. On balance, however, there is less evidence of enduring effects of founders' models on the extent or pace of employment formalization than on the evolution of managerial-administrative intensity.

A question might be raised about whether demonstrating an enduring imprint of founding conditions on technology companies that are almost all still in their first decade provides powerful evidence of path dependence. The issue is an empirical one. As Hannan and Freeman (1984) noted in discussing the tendency toward structural inertia in organizations, one must assess the rate and direction of organizational change relative to trends in the relevant environment(s). Demonstrating strong tendencies toward path-dependent development in the evolution of religious organizations, for instance, would presumably carry little shock value, given the mission and environment of a typical church. In contrast, Baron et al. (1999) contend that the organizations they studied—nascent technology companies in Silicon Valley—are subject in their early years to very turbulent environments, intense product and labor market competition, strong selection pressures, and numerous other influences that should encourage structural isomorphism.

NOTES

1. The variance in the number of telephone companies also increases with the number of political units, a relationship that suggests that the degree of autonomy granted to political units might differ across states.
2. ... The conventional approach to estimating the effects of these covariates involves splitting the spells of risk exposure, updating the covariate values, and treating the spells as censored unless an event is observed.
3. Carroll and Mayer (1986) used Stinchcombe's historical typology of employment systems in industrial sectors in analyzing patterns of individual careers. They found that time of origin of industry affects mobility regimes centuries and decades after founding.
4. Baron et al. (1991) suggest that the effect for the oldest agencies reflects the survivor bias in their data (the set of very old jobs is unusual in having survived for a long time and have been, therefore, perhaps more responsive to environmental pressures).
5. This analysis was based on a survey, completed during 1994/5 by the person in each organization most knowledgeable about human-resource (HR) matters. It indicated whether (and when) a number of employment practices, policies, forms, and documents were adopted. Eleven of these items seem directed at formalizing, standardizing, and/or documenting employment practices: organization chart; standardized employment application; written job descriptions; personnel manual or handbook; written employment tests; written performance evaluations; standard performance evaluation forms; written affirmative action plans; standard employment contract for exempt employees; employee grievance or complaint forms; and human-resources information system.

REFERENCES

Altshuler, Alan, Martin Anderson, Daniel Jones, Daniel Roos, and James Womack.

1984. *The Future of the Automobile*. Cambridge: MIT Press.

Barnett, William P. 1997. "The Dynamics of Competitive Intensity." *Administrative Science Quarterly* 42:128–60.

Barnett, William P., and Glenn R. Carroll. 1993. "How Institutional Constraints Affected the Organization of Early U.S. Telephony." *Journal of Law, Economics, and Organization* 9:98–126.

Barnett, William P., and Morton T. Hansen. 1996. "The Red Queen in Organizational Evolution." *Strategic Management Journal* 17:139–58.

Baron, James N., M. Diane Burton, and Michael T. Hannan. 1999. "Engineering Bureaucracy: The Genesis of Formal Policies, Positions, and Structures in High-Technology Firms." *Journal of Law, Economics, and Organization*, 15:1–41.

Baron, James N., Michael T. Hannan, and M. Diane Burton. 1999. "Building the Iron Cage: Determinants of Managerial Intensity in the Early Years of Organizations." *American Sociological Review*, in press.

Baron, James N., Brian S. Mittman, and Andrew E. Newman. 1991. "Targets of Opportunity: Organizational and Environmental Determinants of Gender Integration Within the California Civil Service, 1979–1985." *American Journal of Sociology* 96:1362–1401.

Baron, James N., and Andrew E. Newman. 1990. "For What It's Worth: Organizations, Occupations, and the Value of Work Done by Women and Non-whites." *American Sociological Review* 55:155–75.

Brooks, John. 1976. *Telephone: The First Hundred Years*. New York: Harper & Row.

Carroll, Glenn R., Lyda Bigelow, Marc-David Seidel, and Lucia Tsai. 1996. "The Fates of De Novo and De Alio Producers in the American Automobile Industry, 1885–1982." *Strategic Management Journal* 17:117–37.

Carroll, Glenn R., Jacques Delacroix, and Jerry Goodstein. 1988. "The Political Environments of Organizations: An Ecological View." Pp. 359–92 in *Research in Organizational Behavior*, Volume 10, edited by B. Staw and L. Cummings. Greenwich, Conn.: JAI Press.

Carroll, Glenn R., and Karl Ulrich Mayer. 1986. "Job Shift Patterns in the Federal Republic of Germany: The Effects of Social Class, Industrial Sector, and Organizational Size." *American Sociological Review* 51:323–41.

Dosi, Giovanni. 1982. "Technological Paradigms and Technological Trajectories." *Research Policy* 11:147–62.

Durkheim, Emile. 1947. *The Division of Labor in Society*. Glencoe, Ill.: Free Press. [Originally published in 1893].

Fischer, Claude S. 1994. *America Calling: A Social History of the Telephone to 1940*. Berkeley and Los Angeles: University of California Press.

Gabel, Richard. 1969. "The Early Competitive Era in Telephone Communications, 1893–1920." *Law and Contemporary Problems* 34:340–59.

Hannan, Michael T., M. Diane Burton, and James N. Baron. 1996. "Inertia and Change in the Early Years: Employment Relations in Young, High-Technology Firms." *Industrial and Corporate Change* 5:503–36.

Hannan, Michael T., Glenn R. Carroll, Stanislav D. Dobrev, and Joon Han. 1998a. "Organizational Mortality in European and American Automobile Industries, Part I: Revisiting the Effects of Age and Size." *European Sociological Review* 14:279–302.

Hannan, Michael T., and John Freeman. 1977. "The Population Ecology of Organizations." *American Journal of Sociology* 82:929–64.

———1984. "Structural Inertia and Organizational Change." *American Sociological Review* 49:149–64.

Hawley, Amos H. 1950. *Human Ecology: A Theory of Community Structure*. New York: Ronald Press.

Klepper, Steven, and Kenneth L. Simons. 1997. "Technological Extinctions of Industrial Firms: An Inquiry into Their Nature and Causes." *Industrial and Corporate Change* 6:379–460.

Meyer, John W., and Brian Rowan. 1977. "Institutionalized Organizations: Formal Structure as Myth and Ceremony." *American Journal of Sociology* 83:340–63.

Meyer, John W., and W. Richard Scott. 1992. *Organizational Environments: Ritual and Rationality*. Updated edition. Newbury Park, Calif.: Sage.

Meyer, John W., W. Richard Scott, and David Strang. 1987. "Centralization, Fragmentation, and School District Complexity." *Administrative Science Quarterly* 32:186–201.

Olzak, Susan. 1989. "Analysis of Events in Studies of Collective Action." *Annual Review of Sociology* 15:119–41.

Phillips, Charles F. 1985. *The Regulation of Public Utilities: Theory and Practice*. Arlington, Virg.: Public Utilities Reports, Inc.

Stehman, Warren J. 1925. *The Financial History of the American Telephone and Telegraph Company*. New York: Houghton Mifflin.

Stinchcombe, Arthur L. 1965. "Social Structure and Organizations." Pp. 142–93 in *Handbook of Organizations*, edited by J. March. Chicago: Rand McNally.

———1979. "Social Mobility and the Industrial Labor Process." *Acta Sociologica* 22:217–45.

Sutton, John. 1999. *Technology and Market Structure*. Cambridge: MIT Press.

Tushman, Michael, and Philip C. Anderson. 1986. "Technological Discontinuities and Organizational Environments." *Administrative Science Quarterly* 31:439–65.

Utterback, James, and Eduardo Suarez. 1993. "Innovation, Competition and Industry Structure." *Research Policy* 22:1–21.

Weber, Max. 1968. *Economy and Society: An Outline of Interpretive Sociology*. New York: Bedmeister. 3 vols. [Originally published in 1924].